D1566416

Writings of Charles S. Peirce

Volume 2

Observers of the Solar Eclipse of 22 December 1870 near Catania in Sicily. Standing fourth from the left is Charles S. Peirce, fourth from the right his father Benjamin; sitting in front of them is Herbert H. D. Peirce, Charles's younger brother. Photograph courtesy of Mrs. Peirce Prince, Herbert's granddaughter.

Writings of

CHARLES S. PEIRCE

A CHRONOLOGICAL EDITION

Volume 2

1867–1871

EDWARD C. MOORE, *Editor*
MAX H. FISCH, *Consulting Editor*
CHRISTIAN J. W. KLOESEL, *Senior Associate Editor*
DON D. ROBERTS, *Associate Editor*
LYNN A. ZIEGLER, *Textual Editor*

Indiana University Press   Bloomington

Preparation of this volume has been supported in part by grants from the Program for Editions of the National Endowment for the Humanities, an independent federal agency, and the National Science Foundation. Publication of this volume was aided by a grant from the Program for Publications of the National Endowment for the Humanities.

CENTER FOR
SCHOLARLY EDITIONS
AN APPROVED EDITION
MODERN LANGUAGE
ASSOCIATION OF AMERICA

Harvard University Press holds the copyright to those parts of this volume that first appeared in *Collected Papers of Charles Sanders Peirce* (Vols. 1–6 edited by Charles Hartshorne and Paul Weiss, 1931–1935; 7–8 by Arthur W. Burks, 1958); Mouton Publishers to those that first appeared in *The New Elements of Mathematics by Charles S. Peirce* (4 vols. in 5 edited by Carolyn Eisele, 1976). For those portions of the text reproduced from *Thomas of Erfurt,* GRAMMATICA SPECULATIVA (translated by G. L. Bursill-Hall, 1972) and from *Ockham's Theory of Terms: Part I of the* SUMMA LOGICAE (translated by Michael J. Loux, 1974), we gratefully acknowledge permission granted by the respective publishers, Longmans Group Ltd. (London) and University of Notre Dame Press (Notre Dame, IN 46556).

Library of Congress Cataloging in Publication Data
(Revised for volume 2)
Peirce, Charles Santiago Sanders, 1839–1914.
   Writings of Charles S. Peirce.

   Vol. 2-   : Edward C. Moore, editor . . . et al.
   CONTENTS: —V. 2. 1867–1871.
   Includes bibliographical references and indexes.
   1. Philosophy—Collected works. I. Moore, Edward C.
B945.P4 1982   191   79-1993
ISBN 0-253-37201-1 (v. 1)
ISBN 0-253-37202-X (v. 2)

Contents

Preface

In an assessment of Charles Peirce as a philosopher, Ernest Nagel wrote that "there is a fair consensus among historians of ideas that Charles Sanders Peirce remains the most original, versatile, and comprehensive philosophical mind this country has yet produced."[1] Although Peirce published a wide variety of papers and reviews, he published only one major work (*Photometric Researches,* Leipzig, 1878) and that was not in philosophy. In 1923, Morris R. Cohen edited a volume, collecting two series of Peirce's published papers, under the title of *Chance, Love and Logic,* but it was not until Harvard University Press published volumes 1 through 6 of the *Collected Papers of Charles Sanders Peirce* from 1931 to 1935 under the editorship of Charles Hartshorne and Paul Weiss and volumes 7 and 8 in 1958 under the editorship of Arthur W. Burks that American philosophers began to be aware of the range and depth of Peirce's work.

Although Peirce is best known as the founder of the philosophical doctrine known as pragmatism, it is becoming increasingly clear that the philosophical problems that interested him the most were those of the scientist. Peirce's father, Benjamin Peirce (1809–1880), was a distinguished professor of mathematics and astronomy at Harvard University; Peirce himself received a bachelor of arts degree from Harvard in 1859, a master of arts in 1862, and a bachelor of science in chemistry in 1863.

He was employed for over thirty years by the United States Coast and Geodetic Survey as a scientist. In 1963 the Survey commissioned the CSS *Peirce.* At that time the Director of the Coast and Geodetic Survey, Rear Admiral H. Arnold Karo, wrote me that, "In addition

[1]Ernest Nagel, *Scientific American,* 200(1959):185.

to being a logician and philosopher, Peirce made many important scientific and technical contributions to the Coast and Geodetic Survey during his thirty years of service in the bureau."

Incidental to his work for the Coast Survey, Peirce worked as an assistant at the Harvard Observatory from 1869 to 1872 and made a series of astronomical observations from 1872 to 1875 of which Solon I. Bailey says, "The first attempt at the Harvard Observatory to determine the form of the Milky Way, or the galactic system, was made by Charles S. Peirce. . . . The investigation was of a pioneer nature, founded on scant data."[2]

Peirce made major contributions also in mathematics and logic. C. I. Lewis has remarked that, "The head and front of mathematical logic is found in the calculus of propositional functions, as developed by Peirce and Schröder. . . ."[3]

Peirce invented, almost from whole cloth, the study of signs. Ogden and Richards say that, "By far the most elaborate and determined attempt to give an account of signs and their meanings is that of the American logician C. S. Peirce, from whom William James took the idea and the term Pragmatism, and whose Algebra of Dyadic Relations was developed by Schröder."[4]

Peirce was elected a member of the American Academy of Arts and Sciences (1867), the National Academy of Sciences (1877), the London Mathematical Society (1880), and the New York Mathematical Society (later the American Mathematical Society) (1891), but his personality traits were such that he often offended men of eminence and he had difficulty obtaining an academic appointment. He taught for a few years at The Johns Hopkins University and gave several series of public lectures at Harvard and in Boston. Through 1891 most of his income came from his work for the Coast and Geodetic Survey. In the 1880s he inherited enough money to buy a farm house and sixty acres of land along the Delaware River near Milford, Pennsylvania. He lived there from 1888 until his death in 1914. He died in the greatest poverty, unknown except to a few friends. Upon his death his unpublished manuscripts were obtained by Harvard Uni-

---

[2]Solon I. Bailey, *The History and Work of Harvard Observatory, 1839–1927,* Harvard Observatory. Monograph No. 4 (New York: McGraw Hill, 1931), pp. 198–99.
[3]C. I. Lewis and C. H. Langford, *Symbolic Logic* (New York: Century, 1932), p. 21.
[4]C. K. Ogden and I. A. Richards, *The Meaning of Meaning* (London: Routledge and Kegan Paul, 1949), p. 279.

versity. Difficulties in editing the cartons of manuscripts protracted the process of making the papers generally available to scholars. Only in 1964 were most of these handwritten papers reproduced in microfilm by the Harvard University Microreproduction Service. The series, titled "The Microfilm Edition of the Charles S. Peirce Papers in the Houghton Library of Harvard University," consisted originally of thirty rolls of microfilm which were later supplemented by two additional rolls from the papers and a six-roll selection from Peirce's professional correspondence, making thirty-eight rolls in all. Richard S. Robin's *Annotated Catalogue of the Papers of Charles S. Peirce* (Amherst: University of Massachusetts Press, 1967) and his "The Peirce Papers: A Supplementary Catalogue" (*Transactions of the Charles S. Peirce Society* 7[1971]:37–57) serve as guides to that edition.

The writings Peirce himself published run to approximately twelve thousand printed pages. At five hundred pages to the volume, these would make 24 volumes. The known manuscripts that he left unpublished run to approximately eighty thousand handwritten pages. If, on the average, two manuscript pages yield a book page, it would take 80 additional volumes for the unpublished papers and would require 104 volumes for his complete works.

Every previously printed edition of Peirce's writings might therefore fairly be entitled "Selected Papers," with a subtitle indicating the scope of the selection. The present edition is no exception. What follows here is a statement of the aims and the editorial policies that have determined the selections for this edition.

The general aim of our edition is to facilitate the study of the development of Peirce's thought. We believe that it is important to know how a philosopher arrives at his conclusions. For that reason the present edition is chronological. It brings into a single chronological order papers published by Peirce and papers which he left unpublished. With the exception of papers read at conferences, papers published appear in our volumes as of the dates of their publication. Papers left unpublished appear as of the dates of their composition when Peirce himself dated them or when their dates can be determined from other evidence. In the case of papers datable only within a year or two, we permit ourselves some latitude in placing them in relation to dated papers.

The second principal aim of our edition is to make it as easy as possible to determine the degree of coherence and systematic unity which Peirce's thought had at each stage of its development. Accordingly, we depart from the chronological arrangement wherever it is necessary in order to present every series of papers as a unit, uninterrupted by other papers published or composed between the first and last of a series. And, with very few exceptions, we publish no excerpts. We hope by these procedures to preserve the integrity of every effort Peirce made to give an orderly and more or less comprehensive exposition of his views.

Our third principal aim is to include as high a proportion of previously unpublished papers as our other aims permit. We shall be able to attain our first and second aims only by including some material published by Peirce himself or included in previous letterpress editions. However, in all cases of material not published by Peirce himself, we have returned to the original manuscripts and edited them anew. With material which Peirce published, we have returned to the original printing. In our edition as a whole, we aim at one-half to two-thirds new material, not previously published. In another sense, however, we expect that nearly everything in our edition will *seem* new in virtue of the fresh context provided for it by our single chronological sequence.

One further word as to the aims of our edition. Recently an increasing proportion of the readers of Peirce come to him from semiotics, the general theory of signs, and think of him as one of the founders of that science; often as *the* founder, or at least as the American founder. Peirce from the beginning conceived of logic as coming in its entirety within the scope of the general theory of signs. All of his work in logic was done within that framework. At first he conceived of logic as a branch of a branch of semeiotic (his preferred spelling). For a time in his fifties he distinguished a narrow and a broad sense of logic. In the broad sense logic was coextensive with semeiotic. Eventually he abandoned the narrow sense. The comprehensive treatise on which he was working in the last decade of his life was entitled "A System of Logic, considered as Semeiotic." Our edition will be the first to give prominence to this development and to facilitate the tracing of it in detail.

We come finally to the question of how the actual selecting of our particular "Selected Papers of Charles S. Peirce" is done. In general, (a) by giving preference to his more philosophical writings in logic and metaphysics; (b) by including fewer selections from his technical scientific, mathematical and historical writings; and (c) by giving preference among the latter only to those that are more relevant to his philosophical writings.

We rest our case for this procedure on the fact that our aim is to show the development of Peirce's thought, and that development is not shown in his technical scientific papers but in his philosophical papers. However, Peirce wrote "natural philosophy" almost in the tradition of Bacon and Newton. From the beginning, philosophy for Peirce meant primarily those problems in logic and metaphysics that are encompassed today by the philosophy of science. While Peirce was primarily a logician, the most widely accepted division of logic in his time was into the logic of mathematics (deductive logic) on the one hand and the logic of science (inductive logic) on the other. In his own eyes his work in mathematics, in the sciences, and in the history of science, was all for the sake of a logic that included both the logic of mathematics and the logic of science. The development of Peirce's thought, was a development primarily in the philosophy of logic in that inclusive sense.

Nevertheless, our policies of selection are open to the objection that Peirce's professional career was in science, not in philosophy. He made original contributions to an extraordinarily wide range of the special sciences and was not only a mathematical physicist but a pure mathematician who made professional contributions to pure mathematics as well as to mathematical pedagogy, and he was also an historian of science and mathematics. A selection from his writings that encourages its readers to ignore or to forget these facts may be considered to be radically defective.

To counter this objection there are two possible replies. The first is that a selected edition of Peirce's writings cannot be all-inclusive or comprehensive. To attempt to do equal justice to everything would be to do justice to nothing. We believe that twenty volumes will be adequate to the aims we have set for the present edition, but this will necessarily limit our accommodating of other aims.

The second point in reply is that nearly all of Peirce's scientific and some of his mathematical writings were published and are therefore available in the journals in which they originally appeared as well as in a microfiche edition: *Charles Sanders Peirce: Complete Published Works, including Selected Secondary Materials,* edited by Kenneth Laine Ketner, Christian J. W. Kloesel, and Joseph M. Ransdell (Greenwich, CT: Johnson Associates, 1977). The mathematical writings Peirce left unpublished are well represented also in *The*

New Elements of Mathematics by Charles S. Peirce, edited by Carolyn Eisele, 4 volumes in 5 (The Hague: Mouton; Atlantic Highlands,
NJ: Humanities Press, 1976). Professor Eisele also has in preparation
a separate edition of Peirce's writings, both published and unpublished, on the history of science. Finally, the articles and reviews
Peirce wrote for the *Nation* contain much of scientific interest and
are now available in *Charles Sanders Peirce: Contributions to* THE
NATION, compiled and annotated by Kenneth Laine Ketner and
James Edward Cook, 3 volumes (Lubbock: Texas Tech Press, 1975–
78). Our option to concentrate on Peirce's philosophical writings
relies heavily on the fact that these excellent editions of his scientific
work are available, leaving our edition free to meet significant needs
of present and future students of Peirce's work which are not now
met.

Each of these replies is sound and just, but even together they
may not entirely suffice. The solution to which we have finally come
is to include in each volume, immediately after the editorial notes,
a single chronological list of all the papers Peirce either published or
wrote but did not publish within the period covered by the volume.
Papers he wrote but did not publish are listed if they seem to have
been drafted with a view to eventual publication, or for delivery as
lectures, for presentation at professional meetings, or for circulation
to correspondence course students. A few professional letters will
also be included in the list.

Thus any reader wishing to make a thorough study of Peirce's
work during the period covered by a given volume of our edition will
find within that volume itself a guide leading to the papers we omit,
and placing them in relation to the papers we include. The chronological list will thus provide, volume by volume, the only kind of
completeness and comprehensiveness that is open to an edition
whose aims and policies are those we have outlined above.

Each volume will moreover contain a brief historical introduction
giving an account of Peirce's activities within its time span, including
the work he was doing in the sciences, in mathematics, and in the
history of science.

We trust that the historical introduction near the beginning and
the chronological list near the end of each volume will serve to frame
the papers that appear between them, and that reference to these
additional materials will, in turn, enrich and support our comprehensive aim of encouraging the careful study of Charles Peirce's philo-

sophical development by tracing his thought chronologically and in his own words.

The reader should be aware that, so far as editing is concerned, our policy has been one of restraint. Those writings of Peirce which are in handwritten form can be edited to the point where a reader may doubt that he is still reading Peirce. We therefore exercise caution. If a spelling (e.g., proceedure) is shown in the *Oxford English Dictionary* as being in use in the nineteenth century, we leave it in. If Peirce spells it "Compte," we leave it that way (although in the index we show "Comte" because that is where a modern reader would look for it). In short, it is our intent that the reader of our volumes should read what Peirce wrote, not what we thought he should have written. Such emendations as we make are done only where we find the original text to be unclear and where we are relatively certain of Peirce's intentions. We have noted these changes in our emendations list. Our double-reader, multiple proof-readings give us confidence that very few typographical errors will be found in the Peirce text. The eccentricities and anomalies that occur are those of the author.

Our volumes are inspected by the Center for Scholarly Editions, Modern Language Association of America. They are clear-text editions and bear the Center's seal as "An Approved Edition."

EDWARD C. MOORE

Indianapolis
January 1983

Acknowledgments

We are indebted to Indiana University, the National Endowment for the Humanities, and the National Science Foundation, for their continuing support of the Peirce Edition Project; to the Harvard University Department of Philosophy for permission to use the original manuscripts, and to the officers of the Houghton Library, where the Charles S. Peirce Papers are kept, for their cooperation; to the John Rylands University Library of Manchester and the Hoose Library of Philosophy at the University of Southern California for permission to reprint Peirce's letters to W. S. Jevons and W. T. Harris, respectively; to the Interlibrary Loan department of Indiana University-Purdue University at Indianapolis for continued good service; to Jean Umiker-Sebeok and Urszula Niklas for preparing the index; to James A. Moore for invaluable services as research associate in the Project; to Webb Dordick for his research assistance in the Harvard libraries; and to all those scholars who have given us expert help at particular points, especially to Arthur W. Burks, Donald E. Buzzelli, Joseph L. Esposito, Kenneth L. Ketner, Edward H. Madden, John J. O'Meara, Marc Rothenberg, Eleonore Stump, Victor E. Thoren, and Allan B. Wolter.

For permission to use duplicates of its annotated electroprint copy of Peirce's manuscripts—the next best thing to the originals—we are indebted to the Institute for Studies in Pragmaticism at Texas Tech University.

Introduction

I

The Decisive Year and Its Early Consequences

MAX H. FISCH

The most decisive year of Peirce's professional life, and one of the most eventful, was 1867.

Superintendent Bache of the Coast Survey had been incapacitated by a stroke in the summer of 1864. He died on 17 February 1867. Benjamin Peirce became the third Superintendent on 26 February and continued in that position into 1874. He retained his professorship at Harvard and, except for short stays in Washington, he conducted the business of Superintendent from Cambridge. Julius E. Hilgard served as Assistant in Charge of the Survey's Washington office. On 1 July 1867 Charles was promoted from Aide to Assistant, the rank next under that of Superintendent. He continued in that rank for twenty-four and a half years, through 31 December 1891.

National and international awareness of the Survey was extended by two related episodes beginning in 1867. A treaty with Russia for the purchase of Alaska, negotiated by Secretary of State William Henry Seward, was approved by the Senate on 9 April, but the House delayed action on the appropriation necessary to complete the transaction. Superintendent Peirce was asked to have a reconnaissance made of the coast of Alaska, and a compilation of the most reliable information obtainable concerning its natural resources. A party led by Assistant George Davidson sailed from San Francisco on 21 July 1867 and returned 18 November 1867. Davidson's report of 30 November was received by Superintendent Peirce in January, reached President Johnson early in February, and was a principal document in his message of 17 February to the House of Representatives, recommending the appropriation. The bill was finally enacted and signed by the President in July.

Charles's younger brother, Benjamin Mills Peirce, returned in the summer of 1867 from two years at the School of Mines in Paris. Seward wished to explore the possibility of purchasing Iceland and Greenland from Denmark. His expansionist supporter Robert J. Walker consulted Superintendent Peirce, who had his son Ben compile *A Report on the Resources of Iceland and Greenland* which he submitted on 14 December 1867, and which his father submitted to Seward on the 16th. With a foreword by Walker, it was published in book form next year by the Department of State. But congressional interest in *acquiring* the islands was insufficient and no action was taken.[1]

Joseph Winlock had become the third Director of the Harvard College Observatory in 1866, and working relations between the Survey and the Observatory became closer than they had previously been. (Winlock had been associated with the *American Ephemeris and Nautical Almanac* from its beginning in 1852, and for the last several years had been its Superintendent, residing in Cambridge. Benjamin Peirce had been its Consulting Astronomer from the beginning. Charles had done some work for it in recent years. Assistant William Ferrel and he had observed the annular eclipse of the sun at St. Joseph, Missouri, 19 October 1865, and both had submitted written reports to Winlock which are still preserved.) By arrangement with Winlock, Charles began in 1867 to make observations at the Observatory that were reported in subsequent volumes of its *Annals*. In 1869 he was appointed an Assistant in the Observatory, where, as in the Survey, the rank of Assistant was next to that of Director.

In 1867 the Observatory received its first spectroscope. Among the most immediately interesting of the observations it made possible were those of the auroral light. In volume 8 of the *Annals* it was reported that "On April 15, 1869, the positions of seven bright lines were measured in the spectrum of the remarkable aurora seen that evening; the observer being Mr. C. S. Peirce."

By that time, Peirce had begun reviewing scientific, mathematical and philosophical books for the *Nation*. His second review was of Roscoe's *Spectrum Analysis,* on 22 July 1869, and it was both as chemist and as astronomer that he reviewed it. With Winlock's permission, he reported that

---

[1]Ben began a promising career as a mining engineer at Marquette, Michigan, but died near there at the early age of twenty-six, on 22 April 1870.

In addition to the green line usually seen in the aurora, six others were discovered and measured at the Harvard College Observatory during the brilliant display of last spring, and four of these lines were seen again on another occasion. On the 29th of June last, a single narrow band of auroral light extended from east to west, clear over the heavens, at Cambridge, moving from north to south. This was found to have a continuous spectrum; while the fainter auroral light in the north showed the usual green line.[2]

Peirce was a contributor to the *Atlantic Almanac* for several years, beginning with the volume for 1868. In that for 1870 he had, among other things, an article on "The Spectroscope," the last paragraph of which was devoted to the spectrum of the aurora borealis and the newly discovered lines.

As an Assistant both in the Survey and in the Observatory, Peirce was an observer of two total eclipses of the sun, at Bardstown, Kentucky, 7 August 1869, and near Catania, Sicily, 22 December 1870. And as late as 1894 he would write: "Of all the phenomena of nature, a total solar eclipse is incomparably the most sublime. The greatest ocean storm is as nothing to it; and as for an annular eclipse, however close it may come to totality, it approaches a complete eclipse not half so near as a hurdy-gurdy a cathedral organ."

In 1871 the Observatory acquired a Zöllner astrophotometer and Winlock made Peirce responsible for planning its use. More of that in our next volume. And in 1871 Peirce's father obtained authorization from Congress for a transcontinental geodetic survey along the 39th parallel, to connect the Atlantic and Pacific coastal surveys. This led to Charles's becoming a professional geodesist and metrologist; but that too is matter for the third and later volumes. Back now to 1867.

One of the most famous cases that ever came to trial was the Sylvia Ann Howland will case, and the most famous of the many famous things about it was the testimony of the Peirces, 5 and 6 June 1867. The questions at issue were (1) whether Miss Howland's signatures to the two copies of the "second page" codicil of an earlier will were genuine, or were forged by tracing her signature to the will itself, and (2) whether, supposing them genuine, the codicil invalidated a later will much less favorable to her niece, Hetty H. Robinson. The Peirces addressed themselves to the first of these questions. Under his father's direction, Charles examined photographic enlargements of forty-two genuine signatures for coinci-

[2]P. 288 below.

dences of position in their thirty downstrokes. In 25,830 different comparisons of downstrokes, he found 5,325 coincidences, so that the relative frequency of coincidence was about a fifth. Applying the theory of probabilities, his father calculated that a coincidence of genuine signatures as complete as that between the signatures to the codicil, or between either of them and that to the will in question, would occur only once in five-to-the-thirtieth-power times. The judge was not prepared to base his decision on the theory of probabilities, but he decided against Miss Robinson on the second issue.[3] In the *Nation* for 19 September 1867, under the title "Mathematics in Court," there appeared a letter to the editor criticizing Benjamin Peirce's testimony, and a long reply signed *"Ed. Nation"* but written by Chauncey Wright, concluding that "The value of the present testimony depends wholly on the judgment of his son in estimating coincidences, and does not depend on the judgment of either father or son as mathematical experts." In a long article on "The Howland Will Case" in the *American Law Review* for July 1870 it was said that: "Hereafter, the curious stories of Poe will be thought the paltriest imitations."

Through 1867 (and on beyond) Peirce made frequent additions to his library in the history of logic. In March and April he acquired early editions of Duns Scotus. On 1 January 1868 he compiled a "Catalogue of Books on Mediaeval Logic which are available in Cambridge"—more of them in his own library than at Harvard's or anywhere else.

Charles W. Eliot became President of the University on 19 May 1869. Two days later he wrote to George Brush of Yale: "what to build *on top of* the American college. . . . This is what we have all got to think about." His first thought was to try turning the University Lectures into sequences running through the academic year, with optional comprehensive examinations on each sequence at the end of the year. He arranged two such sequences for 1869–70; one in philosophy, the other in modern literature. For philosophy he enlisted Francis Bowen, John Fiske, Peirce, F. H. Hedge, J. Elliott Cabot, Emerson, and G. P. Fisher, in that order. Peirce's fifteen lectures, from 14 December to 15 January, were on the history of logic in Great Britain from Duns Scotus to Mill. William James at-

---

[3]Nevertheless, she married Edward H. Green later in 1867 and, as Hetty Green, was on her way to becoming "the witch of Wall Street."

tended at least his seventh, on nominalism from Ockham to Mill, and wrote next day to his friend Henry P. Bowditch that "It was delivered without notes, and was admirable in matter, manner and clearness of statement. . . . I never saw a man go into things so intensely and thoroughly." The Graduate School was not established until 1890, with James Mills ("Jem") Peirce, Charles's older brother, as Dean; but the experiment of 1869–70 was later called "The Germ of the Graduate School."[4]

Back again to 1867. On 30 January Peirce was elected a Resident Fellow of the American Academy of Arts and Sciences. He presented three papers to the Academy at its meetings of 12 March, 9 April, and 14 May, and two further papers at those of 10 September (read by title only) and 13 November. The volume of the Academy's *Proceedings* which included all five of these papers did not appear until the following year, but by November 1867 Peirce had obtained collective offprints of the first three under the title "Three Papers on Logic" and had begun distributing them. He began receiving responses early in December.[5]

The first philosophical journal in the United States—indeed the first in English anywhere—was the quarterly *Journal of Speculative Philosophy,* published in St. Louis and edited by William Torrey Harris. It began with the issue for January 1867. Peirce subscribed at first anonymously through a bookseller. But as soon as the collective offprints of "Three Papers on Logic" were ready, he sent Harris a copy. Harris responded with a letter dated 10 December 1867. He was especially interested in Peirce's third paper, "On a New List of Categories." (Peirce himself as late as 1905 called it "my one contribution to philosophy.") In response to Harris, Peirce wrote a long letter on Hegel which he did not mail and a short letter dated 1 January 1868 which he did mail. Thus began the correspondence that led to five contributions by Peirce to the second volume of the *Journal:* two anonymous exchanges with the editor, and three articles under his own name in response to the editor's challenge to show how on his nominalistic principles "the validity of the laws of logic can be other than inexplicable." (These five contributions are examined in detail by C. F. Delaney in part II of the present introduction.)

---

[4]In the interim, from 1872 to 1890, there had been a small "Graduate Department" and Jem, as secretary of the Academic Council, had been its administrator.
[5]He later obtained and distributed collective offprints of the fourth and fifth papers.

In giving the title "Nominalism *versus* Realism" to the first exchange, Harris obviously meant to call Peirce a nominalist and Hegel and himself (and other followers of Hegel) realists. Peirce did not disclaim the nominalism. But was he a *professing* nominalist, and did Harris know that he was? And, if so, *how* did he know it?

That question takes us back again to 1867. At the end of the first of his "Three Papers on Logic" Peirce advocated a theory of probability for a fuller account of which he referred to his review of Venn's *Logic of Chance.* In that review he called it the nominalistic theory, as opposed to the realistic and conceptualistic theories. But Venn, though he used the latter two terms, *nowhere* used the terms nominalism, nominalistic, or nominalist. (The terms he did use are "material" and "phenomenalist.") Evidently, therefore, Peirce wished to make his own commitment to nominalism unmistakable.

When did Peirce *become* a professing nominalist? Probably in 1851, about the time of his twelfth birthday, when he read Whately's *Elements of Logic.*

Where is the evidence in volume 1 of the present edition that he was a professing nominalist during the period of that volume? In what he says about the falsity of scholastic realism on pages 307 and 312 and in other relevant passages on pages 287, 306, and 360.[6] And that he was still a professing nominalist when he began drafting his *Journal of Speculative Philosophy* articles, commonly called his "cognition series," appears from what he says on pages 175, 180 and 181 of the present volume: "Thus, we obtain a theory of reality which, while it is nominalistic, inasmuch as it bases universals upon signs, is yet quite opposed to that individualism which is often sup-

[6]This is a good point at which to remind our readers that even a twenty-volume edition of Peirce's writings is only an anthology, and that statements about his views based on the anthology may be falsified (or at least may seem to be falsified) by writings it omits. Our first volume, for very good reasons, omits MS 52 (921). If it had been included, it would have come between pages 33 and 37. Past the middle of it there is a leaf whose recto was headed at first "Of Realism & Nominalism. 1859 July 25." The "& Nominalism" was later deleted. The recto continues:

It is not that Realism is false; but only that the Realists did not advance in the spirit of the scientific age. Certainly our ideas are as real as our sensations. We talk of an unrealized idea. That idea has an existence as neumenon in our minds as certainly as its realization has such an existence out of our minds. They are in the same case. An idea I define to be the neumenon of a conception.

That is all. But on the verso there is a "List of Horrid Things I am." They are: Realist, Materialist, Transcendentalist, Idealist. Why did Peirce delete "& Nominalism"? We can only guess. He was not yet twenty. Perhaps he had confused the sense of realism in which it is opposed to idealism with that in which it is opposed to nominalism, but settled on the former.

posed to be coextensive with nominalism." "Now the nominalistic element of my theory is certainly an admission that nothing out of cognition and signification generally, has any generality. . . ." "If this seems a monstrous doctrine, remember that my nominalism saves me from all absurdity."

But in the published form of the second article, in the paragraph on page 239 of the present volume, Peirce unobtrusively takes his first step from nominalism toward realism.[7] "But it follows that since no cognition of ours is absolutely determinate, generals must have a real existence. Now this scholastic realism is usually set down as a belief in metaphysical fictions"—as Peirce himself had set it down on pages 287, 307, 311 and 312 of our first volume. It is the realism of Scotus to which he now commits himself. He takes a second and much more emphatic step in his Berkeley review three years later. He says there (on page 467 below) that Scotus "was separated from nominalism only by the division of a hair." What *was* the hair that Scotus split, we might ask, and *how* did he split it? Instead, going back once more to 1867 and taking the "New List of Categories" together with the three articles of the cognition series (1868–1869) and the Berkeley review (1871), let us ask what hairs *Peirce* split and how *he* split them.

As we remarked on page xxvi of the introduction to volume 1, Peirce's "is the first list of categories that opens the way to making the general theory of signs fundamental in logic, epistemology, and metaphysics." We may add here that the "New List" together with the cognition series and the Berkeley review—five papers in all, and all five contained in the present volume—are now recognized as constituting the modern founding of semeiotic, the general theory of signs, for *all* the purposes of such a theory.[8]

Now for the hairsplitting. The Berkeley review is much more emphatic than the cognition series on the distinction between the

[7]For details see Max H. Fisch, "Peirce's Progress from Nominalism toward Realism," *Monist* 51(1967):159–78, at 160–65.

[8]For details see Max H. Fisch, "Peirce's General Theory of Signs," in *Sight, Sound, and Sense,* edited by Thomas A. Sebeok (Bloomington: Indiana University Press, 1978), pp. 31–70 at 33–38 and, for Berkeley, pp. 57, 63, 65. For Peirce's early nominalism and its probable derivation from Whately, see also pp. 60–63. (It is worth adding here that Boole in *An Investigation of the Laws of Thought* after an introductory first chapter begins the investigation with Chapter II "Of Signs in General, and of the Signs appropriate to the science of Logic in particular; also of the Laws to which that class of signs are Subject"; and that Chapter III is headed "Derivation of the Laws of the Symbols of Logic from the Laws of the Operations of the Human Mind.")

forward and the backward reference of the term "reality" and the identification of nominalism with the backward and of realism with the forward reference. Which amounts to a semeiotic resolution of the controversy. Of the three central categories, quality is monadic, relation dyadic, and representation irreducibly triadic. The sign represents an object to or for an interpretant. But we may focus on the sign-object or on the sign-interpretant. If the question is whether there are real universals, the nominalists turn backward to the sign-object and do not find them; the realists turn forward to the sign-interpretant and find them (pp. 467 ff. below). That is primarily because the backward reference to the object is more individualistic, and the forward reference to the interpretant is more social. So realism goes with what has been called the social theory of logic, or "logical socialism."[9] If we were selecting key sentences from the Peirce texts in the present volume, they might well include these two: (1) "Thus, the very origin of the conception of reality shows that this conception essentially involves the notion of a COMMUNITY, without definite limits, and capable of an indefinite increase of knowledge" (p. 239). (2) "Whether men really have anything in common, so that the *community* is to be considered as an end in itself, and if so, what the relative value of the two factors is, is the most fundamental practical question in regard to every public institution the constitution of which we have it in our power to influence" (p. 487).

The forward reference and the community emphasis owed something to Charles's wife Zina. By 1865 they were settled in a home of their own at 2 Arrow Street in Cambridge, and it remained their home throughout the period of the present volume. Arrow Street shot eastward from Bow Street into what was then Main Street but is now Massachusetts Avenue. The Arrow Street years were a period of experimentation and productivity for Zina as well as for Charles. Her major concerns were three: (1) reducing the burden of housekeeping drudgery for married women, (2) creating institutions to give women a voice in public affairs without their having to compete with men, and (3) higher education for women. For the first she

---

[9]Karl-Otto Apel, *Charles S. Peirce: From Pragmatism to Pragmaticism,* translated by John Michael Krois (Amherst: University of Massachusetts Press, 1981), pp. 53, 90, 153, 196, 213n107. Gerd Wartenberg, *Logischer Sozialismus: Die Transformation der Kantschen Transzendentalphilosophie durch Charles S. Peirce* (Frankfurt: Suhrkamp, 1971).

advocated "Co-operative Housekeeping" in a series of five articles in the *Atlantic Monthly* from November 1868 through March 1869, when Charles's *Journal of Speculative Philosophy* series was appearing. Her articles reappeared in book form in Edinburgh and London in 1870. She also took a leading part in the organization of the short-lived Cambridge Co-operative Housekeeping Society, which rented the old Meacham House on Bow Street for its meetings as well as for its laundry, store, and kitchen. For her second concern, she was active in the movement for a "Woman's Parliament" and was elected president of its first convention in New York City, on 21 October 1869. That movement was still active under the name of "The Women's Congress" at least as late as 1877. For her third concern, she was one of the organizers of the Woman's Education Association of Boston, and her work in it was part of the pre-history of Radcliffe College.

Though Charles never became active in politics, he was an advocate of proportional representation. Zina made notes of his conversations with her about it, and published his views in two of her later books.

Though Zina was not a scientist, she did become a member of the international scientific community by serving, like Charles, as an observer near Catania in Sicily of the total eclipse of the sun on 22 December 1870 and by the inclusion of her excellent account of it in the annual report of the Coast Survey for that year.

Zina's younger sister Amy Fay was a gifted pianist who, after the best training that could be had in New England, studied in Germany from 1869 to 1875 under several of its best teachers, including Tausig, Kullak, and Deppe in Berlin and Liszt in Weimar. By visiting her in Germany and by reading her long and frequent letters home, Zina and Charles became vicarious members of the international community of musicians. Zina published selections from the letters in the *Atlantic Monthly* for April and October 1874, and later a more comprehensive collection in book form, in a single chronological order, under the title *Music-Study in Germany*. It went through more than twenty editions, was translated into French and German, and is still in print. The first twelve chapters come within the period of the present volume. One of them contains a vivid account of the five days that Amy and Charles spent in Dresden in August 1870.

Within the period of the present volume Peirce became acquainted with modern German experimental psychology, as represented by Weber, Fechner, Wundt, and Helmholtz. By 1869 he was already contemplating experiments of the kind he carried out with Jastrow in 1884, which made him the first modern experimental psychologist on the American continent. He sent Wundt copies of his *Journal of Speculative Philosophy* papers and asked permission to translate Wundt's *Vorlesungen über die Menschen- und Thierseele*, to which he refers in appreciative terms on page 307 below. Wundt's reply thanking him for the papers and granting the permission was dated at Heidelberg 2 May 1869. No translation by Peirce was published, and no drafts have been found. A translation of the much revised edition of 1892 was published by J. E. Creighton and E. B. Titchener in 1894 and reviewed by Peirce in the *Nation*. When Helmholtz visited New York City in 1893, Peirce had a visit with him, and his long obituary of Helmholtz in 1894 was reprinted in Pollak's 1915 anthology of the *Nation*'s first fifty years.

Back now to logic. In his Harvard University Lectures on the logic of science in the spring of 1865, a few months after the death of George Boole, Peirce had said that Boole's 1854 *Investigation of the Laws of Thought* "is destined to mark a great epoch in logic; for it contains a conception which in point of fruitfulness will rival that of Aristotle's *Organon*" (W1:224). In the first of his fifteen Harvard University Lectures of 1869–70 on "British Logicians," before turning to medieval nominalism and realism, Peirce said, according to the notes of one of his students, that there was enough in Boole to "take the whole time" of the course. By 1877 the British mathematician and philosopher W. K. Clifford was ready to say that "Charles Peirce . . . is the greatest living logician, and the second man since Aristotle who has added to the subject something material, the other man being George Boole, author of *The Laws of Thought*."[10]

What was the "something material" that Peirce had added? That takes us back once more to 1867, for it certainly included "On an Improvement in Boole's Calculus of Logic." What else? At the very least, and above everything else, the most difficult and, at least for logicians and for historians of logic, the most important paper in the present volume: "Description of a Notation for the Logic of Relatives, resulting from an Amplification of the Conceptions of Boole's Calculus of Logic" (DNLR).[11] But is it not the case that, though the

---

[10]John Fiske, *Edward Livingston Youmans* (New York: D. Appleton and Co., 1894), p. 340. (From a letter of Youmans reporting a visit with Clifford.)
[11]See part three of the present introduction, by Daniel D. Merrill, and the literature there referred to.

logic of relations can be traced back at least to Aristotle, De Morgan was the first logician to invent a notation for it? And was not that in 1860, a decade before Peirce's memoir? Yes, but as soon as Peirce's memoir began to circulate, there was room for the question whether De Morgan's notation might be a dead end. In his obituary of De Morgan, Peirce said (p. 450 below) "it may at least be confidently predicted that the logic of relatives, which he was the first to investigate extensively, will eventually be recognized as a part of logic." He did *not* predict, however, that it would be in De Morgan's notation that it would achieve that recognition. But was not the Boole-Peirce-Schröder line in logic superseded by the Frege-Peano-Russell-Whitehead line? No; it was only eclipsed.

Even more intimately than with Boole and De Morgan, Peirce associated his DNLR with his father's *Linear Associative Algebra*. The two appeared at almost the same time, midway between two total eclipses of the sun, but the connections between them did not become fully apparent until, after his father's death in 1880, Peirce prepared a second edition of the LAA, with an addendum by his father and two addenda by himself, and with well over a hundred footnotes to the original text, in over sixty of which he supplied translations from the LAA formulas into DNLR formulas.

Peirce's father had been one of the founding members of the National Academy of Sciences in 1863. Beginning in 1867, he presented instalments of the LAA at meetings of the Academy.[12] Charles's focus on the logic of relations went back to his earliest work on his categories. A logician who had only three central categories —Quality, Relation, and Representation—was bound to return again and again to the logic of relations. Recall, for example, his remarks about equiparant and disquiparant relations in volume 1, and note what he says about mathematical syllogisms on 42 f. below. But his earliest published mention of De Morgan's paper of 1860 was written late in 1868 (p. 245n2), and he may not have seen that paper more than a few weeks earlier. So the actual composing of the DNLR may have begun in 1869.

Then, on 7 August 1869, came the first of the two eclipses. It was observed by several teams at several points along the line of totality. Peirce and Shaler were stationed at Bardstown, Kentucky. Their

---

[12]At a meeting of the much older American Academy of Arts and Sciences on 12 October 1869, "Professor Peirce made a communication on his investigations in Linear Algebra."

report, one of the most vivid as well as detailed, was submitted by
Peirce to Winlock, included in Winlock's report to Superintendent
Peirce, and published by him in the Survey's Annual Report. It reap-
pears on pages 290–93 below. A quarter of a century later, in an
unpublished paper entitled "Argon, Helium, and Helium's Partner,"
Peirce gave an equally vivid retrospective account (Robin MS 1036).

I remember, as if it were yesterday, the first time I saw helium. It was in
1869. Astronomical spectroscopy was then in its earliest infancy. . . . It was
impossible in those early days, for the same observer to point his telescope
and to use the spectroscope; so I had brought along with me the Kentuckian
geologist Shaler, a man of nerve and proved in war, to bring successively the
different protuberances of the sun upon the slit of my spectroscope, while
I examined the spectrum and recognized what I could. . . .

The observations of the sun's corona and protuberances by the
Peirce-Shaler and other teams prompted new theories as to the composition of the sun, but there was some skepticism about these theories among European astronomers. The earliest opportunity for a test
of them would be the eclipse of 22 December 1870, whose path of
totality was to pass through the Mediterranean. It was desirable that
as many as possible of the American observers of the 1869 eclipse
should be observers of the 1870 one also, and Peirce's father began
making plans to bring that about. One of these plans was to have
Charles follow the path of totality from east to west several months
in advance, inspecting possible sites for observation parties, reporting to his father and to Winlock, and making tentative preliminary
arrangements. But if Charles was to be in Europe for six or more
months and his father for two or more, those interruptions might be
detrimental to the major works they had in progress. It would be
advantageous to finish them before leaving, and even more advantageous to take published copies with them, each of the other's work
as well as his own, and get them that much sooner into the hands of
the mathematicians and logicians they hoped to be meeting.
    At the 616th meeting of the American Academy, on 26 January
1870, as reported by Chauncey Wright, its Recording Secretary,
"The President . . . communicated by title . . . a paper 'On the
Extension of Boole's System to the Logic of Relations by C. S.
Peirce'." Late in the spring, Peirce supplied final copy; it was set in
type and he was given fifty copies in paperback quarto book form,
dated Cambridge 1870, "Extracted from the Memoirs of the Ameri-

can Academy, Vol. IX," though that volume did not appear until three years later.

Also late in the spring, since the National Academy, only seven years old, had as yet no funds for printing the papers or books its members presented, Julius E. Hilgard, a fellow member of the Academy, took Superintendent Peirce's manuscript, had it copied in a more ornate and legible hand, and then had fifty copies lithographed from it.

When Charles sailed from New York on 18 June 1870, he took with him copies of the lithographed book and the printed memoir. In London on 11 July he delivered one of each, with a covering letter from his father, to De Morgan's residence. On a later day he had a visit with De Morgan, who, unfortunately, was already in the final decline that ended in his death in the following March, eleven days after Charles's return to Cambridge.

Charles presented another copy of the DNLR to W. S. Jevons, from whom he received a letter about it farther along on his eastward journey, to which he replied from Pest on 25 August (pp. 445–47 below).

Directly or indirectly, Robert Harley too received a copy. At the Liverpool meeting of the British Association for the Advancement of Science in September, Harley first presented "Observations on Boole's 'Laws of Thought' by the late R. Leslie Ellis," and then a paper by himself "On Boole's 'Laws of Thought'" (continuing one he had presented four years earlier), in which, after reviewing recent works by Jevons, Tait, and Brodie, he said: "But the most remarkable amplification of Boole's conceptions which the author has hitherto met with is contained in a recent paper by Mr. C. S. Peirce, on the 'Logic of Relatives'." He proceeds to quote the passage on "the three grand classes" of logical terms that appears on pages 364–65 below, and then the sentence that appears on page 359: "Boole's logical algebra has such singular beauty, so far as it goes, that it is interesting to inquire whether it cannot be extended over the whole realm of formal logic, instead of being restricted to that simplest and least useful part of the subject, the logic of absolute terms, which, when he wrote, was the only formal logic known." "The object of Mr. Peirce's paper," he went on, "is to show that this extension is possible," and he gave some account of the notation and processes employed.

So Clifford was not alone in thinking that Peirce was "the second man since Aristotle." He was present at the meeting and spoke "On an Unexplained Contradiction in Geometry." He and Peirce may have met in London in July, and he too may then have received a copy of DNLR. If not, they almost certainly met as eclipse observers near Catania in December. In any case, they became well acquainted not later than 1875.

Two brief examples now of Benjamin Peirce's distribution of copies of LAA. In Berlin, on his way to Sicily in November, he gave two copies to our ambassador, his old friend and former colleague, the historian George Bancroft; one for himself and one to present to the Berlin Academy, of which he was a member. And in January, after the eclipse, he addressed the London Mathematical Society on the methods he had used in his LAA, and presented a copy to the Society. Clifford was present and proposed the name "quadrates" for the class of the algebras that includes quaternions, and the Peirces adopted the proposal.

From London in the last week of July 1870, shortly after the Vatican Council had declared the conditions of papal infallibility, and just as the Franco-Prussian War began, Charles journeyed eastward by way of Rotterdam, Berlin, Dresden, Prague, Vienna, Pest, the Danube, and the Black Sea, to Constantinople. Then he began moving westward along the path of totality in search of eligible sites. (He recommended sites in Sicily and southern Spain, and became himself a member of one of the Sicilian teams.) In Berlin he visited Amy Fay, and she accompanied him to Dresden, chiefly for visits to the great art museum there. In Vienna, the director of the Observatory was hospitable and helpful. From Pest, he wrote the letter to Jevons. In Constantinople he enjoyed the guidance of Edward H. Palmer, "the most charming man" he had so far known, and of Palmer's friend Charles Drake; and he began the study of Arabic. In Thessaly he found the English consul most helpful, and the impressions he formed there he later worked up into "A Tale of Thessaly" of which he gave several readings. From Chambéry in Savoy, after his visit to Spain, he wrote to his mother on 16 November 1870, five weeks before the eclipse, that he had heard eighteen distinct languages spoken, seventeen of them (including Basque) in places where they were the languages of everyday speech.

On the whole, the American observations and inferences of the preceding year were vindicated. This was Peirce's first experience of large-scale international scientific cooperation. He had already committed himself to the social theory of logic, but this experience and those of his four later European sojourns confirmed him in that commitment.

Julius E. Hilgard, the Assistant in Charge of the Survey's Washington Office, which included the Office of Weights and Measures until the creation of the National Bureau of Standards in 1901, was to spend several months in Europe in mid-1872. Among other duties, he was to represent the United States at a Paris conference looking toward the international bureau of weights and measures which was finally established there in 1875. Peirce was to substitute for Hilgard in his absence, and that called for several weeks of previous training under Hilgard's supervision. He spent most of December 1871 and part of January 1872 at the new quarters of the Survey in the elegant Richards Building on Capitol Hill, where the Longworth House Office Building now stands. Hilgard gave good reports of his progress.

Hilgard's European sojourn would of course enhance his qualifications for succeeding Peirce's father as Superintendent of the Survey. Peirce's training and experience would qualify him to succeed Hilgard in case of Hilgard's death or resignation or promotion to Superintendent. It would even qualify him, under conceivable future circumstances, to be considered for the superintendency.

The Philosophical Society of Washington (in whose name, as in that of the American Philosophical Society in Philadelphia, "philosophical" meant scientific) had held its first meeting on 13 March 1871. At its 17th meeting, on 16 December 1871, Charles presented the first of the six wide-ranging papers he presented to that Society. It was "On the Appearance of Encke's Comet as Seen at Harvard College Observatory."

Charles's father was to address the Cambridge Scientific Club on 28 December 1871 on the application of mathematics to certain questions in political economy, such as price and amount of sale, and the conditions of a maximum. Charles undertook to prepare diagrams for his father to exhibit at that meeting, and these were mailed to Cambridge on or about the 19th.

Simon Newcomb, then at the Naval Observatory, called on Charles on the 17th and they conversed about these matters. (Fifteen years later Newcomb published a book entitled *Principles of Political Economy* on which Charles commented adversely.) In the evening after the visit Charles wrote Newcomb a letter explaining what he had meant by saying that the law of supply and demand holds only for unlimited competition, and concluded: "P.S. This is all in Cournot." (On the strength of this letter, Baumol and Goldfeld recently included Peirce among their *Precursors in Mathematical Economics.*) In the same evening, Charles wrote to his wife Zina, who had remained in Cambridge, that he had been spending his evenings on political economy, and gave her some account of the questions he had been pursuing. On the 19th, he wrote a letter to his father, beginning: "There is one point on which I get a different result from Cournot, and it makes me suspect the truth of the proposition that the seller puts his price so as to make his profits a maximum."[13]

Charles's own principal contribution to economics, his 1877 "Note on the Theory of the Economy of Research," will be included in our next volume, but these three letters are evidence that he brought to that particular topic a more general competence in economic theory.

But what, finally, of the Metaphysical Club at Cambridge, in which pragmatism was born? According to the best evidence we now have, it was founded not later than January 1872, after Peirce's return from Washington. The introduction to volume 3 will resume the story at that point. But from a consecutive and careful reading of the present volume it will already be evident that pragmatism was the natural and logical next step.

II

The Journal of Speculative Philosophy Papers

C. F. DELANEY

The *Journal of Speculative Philosophy* papers of 1868–69 fall into two quite distinct groups. The first set is composed of a series of interchanges between C. S. Peirce and W. T. Harris (the editor of the journal) on issues of logic and speculative metaphysics that emerge from the philosophy of Hegel. The second set of papers, quite differ-

---

[13]Cf. Carolyn Eisele, *Studies in the Scientific and Mathematical Philosophy of Charles S. Peirce* (The Hague: Mouton, 1979), pp. 58 f., 251 f., and *The New Elements of Mathematics by Charles S. Peirce,* edited by Carolyn Eisele (The Hague: Mouton, 1976), 3:xxiii–xxvii.

ent in tone, consists of Peirce's classic papers on cognition and reality, and the relatively neglected concluding paper of the series on the grounds of validity of the laws of logic.

1.

The Peirce-Harris exchange on Hegelian logic and metaphysics was occasioned by Harris's review article entitled "Paul Janet and Hegel" which appeared in his own journal. This was a long critical review of Janet's *Etudes sur la dialectique dans Platon et dans Hegel*, published in Paris in 1860. The exchange itself consists of letters from Peirce to Harris, two of which the latter transformed into dialectically structured discussion articles for his journal.

After some extensive preliminaries about the spread of Hegelianism, the original Harris article (like Janet's book that it reviews) focuses on Hegel's logic and follows Janet's tripartite division into "The Beginning," "The Becoming," and "The Dialectic." In the section labeled "The Becoming" Harris takes issue with Janet's account of the relation of Being and Nothing and the consequent genesis of Becoming. This is the problem that interested Peirce, and in his initial letter (24 January 1868) he takes issue with Harris's own account of the matter. These comments, together with his own replies, Harris published under the title "Nominalism *versus* Realism."

Peirce's criticisms take the form of five inquiries seeking clarification. Initially he raises some general questions about Harris's doctrine of abstraction; then he raises three sets of questions about what he understands to be Harris's three arguments for the identity of Being and Nothing; finally he suggests, contrary to what he takes to be Harris's view, that the ordinary logical strictures against contradiction should at least have the presumption in their favor. Harris's response to these criticisms is most interesting, particularly in the light of Peirce's mature philosophy. He maintains that the tone of Peirce's initial set of questions about abstraction suggests that Peirce is committed both to nominalism and to a doctrine of immediacy, and that Peirce's consequent specific criticisms of his three arguments bear his suspicion out. Peirce's specific objections draw on formal logic's strictures against contradiction which, Harris maintains, are only adequate to the immediate world of independent things. But, Harris concludes, if one is to be a true speculative philosopher one must transcend this nominalism and become a realist.

Needless to say, Peirce thought that this response totally missed the point. In his follow-up letter, he makes the suggestion that a great deal of the misunderstanding between them may flow from certain unclarities with regard to the term "determined" as it functions in the discussion of Being and its determinations. He distinguishes several senses of "determine," "abstract," and "contradiction" in an attempt to move the discussion forward. Again, Harris published these comments together with his own terse responses, this time under the title "What Is Meant by 'Determined'."

One of the most obvious characteristics of this interchange on Hegel's logic is the marked difference between Harris's sympathy with the dialectical logic of the Hegelian tradition and Peirce's employment of ordinary formal logic. Harris's request that Peirce do something for his journal on the rationale of the objective validity of the laws of logic is a happy outgrowth of this basic difference between the two. In his letter of 9 April 1868 Peirce responds that he has already devoted considerable time to this subject and could not adequately treat the issue in less than three articles. He enclosed the first of his three classic 1868 papers on cognition.

2.

Peirce's 1868 papers on cognition, reality, and logical validity bring up the questions that were to be central throughout his whole philosophical career. In these he articulates his many-faceted attack on the spirit of Cartesianism, a spirit which he sees dominating most of modern philosophy. The Cartesian concern with skeptical doubt, individual justification, immediate knowledge and certainty (which traits he also saw in the empiricists), he seeks to replace by a view of knowledge that was through and through mediate, that construed knowledge as both an historical and communal human activity. From this perspective on knowledge, he proceeds to work through a concept of intersubjectivity to a full-blown account of objectivity, truth, reality, and the basis of the validity of the laws of logic.

The first piece included here is MS 148, consisting of three separately titled sections listed as "Questions on Reality" in the Contents. The third section, entitled "Questions concerning Reality," is an early version of the first published paper in the series, "Questions Concerning Certain Faculties Claimed for Man," but it is most interesting in its own right. In the first place, it is an heroic attempt to handle in a unified way all the issues that would eventually be divided among the three published papers in the 1868–69 series. The unity of the overall project is brought out forcefully in the introductory paragraph of the piece. Here Peirce makes the point that the logician's initial concern is with *the forms of language* but that he must inevitably push on from here to consider what we think, that is, *the manner of reality itself;* and, as a precondition for this inquiry, must get clear about the proper method for ascertaining *how we think.* His order of treatment, then, is, first, to give an account of cognition; secondly, to give an account of truth and reality; and, finally, to deal with some issues of formal logic. It is instructive to note that all three of these topics are treated under the general heading "Questions concerning Reality," indicating a metaphysical thrust that might be overlooked given the final titles: "Questions Concerning Certain Faculties Claimed for Man," "Some Consequences of Four Incapacities," and "Grounds of Validity of the Laws of Logic: Further Consequences of Four Incapacities."[14] It is further instructive to glance over the twelve questions Peirce poses for himself in the outline given in the first section of MS 148 and observe how they reappear in the three published pieces.

The first six questions have to do with an account of thinking and with the methodology appropriate in generating such an account; and it is these six questions that make up the substance of the first published paper in the series, "Questions Concerning Certain Faculties Claimed for Man." The central issue is whether we have any immediate knowledge at all (of ourselves, our mental states, or the external world) and Peirce answers in the negative. In the process he distinguishes between intuition (cognition not determined by a previous cognition) and introspection (internal cognition not determined by external cognition) and defends an account of knowledge construed as a thoroughly mediated inferential sign process. A linchpin of his argument is a methodological stance that favors any account of mental activity that abides by the normal conventions of theory construction, a stance which shifts the burden of proof to those accounts wherein some special faculties are claimed for man. Peirce concludes by adding as a novel seventh question some sum-

---

[14]It was probably Peirce's intention to use the title "Questions concerning Reality" for his first published article, but Harris advised against this in a letter of about 15 April 1868, and Peirce replied on 20 April: "Your remark upon my title is very just. I will make it 'Questions concerning certain Faculties claimed for man'."

mary material that appears at the end of "Questions concerning
Reality" dealing with some general arguments against the thesis that
there is no cognition not determined by a previous cognition.

There are two short pieces entitled "Potentia ex Impotentia" also
included here. These are early versions of beginnings of the second
published paper, "Some Consequences of Four Incapacities," and
again are interesting in their own right because of some methodological points therein. First, Peirce makes the general comment that on
the one hand we should begin our philosophizing simply with those
beliefs we have no reason to call into question, but, on the other, we
should not maintain an attitude of certainty on matters concerning
which there is real disagreement among competent persons. In
short, our philosophizing should be continuous with our common-
sense ways of dealing with the world about us. Secondly, he makes
a series of provocative statements about the present state of philosophy and the methods of explanation that should be employed in
philosophy. The state of philosophy he likens to the state of dynamics
before Galileo; namely, a theater of disputation and dialectics with
little by way of established results. In this state, he maintains, what
is called for is not conservative caution (as would have been called
for in mechanics where much was truly established) but rather bold
and sweeping theorizing to break new ground and put the area in
order. Peirce does not mean that our metaphysical speculation
should be uncontrolled and irresponsible but that it should be guided
by the various different tangible facts we have at our disposal without
any pretense to demonstration, certainty, or finality. We should content ourselves with the probable forms of reasoning that are so fruitful in physical science and congratulate ourselves if we thereby reduce the uncertainty in metaphysics to one hundred times that of
these sciences. It is in this spirit of speculation that one should view
the sweeping theory of mental activity he articulates in "Some
Consequences of Four Incapacities."

In the first published paper in this series Peirce had suggested, in
opposition to the Cartesian account, that all knowing involved an
inferential sign process. In the second paper in the series he takes up
the task of articulating in some detail his own theory of the structure
of mental activity, that is, the structure of the internal sign process
that is involved in knowing. Constructing this account, he is guided
by his methodological strictures to the effect that any account of the
internal (mental activity) must be in terms of the external (publicly
accessible objects) and that, given the postulation of one structure,

another is not to be introduced into the theory unless there are facts impossible to explain on the basis of the first.

Focusing on our public sign system, that is, language, as the paradigmatic external manifestation of mental activity, Peirce proceeds to construct an account of mental activity in terms of "inner speech." Furthermore, he develops an holistic form of this tradition in which the basic mental unit is not the concept (the mental *word*) or even the judgment (the mental *sentence*) but rather the process of reasoning itself (the mental *syllogism*). Since it is then the structure (rather than the matter) of the sign process that is of primary importance, Peirce accordingly construes the process as one of drawing inferences, as syllogistic in nature. Next, drawing on his formal accounts of deduction, induction, and hypothesis, he proceeds to give an account not only of thinking but also of the other forms of mental activity (sensation, emotion, and attention) in terms of his syllogistic model. His final extrapolation of the model enables him to give a speculative account of the mind itself.

The third paper in the published series, "Grounds of Validity of the Laws of Logic: Further Consequences of Four Incapacities," picks up some of the remaining questions outlined in MS 148 and finally comes to grips with Harris's original challenge which had been the impetus for all three papers, namely, how can Peirce account for the objective validity of the laws of logic? The theories of cognition and reality were developed for the sake of providing just such an account, an account which begins with a justification of deduction and then broadens out to encompass a philosophical grounding of the general logic of science.

The point of continuity with the previous pieces is Peirce's claim that every cognition results from an inference and that the structure of all mental activity is inferential. Can't the question be raised—what reason do we have to believe that the principles of inference are true or correspond to anything in the real world? While not purporting to take seriously the stance of the absolute skeptic, Peirce does think it incumbent upon him to provide an account of the objective validity of the logical principles of inference. He proceeds to give an account of the validity of deduction, induction, and hypothesis; and his proffered "justifications" invoke the characteristic Peircean concepts of *truth* (as the ultimate agreement of investigators), *reality* (as that which is represented in that agreement), and *community* (as the ultimate ground of both logic and reality).

It would be difficult indeed to overstate the importance of these three papers in the Peircean corpus. That Peirce himself saw them as central is clear from his designation of them as Chapters 4, 5, and 6 of one of his major projected works, the 1893 "Search for a Method." Most later commentators have seen them as the key to his overall philosophical orientation.

III

The 1870 Logic of Relatives Memoir

DANIEL D. MERRILL

Peirce's "Description of a Notation for the Logic of Relatives, Resulting from an Amplification of Boole's Calculus of Logic" (DNLR) is one of the most important works in the history of modern logic, for it is the first attempt to expand Boole's algebra of logic to include the logic of relations. The complex mathematical analogies which govern parts of this work make it obscure in spots; but the main thrust of its important innovations may be seen by placing it in the context of Peirce's earlier logical studies, and by relating it to the work of Boole, De Morgan, and Benjamin Peirce.

The logical substructure of DNLR is a modified version of Boole's algebra of classes, in which Peirce had shown an early interest.[15] One modification is the use of the "inclusive" sense of logical addition, which Peirce had introduced by 1867.[16] The other main modification is the replacement of Boole's equality or identity sign ($=$) by the sign of illation or inclusion ($\prec$) as the sign for the fundamental logical relation. While this replacement may have been primarily dictated by formal considerations, it was an important step on the road to a less algebraic approach to the logic of classes.

To this basically Boolean structure, Peirce adds a notation for relations and for operations upon relations, as well as laws governing those operations. Even then, though, the influence of Boole remains strong. While Peirce admits logical relations between relations, he

---

[15]See Emily Michael, "An Examination of the Influence of Boole's Algebra on Peirce's Development in Logic," *Notre Dame Journal of Formal Logic* 20(1979): 801–6.

[16]See "On an Improvement in Boole's Calculus of Logic," item 2 below, pp. 12–23.

most often considers logical relations that hold between class terms of which relation terms form a part.

Peirce's interest in the logic of relations can be traced to several sources.[17] Published and unpublished papers prepared around 1866 show a strong interest in the problems which relation terms present for the theory of categories.[18] They are also concerned with different types of relations, such as the distinction between relations of equiparance and relations of disquiparance. His work at this time also shows an interest in arguments involving relations and multiple subsumptions. Such an argument is "Everyone loves him whom he treats kindly; James treats John kindly; hence, James loves John." Peirce's early treatment of these arguments is rather conservative, either reformulating them so as to apply the usual syllogistic forms, or using some principle of multiple subsumption which is construed as a natural generalization of the syllogism.

Unfortunately, the origins of the more powerful and, indeed, revolutionary techniques of DNLR are more obscure.[19] Only two surviving documents provide a sustained insight into their origins. One is the so-called Logic Notebook (LN), which carries entries from 3 to 15 November 1868 in which several notations are devised and some basic identities are shown. Only the rudiments of DNLR may be found here. The same is true of the other source, a series of notes that Peirce wrote at about the same time to add to a projected republication of his American Academy papers of 1867. Note 4 in this set shows how an algebraic notation may be used to validate the following argument, which De Morgan had claimed could not be shown to be valid by syllogistic means:

> Every man is an animal.
> Therefore, any head of a man is a head of an animal.

Most unfortunately, the surviving parts of LN have no entries from 16 November 1868 through 5 October 1869, nor is there any other document which would allow us to trace the development of these techniques.

---

[17]See Emily Michael, "Peirce's Early Study of the Logic of Relations, 1865–1867," *Transactions of the Charles S. Peirce Society* 10(1974):63–75.

[18]This interest culminates in "On a New List of Categories," item 4 below, pp. 49–59.

[19]See Daniel D. Merrill, "De Morgan, Peirce and the Logic of Relations" *Transactions of the Charles S. Peirce Society* 14(1978):247–84.

Peirce's references to De Morgan in DNLR, as well as an undated comparison (in LN) between his notation and De Morgan's, raise the question of De Morgan's role in stimulating the work which led to DNLR.[20] It must be noted, though, that there is little direct biographical information on this issue, and that Peirce's later recollections are contradictory and even inconsistent with known facts.

Peirce apparently initiated an exchange of papers with De Morgan in late 1867, as a result of which De Morgan received a copy of Peirce's "Three Papers on Logic" (the first three American Academy papers) by May 1868. In a letter dated 14 April 1868, De Morgan had promised to send Peirce a copy of his classic paper of 1860 on the logic of relations,[21] but there is no direct evidence that this was ever sent. Nevertheless, Peirce had seen De Morgan's paper by late December 1868, since he refers to it in another paper sent to the printer at that time.[22] It is thus very likely that Peirce had read De Morgan's paper before he wrote the entries in LN dated November 1868, even though those entries carry no clear references to De Morgan and use quite different examples.

Biographical issues aside, Peirce's initial work in the logic of relations is significantly different from De Morgan's. The most important difference is that while De Morgan was interested primarily in the composition of relations with relations, Peirce is concerned with the composition of relations with classes. Thus, while De Morgan's paradigm is an expression such as "X is a lover of a servant of Y," Peirce is first concerned with such expressions as "lover of a woman." A predilection for class expressions is found even in DNLR, though this is often combined with the composition of relations, as in "lover of a servant of a woman." This emphasis upon class expressions seems to reflect the Boolean frame of reference in which Peirce was working.

De Morgan also considered two types of "quantified relations." The first is "X is an L of every M of Y," which is expressed by Peirce as "involution," or exponentiation. Even here, the LN shows him more concerned with the composition of a relation and a class, as in

---

[20]Ibid. See also R. M. Martin, "Some Comments on De Morgan, Peirce, and the Logic of Relations," *Transactions of the Charles S. Peirce Society* 12(1976):223–30.

[21]Augustus De Morgan, "On the Syllogism, No. IV, and on the Logic of Relations," *Transactions of the Cambridge Philosophical Society* 10(1864):331–58.

[22]"Grounds of Validity of the Laws of Logic: Further Consequences of Four Incapacities," item 23 below, pp. 242–72.

"lover of every woman," than with strictly relational composition. The other form of quantified relation is "X is an L of none but M of Y," a form which Peirce only considers in the section on "backward involution" which he added to DNLR shortly before it was printed (pp. 400–408).

These comparisons between De Morgan and Peirce make their relationship problematic. It becomes more so in view of the fact that some of De Morgan's most dramatic results involve the contrary and the converse of a relation. While Peirce deals with contraries throughout LN and DNLR, he did not consider converses in the 1868 portions of LN, and he only deals with them in that section of the DNLR which he added at the time of printing.

We may conclude that while Peirce probably knew of De Morgan's memoir on relations when he was working out the full notation of DNLR, his own Boolean orientation meant that he was working on these topics in his own way.

While DNLR is primarily a contribution to logic, parts of it may also be related to the developments in algebra to which his father contributed. During the years 1867–69, Benjamin Peirce presented a series of papers to the National Academy of Sciences which resulted in a book entitled *Linear Associative Algebra* (LAA) which was privately published in 1870, and then republished with notes by C. S. Peirce in 1881.[23] In it Benjamin Peirce surveyed all the types of linear associative algebras which can be constructed with up to seven units, enormously generalizing such algebras as that of complex numbers (of the form a · 1 + bi) and Hamilton's quaternions (a · 1 + bi + cj + dk). In the subsection on Elementary Relatives in DNLR, Peirce conjectured that all linear associative algebras could be expressed in terms of elementary relatives, which he then proved in 1875[24] and illustrated in his notes to his father's book. This technique formed the foundation for the method of linear representation of matrices, which is now part of the standard treatment of the subject.

As in the case of the relationship of the DNLR to De Morgan's paper, its relation to his father's LAA is difficult to estimate accurately. Certainly they were working on these long papers at about the same

[23]*American Journal of Mathematics* 4(1881):97–229, and as a separate volume paged 1–133 (New York: D. Van Nostrand, 1882).
[24]"On the Application of Logical Analysis to Multiple Algebra," *Proceedings of the American Academy of Arts and Sciences* n.s. 2(1874–75):392–94, which will be published in volume 3 of the present edition.

time, so that some influence would not be surprising. In a short letter to his father that has been dated 9 January 1870, Peirce writes:

> I think the following may possibly have some interest to you in connection with your algebras. I have been applying Boole's Calculus to the Logic of *Relative Terms* & in doing so have got (among other operations) an associative non commutative multiplication. It is like this. Let k denote *killer, w wife, m man*. Then
>
> kwm denotes the class of killers of wives of men

The letter then concludes with the colleague-and-teacher example which is found in the Elementary Relatives section of DNLR (pp. 408–11). While this letter shows that Peirce was thinking of his father's work as he completed DNLR, it also suggests that the relationship between the two papers may not be very intimate.

DNLR was communicated to the American Academy of Arts and Sciences on 26 January 1870 and printed in the late spring. The exact time of its printing is uncertain, though it must have been printed by 17 June 1870 when Peirce left for Europe. He carried with him a letter of introduction from his father to De Morgan, to whom he apparently delivered copies of his memoir and his father's book. Although there is no contemporary record of Peirce's visiting De Morgan, he planned to do so and recalled such a meeting in later years. But the meeting could not have been a very happy one, since De Morgan was in very poor health by that time and incapable of sustained logical or mathematical discussion.

The Boolean substructure of DNLR consists of inclusion and the usual Boolean operations of addition $(x +\!\!,\ y)$, multiplication (x,y), and class complementation $(1 - x)$, along with their standard laws. To illustrate the relational notation, let s = servant, l = lover, and w = woman. The most important notations are relative multiplication (sl, servant of a lover), relative involution (s^l, servant of every lover), backward involution (s_l, servant of none but a lover), and converse of a relation ($\mathscr{K}s$, master). Invertible forms of several of these operations are also given. Relation expressions and class expressions may be combined, as in "s^w" (servant of every woman) and "$s^{(lw)}$" (servant of every lover of a woman). Boolean operations may be applied to relations as well as to classes, so that, for instance, "$(s +\!\!,\ l)$" means "either a servant or a lover."[25]

---

[25]For analyses and interpretations of DNLR, see Chris Brink, "On Peirce's Notation for the Logic of Relatives," *Transactions of the Charles S. Peirce Society* 14(1978):

While DNLR is largely devoted to the logic of two-place relations, Peirce also includes a rather confusing discussion of "conjugative terms," which stand for three-place relations. This is a marked advance over De Morgan's restriction to two-place relations, but Peirce's attempts to deal with this topic within the framework of DNLR present many problems of interpretation.

In addition to outlining a notation, DNLR contains a great many principles which may be easily interpreted in the modern logic of relations. Some significant identities are

$$s(m \mathbin{+\!\!,} w) = sm \mathbin{+\!\!,} sw$$
$$(l \mathbin{+\!\!,} s)w = lw \mathbin{+\!\!,} sw$$
$$s,l = l,s$$
$$(s^l)^w = s^{(lw)}$$
$$s^{m \mathbin{+\!\!,} w} = s^m, s^w$$
$$(s,l)^w = s^w, l^w.$$

There are also a great many inclusions, such as

If $a \prec b$ then $ca \prec cb$
If $a \prec b$ then $c^b \prec c^a$,

along with chains of inclusions involving combinations of operations, as in

$$s^w \prec sw$$
and $(ls)^w \prec ls w.$

The complement of a relation is treated not only in a Boolean way, but also as an operation upon a relation, as is the operation of forming the converse of a relation. De Morgan's principles governing these operations are given in Peirce's notation. The universal and null relations are introduced, and their laws are stated.

While Peirce does not attempt to develop the laws of his notation in a deductive manner, he does provide demonstrations of a sort for many of his laws, especially in the section entitled "General Method of Working with this Notation" (pp. 387–417). In the first subsection

285–304; R. M. Martin, "Of Servants, Lovers and Benefactors: Peirce's Algebra of Relatives of 1870," *Journal of Philosophical Logic* 7(1978):27–48; Jacqueline Brunning, "Peirce's Development of the Algebra of Relations," diss. Toronto 1981; and Hans G. Herzberger, "Peirce's Remarkable Theorem," in *Pragmatism and Purpose: Essays Presented to Thomas A. Goudge* (Toronto: University of Toronto Press, 1981), pp. 41–58.

on Individual Terms, many intuitively valid laws are demonstrated by reducing inclusions between classes to individual instances. In addition to its discussion of backward involution and conversion, the subsection on Infinitesimal Relatives contains the most elaborate mathematical analogies in the memoir, with very puzzling applications of such mathematical techniques as functional differentiation and the summation of series. The subsection on Elementary Relatives relates his own work to Benjamin Peirce's linear associative algebras.

For all its importance, the Logic of Relatives memoir presents many problems of interpretation. Perhaps the most serious issue is whether Peirce is dealing with relations or with relatives—that is, with the relation of being a servant, or with such classes as the class of servants or the class of servants of women. His choice of the term "relative" suggests a desire to distinguish his project from De Morgan's, but in some cases his terms clearly stand for relations. The situation is complicated by the fact that many terms, such as "servant," can stand for either a relation or a relative, depending upon the context. Perhaps it is safest to say that he deals with both relational and relative terms, but that he usually treats relational terms within the context of relative terms. While this seems true in general, the interpretation of particular formulas still remains puzzling.

Other serious issues concern his treatment of conjugative terms and his elaborate and obscure mathematical analogies. More generally, one may ask whether DNLR is best studied by translating it into standard symbolic logic or by considering it in its own right. With the benefit of hindsight, DNLR cries out for the modern theory of quantifiers, to which Peirce was to make important contributions. Nevertheless, the core of its notation is of considerable power and can be studied separately. It remains of interest to those modern logicians and mathematicians who have taken an algebraic approach to the study of logic.[26]

[26]Alfred Tarski, "On the Calculus of Relations," *Journal of Symbolic Logic* 6(1941):73–89.

Writings of Charles S. Peirce

Volume 2

[The Logic Notebook]

MS 140: March–December 1867

1867 March 23

I cannot explain the deep emotion with which I open this book again. Here I write but never after read what I have written for what I write is done in the process of forming a conception. Yet I cannot forget that here are the germs of the theory of the categories which is (if anything is) the gift I make to the world. That is my child. In it I shall live when oblivion has me—my body.

This matter of the logical principles of the different kinds of inference is a difficult matter. One way of putting it would be this.

Every symbol denotes certain objects and connotes certain characters. The symbol represents each of those objects to have each of those characters. The symbol may be a false one; it may be that the objects it denotes do not have the characters it connotes. But if *S* is *M* in this sense—not merely that *M* is a name for *S* but that it is the name of a class of things among which *S* is and if *M* is *P* not merely in the sense that———

then *S* is *P*.

Here the principle is that

That which is *M* is what *M* is.

Every one of the integrant parts of *m* is an integrant part of each prime aliquot of *m* and vice versa.

A purely contentless principle. As a logical principle should be.

Now let us take up the synthetic arguments.

Whatever is a character of every thing denoted by *M* is a character of *M*. Whatever has every character of *M* is denoted by *m*.

Here are two principles. But they do not apply to induction and hypothesis just as they stand.

Whatever is a common character of many things denoted by M is likely to be a character of m.

That does not quite hit the point. It does not contain the idea that the things must have been taken at random out of those denoted by M.

In what point of view shall we regard this necessity for a random selection?

Suppose we look at the matter thus. Certain things have a certain character in common. It follows that there *must* be some genus of these things which have the character. We cannot take any genus *lower* than that which they are selected as belonging to. To take a higher one would involve a perfectly arbitrary proposition.

I am convinced that this is a very awkward way of taking hold of the matter.

Suppose we take it up another way.

For any subject or predicate we can substitute what?

Only that which this subject or predicate represents—only that which fulfils the function of that subject or predicate—only that which the subject or predicate represents *to the proposition* or to the other terms of it.

Now a subject is a direct symbol of *its* subject to its predicate and a predicate of its predicate to its subject.

But a subject is also an imperfect representation of that genus from which it has been taken—by which it is determined. It is not a *semeion* sign of it as I have said—it is an example of it.

A predicate is a representation of the thing of which it is a random character—a copy of it.

This is horribly vague.

1867 March 25

Here is another point of view.

What is the function of a symbol as subject? To stand for certain things. Then if a predicate be true of all the things that it stands for as yet, that is for all which we yet know it to stand for, the symbol may stand as subject provisionally.

The difficulty with this is that it does not represent the synthetic probability of the inference.

It is however a good idea that a random selection is equivalent to all known—the genus of those two would fit *that*.

We have

M is *P* in the sense that the *actual* denotation or things taken under *M* are *P* (contingent)

and 2nd in the sense that all possible things taken under *M* would be *P* (necessary).

On the same principle

S is *M* in the senses

> 1st that *S* has the qualities taken of *M* (attributive)
> 2nd that *S* has all qualities of *M* (subsumptive)

Still it may be doubted if Hypothesis proceeds by random selection of qualities of the new predicate.

Then the principle would be

> the possible is like most of the actual.

1867 April 1

What is taken—the present—of a class if it has any common character—that character probably belongs to the class, or to the majority of it. And if what is known of the characters of a thing belong to another thing, the second thing has most of the characters of the first, probably.

The reason is that the parts compose the whole and therefore what does not belong to the majority of the whole does not belong to the majority of the parts.

What does not belong to most of the parts does not belong to the parts taken mostly, because the parts to be taken are all the possible parts.

April 12

The distinction must be observed between Induction and Hypothesis as formal operations and between them as leading to truth.

———

1867 September 24

Let me consider a little about the nature of truth.

First. I notice that if we define an image to be a representation completely determined in content so that in it every attribute is affirmed or denied there is probably no image. And is not this what is requisite to make an image? What is an image? There is a good question for dialectical research.

As it seems to me that the world has not yet exhausted the instruction to be derived from Sophisms I shall undertake some analysis of a collocation of them which seems to me to lead at once to a solution of the darkest questions of metaphysics.

In the first place what is meant by a hypothetical proposition, when is it true? Take this one—If the carotid artery of a man is cut, he will die. Or this—if the shadow of the moon is cast on the earth, there is an eclipse of the sun.

Truth may be defined as the concurrence of the extension and comprehension of a representation which has extension and comprehension independent of one another.

Thus if a representation is a *mere* likeness (as no human representations are) which stands for nothing except what it happens fully to agree with in characters; it cannot be false of any thing because it only stands for whatever it fully agrees with. And therefore truth has no meaning in reference to it.

So if a representation merely points out certain things and implies nothing of them.

But if a representation at once indicates certain objects and independently implies certain characters, its truth or falsity depends on whether those characters can be predicated of those objects.

This definition is a bad one—it contains a diallele—but it will answer as a preliminary explanation and even sometimes as a test.

[First apply what has been said to a categorical.]

Now in a hypothetical proposition the function of the protasis is to mark the *sphere* of the representation, which it may do by means of its connotation or otherwise. The apodosis on the other hand conveys the *content* of the representation. And the question whether the proposition is true is the same as whether that *content* belongs in fact to that sphere. Thus in the proposition—If the shadow of the moon is cast on the earth, the sun is eclipsed—the former clause indicates the circumstances to which the statement made in the latter clause is applicable.

Take now another case. If the motion of the earth in its orbit were suddenly arrested and the perturbative effects of other bodies prevented, it would fall in a direct line to the sun. Unless the word *truth* be taken in a quite improper sense, this proposition is true. Yet how? For in this case there are no such circumstances as those indicated, they are even physically impossible, so that this would seem to be a representation like a copy which [. . .]

1867 Sep. 26

Let *x* be that of which I know absolutely nothing
Then I do know that I know nothing of *x*
Therefore *x* is not *x*.

————

I know Greek. Greek is not present to my reminiscence, but occasion will call it up. This then is the essence of knowledge and what no occasion will call up is not known or conceived. I have therefore no conception of the absolutely unknowable.

Now a proposition is true in all its consequences for possible experience that either *constitutes* the truth of the proposition or it is false in reference to something which cannot be known (in which case the unknowable means something) or else it is devoid of meaning.

A proposition is not devoid of meaning which has true consequences.—

1867 Sep. 27

Every quality which we know of is of course either experienced or inferred from experience. We admit that things may have qualities which we do not know but that is because we may conceive of a state of knowledge in which something more is predicable of them But do we mean anything if we say that a thing has a quality which cannot be predicated of it; that is which is unknowable and inconceivable? What can we mean by such a statement? We can imagine such a quality for as Berkeley says were we to imagine it, it would not be unimaginable. Can we have any general or relative notion of it? To have a general notion appears to be, having a habit according to which a certain sort of images will arise on occasion, that is having a capacity of imaging the particulars and the sense of this habit. But here such a thing is impossible.

Let us say then that it means nothing to say that a thing has an inconceivable quality. An inconceivable quality—one inconceivable by every being and absolutely—is no quality.

> That which has no qualities is nothing.
> ∴ That which is absolutely inconceivable is nothing.

Sep. 28

To say that a word has meaning is to say that a conception corresponds to it.

To say that we have a general conception of a triangle for instance is to say that upon the occasion of a triangle being presented to the imagination or in experience a certain feeling complicated in a certain way arises. We have no conception therefore of that of which no determination can be presented in the imagination.

Consequently, though we may undoubtedly mean something by the inconceivable we can mean nothing by an absolutely and in itself inconceivable predicate.

Hence such a predicate is no predicate.

———

To say that we know what a word means is to say not that we can always apply it rightly in fact but that we can always apply it rightly to imagined cases.

On Logical Extension and Comprehension

———

One term is more extensive than another, when it is predicable of all that the latter is and of more, besides. One term is more comprehensive than another when all the characters predicable of the latter are predicable of it and more beside.

From this it is plain, at once, that the greater the extension the less the comprehension and *vice versa*.

We may distinguish real and verbal Comprehension and extension; thus "Englishman" is more extensive than "Surly Englishman" since it includes also Englishmen not surly. But if there is any doubt whether any of the latter exist, it is only verbally more extensive.

So "magnanimous hero" is more comprehensive than "hero" but if there is a doubt whether anything is conveyed by the adjective not already conveyed by the noun then the difference is merely verbal.

A better instance is "man John" and "man."

Confining our attention to Real Comprehension and Extension, we may observe that the predication spoken of may be either

1st such as could be made with no information except the meaning of the word. This I shall term the Essential Extension and Comprehension.

2nd such as could logically be made in a particular supposed state of information. This I shall term the Inferred Extension and Comprehension.

3rd such as could be made if our information were complete. This I shall term the Natural Extension and Comprehension.

Essential Extension and Comprehension

One half of all terms are positive and one half negative. Positive terms are defined, and therefore have an essential Comprehension. But they have no real essential extension. Negative terms are not defined and therefore have no real essential comprehension but they have a real essential extension since it is known that no determinate conception can embrace the whole sphere of being.

Man is a rational animal
Then   Whatever is either irrational or not animal is not man

Two terms cannot be equal in essential extension or comprehension because if they were they would have the same meaning. The relation of two terms in essential comprehension or extension may not be measurable on account of the want of distinctness of one or both of those terms.

Oct. 2

There ought to be a proposition relating to universal and particular terms similar to that relating to affirmatives and negatives. My experience of logical symmetries assures me of it.

Perhaps this is it. A particular term will be found generally to have some natural extension, therefore all the extension implied, but it will not have a comprehension adequate to limiting its extension as it is limited. On the other hand a universal term, will never have an extension capable of limiting its comprehension as it is limited since new propositions will be discovered.

This is not yet very clear to me. But it would seem that as there is an arbitrariness in the extension of particulars so that we may exclude this or that from its extension so as to be able to predicate of it what we cannot predicate of them, so there is an arbitrary element in the comprehension of the universal so that this or that may be omitted from it so that we can predicate it of (imaginary things) of which we could not predicate them.

I think this is it. In a particular there is no concrete thing which must be included under it; in a universal there is no concrete quality which must be included in it.

If some S is P
it does not follow that this S is P

If S is P
it does not follow that it is this P

Ah I think I have it now—

Some S has a complete concrete comprehension
Thus Some Man—is a laugher, a one-eyed man, a cross person, &c.

This cannot be said of *Any man* which is therefore without concrete comprehension.
On the other hand Some man is not completely defined in extension since it is disjunctive alternative while *any man* applies definitely to certain things.

Note the meaning of a particular in the predicate. Some S means Either S' S'' S''' &c. select which I please.

Some S is P, that is let me take as my subject one what one I please of S' S'' S''' &c. and I can make the proposition true.

Now this does not hold for M is some P unless M is completely determined in comprehension just as Any S is P only holds if P has a very wide extension.

We may therefore say

Affirmative Negative	} has no essential	{ extension comprehension
Universal Particular	} has no concrete[1]	{ comprehension extension

Oct. 2

§2. Of the Effect of a Change of Information

———

Suppose it is learned that

Any *S* is *P*

Then *S* receives an addition to its comprehension.

P an addition to its extension.

If we looking at an *S* find it to be *P*

Some *S* is *P*

This adds to the extension of *P*—supposing we know *what S.*

Any *S* is not-*P*

This adds to the comprehension of *S*—supposing we know something of not-*P*.

1867 Nov. 24

I wish to investigate the nature of a simple concept. Such a concept first arises as predicated of some object (occasion of experience)

S is *M*

On the ground of some previous representation of the object. (Not immediate)

1. entirely knowable. Intuitional. Capable of external existence.

The predication of the concept is virtually contained in this previous representation.

———

To say that a simple concept is the immediate apprehension of a quality is but a mode of saying that its meaning is given in the representation which gives rise to it inasmuch as it is as much as to say that that quality is contained in that representation.

1867 Dec. 7

When I conceive a thing as say 'three' or say 'necessary' I necessarily have some concrete object in my imagination. I have some concrete object—'the necessary'. By saying that I have the necessary in my mind, it is not meant that I have all necessary things in mind. Nor that I have simply the **character of necessity.** For what I am thinking is not necessity but the necessary. Then I must have something which I recognize as a general sign of the necessary. But why should that particular feeling which is a sign of the necessary be a sign of that any more than of anything else? Because such is my constitution. Very true.

When I conceive as say "necessary," I have some singular object present to my imagination. I have not all necessary things separately imaged.

———

Doubted whether I ever have an absolutely singular object—

On an Improvement in Boole's Calculus of Logic

P 30: Presented 12 March 1867

The principal use of Boole's Calculus of Logic lies in its application to problems concerning probability. It consists, essentially, in a system of signs to denote the logical relations of classes. The data of any problem may be expressed by means of these signs, if the letters of the alphabet are allowed to stand for the classes themselves. From such expressions, by means of certain rules for transformation, expressions can be obtained for the classes (of events or things) whose frequency is sought in terms of those whose frequency is known. Lastly, if certain relations are known between the logical relations and arithmetical operations, these expressions for events can be converted into expressions for their probability.

It is proposed, first, to exhibit Boole's system in a modified form, and second, to examine the difference between this form and that given by Boole himself.

Let the letters of the alphabet denote classes whether of things or of occurrences. It is obvious that an event may either be singular, as "this sunrise," or general, as "all sunrises." Let the sign of equality with a comma beneath it express numerical identity. Thus $a = b$ is to mean that a and b denote the same class,—the same collection of individuals.

Let $a + b$ denote all the individuals contained under a and b together. The operation here performed will differ from arithmetical addition in two respects: 1st, that it has reference to identity, not to equality; and 2d, that what is common to a and b is not taken into account twice over, as it would be in arithmetic. The first of these differences, however, amounts to nothing, inasmuch as the sign of identity would indicate the distinction in which it is founded; and therefore we may say that

(1.)   If No a is b $a +, b =\mp a + b$

It is plain that

(2.) $a +, a =\mp a$

and also, that the process denoted by $+,$ and which I shall call the process of *logical addition,* is both commutative and associative. That is to say

(3.) $a +, b =\mp b +, a$

and

(4.) $(a +, b) +, c =\mp a +, (b +, c).$

Let a, b denote the individuals contained at once under the classes a and $b;$ those of which a and b are the common species. If a and b were independent events, a, b would denote the event whose probability is the product of the probabilities of each. On the strength of this analogy (to speak of no other), the operation indicated by the comma may be called logical multiplication. It is plain that

(5.) $a, a =\mp a.$

Logical multiplication is evidently a commutative and associative process. That is,

(6.) $a, b =\mp b, a$

(7.) $(a, b), c =\mp a, (b, c).$

Logical addition and logical multiplication are doubly distributive, so that

(8.) $(a +, b), c =\mp a, c +, b, c$

and

(9.) $a, b +, c =\mp (a +, c), (b +, c).$

     Proof.   Let $a =\mp a' + x + y + o$
                         $b =\mp b' + x + z + o$
                         $c =\mp c' + y + z + o$

where any of these letters may vanish. These formulæ comprehend every possible relation of a, b and $c;$ and it follows from them, that

$$a +\!\!, b = a' + b' + x + y + z + o \qquad (a +\!\!, b), c = y + z + o.$$

But

$$a,c = y + o \qquad b,c = z + o \qquad a,c +\!\!, b,c = y + z + o \quad \therefore (8).$$

So

$$a,b = x + o \qquad a,b +\!\!, c = c' + x + y + z + o.$$

But

$$(a +\!\!, c) = a' + c' + x + y + z + o \qquad (b +\!\!, c) = b' + c' + x + y + z + o$$

$$(a +\!\!, c),(b +\!\!, c) = c' + x + y + z + o \quad \therefore (9).$$

Let $\div$ be the sign of logical subtraction; so defined that

(10.) $\qquad\qquad$ If $b +\!\!, x = a \qquad x = a \div b.$

Here it will be observed that x is not completely determinate. It may vary from a to a with b taken away. This minimum may be denoted by $a - b$. It is also to be observed that if the sphere of b reaches at all beyond a, the expression $a \div b$ is uninterpretable. If then we denote the contradictory negative of a class by the letter which denotes the class itself, with a line above it,[1] if we denote by v a wholly indeterminate class, and if we allow $[0 \div 1]$ to be a wholly uninterpretable symbol, we have

(11.) $\qquad\qquad a \div b = v,a,b + a,\overline{b} + [0 \div 1],\overline{a},b$

which is uninterpretable unless

$$\overline{a},b = 0.$$

If we define zero by the following identities, in which x may be any class whatever,

(12.) $\qquad\qquad 0 = x \div x = x - x$

then, *zero* denotes the class which does not go beyond any class, that is *nothing* or nonentity.

Let $a\,;b$ be read a logically divided by b, and be defined by the condition that

(13.) $\qquad\qquad$ If $b,x = a \qquad x = a\,;b$

x is not fully determined by this condition. It will vary from a to

---

1. So that, for example, $\overline{a}$ denotes not-a.

$a + \overline{b}$ and will be uninterpretable if a is not wholly contained under b. Hence, allowing $[1;0]$ to be some uninterpretable symbol,

(14.) $$a;b \doteq a,b + v, \ \overline{a},\overline{b} + [1;0]\, a,\overline{b}$$

which is uninterpretable unless

$$a,\overline{b} \doteq 0.$$

Unity may be defined by the following identities in which x may be any class whatever.

(15.) $$1 \doteq x;x = x:x.$$

Then *unity* denotes the class of which any class is a part; that is, *what is* or *ens*.

It is plain that if for the moment we allow $a:b$ to denote the maximum value of $a;b$, then

(16.) $$\overline{x} \doteq 1 - x \doteq 0:x.$$

So that

(17.) $$x,(1 - x) \doteq 0 \qquad x + 0:x \doteq 1.$$

The rules for the transformation of expressions involving logical subtraction and division would be very complicated. The following method is, therefore, resorted to.

It is plain that any operations consisting solely of logical addition and multiplication, being performed upon interpretable symbols, can result in nothing uninterpretable. Hence, if $\varphi + \times x$ signifies such an operation performed upon symbols of which x is one, we have

$$\varphi + \times x \doteq a,x + b,(1 - x)$$

where a and b are interpretable.

It is plain, also, that all four operations being performed in any way upon any symbols, will, in general, give a result of which one term is interpretable and another not; although either of these terms may disappear. We have then

$$\varphi x \doteq i,x + j,(1 - x).$$

We have seen that if either of these coefficients i and j is uninterpretable, the other factor of the same term is nothing, or else the whole expression is uninterpretable. But

$$\varphi(1) = i \text{ and } \varphi(0) = j.$$

Hence

(18.) $$\varphi x = \varphi(1), x + \varphi(0), (1 - x)$$

$$\varphi(x \text{ and } y) = \varphi(1 \text{ and } 1), x, y + \varphi(1 \text{ and } 0), x, \overline{y}$$
$$+ \varphi(0 \text{ and } 1), \overline{x}, y + \varphi(0 \text{ and } 0), \overline{x}, \overline{y}.$$

(18'.) $$\varphi x = (\varphi(1) + \overline{x}), (\varphi(0) + x)$$

$$\varphi(x \text{ and } y) = (\varphi(1 \text{ and } 1) + \overline{x} + \overline{y}), (\varphi(1 \text{ and } 0) + \overline{x} + y),$$
$$(\varphi(0 \text{ and } 1) + x + \overline{y}), (\varphi(0 \text{ and } 0) + x + y).$$

Developing by (18) $x - y$, we have,

$$x - y = (1 - 1), x, y + (1 - 0), x, \overline{y} + (0 - 1), \overline{x}, y + (0 - 0), \overline{x}, \overline{y}.$$

So that, by (11),

(19.) $(1 - 1) = v$ $1 - 0 = 1$ $0 - 1 = [0 - 1]$ $0 - 0 = 0.$

Developing $x ; y$ in the same way, we have[2]

$$x ; y = 1 ; 1, x, y + 1 ; 0, x, \overline{y} + 0 ; 1, \overline{x}, y + 0 ; 0, \overline{x}, \overline{y}.$$

So that, by (14),

(20.) $1 ; 1 = 1$ $1 ; 0 = [1 ; 0]$ $0 ; 1 = 0$ $0 ; 0 = v.$

Boole gives (20), but not (19).

In solving identities we must remember that

(21.) $$(a + b) - b = a$$

(22.) $$(a - b) + b = a.$$

From $a - b$ the value of b cannot be obtained.

(23.) $$(a, b) \div b = a$$

(24.) $$a ; b, b = a.$$

From $a ; b$ the value of b cannot be determined.

Given the identity $\varphi x = 0.$

Required to eliminate x.

2. $a ; b, c$ must always be taken as $(a ; b), c$, not as $a ; (b, c)$.

$$\varphi(1) = x, \varphi(1) + (1 - x), \varphi(1)$$
$$\varphi(0) = x, \varphi(0) + (1 - x), \varphi(0).$$

Logically multiplying these identities, we get

$$\varphi(1), \varphi(0) = x, \varphi(1), \varphi(0) + (1 - x), \varphi(1), \varphi(0).$$

For two terms disappear because of (17).

But we have, by (18),

$$\varphi(1), x + \varphi(0), (1 - x) = \varphi x = 0.$$

Multiplying logically by x we get

$$\varphi(1), x = 0$$

and by $(1 - x)$ we get

$$\varphi(0), (1 - x) = 0.$$

Substituting these values above, we have

(25.) $\qquad \varphi(1), \varphi(0) = 0$ when $\varphi x = 0$.

Given $\qquad\qquad \varphi x = 1.$

Required to eliminate x.

Let $\qquad\qquad \varphi' x = 1 - \varphi x = 0$

$$\varphi'(1), \varphi'(0) = (1 - \varphi(1)), (1 - \varphi(0)) = 0$$
$$1 - (1 - \varphi(1)), (1 - \varphi(0)) = 1.$$

Now, developing as in (18), only in reference to $\varphi(1)$ and $\varphi(0)$ instead of to x and y,

$$1 - (1 - \varphi(1)), (1 - \varphi(0)) = \varphi(1), \varphi(0) + \varphi(1), (1 - \varphi(0))$$
$$+ \varphi(0), (1 - \varphi(1)).$$

But by (18) we have also,

$$\varphi(1) +, \varphi(0) = \varphi(1), \varphi(0) + \varphi(1), (1 - \varphi(0)) + \varphi(0), (1 - \varphi(1)).$$

So that

(26.) $\qquad \varphi(1) +, \varphi(0) = 1$ when $\varphi x = 1$.

Boole gives (25), but not (26).

We pass now from the consideration of *identities* to that of *equations*.

Let every expression for a class have a second meaning, which is its meaning in an equation. Namely, let it denote the proportion of individuals of that class to be found among all the individuals examined in the long run.

Then we have

(27.)   If $a \doteq b$ $a = b$

(28.) $a + b = (a +\!\!, b) + (a,b)$.

Let b_a denote the frequency of b's among the a's. Then considered as a class, if a and b are events b_a denotes the fact that if a happens b happens.

(29.) $ab_a = a,b$.

It will be convenient to set down some obvious and fundamental properties of the function b_a.

(30.) $ab_a = ba_b$

(31.) $\varphi(b_a \text{ and } c_a) = (\varphi(b \text{ and } c))_a$

(32.) $(1 - b)_a = 1 - b_a$

(33.) $b_a = \frac{b}{a} + b_{(1 - a)} (1 - \frac{1}{a})$

(34.) $a_b = 1 - \frac{1 - a}{b} b_{(1 - a)}$

(35.) $(\varphi a)_a = (\varphi(1))_a$.

The application of the system to probabilities may best be exhibited in a few simple examples, some of which I shall select from Boole's work, in order that the solutions here given may be compared with his.

Example 1. Given the proportion of days upon which it hails, and the proportion of days upon which it thunders. Required the proportion of days upon which it does both.

Let $1 \doteq$ days,
    $p \doteq$ days when it hails,
    $q \doteq$ days when it thunders,
    $r \doteq$ days when it hails and thunders.

$$p,q \doteq r$$

Then by (29), $r \doteq p,q = pq_p = qp_q$.

Answer. The required proportion is an unknown fraction of the least of the two proportions given, not less than $p + q - 1$.

By p might have been denoted the probability of the major, and by q that of the minor premise of a hypothetical syllogism of the following form:—

> *If a noise is heard, an explosion always takes place;*
> *If a match is applied to a barrel of gunpowder, a noise is*
>   *heard;*
> ∴ *If a match is applied to a barrel of gunpowder, an*
>   *explosion always takes place.*

In this case, the value given for r would have represented the probability of the conclusion. Now Boole (p. 284) solves this problem by his unmodified method, and obtains the following answer:—

$$r = pq + a(1 - q)$$

where a is an arbitrary constant. Here, if $q = 1$ and $p = 0$, $r = 0$. That is, his answer implies that if the major premise be false and the minor be true, the conclusion must be false. That this is not really so is shown by the above example. Boole (p. 286) is forced to the conclusion that "propositions which, when true, are equivalent, are not necessarily equivalent when regarded only as probable." This is absurd, because probability belongs to the events denoted, and not to forms of expression. The probability of an event is not altered by translation from one language to another.

Boole, in fact, puts the problem into equations wrongly (an error which it is the chief purpose of a calculus of logic to prevent), and proceeds as if the problem were as follows:—

It being known what would be the probability of Y, if X were to happen, and what would be the probability of Z, if Y were to happen; what would be the probability of Z, if X were to happen?

But even this problem has been wrongly solved by him. For, according to his solution, where

$$p = Y_X \qquad q = Z_Y \qquad r = Z_X,$$

r must be at least as large as the product of p and q. But if X be the event that a certain man is a Negro, Y the event that he is born in Massachusetts, and Z the event that he is a white man, then neither p nor q is *zero,* and yet r vanishes.

This problem may be rightly solved as follows:—

$$\text{Let } p' \,\leftrightharpoons\, Yp \,\leftrightharpoons\, X,Y$$
$$q' \,\leftrightharpoons\, Zq \,\leftrightharpoons\, X,Z$$
$$r' \,\leftrightharpoons\, Zr \,\leftrightharpoons\, X,Z.$$

Then, $r' \,\leftrightharpoons\, p',q'; p' \,\leftrightharpoons\, p',q';q'.$

Developing these expressions by (18) we have

$$r' \,\leftrightharpoons\, p',q' + r'_{p',\bar{q}'}\,(p',\bar{q}') + r'_{\bar{p}',\bar{q}'}\,(\bar{p}',\bar{q}')$$
$$\leftrightharpoons\, p',q' + r'_{\bar{p}',q'}\,(\bar{p}',q') + r'_{\bar{p}',\bar{q}'}\,(\bar{p}',\bar{q}').$$

The comparison of these two identities shows that

$$r' \,\leftrightharpoons\, p',q' + r'_{\bar{p}',\bar{q}'}\,(\bar{p}',\bar{q}').$$

$$\text{Let } V \,\leftrightharpoons\, r'_{\bar{p}',\bar{q}'} \,\leftrightharpoons\, \frac{x,\bar{y},z}{\bar{x},y,z + \bar{y}}$$

Now
$$p',q' \,\leftrightharpoons\, p' - p' \,,\, \bar{q}' \,\leftrightharpoons\, q' - q',\bar{p}'$$
$$\bar{p}',\bar{q}' \,\leftrightharpoons\, \bar{q}' - p' \,,\, \bar{q}' \,\leftrightharpoons\, \bar{p}' - q',\bar{p}'$$

And
$$p',\bar{q}' \,\leftrightharpoons\, p' - p'_{q'}, q' \,\leftrightharpoons\, \bar{q}' - \bar{q}'_{\bar{p}'},\bar{p}'$$
$$\bar{p}',q' \,\leftrightharpoons\, q' - q'_{p'}, p' \,\leftrightharpoons\, \bar{p}' - \bar{p}'_{\bar{q}'},\bar{q}'$$

Then let

$$A \,\leftrightharpoons\, p'_{q'} \,\leftrightharpoons\, \frac{x,y,z}{y,z}$$

$$B \,\leftrightharpoons\, \bar{q}'_{\bar{p}'} \,\leftrightharpoons\, \frac{\bar{x},y,\bar{z} + \bar{x},\bar{y},z + x,\bar{y},z + \bar{x},\bar{y},\bar{z}}{1-x,y}$$

$$C \,\leftrightharpoons\, \bar{p}'_{\bar{q}'} \,\leftrightharpoons\, \frac{\bar{x},y,\bar{z} + \bar{x},\bar{y},z + x,\bar{y},z + \bar{x},\bar{y},\bar{z}}{1-y,z}$$

$$D \,\leftrightharpoons\, q'_{p'} \,\leftrightharpoons\, \frac{x,y,z}{x,y}$$

And we have

$$r = \tfrac{Y}{Z}p + V\!\left(\tfrac{1}{Z}-q\right) - (1+V)\!\left(\tfrac{Y}{Z}p - Aq\right)$$
$$= \tfrac{Y}{Z}p + V\!\left(\tfrac{1}{Z}-q\right) - (1+V)\!\left(\tfrac{1}{Z}-q - B\!\left(\tfrac{1-Yp}{Z}\right)\right)$$
$$= q + V\!\left(\tfrac{1-Yp}{Z}\right) - (1+V)\!\left(\tfrac{1-Yp}{Z} - C\!\left(\tfrac{1}{Z}-q\right)\right)$$
$$= q + V\!\left(\tfrac{1-Yp}{Z}\right) - (1+V)\!\left(q - D\tfrac{Y}{Z}p\right)$$

Ex. 2. (See Boole, p. 276.) Given *r* and *q*; to find *p*.

$$p \,\leftrightharpoons\, r;q \,\leftrightharpoons\, r + v,(1 - q) \text{ because } p \text{ is interpretable.}$$

Ans. The required proportion lies somewhere between the proportion of days upon which it both hails and thunders, and that added to one minus the proportion of days when it thunders.

Ex. 3. (See Boole, p. 279.) Given, out of the number of questions put to two witnesses, and answered by *yes* or *no,* the proportion that each answers truly, and the proportion of those their answers to which disagree. Required, out of those wherein they agree, the proportion they answer truly and the proportion they answer falsely.

Let $1 =$ the questions put to both witnesses,
    $p =$ those which the first answers truly,
    $q =$ those which the second answers truly,
    $r =$ those wherein they disagree,
    $w =$ those which both answer truly,
    $w' =$ those which both answer falsely.

$$w = p,q \qquad w' = \overline{p},\overline{q} \qquad r = p +, q - w = \overline{p} +, \overline{q} - w'.$$

Now by (28.)

$$p +, q = p + q - w \qquad \overline{p} +, \overline{q} = p - p + 1 - q - w'.$$

Substituting and transposing,

$$2w = p + q - r \qquad 2w' = 2 - p - q - r.$$

$$\text{Now } w_{1-r} = \tfrac{w,(1-r)}{1-r} \qquad \text{but } w,(1-r) = w.$$

$$w'_{1-r} = \tfrac{w',(1-r)}{1-r} \qquad \text{but } w',(1-r) = w'$$

$$\therefore w_{(1-r)} = \tfrac{p+q-r}{2(1-r)} \qquad w'_{(1-r)} = \tfrac{2-p-q-r}{2(1-r)}.$$

The differences of Boole's system, as given by himself, from the modification of it given here, are three.

1st. Boole does not make use of the operations here termed logical addition and subtraction. The advantages obtained by the introduction of them are three, viz. they give unity to the system; they greatly abbreviate the labor of working with it; and they enable us to express *particular* propositions. This last point requires illustration. Let i be a class only determined to be such that only some one individual of the class a comes under it. Then $a \div i, a$ is the expression for some $a.$ Boole cannot properly express some $a.$

2d. Boole uses the ordinary sign of multiplication for logical multiplication. This debars him from converting every logical identity into an equality of probabilities. Before the transformation can be made the equation has to be brought into a particular form, and much labor is wasted in bringing it to that form.

3d. Boole has no such function as $a_b.$ This involves him in two difficulties. When the probability of such a function is required, he can only obtain it by a departure from the strictness of his system. And on account of the absence of that symbol, he is led to declare that, without adopting the principle that simple, unconditioned events whose probabilities are given are independent, a calculus of logic applicable to probabilities would be impossible.

The question as to the adoption of this principle is certainly not one of words merely. The manner in which it is answered, however, partly determines the sense in which the term "probability" is taken.

In the propriety of language, the probability of a fact either is, or solely depends upon, the strength of the argument in its favor, supposing all relevant relations of all known facts to constitute that argument. Now, the strength of an argument is only the frequency with which *such* an argument will yield a true conclusion when its premises are true. Hence probability depends solely upon the relative frequency of a specific event (namely, that a certain kind of argument yields a true conclusion from true premises) to a generic event (namely, that that kind of argument occurs with true premises). Thus, when an ordinary man says that it is highly probable that it will rain, he has reference to certain indications of rain,—that is, to a certain kind of argument that it will rain,—and means to say that there is an argument that it will rain, which is of a kind of which but a small proportion fail. "Probability," in the untechnical sense, is therefore a vague word, inasmuch as it does not indicate what one, of the numerous subordinated and co-ordinated genera to which every argument belongs, is the one the relative frequency of the truth of which is expressed. It is usually the case, that there is a tacit understanding upon this point, based perhaps on the notion of an *infima species* of argument. But an *infima species* is a mere fiction in logic. And very often the reference is to a very wide genus.

The sense in which the term should be made a technical one is that which will best subserve the purposes of the calculus in question. Now, the only possible use of a calculation of a probability is security in the long run. But there can be no question that an insurance company, for example, which assumed that events were independent without any reason to think that they really were so, would be subjected to great hazard. Suppose, says Mr. Venn, that an insurance company knew that nine-tenths of the Englishmen who go to Madeira die, and that nine-tenths of the consumptives who go there get well. How should they treat a consumptive Englishman? Mr. Venn has made an error in answering the question, but the illustration puts in a clear light the advantage of ceasing to speak of probability, and of speaking only of the relative frequency of this event to that.[3]

On the Natural Classification of Arguments

P 31: Presented 9 April 1867

PART I. §1. *Essential Parts of an Argument*

In this paper, the term "argument" will denote a body of premises considered as such. The term "premise" will refer exclusively to something laid down (whether in any enduring and communicable form of expression, or only in some imagined sign), and not to anything only *virtually* contained in what is said or thought, and also exclusively to that part of what is laid down which is (or is supposed to be) relevant to the conclusion.

Every inference involves the judgment that, if *such* propositions as the premises are are true, then a proposition related to them, as the conclusion is, must be, or is likely to be, true. The principle implied in this judgment, respecting a genus of argument, is termed the *leading principle* of the argument.

A *valid* argument is one whose leading principle is true.

In order that an argument should determine the necessary or probable truth of its conclusion, both the premises and leading principle must be true.

§2. *Relations between the Premises and Leading Principle*

The leading principle contains, by definition, whatever is considered requisite besides the premises to determine the necessary or

3. See a notice, Venn's *Logic of Chance*, in the *North American Review* for July, 1867.

probable truth of the conclusion. And as it does not contain in itself the subsumption of anything under it, each premise must, in fact, be equivalent to a subsumption under the leading principle.

The leading principle can contain nothing irrelevant or superfluous.

No fact, not superfluous, can be omitted from the premises without being thereby added to the leading principle, and nothing can be eliminated from the leading principle except by being expressed in the premises. Matter may thus be transferred from the premises to the leading principle, and *vice versa.*

There is no argument without premises, nor is there any without a leading principle.

It can be shown that there are arguments no part of whose leading principle can be transferred to the premises, and that every argument can be reduced to such an argument by addition to its premises. For, let the premises of any argument be denoted by P, the conclusion by C, and the leading principle by L. Then, if the whole of the leading principle be expressed as a premise, the argument will become

$$L \text{ and } P$$
$$\therefore C.$$

But this new argument must also have its leading principle, which may be denoted by L'. Now, as L and P (supposing them to be true) contain all that is requisite to determine the probable or necessary truth of C, they contain L'. Thus L' must be contained in the leading principle, whether expressed in the premise or not. Hence every argument has, as portion of its leading principle, a certain principle which cannot be eliminated from its leading principle. Such a principle may be termed a *logical principle.*

An argument whose leading principle contains nothing which can be eliminated is termed a *complete,* in opposition to an *incomplete, rhetorical,* or *enthymematic* argument.[1]

---

1. Neither of these terms is quite satisfactory. Enthymeme is usually defined as a syllogism with a premise suppressed. This seems to determine the same sphere as the definition I have given; but the doctrine of a suppressed premise is objectionable. The sense of a premise which is said to be suppressed is either conveyed in some way, or it is not. If it is, the premise is not suppressed in any sense which concerns the logician; if it is not, it ceases to be a premise altogether. What I mean by the distinction is this. He who is convinced that Sortes is mortal because he is a man (the latter belief

Since it can never be requisite that a fact stated should also be implied in order to justify a conclusion, every *logical principle* considered as a proposition will be found to be quite empty. Considered as regulating the procedure of inference, it is determinate; but considered as expressing truth, it is nothing. It is on this account that that method of investigating logic which works upon syllogistic forms is preferable to that other, which is too often confounded with it, which undertakes to enunciate logical principles.

§3. *Decomposition of Argument*

Since a statement is not an argument for itself, no fact concluded can be stated in any one premise. Thus it is no argument to say All *A* is *B; ergo* Some *A* is *B*.

If one fact has such a relation to another that, if the former is true, the latter is necessarily or probably true, this relation constitutes a determinate fact; and therefore, since the leading principle of a complete argument involves no matter of fact, every complete argument has at least two premises.

Every conclusion may be regarded as a statement substituted for either of its premises, the substitution being justified by the other premises. Nothing is relevant to the other premises, except what is requisite to justify this substitution. Either, therefore, these other premises will by themselves yield a conclusion which, taken as a premise along with the first premise, justifies the final conclusion; or else some part of them, taken with the first premise, will yield a

not only being the cause of the former, but also being felt to be so) necessarily says to himself that all *such* arguments are valid. This genus of argument is either clearly or obscurely recognized. In the former case, the judgment amounts to another premise, because the proposition (for example), "All reasoning from humanity to mortality is certain," only says in other words that every man is mortal. But if the judgment amounts merely to this, that the argument in question belongs to some genus all under which are valid, then in one sense it does, and in another it does not, contain a premise. It does in this sense, that by an act of attention such a proposition may be shown to have been virtually involved in it; it does not in this sense, that the person making the judgment did not *actually* understand this premise to be contained in it. This I express by saying that this proposition is contained in the leading principle, but is not *laid down*. This manner of stating the matter frees us at once from all psychological perplexities; and at the same time we lose nothing, since all that we know of thought is but a reflection of what we know of its expression.

These vague arguments are just such as alone are suitable to oratory or popular discourse, and they are appropriate to no other; and this fact justifies the appellation, "rhetorical argument." There is also authority for this use of the term. "Complete" and "incomplete" are adjectives which I have preferred to "perfect" and "imperfect," as being less misleading when applied to argument, although the latter are the best when syllogism is the noun to be limited.

conclusion which, taken as a premise along with all the others, will again justify the final conclusion. In either case, it follows that every argument of more than two premises can be resolved into a series of arguments of two premises each. This justifies the distinction of *simple* and *complex* arguments.

§4. *Of a General Type of Syllogistic Arguments*

A valid, complete, simple argument will be designated as a *syllogistic* argument.

Every proposition may, in at least one way, be put into the form,

$$S \text{ is } P;$$

the import of which is, that the objects to which S or the *total subject* applies have the characteristics attributed to every object to which P or the *total predicate* applies.

Every term has two powers or significations, according as it is subject or predicate. The former, which will here be termed its *breadth,* comprises the objects to which it is applied; while the latter, which will here be termed its *depth,* comprises the characters which are attributed to every one of the objects to which it can be applied. This breadth and depth must not be confounded with logical extension and comprehension, as these terms are usually taken.

Every substitution of one proposition for another must consist in the substitution of term for term. Such substitution can be justified only so far as the first term represents what is represented by the second. Hence the only possible substitutions are—

1st. The substitution for a term fulfilling the function of a subject of another whose breadth is included in that of the former; and

2d. The substitution for a term fulfilling the function of a predicate of another whose depth is included in that of the former.

If, therefore, in either premise a term appears as subject which does not appear in the conclusion as subject, then the other premise must declare that the breadth of that term includes the breadth of the term which replaces it in the conclusion. But this is to declare that every object of the latter term has every character of the former. The eliminated term, therefore, if it does not fulfil the function of predicate in one premise, does so in the other. But if the eliminated term fulfils the function of predicate in one premise, the other premise must declare that its depth includes that of the term which replaces it in the conclusion. Now, this is to declare that every character of the latter term belongs to every object of the former. Hence, in the other premise, it must fulfil the function of a subject. Hence the general formula of all argument must be

$$M \text{ is } P$$
$$S \text{ is } M$$
$$\therefore S \text{ is } P;$$

which is to be understood in this sense,—that the terms of every syllogistic argument fulfil functions of subject and predicate as here indicated, but not that the argument can be grammatically expressed in this way.

PART II. §1. *Of Apagogical Forms*

If C is true when P is, then P is false when C is. Hence it is always possible to substitute for any premise the denial of the conclusion, provided the denial of that premise be at the same time substituted for the conclusion.[2] Hence, corresponding to every syllogistic argument in the general form,

$$S \text{ is } M; M \text{ is } P;$$
$$S \text{ is } P.$$

There are two others:—

It is false that S is P; M is P;	S is M; it is false that S is P;
It is false that S is M.	It is false that M is P.

§2. *Of Contradiction*

The apagogical forms make it necessary to consider in what way propositions deny one another.

If a proposition be put into the general form,

$$S \text{ is } P,$$

its contradictory has, 1st, as its subject, instead of S, "the S now meant"[3] or "some S"; and has, 2d, as its predicate, instead of P, that which differs from P or "not P."

---

2. This operation will be termed a *contraposition* of the premise and conclusion.
3. What S is meant being generally undetermined.

From these relations of contradictories, from the necessities of the logic of apagogically related arguments, therefore, arises the need of the two divisions of propositions into affirmative and negative on the one hand, and into universal and particular on the other. The contradictory of a universal proposition is particular, and the contradictory of an affirmative proposition is negative. Contradiction is a reciprocal relation, and therefore the contradictory of a particular proposition is universal, and that of a negative proposition is affirmative. The contradiction of particular and negative propositions could not be brought under the general formula, were the distinctions of affirmative and negative absolute and not merely relative; but, in fact, not-not-P is the same as P. And, if it is said that "what is now meant of the part of S meant at another time, is P," since the part of S meant at another time is left to be determined in whatever way the proposition made at another time may determine it, this can only be true if All S is P. Therefore, if one man says "some S is not P," and another replies, "some of that same S is P," this second person, since he allows the first man's some S, which has not been defined, to remain undefined, in effect says that All S is P.

Whether contradictories differ in other respects than these well-known ones is an open question.

§3. *Of Barbara*

Since some S means "the part now meant of S," a particular proposition is equivalent to a universal proposition with another subject; and in the same way a negative proposition is equivalent to an affirmative proposition with another predicate.

The form,

$$S \text{ is } P,$$

therefore, as well as representing propositions in general, particularly represents Universal Affirmative propositions; and thus the general form of syllogism

$$M \text{ is } P; \ S \text{ is } M;$$
$$S \text{ is } P,$$

represents specially the syllogisms of the mood *Barbara*.

§4. *Of the First Figure*

Since, in the general form, S may be any subject and P any predicate, it is possible to modify Barbara by making the major premise and conclusion negative, or by making the minor premise and conclusion particular, or in both these ways at once. Thus we obtain all the modes of the first figure.

It is also possible to have such arguments as these:—

Some M is P,
 S has all the common characters of *that* part of M (whatever
   that part may be, and therefore of each and every M),
 $\therefore S$ is P,

and

All not-M is P,
 S is not M,
 $\therefore S$ is P;

but as the theory of apagogical argument has not obliged us to take account of these peculiar modifications of subject and predicate, these arguments must be considered as belonging to Barbara. In this sense the major premise must always be universal, and the minor affirmative.

Three propositions which are related to one another as though major premise, minor premise, and conclusion of a syllogism of the first figure will be termed respectively *Rule*, *Case*, and *Result*.

§5. *Second and Third Figures*

Let the first figure be written thus:—

Fig. 1

Any **M** $^{\text{is}}_{\text{is not}}$ **P**

$^{\text{Any}}_{\text{Some}}$ **S** is **M**

$^{\text{Any}}_{\text{Some}}$ **S** $^{\text{is}}_{\text{is not}}$ **P**

Then its two apagogical modifications are the second and third figures.

Fig. 2					*Fig.* 3			
Any	M	is is not	P		Some Any	S	is not is	P
Some Any	S	is not is	P		Any Some	S	is	M
Some Any	S	is not	M		Some	M	is not is	P

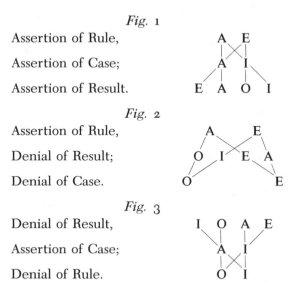

It is customary to enumerate six moods of the third figure instead of four, and the moods Darapti and Felapton appear to be omitted. But a particular proposition is asserted (actually and not merely virtually) by the universal proposition which does not otherwise differ from it; and therefore Darapti is included both under Disamis and Datisi, and Felapton both under Bocardo and Ferison. (De Morgan.)

The second figure, from the assertion of the rule and the denial of the result, infers the denial of the case; the third figure, from the denial of the result and assertion of the case, infers the denial of the rule. Hence we write the moods as follows, by allowing inferences only on the straight lines:—

Fig. 1

Assertion of Rule,

Assertion of Case;

Assertion of Result.

Fig. 2

Assertion of Rule,

Denial of Result;

Denial of Case.

Fig. 3

Denial of Result,

Assertion of Case;

Denial of Rule.

The symmetry of the system of moods of the three figures is also exhibited in the following table.

Enter at the top the proposition asserting or denying the rule; enter at the side the proposition asserting or denying the case; find in the body of the table the proposition asserting or denying the result. In the body of the table, propositions indicated by italics belong to the first figure, those by black-letter to the second figure, and those by script to the third figure.

	I	A	E	O
E		𝕰	𝕬	
A	*𝒮*	A	E	*𝒪*
I	*𝒜*	I	O	*ℰ*
O		𝕺	𝕵	

If, as the denial of the result in the second and third figures, we put the form "Any *N* is *N*," we have—

Fig. 2	*Fig. 3*
No *M* is *N*	Any *N* is *N*
Any *N* is *N*	Some *N* is *M*
∴ No *N* is *M*.	∴ Some *M* is *N*.

These are the formulæ of the two simple conversions. Neither can be expressed syllogistically except in the figures in which they are here put (or in what is called the fourth figure, which we shall consider hereafter). If, for the denial of the result in the second figure, we put "No not-*N* is *N*" (where "not-*N*" has not as yet been defined[4]) we obtain

$$\text{All} \quad M \text{ is } N,$$
$$\text{No not-}N \text{ is } N;$$
$$\therefore \text{No not-}N \text{ is } M.$$

---

4. Except so far as conditioned by the other premise.

In the same way, if we put "Some N is some-N" (where some-N has not been defined[5]) for the denial of the result in the third figure, we have

$$\begin{array}{llll} \text{Some} & N \text{ is} & \text{some-}N \\ \text{All} & N \text{ is} & M \\ \therefore \text{Some} & M \text{ is} & \text{some-}N. \end{array}$$

These are the two ways of contraposing the Universal Affirmative.

There are two ostensive reductions of each mood of the second and third figures. I shall distinguish them as the short reduction and the long reduction. The short reduction is effected by converting or contraposing that premise which is not the denial of the result. The long reduction is effected by transposing the premises, contraposing or converting the denial of the result, and contraposing or converting the conclusion. The alteration thus produced in the order of the terms is shown in the following figure:—

		Short Reduction		Long Reduction	
N	M	M	N	M	Ξ
Ξ	M	Ξ	M	N	M
Ξ	N	Ξ	N	N	Ξ
Σ	Π	Σ	Π	Σ	P
Σ	P	P	Σ	Π	Σ
P	Π	P	Π	Π	P

The names bestowed by Shyreswood, or Petrus Hispanus, upon the moods indicate the possibility of the short reduction in the case of Cesare and Festino of the second figure, and of Datisi and Ferison of the third figure; also the possibility of the long reduction of Camestres of the second figure and of Disamis of the third.

The short reduction of Camestres and Baroco is effected by introducing the term not-P, and defining it as that which S *is* when it is *not* P. Hence for the second premise (Any or some S is not P) we substitute "Any or some S is not-P"; and as the first premise, Any M is P, gives by contraposition Any not-P is not M, the moods

5. Except so far as conditioned by the other premise.

Any   M is P,
Any or some S is not P;
∴ Any or some S is not M,

are reduced to

No   not-P is M,
Any or some S is not-P;
∴ Any or some S is not M.

The short reduction of Disamis and Bocardo is effected by introducing the term some-S, defining it as that part of S which is or is not P when some S is or is not P. We can therefore substitute for the first premise, Some S is or is not P, All some-S is or is not P; while, for the second premise, All S is M can be contraposed into "Some M is some-S": and thus the forms

Some S is (*or* is not) P,
Any S is   M;
∴ Some M is (*or* is not) P,

are reduced to the following:—

Any some-S is (*or* is not) P,
Some M is   some-S;
∴ Some M is (*or* is not) P.

To reduce Cesare, Festino, and Baroco in the long way, it is necessary to introduce the terms not-P and some-S. Not-P is defined as that class to which any M belongs which is not P. Hence for the first premise of Cesare and Festino we can substitute "Any M is not-P." Some-S is defined as that class of S which is (or is not) P, when some S is (or is not) P. Hence for the second premises of Festino and Baroco we can first substitute "Any some-S is (or is not) P"; and then, by contraposition or conversion, we obtain "Any P (or not-P) is not some-S." Then, by the transposition of the premises, we obtain from Cesare, which is

No M is P   Any not-P is not S
Any S is P   Any M is not-P
(∴ No S is M).   ∴ Any M is not-S.

And from the conclusion of this reduced form we obtain the conclusion of Cesare by simple conversion. So Festino and its long reduction are

Any	M	is not	P,		Any	not-P	is not	some-S,
Some	S	is	P;		Any	M	is	not-P;
($\therefore$ Some	S	is not	M.)		$\therefore$ Any	M	is not	some-S;

and the conclusion of Festino is obtained from that of the reduced form by a substitution which may be made syllogistically thus:—

Any M is not some-S,
Some S is   some-S;
$\therefore$ Some S is not M.

Baroco and its long reduction are

Any	M	is	P,		Any P	is not	some-S,	
Some	S	is not	P;		Any M	is		P;
($\therefore$ Some	S	is not	M.)		$\therefore$ Any M	is not	some-S;	

and the conclusion of Baroco is obtained from the conclusion of the reduction in the same way as that of Festino.

In order to reduce Datisi, Bocardo, and Ferison in the long way, we must define Some-S as that S which is M when some S is M, and Not-P as that which some (or any) S *is* when it is *not P*. Hence for "Some S is M" we can substitute "Any some-S is M"; and for "Some (or any) S is not P," "Some (or any) S is not-P." "Some S is not-P" may be converted simply; and "Any S is not-P" may be contraposed so as to become "Some not-P is some-S." Then Datisi and its long reduction are

Any	S is P,		Any	some-S is		M,
Some	S is M;		Some		P is	some-S;
($\therefore$ Some	M is P.)		$\therefore$ Some		P is	M.

And from the conclusion of the reduction, the conclusion of Datisi is obtained by simple conversion. Ferison and its long reduction are

Any	S	is not	P,		Any	some-S is M,
Some	S	is	M;		Some	not-P is some-S;
($\therefore$ Some	M	is not	P.)		$\therefore$ Some	not-P is M.

And from the conclusion of the reduction, the conclusion of Ferison may be obtained by a substitution whose possibility is expressed syllogistically thus:—

$$
\begin{aligned}
&\text{Any} \quad \text{not-}P \text{ is not} \quad P, \\
&\text{Some} \quad \text{not-}P \quad \text{is} \quad M; \\
\therefore\ &\text{Some} \qquad\quad M \text{ is not} \quad P.
\end{aligned}
$$

Bocardo and its long reduction are

$$
\begin{array}{ll}
\text{Some } S \text{ is not } P, & \text{Any} \qquad\quad S \text{ is } M, \\
\text{Any } \; S \quad \text{is} \quad M; & \text{Some } \text{not-}P \text{ is } S; \\
(\therefore \text{ Some } M \text{ is not } P.) & \therefore \text{ Some } \text{not-}P \text{ is } M.
\end{array}
$$

And the conclusion of Bocardo is obtained from that of its reduction in the same way as the conclusion of Ferison.

The ostensive reduction of the indirect or apagogical figures may be considered as the exhibition of them under the general form of syllogism,

$$
\begin{aligned}
&S \text{ is } M; \quad M \text{ is } P: \\
\therefore\ &S \text{ is } P.
\end{aligned}
$$

But, in this sense, it is not truly a reduction if the substitutions made in the process are inferences. But although the possibility of the conversions and contrapositions can be expressed syllogistically, yet this can be done only by taking as one of the premises,

$$
\begin{aligned}
&\text{``All} \qquad\quad N \quad \text{is} \quad N,\text{''} \\
&\text{``Any} \quad \text{not-}N \text{ is not} \quad N,\text{''} \\
\text{or } &\text{``Some} \qquad N \quad \text{is} \quad \text{some-}N.\text{''}
\end{aligned}
$$

Now, these are properly not premises, for they express no facts; they are merely forms of words without meaning. Hence, as no complete argument has less than two premises, the conversions and contrapositions are not inferences. The only other substitutions which have been made have been of not-P and some-S for their definitions. These also can be put into syllogistic form; but a mere modification of language is not an inference. Hence no inferences have been employed in reducing the arguments of the second and third figures to such forms that they are readily perceived to come under the general form of syllogism.

There is, however, an intention in which these substitutions are inferential. For, although the passage from holding for true a fact expressed in the form "No *A* is *B*," to holding its converse, is not an inference, because, these facts being identical, the relation between them is not a fact; yet the passage from one of these forms taken merely as having *some* meaning, but not this or that meaning, to another, since these forms are not identical and their logical relation is a fact, is an inference. This distinction may be expressed by saying that they are not inferences, but substitutions having the *form* of inferences.

Thus the reduction of the second and third figures, considered as mere forms, is inferential; but when we consider only what is meant by any particular argument in an indirect figure, the reduction is a mere change of wording.

The substitutions made use of in the ostensive reductions are shown in the following table, where

e, denotes simple conversion of E;

i, denotes simple conversion of I;

a_2, contraposition of A into E;

a_3, contraposition of A into I;

o_2, the substitution of "Some *S* is not *M*" for "Any *M* is not some-*S*";

o_3, the substitution of "Some *M* is not *P*" for "Some not-*P* is *M*";

e", introduction of not-*P* by definition;

i", introduction of some-*S* by definition.

Reduction of Second Figure		
Name of Mood	Short Reduction	Long Reduction
Cesare	e	$e''\, a_2\, e$
Camestres	$a_2\, e''$	$e\, e$
Festino	e	$e''\, i''\, a_2\, o_2$
Baroco	$a_2\, e''$	$i''\, e\, o_2$

Reduction of Third Figure		
Name of Mood	Short Reduction	Long Reduction
Disamis	$a_3 \, i''$	$i \, i$
Datisi	i	$i'' \, a_3 \, i$
Bocardo	$a_3 \, i''$	$e'' \, i \, o_3$
Ferison	i	$i'' \, e'' \, a_3 \, o_3$

With the exception of the substitutions i'' and e'', which will be considered hereafter, all those which are used in the reduction of the moods of either oblique figure have the form of inferences in the same figure.

The so-called *reductio per impossibile* is the repetition or inversion of that contraposition of propositions by which the indirect figures have been obtained. Now, contradiction arises from a difference both in quantity and quality; but it is to be observed that, in the contraposition which gives the second figure, a change of the *quality* alone, and in that which gives the third figure, a change of the *quantity* alone, of the contraposed propositions, is sufficient. This shows that the two contrapositions are of essentially different kinds, and that the reductions *per impossibile* of the second and third figures respectively involve the following formal inferences.[6]

FIGURE 2

The Result follows from the Case;
∴ The Negative of the Case follows from the Negative of the Result.

FIGURE 3

The Result follows from the Rule;
∴ The Rule changed in Quantity follows from the Result changed in Quantity.

6. A formal inference is a substitution having the form of an inference.

But these inferences may also be expressed as follows:—

FIGURE 2

$$\text{Whatever } (S) \text{ is } M \quad \text{is} \quad {}^{P;}_{\text{not } P;}$$
$$\therefore \text{Whatever } (S) \text{ is } {}^{\text{not } P}_{P} \text{ is not } M.$$

FIGURE 3

$$\text{Any } {}^{S}_{\text{some } S} \text{ is whatever } (P \text{ or not-}P) \quad M \quad \text{is;}$$
$$\therefore \text{Some } M \text{ is whatever } (P \text{ or not-}P) \quad {}^{\text{some } S}_{S} \text{ is.}$$

Now, the limitations in parentheses do not affect the essential nature of the inferences; and omitting them we have,

FIGURE 2

$$\text{Any } M \quad \text{is} \quad {}^{P;}_{\text{not } P;}$$
$$\therefore \text{Any } {}^{\text{not } P}_{P} \text{ is not } M.$$

FIGURE 3

$$\text{Any } {}^{S}_{\text{some } S} \text{ is } M;$$
$$\therefore \text{Some } M \text{ is } {}^{\text{some } S.}_{S.}$$

We have already seen that the former of these is of the form of the second figure, and the latter of the form of the third figure of syllogism.

Hence it appears that no syllogism of an indirect figure can be reduced to the first figure without a substitution which has the form of the very figure from which the syllogism is reduced. In other words, the indirect syllogisms are of an essentially different form from that of the first figure, although in a more general sense they come under that form.

§6. *The Theophrastean Moods*

It is now necessary to consider the five moods of Theophrastus, viz. *Baralipton, Celantes, Dabitis, Fapesmo, Frisesomorum.* Baralipton is included in Dabitis, and Fapesmo in Frisesomorum, in the

same way in which Darapti is included in Disamis and Datisi, and
Felapton in Bocardo and Ferison. The Theophrastean moods are
thus reduced to three, viz.:—

No *X* is *Y,*	No *X* is *Y,*	Some *Y* is *Z,*
All *Z* is *X;*	Some *Y* is *Z;*	All *Z* is *X;*
∴ Any *Y* is not *Z.*	∴ Some *Z* is not *X.*	∴ Some *X* is *Y.*

Suppose we have, 1st, a Rule; 2d, a Case under that rule, which
is itself a Rule; and, 3d, a Case under this second rule, which conflicts
with the first rule. Then it would be easy to prove that these three
propositions must be of the form,

1. No   *X* is *Y.*
2. All   *Z* is *X.*
3. Some *Y* is *Z.*

These three propositions cannot all be true at once; if, then, any
two are asserted, the third must be denied, which is what is done in
the three Theophrastean moods.

These moods are resolved into one another by the contraposition
of propositions, and therefore should be considered as belonging to
different figures.

They can be ostensively reduced to the first Aristotelian figure in
two ways; thus,

	Short Reduction	*Long Reduction*
B A	B A	B Γ
Γ B	Γ B	A B
A Γ	Γ A	A Γ

The verses of Shyreswood show how Celantes and Dabitis are to
be reduced in the short way, and Frisesomorum in the long way.
Celantes and its long reduction are as follows:—

Any *X* is not *Y,*	Any not-*X* is not *Z,*
Any *Z* is *X;*	Any *Y* is not-*X;*
∴ Any *Y* is not *Z.*	∴ Any *Y* is not *Z.*

"Any *X* is not *Y,*" becomes, by conversion, "Any *Y* is not *X.*" The
term "not-*X*" is then introduced, being defined as that which *Y* is

when it is not X. Then "Z is X" becomes "Any not-X is not Z"; and, the premises being transposed, the reduction is effected.

Dabitis and its long reduction are as follows:—

Any	Z is X,		Any	some-Z is		Y,
Some	Y is Z;		Some		X is	some-Z;
∴ Some	X is Y.		∴ Some		X is	Y.

"Some Y is Z" becomes, by conversion, "Some Z is Y." Then the term "some-Z" is introduced, being defined as that Z which is Y if "some Z is Y." Then "Any Z is X" becomes "Some X is some-Z," and, the premises being transposed, the reduction is effected.

Frisesomorum is,

	Some	Y	is	Z,
	Any	X	is not	Y;
∴	Some	Z	is not	X.

Let some-Y be that Y which is Z when some Y is Z; and then we have,

	Some		Y	is	some-Y,
	Any		X	is not	Y;
∴	Some	some-Y		is not	X.

Then let not-X be that which any Y is when some Y is not X, and we have,

Some some-Y is not-X,

which yields by conversion,

Some not-X is some-Y;

and we thus obtain the reduction,

Any	some-Y is		Z,
Some	not-X is	some-Y;	
∴ Some	not-X is		Z.

From the conclusion of this reduction, the conclusion of Frisesomorum is justified as follows:—

$$
\begin{array}{llll}
\text{Some} & \text{not-}X & \text{is} & Z, \\
\text{Any} & X & \text{is not} & \text{not-}X; \\
\therefore \text{Some} & Z & \text{is not} & X.
\end{array}
$$

Another mode of effecting the short reduction of Frisesomorum is this: Let not-Y be that which any X is when no X is Y, and we have

$$
\begin{array}{llll}
\text{Some} & Y & \text{is} & Z, \\
\text{Any} & \text{not-}Y & \text{is not} & Y; \\
\therefore \text{Some} & Z & \text{is not} & \text{not-}Y.
\end{array}
$$

Let some-Z be that Z which is not not-Y when some Z is not-Y, and we have,

$$\text{Any some-}Z \text{ is not not-}Y,$$

and by conversion,

$$\text{Any not-}Y \text{ is not some-}Z.$$

Thus we obtain as the reduced form,

$$
\begin{array}{llll}
\text{Any} & \text{not-}Y & \text{is not} & \text{some-}Z, \\
\text{Any} & X & \text{is} & \text{not-}Y; \\
\therefore \text{Any} & X & \text{is} & \text{some-}Z.
\end{array}
$$

From the conclusion of this reduction, we get that of Frisesomorum thus:—

$$
\begin{array}{llll}
\text{Some} & \text{some-}Z & \text{is} & Z, \\
\text{Any} & X & \text{is not} & \text{some-}Z; \\
\therefore \text{Some} & Z & \text{is not} & X.
\end{array}
$$

In either reduction of Celantes, if we neglect the substitution of terms for their definitions, the substitutions are all of the second syllogistic figure. This of itself shows that Celantes belongs to that figure, and this is confirmed by the fact that it concludes the denial of a Case. In the same way, the reductions of Dabitis involve only substitutions in the third figure, and it concludes the denial of a Rule. Frisesomorum concludes a proposition which is at once the denial of a rule and the denial of a case: its long reduction involves one conversion in the second figure and another in the third, and its short reductions involve conversions in Frisesomorum itself. It therefore belongs to a figure which unites the characters of the second and third, and which may be termed the second-third figure in Theophrastean syllogism.

There are, then, two kinds of syllogism,—the Aristotelian and Theophrastean. In the Aristotelian occur the 1st, 2d, and 3d figures, with four moods of each. In the Theophrastean occur the 2d, 3d, and 2d-3d figures, with one mood of each. The first figure is the fundamental or typical one, and Barbara is the typical mood. There is a strong analogy between the figures of syllogism and the four forms of proposition. A is the fundamental form of proposition, just as the first figure is the fundamental form of syllogism. The second and third figures are derived from the first by the contraposition of propositions, and E and I are derived from A by the contraposition of terms; thus:—

Any *S* is *P.*

Any not-*P* is not *S.*   Some *P* is some-*S.*

O combines the modifications of E and I, just as the 2d-3d figure combines the 2d and 3d. In the second-third figure, only O can be concluded, in the third only I and O, in the second only E and O, in the first either A E I O. Thus A is the first figure of proposition, E the second, I the third, O the second-third.[7]

§7. *Mathematical Syllogisms*

A kind of argument very common in mathematics may be exemplified as follows:—

Every part is less than that of which it is a part,
Boston is a part of the Universe;
∴ Boston is less than the Universe.

---

7. Hypotheticals have not been considered above, the well-known opinion having been adopted that, "If *A,* then *B,*" means the same as "Every state of things in which *A* is true is a state of things in which *B* is (or will be) true."

This may be reduced to syllogistic form thus:—

Any relation of part to whole is a relation of less to greater,
The relation of Boston to the Universe is a relation of part to whole;
∴ The relation of Boston to the Universe is a relation of less to
    greater.

If logic is to take account of the peculiarities of such syllogisms, it would be necessary to consider some propositions as having three terms, subject, predicate, and object; and such propositions would be divided into *active* and *passive*. The varieties in them would be endless.

PART III. §1. *Induction and Hypothesis*

In the syllogism,

$$\text{Any } M \text{ is } P,$$
$$\Sigma' \ S' \text{ is } M;$$
$$\therefore \Sigma' \ S' \text{ is } P;$$

where $\Sigma' \ S'$ denotes the sum of all the classes which come under M, if the second premise and conclusion are known to be true, the first premise is, by enumeration, true. Whence we have, as a valid demonstrative form of inference,

$$\Sigma' \ S' \text{ is } P,$$
$$\Sigma' \ S' \text{ is } M;$$
$$\therefore M \text{ is } P.$$

This is called perfect induction. It would be better to call it formal induction.

In a similar way, from the syllogism,

$$\text{Any } M \text{ is } \Pi' \ P',$$
$$\text{Any } S \text{ is } M;$$
$$\therefore \text{Any } S \text{ is } \Pi' \ P';$$

where $\Pi' \ P'$ denotes the conjunction of all the characters of M, if the conclusion and first premise are true, the second premise is true by definition; so that we have the demonstrative form of argument,

$$\text{Any } M \text{ is } \Pi' \, P',$$
$$\text{Any } S \text{ is } \Pi' \, P';$$
$$\therefore \text{Any } S \text{ is } \quad M.$$

This is reasoning from definition, or, as it may be termed, formal hypothesis.

One half of all possible propositions are true, because every proposition has its contradictory. Moreover, for every true particular proposition there is a true universal proposition, and for every true negative proposition there is a true affirmative proposition. This follows from the fact that the universal affirmative is the type of all propositions. Hence of all possible propositions in either of the forms,

$$\Sigma' \, S' \text{ is } M, \text{ and } M \text{ is } \Pi' \, P',$$

one half are true. In an untrue proposition of either of these forms, some finite ratio of the S's or P's are not true subjects or predicates. Hence, of all propositions of either of these forms which are partly true, some finite ratio more than one half are wholly true. Hence, if in the above formulæ for formal induction or hypothesis, we substitute S' for $\Sigma' \, S'$ and P' for $\Pi' \, P'$ we obtain formulæ of probable inference. This reasoning gives no *determinate* probability to these modes of inference, but it is necessary to consider that, however weak synthetic inference might have been at first, yet if it had the least positive tendency to produce truth, it would continually become stronger, owing to the establishment of more and more secure premises.

The rules for valid induction and hypothesis deducible from this theory are as follows:—

1. The explaining syllogism, that is to say, the deductive syllogism one of whose premises is inductively or hypothetically inferred from the other and from its conclusion, must be valid.

2. The conclusion is not to be held as absolutely true, but only until it can be shown that, in the case of induction, S' was taken from some narrower class than M, or, in the case of hypothesis, that P' was taken from some higher class than M.

3. From the last rule it follows as a corollary that in the case of induction the subject of the premises must be a sum of subjects, and that in the case of hypothesis the predicate of the premises must be a conjunction of predicates.

4. Also, that this aggregate must be of different objects or qualities and not of mere names.

5. Also, that the only principle upon which the instanced subjects or predicates can be selected is that of belonging to M.[8]

---

8. Positivism, apart from its theory of history and of the relations between the sciences, is distinguished from other doctrines by the manner in which it regards hypotheses. Almost all men think that metaphysical theories are valueless, because metaphysicians differ so much among themselves; but the positivists give another reason, namely, that these theories violate the sole condition of all legitimate hypothesis. This condition is that every good hypothesis must be such as is certainly capable of subsequent verification with the degree of certainty proper to the conclusions of the branch of science to which it belongs. There is, it seems to me, a confusion here between the probability of a hypothesis in itself, and its admissibility into any one of those bodies of doctrine which have received distinct names, or have been admitted into a scheme of the sciences, and which admit only conclusions which have a very high probability indeed. I have here to deal with the rule only so far as it is a general canon of the *legitimacy* of hypotheses, and not so far as it determines their *relevancy* to a particular science; and I shall, therefore, consider only another common statement of it; namely, "that no hypothesis is admissible which is not capable of verification by direct observation." The positivist regards an hypothesis, not as an inference, but as a device for stimulating and directing observation. But I have shown above that certain premises will render an hypothesis probable, so that there is such a thing as legitimate hypothetic inference. It may be replied that such conclusions are not hypotheses, but inductions. That the sense in which I have used "hypothesis" is supported by good usage, I could prove by a hundred authorities. The following is from Kant: "An hypothesis is the holding for true of the judgment of the truth of a reason on account of the sufficiency of its consequents." Mill's definition (*Logic,* Book III, Ch. XIV, §4) also nearly coincides with mine. Moreover, an hypothesis in every sense is an inference, because it is adopted for some reason, good or bad, and that reason, in being regarded as such, is regarded as lending the hypothesis some plausibility. The arguments which I term hypothetic are certainly not inductions, for induction is reasoning from particulars to generals, and this does not take place in these cases. The positivist canon for hypotheses is neither sufficient nor necessary. If it is granted that hypotheses are inferred, it will hardly be questioned that the observed facts must follow apodictically from the hypothesis without the aid of subsidiary hypotheses, and that the characters of that which is predicated in the hypothesis, and from which the inference is drawn, must be taken as they occur, and not be picked out in order to make a plausible argument. That the maxim of the positivists is superfluous or worse, is shown, first, by the fact that it is not implied in the proof that hypothetic inference is valid; and next, by the absurdities to which it gives rise when strictly applied to history, which is entirely hypothetical, and is absolutely incapable of verification by direct observation. To this last argument I know of but two answers: first, that this pushes the rule further than was intended, it being considered that history has already been so verified; and second, that the positivist does not pretend to know the world as it absolutely exists, but only the world which appears to him. To the first answer, the rejoinder is that a rule must be pushed to its logical consequences in all cases, until it can be shown that some of these cases differ in some material respect from the others. To the second answer, the rejoinder is double: first, that I mean no more by "is" than the positivist by "appears" in the sense in which he uses it in saying that only what "appears" is known, so that the answer is irrelevant; second, that positivists, like the rest of the world, reject historic testimony sometimes, and in doing so distinguish hypothetically between what is and what in some other sense appears, and yet have no means of verifying the distinction by direct observation.

Another error in reference to hypothesis is, that the antecedent probability of

Hence the formulæ are

Induction

S' S'' S''', &c. are taken at random as M's,
S' S'' S''', &c. are P;
∴ Any M is probably P.

Hypothesis

Any M is, for instance, P' P'' P''', &c.,
S is P' P'' P''', &c.;
∴ S is probably M.

§2. Moods and Figures of Probable Inference

It is obvious that the explaining syllogism of an induction or hypothesis may be of any mood or figure.

It would also seem that the conclusion of an induction or hypothesis may be contraposed with one of the premises.

§3. Analogy

The formula of analogy is as follows:—

S', S'', and S''' are taken at random from such a class that their characters at random are such as P', P'', P'''.
t is P', P'', and P'''.
S', S'', and S''' are q.
∴ t is q.

Such an argument is double. It combines the two following:—

1

S', S'', S''' are taken as being P', P'', P'''.
S', S'', S''' are q.
∴ (By induction) P', P'', P''' is q.

what is testified to cannot affect the probability of the testimony of a good witness. This is as much as to say that probable arguments can neither support nor weaken one another. Mr. Venn goes so far as to maintain the impossibility of a conflict of probabilities. The difficulty is instantly removed by admitting indeterminate probabilities.

t is P', P'', P'''.
∴ (Deductively) t is q.

2

S', S'', S''' are, for instance, P', P'', P'''.
t is P', P'', P'''.
∴ (By hypothesis) t has the common characters of S', S'', S'''.
S', S'', S''' are q.
∴ (Deductively) t is q.

Owing to its double character, analogy is very strong with only a moderate number of instances.

§4. *Formal Relations of the above Forms of Argument*

If we take an identical proposition as the fact to be explained by induction and hypothesis, we obtain the following formulæ.

By Induction

S, S', S'' are taken at random as being M,
S, S', S'' have the characters common to S, S', S''.
∴ Any M has the characters common to S, S', S''.

By Hypothesis

M is, for instance, P, P', P''.
Whatever is at once P, P', and P'' is P, P', P''.
∴ Whatever is at once P, P', and P'' is M.

By means of the substitution thus justified, Induction and Hypothesis can be reduced to the general type of syllogism, thus:—

Induction

S, S', S'' are taken as M,
S, S', S'' are P;
∴ Any M is P.

Reduction

S, S', S'' are P;
Almost any M has the common characters of S, S', S''.
∴ Almost any M is P.

Hypothesis

M is, for instance, P', P'', P''',
S is P', P'', P''';
∴ S is M.

Reduction

Whatever is, at once, P', P'', P''' is like M,
S is P', P'', P''';
∴ S is like M.

Induction may, therefore, be defined as argument which assumes that a whole collection, from which a number of instances have been taken at random, has all the common characters of those instances; hypothesis, as an argument which assumes that a term which necessarily involves a certain number of characters, which have been lighted upon as they occurred, and have not been picked out, may be predicated of any object which has all these characters.

There is a resemblance between the transposition of propositions by which the forms of probable inference are derived and the contraposition by which the indirect figures are derived; in the latter case there is a *denial* or change of modal quality; while in the former there is reduction from certainty to probability, and from the sum of all results to some only, or a change in modal quantity. Thus probable inference is related to apagogical proof, somewhat as the third figure is to the second. Among probable inferences, it is obvious that hypothesis corresponds to the second figure, induction to the third, and analogy to the second-third.

On a New List of Categories

P 32: Presented 14 May 1867

§1. This paper is based upon the theory already established, that the function of conceptions is to reduce the manifold of sensuous impressions to unity, and that the validity of a conception consists in the impossibility of reducing the content of consciousness to unity without the introduction of it.

§2. This theory gives rise to a conception of gradation among those conceptions which are universal. For one such conception may unite the manifold of sense and yet another may be required to unite the conception and the manifold to which it is applied; and so on.

§3. That universal conception which is nearest to sense is that of *the present, in general.* This is a conception, because it is universal. But as the act of *attention* has no connotation at all, but is the pure denotative power of the mind, that is to say, the power which directs the mind to an object, in contradistinction to the power of thinking any predicate of that object,—so the conception of *what is present in general,* which is nothing but the general recognition of what is contained in attention, has no connotation, and therefore no proper unity. This conception of the present in general, or IT in general, is rendered in philosophical language by the word "substance" in one of its meanings. Before any comparison or discrimination can be made between what is present, what is present must have been recognized as such, as *it,* and subsequently the metaphysical parts which are recognized by abstraction are attributed to this *it,* but the *it* cannot itself be made a predicate. This *it* is thus neither predicated of a subject, nor in a subject, and accordingly is identical with the conception of substance.

§4. The unity to which the understanding reduces impressions is the unity of a proposition. This unity consists in the connection of the predicate with the subject; and, therefore, that which is implied in the copula, or the conception of *being,* is that which completes the work of conceptions of reducing the manifold to unity. The copula (or rather the verb which is copula in one of its senses) means either *actually is* or *would be,* as in the two propositions, "There *is* no griffin," and "A griffin *is* a winged quadruped." The conception of *being* contains only that junction of predicate to subject wherein these two verbs agree. The conception of being, therefore, plainly has no content.

If we say "The stove is black," the stove is the *substance,* from which its blackness has not been differentiated, and the *is,* while it leaves the substance just as it was seen, explains its confusedness, by the application to it of *blackness* as a predicate.

Though *being* does not affect the subject, it implies an indefinite determinability of the predicate. For if one could know the copula and predicate of any proposition, as " . . . is a tailed-man," he would know the predicate to be applicable to something supposable, at least. Accordingly, we have propositions whose subjects are entirely indefinite, as "There is a beautiful ellipse," where the subject is merely *something actual or potential;* but we have no propositions whose predicate is entirely indeterminate, for it would be quite senseless to say, "*A* has the common characters of all things," inasmuch as there are no such common characters.

Thus substance and being are the beginning and end of all conception. Substance is inapplicable to a predicate, and being is equally so to a subject.

§5. The terms "prescision" and "abstraction," which were formerly applied to every kind of separation, are now limited, not merely to mental separation, but to that which arises from *attention to* one element and *neglect of* the other. Exclusive attention consists in a definite conception or *supposition* of one part of an object, without any supposition of the other. Abstraction or prescision ought to be carefully distinguished from two other modes of mental separation, which may be termed *discrimination* and *dissociation.* Discrimination has to do merely with the essences of terms, and only draws a distinction in meaning. Dissociation is that separation which, in the absence of a constant association, is permitted by the law of association of images. It is the consciousness of one thing, without the necessary simultaneous consciousness of the other. Abstraction or prescision, therefore, supposes a greater separation than discrimination, but a less separation than dissociation. Thus I can discriminate red from blue, space from color, and color from space, but not red from color. I can prescind red from blue, and space from color (as is manifest from the fact that I actually believe there is an uncolored space between my face and the wall); but I cannot prescind color from space, nor red from color. I can dissociate red from blue, but not space from color, color from space, nor red from color.

Prescision is not a reciprocal process. It is frequently the case, that, while *A* cannot be prescinded from *B*, *B* can be prescinded from *A*. This circumstance is accounted for as follows. Elementary conceptions only arise upon the occasion of experience; that is, they are produced for the first time according to a general law, the condition of which is the existence of certain impressions. Now if a conception does not reduce the impressions upon which it follows to unity, it is a mere arbitrary addition to these latter; and elementary conceptions do not arise thus arbitrarily. But if the impressions could be definitely comprehended without the conception, this latter would not reduce them to unity. Hence, the impressions (or more immediate conceptions) cannot be definitely conceived or attended to, to the neglect of an elementary conception which reduces them to unity. On the other hand, when such a conception has once been obtained, there is, in general, no reason why the premises which have occasioned it should not be neglected, and therefore the explaining conception may frequently be prescinded from the more immediate ones and from the impressions.

§6. The facts now collected afford the basis for a systematic method of searching out whatever universal elementary conceptions there may be intermediate between the manifold of substance and the unity of being. It has been shown that the occasion of the introduction of a universal elementary conception is either the reduction of the manifold of substance to unity, or else the conjunction to substance of another conception. And it has further been shown that the elements conjoined cannot be supposed without the conception, whereas the conception can generally be supposed without these elements. Now, empirical psychology discovers the occasion of the introduction of a conception, and we have only to ascertain what conception already lies in the data which is united to that of substance by the first conception, but which cannot be supposed without this first conception, to have the next conception in order in passing from being to substance.

It may be noticed that, throughout this process, *introspection* is not resorted to. Nothing is assumed respecting the subjective elements of consciousness which cannot be securely inferred from the objective elements.

§7. The conception of *being* arises upon the formation of a proposition. A proposition always has, besides a term to express the substance, another to express the quality of that substance; and the function of the conception of being is to unite the quality to the substance. Quality, therefore, in its very widest sense, is the first conception in order in passing from being to substance.

Quality seems at first sight to be given in the impression. Such results of introspection are untrustworthy. A proposition asserts the applicability of a mediate conception to a more immediate one. Since this is *asserted,* the more mediate conception is clearly regarded independently of this circumstance, for otherwise the two conceptions would not be distinguished, but one would be thought through the other, without this latter being an object of thought, at all. The mediate conception, then, in order to be *asserted* to be applicable to the other, must first be considered without regard to this circumstance, and taken immediately. But, taken immediately, it transcends what is given (the more immediate conception), and its applicability to the latter is hypothetical. Take, for example, the proposition, "This stove is black." Here the conception of *this stove* is the more immediate, that of *black* the more mediate, which latter, to be predicated of the former, must be discriminated from it and considered *in itself,* not as applied to an object, but simply as embodying a quality, *blackness.* Now this *blackness* is a pure species or abstraction, and its application to *this stove* is entirely hypothetical. The same thing is meant by "the stove is black," as by "there is blackness in the stove." *Embodying blackness* is the equivalent of *black.* [1] The proof is this. These conceptions are applied indifferently to precisely the same facts. If, therefore, they were different, the one which was first applied would fulfil every function of the other; so that one of them would be superfluous. Now a superfluous conception is an arbitrary fiction, whereas elementary conceptions arise only upon the requirement of experience; so that a superfluous elementary conception is impossible. Moreover, the conception of a pure abstraction is indispensable, because we cannot comprehend an agreement of two things, except as an agreement in some *respect,*

---

1. This agrees with the author of *De Generibus et Speciebus, Ouvrages Inédits d'Abélard,* p. 528.

and this respect is such a pure abstraction as blackness. Such a pure abstraction, reference to which constitutes a *quality* or general attribute, may be termed a *ground.*

Reference to a ground cannot be prescinded from being, but being can be prescinded from it.

§8. Empirical psychology has established the fact that we can know a quality only by means of its contrast with or similarity to another. By contrast and agreement a thing is referred to a correlate, if this term may be used in a wider sense than usual. The occasion of the introduction of the conception of reference to a ground is the reference to a correlate, and this is, therefore, the next conception in order.

Reference to a correlate cannot be prescinded from reference to a ground; but reference to a ground may be prescinded from reference to a correlate.

§9. The occasion of reference to a correlate is obviously by comparison. This act has not been sufficiently studied by the psychologists, and it will, therefore, be necessary to adduce some examples to show in what it consists. Suppose we wish to compare the letters p and b. We may imagine one of them to be turned over on the line of writing as an axis, then laid upon the other, and finally to become transparent so that the other can be seen through it. In this way we shall form a new image which mediates between the images of the two letters, inasmuch as it represents one of them to be (when turned over) the likeness of the other. Again, suppose we think of a murderer as being in relation to a murdered person; in this case we conceive the act of the murder, and in this conception it is represented that corresponding to every murderer (as well as to every murder) there is a murdered person; and thus we resort again to a mediating representation which represents the relate as standing for a correlate with which the mediating representation is itself in relation. Again, suppose we look out the word *homme* in a French dictionary; we shall find opposite to it the word *man,* which, so placed, represents *homme* as representing the same two-legged creature which *man* itself represents. By a further accumulation of instances, it would be found that every comparison requires, besides the related thing, the ground, and the correlate, also a *mediating representation which represents the relate to be a representation of the same correlate which this mediating representation itself represents.* Such a mediating representation may be termed an *interpretant,* because it fulfils the office of an interpreter, who says that a foreigner says the same thing which he himself says. The term "representation" is here to be understood in a very extended sense, which can be explained by instances better than by a definition. In this sense, a word represents a thing to the conception in the mind of the hearer, a portrait represents the person for whom it is intended to the conception of recognition, a weathercock represents the direction of the wind to the conception of him who understands it, a barrister represents his client to the judge and jury whom he influences.

Every reference to a correlate, then, conjoins to the substance the conception of a reference to an interpretant; and this is, therefore, the next conception in order in passing from being to substance.

Reference to an interpretant cannot be prescinded from reference to a correlate; but the latter can be prescinded from the former.

§10. Reference to an interpretant is rendered possible and justified by that which renders possible and justifies comparison. But that is clearly the diversity of impressions. If we had but one impression, it would not require to be reduced to unity, and would therefore not need to be thought of as referred to an interpretant, and the conception of reference to an interpretant would not arise. But since there is a manifold of impressions, we have a feeling of complication or confusion, which leads us to differentiate this impression from that, and then, having been differentiated, they require to be brought to unity. Now they are not brought to unity until we conceive them together as being *ours*, that is, until we refer them to a conception as their interpretant. Thus, the reference to an interpretant arises upon the holding together of diverse impressions, and therefore it does not join a conception to the substance, as the other two references do, but unites directly the manifold of the substance itself. It is, therefore, the last conception in order in passing from being to substance.

§11. The five conceptions thus obtained, for reasons which will be sufficiently obvious, may be termed *categories*. That is,

> BEING,
>> Quality (Reference to a Ground),
>> Relation (Reference to a Correlate),
>> Representation (Reference to an Interpretant),
> SUBSTANCE.

The three intermediate conceptions may be termed accidents.

§12. This passage from the many to the one is numerical. The conception of a *third* is that of an object which is so related to two others, that one of these must be related to the other in the same way in which the third is related to that other. Now this coincides with the conception of an interpretant. An *other* is plainly equivalent to a *correlate*. The conception of second differs from that of other, in implying the possibility of a third. In the same way, the conception of *self* implies the possibility of an *other*. The *Ground* is the self abstracted from the concreteness which implies the possibility of an other.

§13. Since no one of the categories can be prescinded from those above it, the list of supposable objects which they afford is,

What is.
  Quale—that which refers to a ground,
  Relate—that which refers to ground and correlate,
  Representamen—that which refers to ground, correlate, and
    interpretant.
It.

§14. A quality may have a special determination which prevents its being prescinded from reference to a correlate. Hence there are two kinds of relation.

1st. That of relates whose reference to a ground is a prescindible or internal quality.

2d. That of relates whose reference to a ground is an unprescindible or relative quality.

In the former case, the relation is a mere *concurrence* of the correlates in one character, and the relate and correlate are not distinguished. In the latter case the correlate is set over against the relate, and there is in some sense an *opposition*.

Relates of the first kind are brought into relation simply by their agreement. But mere disagreement (unrecognized) does not constitute relation, and therefore relates of the second kind are only brought into relation by correspondence in fact.

A reference to a ground may also be such that it cannot be prescinded from a reference to an interpretant. In this case it may be termed an *imputed* quality. If the reference of a relate to its ground can be prescinded from reference to an interpretant, its relation to its correlate is a mere concurrence or community in the possession of a quality, and therefore the reference to a correlate can be prescinded from reference to an interpretant. It follows that there are three kinds of representations.

1st. Those whose relation to their objects is a mere community in some quality, and these representations may be termed *Likenesses*.

2d. Those whose relation to their objects consists in a correspondence in fact, and these may be termed *Indices* or *Signs*.

3d. Those the ground of whose relation to their objects is an imputed character, which are the same as *general signs*, and these may be termed *Symbols*.

§15. I shall now show how the three conceptions of reference to a ground, reference to an object, and reference to an interpretant are the fundamental ones of at least one universal science, that of logic. Logic is said to treat of second intentions as applied to first. It would lead me too far away from the matter in hand to discuss the truth of this statement; I shall simply adopt it as one which seems to me to afford a good definition of the subject-genus of this science. Now, second intentions are the objects of the understanding considered as representations, and the first intentions to which they apply are the objects of those representations. The objects of the understanding, considered as representations, are symbols, that is, signs which are at least potentially general. But the rules of logic hold good of any symbols, of those which are written or spoken as well as of those which are thought. They have no immediate application to likenesses or indices, because no arguments can be constructed of these alone, but do apply to all symbols. All symbols, indeed, are in one sense relative to the understanding, but only in the sense in which also all things are relative to the understanding. On this account, therefore, the relation to the understanding need not be expressed in the definition of the sphere of logic, since it determines no limitation of that sphere. But a distinction can be made between concepts which are supposed to have no existence except so far as they are actually present to the understanding, and external symbols which still retain their character of symbols so long as they are only *capable* of being understood. And as the rules of logic apply to these latter as much as to the former (and though only through the former, yet this character, since it belongs to all things, is no limitation), it follows that logic has for its subject-genus all symbols and not merely concepts.[2] We come, therefore, to this, that logic treats of the reference of symbols in general to their objects. In this view it is one of a trivium of conceivable sciences. The first would treat of the formal conditions of symbols having meaning, that is of the reference of symbols in general to their grounds or imputed characters, and this might be called formal grammar; the second, logic, would treat of the formal conditions of the truth of symbols; and the third would treat of the formal conditions of the force of symbols, or their power of appealing to a mind, that is, of their reference in general to interpretants, and this might be called formal rhetoric.

There would be a general division of symbols, common to all these sciences; namely, into,

1°: Symbols which directly determine only their *grounds* or imputed qualities, and are thus but sums of marks or *terms;*

2°: Symbols which also independently determine their *objects* by means of other term or terms, and thus, expressing their own objective validity, become capable of truth or falsehood, that is, are *propositions;* and,

3°: Symbols which also independently determine their *interpretants,* and thus the minds to which they appeal, by premising a proposition or propositions which such a mind is to admit. These are *arguments.*

And it is remarkable that, among all the definitions of the proposition, for example, as the *oratio indicativa,* as the subsumption of an object under a concept, as the expression of the relation of two concepts, and as the indication of the mutable ground of appearance, there is, perhaps, not one in which the conception of reference to an object or correlate is not the important one. In the same way, the conception of reference to an interpretant or third, is always prominent in the definitions of argument.

In a proposition, the term which separately indicates the object of the symbol is termed the subject, and that which indicates the ground is termed the predicate. The objects indicated by the subject (which are always potentially a plurality,—at least, of phases or

2. Herbart says: "Unsre sämmtlichen Gedanken lassen sich von zwei Seiten betrachten; theils als Thätigkeiten unseres Geistes, theils in Hinsicht dessen, *was* durch sie gedacht wird. In letzterer Beziehung heissen sie *Begriffe,* welches Wort, indem es das *Begriffene* bezeichnet, zu abstrahiren gebietet von der Art und Weise, wie wir den Gedanken empfangen, produciren, oder reproduciren mögen." But the whole difference between a concept and an external sign lies in these respects which logic ought, according to Herbart, to abstract from.

appearances) are therefore stated by the proposition to be related to one another on the ground of the character indicated by the predicate. Now this relation may be either a concurrence or an opposition. Propositions of concurrence are those which are usually considered in logic; but I have shown in a paper upon the classification of arguments that it is also necessary to consider separately propositions of opposition, if we are to take account of such arguments as the following:—

Whatever is the half of anything is less than that of which it is the half;

$$A \text{ is half of } B:$$
$$\therefore A \text{ is less than } B.$$

The subject of such a proposition is separated into two terms, a "subject nominative" and an "object accusative."

In an argument, the premises form a representation of the conclusion, because they indicate the interpretant of the argument, or representation representing it to represent its object. The premises may afford a likeness, index, or symbol of the conclusion. In deductive argument, the conclusion is represented by the premises as by a general sign under which it is contained. In hypotheses, something *like* the conclusion is proved, that is, the premises form a likeness of the conclusion. Take, for example, the following argument:—

$$M \text{ is, for instance, } P', P'', P''', \text{ and } P^{iv};$$
$$S \text{ is } P', P'', P''', \text{ and } P^{iv}:$$
$$\therefore S \text{ is } M.$$

Here the first premise amounts to this, that "P', P'', P''', and P^{iv}" is a likeness of M, and thus the premises are or represent a likeness of the conclusion. That it is different with induction another example will show.

$$S', S'', S''', \text{ and } S^{iv} \text{ are taken as samples of the collection } M;$$
$$S', S'', S''', \text{ and } S^{iv} \text{ are } P:$$
$$\therefore \text{ All } M \text{ is } P.$$

Hence the first premise amounts to saying that "S', S'', S''', and S^{iv}" is an index of M. Hence the premises are an index of the conclusion.

The other divisions of terms, propositions, and arguments arise from the distinction of extension and comprehension. I propose to treat this subject in a subsequent paper. But I will so far anticipate that, as to say that there is, first, the direct reference of a symbol to its objects, or its denotation; second, the reference of the symbol to its ground, through its object, that is, its reference to the common characters of its objects, or its connotation; and third, its reference to its interpretants through its object, that is, its reference to all the synthetical propositions in which its objects in common are subject or predicate, and this I term the information it embodies. And as every addition to what it denotes, or to what it connotes, is effected by means of a distinct proposition of this kind, it follows that the extension and comprehension of a term are in an inverse relation, as long as the information remains the same, and that every increase of information is accompanied by an increase of one or other of these two quantities. It may be observed that extension and comprehension are very often taken in other senses in which this last proposition is not true.

This is an imperfect view of the application which the conceptions which, according to our analysis, are the most fundamental ones find in the sphere of logic. It is believed, however, that it is sufficient to show that at least something may be usefully suggested by considering this science in this light.

Upon the Logic of Mathematics

P 33: Presented (by title)
10 September 1867

PART I

The object of the present paper is to show that there are certain general propositions from which the truths of mathematics follow syllogistically, and that these propositions may be taken as definitions of the objects under the consideration of the mathematician without involving any assumption in reference to experience or intuition. That there actually are such objects in experience or pure intuition is not in itself a part of pure mathematics.

Let us first turn our attention to the logical calculus of Boole. I have shown in a previous communication to the Academy, that this calculus involves eight operations, viz. Logical Addition, Arithmetical Addition, Logical Multiplication, Arithmetical Multiplication, and the processes inverse to these.

Definitions

1. *Identity.* $a \doteqdot b$ expresses the two facts that any a is b and any b is a.
2. *Logical Addition.* $a \mathbin{+\!\!\!,} b$ denotes a member of the class which contains under it all the a's and all the b's, and nothing else.
3. *Logical Multiplication.* a,b denotes only whatever is both a and b.
4. *Zero* denotes *nothing,* or the class without extent, by which we mean that if a is any member of any class, $a \mathbin{+\!\!\!,} 0$ is a.
5. *Unity,* denotes *being,* or the class without content, by which we mean that, if a is a member of any class, a is $a,1$.
6. *Arithmetical Addition.* $a + b$, if $a,b \doteqdot 0$ is the same as $a \mathbin{+\!\!\!,} b$, but, if a and b are classes which have any extent in common, it is not a class.
7. *Arithmetical Multiplication.* ab represents an event when a and b are events only if these events are independent of each other, in which case $ab \doteqdot a,b$. By the events being independent is meant that it is possible to take two series of terms, A_1, A_2, A_3, &c., and B_1, B_2, B_3, &c., such that the following conditions will be satisfied. (Here x denotes any individual or class, not nothing; A_m, A_n, B_m, B_n, any members of the two series of terms, and ΣA, ΣB, $\Sigma(A,B)$ logical sums of some of the A_n's, the B_n's, and the (A_n,B_n)'s respectively.)

Condition 1. No A_m is A_n.
         "   2. No B_m is B_n.
         "   3. $x \doteqdot \Sigma(A,B)$.
         "   4. $a \doteqdot \Sigma A$.
         "   5. $b \doteqdot \Sigma B$.
         "   6. Some A_m is B_n.

From these definitions a series of theorems follow syllogistically, the proofs of most of which are omitted on account of their ease and want of interest.

Theorems

I

If $a \doteq b$, then $b \doteq a$.

II

If $a \doteq b$, and $b \doteq c$, then $a \doteq c$.

III

If $a +\!\!, b \doteq c$, then $b +\!\!, a \doteq c$.

IV

If $a +\!\!, b \doteq m$ and $b +\!\!, c \doteq n$ and $a +\!\!, n \doteq x$, then $m +\!\!, c \doteq x$.

Corollary.—These last two theorems hold good also for arithmetical addition.

V

If $a + b \doteq c$ and $a' + b \doteq c$, then $a \doteq a'$, or else there is nothing not b.

This theorem does not hold with logical addition. But from definition 6 it follows that

> No a is b (supposing there is any a)
> No a' is b (supposing there is any a')

neither of which propositions would be implied in the corresponding formulæ of logical addition. Now from definitions 2 and 6,

> Any a is c
> $\therefore$ Any a is c not b

But again from definitions 2 and 6 we have

> Any c not b is a' (if there is any not b)
> $\therefore$ Any a is a' (if there is any not b)

And in a similar way it could be shown that any a' is a (under the same supposition). Hence by definition 1,

$$a \doteq a' \text{ if there is anything not } b.$$

Scholium.—In arithmetic this proposition is limited by the supposition that b is finite. The supposition here though similar to that is not quite the same.

VI

If $a,b \doteq c,$ then $b,a \doteq c.$

VII

If $a,b \doteq m$ and $b,c \doteq n$ and $a,n \doteq x,$ then $m,c \doteq x.$

VIII

If $m,n \doteq b$ and $a +\!\!,\, m \doteq u$ and $a +\!\!,\, n \doteq v$ and $a +\!\!,\, b \doteq x,$ then $u,v \doteq x.$

IX

If $m +\!\!,\, n \doteq b$ and $a,m \doteq u$ and $a,n \doteq v$ and $a,b \doteq x,$ then $u +\!\!,\, v \doteq x.$

The proof of this theorem may be given as an example of the proofs of the rest.

It is required then (by definition 3) to prove three propositions, viz.

1st. That any u is x.
2d. That any v is x.
3d. That any x not u is v.

First Proposition

Since $u \doteq a,m$ by definition 3

Any u is $m,$

and since $m +\!\!,\, n \doteq b$ by definition 2

Any m is $b,$

whence   Any u is b,

But since $u \;=\; a\,,m$ by definition 3

                                Any u is a,

whence   Any u is both a and b,

But since $a\,,b \;=\; x$ by definition 3

                         Whatever is both a and b is x

whence   Any u is x.

Second Proposition

This is proved like the first.

Third Proposition

Since $a\,,m \;=\; u$ by definition 3,

                         Whatever is both a and m is u.

or   Whatever is not u is not both a and m.

or   Whatever is not u is either not a or not m.

or   Whatever is not u and is a is not m.

But since $a\,,b \;=\; x$ by definition 3

                         Any x is a,

whence   Any x not u is not u and is a,

whence   Any x not u is not m.

But since $a\,,b \;=\; x$ by definition 3

                         Any x is b,

whence   Any x not u is b,

                          Any x not u is b not m.

But since $m \mathbin{+\!\!,} n \mathbin{=\!\!\!=} b$ by definition 2

                          Any b not m is n,

whence   Any x not u is n,

and therefore   Any x not u is both a and m.

But since $a, n \mathbin{=\!\!\!=} v$ by definition 3

                          Whatever is both a and u is v,

whence   Any x not u is v.

Corollary 1.—This proposition readily extends itself to arithmetical addition.

Corollary 2.—The converse propositions produced by transposing the last two identities of Theorems VIII and IX are also true.

Corollary 3.—Theorems VI, VII, and IX hold also with arithmetical multiplication. This is sufficiently evident in the case of theorem VI, because by definition 7 we have an additional premise, namely, that a and b are independent, and an additional conclusion which is the same as that premise.

In order to show the extension of the other theorems, I shall begin with the following lemma. If a and b are independent, then corresponding to every pair of individuals, one of which is both a and b, there is just one pair of individuals one of which is a and the other b; and conversely, if the pairs of individuals so correspond, a and b are independent. For, suppose a and b independent, then, by definition 7, condition 3, every class (A_m, B_n) is an individual. If then A_a denotes any A_m which is a, and B_b any B_m which is b, by condition 6 (A_a, B_n) and (A_m, B_b) both exist, and by conditions 4 and 5 the former is any individual a, and the latter any individual b. But given this pair of individuals, both of the pair (A_a, B_b) and (A_m, B_n) exist by condition 6. But one individual of this pair is both a and b. Hence the pairs correspond, as stated above. Next, suppose a and b to be any two classes. Let the series of A_m's be a and not-a; and let the series of B_m's be all individuals separately. Then the first five conditions can always be satisfied. Let us suppose, then, that the sixth alone cannot be satisfied. Then A_p and B_q may be taken such that (A_p,B_q) is nothing. Since A_p and B_q are supposed both to exist, there must be two individuals (A_p,B_n) and (A_m,B_q) which exist. But there is no corresponding pair (A_m,B_n) and (A_p,B_q). Hence, no case in which the sixth condition cannot be satisfied simultaneously with the first five is a case in which the pairs rightly correspond; or, in other words, every case in which the pairs correspond rightly is a case in which the sixth condition can be satisfied, provided the first five can be satisfied. But the first five can always be satisfied. Hence, if the pairs correspond as stated, the classes are independent.

In order to show that Theorem VII may be extended to arithmetical multiplication, we have to prove that if a and b, b and c, and a and (b,c), are independent, then (a,b) and c are independent. Let s denote any individual. Corresponding to every s with (a,b,c), there is an a and (b,c). Hence, corresponding to every s with s and with (a,b,c) (which is a particular case of that pair), there is an s with a and with (b,c). But for every s with (b,c) there is a b with c; hence, corresponding to every a with s and with (b,c), there is an a with b and with c. Hence, for every s with s and with (a,b,c) there is an a with b and with c. For every a with b there is an s with (a,b); hence, for every a with b and with c, there is an s with (a,b) and c. Hence, for every s with s and with (a,b,c) there is an s with (a,b) and with c. Hence, for every s with (a,b,c) there is an (a,b) with c. The converse could be proved in the same way. Hence, &c.

Theorem IX holds with arithmetical addition of whichever sort the multiplication is. For we have the additional premise that "No m is n"; whence since "any u is m" and "any v is n," "no u is v," which is the additional conclusion.

Corollary 2, so far as it relates to Theorem IX, holds with arithmetical addition and multiplication. For, since no m is n, every pair, one of which is a and either m or n, is either a pair, one of which is a and m, or a pair, one of which is a and n, and is not both. Hence, since for every pair one of which is a and m, there is a pair one of which is a and the other m, and since for every pair one of which is a, n there is a pair one of which is a and the other n; for every pair one of which is a and either m or n, there is either a pair one of which is a and the other m, or a pair one of which is a and the other n, and not both; or, in other words, there is a pair one of which is a and the other either m or n.

[It would perhaps have been better to give this complicated proof in its full syllogistic form. But as my principal object is merely to show that the various theorems could be so proved, and as there can be little doubt that if this is true of those which relate to arithmetical addition it is true also of those which relate to arithmetical multiplication, I have thought the above proof (which is quite apodeictic) to be sufficient. The reader should be careful not to confound a proof which needs itself to be experienced with one which requires experience of the object of proof.]

X

If $ab \doteq c$ and $a'b \doteq c$, then $a \doteq a'$, or no b exists.

This does not hold with logical, but does with arithmetical multiplication.

For if a is not identical with a', it may be divided thus

$$a \doteq a,a' + a,\bar{a}'$$

if $\bar{a}'$ denotes not a'. Then

$$a,b \doteq (a,a'),b + (a,\bar{a}'),b$$

and by the definition of independence the last term does not vanish unless $(a,\bar{a}') \doteq 0$ or all a is a'; but since $a,b \doteq a',b \doteq (a,a'),b + (\bar{a},a'),b$, this term does vanish, and, therefore, only a is a', and in a similar way it could be shown that only a' is a.

XI

$1 +, a \doteq 1$.

This is not true of arithmetical addition, for since by definition 7,

$$1x,1 \doteq x1$$

by Theorem IX

$$x,(1 + a) \doteq x(1 + a) \doteq x1 + xa \doteq x + xa$$

Whence $xa \doteqdot 0$, while neither x nor a is zero, which, as will appear directly, is impossible.

XII

$0,a \doteqdot 0$

Proof.—For call $0,a \doteqdot x$. Then by definition 3

x belongs to the class *zero*.

∴ by definition 4 $x \doteqdot 0$.

Corollary 1.—The same reasoning applies to arithmetical multiplication.

Corollary 2.—From Theorem x and the last corollary it follows that if $ab \doteqdot 0$, either $a \doteqdot 0$ or $b \doteqdot 0$.

XIII

$a,a \doteqdot a.$

XIV

$a \mathbin{+\!\!,} a \doteqdot a.$

These do not hold with arithmetical operations.

General Scholium.—This concludes the theorems relating to the direct operations. As the inverse operations have no peculiar logical interest, they are passed over here.

In order to prevent misapprehension, I will remark that I do not undertake to demonstrate the principles of logic themselves. Indeed, as I have shown in a previous paper, these principles considered as speculative truths are absolutely empty and indistinguishable. But what has been proved is the *maxims* of logical procedure, a certain system of signs being given.

The definitions given above for the processes which I have termed arithmetical plainly leave the functions of these operations in many cases uninterpreted. Thus if we write

$$a + b \doteqdot b + a$$
$$a + (b + c) \doteqdot (a + b) + c$$
$$bc \doteqdot cb$$
$$(ab)c \doteqdot a(bc)$$
$$a(m + n) \doteqdot am + an$$

we have a series of identities whose truth or falsity is entirely un-determinable. In order, therefore, *fully to define those operations,* we will say that all propositions, equations, and identities which are in the general case left by the former definitions undetermined as to truth shall be true, provided they are so in all interpretable cases.

On Arithmetic

Equality is a relation of which identity is a species.

If we were to leave equality without further defining it, then by the last scholium all the formal rules of arithmetic would follow from it. And this completes the central design of this paper, as far as arithmetic is concerned.

Still it may be well to consider the matter a little further. Imagine, then, a particular case under Boole's calculus, in which the letters are no longer terms of first intention, but terms of second intention, and that of a special kind. Genus, species, difference, property, and acci-dent, are the well-known terms of second intention. These relate particularly to the *comprehension* of first intentions; that is, they refer to different sorts of predication. Genus and species, however, have at least a secondary reference to the *extension* of first inten-tions. Now let the letters, in the particular application of Boole's calculus now supposed, be terms of second intention which relate exclusively to the extension of first intentions. Let the differences of the characters of things and events be disregarded, and let the letters signify only the differences of classes as wider or narrower. In other words, the only logical comprehension which the letters considered as terms will have is the greater or less divisibility of the classes. Thus, n in another case of Boole's calculus might, for example, denote "New England States"; but in the case now supposed, all the charac-ters which make these States what they are being neglected, it would signify only what essentially belongs to a class which has the same relations to higher and lower classes which the class of New England States has,—that is, a collection of *six.*

In this case, the sign of identity will receive a special meaning. For, if m denotes what essentially belongs to a class of the rank of "sides of a cube," then $m = n$ will imply, not that every New En-gland State is a side of a cube, and conversely, but that whatever essentially belongs to a class of the numerical rank of "New England States" essentially belongs to a class of the rank of "sides of a cube," and conversely. *Identity* of this particular sort may be termed *equal-ity*, and be denoted by the sign $=$.[1] Moreover, since the numerical rank of a *logical sum* depends on the identity or diversity (in first intention) of the integrant parts, and since the numerical rank of a *logical product* depends on the identity or diversity (in first inten-tion) of parts of the factors, logical addition and multiplication can have no place in this system. Arithmetical addition and multiplica-tion, however, will not be destroyed. $ab = c$ will imply that whatever essentially belongs at once to a class of the rank of a, and to another independent class of the rank of b belongs essentially to a class of the rank of c, and conversely. $a + b = c$ implies that whatever belongs essentially to a class which is the logical sum of two mutually exclu-sive classes of the ranks of a and b belongs essentially to a class of the rank of c, and conversely. It is plain that from these definitions the same theorems follow as from those given above. *Zero* and *unity* will, as before, denote the classes which have respectively no extension and no comprehension; only the comprehension here spoken of is, of course, that comprehension which alone belongs to letters in the system now considered, that is, this or that degree of divisibility; and therefore *unity* will be what belongs essentially to a class of any rank independent of its divisibility. These two classes alone are common to the two systems, because the first intentions of these alone deter-mine, and are determined by, their second intentions. Finally, the laws of the Boolian calculus, in its ordinary form, are identical with those of this other so far as the latter apply to *zero* and *unity*, because every class, in its first intention, is either without any extension (that is, is nothing), or belongs essentially to that rank to which every class belongs, whether divisible or not.

These considerations, together with those advanced on page 55 (§12) of this volume, will, I hope, put the relations of logic and arith-metic in a somewhat clearer light than heretofore.

---

1. Thus, in one point of view, *identity* is a species of *equality*, and, in another, the reverse is the case. This is because the Being of the copula may be considered on the one hand (with De Morgan) as a special description of "inconvertible, transitive relation," while, on the other hand, all relation may be considered as a special determi-nation of being. If a Hegelian should be disposed to see a contradiction here, an accurate analysis of the matter will show him that it is only a verbal one.

Upon Logical Comprehension and Extension

P 34: Presented 13 November 1867

§1. *That these Conceptions are not so Modern as has been represented*

The historical account usually given of comprehension and extension is this, "that the distinction, though taken in general terms by Aristotle, and explicitly announced with scientific precision by one, at least, of his Greek commentators, had escaped the marvellous acuteness of the schoolmen, and remained totally overlooked and forgotten till the publication of the *Port-Royal Logic.*"[1] I would offer the following considerations to show that this interpretation of history is not exactly true. In the first place, it is said that a distinction was taken between these attributes, as though they were previously confounded. Now there is not the least evidence of this. A German logician has, indeed, by a subtle misconception, considered extension as a species of comprehension, but, to a mind beginning to reflect, no notions seem more unlike. The mental achievement has been the bringing of them into relation to one another, and the conception of them as factors of the import of a term, and not the separation of them. In the second place it is correctly said that the doctrine taught by the Port Royalists is substantially contained in the work of a Greek commentator. That work is no other than Porphyry's *Isagoge*[2]; and therefore it would be most surprising if the doctrine had been totally overlooked by the schoolmen, for whether their acuteness was as marvellous as Hamilton taught or not, they certainly studied the commentary in question as diligently as they did the Bible. It would seem, indeed, that the tree of Porphyry involves the whole doctrine

---

1. This is quoted from Baynes (*Port-Royal Logic*, 2d ed., p. xxxiii), who says that he is indebted to Sir William Hamilton for the information.
2. Porphyry appears to refer to the doctrine as an ancient one.

of extension and comprehension except the names. Nor were the scholastics without names for these quantities. The *partes subjectives* and *partes essentiales* are frequently opposed; and several other synonymes are mentioned by the Conimbricenses. It is admitted that Porphyry fully enunciates the doctrine; it must also be admitted that the passage in question is fully dealt with and correctly explained by the mediæval commentators. The most that can be said, therefore, is that the doctrine of extension and comprehension was not a prominent one in the mediæval logic.[3]

A like degree of historical error is commonly committed in reference to another point which will come to be treated of in this paper, allied, at least, as it is most intimately, with the subject of comprehension and extension, inasmuch as it also is founded on a conception of a term as a whole composed of parts,—I mean the distinction of clear and distinct. Hamilton tells us "we owe the discrimination to the acuteness of the great Leibniz. By the Cartesians the distinction had not been taken; though the authors of the *Port-Royal Logic* came so near that we may well marvel how they failed explicitly to enounce it." (*Lectures on Logic;* Lecture IX.) Now, in fact, all that the Port Royalists say about this matter[4] is copied from Descartes,[5] and their variations from his wording serve only to confuse what in him is tolerably distinct. As for Leibniz, he himself expressly avows that the distinction drawn by Descartes is the same as his own.[6] Nevertheless, it is very much more clear with Leibniz than with Descartes. A philosophical distinction emerges gradually into consciousness; there is no moment in history before which it is altogether unrecognized, and after which it is perfectly luminous. Before Descartes, the dis-

---

3. The author of *De Generibus et Speciebus* opposes the *integral* and *diffinitive* wholes. John of Salisbury refers to the distinction of comprehension and extension, as something "quod fere in omnium ore celebre est aliud, scilicet esse quod appellativa *significant*, et aliud esse quod *nominant.* Nominantur singularia, sed universalia significantur." (*Metalogicus*, lib. 2, cap. 20. Ed. of 1610, p. 111.)

Vincentius Bellovacensis (*Speculum Doctrinale,* Lib. III, cap. xi.) has the following: "Si vero quæritur utrum hoc universale 'homo' sit in quolibet homine secundum se totum an secundem partem, dicendum est quod secundum se totum, id est secundum quamlibet sui partem diffinitivam. . . . Non autem secundum quamlibet partem subjectivam." William of Auvergne (Prantl's *Geschichte,* Vol. III, p. 77) speaks of "totalitatem istam, quæ est ex partibus rationis seu diffinitionis, et hae partes sunt genus et differentiæ; alio modo partes speciei individua sunt, quoniam ipsam speciem, cum de eis prædicatur, sibi invicem quodammodo partiuntur." If we were to go to later authors, the examples would be endless. See any commentary *Physics,* Lib. I.

4. Part I, chap. ix.

5. *Principia,* Part I, §45 *et seq.*

6. Eighth Letter to Burnet.

tinction of confused and distinct had been thoroughly developed, but the difference between distinctness and clearness is uniformly overlooked. Scotus distinguishes between conceiving confusedly and conceiving the confused, and since any obscure concept necessarily includes more than its proper object, there is always in what is obscurely conceived a conception of something confused; but the schoolmen came no nearer than this to the distinction of Descartes and Leibniz.

§2. *Of the Different Terms applied to the Quantities of Extension and Comprehension*

Extension and *comprehension* are the terms employed by the Port Royalists. Owing to the influence of Hamilton, *intension* is now frequently used for *comprehension;* but it is liable to be confounded with *intensity,* and therefore is an objectionable word. It is derived from the use of cognate words by Cajetan and other early writers. *External* and *internal quantity* are the terms used by many early Kantians. *Scope* and *force* are proposed by De Morgan. *Scope* in ordinary language expresses extension, but *force* does not so much express comprehension as the power of creating a lively representation in the mind of the person to whom a word or speech is addressed. Mr. J. S. Mill has introduced the useful verbs *denote* and *connote,* which have become very familiar. It has been, indeed, the opinion of the best students of the logic of the fourteenth, fifteenth, and sixteenth centuries, that *connotation* was in those ages used exclusively for the reference to a second significate, that is (nearly) for the reference of a relative term (such as *father, brighter,* &c.) to the correlate of the object which it primarily denotes, and was never taken in Mill's sense of the reference of a term to the essential characters implied in its definition.[7] Mr. Mill has, however, considered himself entitled to deny this upon his simple authority, without the citation of a single passage from any writer of that time. After explaining the sense in which he takes the term *connote,* he says:

The schoolmen, to whom we are indebted for the greater part of our logical language, gave us this also, and in this very sense. For though some of their general expressions countenance the use of the word in the more extensive

7. Cf. Morin, *Dictionnaire,* Tome I, p. 685; Chauvin, *Lexicon,* both editions; Eustachius, *Summa,* Part I, Tr. I, qu. 6.

and vague acceptation in which it is taken by Mr. [James] Mill, yet when they had to define it specifically as a technical term, and to fix its meaning as such, with that admirable precision which always characterized their definitions, they clearly explained that nothing was said to be connoted except *forms*, which word may generally, in their writings, be understood as synonymous with *attributes*.

As scholasticism is usually said to come to an end with Occam, this conveys the idea that *connote* was commonly employed by earlier writers. But the celebrated Prantl considers it conclusive proof that a passage in Occam's *Summa* is spurious, that *connotative* is there spoken of as a term in frequent use;[8] and remarks upon a passage of Scotus in which *connotatum* is found, that this conception is here met with for the first time.[9] The term occurs, however, in Alexander of Hales,[10] who makes *nomen connotans* the equivalent of *appellatio relativa*, and takes the relation itself as the object of *connotare*, speaking of *creator* as connoting the relation of creator to creature. Occam's *Summa*[11] contains a chapter devoted to the distinction of absolute and connotative names. The whole deserves to be read, but I have only space to quote the following:

Nomen autem connotativum est illud quod significat aliquid primario et aliquid secundario; et tale nomen proprie habet diffinitionem exprimentem quid nominis et frequenter oportet ponere aliquid illius diffinitionis in recto et aliud in obliquo; sicut est de hoc nomine album, nam habet diffinitionem exprimentem quid nominis in qua una dictio ponitur in recto et alia in obliquo. Unde si queratur quid significat hoc nomen album, dices quod idem quod illa oratio tota "aliquid informatum albedine" vel "aliquid habens albedinem" et patet quod una pars orationis istius ponitur in recto et alia in obliquo. . . . Huiusmodi autem nomina connotativa sunt omnia nomina concreta primo modo dicta, et hoc *quia talia concreta significant unum in recto et aliud in obliquo,* hoc est dictu, in diffinitione exprimente quid nominis debet poni unus rectus significans unam rem et alius obliquus significans aliam rem, sicut patet de omnibus talibus, iustus, albus, animatus, et sic de aliis. Huiusmodi etiam nomina sunt omnia nomina relatiua, quia semper in eorum diffinitionibus ponuntur diversa idem diuersis modis vel diuersa significantia, sicut patet de hoc nomine simile. . . . Mere autem absoluta sunt illa quæ non significant aliquid principaliter et aliud vel idem secundario, sed quicquid significatur per tale nomen æque primo significatur sicut patet de hoc nomine animal.

8. Prantl, *Geschichte*, Vol. III, p. 364.
9. Ibid. p. 134. Scotus also uses the term. *Quodlibeta*, question 13, article 4.
10. *Summa Theologica*, Part I, question 53.
11. Part I, chap. X. (Ed. of 1488, fol. 6, c.)

Eckius, in his comment on Petrus Hispanus, has also some extended remarks on the signification of the term *connote,* which agree in the main with those just quoted.[12] Mr. Mill's historical statement cannot, therefore, be admitted.

Sir William Hamilton has borrowed from certain late Greek writers the terms *breadth* and *depth,* for extension and comprehension respectively.[13] These terms have great merits. They are brief; they are suited to go together; and they are very familiar. Thus, "wide" learning is, in ordinary parlance, learning of many things; "deep" learning, much knowledge of some things. I shall, therefore, give the preference to these terms. Extension is also called *sphere* and *circuit;* and comprehension, *matter* and *content.*

§3. *Of the Different Senses in which the Terms* Extension *and* Comprehension *have been accepted*

The terms *extension* and *comprehension,* and their synonymes, are taken in different senses by different writers. This is partly owing to the fact that while most writers speak only of the extension and comprehension of concepts, others apply these terms equally to concepts and judgments (Rösling), others to any mental representation (Überweg and many French writers), others to cognition generally (Baumgarten), others to "terms" (Fowler, Spalding), others to names (Shedden), others to words (McGregor), others to "meanings" (Jevons), while one writer speaks only of the extension of *classes* and the comprehension of *attributes* (De Morgan in his *Syllabus*).

Comprehension is defined by the Port Royalists as "those attributes which an idea involves in itself, and which cannot be taken away from it without destroying it."

It will be remembered that the *marks* of a term are divided by logicians first into the necessary and the accidental, and that then the necessary marks are subdivided into such as are strictly essential, that is, contained in the definition, and such as are called proper. Thus it is an essential mark of a triangle to have three sides; it is a proper mark to have its three angles equal to two right angles; and it is an accidental mark to be treated of by Euclid.

---

12. Fol. 23. d. See also Tartaretus' *Expositio in Summulas Petri Hispani* towards the end. Ed. of 1509, fol. 91, b.

13. *Logic,* p. 100. In the *Summa Logices* attributed to Aquinas, we read: "Omnis forma sub se habens multa, idest quod universaliter sumitur, habet quandam *latitudinem;* nam invenitur in pluribus, et dicitur de pluribus." (Tr. 1, c. 3.)

The definition of the Port Royalists, therefore, makes comprehension include all necessary marks, whether essential or proper.

The Port Royalists attribute comprehension immediately to any ideas. Very many logicians attribute it immediately only to concepts. Now a concept, as defined by them, is strictly only the essence of an idea; they ought therefore to include in the comprehension only the essential marks of a term. These logicians, however, abstract so entirely from the real world, that it is difficult to see why these essential marks are not at the same time all the marks of the object as they suppose it.

There can, I think, be no doubt that such writers as Gerlach and Sigwart make comprehension include all marks, necessary or accidental, which are universally predicable of the object of the concept.

Again, most German writers regard the comprehension as a sum either of concepts (Drobisch, Bachmann, etc.) or of elements of intuition (Trendelenburg). But many English writers regard it as the sum of real external attributes (Shedden, Spalding, Devey, De Morgan, Jevons, McGregor, Fowler).

According to most writers, comprehension consists of the (necessary) attributes *thought* as common to the objects. Shedden defines it as consisting of all the attributes common to the things denoted.

Again, most logicians consider as marks only such as are virtually[14] predicated; a few, perhaps, only such as are actually thought, and still fewer include those which are habitually thought. Here and there is found an author who makes comprehension include all true attributes, whether thought or not.

There is also a difference in the mode of reckoning up the marks. Most writers count all distinguishable marks, while a few consider coextensive marks as the same.

In the use of the term "extension" the want of a definite convention is still more marked. The Port Royalists define it as "those *subjects* to which the idea applies." It would appear, therefore, that it might include mere fictions.

Others limit the term to *real* species, and at the same time extend it to single beings. This is the case with Watts, and also with Friedrich Fischer.

Others are most emphatic in declaring that they mean by it

---

14. I adopt the admirable distinction of Scotus between actual, habitual, and virtual cognition.

things, and not species, real or imaginary. This is the case with Bachmann, Esser, and Schulze.

Others make it include neither concepts nor things, but singular representations. This is the case with the strict Kantian.

The following table exhibits this diversity:—

Extension embraces

Individual representations	according to	Kant, E. Reinhold, etc.
Representations	" "	Fries, Überweg, etc.
Real external things and species	" "	Watts, Shedden, etc.
Real external individual objects	" "	Bachmann, Devey, etc.
Things	" "	Schulze, Bowen, etc.
Species	" "	Drobisch, De Morgan, etc.
Objects (representations)	" "	Thomson, etc.
Individuals	" "	Mahan.
Concepts	" "	Herbart, Vorländer, etc.
General terms	" "	Spalding.
Psychical concepts	" "	Strümpell.
Variable marks	" "	Ritter.

Again, logicians differ as to whether by extension they mean the concepts, species, things, or representations to which the term is habitually applied in the judgment, or all to which it is truly applicable. The latter position is held by Herbart, Kiesewetter, etc.; the former by Duncan, Spalding, Vorländer, Überweg, etc.

Some logicians include only *actual* things, representations, etc., under extension (Bachmann, Fries, Herbart); others extend it to such as are merely possible (Esser, Ritter, Gerlach).

Finally, some few logicians speak of the two quantities as numerical, while most writers regard them as mere aggregates of diverse objects or marks.

§4. *Denials of the Inverse Proportionality of the two Quantities, and Suggestions of a third Quantity*

Until lately the law of the inverse proportionality of extension and comprehension was universally admitted. It is now questioned on various grounds.

Drobisch says that the comprehension varies arithmetically,

while the extension varies geometrically. This is true, in one sense.

Lotze, after remarking that the only conception of a universal which we can have is the power of imagining singulars under it, urges that the possibility of determining a concept in a way corresponding to each particular under it is a mark of that concept, and that therefore the narrower concepts have as many marks as the wider ones. But, I reply, *these* marks belong to the concept in its second intention, and are not common marks of those things to which it applies, and are therefore no part of the comprehension. They are, in fact, the very marks which constitute the extension. No one ever denied that extension is a mark of a concept; only it is a certain mark of second intention.

Vorländer's objection is much more to the purpose. It is that if from any determinate notion, as that of Napoleon, we abstract all marks, all determination, what remains is merely the conception *something*, which has no more extension than Napoleon. "Something" has an uncertain sphere, meaning either this thing or that or the other, but has no general extension, since it means one thing only. Thus, before a race, we can say that some horse will win, meaning this one, that one, or that one; but by some horse we mean but one, and it therefore has no more extension than would a term definitely indicating which,—although this latter would be more determinate, that is, would have more comprehension. I am not aware that those who adhere to Kant's unmodified doctrine have succeeded in answering this objection.

Überweg has the following remarks.[15]

To the higher representation, since conformably to its definition it contains only the common elements of content of several lower representations, belongs in comparison to each of the lower a more limited content, but a wider circuit. The lower representation, on the contrary, has a richer content but narrower circuit. Yet by no means by every diminution or increase of a given content does the circuit increase or diminish, nor by every increase or diminution of a given circuit does the content diminish or increase.

I am surprised that he does not explain himself further upon this point, which it is the principal object of this paper to develop.

De Morgan says:[16]

15. *Logik*, 2te Aufl., §54.
16. *Formal Logic*, p. 234. His doctrine is different in the *Syllabus*.

According to such statements as I have seen, "man residing in Europe, drawing breath north of the equator, seeing the sun rise before those in America," would be a more intensively quantified notion than "man residing in Europe"; but certainly not less *extensive,* for the third and fourth elements of the notion must belong to those men to whom the first and second belong.

Mr. De Morgan adopts the definitions of extension and comprehension given by the Port Royalists. According to those definitions, if the third and fourth elements necessarily belong to the notion to which the first and second belong, they are parts of the comprehension of that second notion which is composed of the first and second elements, and therefore the two notions are equal in comprehension; but if this is not the case, then the second notion can be predicated of subjects of which the first cannot, for example, of "man residing in Europe drawing breath south of the Equator"; for that there is really no such man will not affect the truth of the proposition, and therefore the second notion is more extensive than the first.

Two logicians, only, as far as I remember, Archbishop Thomson[17] and Dr. W. D. Wilson,[18] while apparently admitting Kant's law, wish to establish a third quantity of concepts. Neither gentleman has defined his third quantity, nor has stated what its relations to the other two are. Thomson calls his Denomination. It seems to be the same as Extension regarded in a particular way. Dr. Wilson terms his new quantity Protension; it has something to do with time, and appears to be generally independent of the other two. It is plain, indeed, that as long as Kant's law holds, and as long as logical quantities can only be compared as being more or less and not directly measured, and as long as the different *kinds* of quantity cannot be compared at all, a third quantity must be directly proportional to one or other of the known quantities, and therefore must measure the same thing, or else must be independent of the other two, and be quite unconnected with them.

§5. *Three Principal Senses in which* Comprehension *and* Extension *will be taken in this Paper*

I shall adopt Hamilton's terms, *breadth* and *depth*, for extension and comprehension respectively, and shall employ them in different senses, which I shall distinguish by different adjectives.

17. *Laws of Thought,* 4th ed., §§52, 80.
18. *Logic,* Part I, chap. ii, §5.

By the *informed breadth* of a term, I shall mean all the real things of which it is predicable, with logical truth on the whole in a supposed state of information. By the phrase "on the whole" I mean to indicate that all the information at hand must be taken into account, and that those things of which there is not on the whole reason to believe that a term is truly predicable are not to be reckoned as part of its breadth.

If T be a term which is predicable only of S', S'', and S''', then the S''s, the S'''s, and the S''''s will constitute the informed breadth of T. If at the same time, S' and S'' are the subjects of which alone another term T' can be predicated, and if it is not known that all S''''s are either S' or S'', then T is said to have a greater informed breadth than T'. If the S''''s are known not to be all among the S''s and S'''s, this excess of breadth may be termed *certain,* and, if this is not known, it may be termed *doubtful.* If there are known to be S''''s, not known to be S''s or S'''s, T is said to have a greater *actual* breadth than T'; but if no S''''s are known except such are known to be S''s, and S'''s (though there may be others), T is said to have a greater *potential* breadth than T'. If T and T' are conceptions in different minds, or in different states of the same mind, and it is known to the mind which conceives T that every S''' is either S'' or S', then T is said to be more *extensively distinct* than T'.[19]

By the informed depth of a term, I mean all the real characters (in contradistinction to mere names) which can be predicated of it[20] (with logical truth, on the whole) in a supposed state of information; no character being counted twice over knowingly in the supposed state of information. The depth, like the breadth, may be certain or doubtful, actual or potential, and there is a comprehensive distinctness corresponding to extensive distinctness.

The informed breadth and depth suppose a state of information which lies somewhere between two imaginary extremes. These are, first, the state in which no fact would be known, but only the meaning of terms; and, second, the state in which the information would amount to an absolute intuition of all there is, so that the things we should know would be the very substances themselves, and the qualities we should know would be the very concrete forms themselves. This suggests two other sorts of breadth and depth corresponding to

19. For the distinction of extensive and comprehensive distinctness, see Scotus, i, dist. 2, qu. 3.

20. That is, of whatever things it is applicable to.

these two states of information, and which I shall term respectively the *essential* and the *substantial* breadth and depth.

By the *essential depth* of a term, then, I mean the really conceivable qualities predicated of it in its definition.

The defined term will not perhaps be applicable to any real objects whatever. Let, for example, the definition of the term T be this,

Any T is both P' and P'' and P''',

then this sums up its whole meaning; and, as it may not be known that there is any such thing as P', the meaning of T does not imply that it exists. On the other hand, we know that neither P', P'', nor P''' is coextensive with the whole sphere of being. For they are determinate qualities, and it is the very meaning of being that it is indeterminate, that is, is more extensive than any determinate term. In fact, P', for example, is a real notion which we never could have except by means of its contrast to something else. Hence we must know that

Whatever is not-P' is not-T,
Whatever is not-P'' is not-T,
and   Whatever is not-P''' is not-T.

Thus if we define the *essential breadth* of a term as those real things of which, according to its very meaning, a term is predicable, not-T has an essential breadth. We may therefore divide all terms into two classes, the essentially affirmative or positive and the essentially negative; of which the former have essential depth, but no essential breadth, and the latter essential breadth, but no essential depth. It must be noted, however, that this division is not the same as the similar one which language makes. For example, *being*, according to this, is an essentially negative term, inasmuch as it means that which can be predicated of whatever you please, and so has an essential breadth; while *nothing* is an essentially positive term, inasmuch as it means that of which you are at liberty to predicate what you please, and therefore has an essential depth. The essential subjects of being cannot be enumerated, nor the essential predicates of nothing.

In essential breadth or depth, no two terms can be equal; for, were that the case, the two terms would have the same meaning, and therefore, for logical purposes, would be the same term. Two terms may have unknown relations in these quantities, on account of one or other of them not being distinctly conceived.

Substantial breadth is the aggregate of real substances of which alone a term is predicable with absolute truth. *Substantial depth* is the real concrete form which belongs to everything of which a term is predicable with absolute truth.

General terms denote several things. Each of these things has in itself no qualities, but only a certain concrete form which belongs to itself alone. This was one of the points brought out in the controversy in reference to the nature of universals.[21] As Sir William Hamilton says, not even the humanity of Leibniz belongs to Newton, but a different humanity. It is only by abstraction, by an oversight, that two things can be said to have common characters. Hence, a general term has no *substantial depth.* On the other hand, particular terms, while they have *substantial depth,* inasmuch as each of the things, one or other of which are predicated of them, has a concrete form, yet have no *substantial breadth,* inasmuch as there is no aggregate of things to which alone they are applicable. In order to place this matter in a clearer light, I must remark, that I, in common with most logicians, take the copula in the sense of a sign of attribution, and not, like Hamilton, in the sense of a sign of equality in extension or comprehension. He exposes the proposition, "man is an animal," thus:—

The extension of man .... *Subject.*
equals .... *Copula.*
a part or all of the extension of animal ... *Predicate.*

And thus he makes the predicate particular. Others interpret it thus:—

Every man .... *Subject.*
has all the attributes common to .... *Copula.*
every animal .... *Predicate.*

It is in this latter sense that the copula is considered in this paper. Now, a particular is, as has been said, an *alternative* subject. Thus, "Some S is M" means, if S', S'', and S''' are the singular S's, that "either S', or else S'', or else S''', has all the attributes belonging to

21. See, for example, *De Generibus et Speciebus,* p. 548.

M." A particular term, then, has a substantial depth, because it may have a predicate which is absolutely concrete, as in the proposition, "Some man is Napoleon." But if we put the particular into the predicate we have such a proposition as this: "*M* has all the attributes belonging to *S'*, or else all those belonging to *S"*, or else all those belonging to *S'''*." And this can never be true unless *M* is a single individual. Now a single individual substance is, I will not say an atom, but the smallest part of an atom, that is, nothing at all. So that a particular can have no *substantial breadth.* Now take the universal term "*S.*" We can say, "Any *S* is *M,*" but not if *M* is a real concrete quality. We cannot say, for instance, "Any man is Napoleon." On the other hand, we can say "Any *M* is *S,*" even if *M* is a real substance or aggregate of substances. Hence a universal term has no *substantial depth,* but has *substantial breadth.* We may therefore divide all terms into substantial universals and substantial particulars.

Two terms may be equal in their substantial breadth and depth, and differ in their essential breadth and depth. But two terms cannot have relations of substantial breadth and depth which are unknown in the state of information supposed, because in that state of information everything is known.

In informed breadth and depth, two terms may be equal, and may have unknown relations. Any term, affirmative or negative, universal or particular, may have informed breadth or depth.

§6. *The Conceptions of Quality, Relation, and Representation, applied to this Subject*

In a paper presented to the Academy last May, I endeavored to show that the three conceptions of reference to a ground, reference to a correlate, and references to an interpretant, are those of which logic must principally make use. I there also introduced the term "symbol," to include both concept and word. Logic treats of the reference of symbols in general to their objects. A symbol, in its reference to its object, has a triple reference:—

1st, Its direct reference to its object, or the real things which it represents;

2d, Its reference to its ground through its object, or the common characters of those objects;

3d, Its reference to its interpretant through its object, or all the facts known about its object.

What are thus referred to, so far as they are known, are:—

1st, The informed *breadth* of the symbol;

2d, The informed *depth* of the symbol;

3d, The sum of synthetical propositions in which the symbol is subject or predicate, or the *information* concerning the symbol.

By breadth and depth, without an adjective, I shall hereafter mean the informed breadth and depth.

It is plain that the breadth and depth of a symbol, so far as they are *not* essential, measure the *information* concerning it, that is, the synthetical propositions of which it is subject or predicate. This follows directly from the definitions of breadth, depth, and information. Hence it follows:—

1st, That, as long as the information remains constant, the greater the breadth, the less the depth;

2d, That every increase of information is accompanied by an increase in depth or breadth, independent of the other quantity;

3d, That, when there is no information, there is either no depth or no breadth, and conversely.

These are the true and obvious relations of breadth and depth. They will be naturally suggested if we term the information the *area,* and write—

$$\text{Breadth} \times \text{Depth} = \text{Area.}$$

If we learn that S is P, then, as a general rule, the depth of S is increased without any decrease of breadth, and the breadth of P is increased without any decrease of depth. Either increase may be *certain* or *doubtful.*

It may be the case that either or both of these increases does not take place. If P is a negative term, it may have no depth, and therefore adds nothing to the depth of S. If S is a particular term, it may have no breadth, and then adds nothing to the breadth of P. This latter case often occurs in metaphysics, and, on account of not-P as well as P being predicated of S, gives rise to an appearance of contradiction where there really is none; for, as a contradiction consists in giving to contradictory terms some breadth in common, it follows that, if the common subject of which they are predicated has no real breadth, there is only a verbal, and not a real contradiction. It is not really contradictory, for example, to say that a boundary is both within and without what it bounds. There is also another important case in which we may learn that "*S* is *P*," without thereby adding to the depth of *S* or the breadth of *P*. This is when, in the very same act by which we learn that *S* is *P*, we also learn that *P* was covertly contained in the previous depth of *S*, and that consequently *S* was a part of the previous breadth of *P*. In this case, *P* gains in extensive distinctness and *S* in comprehensive distinctness.

We are now in condition to examine Vorländer's objection to the inverse proportionality of extension and comprehension. He requires us to think away from an object all its qualities, but not, of course, by thinking it to be without those qualities, that is, by denying those qualities of it in thought. How then? Only by supposing ourselves to be ignorant whether it has qualities or not, that is, by diminishing the supposed information; in which case, as we have seen, the depth can be diminished without increasing the breadth. In the same manner we can suppose ourselves to be ignorant whether any American but one exists, and so diminish the breadth without increasing the depth.

It is only by confusing a movement which is accompanied with a change of information with one which is not so, that people can confound generalization, induction, and abstraction. *Generalization* is an increase of breadth and a decrease of depth, without change of information. *Induction* is a certain increase of breadth without a change of depth, by an increase of believed information. *Abstraction* is a decrease of depth without any change of breadth, by a decrease of conceived information. *Specification* is commonly used (I should say unfortunately) for an increase of depth without any change of breadth, by an increase of asserted information. *Supposition* is used for the same process when there is only a conceived increase of information. *Determination*, for any increase of depth. *Restriction*, for any decrease of breadth; but more particularly without change of depth, by a supposed decrease of information. *Descent*, for a decrease of breadth and increase of depth, without change of information.

Let us next consider the effect of the different kinds of reasoning upon the breadth, depth, and area of the two terms of the conclusion.

In the case of deductive reasoning it would be easy to show, were it necessary, that there is only an increase of the extensive distinctness of the major, and of the comprehensive distinctness of the minor, without any change in information. Of course, when the conclusion is negative or particular, even this may not be effected.

Induction requires more attention. Let us take the following example:—

> S', S'', S''', and S^{iv} have been taken at random from among the M's;
> S', S'', S''', and S^{iv} are P:
> ∴ any M is P.

We have here, usually, an increase of information. M receives an increase of depth, P of breadth. There is, however, a difference between these two increases. A new predicate is actually added to M; one which may, it is true, have been covertly predicated of it before, but which is now actually brought to light. On the other hand, P is not *yet* found to apply to anything but S', S'', S''', and S^{iv}, but only to apply to whatever else may hereafter be found to be contained under M. The induction itself does not make known any such thing. Now take the following example of hypothesis:—

> M is, for instance, P', P'', P''', and P^{iv};
> S is P', P'', P''', and P^{iv}:
> ∴ S is all that M is.

Here again there is an increase of information, if we suppose the premises to represent the state of information before the inferences. S receives an addition to its depth; but only a potential one, since there is nothing to show that the M's have any common characters besides P', P'', P''', and P^{iv}. M, on the other hand, receives an actual increase of breadth in S, although, perhaps, only a *doubtful* one. There is, therefore, this important difference between induction and hypothesis, that the former potentially increases the breadth of one term, and actually increases the depth of another, while the latter potentially increases the depth of one term, and actually increases the breadth of another.

Let us now consider reasoning from definition to definitum, and also the argument from enumeration. A defining proposition has a meaning. It is not, therefore, a merely identical proposition, but there is a difference between the definition and the definitum. According to the received doctrine, this difference consists wholly in the fact that the definition is distinct, while the definitum is confused. But I think that there is another difference. The definitum implies the character of being designated by a word, while the definition, previously to the formation of the word, does not. Thus, the definitum exceeds the definition in depth, although only *verbally*. In the same way, any unanalyzed notion carries with it a feeling,—a constitutional word,—which its analysis does not. If this be so, the definition is the predicate and the definitum the subject, of the defining proposition, and this last cannot be simply converted. In fact, the defining proposition affirms that whatever a certain name is applied to is supposed to have such and such characters; but it does not strictly follow from this, that whatever has such and such characters is actually called by that name, although it certainly *might* be so called. Hence, in reasoning from definition to definitum, there is a verbal increase of depth, and an actual increase of extensive distinctness (which is analogous to breadth). The increase of depth being merely verbal, there is no possibility of error in this procedure. Nevertheless, it seems to me proper, rather to consider this argument as a special modification of hypothesis than as a deduction, such as is reasoning from definitum to definition. A similar line of thought would show that, in the argument from enumeration, there is a verbal increase of breadth, and an actual increase of depth, or rather of comprehensive distinctness, and that therefore it is proper to consider this (as most logicians have done) as a kind of infallible induction. These species of hypothesis and induction are, in fact, merely hypotheses and inductions from the essential parts to the essential whole; this sort of reasoning from parts to whole being demonstrative. On the other hand, reasoning from the substantial parts to the substantial whole is not even a probable argument. No ultimate part of matter fills space, but it does not follow that no matter fills space.

Notes

MS 152: November–December 1868

Note 1

The proof offered that

$$\varphi x \doteqdot \varphi(1),x + \varphi(0),\overline{x}$$

is fallacious. For the identities

$$\varphi(1) \doteqdot i \qquad \varphi(0) \doteqdot j$$

cannot be obtained by simply substituting 1 and 0 for x in the identity

$$\varphi x \doteqdot i,x + j,(1-x)$$

inasmuch as i and j have not been proved to be independent of x. Boole's proof is the same.

It can be proved, however, that i and j are independent of x. For let x be logically multiplied by any factor m_1 and then increased by any term a_1 and we have $m_1,x +, a_1$.

Now when the same pair of processes is performed upon an expression of this form the result is another expression of the same form for

$$m_2,(m_1,x +, a_1) +, a_2 \doteqdot (m_1,m_2),x +, (a_1 +, a_2)$$

Now to multiply by 1 or increase by 0 is the same as omitting to multiply or add at all; and therefore any series of multiplications and additions may by the intercalation of a multiplication by 1 between every pair of successive additions and of an increase by 0 between every pair of successive multiplications, be reduced to a series of alternate additions and multiplications and, therefore, the result of any operation composed only of additions and multiplications is of the form $m, x + a$. Now $m, x + a = (m, 1 + a), x + (m, 0 + a), \bar{x}$. Hence when φ involves only a series of additions and multiplications

$$\varphi x = \varphi(1), x + \varphi(0), \bar{x}$$

But such an expression as a^x does not come under this formula.

It could easily be shown by (11) and (14) that the difference or quotient of two quantities of the form $m, x + a$ is also of this form if it is interpretable and hence the result of any series of additions, subtractions, multiplications, and divisions of x and of terms independent of x, is, if interpretable such that

$$\varphi x = \varphi(1), x + \varphi(0), \bar{x}.$$

Note 2.

Identity (18') is reducible to (18) by developement of the second member by (18).

Note 3.

It should be added that

$$r \geqq p + q - 1$$

For
$$p + q - r + \bar{p}, \bar{q} = 1$$
$$\therefore r = p + q - 1 + \bar{p}, \bar{q}$$

where $\bar{p}, \bar{q}$ cannot be less than nothing. These limits have been treated both by Boole and by De Morgan.

Note 4.

The mode proposed for the expression of particular propositions is weak. What is really wanted is something much more fundamental. Another idea has since occurred to me which I have never worked out but which I can here briefly explain.

If w denotes *wise,* and s denotes Solomon, then the expression w^s cannot be interpreted by (18) or any principle of Boole's calculus.

It might then be used to denote *wiser than Solomon.* Thus, relative terms would be brought into the domain of the calculus. But if we are to have symbols for relative terms, we must have a symbol for *not* or *other than.* Let this be n. Then, n^s will denote *not Solomon.*

But Solomon is a singular. Let m denote man. Then shall w^m denote *wiser than every man* or *wiser than some man?* In either case, n^{wm} will be ambiguous. For it may be taken as $n^{(wm)}$ or as $(n^w)^m$.

Now, if we simply adopt the formula

$$w^{(a\,+,b)} \;\doteqdot\; w^a, w^b$$

which is imitated from algebra, then w^m must be *wiser than every man,* and $(n^w)^m$ must be other than wiser (no more wise) than any man, or other than wiser-than-some-man. So that wiser than some man will be $n^{((nw)^m)}$. So that both conceptions will be susceptible of expression.

Then, we have the familiar-looking formulae

$$w^{a\,+,b} \;\doteqdot\; w^a, w^b$$

But we do *not* have

$$(v^w)^a \;\doteqdot\; v^{w,a}$$

That which we have expressed as n^m can be expressed as $1 - m$ or $0/m$ without any special letter m. Can we not determine the value of n, then? Now n is fully defined by the condition that the logical product of the two expressions x and n^x (whatever x may be) is *zero;* or

$$x, n^x \;\doteqdot\; 0$$

That is to say, if either x or n^x is *zero* the other may be of any value. That is, if $x \doteqdot 0$, n^x need not be zero; or n^0 is not necessarily *zero* or *unity.* And, if n^x is zero, x may have any value; or, in general, when x is *not* zero n^x may be *zero.* Algebraical ideas at once, therefore, suggest that $n \doteqdot 0$; so that *non-man* is expressed by 0^m.

0^0 must be taken as *unity.*

The difference in meaning between $h^{(km)}$ and $(h^k)^m$ is this: if k

means *king* and *h hater* and *m* as before man, the former is hater
of every king over all men and the latter is the hater of every king
of any man.

Hence we have

$$h^{(0((0k)^m))} = (h^k)^m$$

Some examples of the method in which these exponents may be
made use of may now be shown. Let *m* be man, *a* animal. Then,
every man is an animal; or

$$m = m,a$$

or
$$m,0^a = 0$$

or
$$m +, a = a$$

Then,
$$0^a = 0^{m+,a} = 0^m,0^a$$

or
$$0^m = 0^a +, 0^m$$

And in the same way, if *h* denote head,

$$(0^h)^m = (0^h)^a +, (0^h)^m$$

and then

$$0^{(0h)^m} = 0^{(0h)^a +,(0h)^m} = 0^{(0h)^a},0^{(0h)^m}$$

That is, any man's head is an animal's head. This result cannot be
reached by any ordinary forms of Logic or by Boole's Calculus.

The next step requires us to notice an operation to which no
specific name nor symbol has been given in algebra. We have the
series of quantities

$$k \qquad k^k \qquad k^{kk} \qquad k^{kkk} \qquad \&c.$$

Let the nth of this series be denoted by the symbol k_{-n}. Then, $k_0 =$
$1 = k^0 \quad k_1 = 0$.

Then, recurring to our calculus let k denote *one foot longer.* Then

> k^m will be one foot longer than m
> k^{km} or k^m_{-2} will be two feet longer than m
> k^m_{-n} will be n feet longer than m
> k^m_0 will be no longer than m
> k^m_1 will be one foot shorter than m

Now, let k denote *killer.* Then,

> k^m is killer of every m
> k^{km} is killer of every killer of every m
> k^m_0 is Every m
> k^m_1 is killed by every m.

Then, we have, in general,

$$x, k^{(k^x_1)}_{-1} \doteqdot x$$

If, then,

$$a \doteqdot a, k^b$$

$$k^b \doteqdot a +, k^b$$

$$k^{kb}_1 \doteqdot k^{a+,kb}_1 \doteqdot k^a_1, k^{kb}_1$$

$$b, k^{kb}_1 \doteqdot k^a_1, k^{kb}_1, b$$

$$b \doteqdot b, k^a_1$$

The most curious symbol of this system must now be noticed. k_{-1} and k_1 correspond to the *active* and *passive* voices respectively. But now it is also necessary to have a species of non-relative terms derived from relatives, which correspond to the middle voice. This may be indicated by a comma as exponent. Thus, if k denotes killer, k' will be killer of himself. Then we shall have

$$k'_{-1} \doteqdot k'_1$$

$$(k^{h1}_1)_{-1} \doteqdot (h^{k-1}_{-1})_1$$

$$k' \doteqdot k^{(k')}, k'$$

Let p denote parent, l lover, s Sophroniscus, z Socrates. Then, take the premises

$$p \doteqdot l^{p_1}$$

$$s \doteqdot s, p^z$$

The former gives by being multiplied by s

$$s, p \doteqdot l^{p_1 s, p}$$

The second gives

$$z \doteqdot z, p_1^s$$

Hence, $$s \doteqdot s, l^z$$

This symbol is of the utmost importance.

Let ψ^a denote the case in which a does not exist or in which $a \doteqdot 0$.

Then hypothetical propositions are expressed thus:—

If $a \doteqdot 0$, then $b \doteqdot 0$ $\psi^a \doteqdot \psi^a, \psi^b$

Particulars thus:—

Some a is b $\psi^{a,b} \doteqdot 0$
∴ In general if $\psi^{a,b} \doteqdot 0$ $\psi^a \doteqdot 0$

Let us now take the premises

$\psi^{a,b} \doteqdot 0$ Some a is b
$b, c \doteqdot 0$ No b is c

From the latter

$b \doteqdot b, 0^c$
∴ $\psi^{a,0^c,b} \doteqdot 0$
∴ $\psi^{a,0^c} \doteqdot 0$ Some a is not c.

Note 5

An advantageous method of working Boole's calculus is given by Jevons in his *Pure Logic, or the Logic of Quality.*

Note 6

I have discussed this question in the last paper contained in this volume.

Note 7.

Aristotle uses this form to prove the validity of the simple conversion of the universal negative. He says: "If No **B** is **A**, no **A** is **B**. For if not let **Γ** be the **A** which is **B**. Then it is false that no **B** is **A**, for **Γ** is some **B**."

Note 8

The Aristotelean method of writing these would be

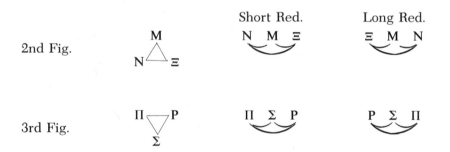

		Short Red.	Long Red.
2nd Fig.	M ∧ N — Ξ	N M Ξ	Ξ M N
3rd Fig.	Π — P ∇ Σ	Π Σ P	P Σ Π

Note 9

Both these reductions are given by Aristotle. Compare 28b14 and 28b20 with 28a24.

Note 10

I neglected to refer afterwards to the form of the substitution of some-*S* and not-*P* for their definitions. But in Part III, §4 I have reduced such arguments to the first figure.

Note 11

Prescision should be spelt with another s as its etymology suggests. But in correcting the proof-sheets Hamilton's *Metaphysics* and Chauvin's *Lexicon* led me astray.

Note 12

It may be doubted whether it was philosophical to rest this matter on empirical psychology. The question is extremely difficult.

Note 13

Theorem VII is the associative principle, the difficulty of the demonstration of which is recognized in quaternions. I give here the demonstration in the text in syllogistic form.

To avoid a very fatiguing prolixity, I employ some abbreviated expressions. If anyone opines that these render the proof nugatory, I shall be happy to go through with him the fullest demonstration. (1). Let (A_m, B_n) be any product of the series described in def. 6. By the principle of Contradiction this includes non-identical classes under it or it does not. If it does, let x denote one of these classes not identical with some other (A_m, B_n).

(2) Then, by cond. 3 of def. 6, x is of the form

$$\Sigma(A, B)$$

By *Barbara*.

(3) The term A_m occurs in this sum or it does not.

(4) If it does the B by which it is multiplied is either B_n or it is not.

(5) If it is, by def. 2, and *Barbara*,

$$\text{Any } (A_m, B_n) \text{ is } x$$

which is contradictory of the supposition in (1) that any x is (A_m, B_n)

$$\text{Some } (A_m, B_n) \text{ is not } x.$$

(6) If this B is not B_n, denote it by B_q. Then by def. 2, and *Barbara*

$$\text{Any } (A_m, B_q) \text{ is } x.$$

(7) But No B_q is B_n, by definition,

(8) And, by def. 3 and *Barbara,*

$$\text{Any } (A_m, B_q) \text{ is } B_q$$

(9) Hence, from (7) and (8), by *Celarent*

$$\text{No } (A_m, B_q) \text{ is } B_n$$

(10) Hence, from (6) and (10), and *Felapton*

$$\text{Some } x \text{ is not } B_n$$

(11) But, by def. 3, and *Barbara,*

$$\text{Any } (A_m, B_n) \text{ is } B_n$$

(12) Hence, from (10) and (11), by *Baroko*

$$\text{Some } x \text{ is not } (A_m, B_n)$$

which is contrary to the definition of x.

(13) This reduces the supposition that A_m occurs in the $\Sigma(A, B)$ defined in (2) to an absurdity. So that A_m does not occur in this sum.

(14) Hence by (2) and Defs. 2 and 3

$$\text{Any } x \text{ is some other } A \text{ than } A_m.$$

(15) Hence, by Def. 7, cond. 1,

$$\text{No } x \text{ is } A_m$$

(16) But by (1)

$$\text{Any } x \text{ is } A_m, B_n$$

(17) Whence, by def. 3,

$$\text{Any } x \text{ is } A_m.$$

(18) And from (15) and (17)

$$\text{Some } A_m \text{ is not } A_m.$$

Which is absurd. Hence

(19) The supposition that A_m, B_n includes mutually coexclusive classes is absurd. Or, every thing of the form (A_m, B_n) is an individual, as stated on p. 64.

(20) Every individual X, that is, whatever does not include under it mutually exclusive classes, by condition 3 of def. 7 can be expressed in the form

$$\Sigma(A, B)$$

(21) Hence, if (A_m, B_n) be a term of $\Sigma(A, B)$ by def. 2

$$\text{Any } (A_m, B_n) \text{ is } X$$

(22) Hence, by definition of an individual

$$\text{Any } X \text{ is } (A_m, B_n)$$

Or any individual can be expressed in the form

$$(A_m, B_n)$$

(23) Let then any individual a be

$$A_a, B_n$$

Then by this definition

$$A_a, B_n \text{ is } a$$

(24) Hence by def. 3

$$\text{Some } A_a \text{ is } a.$$

(25) Hence, by cond. 1 of def. 7,

$$\text{Some } a \text{ is not any other } A.$$

(26) Hence, by cond. 4 of def. 7

$$\text{Any } A_a \text{ is } a.$$

(27) In the same way if (A_m, B_b) is any individual b

$$\text{Any } B_b \text{ is } b.$$

(28) Then (A_a, B_b) belongs to the A which the individual a belongs to. For, by def. 3

$$\text{Any } (A_a, B_b) \text{ is } A_a$$

And by (23) the individual a is A_a, B_n. Whence by def. 3, the individual a is A_a. Whence by cond. 1, of def. 7, the individual a belongs to no other A than A_a.

(29) Similarly (A_a, B_b) belongs to the B to which the individual b belongs.

(30) Moreover by def. 3 and (26) (A_a, B_b) is a.

(31) Similarly it is, also, b.

(32) Moreover by (19) it is an individual.

(33) And by cond. 6 of def. 7 it exists.

(34) In the same way, it could be shown that (A_m, B_n) is an existent individual which belongs to the same A which the individual b belongs to, and the same B which the individual a belongs to.

Thus, for any individuals one a and the other b, there exists an individual which belongs to the same A as a and the same B as b, and an individual which belongs to the same A as b and the same B as a, provided a and b are independent.

This is the first part of our lemma.

[*Venn's* The Logic of Chance]

P 21: North American Review
105(July 1867):317–21

The Logic of Chance. An Essay on the Foundations and Province of the Theory of Probability, with especial Reference to its Application to Moral and Social Science. By John Venn, M.A. London and Cambridge. 1866. 16mo. pp. 370.

Here is a book which should be read by every thinking man. Great changes have taken place of late years in the philosophy of chances. Mr. Venn remarks, with great ingenuity and penetration, that this doctrine has had its realistic, conceptualistic, and nominalistic stages. The logic of the Middle Ages is almost coextensive with demonstrative logic; but our age of science opened with a discussion of probable argument (in the *Novum Organum*), and this part of the subject has given the chief interest to modern studies of logic. What is called the doctrine of chances is, to be sure, but a small part of this field of inquiry; but it is a part where the varieties in the conceptions of probability have been most evident. When this doctrine was first studied, probability seems to have been regarded as something inhering in the singular events, so that it was possible for Bernouilli to enounce it as a *theorem* (and not merely as an identical proposition), that events happen with frequencies proportional to their probabilities. That was a realistic view. Afterwards it was said that probability does not exist in the singular events, but consists in the degree of credence which ought to be reposed in the occurrence of an event. This is conceptualistic. Finally, probability is regarded as the ratio of the number of events in a certain part of an aggregate of them to the number in the whole aggregate. This is the nominalistic view.

This last is the position of Mr. Venn and of the most advanced writers on the subject. The theory was perhaps first put forth by Mr. Stuart Mill; but his head became involved in clouds, and he relapsed into the conceptualistic opinion. Yet the arguments upon the modern side are overwhelming. The question is by no means one of words; but if we were to inquire into the manner in which the terms *probable, likely,* and so forth, have been used, we should find that they always refer to a determination of a genus of argument. See, for example, Locke on the *Understanding,* Book IV, ch. 15, §1. There we find it stated that a thing is probable when it is supported by reasons *such as* lead to a true conclusion. These words *such as* plainly refer to a genus of argument. Now, what constitutes the validity of a genus of argument? The necessity of thinking the conclusion, say the conceptualists. But a madman may be under a necessity of thinking fallaciously, and (as Bacon suggests) all mankind may be mad after one uniform fashion. Hence the nominalist answers the question thus: A genus of argument is valid when from true premises it will yield a true conclusion,—invariably if demonstrative, generally if probable. The conceptualist says, that probability is the degree of credence which *ought* to be placed in the occurrence of an event. Here is an allusion to an entry on the debtor side of man's ledger. What is this entry? What is the meaning of this *ought?* Since probability is not an affair of morals, the *ought* must refer to an alternative to be avoided. Now the reasoner has nothing to fear but error. Probability will accordingly be the degree of credence which it is necessary to repose in a proposition in order to escape error. Conceptualists have not undertaken to say what is meant by "degree of credence." They would probably pronounce it indefinable and indescribable. Their philosophy deals much with the indefinable and indescribable. But propositions are either absolutely true or absolutely false. There is nothing *in the facts* which corresponds at all to a degree of credence, except that a genus of argument may yield a certain proportion of true conclusions from true premises. Thus, the following form of argument would, in the long run, yield (from true premises) a true conclusion two-thirds of the time:—

A is taken at random from among the B's;
$\frac{2}{3}$ of the B's are C;
$\therefore A$ is C.

Truth being, then, the agreement of a representation with its object, and there being nothing *in re* answering to a degree of credence, a modification of a judgment in that respect cannot make it more true, although it may indicate the proportion of *such* judgments which are true *in the long run.* That is, indeed, the precise and only use or significance of these fractions termed probabilities: they give security in the long run. Now, in order that the degree of credence should correspond to any truth in the long run, it must be the representation of a general statistical fact,—a real, objective fact. And then, as it is the fact which is said to be probable, and not the belief, the introduction of "degree of credence" at all into the definition of probability is as superfluous as the introduction of a reflection upon a mental process into any other definition would be,—as though we were to define man as "that which (if the essence of the name is to be apprehended) ought to be conceived as a rational animal."

To say that the conceptualistic and nominalistic theories are both true at once, is mere ignorance, because their numerical results conflict. A conceptualist might hesitate, perhaps, to say that the probability of a proposition of which he knows absolutely nothing is ½, although this would be, in one sense, justifiable for the nominalist, inasmuch as one half of all possible propositions (being contradictions of the other half) are true; but he does not hesitate to assume events to be equally probable when he does not know anything about their probabilities, and this is for the nominalist an utterly unwarrantable procedure. A probability is a statistical fact, and cannot be assumed arbitrarily. Boole first did away with this absurdity, and thereby brought the mathematical doctrine of probabilities into harmony with the modern logical doctrine of probable inference. But Boole (owing to the *needs* of his calculus) admitted the assumption that simple events whose probabilities are given are independent,—an assumption of the same vicious character. Mr. Venn strikes down this last remnant of conceptualism with a very vigorous hand.

He has, however, fallen into some conceptualistic errors of his own; and these are specially manifest in his "applications to moral and social science." The most important of these is contained in the chapter "On the Credibility of Extraordinary Stories"; but it is defended with so much ingenuity as almost to give it the value of a real contribution to science. It is maintained that the credibility of an extraordinary story depends either entirely upon the veracity of the witness, or, in more extraordinary cases, entirely upon the *a priori* credibility of the story; but that these considerations cannot, under any circumstances, be combined, unless arbitrarily. In order to support this opinion, the author invents an illustration. He supposes that statistics were to have shown that nine out of ten consumptives who go to the island of Madeira live through the first year, and that nine out of ten Englishmen who go to the same island die the first year; what, then, would be the just rate of insurance for the first year of a consumptive Englishman who is about to go to that island? There are no certain data for the least approximation to the proportion of consumptive Englishmen who die in Madeira during the first year. But it is certain that an insurance company which insured only Englishmen in Madeira during the first year, or only consumptives under the same circumstances, would be warranted (a certain moral fact being neglected) in taking the consumptive Englishman at its ordinary rate. Hence, Mr. Venn thinks that an insurance company which insured all sorts of men could with safety and fairness insure the consumptive Englishman either as Englishman or as consumptive.[1] Now, the case of an extraordinary story is parallel to this: for such a story is, 1st, told by a certain person, who tells a known proportion of true stories,—say nine out of ten; and, 2d, is of a certain sort (as a fish story), of which a known proportion are true,—say one in ten. Then, as much as before, we come out right, in the long run, by considering such a story under either of the two classes to which it belongs. Hence, says Mr. Venn, we must repose such belief in the story as the veracity of the witness alone, or the antecedent probability alone, requires, or else arbitrarily modify one or other of these degrees of credence. In examining this theory, let us first remark, that there are two principal phrases in which the word *probability* occurs: for, first, we may speak of the probability of an event or proposition, and then we express ourselves incompletely, inasmuch as we refer to the frequency of true conclusions in the genus of arguments by which the event or proposition in question may have

---

1. This is an error. For supposing every man to be insured for the same amount, which we may take as our unit of value, and adopting the notation,

$$(c,e) = \text{number of consumptive Englishmen insured.}$$
$$(c,\bar{e}) = \text{"} \qquad \text{consumptives not English} \quad \text{"}$$
$$(\bar{c},e) = \text{"} \qquad \text{not consumptive English} \quad \text{"}$$

x = unknown ratio of consumptive English who *do not die* in the first year. The amount paid out yearly by the company would be, in the long run,

$$\tfrac{1}{10}(c,\bar{e}) + \tfrac{9}{10}(\bar{c},e) + x(c,e),$$

and x is unknown. This objection to Venn's theory may, however, be waived.

been inferred, without indicating what genus of argument that is; and, secondly, we may speak of the probability that any individual of a certain class has a certain character, when we mean the ratio of the number of those of that class that have that character to the total number in the class. Now it is this latter phrase which we use when we speak of the probability that a story of a certain sort, told by a certain man, is true. And since there is nothing in the data to show what this ratio is, the probability in question is unknown. But a "degree of credence" or "credibility," to be logically determined, must, as we have seen, be an expression of probability in the nominalistic sense; and therefore this "degree of credence" (supposing it to exist) is unknown. "We know not what to believe," is the ordinary and logically correct expression in such cases of perplexity.

Credence and expectation cannot be represented by single numbers. Probability is not always known; and then the probability of each degree of probability must enter into the credence. Perhaps this again is not known; then there will be a probability of each degree of probability of each degree of probability; and so on. In the same way, when a risk is run, the expectation is composed of the probabilities of each possible issue, but is not a single number, as the Petersburg problem shows. Suppose the capitalists of the world were to owe me a hundred dollars, and were to offer to pay in either of the following ways: 1st, a coin should be pitched up until it turned up heads (or else a hundred times, if it did not come up heads sooner), and I should be paid two dollars if the head came up the first time, four if the second time, eight if the third time, &c.; or, 2d, a coin should be turned up a hundred times, and I should receive two dollars for every head. Each of these offers would be worth a hundred dollars, *in the long run;* that is to say, if repeated often enough, I should receive on the average a hundred dollars at each trial. But if the trial were to be made but once, I should infinitely prefer the second alternative, on account of its greater security. Mere certainty is worth a great deal. We wish to know our fate. How much it is worth is a question of political economy. It must go into the market, where its worth is what it will fetch. And since security may be of many kinds (according to the distribution of the probabilities of each sum of money and of each loss, in prospect), the value of the various kinds will fluctuate among one another with the ratio of demand and supply,—the demand varying with the moral and intellectual state of the community,—and thus no single and constant number can represent the value of any kind.

Chapter I. One, Two, and Three

MS 144: Summer–Fall 1867

Logic must begin with analyzing the meanings of certain words, which we shall take up in due order.

The first of these is the word *'is'*, as when we say, Julius Caesar *is* dead, a griffin *is* a fabulous animal, a four-sided triangle *is* an absurdity, height *is* the distance from the ground, nothing *is* that which does not exist. These examples suffice to show that we apply this word to whatever we give a name, whether it really exists or not, or whether we consider it as existing or not.

The word *is* is called by logicians the *copula* because it joins subject and predicate. That which is, in the sense of the copula, was termed *ens* (pl: *entia*) by the schoolmen, and the corresponding abstract noun used was *entitas*. In this as in many other cases, we have taken in English, the abstract noun in a concrete sense, and we can consequently speak of entities. At the same time we have forgotten the very general meaning attached to the word in the middle ages, as denoting whatever can be named, and employ it for what would then have been termed *ens reale*. Thus, we often hear the schoolmen reviled because they considered abstractions to be "entities," but in their sense of the term it admits of no dispute that an abstraction is *ens*. It is true that they frequently use the word *ens* simply when they mean *ens reale*, but only in cases in which there can be no doubt of their meaning; and it was universal to consider *entia* as embracing not only *entia realia* but also *entia rationis*. I propose to restore the term *ens* or *entity* to its original meaning of whatever can be named or talked about. I shall also endeavor as much as possible to reserve the word *being* and other derivatives of *is*, to express this same conception; but these words must be somewhat ambiguous.

It may be observed that *entity* is so extremely general a name that it has no negative over against it. We may talk of a nonentity, but then as we have given it a name it is also an entity.

In contrast with this general being which is conferred by our mere thought of an object, is the being of real things which is quite independent of what we think.

We shall designate this by 'reality', and its cognates; and shall employ 'figment' and 'fiction' to denote that which is non-existent without meaning to imply that the conception has been a deliberate invention.

It is important to observe that the essential difference between a reality and a nonreality, is that the former has an existence entirely independent of what you or I or any number of men may think about it. What I dream, for example, only exists so far as my dreaming imagination creates it. But the fact that I have had such a dream, remains true whether I ever reflect upon that fact or not. The dream, therefore, as a mental phenomenon, is a reality; but the thing dreamed is a figment. If there ever really was such a man as Romulus, he would have existed just the same if history had never mentioned him; but if he is not a reality he exists only in the fables which have been told of the foundation of Rome. When Gray says,

> Full many a gem of purest ray serene
> The dark unfathomed caves of ocean bear;
> Full many a flower is born to blush unseen
> And waste its sweetness on the desert air;

he expresses with precision the essential character of reality. But when we say that the real is that which is independent of how you or I or any number of men think about it, we have still left the conception of independent being to be analyzed. Before making that analysis we must consider the conceptions of *one, two,* and *three.*

We have seen that an *ens* is something to which the copula *is* can be applied. But *is* is a word whose meaning is not complete in itself. It means nothing to say that anything *is* (in the sense of the copula) unless I say what it is; for the only function of the copula is to join subject and predicate. Hence, whatever is, is somehow. This somehow of entity I propose to express by the term *quality.* A *quality* therefore in the very general sense in which I shall use it, denotes whatever can be expressed by all that comes after *is* in a complete assertion. Every ens, then, has some quality for to say that it is an ens is to say that it may be made the subject of an assertion and that assertion must have some predicate. There is no conception so vague that some thing cannot be asserted of the object of it, *for it is the first condition of thought that some quality must be thought in the thought.*

Specimen of a Dictionary of the Terms of Logic and allied Sciences: A to ABS

MS 145: November 1867

This is not supposed to be complete, but only as illustrating the state of my materials, Nov. 1867.

Dictionary A–ABS

A

The first letter of the alphabet is used as a sign in logic.

1. In Aristotle's *Analytics,* A denotes the major extreme of a syllogism of the first figure. He very seldom employs it otherwise.

2. Since the middle of the thirteenth century, it has been usually employed to denote a universal affirmative proposition. E, I, and O, denote the other forms of categoricals, according to the verse,

> Asserit A, negat E, sunt universaliter ambae;
> Asserit I, negat O, sunt particulariter ambae.

It is doubtful whether this use of the vowels originated in the East or in the West. Prantl shows that it had been usual to represent the four forms of propositions by writing simply, πᾶς, οὐδέν, τὶς, and οὐ πᾶς, and he supposes that the A, E, and I, are the accented vowels of the first three words and that the O represents the OY of οὐ πᾶς. Hamilton thinks that the four vowels are the first two of the words *affirmo* and *nego.* The opinion of the last writer that they were invented by Petrus Hispanus can in any case hardly be sustained.

3. A has been used in several other senses which it is unnecessary to specify.

A

A fortiori. See *Argument.*
A majori. See *Argument.*
A minori. See *Argument.*
A parte. See *Argument.*

and indeed the names of arguments mostly begin with an *a.*

A parte ante. In reference to the past.
       See *Universal.*
A parte post. In reference to the future.
       See *Universal.*
A posse. See *Consequence.*
A posteriori. Explained under *A priori.*
A potiori. See *Denomination.*
A priori. This term and *a posteriori* are said to be directly derived from the use by Aristotle of *prior* and *posterior*, πρότερον καὶ ὕστερον. I do not, however, know of the occurrence of these expressions in any writer previous to Cajetan, though *per priora* is found (Aquinas, *Summa,* Prim. prim., quaest. 2, art. 2) in the same sense. The well-authorized senses of these terms are as follows.

1. "Previously to Kant, the terms *a priori* and *a posteriori* were, in a sense which descended from Aristotle, properly and usually employed,—the former to denote a reasoning from cause to effect—the latter, a reasoning from effect to cause." Hamilton, *Reid's Works,* p. 762. See also Trendelenburg, *Elementa Logices Aristoteleae,* §19.

2. By Baumgarten and the Wolffians, *a priori* demonstration was confounded with synthetical demonstration, and *a posteriori* demonstration with analytical demonstration. The terms had previously been used in this way by Le Clerc and others. See Hollmann, Part 3, cap. 3, §517.

3. Finally, there is the metaphysical sense of the terms, now universal, and introduced by Kant. There are some traces of this use before him, as in the two quotations which follow.

"Sense apprehends individual bodies without, by something derived from them, and so *a posteriori,* the senses being last are the images of things. The sensible ideas of things are but umbratile and evanid images of the sensible things, like shadows projected from them; but knowledge is a comprehension of a thing proleptically, and as it were *a priori.*" Cudworth, *Eternal and Immutable Morality,* Ch. 3, §5, p. 99.

"It is easy to see that these two concepts must be taken *relatively.* For if we should make not only immediate experiences but also all that we can discover by means of them *a posteriori,* then the concept *a priori* could only be used in a few of those cases in which we predetermine something by arguments, since in such case we must in no degree depend on any of the premises of experience. And so there would be scarcely anything at all in our cognition which was *a priori.*" Lambert, Book 1, ch. 9, §637, vol. 1, p. 413.

The following passages show Kant's use of the terms. "The rules of logic can therefore be regarded as *a priori,* that is, *independent of all experience,* since they contain merely the conditions of the use of the understanding in general, *without distinction of objects.*" *Logik,* Einleitung I. "Although all our cognition begins *with* experience, it does not necessarily on that account arise *out of* experience. For it might easily be that even our experiential cognition was a compound of that which we receive by impressions and of that which our cognitive faculties (only stimulated by sensuous impressions) bring forth from themselves. . . . Is there such a cognition independent of experience and even of all impressions of sense? One terms such cognitions *a priori,* and distinguishes them from the empirical, which have their sources *a posteriori.*" *Kritik d. reinen Vernunft,* 2nd Ed., Einleitung I.

A priori employment of a synthesis. Its employment in reference to representations which are not empirical. Kant, *Kritik,* p. 99.

A priori knowledge "embraces those principles which, as the conditions of the exercise of the faculties of thought, are, consequently, not the result of that exercise." Hamilton.

A priori possibility. "We know possibility *a priori* when we resolve a notion into its requisites or into other notions of known possibility, and know that there is nothing incompatible in them. We know *a posteriori* the possibility of a thing, when we actually experience its existence." Leibniz, p. 80.

Ab esse. See *Consequence.*

Abdication. Abdicatio. An abdicative judgment. Scotus Erigena.

ABDICATIVE

Applied by Appuleius and Martianus Capella to propositions, in the sense of negative.

ABDUCTION

This is the English form of *abductio,* a word employed by Julius Pacius, as the translation of ἀπαγωγή (*Prior Analytics,* lib. 2, cap. 25), which had been rendered *deductio* by Boëthius and *reductio* and even *inductio* by the schoolmen.

It is a form of argument described by Aristotle as follows:—"Abduction is when it is evident that the first term [that which occurs in the syllogism only as a predicate. See *Analytica Posteriora,* lib. i, ch. 21, p. 82.b.2.] is predicable of the middle, but that the middle is predicable of the last [that which is only subject] is inevident, but is as credible or more so than the conclusion, further if the media of the last and middle are few; for it is being altogether nearer knowledge. Thus, let A be 'what can be taught', while B is 'science', and Γ 'justice'. [A, B, Γ always denote the major, middle, and minor of a syllogism of the first figure.] Now, that science can be taught is plain, but that virtue is science is inevident. If then ΓB is as credible or more so than ΓA, there is an abduction. For by assuming the science of ΓA, we not having it before, are nearer to knowledge. [That is, we come nearer to knowing that justice can be taught, on account of the credibility of justice being a science.] Or again, if the middles of ΓB are few; for thus one is nearer knowledge. As, if Δ were 'capable of being squared', while E were 'rectilinear figure', and Z 'circle'; if there were only one middle of ZE, that a circle becomes equal to a rectilinear figure by menisci, would be near knowledge. But, when ΓB is neither more credible than ΓA nor are the middles few, I do not call it abduction. Nor when ΓB is immediate, for that is knowledge."

It will be seen that abduction has no connection with 'apagogical proof'. See Waitz, *Organon,* i.534.

ABILITY

The power to act in a certain way. See *Moral, Natural.*

ABSENCE

1. The not being in a place.

2. "Mind, since it has no parts whose position can be considered relatively to other corporeal things, is not absent from corporeal things locally, but is absent, according to Thomas and DesCartes, from everything in which it does not operate." Chauvin.

"Such things as, *Draw nigh to God, and he will draw nigh to you,* are said of God in scripture, metaphorically. For as it is said that the sun enters a house or leaves it, in so far as his rays extend to the house, so God is said to approach us or to recede from us, as far as we perceive the influence of his goodness or withdraw from it." Aquinas, prim. prim., quaest. 9, art. 1.

3. "Every privation is a certain negation of the opposite habit, which we designate by the word *absence.*" Burgersdicius.

ABSOLUTE

Absolutum is good Latin. It is now used in a great variety of senses.

1. *Absolutum a restrictione.* Without restriction, in the logical sense. See below, *absolute distribution,* and *absolute scepticism.*

2. *Absolutum a conditione.* Unconditionate. See below, *absolute proposition, absolute necessity,* etc.

3. *Absolutum a causa.* "The Absolute is that which is free from all *necessary* relation, that is, which is free from every relation *as a condition of existence;* but it may exist in relation, provided that relation be not a necessary condition of its existence; that is, provided that relation may be removed without affecting its existence." Calderwood.

Mansel expressly says that this is what he means by 'absolute, in the sense of free from relation'. *Philosophy of Conditioned.* This is its sense in the *Limits of Religious Thought; not sense 4.*

"*Absolutum* means what is *freed* or *loosed;* in which sense the absolute will be what is aloof from relation, comparison, limitation, condition, dependence, etc., and thus is tantamount to τὸ ἀπόλυτον of the lower Greeks. In this meaning the absolute is not opposed to the infinite." Hamilton.

4. "*Absolutum* means *finished, perfected, completed;* in which sense the Absolute will be what is out of relation, &c., as finished,

perfect, complete, total, and thus corresponds to τò ὄλον and τò τέλειον of Aristotle. In this acceptation,—and it is that in which for myself I exclusively use it—the Absolute is diametrically opposed to, is contradictory of the infinite." Hamilton.

"Absolute expresses the attribute of totality (incomposite unity or indivisibility)." F. E. Abbot.

"In our vulgar language, we say a thing is *absolutely* good when it is *perfectly* good." Knox, *History of Reform.* Quoted in Fleming's *Vocabulary.*

5. "The term *absolute* in the sense of *free from relation,* may be used in two applications;—1st, To denote the nature of a thing as it is in itself, as distinguished from its appearance to us. Here it is used in a subordinate sense, as meaning out of relation to human knowledge." Mansel, *Philosophy of Conditioned.*

6. "Eschenmayer asserts that God is infinitely higher than the absolute, which is only the last object of knowledge, while God is only an object of faith, which is infinitely higher than knowledge." Furtmair.

7. *Absolutum a termino.* A term is said to be absolute which can of itself be the subject or predicate of a complete proposition; as *man, tree,* and which implies the existence only of what it denotes. Opposed to connotative or relative terms, such as, *greater, father of.*

8. Without any modifying clause; like the *simpliciter* of the schoolmen.

Absolute adjunct. "An adjunct which belongs to its subject simply and absolutely. . . . Thus, *mortality* is an absolute adjunct of man; *immortality* a limited one; because man is not absolutely immortal, but only so as to his soul." Burgersdicius.

Absolute affection. An affection "which belongs to its subject *per se,*" and not on account of its relation to another. Chauvin.

Absolute beauty. "Beauty has been distinguished into the Free or Absolute, and into the Dependent or Relative. In the former case, it is not necessary to have a notion of what the object ought to be, before we pronounce it beautiful or not; in the latter case such a previous notion is required. Flowers, shells, arabesques, etc. are freely or absolutely beautiful. We judge, for example, a flower to be beautiful though unaware of its destination, and that it contains a complex apparatus of organs all admirably adapted to the propagation of the plant." Hamilton, Metaphysical Lecture 46, p. 624.

Absolute distribution "is the distribution of a term without limitation: as, every man is *Philargyrus.*" Example of the contrary distribution (the limited): "Every animal except the swan dies groaning." Eck, *In summulas Petri Hispani,* fol. 91a.

Absolute good. "The moral good, which concerns the highest interest." Kant, *Kritik d. Urtheilskraft,* §4.

Absolute ground of proof. A ground of proof not itself proved or needing proof, but intuitive.

Absolute horizon. "The congruence of the limits of human cognition with the limits of collective human perfection in general." Kant, *Logik,* Einleitung VI, p. 207. See *Horizon.*

Absolute identity. "The system which reduces mind and matter to phenomenal modifications of the same common substance." Hamilton.

"Nature should be the visible mind, and mind invisible nature. Here, therefore, in the absolute identity of the mind within us, and nature without us, must we solve the problem how it is possible for a nature out of us to be." Schelling.

Absolute impossibility. "The absolutely impossible is that which involves a contradiction; as, that a man is a stone." Burgersdicius.

Absolute independence. "That is said to be absolutely independent which does not owe its being to another; and that, either positively, in which way God alone is independent, or negatively, in which way non-ens owes its being to nothing, inasmuch as it has none." Chauvin.

Absolute indivisibility. "The absolutely indivisible is that which has no parts into which it can be divided, and so is a simple *ens.*"

Absolute intellection. Intellection not performed by means of comparison. "Absolute intellection can only be of some simple object contained under the object of the concept *(intellectus)."* Scotus, *In sententiarum,* lib. 2, dist. 6, qu. 1, vol. 2, p. 242.

Absolute knowledge. Knowledge not relative. See *Relativity of knowledge.*

Absolute liberty. "The absolutely free is free from servitude, from a law established over him by others, from compulsion, and from natural necessity." Burgersdicius, *Institutionum Logicarum,* p. 66.

Absolute locality. "I call absolute locality, provisionally until an apter word occurs, that by which a thing exists alone anywhere, that is, without respect to another thing; of which sort was the locality of God before the foundation of the world, and even now is, out of the circuit of the world, where there are no things." Burgersdicius, *Institutionum Metaphysicarum*, lib. 1, cap. 21.

Absolute motion "is the translation of a body from one absolute place into another." Newton.

Absolute name. Names not connotative. "Merely absolute names are those which do not signify one thing principally and another or the same secondarily, but whatever is signified by such a name is alike primarily signified, as appears concerning this name, 'animal'." Occam. Quoted by Prantl, iii, 364.

Absolute necessity. "The absolutely necessary is that whose negation implies contradiction." Burgersdicius.

Absolute pain. See *absolute pleasure.*

Absolute perfection. Perfection in every respect. "That to which no imperfection of any sort belongs." Burgersdicius.

Absolute philosophy. A philosophy which is absolute knowledge, if true.

Absolute place. "The part of absolute space which a body occupies." Newton.

Absolute pleasure. "Absolute pleasure is all that pleasure which we feel above a state of indifference and which is therefore prized as a good in itself, and not simply as the removal of an evil." Hamilton, Metaphysical Lecture 42.

Absolute power. The power of a despot or autocrat.

Absolute prescience. "Is that by which God knows that things absolutely and without condition will be." Burgersdicius, *Institutionum Metaphysicarum*, lib. 2, cap. 8.

Absolute principle. Absolute principles are those "from which in the construction of a science, cognitions altogether certain not only are, but must be derived." Hamilton.

Absolute problem. Where it is asked whether an attribute belongs to a subject or not, not to which of two subjects it belongs the most. Burgersdicius.

Absolute proposition. A term which Hamilton recommends in place of *categorical proposition.* He cites the authorities of Gassendi and Mocenicus. *Logic,* Lecture 13, p. 165 note.

Absolute reality. Inherence in things as a condition or mark without regard to the forms of human intuition and thought. See Kant's *Kritik d. r. Vernunft,* 1st Ed., p. 35 ad fin.

Absolute scepticism. That is, the very last degree of scepticism. But different writers understand this differently. The simple negation of understanding in inanimate objects is not considered scepticism; neither is idiocy. It is the employment of the reason exclusively "to inquire and debate, but not to fix and determine." It is the adoption of the principle that all possible opinions upon all possible subjects are equally probable,—the adoption of this not as a *doctrine* but as a principle actually determining the state of mind. See Montaigne's *Essays*, Book 2, cap. 12. This is what the *ultima thule* of scepticism really is. But what is usually meant by *absolute scepticism* is one or other of the following dogmas—

1. "Absolute scepticism declares everything to be illusion." Kant, *Logik*, Einleitung X.

2. It is the doctrine "that unconditionally certain knowledge is from its own nature impossible." Seydel, *Logik*, §4.

Absolute space "is that which remains always similar and immovable." Newton.

"The space in which all motion must ultimately be thought, is called pure or absolute space." Kant, *Anfangsgründe der Naturwissenschaft.*

Absolute term "is a term which connotes nothing; as, elephant, cedar." Eck, *In summulas Petri Hispani,* Tractatus 2, text 2, Note 1.

Absolute time. "Absolute, true, and mathematical time, of itself and from its own nature, flows equably without regard to anything external, and is called duration." Newton.

I give the definition of Newton since he invented the term, although it is a little nonsensical.

Absolute truth "is the agreement of the content of cognition with the actuality." Überweg.

Absolute utility. "We may call the higher utility or that conducive to the perfection of a man viewed as an end in himself, by the name of absolute." Hamilton.

ABSOLUTELY

Absolutely first and last. The very first and last.

Absolutely practical. What relates to the absolute good. Kant.

Absolutely proper adjunct. A proper adjunct "which emanates from the essence of the subject; and that either immediately (thus, the faculty of laughing and wondering emanates immediately from the human essence) or by the medium of another property (thus to occupy space emanates from the essence through the quantity of the body)." Burgersdicius.

Absolutely pure. "A cognition is termed absolutely pure in which no experience or impression is mixed." Kant.

ABSTINENCE

"is whereby a man refraineth from anything which he may lawfully take." Elyot, *Governour.* Quoted by Fleming.

ABSTRACT

1. That which signifies or represents an attribute or relation, apart from any reference to a subject.

This appears to be the original meaning of the term. The word is said to be employed by the Roman philosophers and grammarians. It certainly was not in common use in logic before Scotus who uses it frequently. Before him, we meet the expressions, *ex abstractione, per abstractionem, inabstractum, abstrahens, ablatum,* and *remotum,* where *abstractum* might be expected.

2. That which signifies or represents objects in certain of their elements apart from others, whether these latter be the matter, certain forms, or the individuality. See *Abstract concept.*

3. Kant uses this adjective in a peculiar sense. The following is from his elucidator Schmid.

"Abstract concepts are, 2ndly, in particular, abstract concepts in the narrower signification, sensuously abstracted (*Critik d. r. Vernunft,* 2nd Ed., p. 38) that is, such as can arise only in this way and throughout suppose a previous synthesis, since they themselves represent something which is only given by sensuous impressions, something sensible; as, the concept of red colour. In this signification, neither pure intuitions (Space and Time) nor pure intellectual concepts (as Substance, Cause, Totality) are to be termed abstract concepts, since they are not contained as sensuously given constituents in the concrete concepts of sensuous objects, but first make these themselves possible, that is, are conditions which must be present in the cognitive power itself, in order to be empirically intuited or thought by the latter. The prescinded consciousness of them, however, supposes the operation of abstraction, since we at first become acquainted with them only by their immediate application to individual objects, and therefore *in concreto.* Hence arises the illusion of their being sensuously abstracted. That A, from which something else B is abstracted as a mark, we must still be able to represent to

ourselves after the abstraction has taken place. But if, for instance, we abstract space from a body, every other representation which belongs to the body, vanishes along with Space."
See further under the verb *to abstract*.

4. The immediate object of an abstract representation is termed an abstract form or attribute, &c.

See *Logical, Metaphysical, Physical*.

Abstract concept. Abstract, as applied to concept, is commonly used in the second of the above senses. More properly in the first sense; by Kant sometimes in the third.

"The use of some logicians which identifies *abstract* and *universal* is not to be commended. Grammar distinguishes the two sharply. Wolff, also, has the more proper terminology which agrees with that of grammar since he (*Logik*, §110) defines the abstract notion as that which represents something which is in a certain thing (to wit, the attributes, modes, relations, of things) apart from the thing which it is in, but the universal notion as that which represents what is common to several things." Überweg.

Abstract freedom "consists in that indetermination or equality of the *ego* with itself, wherein there is a determination only so far as it makes it its own or puts it into itself." Hegel.

Abstract knowledge. Used by Hamilton (*Reid*, p. 812) in place of *abstractive knowledge*, q.v.

Abstract name. 1. "The question is whether a denominative name signifies the same as an abstract one, to wit, a form only." Scotus, *Quaestiones in Praedicamentis*, Qu. 8. *Abstract* is here used in the first sense.

2. "A practice has grown up in more modern times, which, if not introduced by Locke, has gained currency chiefly from his example, of applying the expression 'abstract name' to all names which are the result of abstraction or generalization, and consequently to all general names, instead of confining it to the names of attributes. The metaphysicians of the Condillac school, . . . have gone on imitating him in this abuse of language, until there is now some difficulty in restoring the word to its original signification. A more wanton alteration of the meaning of a word is rarely to be met with; for the expression 'general name', the exact equivalent of which exists in all languages . . . was already available for the purpose to which *abstract* has been misappropriated, while the misappropriation leaves that important class of words, the names of attributes, without any com-

pact distinctive appellation. The old acceptation, however, has not gone so completely out of use, as to deprive those who still adhere to it of all chance of being understood." Mill, *Logic.*

Abstract Logic "considers the laws of thought as potentially applicable to the objects of all the arts and sciences, but as not actually applied to those of any." Hamilton.

Abstract object. The object of an abstract concept in the first or second sense.

TO ABSTRACT

"It is necessary here to note the very great ambiguity of the word *abstract.* For we should properly say 'to abstract from anything' not 'to abstract anything'. The former denotes that we do not attend in a certain concept to others in any way bound up with it, but the latter that it is not given unless in the concrete and so that it may be separated from the things conjoined with it. Hence, an intellectual concept *abstracts* from all that is sensitive, but *is not abstracted* from sensitive objects; and perhaps it would be more correct to call it *abstrahent* than *abstract.* Wherefore, it is better to name intellectual concepts *pure ideas,* but those which are only given empirically *abstract.*" Kant, *De mundi sensibilis atque intelligibilis forma et principiis.*

It is difficult to see what ground there is for saying that the expression *to abstract anything* has the implication here attributed to it. It is certainly improper to speak, as Berkeley does, of abstracting things apart; but the opinion that some entertain that *mentem* is the understood object of *abstrahere* is neither supported by the original metaphor, τὰ δ'ἀφαιρέσει οἷον ἐκ τοῦ λίθου ὁ Ἑρμῆς, nor by good usage in any age of the world.

The following are examples of the use by Scotus, who chiefly formed the modern custom with reference to the derivatives of *abstractio.* "Intellectus noster in cognoscendo abstrahet ab hic et nunc"; "Prius cognoscit intellectus singulare quam universale; impossibile est enim, quod rationem universalis ab aliquo abstrahet, nisi id, a quo abstrahit, praecognoscat." Of course *ratio* does not here mean reason; *ratio universalis* is the mode of the universal.

ABSTRACTION

Abstractio is the translation by Boëthius of ἀφαίρεσις.

1. Abstraction is the separation in thought of an attribute or relation

from its subject, by neglecting the latter. This seems to be its sense, in Aristotle.

2. Mental separation of any elements by neglect of one and attending to the other; that is, by *supposing* one not to exist.

3. Such a separation of matter and form, or of certain characters from others, but not of one thing from another.

4. Any sort of mental separation.

5. Any separation, mental or real.

6. The power of performing mental abstraction. See *Concrete, Formal, Logical, Mathematical, Metaphysical, Modal, Objective, Partial, Physical, Real, Ultimate.*

ABSTRACTIVE

Abstractive cognition. The distinction between abstractive and intuitive cognition is found in St. Anselm (*Monologium,* Caps. 62, 63, 66, 67), but the word first occurs in Scotus.

1. "In order that I may use brief words, I will call that cognition *abstractive*, which is of the quiddity itself as it is abstracted from existence and non-existence." Scotus, lib. 2, dist. 3, qu. 9, p. 197.

2. "Abstractive knowledge is the cognition of a thing not as it is present; for example, the knowledge by which I know Socrates when absent, and that by which an astronomer in the house considers an eclipse which he does not observe, supposing that he knows that at that time the earth is between the moon and the sun. And also, that by which the philosopher from creatures knows that God is. For although these cognitions are directed to the thing as to its existence, yet they are not so directed to it that the presence of their object is discerned." Conimbricenses, *De Anima,* lib. 2, cap. 6, qu. 3, art. 1.

ABSTRAHENT

This term was often used in the 12th century (see the treatise *De intellectibus.* Cousin, *Fragments Philosophiques,* p. 481). Kant has suggested the revival of the term to denote pure concepts of the understanding.

Abstrahentium non est mendacium. This is an awkward way of saying that a quality which is abstracted from is not denied. If abstraction is not denial, far less is generalization. Yet the two seem to be confounded by Hegel when he says that *being* and *nothing* are the same because they are equally the absence of all determination.

ABSURD

1. That which involves an error obvious to common sense.
2. That which would involve an error, which would offer no illusion or deception whatever; as, That to have a hundred dollars is absolutely the same as to be without it.

ABSURDITY

1. The absurd in either sense.
2. "An absurdity to a particular person is a proposition, true or not, which conflicts with a proposition which has to that person the force of an axiom." Chauvin.
3. The quality of the absurd.
See *Simple*.

ABSURDUM

See *Reductio*.

ABUNDANT

Abundant definition. One which contains derived marks.

List of words, beginning with AC

Academic
Academy
Acatalepsy
Acceptation
Acceptilation
Accident
Accidental—agreement—definition—difference—distinction—form
    —mode—predicable—predication—quality—supposition.
Accidentally—subordinate causes.
Accommodated—distribution
Accountability
Accurate—knowledge
Acedia
Acervus
Achilles

Acousmatic—disciple

Acquired—logic

Acquisitive—faculty

Acrisy

Acroama

Acroamatic—disciple—method—proof

Act

Action

Active—cause—instrument—power

Activity

Actual—cognition—composition—distinction—ens—essence—existence—object—part—whole

ACADEMIC. A platonist.

ACADEMY. The School of Plato.

See *Old, Middle, New.*

ACATALEPSY. Incomprehensibleness, or incapacity of being known with complete certainty.

ACCEPTATION. This is not a very precise term. It means either (1) the sense in which a term is taken, or (2) the manner in which it is used, or (3) the special application of it. The term *suppositio* which was replaced by this term by the purists of the revival, was much better.

See *Collective, Concrete, Distributive, Formal, Material, Simple.*

ACCEPTILATION. Originally a term of the civil Law. Used in theology, for a discharge from an obligation without payment of an equivalent.

ACCIDENT. The word *accidens,* as a noun, occurs first in Quintilian as the translation of συμβεβηκός. This term in its strict sense belongs to Aristotle, but was derived from the ordinary usage of the Greek language.

1. Whatever is *in* substance; that is, whatever cannot be supposed to exist without supposing that something else (the substance) exists. In this sense, it is opposed to *substance.* This is a common sense in Aristotle and in all later philosophers.

2. A quality or mark which does not *necessarily* belong to its subject. In this sense (opposed to *property*), it is also used by Aristotle and all subsequent writers.

"Accident is that which is present and absent without the corruption of its subject."

See *Conversion by Accident, Inseparable, Separable, Abstract, Causal, Concrete, Predicamental, Predicable, Verbal.*

ACCIDENTAL.

Accidental Agreement is agreement in respects extraneous to the essence of the subjects.

Accidental definition. An expression of the nature of a subject by means of its accidents (in the second sense). Occam.

Accidental difference. A difference in respect to accidents, in the second sense.

Accidental distinction. A distinction relating to accidents in the second sense.

Accidental form. A form whose subject may be without it; that is, it is an accident in the second sense.

"Forms are divided into substantial and accidental. A substantial form is one which completes the matter and informs it, and so constitutes the corporeal substance. An accidental form is an addition inhering in the complete substance, and with it constituting the concrete ens, and that which is one *per accidens.* In these definitions, four *discrimina* are expressed, by which these two genera of forms differ from each other. The *first* is, that the substantial form is referred to the matter of the substance, the accidental to the substance itself; and because the matter of substances is of itself imperfect and incomplete in the genus of substances, therefore the substantial form is said to complete the matter in the genus of substances, and to constitute it into a certain species. An Accidental form is not a complement of but an addition to the substance; and this is the *second* point of difference. From this arises the *third,* that the substantial form truly informs the matter, while the accidental form does not inform the complete substance, unless in some general and less proper sense, but rather inheres in it as in a subject. Hence now arises the *fourth* discrimen, that the substantial form makes the substance one *per se,* while the accident makes some concrete Ens, which is one *per accidens,* only." Burgersdicius, *Institutionum Metaphysicarum,* lib. i, cap. 25, §6.

Accidental form of syllogism, "depends on the external expression of the constituent parts of the syllogism, whereby the terms and propositions are variously determined in point of number, position, and consecution." Esser.

Accidental mode. A mode which either modifies an accident, or if it modifies the substance is not included in the notion of the substance. Burgersdicius.

Accidental mode of signifying is one which belongs to a term from any grammatical or logical accident; thus *amo* signifies present time by an accidental mode.

Accidental perfection is 'an addition pertaining to the essence either for causing it to do or to suffer what is fit for it, or for ornament'. Burgersdicius.

Accidental predicable. Property and accident. "They are called accidental because they are not substance, or of the essence of the subjects of which they are predicated. It is to be observed that the real ens is divided into substance and accident; whence taking accident as opposed to substance, property is an accident." Pseudo-Aquinas, *Summa logices.*

Accidental predication.

Accidental quality. An accident in the second sense. Hamilton.

Accidental supposition. A term of the *Parva logicalia;* opposed to natural supposition. "Accidental supposition is the acceptation of a common term for all things, for which its adjunct requires that it be taken." Petrus Hispanus. Thus, in the proposition 'homo erit', homo *supposes* for all future men. "The supposition of a term is accidental in respect to a copula which is not freed from time; as 'homo fame moritur septimo die'." Eck.

[Critique of Positivism]

MS 146: Winter 1867–1868

§1. Statement of the doctrine by which Positivism is distinguished from all other Philosophies.

§2. That this doctrine has a favorable influence upon scientific investigation, and that the Positivists have been clever *savans.*

§3. That this doctrine is fatal to religion, and that the religious side of positivism is its weakness.

§4. That it is possible and usual for scientific men to occupy another position equally advantageous in reference to scientific research and not so destructive of religious faith.

§5. Of Positivism as held by unphilosophic and unscientific persons, not owing to severe thought but to the influence of the "spirit of the age."

§6. That the fundamental position of positivism is false.

§7. The true doctrine and its consequences.

§7½. Of some doctrines allied to positivism.

§8. In what sense positivism has deeply influenced the age and in what sense it has not.

§9. Conclusion.

The first disciples of the positive philosophy (I do not speak now of its doctors) were men interested in carrying the research of what ordinary people call causes into realms which had hitherto been trodden only by the foot of the *metaphysician* or the classifier. Without allowing all its rules for this kind of investigation, we may admit that it has been of real service to those men and through them to the world. Its scientific side is its strength. But now that it has become the fashion, it has been taken up by persons who have neither the stern masculinity proper for positive philosophers nor any business with physical science. By these persons it is regarded in its practical and especially its religious aspect. This is decidedly its weak side. This was perhaps felt by the man who to put it to the test pushed it to its legitimate religious consequences in paradoxes respecting the *grand être,* &c. These modern disciples, however, shrink from these doctrines which offend the Anglosaxon sense and prefer to discard all religious belief altogether. And, then, not being particularly philosophic in temperament they seek to reconcile themselves to the sceptical state by persuading themselves that theism could offer no rational consolation to its believers, even if it could be rationally accepted. Herein they show the secret influence upon them of the capital principle of theism namely that whatever is is best. Only by a covert faith in this could they commit the absurdity of maintaining that God, Freedom, and Immortality would be evils.

Now the pleasantness or unpleasantness of consequences is no argument for or against a speculative opinion. But a man fights the battle of life better under the stimulus of hope; and we ought not to complain, therefore, that men lean toward the hopeful belief. At any rate it is a fact that they do so; and therefore if scepticism can show that the prospects it offers are more cheering than those of theism it is likely to sweep away the latter altogether except from the minds of a few sad thinkers who unfortunately shall be convinced that they are immortal beings under the government of a loving God. But that this never will happen and that scepticism is not so comfortable or inspiriting a state as theistic belief will be shown beyond further controversy in the present paper.

In the first place, then, we are to give no weight to the testimony of an individual sceptic that he finds his scepticism delightful. For apart from the question of veracity (which in such a case is serious for everyone but himself) he may be self-deceived, or may understand by theism a particular determination of it, gloomy on account of what it adds to the fundamental doctrine, or may be of an abnormal constitution in his sentimental part. Nor shall we be convinced by an instance or two of a heroic sceptic, since heroism in these few cases can well be attributed to natural force of character, since for every such instance ten can be adduced of sneaking sceptics, and since on the other hand religion can show a history of whole communities becoming heroic in a way that can only be accounted for by supposing that it can make a hero of almost anybody. The argument might be urged the other way with perfect justness and with a force perfectly convincing to the clear-minded. But since a caviller might easily raise a cloud of dust in reference to such a matter, it will be more adviseable to pass it over.

We prefer to begin with this undoubted fact: All men and all animals love life. This is not a passion produced by theism or any other superstition, but is of all impulses one of the most original, strongest, and ineradicable. If some man says he does not love life, other evidence rather bears down his testimony, and if he really does not he is only an unhappy exception, a miserable abortion, which is not to set aside the result of all experience.

This passion has for its object firstly and primarily ourselves, in a less strong degree our friends, then our blood, then our country, then our race, and finally it is still a deep and lively emotion even in its reference to intellect in general. It may be objected that the love of the life of our family, for example, is not the same passion as the love of our own life. But all I say is, that we have a desire for the continued life of all these objects, and that these desires have this in common that they are all love of life in some form, all are lively emotions, all seem to spring from our original nature and all are in the great body of mankind incapable of being rooted out without shattering the heart almost entirely.

We may wonder why men should care for what is to happen after they are (according to their belief) annihilated; it may be that such a wish implies a lurking of the contrary belief, but it is a fact any man even the merest atheist does not limit his love of life to this side of the grave. He provides for the wellbeing of the world when he is to be no more. Nay, Hume was anxious for his own good reputation among succeeding generations. *The love of life is more than a love of sensuous life:* it is also a love of rational life. For it continues up to the point where our sensations become intolerable agony. Hence, our love of life is not confined within the walls of our own body; but since our reason lives wherever it is active, primarily in our own brains but also secondarily in the brains of those who take up our thoughts and sentiments, it is a part of the love of life, to love our influence upon and fame with succeeding generations. We, also, feel within us in addition to elements peculiar to ourselves, elements also which are common to ourselves and others, among which are personality and intellect. *Personality has two senses, 1st being personal* and *2nd the special idiosyncracy of a particular person.* It is in the first sense that the sympathy we exhibit shows that we feel that it is the same, in others as in ourselves. Hence the love of the life of others is still a passion which centres in ourselves because we love them as having something in common with ourselves, *that is, because a part of them is identical with a part of ourselves.* This would be quite false if these elements were material but as they are general and purely formal objects, there is nothing in nominalism to refute such a sentiment. The more true culture we have, the more we approach that ideal of a man of which we all cherish a more or less vague idea; the more we love our rational life relatively to our sensuous life, and of all the elements of a rational life the more we value those which are fundamental and necessary results of the developement of reason in general relatively to those which are merely the mannerism and idiosyncracy peculiar to ourselves; and consequently the further we advance to what we ought to be, the stronger is our love of reason in general relatively to that of our race, that of our race relatively to that of our country, that of our country relatively to that of our blood, and that of our blood relatively to that of our own persons. These passions then which I have summed up in one *word as the love of life,* are *really intimately bound together and connected in our nature.* These passions go by many different names in common language and some are not named at all, but it will readily be perceived that there is not a single impulse or sentiment of any consequence, which is not among the number, which is not in some sense a love of life. Now let us see what the two doctrines *positivism* and *theism* promise to this passion which is the sum of all longings.

Now some positivists—whom I should certainly adduce as instances of sneaking sceptics—endeavor to conceal the bearing of their doctrine upon religion. They seek to represent that it merely denies the possibility of arriving at scientific certainty with regard to such matters and not the possibility of reaching highly probable conclusions. But this is a miserable falsification. *The doctrine that it implies, that knowing a thing* to be *probable is not knowledge,* is not only unsound in itself, it is so also on positivist principles, and is distinctly recognized as being so by the positivists themselves. Positivists to be consequent should hold that all religious belief is superstition, and that all superstitions which do not come into conflict with any scientifically known fact are on one level of credibility, and should assume the same attitude of mind towards the doctrine that the soul is immortal as to that of Bernardus Carnotensis that universals are beings who marry and have children, "quia albedo significat virginem incorruptam, albet eandem introeuntem thalamum aut cubantem in toro, album vero eandem sed corruptam";—except that one view may be more entertaining than the other. It is true that one of the most eminent American metaphysicians is of opinion that religion might be based on positive philosophy as Comte *defines* it. But though Comte's definition labors under the ambiguity so common in French, all the world understands the term in a sense of which it is an essential part that no theory shall be admitted except in so far as it asserts or denies something with respect to a possible observation. In respect to the continuance of life in this world, positivism is even less favorable. That there always should be intellect in the universe, that there should not come a time when it all dies out forever, not only presents no preponderance of probability but is even perhaps opposed by the fact that all the conditions of the world of which we have any knowledge are mutable.

Life upon the globe is a phase, quite accidental, tending as far as we know to no permanent end, of no sort of use, except in producing a pleasant titillation now and then on the nerves of this or that wayfarer on this weary and purposeless journey—which like a treadmill starts nowhere and goes nowhere, and whose machinery produces nothing at all. There is no good in life but its occasional pleasures; these are mostly delusive, and as like as not will soon utterly pass away.

Let us now turn to theism. The capital principle of this is, that nature is absolutely conformed to an end; or in other words, that there is reason in the nature of things. Now from what has been said before it follows that so far as we attain true culture so far will the sum of all our impulses come to the love of reason as it necessarily is, and therefore so far as we are as we ought to be so far are we perfectly gratified by what according to the nature of things, takes place; which is another way of saying that whatever is is best. Now this is not only a consolation; it is the very sum, quintessence and acme of all consolation. That happens which so far as our own nature is developed, so far as we truly know our own mind, is what delights us most.

Whatever palliatives to the ills of life can be applied by the sceptic are also at the command of the theist and in addition the only true consolation.

I know very well that a great many theists are nearer pessimists than optimists but they are unsound and inconsistent. To say, however, that whatever is is best is not to deny the existence of evil, but only to maintain that if any event is bad in one way it more than counterbalances for it by being good in another and higher way.

Positivists are in the habit of considering positivism and metaphysics as opposed species of philosophy. Now to maintain that the conclusions of metaphysics are as yet very certain would be enthusiastic enough in view of the differences of opinion among metaphysicians. These differences have been growing less and less from one century to another, owing to a gradual clearing up of conceptions. But the whole effective result of metaphysical research hitherto may be described in saying that certain indistinct conceptions have been made distinct. Every great branch of science has once been in the state in which metaphysics is now, that is when its fundamental conceptions were vague and consequently its doctrines utterly unsettled; and there is no reason whatever to despair of metaphysics eventually becoming a real science like the rest; but at present that is not the case. Now the positivist may define metaphysics, as he pleases, but if he deals with conceptions which are indistinct in his mind, he is for all purposes of certainty in the same condition as the metaphysician. *That is precisely what he does do* in *maintaining that we can have no knowledge of any reality except single impressions of sense and their sensible relations. The question what* is reality has a great pertinency here. Suppose we say it is that which is independently of our belief and which could be properly inferred by the most thorough discussion of the sum of all impressions of sense whatever. If that is what the positivist means by reality (and since he does not tell us we must guess for ourselves), then he ought to be not a sceptic but an atheist, for that which we cannot possibly be in a state to infer, is not then a reality at all. And, indeed, *I should be glad to know what the positivist does mean by an existence which cannot possibly be known.* Such an existence must be utterly cut off from everything knowable, for if it was in any way manifested, if it anyhow effected anything knowable, that would be some slight reason for inferring it to be. I can attach no idea to such a reality and I have not been able to find a positivist or other person who could explain it and this confirms me in the opinion that the above definition really expresses what men mean by reality.

If therefore I am asked as a theist what I have to reply to the arguments of the positivist against religion, I reply in the first place, that positivism is only a particular species of metaphysics open to all the uncertainty of metaphysics, and its conclusions are for that reason of not enough weight to disturb any practical belief. We awake to reflection and find ourselves theists. Now those beliefs which come before reflection to all men alike are generally true, and the reason is that the causes which produce fallacies—depend for their operation upon a conscious process of reasoning. But apart from the weight of common sense which must be presumed to attach to theism, the fact that it is my belief itself throws the burden of proof upon its opponents. And metaphysical conclusions ought not in the present state of the science to weigh in practical affairs.

But even if I am asked as a metaphysician whether the objections of positivism to religion seem to me to be valid, I still answer not in the least.

For I object to its logical doctrine that no theory is to be admitted except so far as it asserts or denies something with respect to possible impressions of sense or their sensible relations.

This be it observed is a proposition of positivism which has nothing to do with natural science (the strong side of positivism) which anyway only deals with phenomena. Its principal effect is upon religion with reference to which positivism has rather its comical side. It is true positivists value this proposition as shutting out all metaphysical conclusions, but it appears to me it shuts them out for the wrong reason, that is on account of their object matter instead of on account of the unsatisfactory state of the science as yet.

What is the end of a theory or what is a theory considered as an end? The passionate advocate of positivism will be ready with some hasty answer, but passion and haste are not the way to answer such questions. Were it doubted whether a theory can be considered teleologically, it could be shown that end and theory are almost the same thing; but it is not doubted since positivism expressly defines itself a particular doctrine concerning the end of theory.

I should define the end of a theory as to carry one thread of consciousness through different states of consciousness. But whether this be the end or not, whatever is necessary to accomplishing the end of a theory must be admitted into the theory. Now to admit as a theory is the same as to believe for though in the ordinary use of language we attach more of the notion of a *provisional* character to admitting as a theory, yet as all belief is provisional this is merely a difference of degree which cannot affect the general logical consideration of the matter. We must therefore believe whatever is necessary for accomplishing the end of a theory whether that is capable of observation or not. The only question is whether anything not capable of direct observation is thus necessary.

Now as theories have this in common they are inferences of the unobserved from the observed—from the *present* in experience to the *future* in experience. Now who does not see that the future is not observable except when the present is not, so that we either reason to conclusions which are absolutely unobservable or from facts which are absolutely unobservable. This is the conclusive objection to positivism. If the reader cannot understand it in its pure philosophical statement, let him ask whether *time* can be observed, to flow. All science depends upon record of the past, and a record other than that in the memory is plainly something which cannot be verified by direct observation. The positivist may say if he pleases that memory is an immediate knowledge of the past, but all men admit that it may err. If one man's memory may err, so may ten men's. And though if ten men think they remember the same event there is *really* good ground for believing that they remember rightly, that there is none on the positivist principle that no theory is to be admitted except so far as it concludes something observable, is self-evident. Thus as every theory whatever concludes from the present to the future every theory necessarily concludes more than can possibly be verified by direct observation.

The positivists endeavor to elude this *reductio ad absurdum* by saying that by possible observation they mean that which can be supposed to be made at any time whatever. But they are aware, I suppose, that they cannot force any arbitrary rule of reasoning they please upon the world. They are upon their trial, and if they say that this is their doctrine they must support it by reasons and must hold nothing which shall lead to that further determination of it which we have supposed them to hold and which has been proved absurd. Now they are continually harping upon this: that if a theory concludes more than possible observations, it cannot be verified by direct observation and therefore is wholly baseless and metaphysical. Verification is the watchword of positivism. But it is easy to see that a proposition is no more verifiable by direct observation for being such as we can suppose (by a recognized falsification) to be observed unless it is also such as really can be observed. Their maxim, therefore, must refer to really possible observations not such as are supposably possible, for the proof they give leads to that or to nothing.

But the positivist has another reply to the objection here made to his doctrine. He may say:—"It is very true, that upon my principles I have not the least reason to believe that the record of the facts is true to the facts themselves. I do not pretend to have. The only world of which I have any information or in which I have any interest is the world which appears to me. Whether this represents correctly or otherwise any other world I neither know nor care." This is all very well, but it is plain that the positivist like other men inquires whether his history is right or not. What the significance of his doing so is, it is not necessary to inquire. In any case it follows, that he does somehow discriminate between direct observation and what has not been observed, and indeed if he did not his rule would have no possible application. And as matters of history are not capable of verification by direct observation in any case, some conclusions must be admitted which are not matters of direct observation. Besides, when the positivist assumes the transcendental position, which he is here supposed to do, he must admit that among all the elements present to consciousness, the grounds upon which some are set off as being matters of intuition are as it were conjectural. It is not a question capable of being decided by direct observation, what is and what is not direct observation.

The logical rule, therefore, which is the whole basis of positivism appears to me to be entirely false.

Paul Janet and Hegel, [1] by W. T. Harris

Journal of Speculative Philosophy
1(1867):250–56

[In the following article the passages quoted are turned into English, and the original French is omitted for the sake of brevity and lucid arrangement. As the work reviewed is accessible to most readers, a reference to the pages from which we quote will answer all purposes.—EDITOR.]

Since the death of Hegel in 1831, his philosophy has been making a slow but regular progress into the world at large. At home in Germany it is spoken of as having a right wing, a left wing, and a centre; its disciples are very numerous when one counts such widely different philosophers as Rosenkrantz, Michelet, Kuno Fischer, Erdmann, I. H. Fichte, Strauss, Feuerbach, and their numerous followers. Sometimes when one hears who constitute a "wing" of the Hegelian school, he is reminded of the *"lucus a non"* principle of naming, or rather of misnaming things. But Hegelianism has, as we said, made its way into other countries. In France we have the *Æsthetics* "partly translated and partly analyzed," by Professor Bénard; the logic of the small *Encyclopædia*, translated with copious notes, by Professor Vera, who has gone bravely on, with what seems with him to be a work of love, and given us the *Philosophy of Nature* and the *Philosophy of Spirit*, and promises us the "Philosophy of Religion"—all accompanied with abundant introduction and commentary. We hear of others very much influenced by Hegel: M. Taine, for example, who writes brilliant essays. In English, too, we have a translation of the *Philosophy of History*

---

1. *Etudes sur la dialectique dans Platon et dans Hegel*, par Paul Janet, Membre de L'Institut, professeur à la Faculté des lettres de Paris.—Paris: Ladrange, 1860.

(in Bohn's Library); a kind of translation and analysis of the first part of the third volume of the *Logic* (Sloman & Wallon, London, 1855); and an extensive and elaborate work on *The Secret of Hegel,* by James Hutchison Stirling. We must not forget to mention a translation of Schwegler's *History of Philosophy*—a work drawn principally from Hegel's labors—by our American Professor Seelye; and also (just published) a translation of the same book by the author of the *Secret of Hegel.* Articles treating of Hegel are to be found by the score—seek them in every text-book on philosophy, in every general Cyclopædia, and in numerous works written for or against German Philosophy. Some of these writers tell us in one breath that Hegel was a man of prodigious genius, and in the next they convict him of confounding the plainest of all common-sense distinctions. Some of them find him the profoundest of all thinkers, while others cannot "make a word of sense out of him." There seems to be a general understanding in this country and England on one point: all agree that he was a Pantheist. Theodore Parker, Sir William Hamilton, Mansel, Morell, and even some of the English defenders of Hegelianism admit this. Hegel holds, say some, that God is a *becoming;* others say that he holds God to be *pure being.* These men are careful men apparently—but only *apparently,* for it must be confessed that if Hegel has written any books at all, they are, every one of them, devoted to the task of showing the inadequacy of such abstractions when made the highest principle of things.

The ripest product of the great German movement in philosophy, which took place at the beginning of this century, Hegel's philosophy is likewise the concretest system of thought the world has seen. This is coming to be the conviction of thinkers more and more every day as they get glimpses into particular provinces of his labor. Bénard thinks the *Philosophy of Art* the most wonderful product of modern thinking, and speaks of the *Logic*—which he does not understand—as a futile and perishable production. Another thinks that his *Philosophy of History* is immortal, and a third values extravagantly his *Philosophy of Religion.* But the one who values his *Logic* knows how to value all his labors. *The History of Philosophy* is the work that impresses us most with the unparalleled wealth of his thought; he is able to descend through all history, and give to each philosopher a splendid thought as the centre of his system, and yet never is obliged to confound different systems, or fail in showing the superior depth of modern thought. While we are admiring the depth and clearness of Pythagoras, we are surprised and delighted to find the great thought of Heraclitus, but Anaxagoras is a new surprise; the Sophists come before us bearing a world-historical significance, and Socrates, Plato, and Aristotle lead us successively to heights such as we had not dreamed attainable by any thinking.

But thought is no *immediate* function, like the process of breathing or sleeping, or fancy-making: it is the profoundest mediation of spirit, and he who would get an insight into the speculative thinkers of whatever time, must labor as no mere flesh and blood can labor, but only as spirit can labor: with agony and sweat of blood. A philosophy which should explain the great complex of the universe, could hardly be expected to be transparent to uncultured minds at the first glance. Thus it happens that many critics give us such discouraging reports upon their return from a short excursion into the true wonder-land of philosophy. The Eternal Verities are miraculous only to those eyes which have gazed long upon them after shutting out the glaring sunlight of the senses.

Those who criticise a philosophy must imply a philosophical method of their own, and thus measure themselves while they measure others. A literary man who criticises Goethe, or Shakespeare, or Homer, is very apt to lay himself bare to the shaft of the adversary. There are, however, in our time, a legion of writers who pass judgment as flippantly upon a system of the most comprehensive scope—and which they confess openly their inability to understand—as upon a mere opinion uttered in a "table-talk." Even some men of great reputation give currency to great errors. Sir William Hamilton, in his notes to Reid's Philosophy of "Touch," once quoted the passage from the second part of Fichte's *Bestimmung des Menschen* (wherein one-sided idealism is pushed to its downfall), in order to show that Fichte's Philosophy ended in Nihilism. The *Bestimmung des Menschen* was a mere popular writing in which Fichte adopted the Kantian style of exhibiting the self-refutation of sense and reflection, in order to rest all ultimate truth in the postulates of the Practical Reason. Accordingly he shows the practical results of his own system in the third part of the work in question, and enforces the soundest ethical views of life. He never thought of presenting his theoretical philosophy in that work. Thus, too, in Hamilton's refutation of Cousin and Schelling: he polemicises against all "Doctrines of the Absolute," saying that *to think is to limit; hence to think God would be to determine or limit Him;* and hence is inferred the impossibility of thinking God as he truly is. This, of course, is not pushed to its results by his followers, for then its skeptical tendency would become obvious. Religion demands that we shall do the Will of God; this Will must, therefore, be known. But, again, Will is the realization or self-determination of one's nature— from it the character proceeds. Thus in knowing God's will we know his character or nature. If we cannot do this at all, no religion is possible; and in proportion as Religion is possible, the Knowledge of God is possible.

If it be said that the Absolute is unthinkable, in this assertion it is affirmed that all predicates or categories of thought are inapplicable to the Absolute, for to think is to predicate of some object, the categories of thought; and in so far as these categories apply, to that extent is the Absolute thinkable. Since *Existence* is a category of thought, it follows from this position that to predicate existence of the Absolute is impossible; "a questionable predicament" truly for the Absolute. According to this doctrine—that all thought is limitation—God is made Pure Being, or Pure Thought. This is also the result of Indian Pantheism, and of all Pantheism; this doctrine concerning the mere negative character of thought, in fact, underlies the Oriental tenet that consciousness is finitude. To be consistent, all Hamiltonians should become Brahmins, or, at least, join some sect of modern Spiritualists, and thus embrace a religion that corresponds to their dogma. However, let us not be so unreasonable as to insist upon the removal of inconsistency—it is all the good they have.

After all this preliminary let us proceed at once to examine the work of Professor Paul Janet, which we have named at the head of our article: *Etudes sur la dialectique dans Platon et dans Hegel.*

After considering the Dialectic of Plato in its various aspects, and finding that it rests on the principle of contradiction,

M. Janet grapples Hegel, and makes, in order, the following points:

I. TERMINOLOGY.—He tells us that the great difficulty that lies in the way of comprehending German Philosophy is the abstract terminology employed, which is, in fact, mere scholasticism preserved and applied to modern problems. No nation of modern times, except the Germans, have preserved the scholastic form. He traces the obscurity of modern German philosophy to "Aristotle subtilized by the schools." This he contrasts with the "simple and natural philosophy of the Scotch." [This "simplicity" arises from the fact that the Scotch system holds that immediate sensuous knowing is valid. Of course this implies that they hold that the immediate existence of objects is a true existence—that whatever is, exists thus and so without any further grounds. This is the denial of all philosophy, for it utterly ignores any occasion whatever for it. But it is no less antagonistic to the "natural science" of the physicist: he, the physicist, finds the immediate object of the senses to be no permanent or true phase, but only a transitory one; the object is involved with other beings—even the remotest star—and changes when they change. It is force and matter (two very abstract categories) that are to him the permanent and true existence. But force and matter cannot be seen by the senses; they can only be thought.] Our author proceeds to trace the resemblance between Hegel and Wolff: both consider and analyze the pure concepts, beginning with Being. To M. Janet this resemblance goes for much, but he admits that "Hegel has modified this order (that of Wolff) and rendered it more systematic." If one asks *"How* more systematic?" he will not find the answer. "The scholastic *form* is retained, but not the *thought,"* we are told. That such statements are put forward, even in a book designed for mere surface-readers may well surprise us. That the mathematical method of Wolff or Spinoza—a method which proceeds by definitions and external comparison, holding meanwhile to the principle of contradiction—that such a method should be confounded with that of Hegel which proceeds dialectically, i.e. through the internal movement of the categories to their contradiction or limit, shows the student of philosophy at once that we are dealing with a *littérateur,* and not with a philosopher. So far from retaining the form of Wolff it is the great object of Hegel (see his long prefaces to the *Logik* and the *Phänomenologie des Geistes*) to supplant that form by what he considers the true method—that of the *objective* itself. The objective method is to be distinguished from the arbitrary method of external reflection which selects its point of view somewhere outside of the object considered, and proceeds to draw relations and comparisons which, however edifying, do not give us any exhaustive knowledge. It is also to be distinguished from the method of mere empirical observation which collects without discrimination a mass of characteristics, accidental and necessary, and never arrives at a vivifying soul that unites and subordinates the multiplicity. The objective method seizes somewhat in its definition and traces it through all the phases which necessarily unfold when the object is placed in the form of *relation to itself.* An object which cannot survive the process of self-relation, perishes, i.e. it leads to a more concrete object which is better able to endure. This method, as we shall presently see, is attributed to Plato by M. Janet.

The only resemblance that remains to be noted between the scholastics and Hegel is this: they both treat of subtle distinctions in thought, while our modern "common-sense" system goes only so far as to distinguish very general and obvious differences. This is a questionable merit, and the less ado made about it by such as take pride in it, the better for them.

Our author continues: "The principal difficulty of the system of Kant is our ignorance of the ancient systems of logic. *The Critique of Pure Reason* is modelled on the scholastic system." Could we have a more conclusive refutation of this than the fact that the great professors of the ancient systems grossly misunderstand Kant, and even our essayist himself mistakes the whole purport of the same! Hear him contrast Kant with Hegel: "Kant sees in Being only the form of Thought, while Hegel sees in Thought only the form of Being." This he says is the great difference between the Germans and French, interpreting it to mean: "that the former pursues the route of deduction, and the latter that of experience"!

He wishes to consider Hegel under three heads: 1st, The Beginning; 2d, the dialectical deduction of the Becoming, and 3d, the term *Dialectic.*

II. THE BEGINNING.—According to M. Janet, Hegel must

have used this syllogism in order to find the proper category
with which to commence the *Logic*.

(a) The Beginning should presuppose nothing;
(b) Pure Being presupposes nothing;
(c) Hence Pure Being is the Beginning.

This syllogism he shows to be inconclusive: for there are two
beginnings, (a) in the order of knowledge, (b) in the order of
existence. Are they the same? He answers: "No, the thinking
being—because it thinks—knows itself before it knows the
being which it thinks." Subject and object being identical in
that act, M. Janet in effect says, "it thinks itself before it thinks
itself"—an argument that the scholastics would hardly have
been guilty of! The beginning is really made, he says, with
internal or external *experience*. He quotes (page 316) from
Hegel a passage asserting that *mediation* is essential to knowing. This he construes to mean that "the determined or concrete (the world of experience) is the essential condition of
knowing!" Through his misapprehension of the term "mediation," we are prepared for all the errors that follow, for "mediation in knowing" means with Hegel that it involves a *process*,
and hence can be true only in the form of a system. The "internal and external experience" appertains to what Hegel calls
immediate knowing. It is therefore not to be wondered at that
M. Janet thinks Hegel contradicts himself by holding Pure
Being to be the Beginning, and afterwards affirming mediation
to be necessary. He says (page 317), "In the order of knowing
it is the mediate which is necessarily first, while in the order of
existence the immediate is the commencement." Such a remark shows him to be still laboring on the first problem of
Philosophy, and without any light, for no *Speculative* Philosopher (like Plato, Aristotle, Leibnitz, or Hegel) ever held that
Pure Being—or the immediate—is the first in the order of existence, but rather that God or Spirit (self-thinking, "pure act,"
Noῦς, "Logos," &c.) is the first in the order of existence. In fact,
M. Janet praises Plato and Aristotle for this very thing at the end
of his volume, and thereby exhibits the unconsciousness of his
procedure. Again, "The pure thought is the end of philosophy,
and not its beginning." If he means by this that the culture of

consciousness ends in arriving at pure thought or philosophy, we have no objection to offer, except to the limiting of the application of the term *Philosophy* to its preliminary stage, which is called the Phenomenology of Spirit. The arrival at pure thought marks the beginning of the use of terms in a universal sense, and hence is the beginning of philosophy proper. But M. Janet criticises the distinction made by Hegel between Phenomenology and Psychology, and instances Maine de Biran as one who writes Psychology in the sense Hegel would write Phenomenology. But M. Biran merely manipulates certain unexplained phenomena,—like the Will, for example—in order to derive categories like force, cause, &c. But Hegel shows in his Phenomenology the dialectical unfolding of consciousness through all its phases, starting from the immediate certitude of the senses. He shows how certitude becomes knowledge of truth, and wherein it differs from it. But M. Janet (p. 324) thinks that Hegel's system, beginning in empirical Psychology, climbs to pure thought, "and then draws up the ladder after it."

III. THE BECOMING.—We are told by the author that consciousness determining itself as Being, determines itself as *a* being, and not as *the* being. If this be so we cannot think *pure being* at all. Such an assertion amounts to denying the universal character of the Ego. If the position stated were true, we could think neither being nor any other object.

On page 332, he says, "This contradiction (of Being and non-being) which in the ordinary logic would be the negative of the *posited notion,* is, in the logic of Hegel, only an excitant or stimulus, which somehow determines spirit to find a third somewhat in which it finds the other conciliated." He is not able to see any procedure at all. He sees the two opposites, and thinks that Hegel empirically hunts out a concept which implies both, and substitutes it for them. M. Janet thinks (pp. 336–7) that Hegel has exaggerated the difficulties of conceiving the identity of Being and nought. (P. 338) "If the difference of Being and nought can be neither expressed nor defined, if they are as identical as different—if, in short, the idea of Being is only the idea of the pure void, I will say, not merely that Being transforms itself into Nothing, or passes into its contrary; I will say that there are not two contraries, but only one term which I have falsely called Being in the thesis, but which is in reality only Non-being without restriction—the pure zero." He quotes from Kuno Fischer (p. 340) the following remarks applicable here:

If Being were in reality the pure void as it is ordinarily taken, Non-being would not express the same void a second time; but it would then be the non-void, i.e. the abhorrence of the void, or the immanent contradiction of the void.—

and again from his *Logik und Metaphysik*, II, §29:

The logical Being contradicts itself; for thought vanishes in the immovable repose of Being. But as Being comes only from thought (for it is the act of thought), it contradicts thus itself in destroying thought. Consequently thought manifests itself as the negation of Being—that is to say, as *Non-being*. The Non-being (logical) is not the total suppression of Being—the pure zero—it is not the mathematical opposition of Being to itself as a negative opposed to a positive, but it is the dialectical negative of itself, the immanent contradiction of Being. Being contradicts itself, hence is Non-being, and in the concept of Non-being, thought discovers the immanent contradiction of Being—thought manifests itself at first as Being, and in turn the logical Being manifests itself as Non-being; thought can hence say, "I am the Being which is not."

"Such," continues our author, "is the deduction of M. Fischer. It seems to me very much inferior in clearness to that of Hegel." How he could say this is very mysterious when we find him denying all validity to Hegel's demonstration. Although Fischer's explanation is mixed—partly dialectical and partly psychological—yet, as an explanation, it is correct. But as psychology should not be dragged into Logic, which is the evolution of the forms of pure thinking, we must hold strictly to the dialectic if we would see the "Becoming." The psychological explanation gets no further than the relation of Being and nought as concepts. The Hegelian thought on this point is not widely different from that of Gorgias, as given us by Sextus Empiricus, nor from that of Plato in the *Sophist*. Let us attempt it here:

Being is the pure simple; as such it is considered under the form of self-relation. But as it is wholly undetermined, and has no content, it is pure nought or absolute negation. As such it is the negation by itself or the negation of itself, and hence its own opposite or Being. Thus the simple falls through self-opposition into duality, and this again becomes simple if we attempt to hold it asunder, or give it any validity by itself. Thus if Being is posited as having validity in and by itself without determination *(omnis determinatio est negatio),* it becomes a pure void in nowise different from nought, for difference is determination, and neither Being nor nought possess it. What is the validity of the nought? A negative is a relative, and a negative by itself is a negative related to itself, which is a self-cancelling. Thus Being and nought, posited objectively as having validity, prove dissolving forms and pass over into each other. Being is a *ceasing* and nought is a *beginning,* and these are the two forms of *Becoming.* The Becoming, dialectically considered, proves itself inadequate likewise.

IV. THE DIALECTIC.—To consider an object dialectically we have merely to give it universal validity; if it contradicts itself then, *we* are not in anywise concerned for the result; we will simply stand by and accept the result, without fear that the true will not appear in the end. The negative turned against itself makes short work of itself; it is only when the subjective reflection tries to save it by hypotheses and reservations that a merely negative result is obtained.

(Page 369): "In Spinozism the development of Being is Geometric; in the System of Hegel it is organic." What could have tempted him to use these words, it is impossible to say, unless it was the deep-seated national proclivity for epigrammatic statements. This distinction means nothing less (in the mouth of its original author) than what we have already given as the true difference between Wolff's and Hegel's methods; but M. Janet has long since forgotten his earlier statements. (Page 369) He says, "Hegel's method is a faithful expression of the movement of nature," from which he thinks Hegel derived it empirically!

On page 372 he asks: "Who proves to us that the dialectic stops at *Spirit* as its last term? Why can I not conceive a spirit absolutely superior to mine, in whom the identity between subject and object, the intelligible and intelligence would be more perfect than it is with this great Philosopher [Hegel]? * * * * * In fact, every philosopher is a man, and so far forth is full of obscurity and feebleness." *Spirit* is the last term in philosophy for the reason that it stands in complete self-relation, and hence contains its antithesis within itself; if it could stand in opposition to anything else, then it would contain a contradiction, and be capable of transition into a higher. M. Janet asks in effect: "Who proves that the dialectic stops at God as the highest, and why cannot I conceive a higher?" Judging from his attempt at understanding Hegel, however, he is not in a fair way to conceive "a spirit in whom the identity between subject and object" is more perfect than in Hegel. "What hinders" is his own culture, his own self; *"Du gleichst dem Geist den du begreifst, nicht mir,"* said the World-spirit to Faust.

He asks (p. 374): "When did the 'pure act' commence?" From Eternity; it always commences, and is always complete, says Hegel. "According to Hegel, God is made from nought, by means of the World." Instead of this, Hegel holds that God is self-created, and the world eternally created by him (the Eternally-begotten Son). "What need has God of Nature?" God is Spirit; hence conscious; hence he makes himself an object to himself; in this act he creates nature; hence Nature is His reflection. (P. 386): "The Absolute in Hegel is spirit only on condition that it thinks, and thinks *itself;* hence it is not *essentially* Spirit, but only *accidentally."* To *"think itself"* is to be conscious, and, without this, God would have no personality; and hence if Hegel were to hold any other doctrine than the one attributed to him, he would be a Pantheist. But these things are not mere dogmas with Hegel; they appear as the logical results of the most logical of systems. "But in Plato, God is a Reason *in activity,* a living thought." M. Janet mentions this to show Plato's superiority; he thinks that it is absurd for Hegel to attribute *thinking* to God, but thinks the same thing to be a great merit in Plato. (P. 392): "Behold the Platonic deduction [or dialectic]: being given a pure idea, he shows that this idea, if it were *all alone* [i.e. made universal, or placed in self-relation, or posited as valid for itself] would be contradictory of itself, and consequently could not be. Hence, if it exists, it is on condition that it mingles with another idea. Take, for example, the multiple: by itself, it loses itself in the indiscernible, for it would be impossible without unity." This would do very well for a description of the Dialectic in Hegel if he would lay more stress on the positive side of the result. Not merely does the "pure idea mingle with another"—i.e. pass over to its opposite—but it *returns* into itself by the continuation of its own movement, and thereby reaches a concrete stage. Plato sometimes uses this complete dialectical movement, and ends affirmatively; sometimes he uses only the partial movement and draws negative conclusions.

How much better M. Janet's book might have been—we may be allowed to remark in conclusion—had he possessed the earnest spirit of such men as Vera and Hutchison Stirling! Stimulated by its title, we had hoped to find a book that would kindle a zeal for the study of the profoundest philosophical subject, as treated by the profoundest of thinkers.

Letter, Peirce to W. T. Harris

L 183: W. T. Harris Collection

Cambridge 1868 Jan. 24

Dear Sir

I have to thank you for the fourth number of your excellent Journal. I think you are to be congratulated upon the success of your first volume. There are many things which might be said in the way of praise and blame, but I will not venture upon criticism. Only, the national importance of your undertaking impels me to mention one matter itself of national importance. I think that the terminology used in the journal has occasionally violated usage. I remember, for example, such expressions as, "Locke's primary *properties*" instead of *qualities,* reality as the opposite of potentiality instead of actuality, contemplation (for Anschauung) instead of intuition, comprehension (for Begriff) instead of concept. *Begriff* is a common word and there can be no doubt of its equivalence commonly to concept. Shall we then assign two English words to this one German? Considering the superior richness of the latter language, I fear that this would necessitate our assigning but one word in English to several German ones which ought to be distinguished. If Hegel put up with Begriff, I think that we must get along with Concept. In English a rigid economy of words is requisite which in German is unnecessary, although it could hardly be without its advantages.

I should like to make some inquiries in regard to your meaning in the paragraph beginning 'Being is the pure simple' on p. 140.

I will begin by stating how much of it [. . .]

I have been thus long-winded in order that the nature of my questions in reference to your meaning and position should be unmistakable. I will say again that I do not argue or profess to represent or state the position of Hegelians, but only seek a more explicit statement from one of them.

I have written on one side of the paper only so that if you should think it well to answer my questions in print, you might print them in full with the answers. Should you do this, I should desire (as a mere inquirer) to remain *incognito.* Yours with great respect

C. S. Peirce

Nominalism versus *Realism*

P 25: Journal of
Speculative Philosophy 2(1868):57–61

[We print below some strictures upon the position assumed in our last number with reference to M. Janet's version of Hegel's doctrine of the "Becoming." We hope that these acute statements which have been written, for the most part, in the form of queries, will receive a careful reading, especially by those who have differed from our own views hitherto expressed. They seem to us the most profound and compendious statement of the anti-speculative standpoint as related to the Science of Pure Thought *(Prima Philosophia),* that we have seen. But for this very reason we are fain to believe that the defects of the formalism relied upon are all the more visible. We have endeavored to answer these queries with the same spirit of candor that animates their author.—*Editor.*]

Mr. Editor of the Journal of Speculative Philosophy:

I should like to make some inquiries in regard to your meaning in the paragraph beginning "Being is the pure Simple," p. 140.

I will begin by stating how much of it I already understand, as I believe. I understand that 'Being' and 'Nothing' as used by you, are two abstract, and not two general terms. That Being is the abstraction belonging in common and exclusively to the objects of the concrete term, whose extension is unlimited or all-embracing, and whose comprehension is null. I understand that you use Nothing, also, as an abstract term = nothingness; for otherwise to say that Being is Nothing, is like saying that humanity is non-man, and does not imply at all that Being is in any opposition with itself, since it would only say 'Das Sein ist nicht Seiendes', not 'Sein ist nicht Sein'. By Nothing, then, I understand the abstract term corresponding to a (possible) concrete term, which is the logical contradictory of the concrete term corresponding to 'Being'. And since the logical contradictory of any term has no extension in common with that term, the *concrete* nothing is the term which has no extension. I understand, that, when you say 'Being has no content', and 'Being is wholly undetermined', you mean, simply, that its corresponding concrete has no logical comprehension, or, at least, that what you mean follows from this, and this, conversely, from what you mean.

I come now to what I do not understand, and I have some questions to ask, which I have endeavored so to state that all can see that the Hegelian is bound to answer them, for they simply ask what you mean, whether this or that; they simply ask you to be explicit upon points upon which you have used ambiguous expressions. They are not put forward as arguments, however, but only as inquiries.

1. Abstract terms, according to the doctrine of modern times, are only a device for expressing in another way the meaning of concrete terms. To say that whiteness inheres in an object, is the same as to say that an object is white. To say that whiteness is a color, is the same as to say that the white is colored, and that this is implied in the very meanings of the words.

But, you will undoubtedly admit that there is a difference between a hundred dollars in my pocket, *Being* or *not Being,* and so in any other particular case. You, therefore, admit that there is nothing which is, which is also not. Therefore, it follows that *what is,* and *what is not,* are mutually exclusive and not coëxtensive.

Since, then, you nevertheless say that the corresponding abstractions, Being and Nothingness, are absolutely the same (although you at the same time hold that it is not so, at all), it is plain that you find some other meaning in abstract terms than that which other logicians find. I would, therefore, ask what you mean by an abstraction, and how you propose to find out what is true of abstractions.

[Here we have stated, 1st, what our interrogator thinks he understands, in brief, as follows: *(a)* That Being and Nothing are two abstract, and not two general terms; *(b)* that Being belongs to the concrete term, whose extension is unlimited, and whose comprehension is null; *(c)* that Nothing means *nothingness,* and belongs to the concrete term, whose extension is null.

At this point we will pause, in order to call attention to a vital misapprehension of the signification of Being, as we used the term. If Being were the abstraction corresponding to the concrete term, "whose extension is unlimited and whose comprehension is null," Being would then signify *existence* (not the German *"Seyn,"* but *"Daseyn,"* sometimes called *extant Being*), i.e. it would signify *determined* Being, and not *pure* Being. If Being is taken in this sense, it is not equivalent to Nought, and there is no support given to such an absurdity in any system of Philosophy with which we are acquainted. Therefore, whatever is based on this assumption falls to the ground. But the question may be asked, "If the abstraction corresponding to the most general predicate of individual things is *existence,* by what process of abstraction do you get beyond this most general of predicates to a category transcending it?" We answer, by the simple process of *analysis;* let us try: in the most general predicate, which is *determined Being,* or *existence*—for all things in the Universe are determined beings—we have an evident two-foldness (a composite nature), which allows of a further analysis into pure Being and determination. Now, pure Being, considered apart from all determination, does not correspond to any concrete term, for the reason that *determination,* which alone renders such correspondence possible, has been separated from it by the analysis.

As regards the point *(c),* it is sufficient to remark that we did not use the term "Nothing" for nothingness, in the place referred to, but used the term *"Nought,"* so as to avoid the ambiguity in the term Nothing, to-wit: the confusion arising from its being taken in the sense of no thing, as well as in the sense of the pure void. In analyzing "determined Being," we have two factors: one reduces to pure being, which is the pure void, while the other reduces to pure negation, which is likewise the pure void. Determination is negation, and if determination is isolated it has no substrate; while on the other hand all substrates, or substrate in general when isolated from determination, becomes pure vacuity.

Hence it seems to us that the process of analysis which reflection initiates, does not stop until it comes to the pure simple, which is the turning point where analysis becomes synthesis. Let us see how this synthesis manifests itself: our ultimate abstraction, the pure simple, has two forms, pure Being and pure negation; they coincide, in that they are the pure void. Neither can be determined, and hence neither can possess a distinction from the other. Analytic thought, which sunders the concrete, and never takes note of the link which binds, must always arrive at the abstract simple as the net result of its dualizing process. But arrived at this point it is obliged to consider the *tertium quid,* the *genetic universal,* which it has neglected. For it has arrived at that which is self-contradictory. To seize the pure simple in thought is to cancel it; for by seizing it in thought, we seize it as the negation of the determined, and by so doing we place it in opposition, and thereby determine it. Moreover, it would, objectively considered, involve the same contradiction, for its distinction from existing things determines it likewise. Therefore, *the simple,* which is the limit of analysis, is only a point at which synthesis begins, and hence is a *moment* of a process of self-repulsion, or self-related negation. So long as analysis persists in disregarding the mediation here involved, it can set up this pure immediate for the *ultimatum.* But so soon as it takes it in its truth it allows its mediation to appear, and we learn the synthetic result, which, in its most abstract form, is "the becoming." This we shall also find in another mode of consideration: differentiation and distinguishing are forms of mediation; the simple is the limit at which mediation begins; it (mediation) cancels this limit by beginning; but all mediated somewhats imply, likewise, the simple as the ultimate element upon which determination takes effect. Thus we cannot deny the simple utterly, nor can we posit it affirmatively by itself; it is no sooner reached by analysis than it passes into synthesis.

Again we see the same doctrine verified by seizing the two factors of our analysis in their reflective form, i.e. in their mediation: Being, as the substrate, is the form of identity or self-relation, which, when isolated, becomes empty self-relation, or self-relation in which the negativity of the relation has been left out; this gives a form that collapses into a void. Determination, as the other factor, is the relation to a beyond, or what we call the *relative* proper; it is the self-transcending element, and when isolated so that its relation remains within itself, it falls into the form of the self-related, which is that of substrate, or the form of Being, and this collapses still further into the void, when we continue our demand for the simple; this void (or "hunger," as Boehme called it) is the same relativity that we found determination to be, when isolated, and thus we may follow these abstractions round and round until we find that they are organic phases of ONE PROCESS. Then we have found our synthesis, and have left those abstractions behind us.

We do not pretend to speak for "Hegelians"; we do not know that they would endorse our position. We give this as our own view, merely.

The first query which our interrogator offers contains the following points:

(a) Abstract terms are devices for expressing the meaning of concrete terms.

(b) Difference between a hundred dollars in his pocket being and not being (i.e. that the existence of a hundred dollars in his pocket makes a difference to his wealth) granted, it follows that what is and what is not are mutually exclusive, and not coextensive.

(c) The assertion of the identity of Being and Nothing [nought?] and the simultaneous denial of it indicates some other meaning given to abstract terms than the one he finds.

With regard to the first point, *(a)*, we are ready to say at once, that we could not hold such a doctrine and lay any claim to be speculative philosophers. Nor, indeed, could we consistently hold it and join the class of thinkers which belong to the stage of Reflection—such as the Positivists, the Kantists, the Hamiltonians, &c., &c.,—who agree that we know only phenomena, and hence agree that the immediate world is untrue in itself, and exists only through mediation. For it is evident that the doctrine enunciated by our querist implies that general terms as well as abstract terms are only *"flatus vocis"*—in short, that individual things compose the universe, and that these are valid and true in themselves. On the contrary, we must hold that true actualities must be self-determining totalities, and not mere *things,* for these are always dependent somewhats, and are separated from their true selves. (See chapter VIII of our "Introduction to Philosophy," and, also, chapter X on *The Universal.*) That which abides in the process of origination and decay, which *things* are always undergoing, is the generic; the generic is the total comprehension, the true actuality, or the Universal, and its identity is always preserved, while the mere "thing," which is not self-contained, loses its identity perpetually. The loss of the identity of the *thing,* is the very process that manifests the identity of the total.

Hence, to pre-suppose such a doctrine as formal logic pre-supposes, is to set up the doctrine of immediateness as the only true.

The "hundred dollar" illustration does not relate to the discussion, for the reason, that the question is not that of the identity of *existence* and *non-existence,* but of *pure Being* and *Nought,* as before explained.]

2. You say, in effect,

> Being has no determination;
> *Ergo,* It is nothing.

Now, it certainly appears that the contrary conclusion follows from this premise, namely: that it is not nothingness. I suppose that you have suppressed one of your premises, and that you mean to argue thus:

> Indetermination in respect to any character, is
>   the negation of that character;
> Being is indeterminate in respect to every
>   character;
> *Ergo,* Being is negative of every character.

In short, you seem to imply that to abstract from a character, is to deny it. Is this the manner in which your argument is to be completed, or how else?

3. This suggests another question. You say that nothing has no determination. It is plain that it would not follow from this that Being is nothing, but only that Nothing is being, or rather that Any non-being is a being, thus reducing non-being *(nicht-seiende)* to an absurdity. This would be nothing new (for Albertus Magnus quotes Avicenna to this effect), and in my opinion would be perfectly true. *Non-ens,* or "the not being," is a self-contradictory expression. Still, though I thus see no monstrous consequences of saying that nothing has no determination, I see no proof at all that it is so. It might be said, indeed, that the things which are not have no characters in common, and that therefore *what is not* has no logical comprehension and Being-not no determination. I would ask, then, have you proved that nothing has no determination? Do not suppose that I am endeavoring to drive you into contradiction; for I understand Hegelians profess to be self-contradictory. I only wish to ascertain whether they have an equal disregard for those logical maxims which relate to ambiguities.

4. You say, in effect,

> Difference is determination,
> Being has no determination;
> *Ergo,* Being has no difference from nothing;
> *Ergo,* Being is nothing.

It is incontestable that difference from anything is determination in respect to being or not being that thing. A monkey, in differing from a man, is determined (negatively) in respect to humanity. Difference, then, in any respect, is determination in that respect. This, I take it, is what you mean. Now let us parallel the above argument:

> Difference in any respect is determination in
> that respect;
> Animality, in general, is not determined in
> respect to humanity;
> *Ergo,* Animality, in general, has no difference
> from humanity;
> *Ergo,* Animality, in general, is humanity.

This is plainly sophistical. For to say that an abstraction, in general, is undetermined, has two different senses; one resulting from a strict analysis of the language, and the other reposing upon the ordinary use of language. Strictly, to say that an abstraction is undetermined, would mean that it may be this or may be that abstraction; that is, that the abstract word by which it is expressed may have any one of a variety of meanings. What is ordinarily meant by the phrase, however, is that the object of the corresponding concrete term is undetermined, so that neither of a certain pair of mutually contradictory predicates are *universally* true of that concrete. Now, it is true to say that animality is undetermined in respect to humanity, or that being is not determined at all, only in the latter of these senses, to-wit: that not every animal is a man, and not every animal is not a man, and (in the other case) that there is no predicate which can be truly affirmed or denied of all beings. For in the other sense, we should imply that the abstractions themselves were vague, and that being, for example, has no precise meaning. In the only true sense, therefore, the premise is, in the one case, that "Animal, simply, is undetermined," and in the other, that *"Ens (seiende)* is undetermined"; and what follows is, in the one case, that "not every animal differs from a man," and in the other, that "not every being differs from any nothing." This latter amounts merely to saying that there is nothing from which every being differs, or that a nothing is an absurdity. These correct conclusions do not in the least imply that animality is humanity, or that being is nothingness. To reach the latter conclusions, it would be necessary (in the first place) to use the premises in the other and false sense; but even then, all that would be legitimately inferable would be that "humanity, *in some sense,* is animality," and that "being, *in some sense,* is nothing." Only by a second fallacy could it be concluded that animality, in the sense intended, is humanity, or that being, in the sense intended, is nothing. Now, I would inquire whether you inadvertently fell into these ambiguities, or, if not, wherein the force of your argumentation lies?

[The second point we are requested to answer is involved in the third and fourth, which charges to our account the following syllogism:

Difference is determination; being has no determination; *ergo,* being has no difference from nothing; *ergo,* being is nothing.

This is then paralleled with one in which animality and humanity are confounded; the cause of which is the following oversight: In the article under criticism (p. 141), we said, "Thus, if Being is posited as having validity in and by itself, without determination, it becomes a pure void, in nowise different from nought, for difference is determination, and [N.B.] neither Being nor nought possess it." The ground of their identity is stated to be the lack of determinations in nought as well as in Being.

Again, determination may be quantitative as well as qualitative, and, in the former respect, animality is distinguished from humanity; for to have more extension and less comprehension, certainly distinguishes one concept from another. Two is distinct from three, although contained in the latter. Hence, it is not quite correct to say that "animality, in general, is not determined in respect to humanity." Moreover, if it were correct, its converse "humanity is not determined in respect to animality," would also have to be true to make a case parallel to the one in which Being is asserted to be identical with nothing for the reason that neither is determined in any respect. Were animality and humanity neither determined in respect to the other, they certainly must be identical.

For these reasons, we cannot acknowledge that we "inadvertently fell into these ambiguities," or that we fell into them at all.

And we cannot see the basis of the assertion that "Hegelians profess to be self-contradictory." For they hold that finite things contradict themselves, but that the total preserves itself in its negation. They therefore would consider every one who stakes his faith on the immediate to contradict himself, but that the philosopher who holds only to the absolute mediation, escapes self-contradiction by not attempting to set up non-contradiction as the first principle of things. Hegelians may understand this as they please—to us it seems that the principle of identity is abstract, and only one side of the true principle. If we would comprehend the true principle of the universe, we must be able to seize identity and contradiction in one, and hence to annul both of them. He who comprehends self-determination must be able to do this. The self negates itself, and yet, for the reason that it is the self that does this, the deed is *affirmative,* and hence identity is the result. "The self says to itself, 'thus far shalt thou go, and no farther'; its reply is, 'I am already there, limiting myself'." "When me they fly, I am the wings," says Brahma, and every true Infinite involves this negation, which is at the same time negation of negation or affirmation.

Hence, it seems to us improper to charge self-contradiction upon those who merely assert it of finite things.]

5. Finally, I would inquire whether, in your opinion, the maxims of (ordinary) logic relating to contradictions lack even a *prima facie* presumption in their favor? Whether the burden of proof is or is not upon the Hegelians to show that the assumption of their falsity is a more tenable position than the assumption of their truth? For in the present state of the question, it seems to me more probable that subtle fallacies lurk in the Hegelian reasoning than that such fallacies lurk in all other reasoning whatsoever.

[In answer to the fifth query, we will state that we think the maxims of formal logic are *prima facie* true, for the *prima facie* mode of viewing always gives validity to the immediate phase of things. But Reflection discovers the insufficiency of abstract identity and difference, and comes to their assistance with manifold saving clauses. The speculative insight holds, too, like reflection, that mediation belongs to things, but sees, further, that all mediation is circular, and hence, that self-mediation is the "constant" under all variables.

The whole question of the validity of formal logic and of common sense *vs.* speculative philosophy, can be reduced to this: Do you believe that there are any finite or dependent beings? In other words, Are you a nominalist or a realist?

This is the gist of all philosophizing: If one holds that things are not interdependent, but that each is for itself, he will hold that general terms correspond to no object, and may get along with formal logic; and if he holds that he knows things directly in their essence, he needs no philosophy—common sense is sufficient.

But if he holds that any particular thing is dependent upon what lies beyond its immediate limits, he holds, virtually, that its true being lies beyond it, or, more precisely, that its immediate being is not identical with its total being, and hence, that it is in contradiction with itself, and is therefore *changeable, transitory,* and *evanescent,* regarded from the *immediate* point of view. But regarding the entire or total being (The Generic), we cannot call it changeable or contradictory, for that perpetually abides. It is the "Form of Eternity."]

Letter, Peirce to W. T. Harris

L 183: W. T. Harris Collection

Cambridge 1868 March 16

Dear Sir

I have received the proof sheets of your very courteous reply to my queries. I have strong reasons for thinking that you have understood me as using the adjectives *abstract* and *concrete* in the senses of general or very general and singular; whereas, in fact, by an abstract name I mean such as *entitas, whiteness, immediacy* and by a concrete one such as *ens, white, Immediate.* Further reflection and a reference to your own statement on p. 117 and to Hegel's very careful remarks under the head of *Daseyn,* will I think convince you that being, as I defined it, is not determinate, the reflection that all which is is by negation and determination, not being involved in that definition. Far less, is it *existence,* which you certainly will not maintain to be the same as *Daseyn.* I have thought proper to defer making any remarks upon your reply until you have had an opportunity to amend it in these respects.

There are two unimportant errata in my letter. p 59 2nd column 6th line from the bottom. The dash should be a hyphen. p 60 2nd col. 11th and 12th lines from the top. Omit the words "or that being in the sense intended is humanity."

I have read Mr. Kroeger's pamphlet on Politics with great attention, interest, and general approval. It seems to me that it is in the sphere of morals and politics that the school of Fichte is strongest. I should have been glad to have had more said about the theory of checks and balances which has lately been powerfully attacked and also upon the peculiar modification of the theory of the state of nature contained in the Declaration.

I remain, with great regard
Yours &c.
Charles S. Peirce

What Is Meant by "Determined"

P 28: Journal of
Speculative Philosophy *2(1868):190–91*

[The following discussion, which is a continuation of the one in a former issue called "Nominalism and Realism," may serve a good purpose to clear up any confusion that may exist regarding some of the important technical expressions employed. —EDITOR.]

To the Editor of the Journal of Speculative Philosophy.

SIR:—Your remarks upon my inquiries concerning Being and Nothing are very kind and courteous. Considered as replies, they are less satisfactory than they might have been had I succeeded better in making my difficulties understood.

I suspect that there must be some misunderstanding between us of the meaning of the various terms cognate with "determined." Perhaps, therefore, I shall do well to state more fully than I did before, the manner in which I understand Hegel (in common with all other logicians) to use them. Possibly, the original signification of *bestimmt* was "settled by vote"; or it may have been "pitched to a key." Thus its origin was quite different from that of "determined"; yet I believe that as philosophical terms their equivalence is exact. In general, they mean "fixed to be *this* (or *thus*), in contradistinction to being this, that, or the other (or in some way or other)."[1]—When it is a concept or term, such as is expressed by a concrete noun or adjective which is said to be more determinate than another, the sense sometimes is that the logical extension of the former concept or term is a part and only a part of that of the latter; but more usually the sense is, that the logical comprehension of the latter is a part and only a part of that of the former.

In my former letter (page 151) I sufficiently expressed my own understanding of "determined" as applied to a concept or term such as is expressed by an abstract noun. *Determinate* is also used either in express application or with implicit reference to a second intention or term of second denomination. In such an acceptation, we may speak either of a singular as indeterminate, or of a conception of Being, in general, as determinate. Every singular is in one sense perfectly determinate, since there is no pair of contradictory characters of which it does not possess one. Yet if the extension of the term be limited, not by additions to its comprehension, but *by a reflection upon the term itself*—namely, that it shall denote but one—it is called an indeterminate singular. In this sense, "some one horse" is an indeterminate individual, while "Dexter" is a determinate individual. In a somewhat similar way, every universal conception of Being is quite indeterminate in the sense of not signifying any particular character. Yet, if the reflection is explicitly made *(gesetzt)* that every thing to which it applies has its particular characters, it is called by Hegel, *determinate being.* Hegel teaches that the whole series of categories or universal conceptions can be *evolved* from one—that is, from *Seyn*—by a certain process, the effect of which is to make actually thought that which was virtually latent in the thought. So that this reflection which constitutes *Daseyn* lies implicitly even in *Seyn,* and it is by *explicitly* evolving it from *Seyn* that *Daseyn* is evolved from *Seyn.* (Hegel's *Werke,* Bd. 3, S. 107.) The term "What is" has reference to pure *Seyn* only; the term "What is somehow" has reference to *Daseyn.*

This is my understanding of the term "determinate." It must

---

1. Wherein is the force of this *"in contradistinction to"* which our correspondent employs here? *Determination*—as we understand the Hegelian use of the term—implies all difference, property, mark, quality, attribute, or, in short, any distinction whatever that is thought as belonging to a subject. This would include its "being this, that, or the other." Thus "highness of pitch" and "loudness of sound, in general," are through their determinateness distinct.— EDITOR.

differ from yours, or you would not say that animality, *in general,* is determined in respect to humanity: so when you say that were animality and humanity, in general, undetermined with respect to each other they would be identical, I take the example of "highness of pitch in general" and "loudness of sound in general," and I conclude again that we are taking the word "determine" in different senses. May I ask you to reperuse my 4th question? (p. 151.)

You have apparently understood me as applying the term "abstract" to any concept the result of abstraction. But, as I intimated (p. 145), I adopt that acceptation in which "whiteness" is said to be abstract and "white" concrete. For this use of the terms, I refer to the following authorities: Andrews and Stoddard's Latin Grammar, §26, 5; Scotus, *Super Prædicamenta,* qu. 8; Durandus à Sancto Porciano, *In Sententias,* lib. 1, dist. 34, qu. 1; Ockham, *Summa Logices,* pars 1, cap. 5; Chauvin, *Lexicon Rationale, sub v. Abstractum;* Mill, *Logic,* Bk. 1, cap. 2, §4; Trendelenburg, *Elementa Logices Aristoteleae,* 6th ed., p. 117, note; Überweg, *Logik,* §51 (where Wolff, also, is cited); Hoppe, *Logik,* §§256, 257. This misapprehension affects the relevancy of most of your remarks.

I think that I have not, as you suppose, greatly mistaken the sense in which Hegelians use the term *Pure Being.* At least, my definition seems to be in accord with the explanations of almost all, if not all, the commentators and expositors of Hegel. I would submit respectfully, that your own remarks upon p. 117 of Vol. I of this Journal contradict, almost in terms, what you say (p. 146) in reply to me.[2]

Once or twice you use such expressions as "We do not profess to speak for Hegelians," "Hegelians may understand this as they please," &c. Have I been wrong, then, in supposing that the passage to which my queries related was a professed defence of Hegelian doctrine?[3]

2. The passage here referred to is in Chapter III of the "Introduction to Philosophy," wherein there is no reference whatever to the Hegelian use of the term. It is a psychological investigation of the significance of the first predicate which is a determinate somewhat, and "Being" is used in the popular sense of "something" (i.e. *a* being), and its origin traced to the substantive-making activity of the Ego, which in its first exercise seizes itself as the fundamental basis of all. Just as, according to Kant, Time and Space, the forms of the mind, are made the basis of what the mind sees; so, too, Being as a universal predicate is the pure activity objectified. But *the making it substantive,* at the same time, determines it.—EDITOR.

3. Of course, our correspondent would not consider "a defence of Hegel" as identical with a championship of the Hegelians. It is the latter, only, that we object to, for the reason mentioned in the article on Janet, viz., that the term

I am sorry to learn that I have done you injustice in saying that you profess to be self-contradictory. Yet I do not see in what sense you object to the remark. To say that a *man* is self-contradictory is, of course, but a way of saying that what he believes is self-contradictory. You believe that "finite things contradict themselves"; that is, as I understand it, that contradictions exist. Therefore, what you believe in, appears to be self-contradictory. Nor can I see how a person "escapes self-contradiction by not attempting to set up non-contradiction as the first principle of things"; that is, by not professing to be otherwise than self-contradictory.[4]

I do not see that you notice query 3.[5]

Letter, Peirce to W. T. Harris

L 183: W. T. Harris Collection

Cambridge 1868 Apr. 9

Dear Sir

I have received two letters from you. I will endeavor to find time to write about a page and a half of the journal of remarks upon your printed reply to my letter.

You ask me to consider the rationale of the objective validity of

---

is used so vaguely as to include those who differ essentially from Hegel.—EDITOR.

4. We hasten to assure our correspondent that we do not "believe in the self-contradictory." We are sorry we were so unhappy in our expressions as to convey such a meaning. The *Abiding* or the Total Process is not self-contradictory, neither is it an abstract identity, but is (as we described it on p. 54, 2d col. of this volume) "self-identical through self-distinction." The self-determining is what we believe in, and it alone exists, while the fleeting show whose reality rests on contradiction is (and this is not Hegelian merely, but older than Plato) a mingling of Being and non-Being. One who sets up the principle of contradiction ignores one side of the process, and thus involves himself in that which he tries to avoid.—ED.

5. If any point is involved in question 3d that is not answered in the discussion of the other queries, we fail to seize it.—EDITOR.

logical laws. I have already devoted some attention to that subject. I cannot say what I think in less than three articles of the Journal. I send you a first one—written I regret to say by snatches—in the intervals of business and which I have not time to condense and prune down as I ought to do. I do not know but with more time to think of it—I should cut out the passage beginning page 10 "A similar argument" and extending to the top of page 14 together with the long footnote at the end of it. If I did so it would be not because I question its truth but because it involves a long digression.

I suppose the proof-sheets cannot be sent to me so I must beg that you will take care of my punctuation, &c.

It is very kind in you to offer me a place in your columns. I prefer the Journal to other periodicals or to the American Academy's proceedings for my purposes. In case you should not wish to print this and the two ensuing articles (it may be more than you bargained for) I must beg you to send back my MS so that I can make another use of it.

Please excuse the haste with which I write.

Yours very truly
Charles S. Peirce

[THE *Journal of Speculative Philosophy* SERIES]

Questions on Reality

MS 148: Winter–Spring 1868

Qu. 1. Whether by the simple contemplation of a cognition, we are enabled in any case to declare with considerable certainty that it is an ultimate premise or cognition not determined by any previous cognition, or whether this is only a hypothesis to be resorted to when the facts cannot be explained by the action of known causes? *Ans.* The latter alternative is the true one.

Qu. 2. Whether self-consciousness or our knowledge of ourselves can be accounted for as an inference or whether it is necessary to suppose a peculiar power of immediate self-consciousness? *Answer.* It can be accounted for by the action of known causes. *Error* and *ignorance* being discovered require the supposition of a self. In short, we can discover ourselves by those limitations which distinguish us from the absolute *ego.*

Qu. 3. Whether we have the power of accurately distinguishing by simple contemplation without reasoning or combining many circumstances, between what is seen and what is imagined, what is imagined and what is conceived, what is conceived and what is believed, and, in general, between what is known in one mode and what in another? No.

Qu. 4. Whether in fact it is necessary to suppose that we have any knowledge at all of the internal world except by inference from the external world? No.

Qu. 5. Whether we can think otherwise than in signs? No.

Corollary. Every representation refers to an interpretant.

Qu. 6. Whether any representation, any word, can mean anything from its own nature unknowable. *Ans.* Must consider meaning of universal terms and hypothetical propositions (??) &c. and conclude No.

Qu. 7. Does truth consist in anything but agreement with a conclusion logically inferable from the sum of all information? No.

Qu. 8. And does reality mean anything but the character of the object of a true proposition? No.

Qu. 9. Is a reality necessarily such that a case under it can be ex perienced? No.

Qu. 10. Is matter necessary to reality? No.

Qu. 11. Does contradiction always signify falsity? No.

Qu. 12. Is the previous doctrine opposed to common sense? No.

*[*Questions on Reality (A)*]*

[. . .]

Qu. 6. Is there any cognition which is absolutely incapable of being known?

Since thought is in signs, every thought must address some other which thinks it to be a sign. And the inference from a sign to a thought is always possible. So that there are necessarily grounds for inferring the existence of any thought.

Qu. 7. Have we any intuitions?

The belief in ultimate premises, appears to rest upon two grounds; first upon a believed intuition that certain sensations are intuitive and second upon the principle that there must have been a first cognition of any object which we have not always known.

But the first argument has been already set aside. We have no intuitive power of distinguishing ultimate premises from cognitions determined by previous cognitions. And the second argument is paralleled by the sophism of Achilles and the Tortoise. From the fact that every cognition is determined by a previous one, it follows that there have been an infinite series of finite times previous to any cognition since the latest time when there had been no cognition of the same object but not that there has been an infinitely long time between those two dates. It may perhaps follow that any absolutely determinate cognition does not exist in thought, but that thought is constantly in movement. But that has no bearing upon the present question.

On the other hand, whatever we know, we know only by its relations, and in so far as we know its relations. Now every knowledge of a relation is determined by previous cognitions. But to know a cognition is to know the immediate object of it as it is known in the cognition; hence to know an intuition is to know its object apart from its relations. Hence to know an intuition is impossible. But we have seen that an incognizable cognition does not exist. Hence, no intuition exists.

Moreover, since the object of an intuition is quite without the consciousness it is absolutely unknown except through the knowledge contained in the intuition. Hence, the peculiar character of the intuition cannot be accounted for; because neither is its cause knowable except so far as the knowledge effect itself is a knowledge of it, nor is any law knowable according to which precisely *such* an effect must necessarily be produced from any absolutely unknowable cause. Hence, the proper determination of the intuition is inexplicable. Hence, we have no right to suppose that any cognition is an intuition, for the only justification of a hypothesis is that it explains the facts. But to suppose the facts inexplicable is not to explain them. Now we do not know intuitively that any cognition is an intuition; hence if we do not know it by hypothetic inference we are altogether unwarranted in holding it.

Moreover, any change in an intuition whether by synthesis with others or by analysis results in a cognition determined by previous ones. Hence, as long as an intuition is an intuition it remains what it had been from the moment when it arose. Hence, if there is any finite degree of liveliness of consciousness in it, the passage from no consciousness to a finite consciousness, must have taken place in no time, which is contrary to the general presumption of continuity.

Thus there is no reason at all for admitting intuitions while there are very weighty reasons against it.

Qu. 8. Is there any proposition whose truth or falsity is absolutely incapable of being known?

Questions concerning Reality

As long as the logician contents, himself, with tracing out the forms of propositions and arguments, his science is one of the most exact and satisfactory. It may be confused; it can hardly be erroneous. But logic cannot stop here. It is bound, by its very nature, to push its research into the manner of reality itself, and in doing so can no longer confine its attention to mere forms of language but must inevitably consider how and what we think. This inquiry concerning reality has proved the most difficult as it certainly is in a purely theoretical point of view the most important question which man has ever propounded. Every system of idealism is a proposed solution of this problem.

Since it is necessary to consider how we think, I shall begin by seeking for the proper method of ascertaining how we think.

Question 1. Is there any case in which by the simple contemplation of a cognition, we are enabled to declare, independently of any previous knowledge we may have bearing upon the subject, and without reasoning from signs, that that cognition has not been determined by a previous cognition but refers immediately to its object?

As far as I am aware this question has never been explicitly set forth. The affirmative, however, ought to be maintained, as self-evident, by many philosophers, for the sake of consistency. As long as they assume this (however arbitrarily), they seem to occupy an impregnable position. Only what many well informed and reflecting persons seriously doubt, cannot be said with strict accuracy to be self-evident. It is unnecessary, therefore, to address any argument to those who stuff their ears with "self-evidence," as long as there are persons who are willing to put this pretended faculty of intuitively recognizing an intuition to the test of experience.

I beg those who will do this to consider whether mankind have in all ages regarded the same facts as self-evident. 1° Do we not find, for example, that certain authorities were regarded as self-evident in the middle ages, so that scarcely anyone ever thought of doubting or of defending them, but esteemed an argument from authority as of at least equal weight with an argument from reason. The proposition of Berengarius which was simply this, that the truth of any authority was an inference, was scouted as absurd, impious, and opinionated. 2° Question a child about his knowledge of the vernacular and he will stoutly deny that he derived it as information. He will say that when he became old enough to have sense, he perceived it immediately. 3° The history of opinions on the subject of vision is very instructive in this connection. Before Berkeley, there can be no question that most men were of opinion that the third dimension of space was immediately perceived by them. Now no one maintains it. It was only by a process of reasoning about external things that the error of the supposed internal sense was discovered. Indeed it may be said generally that each age pushes back the boundary of reasoning and shows that what had been taken to be premises were in reality conclusions. 4th If we really can by mere self-contemplation distinguish premises from inferences, let me ask any man not acquainted with physiology whether in looking with one eye, he has at each instant a sensation of a continuous and unbroken space nearly circular or whether this space has the form of a ring. We know that there is in fact a large blind spot nearly in the middle of the retina, so that the continuity of the space we see at each instant must be a matter of inference, of combining in thought the impressions of other times. But who would discover this by intuition? 5th In a similar way any person who has not reflected upon the matter will say that he perceives the pitch of a sound by a power of immediate observation simply without any of that combination of sensations which is called thought. And yet what is immediately experienced must be simply the aggregate of what is experienced in the parts of the time through which we have the experience. But now, pitch depends upon the rapidity with which impressions upon the ear succeed one another. Actual experiment will show that any single one of these impressions will be conveyed to the mind. There can therefore be but little doubt that these impressions are conveyed successively to the mind. It is therefore the relation of these impressions conveyed at different times to the mind upon which the pitch depends, and it is therefore most likely that the sensation of pitch depends upon the apprehension of this relation in a confused manner. In that case, the sensation of pitch arises from the conjunction of previous impressions, and is determined by a previous representation and not immediately by something out of the mind.

It would seem, therefore, that this pretended power fails altogether when put to the test. Moreover, if this power exists, either the subjective elements of consciousness are *per se* objects of consciousness or may be immediately contemplated. In the former case, we could not be conscious of any object without an absolutely certain knowledge of whether it be inferential or otherwise which cannot possibly be maintained to be the case. The latter supposition is impossible for the reason that before we could turn from the objective to the subjective posture of mind the object would cease to be present. *Hoc loquor inde est.*

Question 2. It appears from what has been said that we cannot decide with tolerable certainty by mere introspection whether a cognition is determined by previous cognitions or immediately by an external thing, and that our decision of this question must be an inference. We must examine the facts in each case and see whether there is reason to believe that the cognition can be accounted for or not (for to say that it is immediately produced by something not cognized before and therefore not known except by the cognition in question is to say that the latter cannot be accounted for). I now propose the question whether consciousness or our knowledge of ourselves can be accounted for by the known action of inference or whether it is necessary to suppose a peculiar power of immediate self-consciousness?

In the examination of this question, I would first observe that there is no known self-consciousness to be accounted for in extremely young children. It has already been pointed out by Kant that the late use of the very common word *I* with children, indicates an imperfect self-consciousness in them, and that, therefore, so far as analogy has any weight in the matter it is rather against the existence of any self-consciousness in those who are still younger.

On the other hand it is almost impossible to assign a period when children do not manifest decided powers of thought in directions in which thought is indispensible to their well being. The complicated trigonometry of vision, and the delicate adjustments of coördinated movement, are plainly mastered very young. A similar degree of thought may be supposed in them with reference to themselves.

Very young children may always be observed to watch their own bodies with great attention. There is every reason why it should attract their attention more than other things, because from their point of view it is the most important object in the universe. Only what this body touches has any actual and present feeling; only what it faces has any actual colour; only what is on the tongue has any actual taste.

No one questions that when a sound is heard by a child he thinks not of himself as hearing, but of the bell or other object as sounding. How is it when he wills to move a table? Does he think of himself as desiring or only of the table as fit to be moved? He undoubtedly has the latter thought; the only question is whether he has both or is as ignorant of his own peculiar condition as the angry man who denies that he is in a passion. It seems that the larger supposition is quite unsupported by any fact whatever.

The child, however, must soon discover by observation that things which are thus fit to be changed are apt to be found soon after actually changed after a contact with that peculiarly important body called Willy or Johnny. This consideration makes this body still more important and central since it establishes a correlation between the fitness of a thing to be changed and a tendency in this body to touch it before it is changed.

The child learns to understand the language; that is to say, an association between certain sounds and certain facts becomes established in his mind. He has previously noticed the connection between these sounds and the motions of the lips of bodies somewhat similar to the central one, and has tried the experiment of putting his hand on those lips and has found the sound in that case to be smothered. He thus connects that language with bodies somewhat similar to the central one. By efforts, so unenergetic that they should be called rather instinctive perhaps than tentative, he learns to produce those sounds. So he begins to converse.

About this time, I suppose, he begins to find that what these people about him say is the very best evidence of fact. So much so, that testimony is even a stronger mark of fact than appearances, themselves. I may remark, by the way, that this remains so through life; testimony will convince a man that he himself is mad. The dawning of the conception of testimony is the dawning of self-consciousness. Because testimony relates to a fact which does not appear. Thus, a distinction is established between fact and appearance. For example, suppose a child hears that a stove is hot; it does not seem so to him, but he touches it and finds it so. He, thus, becomes aware of ignorance and it is necessary to suppose an *ego* in whom this ignorance can inhere.

But, further, although appearances generally are either only confirmed or merely supplemented by testimony, yet there is a certain remarkable class of appearances which are constantly contradicted by testimony. These are those predicates which *we* know to be emotional but which *he* distinguishes by their connection with the movements of that central person, himself. These judgments are constantly denied by others. Moreover, he has reason to think that others also have these appearances which are quite denied by all the rest. Thus he adds to the conception of appearance as something other than fact, the conception of it as private, as connected with some one body. In short, *error* appears and it can be explained only by supposing a *self* which is fallible.

Error and ignorance, I may remark, are all that distinguish our private selves from the absolute ego.

This hypothetical account of the developement of self-consciousness can certainly not be defended in all its details. I have made it specific only for the sake of perspicuity. But that, in general, before we otherwise know that children are self-conscious, we know they become aware of ignorance and error and therefore by the exercise of a degree of reason we know them to possess, must become aware of themselves, is a matter of fact, simply. So that it is possible to account for self-consciousness without supposing any original intuitive power of self-consciousness.

On the other hand it may be said that we are more certain of our own existence than of any other fact and that therefore this cannot be inferred since a premise cannot determine a conclusion to be more certain than it is itself. To this I reply that, self-consciousness is more certain than any one other fact, but that there is nothing to prevent a conclusion from being more certain than any one of its premises, as is continually the case in the natural sciences. But to the developed mind of man his own existence is supported by every other fact, and his own existence is not more certain than the truth of a great number of other facts, because the doubt is equally inappreciable in both cases.

I conclude, therefore, that there is no necessity of supposing an intuitive power of self-consciousness, since it may be the result of inference.

Question 3. I will now inquire whether we have the power of

accurately distinguishing by simple contemplation without any reasoning or operation of inference, between what is seen and what is
imagined, what is imagined and what is conceived, what is conceived
and what is believed, and in general, between what is cognized in
one mode and what is cognized in another?

It would seem, at first sight, that there is an overwhelming array
of evidence in favor of such a power. The difference between seeing
a colour and imagining it is immense. There is a vast difference
between the most vivid dream and reality, although it is one which
while we are dreaming we commonly either cannot perceive or else
forget. And if we had no intuitive power of distinguishing between
what we believe and what we merely conceive, we never, it would
seem, could in any way distinguish them; since if we did so by reasoning the question would arise whether the argument itself was believed or conceived, and this must be answered before the conclusion would have any force. And thus there would be a *regressus ad
infinitum.* Besides if we do not know that we believe, then from the
very nature of the case, we do not believe. There is thus a strong
prima facie case in favor of such a faculty.

But be it noted that we do not intuitively know of the existence
of this faculty. For it is an intuitive one, and it has been shown in
answer to the first question that we cannot intuitively know that a
cognition is intuitive. The question is therefore whether it is necessary to suppose the existence of this faculty or whether the facts can
be explained without this supposition.

In the first place, then, with regard to the difference between
what is imagined or dreamt and what is actually experienced, I say
that this is wholly irrelevant to the question. For it is not questioned
that there are distinctions in what is present to the mind; but the
question is whether independently of any such distinction in the
immediate *objects* of consciousness, we have any immediate power
of distinguishing different modes of consciousness. Now the very fact
of the immense difference in the immediate objects of sense and
imagination, sufficiently accounts for our distinguishing those faculties; and instead of being an argument in favor of the existence of an
intuitive power of distinguishing the subjective elements of consciousness, it is a powerful reply to any such argument, so far as the
distinction of sense and imagination is concerned.

Passing then to the distinction of belief and conception, we meet
the statement that the knowledge of belief is essential to its exis-

tence. Now we unquestionably distinguish belief from conception by means of a peculiar feeling of conviction. It is a mere question of words whether we define belief as that judgment which is accompanied by this feeling, or as that judgment from which a man will act. We may term the former sensational and the latter active belief. That neither of these necessarily supposes the other, will surely be admitted without any recital of facts. Taking belief in the sensational sense, the intuitive power of recognizing it will amount simply to the capacity for the sensation which accompanies the judgment. This has nothing at all to do with any intuitive recognition of subjective elements of consciousness, since it is merely an object of consciousness which accompanies the judgment. If, on the other hand, belief is taken in the active sense, it may be discovered by the observation of external facts. Thus, the arguments in favor of this peculiar power of consciousness disappear; and the presumption again is against such a hypothesis. But further to say that subjective elements of consciousness may as such become objects of immediate consciousness appears to involve a contradiction. For this implies that such elements are essentially objects of consciousness, whereas they are essentially that which there is in consciousness besides its objects. It is to be concluded, then, that the faculty in question does not exist.

Question 4. I will now ask whether it is necessary to suppose that we have any power of introspection or internal sense or whether our whole knowledge of the internal world can be accounted for as an inference from facts of external observation?

The affirmative side of the present question has been assumed by almost all and by all the greatest philosophers. We have here no longer to do with any intuitive power of distinction; the question is not whether we can immediately perceive the internal world *as* internal but whether we have any immediate perception whose object is in fact merely internal.

Now there is one sense in which an object of any perception is internal, namely that every sensation is partly determined by internal conditions. Thus, *red* is as it is owing to the constitution of the mind, and in this sense, therefore, it is undeniable that this sensation as well as every other is a sensation of something internal. We may, therefore, derive a knowledge of the mind from the consideration of this sensation, but such a knowledge will in fact be an inference from 'redness' as a predicate of something external. On the other hand there are certain other feelings such as the emotions which appear to arise in the first place, not as predicates of anything at all, and to be referable to the mind only. By means of these, therefore, a knowledge of the mind may be obtained which is not inferred from any character of outward things. The question which I propose here to discuss is whether this is really so. It must be admitted, then, that if a man is angry, his anger implies, in general, no determinate character in the object of his anger. But on the other hand, it can hardly be questioned that there is some relative character in the outward thing which makes him angry, and it will require but a little reflection to see that the essence of anger consists in his saying to himself this thing is wrong, vile, &c. and that it is rather a mark of returning reason to say 'I am angry'. Thus any emotion is a predication concerning some thing, and the chief difference between this and what is commonly called an objective intellectual judgment is that while the latter is relative generally to human nature in general, the former is relative to the particular circumstances and disposition of a particular man at a particular time. What is here said of emotions in general is true in particular of the sense of beauty and of the moral sense. Right and wrong are feelings which first arise as predicates and therefore, since the subjective elements of consciousness are not immediately perceived, are either determined by previous cognitions of the same object or are predicates of the Not-I.

It remains, then, only to inquire whether it is necessary to suppose a particular power of introspection for the sake of accounting for the sense of willing. Now, volition, as distinguished from desire, is nothing but the power of concentrating the attention, of abstracting. Nothing therefore is more natural than to suppose that just as the knowledge of the power of seeing is inferred from coloured objects so the knowledge of the power of abstracting is inferred from abstract objects.

It appears therefore that there is no reason to suppose a power of introspection or special internal sense.

Qu. 5. It has been shown, then, by the preceding discussion that the only way of investigating a psychological question is by inference from external facts. I now proceed to apply this method of research to the solution of the question whether we can think otherwise than in signs.

Thought, says Plato, is a silent speech of the soul with itself. If this be admitted immense consequences follow; quite unrecognized, I believe, hitherto. But it is a vexed question whether this be true; for some respectable philosophers maintain that thought must precede every sign, without admitting for an instant the possibility of an infinite regress. Yet that an infinite is not always impossible is shown by the fact that Achilles does overtake the tortoise. If we seek the light of external facts, we must certainly find only cases of thought in signs; plainly no other thought can be evidenced by external facts. But we have seen that only by external facts can thought be known at all. It appears, then, that the only thought which can possibly be cognized is in signs. But by definition thought which cannot be cognized does not exist. All thought, therefore, must necessarily be in signs. In order to apprehend this reasoning more precisely let us suppose a special case. A man says one thing to himself and then something else which would follow from the former on account of some third thing which he has not however said to himself. Here is a process, apparently, of reasoning. Has the man then not thought that third thing without saying it to himself? Certainly he has done so as far as this goes that he has said that the second thing follows from the first. So far as this is a representation of that third thing he has thought the latter; but that he has done so any further than in so far cannot be pretended. Thought is something supposed from some manifestation of mind. Plainly then it exists so far as it is manifested—is expression. And since it is nothing so far as it is not knowable, it exists no further. Thus the question of whether we must think in signs is decided by a mere syllogism, being no matter of fact but only of meaning.

From this proposition that every *thought* is a *sign* it follows that every thought must address itself to some other, must determine some other, since that is the essence of a sign. And yet this after all is but another form of the old axiom, that in intuition, i.e. in the immediate present, there is no thought. Or to put the thing in another familiar form all that is reflected upon has past. The paradox here is similar to that of motion. The Zenonian may say no thought can be accomplished if there must have been a thought since every thought. But the contradiction here is a merely formal and not a real one. Since any time in the past there have been an infinite series of times. It is only at a date that there has not been an infinite series of times since that date. Now what is here said is that thought cannot happen in a date, but requires a time. That is only another way of saying that every thought must have been interpreted in another thought.

Qu. 6. To approach now more nearly to the question of reality, let us ask whether any representation can mean anything which is from its own nature unknowable? It would seem that it can and that universal and hypothetical propositions are instances of it. Thus the universal proposition, all ruminants are cloven-hoofed, speaks of a possible infinity of animals, and no matter how many ruminants may have been examined the possibility must necessarily remain that there are others which have not been examined. Thus this universal is from its own nature inexhaustible, unknowable, and yet it certainly means something to say that all ruminants are cloven-hoofed. In the case of a hypothetical proposition, the same thing is still more manifest; for such a proposition speaks not merely of the actual state of things but of every possible state of things, all of which are not knowable inasmuch as only one can so much as exist.

On the other hand, since the meaning of a term is the conception which it conveys, and since there is abundant reason to believe that our conceptions derive their origin from experience, in the sense that only by abstractions and combinations of what we learn from judgments concerning facts can we obtain a conception, it cannot be that the meaning of a term should contain anything impossible in its own nature (that is, independently of its not being found to exist).

And in answer to the argument from universal and hypothetical propositions, several conclusive replies may be made. First, that although these cannot be known by complete enumeration, they may be known by induction. Second, that though all the particulars in these cases cannot be experienced, yet in a general way, it may be said that any one of them can so that it is not essentially incognizable. Thirdly, that a hypothetical proposition 'If *A*, *B*' is either equivalent to 'whenever *A*, *B*' or else is simply a deduction from some wider hypothetical proposition. Thus the proposition 'If I were to write with red ink, I should make a red mark', is a deduction from the proposition, 'whenever a person writes with red ink he makes a red mark'. Thus, a hypothetical is only a particular kind of universal. Now a sign essentially signifies some object; but if a universal proposition can find no application at all, real or imaginary, whether a case under it or as a generalization of its contradictory, it has no object and is not a sign.

Thus it appears, that philosophers in endeavoring to erect a division in imitation of that between the I and the not-I, between the objects and things-in-themselves, or the cognizable and the uncognizable, are using words totally without meaning. For as *being* (in the sense of the copula) has no negative, *nothing* being self-contradictory since it would be at once the negative and a determination of being, so that the word is plainly a merely syncategorematic term, so the cognizable in its most general sense is equally without a correlate, since if such a one existed, then a new correlate to these two taken together must on the same principle be assumed and so on *ad infinitum.* In short *thought* and *being* appear to be in their widest sense synonymous terms, and not merely metaphysically the same as the German idealists suppose.

From this an important corollary is deducible (Answer to Q. 7) namely that if a proposition is logically inferable—by deduction, induction, or hypothesis—from the sum of all possible information, past, present, and to come, then it is absolutely true, for it is true in the whole of its meaning.

This, again, brings us at once to the solution of the problem of reality. For the real is the object of an absolutely true proposition. Thus, we obtain a theory of reality which, while it is nominalistic, inasmuch as it bases universals upon signs, is yet quite opposed to that individualism which is often supposed to be coextensive with nominalism. For there is nothing to prevent universal propositions from being absolutely true, and therefore universals may be as real as singulars. But in order to exhibit the relation of this theory to individualism, it will be well to develope it a little further in reference to sensation and individuation.

I will first undertake to prove, then, that no ultimate premise or cognition not determined by a previous cognition exists or ever has existed. We have already seen that it is impossible to know intuitively that a given cognition is not determined by a previous one. The only way in which this can be known, then, is by hypothetic inference from observed facts. But to adduce the cognition by which a given cognition has been determined is to explain that cognition and is the only way of explaining it, since something entirely out of consciousness which may be supposed to determine it can, as such, only be known and therefore only adduced in the determined cognition itself; so that to suppose that a cognition is only determined by something external is simply to suppose that it is incapable of explanation. Now this is a hypothesis which never can be justifiable, inasmuch as the only possible justification of a hypothesis is that it explains the facts, and to say that they are explained by supposing them inexplicable is self-contradictory. But as this reasoning is somewhat too subtle and metaphysical for entire confidence, I will endeavor to put it into somewhat more concrete forms. If we can show that in another and more exact branch of science such an argument would be admissible it follows of course that it is admissible here. Now we have a somewhat similar problem in chemistry. In the early part of this century, almost all the bodies then known were decomposed into certain metallic substances, and certain sulphur-like substances. These so-called elements present as a whole differences from any of the bodies known to be compound. All compound bodies, for example, are either decomposed by electrolysis, or have a very large specific heat for the amounts which would occupy equal volumes in the state of gas, or are decomposed almost spontaneously, by fractional distillation or fractional crystallization, for example. On the other hand, there are but a few of the elements of which this is true. This would seem, then, to be an argument that these bodies never will be decomposed. And yet it is plain that this argument or any other must be inadequate to support such a limitless theory. It is a strong argument to show that they will not be decomposed next year or in the next ten years. It is an argument that they will not be decomposed in the next century, and it even tends slightly to show that they will not be decomposed in the next ten centuries. But to say that it tends however slightly to show that they will never be decomposed is to say that we can jump at once from the finite to the infinite. Some contend that all induction passes from the finite to the infinite. But it does so only in a formal way. When I conclude that 'all ruminants are cloven-hoofed', I really assume that there is some indefinite but finite number of ruminants. Some finite number which I shall find, some finite number which any man will find, and it is of these that I speak. Perhaps an argument concerning elements might tend to show that, if we assume the life of the human race on earth to have a finite duration in the future, no man ever will discover them to be complex. But it does not tend to show that man might not do so if his life on earth were longer. And if no argument can suffice to prove that our present list of elements is ultimate, no argument can ever prove that any future list of elements is ultimate. In short the ultimate is a mere ideal; it does not enter into science.

Now the argument that we never can know any premise to be ultimate is of the same kind as this, only that it is supported by several corroborative circumstances. For, while chemists in decomposing any body always find themselves arrested at the same point and have done so since the early days of the science, every successive age of psychology has as I have said seen the boundary of first cognition pushed one step further back. Moreover, we know in the whole sphere of physics no force by which it seems likely that the present series of elements can be decomposed, whereas in the whole range of mind we know of no power by which an ultimate premise could be cognized. For, in the first place, it is only at the first instant of the existence of a cognition that it would be undetermined by previous cognition, and therefore the apprehension of it must be an event which takes place in no time. And in the second place, every cognition of which we have any conception is relative, is the cognition of a relation, and every cognition of a relation is determined by previous cognition. If the general argument admits of being strengthened it is strengthened by these considerations. But, in fact, it is a fundamental postulate of all hypothetic reasoning that anything which requires explanation, admits of being explained. And there never can be any warrant therefore for supposing that a cognition is not determined by anything otherwise cognized, since that is to suppose that the cognition cannot be explained.

Now if no ultimate premise can be known in any way, it follows from the principle already established that none exists. And even if the principle be not admitted in its whole breadth, it ought to be admitted that a *cognition* which never can be known and never can have been known, has no existence. So that no ultimate premise exists.

Indeed, I have no doubt, that the belief in ultimate premises or cognitions not determined by cognitions, rests on the notion that there *must be a first*. But that this is a wholly sophistical argument, at least in this application, can readily be shown. In retracing our way from conclusions to premises we finally reach a point beyond which in all cases the consciousness in the premises is less lively than the consciousness in the conclusion. We have a less lively consciousness in the cognition which determines our cognition of the third dimension than in the latter cognition itself; a less lively consciousness in the cognition which determines our cognition of a continuous surface (without a blind spot) than in this latter cognition itself; and a less lively consciousness of the impressions which determine the sensation of tone than of that sensation itself. There are many other instances of this sort which will occur to the reader, which seem sufficient to warrant the statement that beyond a certain point this is the general rule. Now let us represent a certain cognition by a horizontal line and let the length of that line serve as a sort of measure or representative of the liveliness of consciousness in that cognition. Then let the external object of that cognition be represented by a point placed below that line. This point will have no length, because the object which it represents is quite out of the consciousness. Let its lower position denote that it determines that cognition and let its finite distance from the line, represent that it is no actual part of that cognition. Now, let us suppose that any other line is drawn between this point and the former line and shorter than that upper line. This new line on these principles will represent another cognition of the same object which is less lively and which determines the cognition represented by the first line. Now let us suppose that we have a triangle resting upon its apex. Then, every horizontal section of that triangle will represent a cognition of the object represented by the apex, determined by any cognition represented by a section below this line, and determining any section above it. By a section I do not mean any line actually drawn, but the place where a line can be drawn. For example, the triangle might be supposed to be pressed down under the surface of water, then the surface of the water would successively make all these sections. It is not impossible that our successive cognitions should be related to one another and to the external object as these surface lines of the water on the triangle are related to one another and to the apex. To say, then, that it is impossible that there should be no cognition not determined by a previous one, is to say that there is no one of these surface lines below which at a finite distance there is not another above the apex. These lines may represent, also, the successive distances of Achilles from the tortoise, supposing only that the triangle is lifted out of the water instead of being dipped in it. And, therefore, it is plain that to say that there must be a *first* cognition is to fall into a sophism exactly similar to this ancient one. Let this sophism be solved as it may, I am satisfied to have the theory of ultimate premises meet the same fate; because I am satisfied that beneath all the logic all the interpretations by which the Zenonian paradoxes are sought to be brought under acknowledged formulae, every philosopher will admit the existence of motion in the phenomenal sense in which I and all the world believe in it. And that is enough for our present purposes. In short, what I

wish to say, is that although the act of perception cannot be represented as whole, by a series of cognitions determining one another,
since it involves the necessity of an infinite series, yet there is no
perception so near to the object that it is not determined by another
which precedes it—for when we reach the point which no determining cognition precedes we find the degree of consciousness there to
be just *zero,* and in short we have reached the external object itself,
and not a representation of it.

I pass now to another consideration, preliminary to the discussion
of individuation.

If we notice the occasion of the occurrence of any of those sensations, such as the sense of beauty, which are readily perceived to be
determined by other cognitions the consciousness of which is lively
enough to be remembered, we shall find that they always arise in
judgments. It is this or that which is beautiful. And it is the same with
the conceptions which are easily seen to be determined by others.
Those sensations which are commonly regarded as intuitive and
those conceptions which are commonly regarded as mere products
of free will, are usually supposed to arise previous to any judgment.
But apart from the analogy between these and the others, there will
be found reason in any special case to consider these as arising in the
same way. Take for example the sensation of tone. This, as we have
seen, arises in all probability, upon the occasion of a series of previous
dim sensations. These previous sensations, then, must have been
attended to, somewhat, as a series. Now this act of attention in itself
gives the conception of an object, a *this,* and the feeling of tone must
arise in conscious conjugation with this *this.* So that we say for example, this is shrill or this is dull. It is, then, an intrinsic part of the
hypothesis whose consequences we are now tracing out—and by the
way until this is done the reader is not asked to accept it—that every
cognition whatever is a judgment. In opposition to this consequence
the philosophic principle might be adduced that subject and object,
ego and non-ego, are correlative and simultaneous notions and that
therefore before self-consciousness is reached there can be no judgment. That generally speaking subject and object are correlative is
a mere grammatical truism; but that *self* and *this* are correlative is
not so plain. *This* is in itself correlative only to *other things. This* and
self, our subsequent knowledge of our selves teaches to have been
correlatives as facts; but that the thoughts of this and self are correlative has never been shown.

We come, now, to the subject of individuality. It is plain that the process we have found to compose any step of perception, a process of the determination of one judgment by another, is one of *inference* in the strict sense. And it is, also, plain that hypothesis must enter into this process everywhere. We have considered principally the predicates of our judgments. But if we were to discuss with equal fulness the act of attention which determines the subject, we should find that this also is determined by previous acts of attention, and that there is no more a first in this case than in the other. It follows that inductions also take place in the process of perception. Hence every cognition we are in possession of is a judgment both whose subject and predicate are general terms. And, therefore, it is not merely the case, as we saw before, that universals have reality on this theory, but also that there are nothing but universals which have an immediate reality. But here it is necessary to distinguish between an individual in the sense of that which has no generality and which here appears as a mere ideal boundary of cognition, and an individual in the far wider sense of that which can be only in one place at one time. It will be convenient to call the former a singular and the latter only an individual. To the former, I have denied all immediate reality. Now the nominalistic element of my theory is certainly an admission that nothing out of cognition and signification generally, has any generality; and therefore this seems to imply that we are not affected by a real external world. But this is not a correct consequence of the principles which I have sought to establish. We have found that if any particular cognition be taken, there is some finite time previous when we had a cognition which completely determined it; but, nevertheless, we also find that if we take the sum of our cognition at any one time, then at any other determinate time before, we were not in possession of cognitions sufficient completely to determine this state of cognitions. I do not propose to examine the grounds of this belief, but accept it with all the world. It is not at all contradictory of the former relation, unless motion itself is self-contradictory. Now a knowledge that cognition is not wholly determined by cognition is a knowledge of something external to the mind, that is the singulars. Singulars therefore have a reality. But singulars in general is not singular but general. We can cognize any part of the singulars however determinate, but however determinate the part it is still general. And therefore what I maintain is that while singulars are real they are so only in their generality; but singulars in their absolute discrimination or singularity are mere ideals. Or in other words that the absolute determination which singularity supposes, can only take place by attribution, which is essentially significative or cognitive, and that therefore it cannot belong to what is wholly out of signification or cognition. In short, those things which we call singulars exist, but the character of singularity which we attribute to them is self-contradictory.

With reference to individuals, I shall only remark that there are certain general terms whose objects can only be in one place at one time, and these are called individuals. They are generals that is, not singulars, because these latter occupy neither time nor space, but can only be at one point and can only be at one date. The subject of individuality, in this sense, therefore, belongs to the theory of space rather than to the theory of logic. But the reader may here inquire whether I believe that there is any reality other than those things which are only in one place at one time. Why, certainly, I should say, there is blackness, if the testimony of our senses is to be credited. But is the blackness of *this,* identical with the blackness of *that?* I cannot see how it can help being; the determinations which accompany it are different but the blackness itself is the same, by supposition. If this seems a monstrous doctrine, remember that my nominalism saves me from all absurdity. This blackness, upon my principles, is purely significative purely cognitive; there is nothing I suppose to prevent signs being applied to different individuals in precisely the same sense. If there be, all language is equivocal. The blackness which the objection seems to imply that I refer to, is the singular determination of the singular; but if our principles are correct blackness in general, is shown to be real, by the testimony of the senses, and its cognitive or significative character does not stand in the way of this, at all. Our principle, indeed, is simply that realities, all realities, are nominal, significative, cognitive. This is simply the pure doctrine of idealism, not of this or that modification of idealism, but the constitutive mark of idealism in general. And idealism is coëxtensive with philosophy, in our days; and has been so, essentially, since Berkeley. But perhaps the day has not yet past, when someone may inquire whether this doctrine of idealism does not make the reality of things dependent on the existence of the *ego,* since a cognition requires a mind and indeed *my* mind in which to inhere. If this were the consequence, it would amount merely to a necessary immortality of the soul, since the dependence would be mutual. But it is not the consequence of idealism; we must not forget that idealism makes the reality of *ideas* as well as of everything else significative or cognitive. From this it follows that there is reason to believe that the world exists as long as there is reason to believe that if a mind were in it that mind would have cognitions.

I believe that the general character of the consequences of this definition of reality or what amounts to the same thing of the doctrine that thought is a silent speech of the soul with itself;—a doctrine which I believe I have given some reasons for believing is the one to which the facts point. I wish, now, to consider one or two special consequences of this theory.

I have said that a true proposition is one which is logically inferable from the sum of all information. But in another paper, I have insisted that a logical inference is to be defined as one which is of such a kind that if the premises are true the conclusion is either necessarily or probably true. Here appears to be a *circulus in definiendo;* but I did not argue that the above was a *definition* of a true proposition but only that it is accurately coëxtensive with it. I may define a true proposition as one which is determined by the sum of all information and which denies no particular of all information. But this definition is something more than a verbal one, and requires some explanation to exhibit its true character.

A proposition might contain a certain amount of information and might also partly be wider than the sum of all information. That is its object might intersect the sphere of information. For example, it might be a hypothetical proposition, whose antecedent might cover some possible or actual cases and some quite non-existent cases. Now those impossible cases would plainly not affect the truth of the proposition in the least degree. Thus take the proposition 'If A is B, C is D' and suppose that A is sometimes a particular species of B, namely BX; and suppose that when it is so C is D. Then the proposition, 'If A is B, C is D' is perfectly true and the fact that A never is another species of B, as B not X, does not affect its truth in the least. But what in this case shall be said to the proposition 'If A is B not X, C is D' where the antecedent is one which never can or never does take place at all? Such propositions are constantly used, so much so, that we have a special syntactical construction for expressing them. The universal conviction therefore is that they have meaning and may have truth. Consider, on the other hand, such a proposition as this 'If the man in the moon were king of New Jersey he would certainly come in conflict with Gog and Magog'. This proposition has absolutely no meaning at all, for as we have seen a sign which refers to something absolutely incognizable only, means nothing. Now the question is whether it is not also the case with the proposition 'If *A* is *B* which is not-*X*, *C* is *D*' that it says nothing at all and has no meaning. The answer which I would propose distinguishes between these two expressions. It says nothing at all, but it has a meaning. That is to say, it determines no particular of the sum of all information, but it is itself determinable by the information. It is even true, because it is affirmatively determinable by the sum of all information. There is nothing arbitrary in it.

I would, therefore, say

1° that a proposition has *meaning* which is determinable (affirmatively or negatively) by the sum of information.

2° that a proposition has *content,*—is not identical—when it is *not* determinable by each part of the sum of information.

3° that it has *sphere,* when it helps to determine some particular of the sum of information.

4° that it is *true,* when it is affirmatively determined by the sum of information.

The sophisms relating to motion, the liar, and others which seem to show that the principle of contradiction is in conflict with appearances, and which form on the whole the most difficult problem in logic or metaphysics, derive their peculiar character from the propositions without sphere which they contain. Everybody is familiar with such arguments as the following. I should never drop an inkstand, if the ink would thereby be spilt; or in other words

	If I should drop this inkstand, the ink would not be spilt.
Yet certainly	If I should drop this inkstand the ink would be spilt.
And the conclusion is	I shall not drop the inkstand.

Now these premises are formally contrary to one another. Such propositions are virtually contained in every dilemma; for of the two propositions,

| | If *A* happens, then *B* happens, |
| and | If *A* does not happen, then *B* happens; |

the former is equivalent to this,

If *B* does not happen, *A* does not happen

and the latter to this

If *B* does not happen, *A* does happen.

Now it can be shown beyond any shadow of doubt that the contradictions of the Zenonian sophisms are precisely of this sort, and therefore Herbart's explanation that motion does not exist falls to the ground. On the contrary it is perfectly certain that the principle of contradiction in its crude form, in which it implies that of the two propositions—

Any *S* would be *P*   and   Any *S* would not be *P*

one is false, must receive some modification, adjustment, or limitation. Some logicians wish to cut the Gordian Knot by saying that there are no propositions except such as imply the existence of their subjects, which is to cut us off from the subjunctive mood altogether. They propose to interpret the subjunctive mood. The proposition

A dragon would breathe fire,

they would *expose* thus

The name of a *dragon* is a name for what breathes fire.

This answers well enough because the proposition which here serves as an example is explicatory or analytical. It deals with the implication of words and not with what is found in experience. But it is a great mistake to suppose that all propositions with a 'would be' speak only of the meanings of words. When I said, 'If I should drop this inkstand, the ink would not be spilt', I by no means meant to say as much as that 'to *say* that I drop this inkstand is itself to say or imply that the ink is not spilt'. But what I meant was that 'On whatever occasion my dropping the inkstand may appear in the world of phenomena (whether it ever actually appears or not) the ink's not being spilt may be found among phenomena', I am speaking of facts

—although hypothetical ones,—and not of names, at all. When, therefore, Mill proposes to solve the sophism

> Every dragon is an animal,
> Every dragon breathes fire;
> ∴ Some animal breathes fire.

by substituting 'the name of ———' for every term, although he avoids the difficulty in this particular case, well enough, he overlooks the circumstance that there are many other sophisms of precisely this form (i.e. Darapti and Felapton, where the middle term denotes what may not exist) where this method of solution will not apply. In place of saying that every proposition implies the existence of its subject, Leibnitz proposes to say that every *particular* proposition does so. One of two contradictories is particular, and hence if the 'some' means 'something capable of being given in perception', there is no contradiction between propositions whose subject may not exist and *Darapti* and *Felapton* must be omitted from the moods of the third figure, as I have seen fit to do for other reasons in my paper on the classification of arguments. The objections to this theory are; first, that according to it the particular is not implied in its universal, and thus disturbs the whole system of syllogistic, and, second, that particular propositions which do not imply the existence of their subject are quite possible, as 'Of men who should of their own free-will be left in a boat or boats in open sea without other food than each other's bodies, and should not be rescued, some would die in a month'. If we yield to the force of these objections, it will be necessary to divide all propositions, universal and particular, into two classes, those which imply that their subjects have spheres and those which do not imply this. And on account of the complete symmetry in all its parts which syllogistic presents, we shall also be led to divide propositions into such as imply that they have a content, and into such as do not. Those which imply that their subjects have spheres, speak of course only of the actual state of things and are *contingent.* Those, which do not imply this, speak of every possible state of things, and are *necessary.* These necessary propositions are always the result of an apodictic deductive inference. They come to speak of every possible state of things, simply by losing the implication that their subjects exist. Nevertheless, it is evident, that a contingent proposition says something that the corresponding necessary one does not, and that a necessary proposition says something that the corresponding contingent one does not. Thus they are opposed to one another, like affirmatives a/nd/ negatives but result from different determinations of the subject like universals and particulars. On the other hand the proposition which does not imply that its predicate is not essentially contained in its subject—(which I shall term an *attributive* proposition) says nothing which is not said by the corresponding proposition which does imply this (which I shall call a *subsumptive* proposition). And thus these are related to one another as universals and particulars although they arise from determinations of the predicate like affirmatives and negatives. Thus instead of two respects in which propositions differ, there will be four; and instead of four forms of propositions, there will be sixteen. It is plain that contradictory propositions will differ in all four respects. Let us next see what modifications this theory requires in the doctrine of syllogism.

In the first place then it is plain that in the third figure both premises cannot be necessary, and also that in the first figure the conclusion must agree with the case in being necessary or contingent. On the other hand both premises may be contingent in the third figure. Here is already a difficulty; for by the contraposition of the propositions of such a syllogism in the third figure we should get a syllogism in the first figure having a contingent case and necessary result. Take, for example, the syllogism

S exists and every actual S is P,
S exists and some actual S is M;
∴ M exists and some actual M is P.

The denial of the conclusion is

Either M does not exist or no actual M is P

which is the same as to say

If M exists, any M is not P.

The denial of the first premise is in the same way

If S exists, some S is not P

And the syllogism must be good,

> If *M* exists, any *M* is not *P*,
> *S* exists and some actual *S* is *M;*
> ∴ If *S* exists, some *S* is not *P*.

It must be therefore that the necessary proposition is implied in the corresponding contingent one.

> *A* is *P*
> ∴ *A* would be *P*.

Thus the symmetry of syllogistic is broken up, unless some other distinction can be substituted for our present one between subsumptives and attributives. The *rule* in the first and second figures need only be necessary, and the conclusion of the third figure may always be contingent.

Potentia ex Impotentia

MS 149: Summer 1868

In the last number of this Journal, we instituted some inquiries "concerning certain faculties claimed for man." The degree of probability to which any metaphysical or psychological conclusions can at present attain, is unfortunately as compared with the results of several other sciences, not very high. It is of no avail that philosophers adopt strictly demonstrative forms of argument as long as they cannot, after all, come to agreement upon conclusions. //What competent men disagree about is not certain./That is not certain upon which competent men disagree.// I was content, therefore, in discussing those questions in the last number, to use inductive and hypothetic reasoning, which are the processes of natural science, thinking that, perhaps, there is nothing in such merely presumptive evidence which need render my conclusions less certain than those which have been deduced from first principles, by other psychologists. Nor did I think fit to engage in the vain attempt to hedge about my inferences with all the safeguards and precautions used in astronomy and physics. When a science first enters upon the inductive road the caution, afterwards so healthful, amounts to fruitless and indolent scepticism. The thousand confirmations which make mechanics, for example, so secure, have been the result of generations of labour, consequent upon the adoption of the theories, themselves. The proposition that a body left to itself would move on forever in a straight line, was, when first enunciated by Galileo, something more, indeed, than a shrewd guess. It was a regular and deliberate inference, but not supported upon all sides, as a new theory must be before it can claim a place among the body of truths of regularly instituted science of mechanics. Now, dynamics just before the time of Galileo was in a state not dissimilar to that in which philosophy now is. It had been studied from the earliest times without any certain results. It had been the grand theatre of disputation and of dialectical subtilety; but it had lately manifested symptoms of emergence from this condition (consisting partly, it is true, in the multiplication of jarring theories) and the quite arbitrary and mystical dogma of the indifferentists that reasonable certainty was unattainable in this science did not find quite so unyielding an acquiescence among sensible men as it had a little while before. If metaphysics has the happy future before it which dynamics then had, it must be content to rest upon tangible external facts and to begin with theories not supported by any great multitude of different considerations or held with absolute confidence. When these first theories have been systematically traced to their consequences, we can see how many facts they serve to explain, and which are the ones which require to be retained. Meanwhile, I think it becoming neither to contemn the views of others nor to hold too confidently to my own, regarding them rather as things yet to be inquired into further, than as //facts/beliefs// which are to influence my faith or my hopes.

In this spirit, I purpose to take up the conclusions of my former paper, which must probably stand or fall together, and see what are their bearings upon the reality of knowledge, the validity of logic, the instincts of religion, and other matters of common sense or common prejudice. In the present paper, I shall confine myself more particularly to the question of reality.

Potentia ex Impotentia

To consider from what point we shall take our departure in philosophy seems to be unnecessary, inasmuch as we cannot start from any other condition than that in which we actually are. To attempt such a solution of the problem as Hegel has done, seems like going to China by proceeding first due north to the pole and thence due south to China—a method which certainly has the merit of being highly systematic, and has also a pleasing paradoxical appearance, but which would present certain inconveniences in practice. We really *believe* many things, and, therefore, philosophic doubts upon such matters must be mere pretence and can result in nothing but a show of demonstration of things really taken for granted. Nothing can be gained by gratuitous and fictitious doubts, nor can any conclusions be reached without premises. Now whatever is doubted by men whom there is reason to think competent judges, is so far doubtful; and, therefore, a certain shade of doubt will hang over almost all psychological or very general propositions. It is, therefore, proper to rest philosophy,—upon what every real science must rest—namely those ordinary facts of which (in a general way) we are actually assured and therefore *cannot*, if we would, mistrust. Moreover, to hold your own system to be certain when intelligent, candid, and well-informed persons cannot agree with you, is a thing to be ashamed of and to be eradicated, as a sin; and on that principle metaphysics must be held to be very uncertain. Thus, the strictly demonstrative style of argumentation usually adopted by philosophers has utterly failed of its purpose, and we might as well content ourselves with such probable inferences as support astronomy and chemistry, since if we can only reduce the uncertainty of metaphysics to a hundred times that appertaining to those sciences, we shall have much to congratulate ourselves upon. Nor ought we to aspire at first to the rigidness of proof which pertains to the physical sciences in their developed state, but should rather take as our examples those less complicated reasonings upon which Galileo established the laws of motion and Copernicus the order of the solar system. It was upon these principles, that in the last number of this journal, in a paper entitled "Questions concerning certain faculties claimed for man," I endeavored to establish with the degree of probability which the subject admits of at present the following propositions—

1st, We have no intuitive power of distinguishing intuitive from mediate cognitions;

2nd, We have no intuitive self-consciousness;

3rd, Subjective elements of consciousness are not immediate objects of consciousness.

4th, We have no power of introspection.

5th, All thought is in signs.

6th, No sign consistently means anything essentially incognizable.

7th, There is no intuitive cognition.

For the further support of the 6th proposition the two following arguments may be added. In the first place, every character which belongs to the immediate object of cognition is essentially cognizable, since the character means nothing else than the possibility of the cognition. It is indeed, not denied that an inaudible sound or an invisible colour, is an absurdity. But it is held that since *thought* is *active* and not dependent only on the presence of an outward object, it is sufficient that a *relation* for example, should be *thinkable* and that it need not be *inferrable*. But thought is no more active than imagination, since all thoughts are but combinations of conceptions abstracted from experience, and it would be impossible to name any other. Now abstraction takes place only by generalization. Hence nothing essentially foreign to experience can enter into any thought. Take, for example, the conception of *other*. This can only arise, by abstraction, from the various particular cognized others; consequently *other* must mean with us *cognizable other*, and therefore 'other than the cognizable', can only consistently mean one cognizable other than another cognizable, for the incognizable other would be the incognizable cognizable.

Let us now go on to trace out the consequences of the above seven propositions, with a view partly to test them further, partly to obtain new truths, and in great measure also simply to discover unsuspected alternatives which philosophers must refute before they can establish any theory.

The representationists tell us that we can have no knowledge of things-in-themselves. But we go further and deny that we can so much as attach any consistent meaning to the 'absolutely incognizable'. Hence if we mean anything by the very things themselves, they are cognizable. So that a still more rigid criticism than that of the representationists restores the most important faculty which they have denied to us.

Therefore, there is nothing absolutely out of the mind, but the first impression of sense is the most external thing in existence. Here we touch material idealism. But we have adopted, also, another idealistic //conclusion/doctrine//, that there is no intuitive cognition. It follows that the first impression of sense is not cognition but only the limit of cognition. It may therefore be said to be so far out of the mind, that it is as much external as internal. Our experience of any object is developed by a process continuous from the very first, of change of the cognition and increase in the liveliness of consciousness. At the very first instant of this process, there is no consciousness but only the beginning of becoming conscious. It is also not a real state of mind because it instantaneously passes away.

There is a paradox here. But so there is in respect to any beginning or other limit of anything continuous. Does the line of separation between contiguous black and white surfaces lie within the black or the white? Since the surfaces are contiguous, points on this line lie within one or the other, for the black covers by definition all points with a certain space not covered by the white and no others. But these points are no more in one surface than in the other. Whatever may be the solution of this antinomy, it is plain that the apparent contradiction respecting our beginning of consciousness is of the same nature.

Thus the first impression is out of the mind in the sense that the degree of consciousness in it is *zero*. But there is another far more important use of the term *externality* as synonymous with *reality* and opposed to *figment*.

Letter, Peirce to W. T. Harris

L 183: W. T. Harris Collection

Cambridge 1868 Nov. 30

Dear Sir

I send to you today two proof-sheets. I should have sent the first one on some days ago but was ill when it came.

I suppose you saw that I struck out the paragraph referring to Hegelians. I intended no *slur* on them, or any appeal to the ignorant against them. What I meant was to protest respectfully but energetically *to* them against a certain tendency in their philosophy. In fact with all the disposition of this school to find every philosophical doctrine true for its time and stage of developement, yet if their categories should happen not to be true it is plain that to classify men according to them may be one of the most unfair things in the world.

I have considered your remark that you do not see the drift of my making man entirely ignorant of his own states of mind. I suppose I have not written very clearly for one thing,—and that I have tried to correct in the proof. But the real difficulty is that the article is truncated. I had intended to wind up with a long discussion about the metaphysics—the ontology of the soul. I left this off on account of the length of the article. But now I find by your criticism that it is wanted, and I have endeavored to put it into the briefest and most meagre form and send it to you, in hopes you will be able to tack it on to the end of the article.

I do not say that we are ignorant of our states of mind. What I say is that the mind is virtual, not in a series of moments, not capable of existing except in a space of time—nothing so far as it is at any one moment.

Yrs. very truly
C. S. Peirce

Questions Concerning Certain Faculties Claimed for Man

P 26: Journal of
Speculative Philosophy *2(1868):103–14*

QUESTION 1. *Whether by the simple contemplation of a cognition, independently of any previous knowledge and without reasoning from signs, we are enabled rightly to judge whether that cognition has been determined by a previous cognition or whether it refers immediately to its object.*

Throughout this paper, the term *intuition* will be taken as signifying a cognition not determined by a previous cognition of the same object, and therefore so determined by something out of the consciousness.[1] Let me request the reader to note this. *Intuition* here will be nearly the same as "premise not itself a conclusion"; the only difference being that premises and conclusions are judgments, whereas an intuition may, as far as its definition states, be any kind of cognition whatever. But just as a conclusion (good or bad) is determined in the mind of the reasoner by its premise, so cognitions not judgments may be determined by previous cognitions; and a cogni-

---

1. The word *intuitus* first occurs as a technical term in St. Anselm's *Monologium.* He wished to distinguish between our knowledge of God and our knowledge of finite things (and, in the next world, of God, also); and thinking of the saying of St. Paul, *Videmus nunc per speculum in ænigmate: tunc autem facie ad faciem,* he called the former *speculation* and the latter *intuition.* This use of "speculation" did not take root, because that word already had another exact and widely different meaning. In the middle ages, the term "intuitive cognition" had two principal senses, 1st, as opposed to abstractive cognition, it meant the knowledge of the present as present, and this is its meaning in Anselm; but 2d, as no intuitive cognition was allowed to be determined by a previous cognition, it came to be used as the opposite of discursive cognition (see Scotus, *In sententias,* lib. 2, dist. 3, qu. 9), and this is nearly the sense in which I employ it. This is also nearly the sense in which Kant uses it, the former distinction being expressed by his *sensuous* and *non-sensuous.* (See *Werke,* herausg. Rosenkrantz, Thl. 2, S. 713, 31, 41, 100, u. s. w.) An enumeration of six meanings of intuition may be found in Hamilton's *Reid,* p. 759.

tion not so determined, and therefore determined directly by the transcendental object, is to be termed an *intuition*.

Now, it is plainly one thing to have an intuition and another to know intuitively that it is an intuition, and the question is whether these two things, distinguishable in thought, are, in fact, invariably connected, so that we can always intuitively distinguish between an intuition and a cognition determined by another. Every cognition, as something present, is, of course, an intuition of itself. But the determination of a cognition by another cognition or by a transcendental object is not, at least so far as appears obviously at first, a part of the immediate content of that cognition, although it would appear to be an element of the action or passion of the transcendental *ego*, which is not, perhaps, in consciousness immediately; and yet this transcendental action or passion may invariably determine a cognition of itself, so that, in fact, the determination or non-determination of the cognition by another may be a part of the cognition. In this case, I should say that we had an intuitive power of distinguishing an intuition from another cognition.

There is no evidence that we have this faculty, except that we seem to *feel* that we have it. But the weight of that testimony depends entirely on our being supposed to have the power of distinguishing in this feeling whether the feeling be the result of education, old associations, etc., or whether it is an intuitive cognition; or, in other words, it depends on presupposing the very matter testified to. Is this feeling infallible? And is this judgment concerning it infallible and so on, *ad infinitum?* Supposing that a man really could shut himself up in such a faith, he would be, of course, impervious to the truth, "evidence-proof."

But let us compare the theory with the historic facts. The power of intuitively distinguishing intuitions from other cognitions has not prevented men from disputing very warmly as to which cognitions are intuitive. In the middle ages, reason and external authority were regarded as two coördinate sources of knowledge, just as reason and the authority of intuition are now; only the happy device of considering the enunciations of authority to be essentially indemonstrable had not yet been hit upon. All authorities were not considered as infallible, any more than all reasons; but when Berengarius said that the authoritativeness of any particular authority must rest upon reason, the proposition was scouted as opinionated, impious, and absurd. Thus, the credibility of authority was regarded by men of that time simply as an ultimate premise, as a cognition not determined by a previous cognition of the same object, or, in our terms, as an intuition. It is strange that they should have thought so, if, as the theory now under discussion supposes, by merely contemplating the credibility of the authority, as a Fakir does his God, they could have seen that it was not an ultimate premise! Now, what if our *internal* authority should meet the same fate, in the history of opinions, as that external authority has met? Can that be said to be absolutely certain which many sane, well-informed, and thoughtful men already doubt?[2]

Every lawyer knows how difficult it is for witnesses to distinguish between what they have seen and what they have inferred. This is particularly noticeable in the case of a person who is describing the performances of a spiritual medium or of a professed juggler. The difficulty is so great that the juggler himself is often astonished at the discrepancy between the actual facts and the statement of an intelligent witness who has not understood the trick. A part of the very complicated trick of the Chinese rings consists in taking two solid rings linked together, talking about them as though they were sepa-

---

2. The proposition of Berengarius is contained in the following quotation from his *De Sacra Cœna: "Maximi plane cordis est, per omnia ad dialecticam confugere, quia confugere ad eam ad rationem est confugere, quo qui non confugit, cum secundum rationem sit factus ad imaginem dei, suum honorem reliquit, nec potest renovari de die in diem ad imaginem dei."* The most striking characteristic of medieval reasoning, in general, is the perpetual resort to authority. When Fredegisus and others wish to prove that darkness is a thing, although they have evidently derived the opinion from nominalistic-Platonistic meditations, they argue the matter thus: "God called the darkness, night"; then, certainly, it is a thing, for otherwise before it had a name, there would have been nothing, not even a fiction to name. Abelard thinks it worth while to cite Boëthius, when he says that space has three dimensions, and when he says that an individual cannot be in two places at once. The author of *De Generibus et Speciebus,* a work of a superior order, in arguing against a Platonic doctrine, says that if whatever is universal is eternal, the *form* and matter of Socrates, being severally universal, are both eternal, and that, therefore, Socrates was not created by God, but only put together, *"quod quantum a vero deviet, palam est."* The authority is the final court of appeal. The same author, where in one place he doubts a statement of Boëthius, finds it necessary to assign a special reason why in this case it is not absurd to do so. *Exceptio probat regulam in casibus non exceptis.* Recognized authorities were certainly sometimes disputed in the twelfth century; their mutual contradictions insured that; and the authority of philosophers was regarded as inferior to that of theologians. Still, it would be impossible to find a passage where the authority of Aristotle is directly denied upon any logical question. *"Sunt et multi errores eius,"* says John of Salisbury, *"qui in scripturis tam Ethnicis, quam fidelibus poterunt inveniri: verum in logica parem habuisse non legitur." "Sed nihil adversus Aristotelem,"* says Abelard, and in another place, *"Sed si Aristotelem Peripateticorum principem culpare possumus, quam amplius in hac arte recepimus?"* The idea of going without an authority, or of subordinating authority to reason, does not occur to him.

rate—taking it for granted, as it were—then pretending to put them together, and handing them immediately to the spectator that he may see that they are solid. The art of this consists in raising, at first, the strong suspicion that one is broken. I have seen McAlister do this with such success, that a person sitting close to him, with all his faculties straining to detect the illusion, would have been ready to swear that he saw the rings put together, and, perhaps, if the juggler had not professedly practised deception, would have considered a doubt of it as a doubt of his own veracity. This certainly seems to show that it is not always very easy to distinguish between a premise and a conclusion, that we have no infallible power of doing so, and that in fact our only security in difficult cases is in some signs from which we can infer that a given fact must have been seen or must have been inferred. In trying to give an account of a dream, every accurate person must often have felt that it was a hopeless undertaking to attempt to disentangle waking interpretations and fillings out from the fragmentary images of the dream itself.

The mention of dreams suggests another argument. A dream, as far as its own content goes, is exactly like an actual experience. It is mistaken for one. And yet all the world believes that dreams are determined, according to the laws of the association of ideas, &c., by previous cognitions. If it be said that the faculty of intuitively recognizing intuitions is asleep, I reply that this is a mere supposition, without other support. Besides, even when we wake up, we do not find that the dream differed from reality, except by certain *marks*, darkness and fragmentariness. Not unfrequently a dream is so vivid that the memory of it is mistaken for the memory of an actual occurrence.

A child has, as far as we know, all the perceptive powers of a man. Yet question him a little as to *how* he knows what he does. In many cases, he will tell you that he never learned his mother-tongue; he always knew it, or he knew it as soon as he came to have sense. It appears, then, that *he* does not possess the faculty of distinguishing, by simple contemplation, between an intuition and a cognition determined by others.

There can be no doubt that before the publication of Berkeley's book on Vision, it had generally been believed that the third dimension of space was immediately intuited, although, at present, nearly all admit that it is known by inference. We had been *contemplating* the object since the very creation of man, but this discovery was not made until we began to *reason* about it.

Does the reader know of the blind spot on the retina? Take a number of this journal, turn over the cover so as to expose the white paper, lay it sideways upon the table before which you must sit, and put two cents upon it, one near the left-hand edge, and the other to the right. Put your left hand over your left eye, and with the right eye look *steadily* at the left-hand cent. Then, with your right hand, move the right-hand cent (which is now plainly seen) *towards* the left hand. When it comes to a place near the middle of the page it will disappear—you cannot see it without turning your eye. Bring it nearer to the other cent, or carry it further away, and it will reappear; but at that particular spot it cannot be seen. Thus it appears that there is a blind spot nearly in the middle of the retina; and this is confirmed by anatomy. It follows that the space we immediately see (when one eye is closed) is not, as we had imagined, a continuous oval, but is a ring, the filling up of which must be the work of the intellect. What more striking example could be desired of the impossibility of distinguishing intellectual results from intuitional data, by mere contemplation?

A man can distinguish different textures of cloth by feeling; but not immediately, for he requires to move his fingers over the cloth, which shows that he is obliged to compare the sensations of one instant with those of another.

The pitch of a tone depends upon the rapidity of the succession of the vibrations which reach the ear. Each of those vibrations produces an impulse upon the ear. Let a single such impulse be made upon the ear, and we know, experimentally, that it is perceived. There is, therefore, good reason to believe that each of the impulses forming a tone is perceived. Nor is there any reason to the contrary. So that this is the only admissible supposition. Therefore, the pitch of a tone depends upon the rapidity with which certain impressions are successively conveyed to the mind. These impressions must exist previously to any tone; hence, the sensation of pitch is determined by previous cognitions. Nevertheless, this would never have been discovered by the mere contemplation of that feeling.

A similar argument may be urged in reference to the perception of two dimensions of space. This appears to be an immediate intuition. But if we were to *see* immediately an extended surface, our retinas must be spread out in an extended surface. Instead of that, the retina consists of innumerable needles pointing towards the light, and whose distances from one another are decidedly greater than the *minimum visibile*. Suppose each of those nerve-points conveys the sensation of a little colored surface. Still, what we immediately see must even then be, not a continuous surface, but a collection of spots. Who could discover this by mere intuition? But all the analogies of the nervous system are against the supposition that the excitation of a single nerve can produce an idea as complicated as that of a space, however small. If the excitation of no one of these nerve-points can immediately convey the impression of space, the excitation of all cannot do so. For, the excitation of each produces some impression (according to the analogies of the nervous system), hence, the sum of these impressions is a necessary condition of any perception produced by the excitation of all; or, in other terms, a perception produced by the excitation of all is determined by the mental impressions produced by the excitation of every one. This argument is confirmed by the fact that the existence of the perception of space can be fully accounted for by the action of faculties known to exist, without supposing it to be an immediate impression. For this purpose, we must bear in mind the following facts of physio-psychology: 1. The excitation of a nerve does not of itself inform us where the extremity of it is situated. If, by a surgical operation, certain nerves are displaced, our sensations from those nerves do not inform us of the displacement. 2. A single sensation does not inform us how many nerves or nerve-points are excited. 3. We can distinguish between the impressions produced by the excitations of different nerve-points. 4. The differences of impressions produced by different excitations of similar nerve-points are similar. Let a momentary image be made upon the retina. By No. 2, the impression thereby produced will be indistinguishable from what might be produced by the excitation of some conceivable single nerve. It is not conceivable that the momentary excitation of a single nerve should give the sensation of space. Therefore, the momentary excitation of all the nerve-points of the retina cannot, immediately or mediately, produce the sensation of space. The same argument would apply to any unchanging image on the retina. Suppose, however, that the image moves over the retina. Then the peculiar excitation which at one instant affects one nerve-point, at a later instant will affect another. These will convey impressions which are very similar by 4, and yet which are distinguishable by 3. Hence, the conditions for the recognition of a relation between these impressions are present. There being, however, a very great number of nerve-points affected by a very great number of successive excitations, the relations of the resulting impressions will be almost inconceivably complicated. Now, it is a known law of mind, that when phenomena of an extreme complexity are presented, which yet would be reduced to *order* or mediate simplicity by the application of a certain conception, that conception sooner or later arises in application to those phenomena. In the case under consideration, the conception of extension would reduce the phenomena to unity, and, therefore, its genesis is fully accounted for. It remains only to explain why the previous cognitions which determine it are not more clearly apprehended. For this explanation, I shall refer to a paper upon a new list of categories, §5,[3] merely adding that just as we are able to recognize our friends by certain appearances, although we cannot possibly say what those appearances are and are quite unconscious of any process of reasoning, so in any case when the reasoning is easy and natural to us, however complex may be the premises, they sink into insignificance and oblivion proportionately to the satisfactoriness of the theory based upon them. This theory of space is confirmed by the circumstance that an exactly similar theory is imperatively demanded by the facts in reference to time. That the course of time should be immediately felt is obviously impossible. For, in that case, there must be an element of this feeling at each instant. But in an instant there is no duration and hence no immediate feeling of duration. Hence, no one of these elementary feelings is an immediate feeling of duration; and, hence the sum of all is not. On the other hand, the impressions of any moment are very complicated,—containing all the images (or the elements of the images) of sense and memory, which complexity is reducible to mediate simplicity by means of the conception of time.[4]

3. *Proceedings of the American Academy,* May 14, 1867.
4. The above theory of space and time does not conflict with that of Kant so much as it appears to do. They are in fact the solutions of different questions. Kant, it is true, makes space and time intuitions, or rather forms of intuition, but it is not essential to his theory that intuition should mean more than "individual representation." The apprehension of space and time results, according to him, from a mental *process,*—the "Synthesis der Apprehension in der Anschauung." (See *Critik d. reinen Vernunft.* Ed. 1781, pp. 98 *et seq.*) My theory is merely an account of this synthesis.
The gist of Kant's "Transcendental Æsthetic" is contained in two principles. First, that universal and necessary propositions are not given in experience. Second, that universal and necessary facts are determined by the conditions of experience in

We have, therefore, a variety of facts, all of which are most readily explained on the supposition that we have no intuitive faculty of distinguishing intuitive from mediate cognitions. Some arbitrary hypothesis may otherwise explain any one of these facts; this is the only theory which brings them to support one another. Moreover, no facts require the supposition of the faculty in question. Whoever has studied the nature of proof will see, then, that there are here very strong reasons for disbelieving the existence of this faculty. These will become still stronger when the consequences of rejecting it have, in this paper and in a following one, been more fully traced out.

QUESTION 2. *Whether we have an intuitive self-consciousness.*

Self-consciousness, as the term is here used, is to be distinguished both from consciousness generally, from the internal sense, and from pure apperception. Any cognition is a consciousness of the object as represented; by self-consciousness is meant a knowledge of our-

---

general. By a universal proposition is meant merely, one which asserts something of *all* of a sphere,—not necessarily one which all men believe. By a necessary proposition, is meant one which asserts what it does, not merely of the actual condition of things, but of every possible state of things; it is not meant that the proposition is one which we cannot help believing. Experience, in Kant's first principle, cannot be used for a product of the objective understanding, but must be taken for the first impressions of sense with consciousness conjoined and worked up by the imagination into images, together with all which is logically deducible therefrom. In this sense, it may be admitted that universal and necessary propositions are not given in experience. But, in that case, neither are any inductive conclusions which might be drawn from experience, given in it. In fact, it is the peculiar function of induction to produce universal and necessary propositions. Kant points out, indeed, that the universality and necessity of scientific inductions are but the analogues of philosophic universality and necessity; and this is true, in so far as it is never allowable to accept a scientific conclusion without a certain indefinite drawback. But this is owing to the insufficiency in the number of the instances; and whenever instances may be had in as large numbers as we please, *ad infinitum,* a truly universal and necessary proposition is inferable. As for Kant's second principle, that the truth of universal and necessary propositions is dependent upon the conditions of the general experience, it is no more nor less than the principle of Induction. I go to a fair and draw from the "grab-bag" twelve packages. Upon opening them, I find that every one contains a red ball. Here is a universal fact. It depends, then, on the condition of the experience. What is the condition of the experience? It is solely that the balls are the contents of packages drawn from that bag, that is, the only thing which determined the experience, was the drawing from the bag. I infer, then, according to the principle of Kant, that what is drawn from the bag will contain a red ball. This is induction. Apply induction not to any limited experience but to all human experience and you have the Kantian philosophy, so far as it is correctly developed.

Kant's successors, however, have not been content with his doctrine. Nor ought they to have been. For, there is this third principle: "Absolutely universal propositions must be analytic." For whatever is absolutely universal is devoid of all content or determination, for all determination is by negation. The problem, therefore, is not how universal propositions can be synthetical, but how universal propositions appearing to be synthetical can be evolved by thought alone from the purely indeterminate.

selves. Not a mere feeling of subjective conditions of consciousness, but of our personal selves. Pure apperception is the self-assertion of THE *ego;* the self-consciousness here meant is the recognition of my *private* self. I know that *I* (not merely *the* I) exist. The question is, how do I know it; by a special intuitive faculty, or is it determined by previous cognitions?

Now, it is not self-evident that we have such an intuitive faculty, for it has just been shown that we have no intuitive power of distinguishing an intuition from a cognition determined by others. Therefore, the existence or non-existence of this power is to be determined upon evidence, and the question is whether self-consciousness can be explained by the action of known faculties under conditions known to exist, or whether it is necessary to suppose an unknown cause for this cognition, and, in the latter case, whether an intuitive faculty of self-consciousness is the most probable cause which can be supposed.

It is first to be observed that there is no known self-consciousness to be accounted for in extremely young children. It has already been pointed out by Kant[5] that the late use of the very common word "I" with children indicates an imperfect self-consciousness in them, and that, therefore, so far as it is admissible for us to draw any conclusion in regard to the mental state of those who are still younger, it must be against the existence of any self-consciousness in them.

On the other hand, children manifest powers of thought much earlier. Indeed, it is almost impossible to assign a period at which children do not already exhibit decided intellectual activity in directions in which thought is indispensable to their well-being. The complicated trigonometry of vision, and the delicate adjustments of coördinated movement, are plainly mastered very early. There is no reason to question a similar degree of thought in reference to themselves.

A very young child may always be observed to watch its own body with great attention. There is every reason why this should be so, for from the child's point of view this body is the most important thing in the universe. Only what it touches has any actual and present feeling; only what it faces has any actual color; only what is on its tongue has any actual taste.

No one questions that, when a sound is heard by a child, he thinks, not of himself as hearing, but of the bell or other object as sounding.

5. *Werke,* vii (2), 11.

How when he wills to move a table? Does he then think of himself as desiring, or only of the table as fit to be moved? That he has the latter thought, is beyond question; that he has the former, must, until the existence of an intuitive self-consciousness is proved, remain an arbitrary and baseless supposition. There is no good reason for thinking that he is less ignorant of his own peculiar condition than the angry adult who denies that he is in a passion.

The child, however, must soon discover by observation that things which are thus fit to be changed are apt actually to undergo this change, after a contact with that peculiarly important body called Willy or Johnny. This consideration makes this body still more important and central, since it establishes a connection between the fitness of a thing to be changed and a tendency in this body to touch it before it is changed.

The child learns to understand the language; that is to say, a connection between certain sounds and certain facts becomes established in his mind. He has previously noticed the connection between these sounds and the motions of the lips of bodies somewhat similar to the central one, and has tried the experiment of putting his hand on those lips and has found the sound in that case to be smothered. He thus connects that language with bodies somewhat similar to the central one. By efforts, so unenergetic that they should be called rather instinctive, perhaps, than tentative, he learns to produce those sounds. So he begins to converse.

It must be about this time that he begins to find that what these people about him say is the very best evidence of fact. So much so, that testimony is even a stronger mark of fact than *the facts themselves,* or rather than what must now be thought of as the *appearances* themselves. (I may remark, by the way, that this remains so through life; testimony will convince a man that he himself is mad.) A child hears it said that the stove is hot. But it is not, he says; and, indeed, that central body is not touching it, and only what that touches is hot or cold. But he touches it, and finds the testimony confirmed in a striking way. Thus, he becomes aware of ignorance, and it is necessary to suppose a *self* in which this ignorance can inhere. So testimony gives the first dawning of self-consciousness.

But, further, although usually appearances are either only confirmed or merely supplemented by testimony, yet there is a certain remarkable class of appearances which are continually contradicted by testimony. These are those predicates which *we* know to be emotional, but which *he* distinguishes by their connection with the movements of that central person, himself (that the table wants moving, etc.). These judgments are generally denied by others. Moreover, he has reason to think that others, also, have such judgments which are quite denied by all the rest. Thus, he adds to the conception of appearance as the actualization of fact, the conception of it as something *private* and valid only for one body. In short, *error* appears, and it can be explained only by supposing a *self* which is fallible.

Ignorance and error are all that distinguish our private selves from the absolute *ego* of pure apperception.

Now, the theory which, for the sake of perspicuity, has thus been stated in a specific form, may be summed up as follows: At the age at which we know children to be self-conscious, we know that they have been made aware of ignorance and error; and we know them to possess at that age powers of understanding sufficient to enable them then to infer from ignorance and error their own existence. Thus we find that known faculties, acting under conditions known to exist, would rise to self-consciousness. The only essential defect in this account of the matter is, that while we know that children exercise *as much* understanding as is here supposed, we do not know that they exercise it in precisely this way. Still the supposition that they do so is infinitely more supported by facts, than the supposition of a wholly peculiar faculty of the mind.

The only argument worth noticing for the existence of an intuitive self-consciousness is this. We are more certain of our own existence than of any other fact; a premise cannot determine a conclusion to be more certain than it is itself; hence, our own existence cannot have been inferred from any other fact. The first premise must be admitted, but the second premise is founded on an exploded theory of logic. A conclusion cannot be more certain than that some one of the facts which support it is true, but it may easily be more certain than any one of those facts. Let us suppose, for example, that a dozen witnesses testify to an occurrence. Then my belief in that occurrence rests on the belief that each of those men is generally to be believed upon oath. Yet the fact testified to is made more certain than that any one of those men is generally to be believed. In the same way, to the developed mind of man, his own existence is supported by *every other fact,* and is, therefore, incomparably more certain than any one of these facts. But it cannot be said to be more certain than that there is another fact, since there is no doubt perceptible in either case.

It is to be concluded, then, that there is no necessity of supposing an intuitive self-consciousness, since self-consciousness may easily be the result of inference.

QUESTION 3. *Whether we have an intuitive power of distinguishing between the subjective elements of different kinds of cognitions.*

Every cognition involves something represented, or that of which we are conscious, and some action or passion of the self whereby it becomes represented. The former shall be termed the objective, the latter the subjective, element of the cognition. The cognition itself is an intuition of its objective element, which may therefore be called, also, the immediate object. The subjective element is not necessarily immediately known, but it is possible that such an intuition of the subjective element of a cognition of its character, whether that of dreaming, imagining, conceiving, believing, etc., should accompany every cognition. The question is whether this is so.

It would appear, at first sight, that there is an overwhelming array of evidence in favor of the existence of such a power. The difference between seeing a color and imagining it is immense. There is a vast difference between the most vivid dream and reality. And if we had no intuitive power of distinguishing between what we believe and what we merely conceive, we never, it would seem, could in any way distinguish them; since if we did so by reasoning, the question would arise whether the argument itself was believed or conceived, and this must be answered before the conclusion could have any force. And thus there would be a *regressus ad infinitum.* Besides, if we do not know that we believe, then, from the nature of the case, we do not believe.

But be it noted that we do not intuitively know the existence of this faculty. For it is an intuitive one, and we cannot intuitively know that a cognition is intuitive. The question is, therefore, whether it is necessary to suppose the existence of this faculty, or whether then the facts can be explained without this supposition.

In the first place, then, the difference between what is imagined or dreamed and what is actually experienced, is no argument in favor of the existence of such a faculty. For it is not questioned that there are distinctions in what is present to the mind, but the question is, whether independently of any such distinctions in the immediate *objects* of consciousness, we have any immediate power of distinguishing different modes of consciousness. Now, the very fact of the immense difference in the immediate objects of sense and imagination, sufficiently accounts for our distinguishing those faculties; and instead of being an argument in favor of the existence of an intuitive power of distinguishing the subjective elements of consciousness, it is a powerful reply to any such argument, so far as the distinction of sense and imagination is concerned.

Passing to the distinction of belief and conception, we meet the statement that the knowledge of belief is essential to its existence. Now, we can unquestionably distinguish a belief from a conception, in most cases, by means of a peculiar feeling of conviction; and it is a mere question of words whether we define belief as that judgment which is accompanied by this feeling, or as that judgment from which a man will act. We may conveniently call the former *sensational*, the latter *active* belief. That neither of these necessarily involves the other, will surely be admitted without any recital of facts. Taking belief in the sensational sense, the intuitive power of reorganizing it will amount simply to the capacity for the sensation which accompanies the judgment. This sensation, like any other, is an object of consciousness; and therefore the capacity for it implies no intuitive recognition of subjective elements of consciousness. If belief is taken in the active sense, it may be discovered by the observation of external facts and by inference from the sensation of conviction which usually accompanies it.

Thus, the arguments in favor of this peculiar power of consciousness disappear, and the presumption is again against such a hypothesis. Moreover, as the immediate objects of any two faculties must be admitted to be different, the facts do not render such a supposition in any degree necessary.

QUESTION 4. *Whether we have any power of introspection, or whether our whole knowledge of the internal world is derived from the observation of external facts.*

It is not intended here to assume the reality of the external world. Only, there is a certain set of facts which are ordinarily regarded as external, while others are regarded as internal. The question is whether the latter are known otherwise than by inference from the former. By introspection, I mean a direct perception of the internal world, but not necessarily a perception of it *as* internal. Nor do I mean to limit the signification of the word to intuition, but would extend it to any knowledge of the internal world not derived from external observation.

There is one sense in which any perception has an internal object, namely, that every sensation is partly determined by internal conditions. Thus, the sensation of redness is as it is, owing to the constitution of the mind; and in this sense it is a sensation of something internal. Hence, we may derive a knowledge of the mind from a consideration of this sensation, but that knowledge would, in fact, be an inference from redness as a predicate of something external. On the other hand, there are certain other feelings—the emotions, for example—which appear to arise in the first place, not as predicates at all, and to be referable to the mind alone. It would seem, then, that by means of these, a knowledge of the mind may be obtained, which is not inferred from any character of outward things. The question is whether this is really so.

Although introspection is not necessarily intuitive, it is not self-evident that we possess this capacity; for we have no intuitive faculty of distinguishing different subjective modes of consciousness. The power, if it exists, must be known by the circumstance that the facts cannot be explained without it.

In reference to the above argument from the emotions, it must be admitted that if a man is angry, his anger implies, in general, no determinate and constant character in its object. But, on the other hand, it can hardly be questioned that there is some relative character in the outward thing which makes him angry, and a little reflection will serve to show that his anger consists in his saying to himself, "this thing is vile, abominable, etc.," and that it is rather a mark of returning reason to say, "I am angry." In the same way any emotion is a predication concerning some object, and the chief difference between this and an objective intellectual judgment is that while the latter is relative to human nature or to mind in general, the former is relative to the particular circumstances and disposition of a particular man at a particular time. What is here said of emotions in general, is true in particular of the sense of beauty and of the moral sense. Good and bad are feelings which first arise as predicates, and therefore are either predicates of the not-I, or are determined by previous cognitions (there being no intuitive power of distinguishing subjective elements of consciousness).

It remains, then, only to inquire whether it is necessary to suppose a particular power of introspection for the sake of accounting for the sense of willing. Now, volition, as distinguished from desire, is nothing but the power of concentrating the attention, of abstracting. Hence, the knowledge of the power of abstracting may be inferred from abstract objects, just as the knowledge of the power of seeing is inferred from colored objects.

It appears, therefore, that there is no reason for supposing a power of introspection; and, consequently, the only way of investigating a psychological question is by inference from external facts.

QUESTION 5. *Whether we can think without signs.*

This is a familiar question, but there is, to this day, no better argument in the affirmative than that thought must precede every sign. This assumes the impossibility of an infinite series. But Achilles, as a fact, will overtake the tortoise. *How* this happens, is a question not necessary to be answered at present, as long as it certainly does happen.

If we seek the light of external facts, the only cases of thought which we can find are of thought in signs. Plainly, no other thought can be evidenced by external facts. But we have seen that only by external facts can thought be known at all. The only thought, then, which can possibly be cognized is thought in signs. But thought which cannot be cognized does not exist. All thought, therefore, must necessarily be in signs.

A man says to himself, "Aristotle is a man; *therefore,* he is fallible." Has he not, then, thought what he has not said to himself, that all men are fallible? The answer is, that he has done so, so far as this is said in his *therefore.* According to this, our question does not relate to *fact,* but is a mere asking for distinctness of thought.

From the proposition that every thought is a sign, it follows that every thought must address itself to some other, must determine some other, since that is the essence of a sign. This, after all, is but another form of the familiar axiom, that in intuition, i.e. in the immediate present, there is no thought, or, that all which is reflected upon has past. *Hinc loquor inde est.* That, since any thought, there must have been a thought, has its analogue in the fact that, since any past time, there must have been an infinite series of times. To say, therefore, that thought cannot happen in an instant, but requires a time, is but another way of saying that every thought must be interpreted in another, or that all thought is in signs.

QUESTION 6. *Whether a sign can have any meaning, if by its definition it is the sign of something absolutely incognizable.*

It would seem that it can, and that universal and hypothetical propositions are instances of it. Thus, the universal proposition, "all ruminants are cloven-hoofed," speaks of a possible infinity of animals, and no matter how many ruminants may have been examined, the possibility must remain that there are others which have not been examined. In the case of a hypothetical proposition, the same thing is still more manifest; for such a proposition speaks not merely of the actual state of things, but of every possible state of things, all of which are not knowable, inasmuch as only one can so much as exist.

On the other hand, all our conceptions are obtained by abstractions and combinations of cognitions first occurring in judgments of experience. Accordingly, there can be no conception of the absolutely incognizable, since nothing of that sort occurs in experience. But the meaning of a term is the conception which it conveys. Hence, a term can have no such meaning.

If it be said that the incognizable is a concept compounded of the concept *not* and *cognizable*, it may be replied that *not* is a mere syncategorematic term and not a concept by itself.

If I think "white," I will not go so far as Berkeley and say that I think of a person seeing, but I will say that what I think is of the nature of a cognition, and so of anything else which can be experienced. Consequently, the highest concept which can be reached by abstractions from judgments of experience—and therefore, the highest concept which can be reached at all—is the concept of something of the nature of a cognition. *Not,* then, or *what is other than,* if a concept, is a concept of the cognizable. Hence, not-cognizable, if a concept, is a concept of the form "*A*, not-*A*," and is, at least, self-contradictory. Thus, ignorance and error can only be conceived as correlative to a real knowledge and truth, which latter are of the nature of cognitions. Over against any cognition, there is an unknown but knowable reality; but over against all possible cognition, there is only the self-contradictory. In short, *cognizability* (in its widest sense) and *being* are not merely metaphysically the same, but are synonymous terms.

To the argument from universal and hypothetical propositions, the reply is, that though their truth cannot be cognized with absolute certainty, it may be probably known by induction.

QUESTION 7. *Whether there is any cognition not determined by a previous cognition.*

It would seem that there is or has been; for since we are in possession of cognitions, which are all determined by previous ones, and these by cognitions earlier still, there must have been a *first* in this series or else our state of cognition at any time is completely determined, according to logical laws, by our state at any previous time. But there are many facts against the last supposition, and therefore in favor of intuitive cognitions.

On the other hand, since it is impossible to know intuitively that a given cognition is not determined by a previous one, the only way in which this can be known is by hypothetic inference from observed facts. But to adduce the cognition by which a given cognition has been determined is to explain the determinations of that cognition. And it is the only way of explaining them. For something entirely out of consciousness which may be supposed to determine it, can, as such, only be known and only adduced in the determinate cognition in question. So, that to suppose that a cognition is determined solely by something absolutely external, is to suppose its determinations incapable of explanation. Now, this is a hypothesis which is warranted under no circumstances, inasmuch as the only possible justification for a hypothesis is that it explains the facts, and to say that they are explained and at the same time to suppose them inexplicable is self-contradictory.

If it be objected that the peculiar character of *red* is not determined by any previous cognition, I reply that that character is not a character of red as a cognition; for if there be a man to whom red things look as blue ones do to me and *vice versa,* that man's eyes teach him the same facts that they would if he were like me.

Moreover, we know of no power by which an intuition could be known. For, as the cognition is beginning, and therefore in a state of change, at only the first instant would it be intuition. And, therefore, the apprehension of it must take place in no time and be an event occupying no time.[6] Besides, all the cognitive faculties we know of are relative, and consequently their products are relations. But the

---

6. This argument, however, only covers a part of the question. It does not go to show that there is no cognition undetermined except by another like it.

cognition of a relation is determined by previous cognitions. No cognition not determined by a previous cognition, then, can be known. It does not exist, then, first, because it is absolutely incognizable, and second, because a cognition only exists so far as it is known.

The reply to the argument that there must be a first is as follows: In retracing our way from conclusions to premises, or from determined cognitions to those which determine them, we finally reach, in all cases, a point beyond which the consciousness in the determined cognition is more lively than in the cognition which determines it. We have a less lively consciousness in the cognition which determines our cognition of the third dimension than in the latter cognition itself; a less lively consciousness in the cognition which determines our cognition of a continuous surface (without a blind spot) than in this latter cognition itself; and a less lively consciousness of the impressions which determine the sensation of tone than of that sensation itself. Indeed, when we get near enough to the external this is the universal rule. Now let any horizontal line represent a cognition, and let the length of the line serve to measure (so to speak) the liveliness of consciousness in that cognition. A point, having no length, will, on this principle, represent an object quite out of consciousness. Let one horizontal line below another represent a cognition which determines the cognition represented by that other and which has the same object as the latter. Let the finite distance between two such lines represent that they are two different cognitions. With this aid to thinking, let us see whether "there must be a first." Suppose an inverted triangle ▽ to be gradually dipped into water. At any date or instant, the surface of the water makes a horizontal line across that triangle. This line represents a cognition. At a subsequent date, there is a sectional line so made, higher upon the triangle. This represents another cognition of the same object determined by the former, and having a livelier consciousness. The apex of the triangle represents the object external to the mind which determines both these cognitions. The state of the triangle before it reaches the water, represents a state of cognition which contains nothing which determines these subsequent cognitions. To say, then, that if there be a state of cognition by which all subsequent cognitions of a certain object are not determined, there must subsequently be some cognition of that object not determined by previous cognitions of the same object, is to say that when that triangle is dipped into the water there must be a sectional line made by the surface of the water lower than which no surface line had been made in that way. But draw the horizontal line where you will, as many horizontal lines as you please can be assigned at finite distances below it and below one another. For any such section is at some distance above the apex, otherwise it is not a line. Let this distance be *a*. Then there have been similar sections at the distances $\frac{1}{2}a$, $\frac{1}{4}a$, $\frac{1}{8}a$, $\frac{1}{16}a$, above the apex, and so on as far as you please. So that it is not true that there must be a first. Explicate the logical difficulties of this paradox (they are identical with those of the Achilles) in whatever way you may. I am content with the result, as long as your principles are fully applied to the particular case of cognitions determining one another. Deny motion, if it seems proper to do so; only then deny the process of determination of one cognition by another. Say that instants and lines are fictions; only say, also, that states of cognition and judgments are fictions. The point here insisted on is not this or that logical solution of the difficulty, but merely that cognition arises by a *process* of beginning, as any other change comes to pass.

In a subsequent paper, I shall trace the consequences of these principles, in reference to the questions of reality, of individuality, and of the validity of the laws of logic.

Some Consequences of Four Incapacities

P 27: Journal of
Speculative Philosophy *2(1868):140–57*

Descartes is the father of modern philosophy, and the spirit of Cartesianism—that which principally distinguishes it from the scholasticism which it displaced—may be compendiously stated as follows:

1. It teaches that philosophy must begin with universal doubt; whereas scholasticism had never questioned fundamentals.

2. It teaches that the ultimate test of certainty is to be found in the individual consciousness; whereas scholasticism had rested on the testimony of sages and of the Catholic Church.

3. The multiform argumentation of the middle ages is replaced by

a single thread of inference depending often upon inconspicuous premises.

4. Scholasticism had its mysteries of faith, but undertook to explain all created things. But there are many facts which Cartesianism not only does not explain, but renders absolutely inexplicable, unless to say that "God makes them so" is to be regarded as an explanation.

In some, or all of these respects, most modern philosophers have been, in effect, Cartesians. Now without wishing to return to scholasticism, it seems to me that modern science and modern logic require us to stand upon a very different platform from this.

1. We cannot begin with complete doubt. We must begin with all the prejudices which we actually have when we enter upon the study of philosophy. These prejudices are not to be dispelled by a maxim, for they are things which it does not occur to us *can* be questioned. Hence this initial scepticism will be a mere self-deception, and not real doubt; and no one who follows the Cartesian method will ever be satisfied until he has formally recovered all those beliefs which in form he has given up. It is, therefore, as useless a preliminary as going to the North Pole would be in order to get to Constantinople by coming down regularly upon a meridian. A person may, it is true, in the course of his studies, find reason to doubt what he began by believing; but in that case he doubts because he has a positive reason for it, and not on account of the Cartesian maxim. Let us not pretend to doubt in philosophy what we do not doubt in our hearts.

2. The same formalism appears in the Cartesian criterion, which amounts to this: "Whatever I am clearly convinced of, is true." If I were really convinced, I should have done with reasoning, and should require no test of certainty. But thus to make single individuals absolute judges of truth is most pernicious. The result is that metaphysicians will all agree that metaphysics has reached a pitch of certainty far beyond that of the physical sciences;—only they can agree upon nothing else. In sciences in which men come to agreement, when a theory has been broached, it is considered to be on probation until this agreement is reached. After it is reached, the question of certainty becomes an idle one, because there is no one left who doubts it. We individually cannot reasonably hope to attain the ultimate philosophy which we pursue; we can only seek it, therefore, for the *community* of philosophers. Hence, if disciplined and candid minds carefully examine a theory and refuse to accept it, this ought to create doubts in the mind of the author of the theory himself.

3. Philosophy ought to imitate the successful sciences in its methods, so far as to proceed only from tangible premises which can be subjected to careful scrutiny, and to trust rather to the multitude and variety of its arguments than to the conclusiveness of any one. Its reasoning should not form a chain which is no stronger than its weakest link, but a cable whose fibres may be ever so slender, provided they are sufficiently numerous and intimately connected.

4. Every unidealistic philosophy supposes some absolutely inexplicable, unanalyzable ultimate; in short, something resulting from mediation itself not susceptible of mediation. Now that anything *is* thus inexplicable can only be known by reasoning from signs. But the only justification of an inference from signs is that the conclusion explains the fact. To suppose the fact absolutely inexplicable, is not to explain it, and hence this supposition is never allowable.

In the last number of this journal will be found a piece entitled "Questions concerning certain Faculties claimed for Man," which has been written in this spirit of opposition to Cartesianism. That criticism of certain faculties resulted in four denials, which for convenience may here be repeated:

1. We have no power of Introspection, but all knowledge of the internal world is derived by hypothetical reasoning from our knowledge of external facts.

2. We have no power of Intuition, but every cognition is determined logically by previous cognitions.

3. We have no power of thinking without signs.

4. We have no conception of the absolutely incognizable.

These propositions cannot be regarded as certain; and, in order to bring them to a further test, it is now proposed to trace them out to their consequences. We may first consider the first alone; then trace the consequences of the first and second; then see what else will result from assuming the third also; and, finally, add the fourth to our hypothetical premises.

In accepting the first proposition, we must put aside all prejudices derived from a philosophy which bases our knowledge of the external world on our self-consciousness. We can admit no statement concerning what passes within us except as a hypothesis necessary to explain what takes place in what we commonly call the external world. Moreover when we have upon such grounds assumed one faculty or mode of action of the mind, we cannot, of course, adopt any other hypothesis for the purpose of explaining any fact which can be explained by our first supposition, but must carry the latter as far as it will go. In other words, we must, as far as we can do so without additional hypotheses, reduce all kinds of mental action to one general type.

The class of modifications of consciousness with which we must commence our inquiry must be one whose existence is indubitable, and whose laws are best known, and, therefore (since this knowledge comes from the outside), which most closely follows external facts; that is, it must be some kind of cognition. Here we may hypothetically admit the second proposition of the former paper, according to which there is no absolutely first cognition of any object, but cognition arises by a continuous process. We must begin, then, with a *process* of cognition, and with that process whose laws are best understood and most closely follow external facts. This is no other than the process of valid inference, which proceeds from its premise, *A*, to its conclusion, *B*, only if, as a matter of fact, such a proposition as *B* is always or usually true when such a proposition as *A* is true. It is a consequence, then, of the first two principles whose results we are to trace out, that we must, as far as we can, without any other supposition than that the mind reasons, reduce all mental action to the formula of valid reasoning.

But does the mind in fact go through the syllogistic process? It is certainly very doubtful whether a conclusion—as something existing in the mind independently, like an image—suddenly displaces two premises existing in the mind in a similar way. But it is a matter of constant experience, that if a man is made to believe in the premises, in the sense that he will act from them and will say that they are true, under favorable conditions he will also be ready to act from the conclusion and to say that that is true. Something, therefore, takes place within the organism which is equivalent to the syllogistic process.

A valid inference is either *complete* or *incomplete*. An incomplete inference is one whose validity depends upon some matter of fact not contained in the premises. This implied fact might have been stated as a premise, and its relation to the conclusion is the same whether it is explicitly posited or not, since it is at least virtually taken for granted; so that every valid incomplete argument is virtually complete. Complete arguments are divided into *simple* and *complex*. A complex argument is one which from three or more premises concludes what might have been concluded by successive steps in reasonings each of which is simple. Thus, a complex inference comes to the same thing in the end as a succession of simple inferences.

A complete, simple, and valid argument, or syllogism, is either *apodictic* or *probable*. An apodictic or deductive syllogism is one whose validity depends unconditionally upon the relation of the fact inferred to the facts posited in the premises. A syllogism whose validity should depend not merely upon its premises, but upon the existence of some other knowledge, would be impossible; for either this other knowledge would be posited, in which case it would be a part of the premises, or it would be implicitly assumed, in which case the inference would be incomplete. But a syllogism whose validity depends partly upon the *non-existence* of some other knowledge, is a *probable* syllogism.

A few examples will render this plain. The two following arguments are apodictic or deductive:

1. No series of days of which the first and last are different days of the week exceeds by one a multiple of seven days; now the first and last days of any leap-year are different days of the week, and therefore no leap-year consists of a number of days one greater than a multiple of seven.

2. Among the vowels there are no double letters; but one of the double letters *(w)* is compounded of two vowels: hence, a letter compounded of two vowels is not necessarily itself a vowel.

In both these cases, it is plain that as long as the premises are true, however other facts may be, the conclusions will be true. On the other hand, suppose that we reason as follows:—"A certain man had the Asiatic cholera. He was in a state of collapse, livid, quite cold, and without perceptible pulse. He was bled copiously. During the process he came out of collapse, and the next morning was well enough to be about. Therefore, bleeding tends to cure the cholera." This is a fair probable inference, provided that the premises represent our whole knowledge of the matter. But if we knew, for example, that recoveries from cholera were apt to be sudden, and that the physician who had reported this case had known of a hundred other trials of the remedy without communicating the result, then the inference would lose all its validity.

The absence of knowledge which is essential to the validity of any probable argument relates to some question which is determined by the argument itself. This question, like every other, is whether certain objects have certain characters. Hence, the absence of knowledge is either whether besides the objects which, according to the premises, possess certain characters, any other objects possess them; or, whether besides the characters which, according to the premises, belong to certain objects, any other characters not necessarily involved in these belong to the same objects. In the former case, the reasoning proceeds as though all the objects which have certain characters were known, and this is *induction;* in the latter case, the inference proceeds as though all the characters requisite to the determination of a certain object or class were known, and this is *hypothesis.* This distinction, also, may be made more plain by examples.

Suppose we count the number of occurrences of the different letters in a certain English book, which we may call *A.* Of course, every new letter which we add to our count will alter the relative number of occurrences of the different letters; but as we proceed with our counting, this change will be less and less. Suppose that we find that as we increase the number of letters counted, the relative number of *e*'s approaches nearly 11¼ *per cent* of the whole, that of the *t*'s 8½ *per cent,* that of the *a*'s 8 *per cent,* that of the *s*'s 7½ *per cent,* &c. Suppose we repeat the same observations with half a dozen other English writings (which we may designate as *B, C, D, E, F, G*) with the like result. Then we may infer that in every English writing of some length, the different letters occur with nearly those relative frequencies.

Now this argument depends for its validity upon our *not* knowing the proportion of letters in any English writing besides *A, B, C, D, E, F,* and *G.* For if we know it in respect to *H,* and it is not nearly the same as in the others, our conclusion is destroyed at once; if it is the same, then the legitimate inference is from *A, B, C, D, E, F, G,* and *H,* and not from the first seven alone. This, therefore, is an *induction.*

Suppose, next, that a piece of writing in cypher is presented to us, without the key. Suppose we find that it contains something less than 26 characters, one of which occurs about 11 *per cent* of all the times, another 8½ *per cent,* another 8 *per cent,* and another 7½ *per cent.* Suppose that when we substitute for these *e, t, a,* and *s,* respectively, we are able to see how single letters may be substituted for each of the other characters so as to make sense in English, provided, however, that we allow the spelling to be wrong in some cases. If the writing is of any considerable length, we may infer with great probability that this is the meaning of the cipher.

The validity of this argument depends upon there being no other known characters of the writing in cipher which would have any weight in the matter; for if there are—if we know, for example, whether or not there is any other solution of it—this must be allowed its effect in supporting or weakening the conclusion. This, then, is *hypothesis.*

All valid reasoning is either deductive, inductive, or hypothetic; or else it combines two or more of these characters. Deduction is pretty well treated in most logical text-books; but it will be necessary to say a few words about induction and hypothesis in order to render what follows more intelligible.

Induction may be defined as an argument which proceeds upon the assumption that all the members of a class or aggregate have all the characters which are common to all those members of this class concerning which it is known, whether they have these characters or not; or, in other words, which assumes that that is true of a whole collection which is true of a number of instances taken from it at random. This might be called statistical argument. In the long run, it must generally afford pretty correct conclusions from true premises. If we have a bag of beans partly black and partly white, by counting the relative proportions of the two colors in several different handfuls, we can approximate more or less to the relative proportions in the whole bag, since a sufficient number of handfuls would constitute all the beans in the bag. The central characteristic and key to induction is, that by taking the conclusion so reached as major premise of a syllogism, and the proposition stating that such and such objects are taken from the class in question as the minor premise, the other premise of the induction will follow from them deductively. Thus, in the above example we concluded that all books in English have about 11¼ *per cent* of their letters *e*'s. From that as major premise, together with the proposition that *A, B, C, D, E, F,* and *G* are books in English, it follows deductively that *A, B, C, D, E, F,* and *G* have about 11¼ *per cent* of their letters *e*'s. Accordingly, induction has been defined by Aristotle as the inference of the major premise of a syllogism from its minor premise and conclusion. The function of an induction is to substitute for a series of many subjects, a single one which embraces them and an indefinite number of others. Thus it is a species of "reduction of the manifold to unity."

Hypothesis may be defined as an argument which proceeds upon the assumption that a character which is known necessarily to involve a certain number of others, may be probably predicated of any object which has all the characters which this character is known to involve. Just as induction may be regarded as the inference of the major premise of a syllogism, so hypothesis may be regarded as the inference of the minor premise, from the other two propositions. Thus, the example taken above consists of two such inferences of the minor premises of the following syllogisms:

1. Every English writing of some length in which such and such characters denote *e, t, a,* and *s,* has about 11¼ *per cent* of the first sort of marks, 8½ of the second, 8 of the third, and 7½ of the fourth;

This secret writing is an English writing of some length, in which such and such characters denote *e, t, a,* and *s,* respectively:

∴ This secret writing has about 11¼ *per cent* of its characters of the first kind, 8½ of the second, 8 of the third, and 7½ of the fourth.

2. A passage written with such an alphabet makes sense when such and such letters are severally substituted for such and such characters.

This secret writing is written with such an alphabet.

∴ This secret writing makes sense when such and such substitutions are made.

The function of hypothesis is to substitute for a great series of predicates forming no unity in themselves, a single one (or small number) which involves them all, together (perhaps) with an indefinite number of others. It is, therefore, also a reduction of a manifold to unity.[1] Every deductive syllogism may be put into the form

---

1. Several persons versed in logic have objected that I have here quite misapplied the term *hypothesis,* and that what I so designate is an argument from *analogy.* It is a sufficient reply to say that the example of the cipher has been given as an apt illustration of hypothesis by Descartes (Rule 10, *Œuvres choisies:* Paris, 1865, page 334), by Leibniz (*Nouveaux Essais,* lib. 4, ch. 12, §13, Ed. Erdmann, p. 383 *b*), and (as I learn from D. Stewart; *Works,* vol. 3, pp. 305 et seqq.) by Gravesande, Boscovich, Hartley, and G. L. Le Sage. The term *Hypothesis* has been used in the following senses:—1. For the theme or proposition forming the subject of discourse. 2. For an assumption. Aristotle divides *theses* or propositions adopted without any reason into definitions and hypotheses. The latter are propositions stating the existence of something. Thus the geometer says, "Let there be a triangle." 3. For a condition in a general sense. We are said to seek other things than happiness ἐξ ὑποθέσεως, conditionally. The best republic is the ideally perfect, the second the best on earth, the third the best ἐξ ὑποθέσεως, under the circumstances. Freedom is the ὑπόθεσις or condition of democracy. 4. For the antecedent of a hypothetical proposition. 5. For an oratorical question which assumes facts. 6. In the *Synopsis* of Psellus, for the reference of a

If *A*, then *B*;
But *A*:
∴ *B*.

---

subject to the things it denotes. 7. Most commonly in modern times, for the conclusion of an argument from consequence and consequent to antecedent. This is my use of the term. 8. For such a conclusion when too weak to be a theory accepted into the body of a science.

I give a few authorities to support the seventh use:

Chauvin.—Lexicon Rationale, 1st Ed.—"Hypothesis est propositio, quæ assumitur ad probandam aliam veritatem incognitam. Requirunt multi, ut hæc hypothesis vera esse cognoscatur, etiam antequam appareat, an alia ex eâ deduci possint. Verum aiunt alii, hoc unum desiderari, ut hypothesis pro vera admittatur, quod nempe ex hac talia deducitur, quæ respondent phænomenis, et satisfaciunt omnibus difficultatibus, quæ hac parte in re, et in iis quæ de ea apparent, occurrebant."

Newton.—"Hactenus phænomena cœlorum et maris nostri per vim gravitatis exposui, sed causam gravitatis nondum assignavi. . . . Rationem vero harum gravitatis proprietatum ex phænomenis nondum potui deducere, et hypotheses non fingo. Quicquid enim ex phænomenis non deducitur, *hypothesis* vocanda est. . . . In hâc Philosophiâ Propositiones deducuntur ex phænomenis, et redduntur generales per inductionem." *Principia. Ad fin.*

Sir Wm. Hamilton.—"*Hypotheses,* that is, propositions which are assumed with probability, in order to explain or prove something else which cannot otherwise be explained or proved."—*Lectures on Logic* (Am. Ed.), p. 188.

"The name of *hypothesis* is more emphatically given to provisory suppositions, which serve to explain the phenomena in so far as observed, but which are only asserted to be true, if ultimately confirmed by a complete induction."—Ibid., p. 364.

"When a phenomenon is presented which can be explained by no principle afforded through experience, we feel discontented and uneasy; and there arises an effort to discover some cause which may, at least provisionally, account for the outstanding phenomenon; and this cause is finally recognized as valid and true, if, through it, the given phenomenon is found to obtain a full and perfect explanation. The judgment in which a phenomenon is referred to such a problematic cause, is called a *Hypothesis.*"—Ibid., pp. 449, 450. See also *Lectures on Metaphysics,* p. 117.

J. S. Mill.—"An hypothesis is any supposition which we make (either without actual evidence, or on evidence avowedly insufficient), in order to endeavor to deduce from it conclusions in accordance with facts which are known to be real; under the idea that if the conclusions to which the hypothesis leads are known truths, the hypothesis itself either must be, or at least is likely to be true."—*Logic* (6th Ed.), vol. 2, p. 8.

Kant.—"*If all the consequents of a cognition are true, the cognition itself is true.* . . . It is allowable, therefore, to conclude from consequent to *a* reason, but without being able to determine this reason. From the complexus of all consequents alone can we conclude the truth of a determinate reason. . . . The difficulty with this *positive* and *direct* mode of inference *(modus ponens)* is that the totality of the consequents cannot be apodeictically recognized, and that we are therefore led by this mode of inference only to a probable and *hypothetically* true cognition *(Hypotheses).*"—*Logik* by Jäsche, *Werke,* ed. Rosenkranz and Schubert, vol. 3, p. 221.

"A hypothesis is the judgment of the truth of a reason on account of the sufficiency of the consequents."—Ibid., p. 262.

Herbart.—"We can make hypotheses, thence deduce consequents, and afterwards see whether the latter accord with experience. Such suppositions are termed hypotheses."—*Einleitung; Werke,* vol. 1, p. 53.

Beneke.—"Affirmative inferences from consequent to antecedent, or hypotheses."—*System der Logik,* vol. 2, p. 103.

There would be no difficulty in greatly multiplying these citations.

And as the minor premise in this form appears as antecedent or reason of a hypothetical proposition, hypothetic inference may be called reasoning from consequent to antecedent.

The argument from analogy, which a popular writer upon logic calls reasoning from particulars to particulars, derives its validity from its combining the characters of induction and hypothesis, being analyzable either into a deduction or an induction, or a deduction and a hypothesis.

But though inference is thus of three essentially different species, it also belongs to one genus. We have seen that no conclusion can be legitimately derived which could not have been reached by successions of arguments having two premises each, and implying no fact not asserted.

Either of these premises is a proposition asserting that certain objects have certain characters. Every term of such a proposition stands either for certain objects or for certain characters. The conclusion may be regarded as a proposition substituted in place of either premise, the substitution being justified by the fact stated in the other premise. The conclusion is accordingly derived from either premise by substituting either a new subject for the subject of the premise, or a new predicate for the predicate of the premise, or by both substitutions. Now the substitution of one term for another can be justified only so far as the term substituted represents only what is represented in the term replaced. If, therefore, the conclusion be denoted by the formula,

$$S \text{ is } P;$$

and this conclusion be derived, by a change of subject, from a premise which may on this account be expressed by the formula,

$$M \text{ is } P,$$

then the other premise must assert that whatever thing is represented by S is represented by M, or that

$$\text{Every } S \text{ is an } M;$$

while, if the conclusion, S is P, is derived from either premise by a change of predicate, that premise may be written

$$S \text{ is } M;$$

and the other premise must assert that whatever characters are implied in P are implied in M, or that

$$\text{Whatever is } M \text{ is } P.$$

In either case, therefore, the syllogism must be capable of expression in the form,

$$S \text{ is } M; M \text{ is } P:$$
$$\therefore S \text{ is } P.$$

Finally, if the conclusion differs from either of its premises, both in subject and predicate, the form of statement of conclusion and premise may be so altered that they shall have a common term. This can always be done, for if P is the premise and C the conclusion, they may be stated thus:

$$\text{The state of things represented in } P \text{ is real,}$$
$$\text{and}$$
$$\text{The state of things represented in } C \text{ is real.}$$

In this case the other premise must in some form virtually assert that every state of things such as is represented by C is the state of things represented in P.

All valid reasoning, therefore, is of one general form; and in seeking to reduce all mental action to the formulæ of valid inference, we seek to reduce it to one single type.

An apparent obstacle to the reduction of all mental action to the type of valid inferences is the existence of fallacious reasoning. Every argument implies the truth of a general principle of inferential procedure (whether involving some matter of fact concerning the subject of argument, or merely a maxim relating to a system of signs), according to which it is a valid argument. If this principle is false, the argument is a fallacy; but neither a valid argument from false premises, nor an exceedingly weak, but not altogether illegitimate, induction or hypothesis, however its force may be over-estimated, however false its conclusion, is a fallacy.

Now words, taken just as they stand, if in the form of an argument, thereby do imply whatever fact may be necessary to make the argument conclusive; so that to the formal logician, who has to do only with the meaning of the words according to the proper principles of interpretation, and not with the intention of the speaker as guessed at from other indications, the only fallacies should be such as are simply absurd and contradictory, either because their conclusions are absolutely inconsistent with their premises, or because they connect propositions by a species of illative conjunction, by which they cannot under any circumstances be validly connected.

But to the psychologist an argument is valid only if the premises from which the mental conclusion is derived would be sufficient, if true, to justify it, either by themselves, or by the aid of other propositions which had previously been held for true. But it is easy to show that all inferences made by man, which are not valid in this sense, belong to four classes, viz.: 1. Those whose premises are false; 2. Those which have some little force, though only a little; 3. Those which result from confusion of one proposition with another; 4. Those which result from the indistinct apprehension, wrong application, or falsity, of a rule of inference. For, if a man were to commit a fallacy not of either of these classes, he would, from true premises conceived with perfect distinctness, without being led astray by any prejudice or other judgment serving as a rule of inference, draw a conclusion which had really not the least relevancy. If this could happen, calm consideration and care could be of little use in thinking, for caution only serves to insure our taking all the facts into account, and to make those which we do take account of, distinct; nor can coolness do anything more than to enable us to be cautious, and also to prevent our being affected by a passion in inferring that to be true which we wish were true, or which we fear may be true, or in following some other wrong rule of inference. But experience shows that the calm and careful consideration of the same distinctly conceived premises (including prejudices) will insure the pronouncement of the same judgment by all men. Now if a fallacy belongs to the first of these four classes and its premises are false, it is to be presumed that the procedure of the mind from these premises to the conclusion is either correct, or errs in one of the other three ways; for it cannot be supposed that the mere falsity of the premises should affect the procedure of reason when that falsity is not known to reason. If the fallacy belongs to the second class and has some force, however little, it is a legitimate probable argument, and belongs to the type of valid inference. If it is of the third class and results from the confusion of one proposition with another, this confusion must be owing to a resemblance between the two propositions; that is to say, the person reasoning, seeing that one proposition has some of the characters which belong to the other, concludes that it has all the essential characters of the other, and is equivalent to it. Now this is a hypothetic inference, which though it may be weak, and though its conclusion happens to be false, belongs to the type of valid inferences; and, therefore, as the *nodus* of the fallacy lies in this confusion, the procedure of the mind in these fallacies of the third class conforms to the formula of valid inference. If the fallacy belongs to the fourth class, it either results from wrongly applying or misapprehending a rule of inference, and so is a fallacy of confusion, or it results from adopting a wrong rule of inference. In this latter case, this rule is in fact taken as a premise, and therefore the false conclusion is owing merely to the falsity of a premise. In every fallacy, therefore, possible to the mind of man, the procedure of the mind conforms to the formula of valid inference.

The third principle whose consequences we have to deduce is, that, whenever we think, we have present to the consciousness some feeling, image, conception, or other representation, which serves as a sign. But it follows from our own existence (which is proved by the occurrence of ignorance and error) that everything which is present to us is a phenomenal manifestation of ourselves. This does not prevent its being a phenomenon of something without us, just as a rainbow is at once a manifestation both of the sun and of the rain. When we think, then, we ourselves, as we are at that moment, appear as a sign. Now a sign has, as such, three references: 1st, it is a sign *to* some thought which interprets it; 2d, it is a sign *for* some object to which in that thought it is equivalent; 3d, it is a sign, *in* some respect or quality, which brings it into connection with its object. Let us ask what the three correlates are to which a thought-sign refers.

1. When we think, to what thought does that thought-sign which is ourself address itself? It may, through the medium of outward expression, which it reaches perhaps only after considerable internal development, come to address itself to thought of another person. But whether this happens or not, it is always interpreted by a subsequent thought of our own. If, after any thought, the current of ideas flows on freely, it follows the law of mental association. In that case,

each former thought suggests something to the thought which follows it, i.e. is the sign of something to this latter. Our train of thought may, it is true, be interrupted. But we must remember that, in addition to the principal element of thought at any moment, there are a hundred things in our mind to which but a small fraction of attention or consciousness is conceded. It does not, therefore, follow, because a new constituent of thought gets the uppermost, that the train of thought which it displaces is broken off altogether. On the contrary, from our second principle, that there is no intuition or cognition not determined by previous cognitions, it follows that the striking in of a new experience is never an instantaneous affair, but is an *event* occupying time, and coming to pass by a continuous process. Its prominence in consciousness, therefore, must probably be the consummation of a growing process; and if so, there is no sufficient cause for the thought which had been the leading one just before, to cease abruptly and instantaneously. But if a train of thought ceases by gradually dying out, it freely follows its own law of association as long as it lasts, and there is no moment at which there is a thought belonging to this series, subsequently to which there is not a thought which interprets or repeats it. There is no exception, therefore, to the law that every thought-sign is translated or interpreted in a subsequent one, unless it be that all thought comes to an abrupt and final end in death.

2. The next question is: For what does the thought-sign stand— what does it name—what is its *suppositum?* The outward thing, undoubtedly, when a real outward thing is thought of. But still, as the thought is determined by a previous thought of the same object, it only refers to the thing through denoting this previous thought. Let us suppose, for example, that Toussaint is thought of, and first thought of as a *Negro,* but not distinctly as a man. If this distinctness is afterwards added, it is through the thought that a *Negro* is a *man;* that is to say, the subsequent thought, *man,* refers to the outward thing by being predicated of that previous thought, *Negro,* which has been had of that thing. If we afterwards think of Toussaint as a general, then we think that this Negro, this man, was a general. And so in every case the subsequent thought denotes what was thought in the previous thought.

3. The thought-sign stands for its object in the respect which is thought; that is to say, this respect is the immediate object of consciousness in the thought, or, in other words, it is the thought itself,

or at least what the thought is thought to be in the subsequent thought to which it is a sign.

We must now consider two other properties of signs which are of great importance in the theory of cognition. Since a sign is not identical with the thing signified, but differs from the latter in some respects, it must plainly have some characters which belong to it in itself, and have nothing to do with its representative function. These I call the *material* qualities of the sign. As examples of such qualities, take in the word "man" its consisting of three letters—in a picture, its being flat and without relief. In the second place, a sign must be capable of being connected (not in the reason but really) with another sign of the same object, or with the object itself. Thus, words would be of no value at all unless they could be connected into sentences by means of a real copula which joins signs of the same thing. The usefulness of some signs—as a weathercock, a tally, &c.— consists wholly in their being really connected with the very things they signify. In the case of a picture such a connection is not evident, but it exists in the power of association which connects the picture with the brain-sign which labels it. This real, physical connection of a sign with its object, either immediately or by its connection with another sign, I call the *pure demonstrative application* of the sign. Now the representative function of a sign lies neither in its material quality nor in its pure demonstrative application; because it is something which the sign is, not in itself or in a real relation to its object, but which it is *to a thought*, while both of the characters just defined belong to the sign independently of its addressing any thought. And yet if I take all the things which have certain qualities and physically connect them with another series of things, each to each, they become fit to be signs. If they are not regarded as such they are not actually signs, but they are so in the same sense, for example, in which an unseen flower can be said to be *red*, this being also a term relative to a mental affection.

Consider a state of mind which is a conception. It is a conception by virtue of having a *meaning*, a logical comprehension; and if it is applicable to any object, it is because that object has the characters contained in the comprehension of this conception. Now the logical comprehension of a thought is usually said to consist of the thoughts contained in it; but thoughts are events, acts of the mind. Two thoughts are two events separated in time, and one cannot literally be contained in the other. It may be said that all thoughts exactly similar are regarded as one; and that to say that one thought contains another, means that it contains one exactly similar to that other. But how can two thoughts be similar? Two objects can only be *regarded* as similar if they are compared and brought together in the mind. Thoughts have no existence except in the mind; only as they are regarded do they exist. Hence, two thoughts cannot *be* similar unless they are brought together in the mind. But, as to their existence, two thoughts are separated by an interval of time. We are too apt to imagine that we can frame a thought similar to a past thought, by matching it with the latter, as though this past thought were still present to us. But it is plain that the knowledge that one thought is similar to or in any way truly representative of another, cannot be derived from immediate perception, but must be an hypothesis (unquestionably fully justifiable by facts), and that therefore the formation of such a representing thought must be dependent upon a real effective force behind consciousness, and not merely upon a mental comparison. What we must mean, therefore, by saying that one concept is contained in another, is that we normally represent one to be in the other; that is, that we form a particular kind of judgment,[2] of which the subject signifies one concept and the predicate the other.

No thought in itself, then, no feeling in itself, contains any others, but is absolutely simple and unanalyzable; and to say that it is composed of other thoughts and feelings, is like saying that a movement upon a straight line is composed of the two movements of which it is the resultant; that is to say, it is a metaphor, or fiction, parallel to the truth. Every thought, however artificial and complex, is, so far as it is immediately present, a mere sensation without parts, and therefore, in itself, without similarity to any other, but incomparable with any other and absolutely *sui generis.*[3] Whatever is wholly incomparable with anything else is wholly inexplicable, because explanation consists in bringing things under general laws or under natural classes. Hence every thought, in so far as it is a feeling of a peculiar

2. A judgment concerning a minimum of information, for the theory of which see my paper on Comprehension and Extension, in the *Proceedings of the American Academy of Arts and Sciences,* vol. 7, p. 426.

3. Observe that I say *in itself.* I am not so wild as to deny that my sensation of red to-day is like my sensation of red yesterday. I only say that the similarity can *consist* only in the physiological force behind consciousness,—which leads me to say, I recognize this feeling the same as the former one, and so does not consist in a community of sensation.

sort, is simply an ultimate, inexplicable fact. Yet this does not conflict with my postulate that that fact should be allowed to stand as inexplicable; for, on the one hand, we never can think, "This is present to me," since, before we have time to make the reflection, the sensation is past, and, on the other hand, when once past, we can never bring back the quality of the feeling as it was *in and for itself,* or know what it was like *in itself,* or even discover the existence of this quality except by a corollary from our general theory of ourselves, and then not in its idiosyncrasy, but only as something present. But, as something present, feelings are all alike and require no explanation, since they contain only what is universal. So that nothing which we can truly predicate of feelings is left inexplicable, but only something which we cannot reflectively know. So that we do not fall into the contradiction of making the Mediate immediable. Finally, no present actual thought (which is a mere feeling) has any meaning, any intellectual value; for this lies not in what is actually thought, but in what this thought may be connected with in representation by subsequent thoughts; so that the meaning of a thought is altogether something virtual. It may be objected, that if no thought has any meaning, all thought is without meaning. But this is a fallacy similar to saying, that, if in no one of the successive spaces which a body fills there is room for motion, there is no room for motion throughout the whole. At no one instant in my state of mind is there cognition or representation, but in the relation of my states of mind at different instants there is.[4] In short, the Immediate (and therefore in itself unsusceptible of mediation—the Unanalyzable, the Inexplicable, the Unintellectual) runs in a continuous stream through our lives; it is the sum total of consciousness, whose mediation, which is the continuity of it, is brought about by a real effective force behind consciousness.

Thus, we have in thought three elements: 1st, the representative function which makes it a *representation;* 2d, the pure denotative application, or real connection, which brings one thought into *relation* with another; and 3d, the material quality, or how it feels, which gives thought its *quality.*[5]

That a sensation is not necessarily an intuition, or first impression of sense, is very evident in the case of the sense of beauty; and has

4. Accordingly, just as we say that a body is in motion, and not that motion is in a body we ought to say that we are in thought, and not that thoughts are in us.

5. On quality, relation, and representation, see *Proceedings of the American Academy of Arts and Sciences,* vol. 7, p. 293.

been shown, upon page 197, in the case of sound. When the sensation beautiful is determined by previous cognitions, it always arises as a predicate; that is, we think that something is beautiful. Whenever a sensation thus arises in consequence of others, induction shows that those others are more or less complicated. Thus, the sensation of a particular kind of sound arises in consequence of impressions upon the various nerves of the ear being combined in a particular way, and following one another with a certain rapidity. A sensation of color depends upon impressions upon the eye following one another in a regular manner, and with a certain rapidity. The sensation of beauty arises upon a manifold of other impressions. And this will be found to hold good in all cases. Secondly, all these sensations are in themselves simple, or more so than the sensations which give rise to them. Accordingly, a sensation is a simple predicate taken in place of a complex predicate; in other words, it fulfils the function of an hypothesis. But the general principle that every thing to which such and such a sensation belongs, has such and such a complicated series of predicates, is not one determined by reason (as we have seen), but is of an arbitrary nature. Hence, the class of hypothetic inferences which the arising of a sensation resembles, is that of reasoning from definition to definitum, in which the major premise is of an arbitrary nature. Only in this mode of reasoning, this premise is determined by the conventions of language, and expresses the occasion upon which a word is to be used; and in the formation of a sensation, it is determined by the constitution of our nature, and expresses the occasions upon which sensation, or a natural mental sign, arises. Thus, the sensation, so far as it represents something, is determined, according to a logical law, by previous cognitions; that is to say, these cognitions determine that there shall be a sensation. But so far as the sensation is a mere feeling of a particular sort, it is determined only by an inexplicable, occult power; and so far, it is not a representation, but only the material quality of a representation. For just as in reasoning from definition to definitum, it is indifferent to the logician how the defined word shall sound, or how many letters it shall contain, so in the case of this constitutional word, it is not determined by an inward law how it shall feel in itself. A feeling, therefore, as a feeling, is merely the *material quality* of a mental sign.

But there is no feeling which is not also a representation, a predicate of something determined logically by the feelings which precede it. For if there are any such feelings not predicates, they are the emotions. Now every emotion has a subject. If a man is angry, he is saying to himself that this or that is vile and outrageous. If he is in joy, he is saying "this is delicious." If he is wondering, he is saying "this is strange." In short, whenever a man feels, he is thinking of *something*. Even those passions which have no definite object—as melancholy—only come to consciousness through tinging the *objects of thought*. That which makes us look upon the emotions more as affections of self than other cognitions, is that we have found them more dependent upon our accidental situation at the moment than other cognitions; but that is only to say that they are cognitions too narrow to be useful. The emotions, as a little observation will show, arise when our attention is strongly drawn to complex and inconceivable circumstances. Fear arises when we cannot predict our fate; joy, in the case of certain indescribable and peculiarly complex sensations. If there are some indications that something greatly for my interest, and which I have anticipated would happen, may not happen; and if, after weighing probabilities, and inventing safeguards, and straining for further information, I find myself unable to come to any fixed conclusion in reference to the future, in the place of that intellectual hypothetic inference which I seek, the feeling of *anxiety* arises. When something happens for which I cannot account, I *wonder*. When I endeavor to realize to myself what I never can do, a pleasure in the future, I *hope*. "I do not understand you," is the phrase of an angry man. The indescribable, the ineffable, the incomprehensible, commonly excite emotion; but nothing is so chilling as a scientific explanation. Thus an emotion is always a simple predicate substituted by an operation of the mind for a highly complicated predicate. Now if we consider that a very complex predicate demands explanation by means of an hypothesis, that that hypothesis must be a simpler predicate substituted for that complex one; and that when we have an emotion, an hypothesis, strictly speaking, is hardly possible—the analogy of the parts played by emotion and hypothesis is very striking. There is, it is true, this difference between an emotion and an intellectual hypothesis, that we have reason to say in the case of the latter, that to whatever the simple hypothetic predicate can be applied, of that the complex predicate is true; whereas, in the case of an emotion this is a proposition for which no reason can be given, but which is determined merely by our emotional constitution. But this corresponds precisely to the difference between hypothesis and reasoning from definition to definitum, and thus it would appear that emotion is nothing but sensation. There appears to be a difference, however, between emotion and sensation, and I would state it as follows:

There is some reason to think that, corresponding to every feeling within us, some motion takes place in our bodies. This property of the thought-sign, since it has no rational dependence upon the meaning of the sign, may be compared with what I have called the material quality of the sign; but it differs from the latter inasmuch as it is not essentially necessary that it should be felt in order that there should be any thought-sign. In the case of a sensation, the manifold of impressions which precede and determine it are not of a kind, the bodily motion corresponding to which comes from any large ganglion or from the brain, and probably for this reason the sensation produces no great commotion in the bodily organism; and the sensation itself is not a thought which has a very strong influence upon the current of thought except by virtue of the information it may serve to afford. An emotion, on the other hand, comes much later in the development of thought—I mean, further from the first beginning of the cognition of its object—and the thoughts which determine it already have motions corresponding to them in the brain, or the chief ganglion; consequently, it produces large movements in the body, and independently of its representative value, strongly affects the current of thought. The animal motions to which I allude, are, in the first place and obviously, blushing, blenching, staring, smiling, scowling, pouting, laughing, weeping, sobbing, wriggling, flinching, trembling, being petrified, sighing, sniffing, shrugging, groaning, heartsinking, trepidation, swelling of the heart, etc., etc. To these may, perhaps, be added, in the second place, other more complicated actions, which nevertheless spring from a direct impulse and not from deliberation.

That which distinguishes both sensations proper and emotions from the feeling of a thought, is that in the case of the two former the material quality is made prominent, because the thought has no relation of reason to the thoughts which determine it, which exists in the last case and detracts from the attention given to the mere feeling. By there being no relation of reason to the determining thoughts, I mean that there is nothing in the content of the thought which explains why it should arise only on occasion of these determining thoughts. If there is such a relation of reason, if the thought is essentially limited in its application to these objects, then the thought comprehends a thought other than itself; in other words, it is then a complex thought. An incomplex thought can, therefore, be nothing but a sensation or emotion, having no rational character. This is very different from the ordinary doctrine, according to which the very highest and most metaphysical conceptions are absolutely simple. I shall be asked how such a conception of a *being* is to be analyzed, or whether I can ever define *one, two,* and *three,* without a diallele. Now I shall admit at once that neither of these conceptions can be separated into two others higher than itself; and in that sense, therefore, I fully admit that certain very metaphysical and eminently intellectual notions are absolutely simple. But though these concepts cannot be defined by genus and difference, there is another way in which they can be defined. All determination is by negation; we can first recognize any character only by putting an object which possesses it into comparison with an object which possesses it not. A conception, therefore, which was quite universal in every respect would be unrecognizable and impossible. We do not obtain the conception of Being, in the sense implied in the copula, by observing that all the things which we can think of have something in common, for there is no such thing to be observed. We get it by reflecting upon signs—words or thoughts;—we observe that different predicates may be attached to the same subject, and that each makes some conception applicable to the subject; then we imagine that a subject has something true of it merely because a predicate (no matter what) is attached to it,—and that we call Being. The conception of being is, therefore, a conception about a sign—a thought, or word;—and since it is not applicable to every sign, it is not primarily universal, although it is so in its mediate application to things. Being, therefore, may be defined; it may be defined, for example, as that which is common to the objects included in any class, and to the objects not included in the same class. But it is nothing new to say that metaphysical conceptions are primarily and at bottom thoughts about words, or thoughts about thoughts; it is the doctrine both of Aristotle (whose categories are parts of speech) and of Kant (whose categories are the characters of different kinds of propositions).

Sensation and the power of abstraction or attention may be regarded as, in one sense, the sole constituents of all thought. Having considered the former, let us now attempt some analysis of the latter. By the force of attention, an emphasis is put upon one of the objective elements of consciousness. This emphasis is, therefore, not itself an object of immediate consciousness; and in this respect it differs entirely from a feeling. Therefore, since the emphasis, nevertheless, consists in some effect upon consciousness, and so can exist only so far as it affects our knowledge; and since an act cannot be supposed to determine that which precedes it in time, this act can consist only in the capacity which the cognition emphasized has for producing an effect upon memory, or otherwise influencing subsequent thought. This is confirmed by the fact that attention is a matter of continuous quantity; for continuous quantity, so far as we know it, reduces itself in the last analysis to time. Accordingly, we find that attention does, in fact, produce a very great effect upon subsequent thought. In the first place, it strongly affects memory, a thought being remembered for a longer time the greater the attention originally paid to it. In the second place, the greater the attention, the closer the connection and the more accurate the logical sequence of thought. In the third place, by attention a thought may be recovered which has been forgotten. From these facts, we gather that attention is the power by which thought at one time is connected with and made to relate to thought at another time; or, to apply the conception of thought as a sign, that it is the *pure demonstrative application* of a thought-sign.

Attention is roused when the same phenomenon presents itself repeatedly on different occasions, or the same predicate in different subjects. We see that A has a certain character, that B has the same, C has the same; and this excites our attention, so that we say, *"These have this character."* Thus attention is an act of induction; but it is an induction which does not increase our knowledge, because our "these" covers nothing but the instances experienced. It is, in short, an argument from enumeration.

Attention produces effects upon the nervous system. These effects are habits, or nervous associations. A habit arises, when, having had the sensation of performing a certain act, m, on several occasions a, b, c, we come to do it upon every occurrence of the general event, l, of which a, b, and c are special cases. That is to say, by the cognition that

Every case of a, b, or c, is a case of m,

is determined the cognition that

Every case of l is a case of m.

Thus the formation of a habit is an induction, and is therefore neces-sarily connected with attention or abstraction. Voluntary actions re-sult from the sensations produced by habits, as instinctive actions result from our original nature.

We have thus seen that every sort of modification of consciousness —Attention, Sensation, and Understanding—is an inference. But the objection may be made that inference deals only with general terms, and that an image, or absolutely singular representation, cannot therefore be inferred.

"Singular" and "individual" are equivocal terms. A singular may mean that which can be but in one place at one time. In this sense it is not opposed to general. *The sun* is a singular in this sense, but, as is explained in every good treatise on logic, it is a general term. I may have a very general conception of Hermolaus Barbarus, but still I conceive him only as able to be in one place at one time. When an image is said to be singular, it is meant that it is absolutely determi-nate in all respects. Every possible character, or the negative thereof, must be true of such an image. In the words of the most eminent expounder of the doctrine, the image of a man "must be either of a white, or a black, or a tawny; a straight, or a crooked; a tall, or a low, or a middle-sized man." It must be of a man with his mouth open or his mouth shut, whose hair is precisely of such and such a shade, and whose figure has precisely such and such proportions. No statement of Locke has been so scouted by all friends of images as his denial that the "idea" of a triangle must be either of an obtuse-angled, right-angled, or acute-angled triangle. In fact, the image of a triangle must be of one, each of whose angles is of a certain number of degrees, minutes, and seconds.

This being so, it is apparent that no man has a *true* image of the road to his office, or of any other real thing. Indeed he has no image of it at all unless he can not only recognize it, but imagines it (truly or falsely) in all its infinite details. This being the case, it becomes very doubtful whether we ever have any such thing as an image in our imagination. Please, reader, to look at a bright red book, or other brightly colored object, and then to shut your eyes and say whether you *see* that color, whether brightly or faintly—whether, indeed, there is anything like sight there. Hume and the other followers of Berkeley maintain that there is no difference between the sight and the memory of the red book except in "their different degrees of force and vivacity." "The colors which the memory employs," says

Hume, "are faint and dull compared with those in which our original perceptions are clothed." If this were a correct statement of the difference, we should remember the book as being less red than it is; whereas, in fact, we remember the color with very great precision for a few moments [please to test this point, reader], although we do not see any thing like it. We carry away absolutely nothing of the color except the *consciousness that we could recognize it.* As a further proof of this, I will request the reader to try a little experiment. Let him call up, if he can, the image of a horse—not of one which he has ever seen, but of an imaginary one,—and before reading further let him by contemplation[6] fix the image in his memory . . . . . Has the reader done as requested? for I protest that it is not fair play to read further without doing so.—Now, the reader can say in general of what color that horse was, whether grey, bay, or black. But he probably cannot say *precisely* of what shade it was. He cannot state this as exactly as he could just after having *seen* such a horse. But why, if he had an image in his mind which no more had the general color than it had the particular shade, has the latter vanished so instantaneously from his memory while the former still remains? It may be replied, that we always forget the details before we do the more general characters; but that this answer is insufficient is, I think, shown by the extreme disproportion between the length of time that the exact shade of something looked at is remembered as compared

6. No person whose native tongue is English will need to be informed that contemplation is essentially (1) protracted (2) voluntary, and (3) an action, and that it is never used for that which is set forth to the mind in this act. A foreigner can convince himself of this by the proper study of English writers. Thus, Locke (*Essay concerning Human Understanding,* Book II, chap. 19, §1) says, "If it [an idea] be held there [in view] long under attentive consideration, 'tis *Contemplation";* and again (*Ibid.,* Book II, chap. 10, §1), "Keeping the *Idea,* which is brought into it [the mind] for some time actually in view, which is called *Contemplation."* This term is therefore unfitted to translate *Anschauung;* for this latter does not imply an act which is necessarily protracted or voluntary, and denotes most usually a mental presentation, sometimes a faculty, less often the reception of an impression in the mind, and seldom, if ever, an action. To the translation of *Anschauung* by intuition, there is, at least, no such insuperable objection. Etymologically the two words precisely correspond. The original philosophical meaning of intuition was a cognition of the present manifold in that character; and it is now commonly used, as a modern writer says, "to include all the products of the perceptive (external or internal) and imaginative faculties; every act of consciousness, in short, of which the immediate object is an *individual,* thing, act, or state of mind, presented under the condition of distinct existence in space and time." Finally, we have the authority of Kant's own example for translating his *Anschauung* by *Intuitus;* and, indeed, this is the common usage of Germans writing Latin. Moreover, *intuitiv* frequently replaces *anschauend* or *anschaulich.* If this constitutes a misunderstanding of Kant, it is one which is shared by himself and nearly all his countrymen.

with that instantaneous oblivion to the exact shade of the thing imagined, and the but slightly superior vividness of the memory of the thing seen as compared with the memory of the thing imagined.

The nominalists, I suspect, confound together thinking a triangle without thinking that it is either equilateral, isosceles, or scalene, and thinking a triangle without thinking whether it is equilateral, isosceles, or scalene.

It is important to remember that we have no intuitive power of distinguishing between one subjective mode of cognition and another; and hence often think that something is presented to us as a picture, while it is really constructed from slight data by the understanding. This is the case with dreams, as is shown by the frequent impossibility of giving an intelligible account of one without adding something which we feel was not in the dream itself. Many dreams, of which the waking memory makes elaborate and consistent stories, must probably have been in fact mere jumbles of these feelings of the ability to recognize this and that which I have just alluded to.

I will now go so far as to say that we have no images even in actual perception. It will be sufficient to prove this in the case of vision; for if no picture is seen when we look at an object, it will not be claimed that hearing, touch, and the other senses, are superior to sight in this respect. That the picture is not painted on the nerves of the retina is absolutely certain, if, as physiologists inform us, these nerves are needle-points pointing to the light and at distances considerably greater than the *minimum visibile.* The same thing is shown by our not being able to perceive that there is a large blind spot near the middle of the retina. If, then, we have a picture before us when we see, it is one constructed by the mind at the suggestion of previous sensations. Supposing these sensations to be signs, the understanding by reasoning from them could attain all the knowledge of outward things which we derive from sight, while the sensations are quite inadequate to forming an image or representation absolutely determinate. If we have such an image or picture, we must have in our minds a representation of a surface which is only a part of every surface we see, and we must see that each part, however small, has such and such a color. If we look from some distance at a speckled surface, it seems as if we did not see whether it were speckled or not; but if we have an image before us, it must appear to us either as speckled, or as not speckled. Again, the eye by education comes to distinguish minute differences of color; but if we see only absolutely determinate images, we must, no less before our eyes are trained than afterwards, see each color as particularly such and such a shade. Thus to suppose that we have an image before us when we see, is not only a hypothesis which explains nothing whatever, but is one which actually creates difficulties which require new hypotheses in order to explain them away.

One of these difficulties arises from the fact that the details are less easily distinguished than, and forgotten before, the general circumstances. Upon this theory, the general features exist in the details: the details are, in fact, the whole picture. It seems, then, very strange that that which exists only secondarily in the picture should make more impression than the picture itself. It is true that in an old painting the details are not easily made out; but this is because we know that the blackness is the result of time, and is no part of the picture itself. There is no difficulty in making out the details of the picture as it looks at present; the only difficulty is in guessing what it used to be. But if we have a picture on the retina, the minutest details are there as much as, nay, more than, the general outline and significancy of it. Yet that which must actually be seen, it is extremely difficult to recognize; while that which is only abstracted from what is seen is very obvious.

But the conclusive argument against our having any images, or absolutely determinate representations in perception, is that in that case we have the materials in each such representation for an infinite amount of conscious cognition, which we yet never become aware of. Now there is no meaning in saying that we have something in our minds which never has the least effect on what we are conscious of knowing. The most that can be said is, that when we see we are put in a condition in which we are able to get a very large and perhaps indefinitely great amount of knowledge of the visible qualities of objects.

Moreover, that perceptions are not absolutely determinate and singular is obvious from the fact that each sense is an abstracting mechanism. Sight by itself informs us only of colors and forms. No one can pretend that the images of sight are determinate in reference to taste. They are, therefore, so far general that they are neither sweet nor non-sweet, bitter nor non-bitter, having savor or insipid.

The next question is whether we have any general conceptions except in judgments. In perception, where we know a thing as existing, it is plain that there is a judgment that the thing exists, since a mere general concept of a thing is in no case a cognition of it as existing. It has usually been said, however, that we can call up any concept without making any judgment; but it seems that in this case we only arbitrarily suppose ourselves to have an experience. In order to conceive the number 7, I suppose, that is, I arbitrarily make the hypothesis or judgment, that there are certain points before my eyes, and I judge that these are seven. This seems to be the most simple and rational view of the matter, and I may add that it is the one which has been adopted by the best logicians. If this be the case, what goes by the name of the association of images is in reality an association of judgments. The association of ideas is said to proceed according to three principles—those of resemblance, of contiguity, and of causality. But it would be equally true to say that signs denote what they do on the three principles of resemblance, contiguity, and causality. There can be no question that anything *is* a sign of whatever is associated with it by resemblance, by contiguity, or by causality: nor can there be any doubt that any sign recalls the thing signified. So, then, the association of ideas consists in this, that a judgment occasions another judgment, of which it is the sign. Now this is nothing less nor more than inference.

Everything in which we take the least interest creates in us its own particular emotion, however slight this may be. This emotion is a sign and a predicate of the thing. Now, when a thing resembling this thing is presented to us, a similar emotion arises; hence, we immediately infer that the latter is like the former. A formal logician of the old school may say, that in logic no term can enter into the conclusion which had not been contained in the premises, and that therefore the suggestion of something new must be essentially different from inference. But I reply that that rule of logic applies only to those arguments which are technically called completed. We can and do reason—

> Elias was a man;
> ∴ He was mortal.

And this argument is just as valid as the full syllogism, although it is so only because the major premise of the latter happens to be true. If to pass from the judgment "Elias was a man" to the judgment "Elias was mortal," without actually saying to one's self that "All men are mortal," is not inference, then the term "inference" is used in so restricted a sense that inferences hardly occur outside of a logic-book.

What is here said of association by resemblance is true of all association. All association is by signs. Everything has its subjective or emotional qualities, which are attributed either absolutely or relatively, or by conventional imputation to anything which is a sign of it. And so we reason,

> The sign is such and such;
> ∴ The sign is that thing.

This conclusion receiving, however, a modification, owing to other considerations, so as to become—

> The sign is almost (is representative of) that thing.

We come now to the consideration of the last of the four principles whose consequences we were to trace; namely, that the absolutely incognizable is absolutely inconceivable. That upon Cartesian principles the very realities of things can never be known in the least, most competent persons must long ago have been convinced. Hence the breaking forth of idealism, which is essentially anti-Cartesian, in every direction, whether among empiricists (Berkeley, Hume), or among noologists (Hegel, Fichte). The principle now brought under discussion is directly idealistic; for, since the meaning of a word is the conception it conveys, the absolutely incognizable has no meaning because no conception attaches to it. It is, therefore, a meaningless word; and, consequently, whatever is meant by any term as "the real" is cognizable in some degree, and so is of the nature of a cognition, in the objective sense of that term.

At any moment we are in possession of certain information, that is, of cognitions which have been logically derived by induction and hypothesis from previous cognitions which are less general, less distinct, and of which we have a less lively consciousness. These in their turn have been derived from others still less general, less distinct, and less vivid; and so on back to the ideal[7] first, which is quite singular, and quite out of consciousness. This ideal first is the particular thing-in-itself. It does not exist *as such*. That is, there is no thing

7. By an ideal, I mean the limit which the possible cannot attain.

which is in-itself in the sense of not being relative to the mind, though things which are relative to the mind doubtless are, apart from that relation. The cognitions which thus reach us by this infinite series of inductions and hypotheses (which though infinite *a parte ante logice,* is yet as one continuous process not without a beginning *in time*) are of two kinds, the true and the untrue, or cognitions whose objects are *real* and those whose objects are *unreal.* And what do we mean by the real? It is a conception which we must first have had when we discovered that there was an unreal, an illusion; that is, when we first corrected ourselves. Now the distinction for which alone this fact logically called, was between an *ens* relative to private inward determinations, to the negations belonging to idiosyncrasy, and an *ens* such as would stand in the long run. The real, then, is that which, sooner or later, information and reasoning would finally result in, and which is therefore independent of the vagaries of me and you. Thus, the very origin of the conception of reality shows that this conception essentially involves the notion of a COMMUNITY, without definite limits, and capable of an indefinite increase of knowledge. And so those two series of cognitions—the real and the unreal —consist of those which, at a time sufficiently future, the community will always continue to reaffirm; and of those which, under the same conditions, will ever after be denied. Now, a proposition whose falsity can never be discovered, and the error of which therefore is absolutely incognizable, contains, upon our principle, absolutely no error. Consequently, that which is thought in these cognitions is the real, as it really is. There is nothing, then, to prevent our knowing outward things as they really are, and it is most likely that we do thus know them in numberless cases, although we can never be absolutely certain of doing so in any special case.

But it follows that since no cognition of ours is absolutely determinate, generals must have a real existence. Now this scholastic realism is usually set down as a belief in metaphysical fictions. But, in fact, a realist is simply one who knows no more recondite reality than that which is represented in a true representation. Since, therefore, the word "man" is true of something, that which "man" means is real. The nominalist must admit that man is truly applicable to something; but he believes that there is beneath this a thing in itself, an incognizable reality. His is the metaphysical figment. Modern nominalists are mostly superficial men, who do not know, as the more thorough Roscellinus and Occam did, that a reality which has no representation is one which has no relation and no quality. The great argument for nominalism is that there is no man unless there is some particular man. That, however, does not affect the realism of Scotus; for although there is no man of whom all further determination can be denied, yet there is a man, abstraction being made of all further determination. There is a real difference between man irrespective of what the other determinations may be, and man with this or that particular series of determinations, although undoubtedly this difference is only relative to the mind and not *in re.* Such is the position of Scotus.[8] Occam's great objection is, there can be no real distinction which is not *in re,* in the thing-in-itself; but this begs the question, for it is itself based only on the notion that reality is something independent of representative relation.[9]

Such being the nature of reality in general, in what does the reality of the mind consist? We have seen that the content of consciousness, the entire phenomenal manifestation of mind, is a sign resulting from inference. Upon our principle, therefore, that the absolutely incognizable does not exist, so that the phenomenal manifestation of a substance is the substance, we must conclude that the mind is a sign developing according to the laws of inference. What distinguishes a man from a word? There is a distinction doubtless. The material qualities, the forces which constitute the pure denotative application, and the meaning of the human sign, are all exceedingly complicated in comparison with those of the word. But these differences are only relative. What other is there? It may be said that man is conscious, while a word is not. But consciousness is a very vague term. It may mean that emotion which accompanies the reflection that we have animal life. This is a consciousness which is dimmed when animal life is at its ebb in old age, or sleep, but which is not dimmed when the spiritual life is at its ebb; which is the more lively the better *animal* a man is, but which is not so, the better *man* he is. We do not attribute this sensation to words, because we have reason to believe that it is dependent upon the possession of an animal body. But this consciousness, being a mere sensation, is only a part of the *material quality* of the man-sign. Again, consciousness is sometimes used to signify the *I think,* or unity in thought; but this

8. "Eadem natura est, quæ in existentia per gradum singularitatis est determinata, et in intellectu, hoc est ut habet relationem ad intellectum ut cognitum ad cognoscens, est indeterminata."—*Quæstiones Subtillissimæ,* lib. 7, qu. 18.
9. See his argument *Summa logices,* part 1, cap. 16.

unity is nothing but consistency, or the recognition of it. Consistency belongs to every sign, so far as it is a sign; and therefore every sign, since it signifies primarily that it is a sign, signifies its own consistency. The man-sign acquires information, and comes to mean more than he did before. But so do words. Does not electricity mean more now than it did in the days of Franklin? Man makes the word, and the word means nothing which the man has not made it mean, and that only to some man. But since man can think only by means of words or other external symbols, these might turn round and say: "You mean nothing which we have not taught you, and then only so far as you address some word as the interpretant of your thought." In fact, therefore, men and words reciprocally educate each other; each increase of a man's information involves and is involved by, a corresponding increase of a word's information.

Without fatiguing the reader by stretching this parallelism too far, it is sufficient to say that there is no element whatever of man's consciousness which has not something corresponding to it in the word; and the reason is obvious. It is that the word or sign which man uses *is* the man himself. For, as the fact that every thought is a sign, taken in conjunction with the fact that life is a train of thought, proves that man is a sign; so, that every thought is an *external* sign, proves that man is an external sign. That is to say, the man and the external sign are identical, in the same sense in which the words *homo* and *man* are identical. Thus my language is the sum total of myself; for the man is the thought.

It is hard for man to understand this, because he persists in identifying himself with his will, his power over the animal organism, with brute force. Now the organism is only an instrument of thought. But the identity of a man consists in the *consistency* of what he does and thinks, and consistency is the intellectual character of a thing; that is, is its expressing something.

Finally, as what anything really is, is what it may finally come to be known to be in the ideal state of complete information, so that reality depends on the ultimate decision of the community; so thought is what it is, only by virtue of its addressing a future thought which is in its value as thought identical with it, though more developed. In this way, the existence of thought now, depends on what is to be hereafter; so that it has only a potential existence, dependent on the future thought of the community.

The individual man, since his separate existence is manifested

only by ignorance and error, so far as he is anything apart from his
fellows, and from what he and they are to be, is only a negation. This
is man,

> proud man,
> Most ignorant of what he's most assured,
> His glassy essence.

Grounds of Validity of the Laws of Logic: Further Consequences of Four Incapacities

P 41: Journal of
Speculative Philosophy *2(1869):193–208*

If, as I maintained in an article in the last number of this Journal,
every judgment results from inference, to doubt every inference is
to doubt everything. It has often been argued that absolute scepticism is self-contradictory; but this is a mistake: and even if it were not
so, it would be no argument against the absolute sceptic, inasmuch
as he does not admit that no contradictory propositions are true.
Indeed, it would be impossible to move such a man, for his scepticism
consists in considering every argument and never deciding upon its
validity; he would, therefore, act in this way in reference to the
arguments brought against him.

But then there are no such beings as absolute sceptics. Every
exercise of the mind consists in inference, and so, though there are
inanimate objects without beliefs, there are no intelligent beings in
that condition.

Yet it is quite possible that a person should doubt every principle
of inference. He may not have studied logic, and though a logical
formula may sound very obviously true to him, he may feel a little
uncertain whether some subtle deception may not lurk in it. Indeed,
I certainly shall have, among the most cultivated and respected of my

readers, those who deny that those laws of logic which men generally admit have universal validity. But I address myself, also, to those who have no such doubts, for even to them it may be interesting to consider how it is that these principles come to be true. Finally, having put forth in former numbers of this Journal some rather heretical principles of philosophical research, one of which is that nothing can be admitted to be absolutely inexplicable, it behooves me to take up a challenge which has been given me to show how upon my principles the validity of the laws of logic can be other than inexplicable.

I shall be arrested, at the outset, by a sweeping objection to my whole undertaking. It will be said that my deduction of logical principles, being itself an argument, depends for its whole virtue upon the truth of the very principles in question; so that whatever my proof may be, it must take for granted the very things to be proved. But to this I reply, that I am neither addressing absolute sceptics, nor men in any state of fictitious doubt whatever. I require the reader to be candid; and if he becomes convinced of a conclusion, to admit it. There is nothing to prevent a man's perceiving the force of certain special arguments, although he does not yet know that a certain general law of arguments holds good; for the general rule may hold good in some cases and not in others. A man may reason well without understanding the principles of reasoning, just as he may play billiards well without understanding analytical mechanics. If you, the reader, actually find that my arguments have a convincing force with you, it is a mere pretence to call them illogical.

That if one sign denotes generally everything denoted by a second, and this second denotes generally everything denoted by a third, then the first denotes generally everything denoted by the third, is not doubted by anybody who distinctly apprehends the meaning of these words. The deduction of the general form of syllogism, therefore, will consist only of an explanation of the *suppositio communis.*[1] Now, what the formal logician means by an expression

---

1. The word *suppositio* is one of the useful technical terms of the middle ages which was condemned by the purists of the *renaissance* as incorrect. The early logicians made a distinction between *significatio* and *suppositio. Significatio* is defined as "rei per vocem secundum placitum representatio." It is a mere affair of lexicography, and depends on a special convention *(secundum placitum),* and not on a general principle. *Suppositio* belongs, not directly to the *vox,* but to the *vox* as having this or that *significatio.* "Unde significatio prior est suppositione et differunt in hoc, quia significatio est vocis, suppositio vero est termini jam compositi ex voce et significa-

of the form, "Every *M* is *P*," is that anything of which *M* is predicable is *P*; thus, if *S* is *M*, that *S* is *P*. The premise that "Every *M* is *P*" may, therefore, be denied; but to admit it, unambiguously, in the sense intended, is to admit that the inference is good that *S* is *P* if *S* is *M*. He, therefore, who does not deny that *S* is *P*—*M*, *S*, *P*, being any terms such that *S* is *M* and every *M* is *P*—denies nothing that the formal logician maintains in reference to this matter; and he who does deny this, simply is deceived by an ambiguity of language. How we come to make any judgments in the sense of the above "Every *M* is *P*," may be understood from the theory of reality put forth in the article in the last number. It was there shown that real things are of a cognitive and therefore significative nature, so that the real is that which signifies something real. Consequently, to predicate anything of anything real is to predicate it of that of which that subject [the real] is itself predicated; for to predicate one thing of another is to state that the former is a sign of the latter.

These considerations show the reason of the validity of the formula,

$$S \text{ is } M; \ M \text{ is } P:$$
$$\therefore S \text{ is } P.$$

They hold good whatever *S* and *P* may be, provided that they be such that any middle term between them can be found. That *P* should be a negative term, therefore, or that *S* should be a particular term, would not interfere at all with the validity of this formula. Hence, the following formulæ are also valid:

$$S \text{ is } M; \ M \text{ is not } P:$$
$$\therefore S \text{ is not } P.$$

---

tione." The various *suppositiones* which may belong to one word with one *significatio* are the different senses in which the word may be taken, according to the general principles of the language or of logic. Thus, the word *table* has different *significationes* in the expressions "table of logarithms" and "writing-table"; but the word *man* has one and the same *significatio*, and only different *suppositiones*, in the following sentences: "A man is an animal," "a butcher is a man," "man cooks his food," "man appeared upon the earth at such a date," &c. Some later writers have endeavored to make *"acceptio"* do service for *"suppositio";* but it seems to me better, now that scientific terminology is no longer forbidden, to revive *supposition.* I should add that as the principles of logic and language for the different uses of the different parts of speech are different, *supposition* must be restricted to the acceptation of a *substantive.* The term *copulatio* was used for the acceptation of an adjective or verb.

Some *S* is *M; M* is *P:*
∴ Some *S* is *P.*

Some *S* is *M; M* is not *P:*
∴ Some *S* is not *P.*

Moreover, as all that class of inferences which depend upon the introduction of relative terms can be reduced to the general form, they also are shown to be valid. Thus, it is proved to be correct to reason thus:

Every relation of a subject to its predicate is
a relation of the relative "not *X*'d, except
by the *X* of some," to its correlate, where *X*
is any relative I please.

Every relation of "man" to "animal" is a
relation of a subject to its predicate.
∴ Every relation of "man" to "animal" is a relation
of the relative "not *X*'d, except by the *X* of
some," to its correlate, where *X* is any
relative I please.

Every relation of the relative "not *X*'d, except
by the *X* of some," to its correlate, where *X*
is any relative I please, is a relation of the
relative "not *headed,* except by the *head* of
some," to its correlate.
∴ Every relation of "man" to "animal" is a relation
of the relative "not headed, except by the
head of some," to its correlate.[2]

At the same time, as will be seen from this example, the proof of the validity of these inferences depends upon the assumption of the truth of certain general statements concerning relatives. These formulæ can all be deduced from the principle, that in a system of signs in which no sign is taken in two different senses, two signs which

2. "If any one will by ordinary syllogism prove that because every man is an animal, therefore every head of a man is a head of an animal, I shall be ready to—set him another question."—*De Morgan:* "On the Syllogism No. IV, and on the Logic of Relations."

differ only in their manner of representing their object, but which are equivalent in meaning, can always be substituted for one another. Any case of the falsification of this principle would be a case of the dependence of the mode of existence of the thing represented upon the mode of this or that representation of it, which, as has been shown in the article in the last number, is contrary to the nature of reality.

The next formula of syllogism to be considered is the following:

$$S \text{ is other than } P; \ M \text{ is } P:$$
$$\therefore S \text{ is other than } M.$$

The meaning of "not" or "other than" seems to have greatly perplexed the German logicians, and it may be, therefore, that it is used in different senses. If so, I propose to defend the validity of the above formula only when *other than* is used in a particular sense. By saying that one thing or class is other than a second, I mean that any third whatever is identical with the class which is composed of that third and of whatever is, at once, the first and second. For example, if I say that rats are not mice, I mean that any third class as dogs is identical with dogs and rats-which-are-mice; that is to say, the addition of rats-which-are-mice, to anything, leaves the latter just what it was before. This being all that I mean by S is other than P, I mean absolutely the same thing when I say that S is other than P, that I do when I say that P is other than S; and the same when I say that S is other than M, that I do when I say that M is other than S. Hence the above formula is only another way of writing the following:

$$M \text{ is } P; \ P \text{ is not } S:$$
$$\therefore M \text{ is not } S.$$

But we have already seen that this is valid.

A very similar formula to the above is the following:

$$S \text{ is } M; \ \text{some } S \text{ is } P:$$
$$\therefore \text{Some } M \text{ is } P.$$

By saying that some of a class is of any character, I mean simply that no statement which implies that none of that class is of that character is true. But to say that none of that class is of that character, is, as I take the word "not," to say that nothing of that character is of that class. Consequently, to say that some of *A* is *B*, is, as I understand words and in the only sense in which I defend this formula, to say that some *B* is *A*. In this way the formula is reduced to the following, which has already been shown to be valid:

$$\text{Some } P \text{ is } S; S \text{ is } M:$$
$$\therefore \text{Some } P \text{ is } M.$$

The only demonstrative syllogisms which are not included among the above forms are the Theophrastean moods, which are all easily reduced by means of simple conversions.

Let us now consider what can be said against all this, and let us take up the objections which have actually been made to the syllogistic formulæ, beginning with those which are of a general nature and then examining those sophisms which have been pronounced irresolvable by the rules of ordinary logic.

It is a very ancient notion that no proof can be of any value, because it rests on premises which themselves equally require proof, which again must rest on other premises, and so back to infinity. This really does show that nothing can be proved beyond the possibility of a doubt; that no argument could be legitimately used against an absolute sceptic; and that inference is only a transition from one cognition to another, and not the creation of a cognition. But the objection is intended to go much further than this, and to show (as it certainly seems to do) that inference not only cannot produce *infallible* cognition, but that it cannot *produce* cognition at all. It is true, that since some judgment precedes every judgment inferred, either the first premises were not inferred, or there have been no first premises. But it does not follow that because there has been no first in a series, therefore that series has had no beginning in time; for the series may be *continuous,* and may have begun gradually, as was shown in an article in No. 3 of this volume, where this difficulty has already been resolved.

A somewhat similar objection has been made by Locke and others, to the effect that the ordinary demonstrative syllogism is a *petitio principii,* inasmuch as the conclusion is already implicitly stated in the major premise. Take, for example, the syllogism,

All men are mortal;
Socrates is a man:
∴ Socrates is mortal.

This attempt to prove that Socrates is mortal begs the question, it is said, since if the conclusion is denied by any one, he thereby denies that all men are mortal. But what such considerations really prove is that the syllogism is demonstrative. To call it a *petitio principii* is a mere confusion of language. It is strange that philosophers, who are so suspicious of the words *virtual* and *potential,* should have allowed this "implicit" to pass unchallenged. A *petitio principii* consists in reasoning from the unknown to the unknown. Hence, a logician who is simply engaged in stating what general forms of argument are valid, can, at most, have nothing more to do with the consideration of this fallacy than to note those cases in which from logical principles a premise of a certain form cannot be better known than a conclusion of the corresponding form. But it is plainly beyond the province of the logician, who has only proposed to state what forms of facts involve what others, to inquire whether man can have a knowledge of universal propositions without a knowledge of every particular contained under them, by means of natural insight, divine revelation, induction, or testimony. The only *petitio principii,* therefore, which he can notice is the assumption of the conclusion itself in the premise; and this, no doubt, those who call the syllogism a *petitio principii* believe is done in that formula. But the proposition "All men are mortal" does not in itself involve the statement that Socrates is mortal, but only that "whatever has man truly predicated of it is mortal." In other words, the *conclusion* is not involved in the meaning of the premise, but only the *validity of the syllogism.* So that this objection merely amounts to arguing that the syllogism is not valid, because it is demonstrative.[3]

A much more interesting objection is that a syllogism is a purely mechanical process. It proceeds according to a bare rule or formula; and a machine might be constructed which would so transpose the terms of premises. This being so (and it is so), it is argued that this cannot be *thought;* that there is no life in it. Swift has ridiculed the

3. Mr. Mill thinks the syllogism is merely a formula for recalling forgotten facts. Whether he means to deny, what all logicians since Kant have held, that the syllogism serves to render confused thoughts distinct, or whether he does not know that this is the usual doctrine, does not appear.

syllogism in the "Voyage to Laputa," by describing a machine for making science:

> By this contrivance, the most ignorant person, at a reasonable charge, and with little bodily labor, might write books in philosophy, poetry, politics, laws, mathematics, and theology, without the least assistance from genius or study.

The idea involved in this objection seems to be that it requires mind to apply any formula or use any machine. If, then, this mind is itself only another formula, it requires another mind behind it to set it into operation, and so on *ad infinitum*. This objection fails in much the same way that the first one which we considered failed. It is as though a man should address a land surveyor as follows:—"You do not make a true representation of the land; you only measure lengths from point to point—that is to say, lines. If you observe angles, it is only to solve triangles and obtain the lengths of their sides. And when you come to make your map, you use a pencil which can only make lines, again. So, you have to do solely with lines. But the land is a surface; and no number of lines, however great, will make any surface, however small. You, therefore, fail entirely to represent the land." The surveyor, I think, would reply, "Sir, you have proved that my lines cannot make up the land, and that, therefore, my map *is not* the land. I never pretended that it was. But that does not prevent it from truly representing the land, as far as it goes. It cannot, indeed, represent every blade of grass; but it does not represent that there is not a blade of grass where there is. To abstract from a circumstance is not to deny it." Suppose the objector were, at this point, to say, "To abstract from a circumstance *is* to deny it. Wherever your map does not represent a blade of grass, it represents there is no blade of grass. Let us take things on their own valuation." Would not the surveyor reply: "This map is my description of the country. Its own valuation can be nothing but what I say, and all the world understands, that I mean by it. Is it very unreasonable that I should demand to be taken as I mean, especially when I succeed in making myself understood?" What the objector's reply to this question would be, I leave it to any one to say who thinks his position well taken. Now this line of objection is parallel to that which is made against the syllogism. It is shown that no number of syllogisms can constitute the sum total of any mental action, however restricted. This may be freely granted, and yet it will not follow that the syllogism does not truly represent the mental action, as far as it purports to represent it at all. There is reason to believe that the action of the mind is, as it were, a continuous movement. Now the doctrine embodied in syllogistic formulæ (so far as it applies to the mind at all) is, that if two successive positions, occupied by the mind in this movement, be taken, they will be found to have certain relations. It is true that no number of successions of positions can make up a continuous movement; and this, I suppose, is what is meant by saying that a syllogism is a dead formula, while thinking is a living process. But the reply is that the syllogism is not intended to represent the mind, as to its life or deadness, but only as to the relation of its different judgments concerning the same thing. And it should be added that the relation between syllogism and thought does not spring from considerations of formal logic, but from those of psychology. All that the formal logician has to say is, that if facts capable of expression in such and such forms of words are true, another fact whose expression is related in a certain way to the expression of these others is also true.

Hegel taught that ordinary reasoning is "one-sided." A part of what he meant was that by such inference a part only of all that is true of an object can be learned, owing to the generality or abstractedness of the predicates inferred. This objection is, therefore, somewhat similar to the last; for the point of it is that no number of syllogisms would give a complete knowledge of the object. This, however, presents a difficulty which the other did not; namely, that if nothing incognizable exists, and all knowledge is by mental action, by mental action everything is cognizable. So that if by syllogism everything is not cognizable, syllogism does not exhaust the modes of mental action. But grant the validity of this argument and it proves too much; for it makes, not the syllogism particularly, but all finite knowledge to be worthless. However much we know, more may come to be found out. Hence, all can never be known. This seems to contradict the fact that nothing is absolutely incognizable; and it would really do so *if our knowledge* were something absolutely limited. For, to say that all can never be known, means that information may increase beyond any assignable point; that is, that an absolute termination of all increase of knowledge is absolutely incognizable, and therefore does not exist. In other words, the proposition merely means that the sum of all that will be known up to any time, however advanced, into the future, has a ratio less than any assignable ratio to all that may be known at a time still more advanced. This does not contradict the fact that everything is cognizable; it only contradicts a proposition, which no one can maintain, that everything will be known at some time some number of years into the future. It may, however, very justly be said that the difficulty still remains, how at every future time, however late, there can be something yet to happen. It is no longer a contradiction, but it is a difficulty; that is to say, *lengths of time* are shown not to afford an adequate conception of futurity in general; and the question arises, in what other way we are to conceive of it. I might indeed, perhaps, fairly drop the question here, and say that the difficulty had become so entirely removed from the syllogism in particular, that the formal logician need not feel himself specially called on to consider it. The solution, however, is very simple. It is that we conceive of the future, as a whole, by considering that this *word*, like any other general term, as "inhabitant of St. Louis," may be taken distributively or collectively. We conceive of the infinite, therefore, not directly or on the side of its infinity, but by means of a consideration concerning words or a second intention.

Another objection to the syllogism is that its "therefore" is merely subjective; that, because a certain conclusion syllogistically follows from a premise, it does not follow that the fact denoted by the conclusion really depends upon the fact denoted by the premise, so that the syllogism does not represent things as they really are. But it has been fully shown that if the facts are as the premises represent, they are also as the conclusion represents. Now this is a purely objective statement: therefore, there is a real connection between the facts stated as premises and those stated as conclusion. It is true that there is often an appearance of reasoning deductively from effects to causes. Thus we may reason as follows:—"There is smoke; there is never smoke without fire: hence, there has been fire." Yet smoke is not the cause of fire, but the effect of it. Indeed, it is evident, that in many cases an event is a demonstrative sign of a certain previous event having occurred. Hence, we can reason deductively from relatively future to relatively past, whereas causation really determines events in the direct order of time. Nevertheless, if we can thus reason against the stream of time, it is because there really are such facts as that "If there is smoke, there has been fire," in which the following event is the antecedent. Indeed, if we consider the manner in which such a proposition became known to us, we shall find that what it really means is that "If we find smoke, we *shall* find evidence on the whole that there has been fire"; and this, if reality consists in the agreement that the whole community would eventually come to, is the very same thing as to say that there really has been fire. In short, the whole present difficulty is resolved instantly by this theory of reality, because it makes all reality something which is constituted by an event indefinitely future.

Another objection, for which I am quite willing to allow a great German philosopher the whole credit, is that sometimes the conclusion is false, although both the premises and the syllogistic form are correct.[4] Of this he gives the following examples. From the middle term that a wall has been painted blue, it may correctly be concluded that it is blue; but notwithstanding this syllogism it may be green if it has also received a coat of yellow, from which last circumstance by itself it would follow that it is yellow. If from the middle term of the sensuous faculty it be concluded that man is neither good nor bad, since neither can be predicated of the sensuous, the syllogism is correct; but the conclusion is false, since of man in the concrete, spirituality is equally true, and may serve as middle term in an opposite syllogism. From the middle term of the gravitation of the planets, satellites, and comets, towards the sun, it follows correctly that these bodies fall into the sun; but they do not fall into it, because (!) they equally gravitate to their own centres, or, in other words (!!), they are supported by centrifugal force. Now, does Hegel mean to say that these syllogisms satisfy the rules for syllogism given by those who defend syllogism? or does he mean to grant that they do not satisfy *those* rules, but to set up some rules of his own for syllogism which shall insure its yielding false conclusions from true premises? If the latter, he ignores the real issue, which is whether the syllogism as defined by the rules of formal logic is correct, and not whether the syllogism as represented by Hegel is correct. But if he means that the above examples satisfy the usual definition of a true syllogism, he is mistaken. The first, stated in form, is as follows:

> Whatever has been painted blue is blue;
> This wall has been painted blue:
> ∴ This wall is blue.

4. "So zeigt sich jener Schlussatz dadurch als falsch, obgleich für sich dessen Prämissen und ebenso dessen Consequenz ganz richtig sind."—Hegel's *Werke*, vol. v, p. 124.

Now "painted blue" may mean painted with blue paint, or painted so as to be blue. If, in the example, the former were meant, the major premise would be false. As he has stated that it is true, the latter meaning of "painted blue" must be the one intended. Again, "blue" may mean blue at some time, or blue at this time. If the latter be meant, the major premise is plainly false; therefore, the former is meant. But the conclusion is said to contradict the statement that the wall is yellow. If blue were here taken in the more general sense, there would be no such contradiction. Hence, he means in the conclusion that this wall is now blue; that is to say, he reasons thus:

> Whatever has been made blue has been blue;
> This has been made blue:
> ∴ This is blue now.

Now substituting letters for the subjects and predicates, we get the form,

$$M \text{ is } P;$$
$$S \text{ is } M:$$
$$\therefore S \text{ is } Q.$$

This is not a syllogism in the ordinary sense of that term, or in any sense in which anybody maintains that the syllogism is valid.

The second example given by Hegel, when written out in full, is as follows:

> Sensuality is neither good nor bad;
> Man *has* (not *is*) sensuality:
> ∴ Man is neither good nor bad.

Or, the same argument may be stated as follows:

> The sensuous, *as such,* is neither good nor bad;
> Man is sensuous:
> ∴ Man is neither good nor bad.

When letters are substituted for subject and predicate in either of these arguments, it takes the form,

$$M \text{ is } P;$$
$$S \text{ is } N:$$
$$\therefore S \text{ is } P.$$

This, again, bears but a very slight resemblance to a syllogism.

The third example, when stated at full length, is as follows:

Whatever tends towards the sun, *on*
the whole, falls into the sun;
The planets tend toward the sun:
∴ The planets fall into the sun.

This is a fallacy similar to the last.

I wonder that this eminent logician did not add to his list of examples of correct syllogism the following:

It either rains, or it does not rain;
It does not rain:
∴ It rains.

This is fully as deserving of serious consideration as any of those which he has brought forward. The rainy day and the pleasant day are both, in the first place, day. Secondly, each is the negation of a day. It is indifferent which be regarded as the positive. The pleasant is Other to the rainy, and the rainy is in like manner Other to the pleasant. Thus, both are equally Others. Both are Others of each other, or each is Other for itself. So this day being other than rainy, that to which it is Other is itself. But it is Other than itself. Hence, it is itself Rainy.

Some sophisms have, however, been adduced, mostly by the Eleatics and Sophists, which really are extremely difficult to resolve by syllogistic rules; and according to some modern authors this is actually impossible. These sophisms fall into three classes: *1st,* those which relate to continuity; *2d,* those which relate to consequences of supposing things to be other than they are; *3d,* those which relate to propositions which imply their own falsity. Of the first class, the most celebrated are Zeno's arguments concerning motion. One of these is, that if Achilles overtakes a tortoise in any finite time, and the tortoise has the start of him by a distance which may be called *a,* then

Achilles has to pass over the sum of distances represented by the polynomial

$$\tfrac{1}{2}a \;+\; \tfrac{1}{4}a \;+\; \tfrac{1}{8}a \;+\; \tfrac{1}{16}a \;+\; \tfrac{1}{32}a \;\textit{&c.}$$

up to infinity. Every term of this polynomial is finite, and it has an infinite number of terms; consequently, Achilles must in a finite time pass over a distance equal to the sum of an infinite number of finite distances. Now this distance must be infinite, because no finite distance, however small, can be multiplied by an infinite number without giving an infinite distance. So that even if none of these finite distances were larger than the smallest (which is finite since all are finite), the sum of the whole would be infinite. But Achilles cannot pass over an infinite distance in a finite time; therefore, he cannot overtake the tortoise in any time, however great.

The solution of this fallacy is as follows: The conclusion is dependent on the fact that Achilles cannot overtake the tortoise without passing over an infinite number of terms of that series of finite distances. That is, no case of his overtaking the tortoise would be a case of his not passing over a non-finite number of terms; that is (by simple conversion), no case of his not passing over a non-finite number of terms would be a case of his overtaking the tortoise. But if he does not pass over a non-finite number of terms, he either passes over a finite number, or he passes over none; and conversely. Consequently, nothing more has been said than that every case of his passing over only a finite number of terms, or of his not passing over any, is a case of his not overtaking the tortoise. Consequently, nothing more can be concluded than that he passes over a distance greater than the sum of any finite number of the above series of terms. But because a quantity is greater than any quantity of a certain series, it does not follow that it is greater than any quantity.

In fact, the reasoning in this sophism may be exhibited as follows: —We start with the series of numbers,

$$\tfrac{1}{2}a$$
$$\tfrac{1}{2}a \;+\; \tfrac{1}{4}a$$
$$\tfrac{1}{2}a \;+\; \tfrac{1}{4}a \;+\; \tfrac{1}{8}a$$
$$\tfrac{1}{2}a \;+\; \tfrac{1}{4}a \;+\; \tfrac{1}{8}a \;+\; \tfrac{1}{16}a$$
$$\textit{&c.} \;\; \textit{&c.} \;\; \textit{&c.}$$

Then, the implied argument is

> Any number of this series is less than a;
> But any number you please is less than the number of terms
>   of this series:
> Hence, any number you please is less than a.

This involves an obvious confusion between the number of terms and the value of the greatest term.

Another argument by Zeno against motion, is that a body fills a space no larger than itself. In that place there is no room for motion. Hence, while in the place where it is, it does not move. But it never is other than in the place where it is. Hence, it never moves. Putting this into form, it will read:

> No body in a place no larger than itself is moving;
> But every body is a body in a place no larger than itself:
> ∴ No body is moving.

The error of this consists in the fact that the minor premise is only true in the sense that during a time sufficiently short the space occupied by a body is as little larger than itself as you please. All that can be inferred from this is, that during no time a body will move no distance.

All the arguments of Zeno depend on supposing that a *continuum* has ultimate parts. But a *continuum* is precisely that, every part of which has parts, in the same sense. Hence, he makes out his contradictions only by making a self-contradictory supposition. In ordinary and mathematical language, we allow ourselves to speak of such parts —*points*—and whenever we are led into contradiction thereby, we have simply to express ourselves more accurately to resolve the difficulty.

Suppose a piece of glass to be laid on a sheet of paper so as to cover half of it. Then, every part of the paper is *covered*, or *not covered*; for "not" means merely outside of, or other than. But is the line under the edge of the glass covered or not? It is no more on one side of the edge than it is on the other. Therefore, it is either on both sides, or neither side. It is not on neither side; for if it were it would be *not* on either side, therefore not on the covered side, therefore not covered, therefore on the uncovered side. It is not partly on one side and partly on the other, because it has no width. Hence, it is wholly on both sides, or both covered and not covered.

The solution of this is, that we have supposed a part too narrow to be partly uncovered and partly covered; that is to say, a part which has no parts in a continuous surface, which by definition has no such parts. The reasoning, therefore, simply serves to reduce this supposition to an absurdity.

It may be said that there really is such a thing as a line. If a shadow falls on a surface, there really is a division between the light and the darkness. That is true. But it does not follow that because we attach a definite meaning to the part of a surface being covered, therefore we know what we mean when we say that a line is covered. We may define a covered line as one which separates two surfaces both of which are covered, or as one which separates two surfaces *either* of which is covered. In the former case, the line under the edge is uncovered; in the latter case, it is covered.

In the sophisms thus far considered, the appearance of contradiction depends mostly upon an ambiguity; in those which we are now to consider, two true propositions really do in form conflict with one another. We are apt to think that formal logic forbids this, whereas a familiar argument, the *reductio ad absurdum,* depends on showing that contrary predicates are true of a subject, and *that therefore that subject does not exist.* Many logicians, it is true, make affirmative propositions assert the existence of their subjects.[5] The objection to this is that it cannot be extended to hypotheticals. The proposition

If *A* then *B*

may conveniently be regarded as equivalent to

Every case of the truth of *A* is a case of the truth of *B*.

But this cannot be done if the latter proposition asserts the existence of its subject; that is, asserts that *A* really happens. If, however, a categorical affirmative be regarded as asserting the existence of its subject, the principle of the *reductio ad absurdum* is that two propositions of the forms,

If *A* were true, *B* would not be true,

5. The usage of ordinary language has no relevancy in the matter.

and

> If *A* were true, *B* would be true,

may both be true at once; and that if they are so, *A* is not true. It will be well, perhaps, to illustrate this point. No man of common sense would deliberately upset his inkstand if there were ink in it; that is, if any ink would run out. Hence, by simple conversion,

> If he were deliberately to upset his inkstand, no ink would be spilt.

But suppose there is ink in it. Then, it is also true, that

> If he were deliberately to upset his inkstand, the ink would be spilt.

These propositions are both true, and the law of contradiction is not violated which asserts only that nothing has contradictory predicates: only, it follows from these propositions that the man will not deliberately overturn his inkstand.

There are two ways in which deceptive sophisms may result from this circumstance. In the first place, contradictory propositions are never both true. Now, as a universal proposition may be true when the subject does not exist, it follows that the contradictory of a universal—that is, a particular—cannot be taken in such a sense as to be true when the subject does not exist. But a particular simply asserts a part of what is asserted in the universal over it; therefore, the universal over it asserts the subject to exist. Consequently, there are two kinds of universals, those which do not assert the subject to exist, and these have no particular propositions under them, and those which do assert that the subject exists, and these strictly speaking have no contradictories. For example, there is no use of such a form of proposition as "Some griffins would be dreadful animals," as particular under the useful form "The griffin would be a dreadful animal"; and the apparent contradictories "All of John Smith's family are ill," and "Some of John Smith's family are not ill," are both false at once if John Smith has no family. Here, though an inference from a universal to the particular under it is always valid, yet a procedure which greatly resembles this would be sophistical if the universal were one of those propositions which does not assert the existence of its subject. The following sophism depends upon this; I call it the True Gorgias:

Gorgias. What say you, Socrates, of black? Is any black, white?
Socrates. No, by Zeus!
Gor. Do you say, then, that no black is white? *Soc.* None at all.
Gor. But is everything either black or non-black? *Soc.* Of course.
Gor. And everything either white or non-white? *Soc.* Yes.
Gor. And everything either rough or smooth? *Soc.* Yes.
Gor. And everything either real or unreal? *Soc.* Oh, bother! yes.
Gor. Do you say, then, that all black is either rough black or smooth black? *Soc.* Yes.
Gor. And that all white is either real white or unreal white? *Soc.* Yes.
Gor. And yet is no black, white? *Soc.* None at all.
Gor. Nor no white, black? *Soc.* By no means.
Gor. What? Is no smooth black, white? *Soc.* No; you cannot prove that, Gorgias.
Gor. Nor no rough black, white? *Soc.* Neither.
Gor. Nor no real white, black? *Soc.* No.
Gor. Nor no unreal white, black? *Soc.* No, I say. No white at all is black.
Gor. What if black is smooth, is it not white? *Soc.* Not in the least.
Gor. And if the last is false, is the first false? *Soc.* It follows.
Gor. If, then, black is white, does it follow, that black is not smooth? *Soc.* It does.
Gor. Black-white is not smooth? *Soc.* What do you mean?
Gor. Can any dead man speak? *Soc.* No, indeed.
Gor. And is any speaking man dead? *Soc.* I say, no.
Gor. And is any good king tyrannical? *Soc.* No.
Gor. And is any tyrannical king good? *Soc.* I just said no.
Gor. And you said, too, that no rough black is white, did you not? *Soc.* Yes.
Gor. Then, is any black-white, rough? *Soc.* No.
Gor. And is any unreal black, white? *Soc.* No.
Gor. Then, is any black-white unreal? *Soc.* No.

Gor. No black-white is rough? *Soc.* None.

Gor. All black-white, then, is non-rough? *Soc.* Yes.

Gor. And all black-white, non-unreal? *Soc.* Yes.

Gor. All black-white is then smooth? *Soc.* Yes.

Gor. And all real? *Soc.* Yes.

Gor. Some smooth, then, is black-white? *Soc.* Of course.

Gor. And some real is black-white? *Soc.* So it seems.

Gor. Some black-white smooth is black-white? *Soc.* Yes.

Gor. Some black smooth is black-white? *Soc.* Yes.

Gor. Some black smooth is white. *Soc.* Yes.

Gor. Some black real is black-white? *Soc.* Yes.

Gor. Some black real is white? *Soc.* Yes.

Gor. Some real black is white? *Soc.* Yes.

Gor. And some smooth black is white? *Soc.* Yes.

Gor. Then, some black is white? *Soc.* I think so myself.

The principle of the *reductio ad absurdum* also occasions deceptions in another way, owing to the fact that we have many words, such as *can, may, must,* &c., which imply more or less vaguely an otherwise unexpressed condition, so that these propositions are in fact hypotheticals. Accordingly, if the unexpressed condition is some state of things which does not actually come to pass, the two propositions may appear to be contrary to one another. Thus, the moralist says, "You ought to do this, and you can do it." This "You can do it" is principally hortatory in its force: so far as it is a statement of fact, it means merely, "If you try, you will do it." Now, if the act is an outward one and the act is not performed, the scientific man, in view of the fact that every event in the physical world depends exclusively on physical antecedents, says that in this case the laws of nature prevented the thing from being done, and that therefore, "Even if you had tried, you would not have done it." Yet the reproachful conscience still says you might have done it; that is, that "If you had tried, you would have done it." This is called the paradox of freedom and fate; and it is usually supposed that one of these propositions must be true and the other false. But since, in fact, you have not tried, there is no reason why the supposition that you have tried should not be reduced to an absurdity. In the same way, if you had tried and had performed the action, the conscience might say, "If you had not tried, you would not have done it"; while the understanding would say, "Even if you had not tried, you would have done it." These propositions are perfectly consistent, and only serve to reduce the supposition that you did not try to an absurdity.[6]

The third class of sophisms consists of the so-called *Insolubilia*. Here is an example of one of them with its resolution:

THIS PROPOSITION IS NOT TRUE.
IS IT TRUE OR NOT?

Suppose it true.	Suppose it not true.
Then,	Then,
The proposition is true;	It is not true.
But, that it is not true is the proposition:	∴ It is true that it is not true.
∴ That it is not true is true;	But, the proposition is that it is not true.
∴ It is not true.	∴ The proposition is true.
Besides,	Besides,
It is true.	The proposition is not true.
∴ It is true that it is true,	But that it is not true is the proposition.
∴ It is not true that it is not true;	∴ That it is not true, is not true.
But, the proposition is that it is not true,	∴ That it is true, is true.
∴ The proposition is not true.	∴ It is true.

∴ Whether it is true or not, it is both true and not.
∴ It is both true and not,
which is absurd.

---

6. This seems to me to be the main difficulty of freedom and fate. But the question is overlaid with many others. The Necessitarians seem now to maintain less that every physical event is completely determined by physical causes (which seems to me irrefragable), than that every act of will is determined by the strongest motive. This has never been proved. Its advocates seem to think that it follows from universal causation, but why need the cause of an act lie within the consciousness at all? If I act from a reason at all, I act voluntarily; but which of two reasons shall appear strongest to me on a particular occasion may be owing to what I have eaten for dinner. Unless there is a perfect regularity as to what is the strongest motive with me, to say that I act from the strongest motive is mere tautology. If there is no calculating how a man will act except by taking into account external facts, the character of his motives does not determine how he acts. Mill and others have, therefore, not shown that a man always acts from the strongest motive. Hobbes maintained that a man always acts from a reflection upon what will please him most. This is a very crude opinion. Men are not always thinking of themselves.

Self-control seems to be the capacity for rising to an extended view of a practical subject instead of seeing only temporary urgency. This is the only freedom of which man has any reason to be proud; and it is because love of what is good for all on the whole, which is the widest possible consideration, is the essence of Christianity, that it is said that the service of Christ is perfect freedom.

Since the conclusion is false, the reasoning is bad, or the premises are not all true. But the reasoning is a dilemma; either, then, the disjunctive principle that it is either true or not is false, or the reasoning under one or the other branch is bad, or the reasoning is altogether valid. If the principle that it is either true or not is false, it is other than true and other than not true; that is, not true and not not true; that is, not true and true. But this is absurd. Hence, the disjunctive principle is valid. There are two arguments under each horn of the dilemma; both the arguments under one or the other branch must be false. But, in each case, the second argument involves all the premises and forms of inference involved in the first; hence, if the first is false, the second necessarily is so. We may, therefore, confine our attention to the first arguments in the two branches. The forms of argument contained in these are two: first, the simple syllogism in Barbara, and, second, the consequence from the truth of a proposition to the proposition itself. These are both correct. Hence, the whole form of reasoning is correct, and nothing remains to be false but a premise. But since the repetition of an alternative supposition is not a premise, there is, properly speaking, but one premise in the whole. This is that the proposition is the same as that that proposition is not true. This, then, must be false. Hence the proposition signifies either less or more than this. If it does not signify as much as this, it signifies nothing, and hence it is not true, and hence another proposition which says of it what it says of itself is true. But if the proposition in question signifies something more than that it is itself not true, then the premise that

Whatever is said in the proposition is that it is not true,

is not true. And as a proposition is true only if whatever is said in it is true, but is false if anything said in it is false, the first argument on the second side of the dilemma contains a false premise, and the second an undistributed middle. But the first argument on the first side remains good. Hence, if the proposition means more than that it is not true, it is not true, and another proposition which repeats this of it is true. Hence, whether the proposition does or does not mean that it is not true, it is not true, and a proposition which repeats this of it is true.

Since this repeating proposition is true, it has a meaning. Now, a proposition has a meaning if any part of it has a meaning. Hence the original proposition (a part of which repeated has a meaning) has itself a meaning. Hence, it must imply something besides that which it explicitly states. But it has no particular determination to any further implication. Hence, what more it signifies it must signify by virtue of being a proposition at all. That is to say, every proposition must imply something analogous to what this implies. Now, the repetition of this proposition does not contain this implication, for otherwise it could not be true; hence, what every proposition implies must be something concerning itself. What every proposition implies concerning itself must be something which is false of the proposition now under discussion, for the whole falsity of this proposition lies therein, since all that it explicitly lays down is true. It must be something which would not be false if the proposition were true, for in that case some true proposition would be false. Hence, it must be that it is itself true. That is, *every proposition asserts its own truth.*

The proposition in question, therefore, is true in all other respects but its implication of its own truth.[7]

The difficulty of showing how the law of deductive reasoning is true depends upon our inability to conceive of its not being true. In the case of probable reasoning the difficulty is of quite another kind; here, where we see precisely what the procedure is, we wonder how such a process can have any validity at all. How magical it is that by examining a part of a class we can know what is true of the whole of the class, and by study of the past can know the future; in short, that we can know what we have not experienced!

Is not this an intellectual intuition! Is it not that besides ordinary experience which is dependent on there being a certain physical connection between our organs and the thing experienced, there is a second avenue of truth dependent only on there being a certain intellectual connection between our previous knowledge and what

7. This is the principle which was most usually made the basis of the resolution of the *Insolubilia*. See, for example, *Pauli Veneti Sophismata Aurea*. Sophisma 50. The authority of Aristotle is claimed for this mode of solution. *Sophistici Elenchi*, cap. 25. The principal objection which was made to this mode of solution, viz., that the principle that every proposition implies its own truth, cannot be proved, I believe that I have removed. The only arguments against the truth of this principle were based on the imperfect doctrines of *modales* and *obligationes*. Other methods of solution suppose that a part of a proposition cannot denote the whole proposition, or that no intellection is a formal cognition of itself. A solution of this sort will be found in Occam's *Summa Totius Logices*, 3d part of 3d part, cap. 38. Such modern authors as think the solution "very easy" do not understand its difficulties. See Mansel's Aldrich, p. 145.

we learn in that way? Yes, this is true. Man has this faculty, just as opium has a somnific virtue; but some further questions may be asked, nevertheless. How is the existence of this faculty accounted for? In one sense, no doubt, by natural selection. Since it is absolutely essential to the preservation of so delicate an organism as man's, no race which had it not has been able to sustain itself. This accounts for the prevalence of this faculty, provided it was only a possible one. But how can it be possible? What could enable the mind to know physical things which do not physically influence it and which it does not influence? The question cannot be answered by any statement concerning the human mind, for it is equivalent to asking what makes the facts usually to be, as inductive and hypothetic conclusions from true premises represent them to be? Facts of a certain kind are usually true when facts having certain relations to them are true; what is the cause of this? That is the question.

The usual reply is that nature is everywhere regular; as things have been, so they will be; as one part of nature is, so is every other. But this explanation will not do. Nature is not regular. No disorder would be less orderly than the existing arrangement. It is true that the special laws and regularities are innumerable; but nobody thinks of the irregularities, which are infinitely more frequent. Every fact true of any one thing in the universe is related to every fact true of every other. But the immense majority of these relations are fortuitous and irregular. A man in China bought a cow three days and five minutes after a Greenlander had sneezed. Is that abstract circumstance connected with any regularity whatever? And are not such relations infinitely more frequent than those which are regular? But if a very large number of qualities were to be distributed among a very large number of things in almost any way, there would chance to be some few regularities. If, for example, upon a checker-board of an enormous number of squares, painted all sorts of colors, myriads of dice were to be thrown, it could hardly fail to happen, that upon some color, or shade of color, out of so many, some one of the six numbers should not be uppermost on any die. This would be a regularity; for, the universal proposition would be true that upon that color that number is never turned up. But suppose this regularity abolished, then a far more remarkable regularity would be created, namely, that on every color every number is turned up. Either way, therefore, a regularity must occur. Indeed, a little reflection will show that although we have here only variations of color and of the numbers of the dice, many regularities must occur. And the greater the number of objects, the more respects in which they vary, and the greater the number of varieties in each respect, the greater will be the number of regularities. Now, in the universe, all these numbers are infinite. Therefore, however disorderly the chaos, the *number* of regularities must be infinite. The orderliness of the universe, therefore, if it exists, must consist in the large *proportion* of relations which present a regularity to those which are quite irregular. But this proportion in the actual universe is, as we have seen, as small as it can be; and, therefore, the orderliness of the universe is as little as that of any arrangement whatever.

But even if there were such an orderliness in things, it never could be discovered. For it would belong to things either collectively or distributively. If it belonged to things collectively, that is to say, if things formed a system the difficulty would be that a system can only be known by seeing some considerable proportion of the whole. Now we never can know how great a part of the whole of nature we have discovered. If the order were distributive, that is, belonged to all things only by belonging to each thing, the difficulty would be that a character can only be known by comparing something which has with it something which has it not. *Being, quality, relation,* and other universals are not known except as characters of words or other signs, attributed by a figure of speech to things. Thus, in neither case could the order of things be known. But the order of things would not help the validity of our reasoning—that is, would not help us to reason correctly—unless we knew what the order of things required the relation between the known reasoned *from* to the unknown reasoned *to,* to be.

But even if this order both existed and were known, the knowledge would be of no use except as a general principle, from which things could be deduced. It would not explain how knowledge could be increased (in contradistinction to being rendered more distinct), and so it would not explain how it could itself have been acquired.

Finally, if the validity of induction and hypothesis were dependent on a particular constitution of the universe, we could imagine a universe in which these modes of inference should not be valid, just as we can imagine a universe in which there would be no attraction, but things should merely drift about. Accordingly, J. S. Mill, who explains the validity of induction by the uniformity of nature,[8] maintains that he can imagine a universe without any regularity, so that no probable inference would be valid in it.[9] In the universe as it is, probable arguments sometimes fail, nor can any definite proportion of cases be stated in which they hold good; all that can be said is that in the long run they prove approximately correct. Can a universe be imagined in which this would not be the case? It must be a universe where probable argument can have some application, in order that it may fail half the time. It must, therefore, be a universe experienced. Of the finite number of propositions true of a finite amount of experience of such a universe, no one would be universal in form, unless the subject of it were an individual. For if there were a plural universal proposition, inferences by analogy from one particular to another would hold good invariably in reference to that subject. So that these arguments might be no better than guesses in reference to other parts of the universe, but they would invariably hold good in a finite proportion of it, and so would on the whole be somewhat better than guesses. There could, also, be no individuals in that universe, for there must be some general class—that is, there must be some things more or less alike—or probable argument would find no premises there; therefore, there must be two mutually exclusive classes, since every class has a residue outside of it; hence, if there were any individual, that individual would be wholly excluded from one or other of these classes. Hence, the universal plural proposition would be true, that no one of a certain class was that individual. Hence, no universal proposition would be true. Accordingly, every combination of characters would occur in such a universe. But this would not be disorder, but the simplest order; it would not be unintelligible, but, on the contrary, everything conceivable would be found in it with equal frequency. The notion, therefore, of a universe

---

8. *Logic*, Book 3, chap. 3, sec. 1.

9. *Ibid.* Book 3, chap. 21, sec. 1. "I am convinced that any one accustomed to abstraction and analysis, who will fairly exert his faculties for the purpose, will, when his imagination has once learnt to entertain the notion, find no difficulty in conceiving that in some one, for instance, of the many firmaments into which sidereal astronomy divides the universe, events may succeed one another at random, without any fixed law; nor can anything in our experience or mental nature constitute a sufficient, or indeed any, reason for believing that this is nowhere the case.

"Were we to suppose (what it is perfectly possible to imagine) that the present order of the universe were brought to an end, and that a chaos succeeded, in which there was no fixed succession of events, and the past gave no assurance of the future," &c.

in which probable arguments should fail as often as hold true, is absurd. We can suppose it in general terms, but we cannot specify how it should be other than self-contradictory.[10]

Since we cannot conceive of probable inferences as not generally holding good, and since no special supposition will serve to explain their validity, many logicians have sought to base this validity on that of deduction, and that in a variety of ways. The only attempt of this sort, however, which deserves to be noticed is that which seeks to determine the probability of a future event by the theory of probabilities, from the fact that a certain number of similar events have been observed. Whether this can be done or not depends on the meaning assigned to the word *probability*. But if this word is to be taken in such a sense that a form of conclusion which is probable is valid; since the validity of an inference (or its correspondence with facts) consists solely in this, that when such premises are true, such a conclusion is generally true, then probability can mean nothing but the ratio of the frequency of occurrence of a specific event to a general one over it. In this sense of the term, it is plain that the probability of an inductive conclusion cannot be *deduced* from the premises; for from the inductive premises

$$S', S'', S''' \text{ are } M,$$
$$S', S'', S''', \text{ are } P,$$

nothing follows deductively, except that any M, which is S', or S'', or S''' is P; or, less explicitly, that some M is P.

Thus, we seem to be driven to this point. On the one hand, no determination of things, no *fact*, can result in the validity of probable argument; nor, on the other hand, is such argument reducible to that form which holds good, however the facts may be. This seems very much like a reduction to absurdity of the validity of such reasoning; and a paradox of the greatest difficulty is presented for solution.

There can be no doubt of the importance of this problem. According to Kant, the central question of philosophy is "How are syntheti-

---

10. Boole (*Laws of Thought*, p. 370) has shown, in a very simple and elegant manner, that an *infinite* number of balls may have characters distributed in such a way, that from the characters of the balls already drawn, we could infer nothing in regard to that of the characters of the next one. The same is true of some arrangements of a finite number of balls, provided the inference takes place after a fixed number of drawings. But this does not invalidate the reasoning above, although it is an important fact without doubt.

cal judgments *a priori* possible?" But antecedently to this comes the question how synthetical judgments in general, and still more generally, how synthetical reasoning is possible at all. When the answer to the general problem has been obtained, the particular one will be comparatively simple. This is the lock upon the door of philosophy.

All probable inference, whether induction or hypothesis, is inference from the parts to the whole. It is essentially the same, therefore, as statistical inference. Out of a bag of black and white beans I take a few handfuls, and from this sample I can judge approximately the proportions of black and white in the whole. This is identical with induction. Now we know upon what the validity of this inference depends. It depends upon the fact that in the long run, any one bean would be taken out as often as any other. For were this not so, the mean of a large number of results of such testings of the contents of the bag would not be precisely the ratio of the numbers of the two colors of beans in the bag. Now we may divide the question of the validity of induction into two parts: 1st, why of all inductions, premises for which occur, the generality should hold good, and 2d, why men are not fated always to light upon the small proportion of worthless inductions. Then, the first of these two questions is readily answered. For since all the members of any class are the same as all that are to be known; and since from any part of those which are to be known an induction is competent to the rest, in the long run any one member of a class will occur as the subject of a premise of a possible induction as often as any other, and, therefore, the validity of induction depends simply upon the fact that the parts make up and constitute the whole. This in its turn depends simply upon there being such a state of things that any general terms are possible. But it has been shown, p. 239, that being at all is being in general. And thus this part of the validity of induction depends merely on there being any reality.

From this it appears that we cannot say that the generality of inductions are true, but only that in the long run they approximate to the truth. This is the truth of the statement, that the universality of an inference from induction is only the analogue of true universality. Hence, also, it cannot be said that we know an inductive conclusion to be true, however loosely we state it; we only know that by accepting inductive conclusions, in the long run our errors balance one another. In fact, insurance companies proceed upon induction;

—they do not know what will happen to this or that policy-holder; they only know that they are secure in the long run.

The other question relative to the validity of induction, is why men are not fated always to light upon those inductions which are highly deceptive. The explanation of the former branch of the problem we have seen to be that there is something real. Now, since if there is anything real, then (on account of this reality consisting in the ultimate agreement of all men, and on account of the fact that reasoning from parts to whole, is the only kind of synthetic reasoning which men possess) it follows necessarily that a sufficiently long succession of inferences from parts to whole will lead men to a knowledge of it, so that in that case they cannot be fated on the whole to be thoroughly unlucky in their inductions. This second branch of the problem is in fact equivalent to asking why there is anything real, and thus its solution will carry the solution of the former branch one step further.

The answer to this question may be put into a general and abstract, or a special detailed form. If men were not to be able to learn from induction, it must be because as a general rule, when they had made an induction, the order of things (as they appear in experience), would then undergo a revolution. Just herein would the unreality of such a universe consist; namely, that the order of the universe should depend on how much men should know of it. But this general rule would be capable of being itself discovered by induction; and so it must be a law of such a universe, that when this was discovered it would cease to operate. But this second law would itself be capable of discovery. And so in such a universe there would be nothing which would not sooner or later be known; and it would have an order capable of discovery by a sufficiently long course of reasoning. But this is contrary to the hypothesis, and therefore that hypothesis is absurd. This is the particular answer. But we may also say, in general, that if nothing real exists, then, since every question supposes that something exists—for it maintains its own urgency—it supposes only illusions to exist. But the existence even of an illusion is a reality; for an illusion affects all men, or it does not. In the former case, it is a reality according to our theory of reality; in the latter case, it is independent of the state of mind of any individuals except those whom it happens to affect. So that the answer to the question, Why is anything real? is this: That question means, "supposing anything to exist, why is something real?" The answer is, that that very existence is reality by definition.

All that has here been said, particularly of induction, applies to all inference from parts to whole, and therefore to hypothesis, and so to all probable inference.

Thus, I claim to have shown, in the first place, that it is possible to hold a consistent theory of the validity of the laws of ordinary logic.

But now let us suppose the idealistic theory of reality, which I have in this paper taken for granted to be false. In that case, inductions would not be true unless the world were so constituted that every object should be presented in experience as often as any other; and further, unless we were so constituted that we had no more tendency to make bad inductions than good ones. These facts might be explained by the benevolence of the Creator; but, as has already been argued, they could not explain, but are absolutely refuted by the fact that no state of things can be conceived in which probable arguments should not lead to the truth. This affords a most important argument in favor of that theory of reality, and thus of those denials of certain faculties from which it was deduced, as well as of the general style of philosophizing by which those denials were reached.

Upon our theory of reality and of logic, it can be shown that no inference of any individual can be thoroughly logical without certain determinations of his mind which do not concern any one inference immediately; for we have seen that that mode of inference which alone can teach us anything, or carry us at all beyond what was implied in our premises—in fact, does not give us to know any more than we knew before; only, we know that, by faithfully adhering to that mode of inference, we shall, on the whole, approximate to the truth. Each of us is an insurance company, in short. But, now, suppose that an insurance company, among its risks, should take one exceeding in amount the sum of all the others. Plainly, it would then have no security whatever. Now, has not every single man such a risk? What shall it profit a man if he shall gain the whole world and lose his own soul? If a man has a transcendent personal interest infinitely outweighing all others, then, upon the theory of validity of inference just developed, he is devoid of all security, and can make no valid inference whatever. What follows? That logic rigidly requires, before all else, that no determinate fact, nothing which can happen to a man's self, should be of more consequence to him than everything else. He who would not sacrifice his own soul to save the whole world, is illogical in all his inferences, collectively. So the social principle is rooted intrinsically in logic.

That being the case, it becomes interesting to inquire how it is with men as a matter of fact. There is a psychological theory that man cannot act without a view to his own pleasure. This theory is based on a falsely assumed subjectivism. Upon our principles of the objectivity of knowledge, it could not be based, and if they are correct it is reduced to an absurdity. It seems to me that the usual opinion of the selfishness of man is based in large measure upon this false theory. I do not think that the facts bear out the usual opinion. The immense self-sacrifices which the most wilful men often make, show that wilfulness is a very different thing from selfishness. The care that men have for what is to happen after they are dead, cannot be selfish. And finally and chiefly, the constant use of the word *"we"*—as when we speak of our possessions on the Pacific—our destiny as a republic —in cases in which no personal interests at all are involved, show conclusively that men do not make their personal interests their only ones, and therefore may, at least, subordinate them to the interests of the community.

But just the revelation of the possibility of this complete self-sacrifice in man, and the belief in its saving power, will serve to redeem the logicality of all men. For he who recognizes the logical necessity of complete self-identification of one's own interests with those of the community, and its potential existence in man, even if he has it not himself, will perceive that only the inferences of that man who has it are logical, and so views his own inferences as being valid only so far as they would be accepted by that man. But so far as he has this belief, he becomes identified with that man. And that ideal perfection of knowledge by which we have seen that reality is constituted must thus belong to a community in which this identification is complete.

This would serve as a complete establishment of private logicality, were it not that the assumption that man or the community (which may be wider than man) shall ever arrive at a state of information greater than some definite finite information, is entirely unsupported by reasons. There cannot be a scintilla of evidence to show that at some time all living beings shall not be annihilated at once, and that forever after there shall be throughout the universe any intelligence whatever. Indeed, this very assumption involves itself a transcendent and supreme interest, and therefore from its very nature is unsusceptible of any support from reasons. This infinite hope which we all have (for even the atheist will constantly betray his calm expectation that what is Best will come about) is something so august and momentous, that all reasoning in reference to it is a trifling impertinence. We do not want to know what are the weights of reasons *pro* and *con*—that is, how much *odds* we should wish to receive on such a venture in the long run—because there is no long run in the case; the question is single and supreme, and ALL is at stake upon it. We are in the condition of a man in a life and death struggle; if he have not sufficient strength, it is wholly indifferent to him how he acts, so that the only assumption upon which he can act rationally is the hope of success. So this sentiment is rigidly demanded by logic. If its object were any determinate fact, any private interest, it might conflict with the results of knowledge and so with itself; but when its object is of a nature as wide as the community can turn out to be, it is always a hypothesis uncontradicted by facts and justified by its indispensibleness for making any action rational.

Professor Porter's Human Intellect[1]

P 43: Nation 8(18 March 1869):211–13

The Rev. Dr. Porter, of Yale College, has published an important work upon that branch of psychology which relates to the faculties of cognition. Whatever be the judgment pronounced upon this treatise, no man can withhold his respect for the self-denying labor, both in the way of study and of composition, which has been devoted to its production. The size of the book is something stupendous. It is a large octavo of nearly seven hundred pages (printed, we regret to say, upon that harsh, cottony paper in which New York publishers seem to delight), in three sizes of print, of which the largest would not be unusual for a duodecimo while the smallest is painful to read. The work is designed primarily for a text-book, and the part in the largest type "is somewhat technically phrased and formally propounded in order that it may be learned more readily for the examinations of the class-room." But as the philosophical world was also to be addressed and the discussion must accordingly be carried in many places beyond the depth of learners, and inasmuch also as the author wisely thought it well to put more information into the hands of his scholars than they were to be positively required to master, the book has been more than doubled by the addition of matter in two sizes of small print, that in the middle-sized type being suitable for general students, and that in the smallest consisting chiefly of historical and critical notices.

General readers in metaphysics will hardly find the book to their taste. The appearance of it is not inviting; the type is too small, the volume too large, and the paper disagreeable. A style studiously technical and formal, even if it were not stiff and awkward and of a magisterial tone, would not attract them. Nor is a compendium of

1. *The Human Intellect; with an Introduction upon Psychology and the Soul.* By Noah Porter, D.D., Clarke Professor of Moral Philosophy and Metaphysics in Yale College. New York: Charles Scribner & Co. 1868. 8vo, pp. 673.

699 numbered sections, with scarcely any unity of conception developing through them all, precisely what such readers desire. But it is admirably fitted for a college text-book. The formal and bald manner in which the arguments on either side are laid down is eminently adapted to nourish the logical power of the student. Great pains have been taken to give a full and rigidly precise account of the meaning of the principal terms employed, thus inculcating one of the most essential requisites for accurate thinking upon abstract subjects. The author's talent for explaining words is well illustrated in the chapter upon consciousness. He shows somewhat more favor to modern German terminology than we should approve. For example, "sense-perception," instead of external perception, seems to us to have little to recommend it. The scholastic terminology forms a system at once precise and elastic. New terms can be constructed in accordance with the principles of it which may be understood by any one who is acquainted with these principles. This system, together with the accretions which it received in the seventeenth century, has the character of a somewhat obsolete but yet universal language; it is not confined to the philosophers of any particular nation, but is equally the possession of all. It is the basis of the actual English terminology, and has even passed in great degree into ordinary English speech. The modern German terminology, on the other hand, is unsettled and unsystematic; most of its single words correspond precisely to no single English words, and its method of compounding them is foreign to our conceptions of grammar. For these reasons, we think that the basis of English terminology should be allowed to remain as it actually is, scholastic; and certainly no one who favors a movement in the direction of Aristotelianism, as Dr. Porter partly does, should oppose this position. But once admit that such should be the basis of our terminology, and no doubt we should adhere to it consistently, except in cases in which it altogether fails us. In the present case it has not failed us. The phrase "external perception" would be quite intelligible to any educated person, even if it were a newly invented term. But in point of fact it is quite familiar both in English and in German. If it be objected that some persons believe in an external perception not through the senses, still Dr. Porter is not one of these; but even if it were judged proper to take account of that mystical and fictitious faculty, the term "external sensuous perception" might be adopted. Dr. Porter's using "representation" for imagination and memory appears to be another case of borrowing from the German.

Representation is wanted in a general unpsychological sense, and as a psychological term it has already been used in two other senses besides that in which Dr. Porter takes it. Either "the representative faculty" or the "imagination" might have been employed advantageously in the last sense, as they were, in fact, by Hamilton. In using words cognate with "activity" we are inclined to suspect that Dr. Porter has been somewhat influenced by German usage, although we do not find that he anywhere defines any of these words, the ambiguity of which has often led writers into fallacies.

Another character of the work which makes it suitable for purposes of instruction is the impartiality with which the whole ground is gone over, no one or more faculties or phenomena being dwelt upon at such inordinate length as to encroach upon the space due to the others. The student will consequently receive the best armor against plausible theories which answer well for the facts that concern one mental process, but which may conflict with those that concern another. Another merit is that in the smaller type the student will generally find some notice of doctrines not contained in the text he is required to learn, and some references to the books in which those doctrines are maintained. Accordingly, when he has once become thoroughly familiar with this treatise by a year's study of it, it will always serve him as an invaluable index of reference in any further psychological studies which he may choose to pursue. We must not omit to say that the doctrines which it teaches are entirely conformable to orthodox theology, and quite free from any materialistic leanings. A young mind thoroughly imbued with Dr. Porter's teachings will be likely to get its philosophy so bound up with its religion that it cannot part with either unless it parts with the other.

The historical notices are full and valuable. They do not cover every important question, and in some places, as where psychology trends upon logic, are comparatively meagre; but some account is given of most of the more prominent discussions. These notices, considered as criticisms, will be thought by some to carry but little weight and to present no very noticeable characteristics. Considered as statements of fact, they are learned. The accounts of ancient opinions have evidently not been written without a study of the latest commentaries. In what relates to the history of the Scotch and English schools, even professed students of philosophy will find much that is fresh and instructive. The great defect of this part of the book is that, as a general rule, no account whatever is given of recent works, these being cited only by title. This omission detracts very seriously in some cases from the value of the book. Twenty-five pages of the finest print are devoted to an account of the various theories of perception without the least mention, except by title, of the writings of Fechner, Wundt, Trendelenburg, George, Lotze, and others, whose investigations may truly be said to be of more value than all the others put together.

Mediæval doctrines, which are seldom intelligibly treated, are not treated intelligibly here. The reader is for the most part expected to gather the opinions of the masters and doctors from single quoted sentences, which are often utterly meaningless or even misleading to those who have not given special attention to scholastic philosophy. Take for example the account of nominalism and realism on pages 405–407. What is a person not already acquainted with the subject to make of the statement that a certain master taught that a universal is "indifferenter" in all the singulars under it? How correct a notion is he likely to form of Abelard's doctrine from being told that he "*sermones* intuetur et ad illos detorquet quicquid alicubi de universalibus meminit scriptum"? Will he understand, as he should, that the *sermo* means a word actually in application by the mind as a predicate? Considering the historical importance of Roscellin, and considering the fact that, though an extreme nominalist, his doctrines were associated with those of Scotus Erigena, who was a sort of Platonistic idealist, is it quite sufficiently explaining his views to quote that sentence of Anselm's in which he is said to have thought that universal substances are the breath of the voice, that the wisdom of man is the soul, and that color is the colored body? It would have been easy to explain, first, that the *vox* was regarded by grammarians of that age as something incorporeal, because it is *produced* by the percussion of the palate and the air, but *is* not either, and because a natural motion cannot produce a new body, and also because the *vox* is in several ears at once, whereas a body can only be in one place at one time; that we have positive reason to think that Roscellin believed this; that, in the second place, reasoning (as we may suppose) like others in that age from such facts as that the same line which, when measured by one measure (a foot) is equal to *two,* when measured by another (an inch) is equal to *twenty-four,* and that the wall of a house is on the one hand a whole in itself and on the other a part of a house, he came to believe (as we are positively informed) that all mathematical relations—that is, all relations of parts and whole—exist not in the body itself, but only in the incorporeal words which may be applied to it; and that, thirdly, he thence inferred that those universal essences of things, genera and species, since they essentially have parts and are parts, themselves are not things, but incorporeal *voces*. Of any interruption in the course of the controversy between the twelfth and thirteenth centuries our author tells us nothing, although the discovery of all the works of Aristotle except the two short treatises already known, and of the writings of the Arabian commentators, had in the interval between Abelard and Albertus so changed the whole face of scholasticism that it is rarely indeed that any writer of the twelfth century except Peter Lombard and Gilbertus Porretanus is quoted at all in the thirteenth. The facts that Albertus had properly no opinion of his own and that that of St. Thomas was very vacillating (as was notorious in the fourteenth century) are not mentioned. Scotus's realism is said to be identical with that of these writers except as to the *hæcceity;* but the difference is more important. The Thomistic view was that of the two elements of the individual thing—that is to say, the matter and the form, or that which makes it to be, and that which makes it, if it is to be, to be *as* as it is—the form is always universal, the matter, or at least signate matter (this or that matter), is always singular. Their union is an individual, but it is a union in which the form is as such actually universal in itself. Scotus admitted that in the singular thing there is nothing actually universal; all generality results from a relation of reason. Nevertheless, when a general predicate is attached by the mind to a thing, the proposition so formed may be true, and since the *same* predicate may also be truly asserted of other things, it is true that there is something in the thing which, though actually contracted to the grade of singularity, is in its own nature not repugnant to being predicated of many. There is, then, a distinction between a predicate predicated of many and the singular forms in the several things by virtue of which the same general predicate is true. Yet since this general predicate *is* true, it really is in the several things, although it is there in the grade of singularity and identified with these singular forms. Thus there is a really, but only potentially, general form in the singular thing which yet in that thing in itself does not differ from the singular thing. This is the famous doctrine of formal distinctions, which is the central idea of the whole Scotistic philosophy. This formed also the very point of Occam's attack, for his whole notion of a reality was that of a thing which is in itself whatever it really is. This he was able to see must be something devoid of all quality and all relations. All qualities and relations, according to him, are *terms,* subjects and predicates of written, spoken, or thought propositions; and the qualities and relations of things can consist in nothing except that the mind naturally applies to them such and such *terms.* Prof. Porter says the controversy came to a close early in the fourteenth century, but Occam did not die until 1347, and it certainly raged with the greatest fury after his death.

The Scotch school of philosophy, to which this work belongs, is too old a tree to bear good fruit. Its method consists in an appeal to consciousness—that is to say, to what all men know and know that they know (p. 113)—supported by some familiar facts and occasional anecdotes. Such a procedure is not wholly useless. The common sense of mankind has so little impulse to seek explanations of facts that it is hardly tempted to twist them, and he who busies himself with reproducing ordinary beliefs is free from so deep an absorption in laborious experiments and observations as to overlook what lies upon the surface. The great mistake of writers of this sort has been that they have had an ambition to be more than accurate describers of common beliefs and unanalyzed facts. That natural self-consciousness, when heightened by direct effort, becomes a scientific knowledge of the soul, is not the doctrine of modern psychology. This opinion is disappearing, and with it will probably disappear some of that morbid tendency to introspection, the prevalence of which justified the advice given by the editor of a magazine to a contributor, "Should you ever be drowned or hung, be sure and make a note of your sensations; they will be worth to you ten guineas a sheet." The efforts which Dr. Porter recommends, "to hope and fear again and again, simply that we may know more exactly how it seems or what it is to perform [*sic*] or experience these states," to say nothing of their double futility (for we cannot so hope and fear, and if we could it would teach us little of the essence of these emotions), are very unwholesome.

Within the Scottish school we should suppose that this book must take a very high rank. Indeed, as long as Mr. Mansel (even if he properly belongs to that school) produces nothing more, we do not see what living writer, unless it be Dr. McCosh, is to dispute with Dr. Porter the honor of the very first place. In the character of his genius and learning more like Dugald Stewart than any of the other *coryphæi* of that philosophy, Dr. Porter's relation to Scotch psychology is somewhat similar to that of Hamilton, inasmuch as he modifies the pure Scotch opinions by an admixture of the prevalent German views. As Hamilton treated high metaphysics upon modified Kantian principles, so Porter imports into the same branch of philosophy considerations which have been derived in large measure from the study of Trendelenburg. His metaphysic starts, as it ought, with a theory of inductive reasoning. He holds that the reason why an innumerable number of instances will not justify the inference that all swans are white, while a single instance would suffice to show that all men's heads are placed upon their shoulders, is because a failure of the latter induction, unlike a failure of the former, would be "entirely incompatible with the ideal of beauty and convenience to which we assume that nature would certainly conform." Since then the validity of induction rests upon certain assumptions of this sort, these assumptions are not themselves demonstrable either by induction or otherwise, but are original and self-evident truths. These intuitions are as follows: 1st, that an object is either substance or attribute; 2d, that objects originate by a causative energy; 3d, that objects are in space and time; 4th, that properties and laws which are known *indicate* and *signify* other properties and laws; 5th, that *nature adapts objects and powers to certain ends;* and 6th, that the *rational methods of the divine and human minds are similar.* These ultimate facts and relations are not learned by the ordinary processes of thought, imagination, and perception. They are "not *apprehended by,* but *involved in,* these processes," and must, therefore, be referred to a separate faculty. They are first apprehended in a concrete, not in an abstract, form. We do not set out with the universal belief that every event has a cause, but as we apprehend each separate object by perception or consciousness we apprehend it as caused. Such apprehension is a proposition, and from such propositions are derived the various concepts, substance and attribute, cause and effect, means and end, etc. These concepts being apprehended abstractly and compared with the processes of cognition are found to be essentially involved in them all. Finally, it is perceived that over against all objects of experience, as having these various relations of dependence, there must be some independent correlates upon which they depend. Thus all things being extended, there must be a space; in correlation with all things as being caused there must be a First Cause, etc. The whole argument upon this subject, which occupies some two hundred pages, is followed out with great ability.

It will be perceived that this theory of intuition has a general resemblance to that of Dr. McCosh.

It is easy to see upon what side such a theory may expect attack. Its essence is that the process by which we attain our first knowledge of these fundamental ideas is essentially different from the other processes of the mind. Now, if it were shown that all the other mental processes, whether of cognition, emotion, or action, were essentially one, it would be hard to prevent men from believing that this process alone did not conform to their common formula. Accordingly, it is not surprising that we find throughout Dr. Porter's work a tendency to exaggerate the distinctions between the faculties and to overrate the importance of these distinctions, and to explain facts by the general supposition of a peculiar faculty even when such a supposition requires it to be as complex as the facts themselves, in order to explain them in detail. But though the reader of this book would scarcely suspect it, there is a movement which is steadily coming to a head towards identifying all the faculties. It is the motive of all sensualism, it is the latest mood of psycho-physical inquirers, and it is beginning to be consciously felt even in this country. If that doctrine should once be established, it would not avail Dr. Porter's theory that he had correctly answered the question why the inference that all men carry their heads upon their shoulders is so strong, because it would appear that the principle of design which effects this inference is only a derivative one, and that the only assumption which can enter into every induction is no assumption about the things reasoned upon at all. Dr. Porter's opinion is, that the assumptions involved in induction are the only basis of religion; but the only assumption which can be essentially involved in scientific inference is the assumption of the validity of scientific inference. But to make the validity of scientific inference the only possible basis of religion approaches very near to pure rationalism—a doctrine that is not in the interest of religion, because it subordinates religion to science. We are inclined to suspect that the metaphysician, whether spiritualist or materialist, is in this dilemma; either he must look upon his problems with the cold eye of science, and have no other feeling for the eternal interests of man than the curiosity with which he would examine a trilobite; and then, being in a state of mind essentially irreligious, he can arrive at no result that would really help religion, for at most he can only say to mortal man that it is most likely that there is a God, which is no assurance; or he must bring the feelings of a religious man into the inquiry, and then he is as incompetent to treat the problem as a physician is to judge of his own case. Can it possibly be, that the directest and most uncritical faith in the object which commands one's adoration—the faith of a little child—is the only actual motive to religion which there ever has been or ever will be, and that all reasonings *pro* or *con* upon the fundamental proposition of religion must be entirely irrelevant and unsatisfactory?

The Pairing of the Elements

P 40: Chemical News 4*(June 1869):339–40*

Your remarks on atomic weights in the April Number of *Chemical News* have suggested to me the enclosed table. You perceive that I have put the different elements at heights representing their atomic weights, and those of one series in columns together. The regularity observable is certainly a very rude one. But considering that every different combination of molecular elasticities (as shown by spectral lines) must give a new set of chemical properties, and considering that only about sixty elementary substances, out of the myriads which there might probably be, are known to us, we ought to expect no more accurate a classification of them than could be made of the animal kingdom, if only sixty animals were known.

You will perceive, however, that the atomic weights seem to arrange themselves on the diagram in parallel shelving lines. Also, that there is a correspondence between the series of artiads and perissads which have the highest atomic weight—that is to say, Na, K, Rb, Cs, Tl, on the one hand, and Mg, Ca, Sr, Ba, Pb, on the other, inasmuch as they form strong bases and peroxides, but no suboxides or acids. A correspondence is also to be traced between the two series having the next highest atomic weights; that is to say, Fl, Cl, Br, I, and O, S, Se, Te, inasmuch as they have a strong tendency to unite in simple proportions with the members of the two groups just mentioned, forming definite and distinct compounds, and also form strong acids with oxygen, but never bases. There is also some correspondence between the next highest groups on each side, that is between N, P, As, Sb, Bi, and C, Si, Ti, Zr, Sn, Pt, inasmuch as they form acids which unite in the most complicated proportions with bases, putting types at defiance, and also (as far as the higher members of each series are concerned) have some tendency to form weak bases.

I also notice that there is a much greater difference in chemical characters between K and Na (not isomorphous), between Fl and Cl (the fluorides being very insoluble), between N and P (N_2O_5 being monobasic), between O and S, between C and Si, and between Gl and Mg, than between any other two adjacent members of their respective series. Also that the maximum of resemblance is between As and Sb, Br and I, Rb and Cs, Sr and Ba, Se and Te, Zn and Cd.

Finally, there is, as you point out, special resemblance between elements occupying corresponding places in the series, as between C and B, O and Fl, S and P, Ca and K, Se and As, Sr and Rb, Ag and Pd, Au and Os, Tl and Pb, &c.

Perissads   Artiads

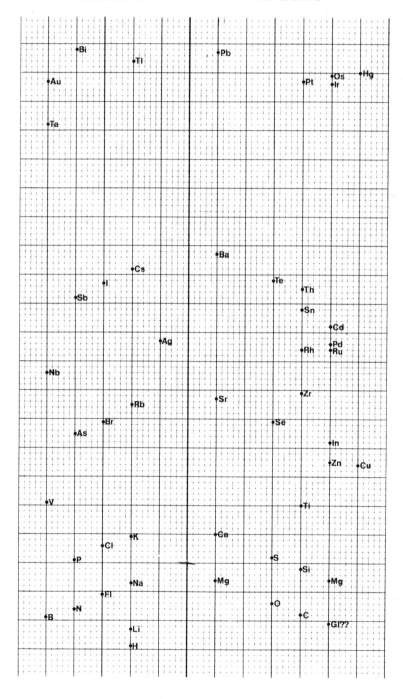

Roscoe's Spectrum Analysis[1]

P 44: Nation *9(22 July 1869):73–74*

The sudden impulse which spectroscopic researchers received in 1860, and which has resulted in several brilliant discoveries in chemistry and astronomy, affords a singular problem in the history of scientific progress. There was nothing absolutely new in the method of Kirchhoff and Bunsen. It consisted essentially in observing the spectra of the colorations imparted by different substances to the non-luminous gas-flame generally used in laboratories. Colored flames had been used since an early period in the history of chemistry for distinguishing the different alkalies and alkaline earths; and J. F. W. Herschel in 1822, W. H. F. Talbot in 1826, and W. A. Miller in 1845, had made some study of the spectra of these flames with reference to chemical analysis. The black lines of the spectra of some of the stars had been examined by Fraunhofer, and found to differ from those of the spectrum common to the sun, moon, and planets. The absorption-lines produced by some gases had been studied by Brewster; and Stokes had pointed out the use of absorption-bands in detecting certain metals in solution. The coincidence of the bright line of incandescent sodium vapor with the D line of the solar spectrum had been noticed by Fraunhofer; and Stokes and William Thomson thence inferred that sodium was contained in the atmosphere of the sun, because a substance can only emit what it is capable of absorbing.

These investigations appertain to all parts of spectral analysis. Why, then, did they remain comparatively unfruitful while the very first memoir of Kirchhoff and Bunsen created a sensation such as the scientific world had not felt since the discovery of Neptune? Kirchhoff himself seems to think that it was because he and Bunsen first

---

1. *Spectrum Analysis. Six Lectures delivered in 1868, before the Society of Apothecaries of London.* By Henry E. Roscoe, B.A., Ph.D., F.R.S., Professor of Chemistry in Owens College, Manchester. New York: D. Appleton & Co. 1869.

clearly showed that the positions of the spectral lines depend solely upon the chemical constituents of the glowing gases. No doubt, the effect upon the imagination of so broad a proposition upon a new matter of science is great, yet the habitual reliance by chemists upon the flame reaction of sodium seems to show that this law had been implicitly assumed upon all hands to be true in practice. Perhaps the chief causes of the profound impression produced by Kirchhoff and Bunsen's papers were these three: 1st, The flame of the Bunsen burner, which was employed by them, was capable from its intense heat and small lighting power of giving much more satisfactory results than the alcohol flames used by the early experimenters; 2d, The new investigations were conducted with a tact and thoroughness which commanded admiration; and 3d, Bunsen had the good fortune and the skill to detect by the new method two metals—rubidium and cæsium—before unknown, in some mineral water he was analyzing, the mixed chlorides of these metals being contained in the proportion of about a drachm in twenty tons of the water.

Bunsen not only discovered these elements, but studied them so well (working partly in company with Kirchhoff) that they are now among those whose chemical relations are the best understood. They have been found to be somewhat widely distributed through the mineral kingdom in very small quantities. An Italian mineral, which had formerly been analyzed by the celebrated mineralogist Plattner, has been found to contain 34 per cent of the oxide of cæsium, which had been mistaken for potassa. Plattner's analysis did not add up 100 per cent at all correctly, owing to the great difference in the combining numbers of potassa and cæsium. Many a chemist would have been ashamed to own such an analysis; Plattner was willing to publish a work which there was no other reason for condemning than one which was perfectly patent, and the result is that time has shown that his experiments were correctly performed. In 1861, an English chemist, Crookes, hardly known before, discovered by means of the spectroscope another metal (thallium) of very singular chemical characters; and this is a discovery which may lead to others, for with thallium a glass has been made which is reported as wonderfully adapted for prisms. In 1863, a fourth metal—indium—resembling zinc was discovered by means of the spectroscope in the zincblende of Freiberg.

The study of the celestial spectra has afforded important information concerning the sun, the stars, the nebulas, some comets, and the aurora borealis. We have learned that many chemical elements which are found upon the earth exist in the atmosphere of the sun, including nearly all of those which form a large proportion of the earth's crust. We have also ascertained, what might have been known *à priori*, that the most elastic of the gases (hydrogen) extends higher from the sun's centre than any of the other substances. The solar spots are getting examined; and if some observations lately reported are confirmed, we shall have some of the theories upon this subject brought to a test. In the stars have been recognized a number of the chemical elements which we know; yet in many of them some of the commonest substances here, and those most essential to life as we know it, are altogether wanting. A displacement of one of the hydrogen lines in the spectrum of Sirius is held to prove that that star is moving rapidly towards our system. The nebulas have been found to be of two entirely different kinds; for the spectra of some of them have been found to consist of isolated bright lines, showing that these nebulas are gaseous, while by far the larger proportion show the continuous spectrum which is seldom produced by an incandescent gas. This difference between the spectra corresponds strictly to a difference between the ordinary telescopic appearances of the nebulas. This is the more interesting, as the first proposition upon which Sir William Herschel founded his nebula hypothesis was that there was no natural classification among nebulas. None of the nebulas have been proved to contain any substance otherwise known to us. Several minute comets have been subjected to spectroscopic examination, and two of them have been shown to contain carbon in some gaseous state. The spectrum of the aurora, as usually seen, consists of a single yellowish-green line, which belongs to no substance with which we are acquainted. As the aurora is held to be above the ordinary atmosphere (and this is confirmed by its showing no nitrogen lines), it follows that there is some unknown gas reaching above the other constituents of the atmosphere. According to the laws of gravity and of diffusion of gases, this substance must extend down to the surface of the earth. Why, then, have not chemists discovered it? It must be a very light elastic gas to reach so high. Now, the atomic weights of elementary gases are proportional to their density. It must, then, have a very small atomic weight. It *may* be as much lighter than hydrogen as hydrogen is than air. In that case, its atomic weight would be so small that, supposing it to have an oxide on the type of water, this oxide would contain less than one per cent of it,

and in general it would enter into its compounds in such small proportions as almost infallibly to escape detection. In addition to the
green line usually seen in the aurora, six others were discovered and
measured at the Harvard College Observatory during the brilliant
display of last spring, and four of these lines were seen again on
another occasion. On the 29th of June last, a single narrow band of
auroral light extended from east to west, clear over the heavens, at
Cambridge, moving from north to south. This was found to have a
continuous spectrum; while the fainter auroral light in the north
showed the usual green line.[2]

Professor Roscoe's book contains an interesting and very thorough account of spectrum analysis. The paper, ink, type, and plates
are beautiful. In his style, Mr. Roscoe neither aims at sensational
effect, nor so strains after simplicity as to verge upon baby-talk. And
these are the two commonest faults of popular science. The only
exaggeration which we have noticed is in the chromo-lithograph of
the spectrum of a nebula. If the book be taken into a nearly dark
room, so that at first glance nothing is seen but the dark oblong
shapes of the whole spectra of that plate, the figure in question *will*
"serve to give some idea of the peculiar beauty of the phenomenon
in question." The lines in the spectrum of Sirius, on the same plate,
are made much too distinct, both absolutely and relatively to the
other stars.

The practical spectroscopists will find here an exceedingly convenient repertory of facts. Kirchhoff's chart of the solar spectrum, with
the extension of Angström and Thalén, is very beautifully reproduced in miniature. Huggins's maps of the metal lines are given in
a form far more convenient for use at the spectroscope than the two
folding sheets in a huge quarto in which alone they have hitherto
been published. The numerical tables in full accompany both sets of
maps. It is much to be regretted that Dr. Gibbs's important tables for
the comparison of Kirchhoff's, Huggins's, and the Normal scales have
not been given. We should also have been glad to have Thalén's
metallic spectra. At the end of the book there is a "List of Memoirs,
etc., upon Spectrum Analysis." This is certainly valuable, and appears
to be full. We observe, however, the omission of Stokes's paper upon
the absorption-bands as a reagent, and also of Secchi's catalogue of

---

2. We have received permission from Prof. Winlock to state this singular fact,
which has not been published before.

the spectra of the stars. As the work contains little about the spectra of particular celestial objects, the last-named paper might well have been translated and inserted in full, with notes.

Professor Roscoe's book may truly be said to be popular and scientific at the same time. And we call it scientific, not only because it is a thorough account of the facts, but also because it contains long extracts from the original memoirs of the serious workers in this branch of science. There is, doubtless, a vast difference between that knowledge of scientific research which comes of actual practice and that which recommends this book to general readers. No one need be scared by a fear that it is mathematical, for everything which borders upon that subject is omitted. There is nothing about the angles of prisms, the theory of exchanges, or the theory of the displacement of lines owing to the motion of the source of light.

[*The Solar Eclipse of 7 August 1869*]

P 70: Coast Survey Report 1869, *126–27*

Cambridge, August 20, 1869

SIR: In accordance with your instructions I transmit to you the following account of the observations made by me on the solar eclipse of August 7. The station which you selected for me was Bardstown, Kentucky, a little southwest of the central line of the eclipse.

I was furnished with an elegant equatorial telescope of four inches clear aperture, and five feet focal length. Upon opposite sides of the tube of this telescope, and parallel to it, were attached two brass rods at the eye-end of the tube, and reaching about a foot beyond it. Upon these rods was fixed the spectroscope, and in such a manner that the slit was plainly visible. I found this arrangement of yours all that could be desired. With it I had little need of a finder. Pieces of white paper were pasted upon the brass-work of the slit to receive the image of the sun, which, during totality, could not well have been seen upon the polished brass. There was some danger of detaching this paper in opening and closing the slit, and I therefore wished to change the width of the slit as few times as possible during totality. The spectroscope attached to my telescope contained a single flint-glass prism and a three-prism direct-vision spectroscope screwed in in place of its telescope. There were no means of measuring the positions of the lines. In order to bring different parts of the spectrum into view it was necessary to unscrew a binding-screw, which then left the somewhat heavy arm which carried the direct-vision spectro-scope entirely loose, and then to move this arm with the hand and tighten up the screw. When this was done the arm would fall a little, and it was only by looking at the spectrum, and estimating how much the arm would fall that it was possible to set upon any part of the spectrum. During totality there might be no light in the field if the observer were to move away from a protuberance, and, therefore, no means of knowing to what part of the spectrum, if any, the arm was set. If the slit was opened to give full light, the paper pasted on it might become detached and render it impossible to set the slit on a protuberance. There was no clock-work on the telescope, and the observers were in continual apprehension of some disturbance in the crowd of mostly ignorant spectators, and therefore an attempt to move this arm was a thing to be dreaded. On the other hand, it could be so set as to afford a view of the spectrum from its red extremity up to half-way between F and G. Under the circumstances I would not venture to move it. If I had been alone, and consequently at my ease, I should have done so.

My telescope was pointed for me by Mr. N. S. Shaler, the geologist, who generously relinquished his opportunity of witnessing the sublime phenomenon undisturbed, and offered his assistance in the astronomical observations. My telescope was, therefore, managed for me with perfect skill and coolness.

Upon the morning of the 6th I set up my instrument and searched for protuberances. I found only one, which was upon the following side of the sun, and was very yellow, that is to say, the yellow line near D was relatively very bright in it. Indeed, I could not see the F line at all. On the morning of the 7th I examined the sun with greater care, and noted several protuberances (which were afterward plainly seen at totality), but none of these were as brilliant as the one which had been seen the day before continued to be; and this was now less high, extended over a larger arc on the disk of the sun, and was still more yellow than it had previously appeared.

At the instant of totality my telescope was pointed on this protuberance and my slit was rather narrow. At that instant the continuous spectrum vanished, and five lines, brilliantly colored, became visible. These were F, *b*, another dimmer and broader line, say one-fourth of the distance from *b* to D, the well-known yellow line near D and C. After observing the spectrum of this protuberance at different positions, I looked at the sun, and was pleased to find my conceptions of the shape and color of this protuberance entirely confirmed.

The same glance showed me upon the southwestern limb of the sun (where my business chiefly lay) a well-marked rose-colored protuberance. I first observed the spectrum of another red protuberance on the southern edge, and then that of the one just mentioned. I found the spectra of the red protuberances to be alike; they differed from that of the yellow one only in the relative greater brilliancy of the red, yellow, and blue lines in the former, the fainter green being especially much fainter. I have no doubt, from my previous observations, that the yellow line was also less bright in the red protuberances, but it appeared so bright that I could not perceive that it was less bright than in the yellow protuberance.

Mr. Shaler then pointed for me on the corona, and I was just opening the slit to get more light when the sun burst forth and put an end to my observations. Two seconds more, or a little more privacy, would have enabled me to get it.

During the eclipse the following miscellaneous observations were made by Mr. Shaler and me:

The protuberances were of two distinct kinds: one sort was low, long, and yellow; the other high, short, and red.

Mr. Shaler saw the disk of the sun break into beads at the moment of totality. The appearance lasted only an instant, and seemed as if it were the effect of irregularities of the limb of the moon. About a month before, Mr. Shaler had observed on the limb of the moon a serrated appearance occasioned by a range of mountains.

Mr. Shaler observed that the corona formed a quadrangle, with concave sides vertical and horizontal, the latter being the longest. He estimated its mean breadth at one and a half the diameter of the sun. He found that it did not fade gradually away, but had a sharply defined edge.

I noticed the following points in reference to colors. While the eclipse was coming on there was no change in the colors of the landscape or of people's faces, but the light had a singular theatrical effect, owing to the sharpness of the shadows. During totality, the light on the landscape was like the gray of twilight. The moon, at this time, was not black, but of a deep, dull, and somewhat purplish blue, darker than the sky. Mr. Shaler confirmed this. The sky was of a dark purplish blue. It was not lighter near the corona. The corona was quite white and not bluish. The yellow protuberances were greenish like the aurora, and intensely brilliant. The red ones had much the color of the light from hydrogen in a Geissler tube. Upon the south, and also (as Mr. Shaler says) on the north, was a salmon-colored light upon the horizon, reaching up some five degrees or more. Venus and Mercury looked as white as Vega ever looks.

Mr. Shaler says: "Little effect was visible on animated nature until the last five minutes before totality, except that the cocks all began to crow, at several points, with the sleepy crow of early morning and not the exultation of full day. The birds began to make their nesting-cries as the light rapidly waned. Cattle were evidently much alarmed, and ran, with tails up and heads erect, across the fields almost in stampede. At the close of the eclipse a hen was found, with her chickens under her wings. Four months' old chickens were seen, within ten minutes of the total eclipse, quietly feeding. They then disappeared. The crowd was placed, at the request of the observer, beyond a fence, distant about thirty feet from the telescope. At the moment of totality a hollow sound, half of fear, half of admiration, called attention to their faces, with dropped jaws and look of horror, which were turned toward the wreck of the sun. There is no doubt that exceeding fear took possession of the whole people. The many who were present slipped away quietly; the few who staid after totality seemed singularly quiet, evidently recovering from a considerable nervous shock."

All of which is respectfully submitted, &c.

CHARLES S. PEIRCE.

Preliminary Sketch of Logic

MS 154: Fall 1869

§1. *Logic* is the science needed in order to test arguments.

The science required for any testing is one which merely divides its object into its natural kinds and describes the characters of each kind. Thus a "Bank-Note Detector" affords the knowledge requisite to testing bank-notes and it describes each kind of bank-note merely, without entering into an account of its manufacture. Such a knowledge will be termed a *classificatory* in opposition to a *causal* or *demonstrative* science.

§2. An *argument* is a statement supposed to *appeal* to some person. Appealing is having such a relation to a person that he will regard the statement as if he would admit that every set of facts, taken as those stated have been taken, determines by certain relations another possible statement, and that this would be more apt to be true in the long run when the facts stated are true, than a random assertion would be.[1]

That which is laid down is termed the *premiss* or *premises;* the determinate proposition to which the *premise* or premises are related is termed the *conclusion;* and the implication that such a conclusion is usually true if the premises are is termed the *leading principle.*

§3. A *valid* argument (opposed to a *fallacious* argument or *fallacy*) is one whose leading principle is true.

A *demonstrative* (opposed to a merely *probable*) argument is one whose leading principle would make *every* such conclusion true and not merely the greater number of them.

§4. An argument determines its conclusion to be true, only if both leading principle and premisses are true. Whatever is required be-

---

1. This sufficiently sets forth the essential elements of an argument; but does not define it, since in introducing the conception of truth it commits a diallele.

sides the premises to determine the truth of the conclusion is *ipso facto* implied in the leading principle. Hence whatever fact (not superfluous) is dropped from the premises is added to the leading principle; and no fact can be eliminated from the leading principle without having been added to the premises. All that is in the premisses cannot however be thrown into the leading principle, since there is no argument which states nothing. Nor is there an argument without a leading principle, for if nothing is implied the conclusion is already stated in the premisses. But a mere statement is not an argument.

§5. That there is a certain minimum leading principle, that cannot be got rid of may be illustrated as follows. Let a certain argument be *A* and its conclusion, *B*. Then we may say that the leading principle is that "If *A* is true *B* is true." Take this as an additional premiss and the argument becomes—

> If *A*, *B*
> But *A*
> *Ergo B.*

The leading principle of this plainly is that if two facts are related as reason and consequent and the reason be true the consequent is true. Make another premise of this and the argument becomes—

If one statement be related to another so that if the former is true the latter is and if the former is true, the latter is.

A is so related to *B* and is true

Ergo B is true.

Now the leading principle of this is plainly the same as that of the last previous form of the argument. Here, therefore, is a leading principle which is not dispensed with by being thrown into the premiss. And as it is absurd to say that anything can be eliminated from the leading principle by taking away anything from the premises, it is plain this principle must have lurked in the leading principle even of the first form of the argument.

An argument in which everything has been eliminated from the leading principle which can be so eliminated is termed a *complete* in opposition to an *incomplete* or *rhetorical* argument or *enthymeme.*[2]

---

2. Aristotle makes the rhetorical argument the same as the probable one. This is an error.

Logic is, of course, not the encyclopaedia. Those things which can possibly be required to be stated have as such no truth in common and are in detail the object of the various sciences. Hence logic does not take account of the truth of premisses, or of anything which would appear as a premiss if the argument were put into the complete form. On the other hand whatever cannot be eliminated from the leading principle is taken for granted by every other science and not laid down; hence logic does take account of these things. Logic might, indeed, be defined as the science of the leading principles of complete arguments; and such leading principles are properly termed *logical principles.*

The example of a logical principle given above illustrates an important character of all such principles; namely, that they not only cannot be stated in arguments without superfluity but that in one sense they cannot be stated at all. The statement which contains only a logical principle contains no fact. In order to infer so as to conform to logical principles we must infer a determinate conclusion, but in order to *state* what shall imply a logical principle we are not obliged to make any definite statement at all.

§6. A *proposition* is a collocation of significant terms so put as to state something.

To *state* is to purport to represent an object—or in other words, to represent that whatever a certain significant term represents is represented by another significant term.

The manner in which the significant terms are put together—or the sign that they are so put together—is termed the *copula.* This is essentially the same for all propositions.

The term whose object is said to be represented by another may be called the *true subject;* that which is said to represent the object of the other may be called the true predicate.

§7. A *significant term* is something which stands for an object, by means of its relation to a certain symbol or symbols.

A *symbol* is something to which a certain character is *imputed,* that is which stands for whatever object may have that character.

§8. Mere iteration is not argument, for it could not appeal to any mind that did not admit the fact asserted, and one that already admitted it it would not affect. In short, it does not fall strictly under the definition of argument nor is it analogous to it. Every conclusion therefore states something different from any one of its premisses. But the copula is the same for all propositions. Hence the conclusion must be obtained from any premiss by the substitution of a significant term or terms.

That another significant term or terms may be substituted for a term or terms of a premise, requires to be put into another premise in a complete argument, unless the substitution is wholly determined by a principle implied by every such argumentative substitution. But in this case the principle would be implied in the very premiss itself and therefore the conclusion would merely repeat a part of what is implied in the premise, which we have just seen is impossible. In all cases, therefore, a second premiss is required to express the condition which makes it possible to substitute the conclusion for the first premise.

If more premisses than one are required to express the fact that the conclusion can be substituted for any given premise, either these other premisses by themselves yield one conclusion which expresses this fact or successive substitutions can be made by single propositions. Hence every argument of more than two premisses can be broken up into arguments of two premisses. Such arguments are called *simple* arguments in opposition to *complex* ones.

§9. The substitution of conclusion for a premiss is as we have seen the substitution of one term for another.

Now, it is evident that the only such substitution which necessarily yields a true conclusion from true premises is the substitution for a subject or predicate of another term which has as subject or predicate no function or value beyond that of the term for which it is substituted.

We thus get such an argument as this—

$$S \text{ has no force as subject beyond } M$$
$$P \text{ has no force as predicate beyond } M$$
$$\therefore S \text{ is } P$$

or in other language S is denoted by M
                            M connotes P
                            $\therefore S$ is P

This principle is that of *deduction*.

§10. Passing over for the present the divisions of mood and figure, also over the question whether there is any other form of predication except that in which the predicate is said to denote and to be connoted by the subject, we come to another principle of inference.

[The Logic Notebook]

MS 155: October 1869

1869 Oct. 6

Combination of Arithmetic and Boole's Calculus

Given $\quad pa,\overline{m} \doteqdot 0 \quad$ where $p = \frac{1}{2}$

$\qquad\qquad qa,\overline{n} \doteqdot 0 \qquad$ " $\quad q = \frac{1}{2}$

$\qquad\qquad m,n \doteqdot 0$

$\qquad\qquad x,m \doteqdot 0$

$\qquad\qquad x,\overline{a} \doteqdot 0$

We have by ordinary processes

(1) $\qquad\qquad qa,\overline{n} \;[+]\; pa,n + pa,x + x,\overline{a} \doteqdot 0$

And from this

(2) $\qquad\qquad\qquad pa,qa \doteqdot 0$

But $\qquad\qquad\qquad p \mathbin{+\!\!,} q \doteqdot p + q - p,q$

$\qquad\qquad \therefore p \mathbin{+\!\!,} q = p + q - p,q$

$\qquad\qquad$ and since $p + q = 1$

$\qquad\qquad\qquad p \mathbin{+\!\!,} q = 1 - p,q$

$\qquad\qquad$ But $p \mathbin{+\!\!,} q \doteqdot 1 - \overline{p},\overline{q}$

$\qquad\qquad\qquad\qquad = 1 - \overline{p},\overline{q}$

$\qquad\qquad$ Hence $p,q = \overline{p},\overline{q}$

$\qquad\qquad$ Hence $pa,qa \doteqdot 0 \doteqdot \overline{p}a,\overline{q}a$

Hence adding this to (1) we have

(3) $\qquad qa,\overline{n} \mathbin{+\!\!,} pa,n \mathbin{+\!\!,} pa,x \mathbin{+\!\!,} x,\overline{a} \mathbin{+\!\!,} \overline{p}a,\overline{q}a \doteqdot 0$

But $\qquad qa(1-a) \doteq 0$

$\qquad\qquad\quad pa(1-a) \doteq 0$

Hence $\qquad x,\bar{a} \;+_,\; \overline{pa},\overline{qa} \doteq \overline{pa},\overline{qa}$

So that (3) becomes

$$qa,\bar{n} \;+_,\; pa,n \;+_,\; pa,x \;+_,\; \overline{pa},\overline{qa} \doteq 0$$

which gives $\qquad\qquad\qquad x,\bar{n} \doteq 0$

$\qquad\qquad\qquad\qquad\qquad\qquad\qquad$ Oct. 6

Example of an application of the forms l^x

———

How many colours are required to paint a map?

Let *a, b, c, d,* &c. be the countries.

Let *l* be like in colour.

Then since there is but one *a* &c.

$$(1-l)^a = 1 - l^a$$
$$(1-l)^b = 1 - l^b \text{ \&c.}$$

Also $\quad l^{l^x} = l^x \qquad l^x_v = l^x \qquad \left(\begin{array}{l} l^{(1-l)x}\,(1-(1-l)^x) \doteq 0 \\ \text{or } l^{(1-l)x}l^x \doteq 0 \\ \text{or} \\ \text{For } (1-l)^x + l^x \doteq 1 \end{array} \right)$

Also since the earth has no hole in it

If $\quad l^a,l^b \doteq 0 \quad l^a,l^c \doteq 0 \quad l^b,l^c \doteq 0 \quad$ *Then* $l^c l^d \doteq 0$}

$\qquad\qquad\qquad l^a,l^d \doteq 0 \quad l^b,l^d \doteq 0 \quad$ are equations given, and no

$\qquad\qquad\qquad\qquad\qquad\qquad\qquad$ others of the form $l^a l^e + l^b l^e$

$\qquad\qquad\qquad\qquad\qquad\qquad\qquad \doteq 0$ are given

Let us write *A B C* &c. for $l^a\ l^b\ l^c$ &c.

Then the above principle is that

if $A,B \doteq 0 \quad A,C \doteq 0 \quad B,C \doteq 0$ are among the given equations

(by *given* equations I mean those determined by direct touching of one country on another)

and if F^A F^B &c. denote factors a b &c.

other than a b &c. in the given equations

$$F^A, F^B = 1 \text{ denote it by } D \text{ or } l^d$$

Let L denote the sum of terms in given equations which contain neither A, B, or C. (The given equations are all of the form $(l^g, l^h \doteq 0)$.)

Let us now eliminate A, B, and C from the given equations. Since $AB = 0$, $AC = 0$, $BC = 0$ are given equations when 2 or 3 of the three letters A, B, C is put $= 1$ then the sum of the equations $= 1$.

When $A = 1$ $B = 0$ $C = 0$ The sum of equations becomes $F^A \dotplus L$

" $A = 0$ $B = 1$ "   "   "   "   "   " $F^B \dotplus L$

" A " $B = 0$ $C = 1$ "   "   "   "   " $F^C \dotplus L$

The product is

$$F^A F^B F^C + L \doteq 0$$

Denote $L \doteq D\Sigma M \dotplus \Sigma N$ where D has the signification mentioned above.

Thence it is easy to deduce that if $(1 - A)(1 - B)(1 - C) \doteq 0$ or if only 3 colours are used

$$D = C$$
$$\text{But } D = F^A F^B$$
$$\text{when } D, F^C = 0$$

That is D cannot touch C.

But from the given equations alone this cannot be deduced. Hence not in every case will 3 colours serve.

Now let us suppose $(1 - A)(1 - B)(1 - C)(1 - l^{(1-l)^{a} \dotplus b \dotplus c}) \doteq 0$ or that 4 colours are used.

Then if $D = C$ Nothing follows from this proposition.

If $D, C = 0$ then $D = (1 - A)(1 - B)(1 - C)$.

But there is nothing in the given equations to contradict it.

If

every a is   lower   than   every b
" b "   higher   "   " a and *vice versa*
$\therefore$ If every a is not lower   than   every b
" b "   "   higher   "   " a

$$l^1 \doteqdot 0 \quad \textit{usually.}$$
$$l^0 \doteqdot 1 \quad \textit{invariably, I think.}$$

If $a < l^b$ $b < \log_l a$

      or $b < l^a_v$

If $b < l^a_v$ $a < \log_{l_v} b$

      or $a < (l_v)^b_v$

EUREKA
$(l^a)^b$ is not the same as $l^{a,b}$.
Hence, $(l')^a$ is not the same as l^a.
    Hence, l is not the same as l'.
For $(l)^a \doteqdot l^a$ but $(l')^a$ is not.
    Hence, $l < m$
may be taken for the expression that

$$l^a < m^a$$
$$l^b < m^b \text{ &c. &c.}$$

The English Doctrine of Ideas [1]

P 45: Nation 9(25 November 1869):461–62

James Mill's *Analysis of the Human Mind* has long been known as one of the most original and characteristic productions of English thought. It now appears in a second edition, enlarged by many long notes by the author's disciples, who are to-day the most eminent representatives of the English school. These notes are chiefly of interest as forming the clearest exposition of the present state of opinion in that school, and of the changes which it has undergone since 1829.

It is a timely publication, because the peculiarities of the English mind are so sharply cut in James Mill that it will help to awaken that numerous class of general readers who have become impregnated with the ideas of Stuart Mill's logic into self-consciousness in reference to the intellectual habit which they have contracted. A philosophy or method of thinking which is held in control—the mind rising above it, and understanding its limitations—is a valuable instrument; but a method in which one is simply immersed, without seeing how things can be otherwise rationally regarded, is a sheer restriction of the mental powers. In this point of view, it is a fact of interest to the adherent of the English school that it is not a particularly learned body, and that its more modern leaders at least have not generally been remarkable for an interior understanding of opposing systems, nor even for a wide acquaintance with results the most analogous to their own which have been obtained in other countries. It is a familiar logical maxim that nothing can be comprehended without comparing it with other things; and this is so true in regard to philosophies that a great German metaphysician has said that whoever has reached a thorough comprehension of a philosophical system has

---

1. *Analysis of the Phenomena of the Human Mind.* By James Mill. A new edition, with notes, illustrative and critical, by Alexander Bain, Andrew Findlater, and George Grote; edited with additional notes by John Stuart Mill. 2 vols. 8vo. London: Longmans, 1869.

outgrown it. Accordingly, we think that we discern in English philosophers an unconsciousness of their own peculiarities, and a tendency to describe them in language much too wide; in consequence of which the student has to gather the essential characters of their thought by a comparison with different systems, and cannot derive any real understanding of them from anything which lies wholly within their horizon alone.

This somewhat insular group of thinkers are now often called Positivists. If this means that they are the philosophers of exact experience, it is too much to say of them; if it means that they are followers of M. Comte, it is too little. They seem to us to be what remains of that *sacra schola invictissimorum nominalium,* of which the English Ockham was the "venerable beginner." Many pages of this *Analysis* might, if somewhat changed in language, easily be mistaken for Ockham's.

The chief methodical characteristic of their thought is "analysis." And what is analysis? The application of Ockham's razor—that is to say, the principle of reducing the expression of the nature of things and of the mind to its simplest terms by lopping off everything which looks like a metaphysical superfluity. By mental analysis the English mean the separation of a compound idea or sensation into its constituent ideas or sensations. Thus, they would say that the sensation of white had no distinct existence; it is merely the concurrence of the three sensations of blue, red, and yellow. So, James Mill says that virtue is the habit of associating with the actions from which men derive advantage the pleasures which result from them. It is plain that such analysis reduces the number of distinct constituents of human nature. The same thinkers reason in a manner entirely analogous when they are not dealing with the mind at all; and in general their method may be described as simplifying existing hypotheses and then endeavoring to show that known facts may be accounted for by these simplified hypotheses. In this way, a highly elegant and instructive system has been created; but it is not pre-eminently scientific. It might be scientific if these philosophers occupied themselves with subjecting their modified theories to the test of exact experience in every possible way, and spent their time in a systematic course of observations and measurements, as some German psychologists have done. But that is not their business; they are writers. Their energies are occupied in adjusting their theories to the facts, and not in ascertaining the certainty of their theories. This cannot be said to hold good fully in the case of Mr. Bain; his books are largely occupied with correcting and limiting theories; but so far he appears quite different from the English school generally, to which, however, he certainly belongs. Desultory experience is what they all build on, and on that basis no true science can be reared.

James Mill's psychological theory is this: All that is in the mind is sensations, and copies of sensations; and whatever *order* there is in these copies is merely a reproduction of the order which there was in their originals. To have a feeling (a sensation, or the copy of one), and to know that we have it, and what its characters are; or to have two feelings, and to know their mutual relations and agreements, are not two things, but one and the same thing. These principles are held to be sufficient to explain all the phenomena of mind.

The beauty of this theory appears when we consider that it is as much as to say simply that *ideas* in *consciousness* are concrete images of *things* in *existence*. For a thing to exist, and for it to have all its characters; or for two things to exist, and for them to have all their relations of existence to each other, are not two facts, but one. A book which thoroughly follows out such a hypothesis is a great contribution to human knowledge, even if the hypothesis does not satisfy the facts. For it clears up our conceptions greatly to understand precisely how far a simple, single supposition like this will go, and where it will fail.

The theory is of the most markedly English character. Though it is a single supposition which cannot logically be broken, yet we may say that its chief points are these three:

1. Every idea is the mere copy of a sensation.

2. Whatever is in the mind is known.

3. The order of ideas is a mere reproduction of the order of sensations.

That every idea is the copy of a sensation has always been recognized as the chief point of English psychology. Hume expresses it in the clearest language, saying that the difference between an idea and a sensation is, that the former is faint and the latter lively. This involves the opinion that all our ideas are singular, or devoid of generality; that is, that just as every existing thing either has or has not each conceivable quality, so every idea is an idea of the presence or absence of every quality. As Berkeley says, my idea of a man "must be either of a white or a black or a tawny, a straight or a crooked, a tall or a low or a middle-sized man." Accordingly, it is obvious that

one of the difficulties in the way of these philosophers is to explain
our seeming to attach a general meaning to words; for if we have
nothing in our minds but sensations and ideas, both of which are
singular, we cannot really take a word in a general sense. So, if I
compare a red book and a red cushion, there is, according to them,
no general sensation *red* which enters into both these images, nor is
there any idea of a general respect, color, in which they agree; and
their similarity can consist in nothing whatsoever, except that they
have the same general name attached to them; and there is no possible reason for their being associated together under one name
(which these philosophers can consistently give) than one at which
James Mill hints, and which follows from his principles—namely, that
the corresponding sensations have been frequently associated together in experience. This was perfectly appreciated in the days
when nominalism was actively discussed, but now the nominalists do
not seem to look it in the face. We will, therefore, put some passages
from the present work in juxtaposition, to show that James Mill did
feel, obscurely perhaps, this difficulty. "Every color is an individual
color, every size an individual size, every shape an individual shape.
But things have no individual color in common, no individual shape
in common, no individual size in common; that is to say, they have
neither shape, color, nor size in common" (vol. i, p. 249). He here
speaks of things; but as things are only sensations or ideas with him,
all this holds good of ideas. "It is easy to see, among the principles
of association, what particular principle it is which is mainly concerned in classification. . . . That principle is resemblance." "Having
the sensation. . . . what happens in recognizing that it is similar to a
former sensation? Besides the *sensation,* in this case, there is an *idea.*
The idea of the former sensation is called up by, that is, is associated
with, the new sensation. As having a sensation, and a sensation, and
knowing them, that is, distinguishing them, are the same thing; and
having an idea, and an idea, is knowing them; so, having an idea and
a sensation, and distinguishing the one from the other, are the same
thing. But to know that I have the idea and the sensation, in this case,
is not all. I observe that the sensation is like the idea. What is this
observation of likeness? Is it anything but that distinguishing of one
feeling from another which we have recognized to be the same thing
as having two feelings? As change of sensation is sensation; as change
from a sensation to an idea differs from change to a sensation in
nothing but this, that the second feeling in the latter change is an

idea, not a sensation; and as the passing from one feeling to another is distinguishing, the whole difficulty seems to be resolved, for undoubtedly the distinguishing differences and similarities is the same thing—a similarity being nothing but a slight difference" (vol. ii, p. 15). Evidently, if a similarity is a difference, the line of demarcation between the two is to be drawn where our language happens to draw it. But to ascertain why two similar sensations are associated under one name, we must recur to his general law of association, which is given in these words: "Our ideas spring up or exist in the order in which the sensations existed, of which they are the copies. This is the general law of the 'Association of Ideas' " (vol. i, p. 78). "Resemblance only remains as an alleged principle of association, and it is necessary to enquire whether it is included in the laws which have been above expounded. I believe it will be found that we are accustomed to see like things together. When we see a tree, we generally see more trees than one; when we see an ox, we generally see more oxen than one; a sheep, more sheep than one; a man, more men than one. From this observation, I think we may refer resemblance to the law of frequency, of which it seems to form only a particular case" (vol. i, p. 111). This is what he says upon the subject of similarity. As an attempt at analyzing that idea, it is a complete failure, and with it the whole system falls. Stuart Mill is gravely mistaken in supposing that his father's rejection of resemblance as a guiding principle of association was an unimportant part of his theory. Association by resemblance stood in the way of his doctrine that the order of ideas is nothing but the order of sensations, and to grant the mind a power of giving an inwardly determined order to its ideas would be to grant that there is something in the mind besides sensations and their copies. Moreover, upon nominalistic principles similarity can *consist* in nothing but the association of two ideas with one name, and therefore James Mill must say, with Ockham, that such association is without any reason or cause, or must explain it as he attempts to do. The doctrine that an idea is the copy of a sensation has obviously not been derived from exact observation. It has been adopted because it has been thought that it *must be so;* in fact, because it was a corollary from the notion (which its authors could not free themselves from) that ideas were in consciousness just as things are in existence. It thus forms a striking illustration of Wundt's remark that the chief difference between modern attempts to put psychology upon a basis like that of the physical sciences and earlier speculative systems, is that speculations are now put forth as results of scientific research, while formerly facts of observation were frequently represented as deductions of pure thought.

The same thing may be said of the doctrine that to feel and to be aware of the feeling are the same thing. James Mill plainly cannot conceive of the opposite supposition. With him, therefore, it is a mere result of defective reading. It is not only not supported by exact observation, but it is directly refuted in that way.

The English school are accustomed to claim the doctrine of the association of ideas as their own discovery, but Hamilton has proved that it is not only given by Aristotle, but that, as to its main features, the knowledge of it by the English was derived from him. This, therefore, does not constitute a valid claim to the scientific character; yet it is the only claim they have. At present, the doctrine has received a transformation at the hands of Wundt of the most fundamental description. He has solved the perplexing questions concerning the principles of association by showing that every train of thought is essentially inferential in its character, and is, therefore, regulated by the principles of inference.[2] But this conception is also found in Aristotle.

The *Analysis* is written in an unusually forcible, perspicuous, and agreeable style—a character which belongs to most of the English philosophers more or less, but to none in a higher degree than to James Mill. One wishes that such a master of language had a doctrine to enunciate which would test his powers more than this simple English psychology. The fewer elements a hypothesis involves, the less complication and consequent obscurity will appear in its development.

2. This idea is fully explained in his very important and agreeably written *Vorlesungen über die Menschen- und Thierseele.*

[LECTURES ON BRITISH LOGICIANS]

Lecture I. Early nominalism and realism

MS 158: November–December 1869

The president requested me to deliver nine lectures upon the history of logic. I have limited the subject to British Logicians, but even with this limitation I have a subject which would require for an adequate treatment not less than ten times the number of lectures I have to give. I am under the necessity therefore of treating it in an altogether fragmentary manner and you must not be surprized that I leave quite out of account some of the most famous names.

Let it be understood in the first place that I do not come here to air my own opinions or even to talk about logic at all but purely and solely about a branch of history,—the history of logical thought in the British Islands. In such imperfect manner as the time will allow I shall endeavor to show you how this subject appeared to the chief thinkers in England and reproduce their state of mind. But whether they were right or wrong will be for you and me a question altogether to be neglected, for that is a question of philosophy and not of history.

This history of logic is not altogether without an interest as a branch of history. For so far as the logic of an age adequately represents the methods of thought of that age, its history is a history of the human mind in its most essential relation,—that is to say with reference to its power of investigating truth. But the chief value of the study of historical philosophy is that it disciplines the mind to regard philosophy in a cold and scientific eye and not with passion as though philosophers were contestants.

British Logic is a subject of some particular interest inasmuch as some peculiar lines of thought have always been predominant in those islands, giving their logicians a certain family resemblance, which already begins to appear in very early times. The most striking characteristic of British thinkers is their nominalistic tendency. This has always been and is now very marked. So much so that in England and in England alone are there many thinkers more distinguished at this day as being nominalistic than as holding any other doctrines. William Ockham or Oakum, an Englishman, is beyond question the greatest nominalist that ever lived; while Duns Scotus, another British name, it is equally certain is the subtilest advocate of the opposite opinion. These two men Duns Scotus and William Ockham are decidedly the greatest speculative minds of the middle ages, as well as two of the profoundest metaphysicians that ever lived. Another circumstance which makes Logic of the British Islands interesting is that there more than elsewhere have the studies of the logic of the natural sciences been made. Already we find some evidence of English thought running in that direction, when we meet with that singular phenomenon Roger Bacon,—a man who was scientific before science began. At the first dawn of the age of science, Francis Bacon wrote that professedly and really logical treatise the *Novum Organum,* a work the celebrity of which perhaps exceeds its real merits. In our own day, the writings of Whewell, Mill, and Herschel afford some of the finest accounts of the method of thought in science. Another direction in which logical thought has gone farther in England than elsewhere is in mathematico-formal logic,—the chief writers on which are Boole, De Morgan, and the Scotch Sir Wm. Hamilton,— for although Hamilton was so bitter against mathematics, that his own doctrine of the quantified predicate is essentially mathematical is beyond intelligent dispute. This fondness for the formal part of logic already appeared in the middle ages, when the nominalistic school of Ockham—the most extremely scholastic of the scholastics —and next to them the school of Scotus—carried to the utmost the doctrines of the *Parva Logicalia* which were the contribution of those ages to this branch of the science. And those *Parva Logicalia* may themselves have had an English origin for the earliest known writer upon the subject—unless the *Synopsis* Ἀριστοτελοῦς Ὀργάνου be attributed to Psellus—is an Englishman, William of Sherwood.

You perceive therefore how intimately modern and medieval thought are connected in England—more so than in Germany or France; and therefore how indispensable it is that we should begin our history at a very early date. But here comes a stupendous difficulty. If I were to devote the whole of my nine lectures to medieval philosophy I could not enable you to read a page of Scotus or of

Ockham understandingly nor even give you a good general idea of
their historical position. I shall content myself therefore with some
remarks upon their nominalism and realism with special reference
to their relations to modern doctrines concerning generals. And as
preliminary to those remarks I will in this lecture give a very slight
sketch of the great strife between the nominalists and realists which
took place in the 12th century.

All real acquaintance with Scholasticism died out in the 17th
century, and it was not till late in our own that the study of it was
taken up again. Even now the later ages are little understood but the
great logical controversies of the 12th century have been pretty well
studied. Cousin began the investigation, by publishing some logical
works of Abaelard, together with other works which he wrongly
attributed to the author, and by writing an introduction to them in
which he gave his conception of the dispute. These contributions of
Cousin are contained in his *Ouvrages Inédits d'Abélard,* which forms
one of the volumes of the *Documents relatives à l'Histoire de France*
and in the second edition of his *Fragments Philosophiques: Philosophie Scholastique.* Hauréau in his *Histoire de la philosophie scholastique,* de Rémusat in his *Abélard,* Jourdain in his *Recherches critiques
sur la connaissance d'Aristote dans le moyen age,* and Barach in his
Nominalismus vor Roscellinus have brought to light other important
documents relative to this subject. The works of Anselm, John of
Salisbury, and Alanus of Lille, the *Liber sex principiorum* of Gilbertus, the same author's commentary on the three books *De Trinitate*
falsely attributed to Boethius, and Abaelard's letters to Heloise and
his *Introductio in Theologiam*—works having an important bearing
upon this part of logical history—were already in our possession. The
best account of the dispute is contained in Prantl's great *Geschichte
der Logik im Abendlande,* chapter 14.

The most striking characteristic of medieval thought is the importance attributed to authority. It was held that authority and reason
were two coördinate methods of arriving at truth, and far from holding that authority was secondary to reason, the scholastics were much
more apt to place it quite above reason. When Berengarius in his
dispute with Lanfranc remarked that the whole of an affirmation
does not stand after a part is subverted, his adversary replied: "The
sacred authorities being relinquished you take refuge in dialectic,
and when I am to hear and to answer concerning the ministry of the
Faith, I prefer to hear and to answer the sacred authorities which are

supposed to relate to the subject than dialectical reasons." To this Berengarius replied that St. Augustine in his book *De doctrina chris-tiana* says that what he said concerning an affirmation is bound up indissolubly with that very eternity of truth which is God. But added "Maximi plane cordis est, per omnia ad dialecticam confugere, quia confugere ad eam ad rationem est confugere, quo qui non confugit, cum secundum rationem sit factus ad imaginem Dei, suum honorem reliquit, nec potest renovari de die in diem ad imaginem Dei." Next to sacred authorities—the Bible, the church, and the fathers,—that of Aristotle of course ranked the highest. It could be denied, but the presumption was immense against his being wrong on any particular point.

Such a weight being attached to authority,—a weight which would be excessive were not the human mind at that time in so uneducated a state that it could not do better than follow masters since it was totally incompetent to solve metaphysical problems for itself,—it follows naturally that originality of thought was not greatly admired but that on the contrary the admirable mind was his who succeeded in interpreting consistently the dicta of Aristotle, Por-phyry, and Boethius. Vanity, therefore, the vanity of cleverness was a vice from which the schoolmen were remarkably free. They were minute and thorough in their knowledge of such authorities as they had, and they were equally minute and thorough in their treatment of every question which came up.

All these characters remind us less of the philosophers of our day than of the men of science. I do not hesitate to say that scientific men now think much more of authority than do metaphysicians; for in science a question is not regarded as settled or its solution as certain until all intelligent and informed doubt has ceased and all competent persons have come to a catholic agreement, whereas 50 metaphysi-cians each holding opinions that no one of the other 49 can admit, will nevertheless severally regard their 50 opposite opinions as more certain than that the sun will rise tomorrow. This is to have what seems an absurd disregard for others' opinions; the man of science attaches a positive value to the opinion of every man as competent as himself so that he cannot but have a doubt of a conclusion which he would adopt were it not that a competent man opposes it; but on the other hand, he will regard a sufficient divergence from the con-victions of the great body of scientific men as tending of itself to argue incompetence and he will generally attach little weight to the

314 WRITINGS OF CHARLES S. PEIRCE, 1867–1871

opinions of men who have long been dead and were ignorant of much that has been since discovered which bears upon the question in hand. The schoolmen however attached the greatest authority to men long since dead and there they were right for in the dark ages it was not true that the later state of human knowledge was the most perfect but on the contrary. I think it may be said then that the schoolmen did not attach too much weight to authority although they attached much more to it than we ought to do or than ought or could be attached to it in any age in which science is pursuing a successful and onward course—and of course infinitely more than is attached to it by those intellectual nomads the modern metaphysicians, including the positivists. In the slight importance they attached to a brilliant theory, the schoolmen also resembled modern scientific men, who cannot be comprehended in this respect at all by men not scientific. The followers of Herbert Spencer, for example, cannot comprehend why scientific men place Darwin so infinitely above Spencer, since the theories of the latter are so much grander and more comprehensive. They cannot understand that it is not the sublimity of Darwin's theories which makes him admired by men of science, but that it is rather his minute, systematic, extensive, and strict scientific researches which have given his theories a more favorable reception—theories which in themselves would barely command scientific respect. And this misunderstanding belongs to all those metaphysicians who fancy themselves men of science on account of their metaphysics. This same scientific spirit has been equally misunderstood as it is found in the schoolmen. They have been above all things found fault with because they do not write a literary style and do not "study in a literary spirit." The men who make this objection can not possibly comprehend the real merits of modern science. If the words *quidditas, entitas,* and *haecceitas,* are to excite our disgust, what shall we say of the Latin of the botanists, and the style of any technically scientific work. As for that phrase "studying in a literary spirit" it is impossible to express how nauseating it is to any scientific man, yes even to the scientific linguist. But above all things it is the searching thoroughness of the schoolmen which affiliates them with men of science and separates them, worldwide, from modern so-called philosophers. The thoroughness I allude to consists in this that in adopting any theory, they go about everywhere, they devote their whole energies and lives, in putting it to tests *bona fide*—not such as shall merely add a new spangle to the glitter of their proofs but such as shall really go towards satisfying their restless insatiable impulse to put their opinions to the *test.* Having a theory they must apply it to every subject and to every branch of every subject to see whether it produces a result in accordance with the only criteria they were able to apply—the truth of the catholic faith and the teaching of the Prince of Philosophers. Mr. George Henry Lewes in his work on Aristotle seems to me to have come pretty near to stating the true cause of the success of modern science when he has said that it was *Verification.* I should express it in this way: modern students of science have been successful, because they have spent their lives not in their libraries and museums but in their laboratories and in the field—and while in their laboratories and in the field they have been not gazing on nature with a vacant eye, that is in passive perception unassisted by thought—but have been *observing*—that is perceiving by the aid of analysis,—and testing suggestions of theories. The cause of their success has been that the motive which has carried them to the laboratory and the field has been a craving to know how things really were and an interest in finding out whether or not general propositions actually held good—which has overbalanced all prejudice, all vanity, and all passion. Now it is plainly not an essential part of this method in general, that the tests were made by the observation of natural objects. For the immense progress which modern mathematics has made is also to be explained by the same intense interest in testing general propositions and particular cases—only the tests were applied by means of particular demonstrations. This is observation, still, for as the great mathematician Gauss has declared—Algebra is a science of the eye,—only it is observation of artificial objects and of a highly recondite character. Now this same unwearied interest in testing general propositions is what produced those long rows of folios of the schoolmen,—and if the test which they employed is of only limited validity so that they could not unhampered go on indefinitely to further discoveries, yet the *spirit,* which is the most essential thing—the *motive,* was nearly the same. And how different this spirit is from that of the major part, though not all, of modern philosophers—even of those who have called themselves empirical, no man who is actuated by it can fail to perceive.

One consequence of the dependence of logical thought in the middle ages upon Aristotle is that the state of development of logic at any time may be measured by the amount of Aristotle's writings which were known to the Western world. At the time of the great discussion between the nominalists and realists in the 12th century the only works of Aristotle which were thoroughly known were the *Categories* and *Peri Hermeneias,* two small treatises forming less than a sixtieth of his works as we now know them and of course a much smaller proportion of them as they originally existed. There was also some knowledge of the *Prior Analytics* but not much. Porphyry's introduction to the categories was well known and the authority of it was nearly equal to that of Aristotle. This treatise concerns the logical nature of genus, species, difference, property, and accident; and is a work of great value and interest. A sentence of this book is said by Cousin to have created scholastic philosophy, which is as true as such eminently French statements usually are. It is however correct that it was in great measure the study of this book which resulted in course of time in the discussion concerning nominalism and realism; but to mistake this discussion for all scholastic philosophy argues great ignorance of the subject,—an ignorance excusable when Cousin wrote but not now.

Before we come to this dispute it will be well to give a glance at the state of opinions upon the subject before the dispute began and as these opinions were much influenced by Scotus Erigena, I will say a word or two about this man.

Scotus Erigena was an Irishman who lived in the ninth century, —when Ireland was very far beyond the rest of Western Europe in intellectual culture,—when in fact Ireland alone had any learning,— and was sending missionaries to France, England, and Germany who first roused these countries from utter barbarism. He has excited great interest in our own day and many books have been written about him. Various editions of his different works have been published of which the most important is his *De Divisione Naturae.* Hauréau has in the 21st volume of the *Notices* of manuscripts of the French academy published some extracts from a gloss supposed to be by him upon Porphyry. Works upon his Life and Writings of Scotus have been published by Hjort, Staudenmaier, Taillandier, Möller, Christlieb, and Huber. Although he is not chiefly a logician his writings are of great interest for this history of logic and I should gladly devote several lectures to the consideration of them. This pleasure I must deny myself and shall speak of Scotus Erigena not to explain his position but only to throw a light on those who followed after him and were influenced by him. He is usually and rightly reckoned as an extreme realist and yet the extremest nominalists such as Roscellin were regarded as his followers. How could this be?

For one thing we perceive that Erigena attaches a vast importance to words. In consequence of this he seems to suppose that non-existences are as real as existences. He begins his work *De divisione naturae* by dividing all things into those which are and those which are not. In another place he declares that no philosopher rightly denies that possibles and impossibles are to be reckoned among the number of things. And such expressions are in fact constantly met with in his works. He does not seem to see that as the ancient philosopher said "Being only is and nothing is altogether not." Thus he says that the name *Nothing* signifies the ineffable, incomprehensible, and inaccessible brightness of the Divine nature which is unknown to every understanding of man or of Angel, which "dum per se ipsam cogitatur" neither is nor was nor will be. And he describes creation as the production out of the negations of things which are and which are not, the affirmations of all things which are and which are not. Again he says "Darkness is not nothing but something; otherwise the Scripture would not say 'and God called the light day and the darkness he called night'." Thus you perceive he has the idea that the immediate immaterial object of a name is something.

Ockam. Lecture 3

MS 160: November–December 1869

As Scotus was the chief of the *formalists* who were the most consistent realists; so William of Ockam was the head of the *terminists* who were the most consistent of *nominalists.*

The chief peculiarity of Scotus was the importance he attached to *formalitates* or modes of conception; that of Ockam was the importance he attached to *terms,* in the logical sense.

I shall begin what I have to say about Ockam by reading with you the first few pages of his textual logic. He has departed here from the usual method, that of writing commentaries, because he wished to present his thoughts in an order chosen by himself and therefore the order which he adopts becomes of more than usual consequence.

This logic is divided in 3 parts and each part into chapters. I propose to run over the first 17 chapters, giving you the substance of each.

Chapter 1

"Omnes logice tractatores intendunt astruere per argumenta quod sillogismi ex propositionibus et propositiones ex terminis componuntur. Unde terminus aliud non est quam pars propinqua propositionis."

All systematical writers on logic conceive that they discover by means of arguments that syllogisms of propositions, propositions of terms are composed. So a term is nothing but one of the parts into which a proposition may be directly resolved.

In order however that we may have a perfectly distinct conception of this important subject, he draws a distinction in reference to terms which plays a large part in nominalism.

Terms are *written, spoken,* or *conceived.* "Triplex est terminus, scriptus, prolatus, et conceptus."

The written term is a part of a proposition which has been inscribed on something material and is capable of being seen by the bodily eye. The spoken term is a part of a proposition which has been uttered aloud and is capable of being heard with the bodily ear. The conceptual term is an intention or impression of the soul which signifies or consignifies something naturally and is capable of being a part of mental proposition and of suppositing in such a proposition for the thing it signifies. Thus, these conceptual terms and the propositions composed of them are the mental words which, according to St. Augustine in chapter 15 of *De Trinitate,* belong to no language. They reside in the intellect alone and are incapable of being uttered aloud, although the spoken words which are subordinated to them as signs are uttered aloud.

I say that spoken words are signs subordinated to concepts or intentions of the soul not because in the strict sense of 'signify' they always signify the concepts of the soul primarily and properly. The point is rather that spoken words are used to signify the very things that are signified by concepts of the mind, so that a concept primarily and naturally signifies something and a spoken word signifies the same thing secondarily. Thus, suppose a spoken word is used to signify something signified by a particular concept of the mind. If that concept were to change its signification, by that fact alone it would happen that the spoken word would change its signification, even in the absence of any new linguistic convention.

This is all that Aristotle means when he says that spoken words are signs of the impressions of the soul and Boethius means the same thing when he says that spoken words signify concepts. In general, whenever writers say that all spoken words signify or serve as signs of impressions, they only mean that spoken words secondarily signify the things impressions of the soul primarily signify. Nonetheless, it is true that some spoken words primarily designate impressions of the soul or concepts, but these words secondarily designate other intentions of the soul as will be shown later.

The same sort of relation I have claimed to hold between spoken words and impressions or intentions or concepts holds between written words and spoken words.

Now, there are certain differences among these three kinds of terms. For one thing the concept or impression of the soul signifies naturally; whereas the spoken or written term signifies only conventionally. This difference gives rise to a further difference. We can decide to alter the signification of a spoken or written term, but no decision or agreement on the part of anyone can have the effect of altering the signification of a conceptual term.

Nevertheless, to silence hairsplitters it should be pointed out that the word 'sign' has two different senses. In one sense a sign is anything which when apprehended brings something else to mind. Here, a sign need not, as has been shown elsewhere, enable us to grasp the thing signified for the first time, but only after we have some sort of habitual knowledge of the thing. In this sense of 'sign' the spoken word is a natural sign of a thing, the effect is a sign of its cause, and the barrel-hoop is a sign of wine in the tavern. However, I have not been using the term 'sign' in this wide sense. In another sense a sign is anything which (1) brings something to mind and can supposit for that thing; (2) can be added to a sign of this sort in a proposition (e.g., syncategorematic expressions, verbs, and other parts of speech lacking a determinate signification); or (3) can be composed of things that are signs of either sort (e.g., propositions). Taking the term 'sign' in this sense the spoken word is not the natural sign of anything.

Chapter 2

This is of little importance. He observes that a term may be taken in three senses.

1st For all that can be copula or extreme of a categorical proposition. In which sense a proposition is a term since it may be the subject of a proposition.

2nd It may be taken so as to exclude propositions.

3rd Precisely and more strictly for that which *significatively* taken can be the subject or predicate of a proposition.

In this sense when we say *of* is a preposition—*of* is not a term because it is not significatively taken, *significative sumptum* but only *simpliciter* or *materialit[er]* in scholastic phraseology.

On Chapter 3. He remarks that not only are terms divided into written, spoken, and conceived, but also that these are up to a certain point subdivided together. For example not only are written and vocal terms divided into Nouns and Verbs—but Mental terms are also divided in Mental nouns and verbs.

There are therefore some grammatical distinctions which belong at once to written, vocal, and mental terms.

But there are others which belong only to written and vocal terms and not to mental terms.

For instance there may be a doubt whether the distinction between *verbs* and *participles* exists in mental terms since a participle with *est* expresses sufficiently the same meaning as the *verb: is running* is the same as *runs.* This being the case there does not seem to be any great necessity of supposing such a plurality in the mental propositions and terms as there is in the vocal propositions and terms.

And he lays down the principle that those distinctions of words which have been invented not on account of a need of signifying but for ornament are not to be supposed to exist in mental terms.

He then runs rapidly through the various grammatical accidents and states what ones he conceives to be mental and what ones merely vocal.

This chapter has a significance which one who did not thoroughly understand the distinction between nominalism and realism would hardly suspect. And I will ask you to consider it a moment. Ockam endeavors to say what is and what is not a mental distinction. And his only means of determining it is by ascertaining what distinction is required by the necessity of signification. But this test can only determine whether a distinction *must be* mental or whether it *need not be.* And this he himself recognizes apparently, for he says "Utrum autem participiis vocalibus et scriptis correspondeant in mente quedam intentiones a verbis distincte *potest esse dubium* eo quod non videtur magna *necessitas* talem pluralitatem ponere in propositionibus mentalibus sine terminis."

It may be that the *mental* grammatical accidents are precisely those which belong to the Latin language or it may be that they are more various than and altogether different from those of any known language. And therefore it may be that the list of mental grammatical accidents which Ockam by his method obtains bears but a slight resemblance to the true list.

Yet if this be so it remains certain that the list which he ought to obtain by his method comprises the only ones which need be considered in logic, those omitted being mere accidental variations of our mental language and not springing from the necessity of signification.

There is then a peculiar importance in those distinctions which arise from the needs of signifying, over and above such importance as they may derive from their being mental distinctions. Yet these distinctions are not such as there are between different things. You cannot divide things into those that are signified by nouns and those that are signified by verbs—yet the distinction between noun and verb arises from the needs of signifying. So does most certainly that between a noun and a pronoun but you cannot divide things into those pointed out by nouns and those pointed out by pronouns. So does that between singular and plural but you cannot separate men into singular men and plural men.

Thus it appears that there is a distinction greater than a distinction merely *in mentalibus* and yet less than a distinction between different things or a *distinctio realis.* In other words there is such a distinction as the Scotistic *distinctio formalis.*

You will understand that I say this not because I believe it to be true or wish you to do so,—for throughout this course I care nothing whatever for the truth of logical doctrines—but only because I want to point out how differently a Scotist would regard this matter from what Ockam does.

In point of fact this chapter of Ockam's is distinctly anti-Scotistical and if he refutes the realistic position on the basis of the conclusions of this chapter, a Scotist might say that his reasoning was vitiated here.

Scotus's earliest work probably was his *Grammatica Speculativa* which is I suppose the earliest attempt at a Philosophy of Grammar. In this work he has discussed the same question here treated by Ockam.

Of this work I will read the first six chapters.

THE AUTHOR'S PREAMBLE

1 *The rationale of the method.* In all science, understanding and knowledge derive from a recognition of its principles, as stated in I *Physicorum, Text*

Comment 1; we therefore, wishing to know the science of grammar, insist that it is necessary first of all to know its principles which are the modes of signifying. But before we enquire into their particular features, we must first set forth some of their general features without which it is not possible to obtain the fullest understanding of them.

Of these, the first and most important is, in what way is a mode of signifying divided and described? The second is, what does the mode of signifying basically originate from? Thirdly, what is the mode of signifying directly derived from? Fourthly, in what way are the mode of signifying, the mode of understanding, and the mode of being differentiated? The fifth is, in what way is the mode of signifying subjectively arrived at? The sixth is, what order obtains for the following terms in relation to one another, *ie* sign, word, part of speech, and terminus?

CHAPTER I

How the mode of signifying is to be divided and described.

2 *The mode of signifying introduces two factors. The active and passive modes of signifying.* Concerning the first, it must be said that the mode of signifying introduces equal factors which are called the active and passive modes of signifying. The active mode of signifying is the mode or property of the expression vouchsafed by the intellect to itself by means of which the expression signifies the property of the *thing.* The passive mode of signifying is the mode or property of the thing as signified by the expression. And because 'signifying and consignifying' imply being active and 'being signified' and 'being consignified' imply being acted upon, hence we can say that the mode or property of the expression by means of which the expression actively signifies the property of the thing is called the active mode of signifying; but the mode or property of the thing, in as much as it is signified passively by expressions, is called the passive mode of signifying.

3 *The intellect attributes a double faculty to the expression.* In addition, it must be noted that, since the intellect uses the expression for signifying and consignifying, it attributes to it a double faculty, [*a*] the faculty of signifying, which can be called signification by means of which a sign or significant is effected, and so it is formally a word; and [*b*] the faculty of consignifying which is called the active mode of signifying by means of which the signifying expression creates the cosign or consignificant, and so it is formally a part of speech. Therefore, a part of speech is such accordingly by means of this faculty of consignifying or active mode of signifying according to an instance of the formal principle; however, it is a part of speech in relation to other parts of speech by virtue of this same active faculty of consignifying according to the intrinsic efficient principle.

From which, it is clear that the active faculties of consignifying or active modes of signifying in and of themselves refer primarily to grammar, inasmuch that they are principles relevant to grammar. But the passive faculties of consignifying or passive modes of signifying are not relevant, except accidentally, to grammar, because they are neither a formal nor an efficient principle of a part of a speech, since they may be properties of things; they may be relevant only insofar as their formal aspect is concerned, since in this way they do not differ greatly from the active modes of signifying, as we shall see.

CHAPTER II

From what does the mode of signifying basically originate.

4 *Every active mode of signifying comes from some property of the thing.* It should be noted immediately that since faculties of this kind or active modes of signifying are not fictions, it follows necessarily that every active mode of signifying must originate basically from some property of the thing. It is clear therefore, that since the intellect classifies the expression for the purpose of signifying under some active mode of signifying, it is referring to the property itself of the thing from which it originally derives the active mode of signifying; it is also clear that the understanding, since it may be a passive capacity undefined by itself, does not apply to the prescribed act unless it is determined from another source. Hence since it classifies the expression for the purpose of signifying by means of a prescribed active mode of signifying, it is necessarily occasioned by a prescribed property of the thing. Therefore some property or mode of being of the thing corresponds to some active mode of signifying or other.

5 But if the objection to this is made that, since a significative expression such as *deitas* has feminine gender which is a passive mode of signifying, nevertheless the property is not mutually correspondent in the thing signified, because it is a property of being acted upon, and feminine gender arises from this. Similarly, negations and fictions fall under no properties whatsoever since they are not entities, and yet the significative expressions of negations and fictions have active modes of signifying, *eg: caecitas* (blindness), *chimaera* (chimera), etc.

It must be said that it does not follow that the active mode of signifying of a word is always drawn from the property of the thing of that word of which it is a mode of signifying, but it can be derived from a property of the thing of another word and attributed to the thing of that word, and it suffices that these should not be incompatible. And because we do not understand separate substances unless perceived by the senses, therefore we give names to them by means of the properties of the senses and assign active modes of signifying to their names. Hence, there is, in reality, no passive property in God, yet we imagine Him, as it were, being acted upon by our prayers.

Similarly we understand negations from their features, therefore we classify their names under the properties of their features and assign active modes of signifying to their names. Similarly in relation to the names of figments, the active modes of signifying are taken from the properties of the parts from which, for example, we imagine *Chimaera* to be composed, in that we imagine it to be composed of the head of a lion and the tail of a dragon; and so on.

6 And if it is insisted, that if the active modes of signifying in relation to the names of negations are taken from the modes of being of their features, then they designate the names of the actual existing feature and not of the negations. From such a standpoint, the names of the negations by means of their own active modes of signifying will be false from the point of view of consignification.

It must be said that it is not true, that the names of the negations, certainly do not by means of their active modes of signifying, designate with reference to the negations the modes of understanding of the negations which are their modes of being. In consequence of which it can be stated that although negations may not be positive entities outside the mind, they are however positive entities in the mind, as is shown in IV *Met. Text 9,* and are entities according to the mind. And because their conceptualisation constitutes their existence, therefore their modes of understanding will be their modes of being. Hence the names of negations will not be wrongly consignified by means of their active modes of signifying, because since the modes of understanding of negations can be reduced to the modes of understanding of the feature (since a negation is not known except by its feature), therefore the modes of being of the negations can after all be reduced to the modes of being of the feature.

CHAPTER III

From what is the mode of signifying directly derived.

7 *The modes of signifying and understanding are bipartite.* The third fact to be noted is that the active modes of signifying are directly derived from the passive modes of understanding. As a consequence it must be stated that, just as the mode of signifying is bipartite, *ie* active and passive, so too is the mode of understanding, *ie* active and passive. The active mode of understanding is the faculty of conceptualising by means of which the intellect signifies, conceives or comprehends the properties of the thing. But the passive mode of understanding is the property of the thing as comprehended by the mind.

From which properties are the active modes of signifying derived. It can therefore be said that the active modes of signifying are derived directly from the passive modes of understanding, because the active modes of signifying are not derived from the modes of being unless these modes of being have been comprehended by the mind. But the modes of being, as they are understood by the mind, are called the passive modes of understanding, therefore the active modes of signifying are derived from the modes of being by means of the passive modes of understanding, and therefore the active modes of signifying are derived directly from the passive modes of understanding.

CHAPTER IV

How the mode of signifying is distinguished from the mode of understanding and the mode of being.

8 *What are the modes of being, understanding, and signifying.* The fourth point to be noted is that the modes of being, the passive modes of understanding, and the passive modes of signifying are the same materially and in reality but differ formally, because the mode of being is the property of the thing as such, the passive mode of understanding is also that property of the thing as apprehended by the mind, and the passive mode of signifying is the property of the same thing inasmuch as it is consignified by the expression. They are the same materially and in reality, because whatever the mode of being expresses absolutely, the passive mode of understanding expresses inasmuch as is relevant to the intellect, and whatever the passive mode of understanding expresses, so does the passive mode of signifying inasmuch as it is relevant to the expression. Therefore they are the same materially. However, they differ formally, which can be shown thus: whatever implies the mode of being expresses the property of the thing absolutely or under the rubric of existing, but whatever implies the passive mode of understanding expresses the same property of the thing as something material, and the faculty of understanding or conceptualising, as something formal; whatever specifies the passive mode of signifying expresses the same property of the thing as something material and the faculty of consignifying as something formal. And since there may be one faculty of being, another of understanding, and another of signifying, they differ in terms of their formal faculties.

But they agree in terms of reality, for the mode of being expresses the property of the thing absolutely, the passive mode of understanding expresses the property of the thing by means of the mode of understanding, and the passive mode of signifying states the property of the thing by means of the faculty of consignifying. But it is the same property of the thing as perceived absolutely together with the mode of understanding and the mode of consignifying.

In what way do the mode of being, the active mode of understanding, and the active mode of signifying differ. Similarly it should be realised that the mode of being, the active mode of understanding, and the active mode of signifying differ formally and materially, because the mode of being expresses the property of the thing in absolute terms or by means of the faculty of existing, as was stated earlier, but the active mode of understanding expresses the property of the mind which is the faculty of understanding or conceptualising, and the active mode of signifying states the property of the expression which is the faculty of consignifying. But, one is the property of the thing extraneous to the mind, another the property of the intellect, and yet another a property of the expression, and therefore, one is the faculty of being, the others the faculties of understanding, and of consignifying; therefore the mode of being, the active mode of understanding, and the active mode of signifying differ both ways.

In what way do the active and passive modes of understanding differ and agree. Similarly it should be appreciated that the active mode of understanding and the passive mode of understanding differ materially and agree formally, for the passive mode of understanding expresses the property of the thing by means of the passive faculty of understanding, but the active mode of understanding expresses the property of the intellect which is the active faculty of understanding. It is the same faculty of understanding by means of which the intellect understands the property of the thing actively and by means of which the property of the thing is understood passively. Therefore the properties are different but the faculty is the same, and therefore they differ materially and are the same formally.

In what way do the active and passive modes of signifying differ and agree. Similarly it should be known that the active and passive modes of signifying differ materially and are the same formally, because the passive mode of signifying expresses the property of the thing by means of the passive faculty of consignifying but the active mode of signifying states the property of the expression which is the active faculty of consignifying. But the potentiality is the same as that by means of which the expression is capable of signifying in an active manner and by means of which the property of the thing is signified in a passive manner; materially they are different, but formally the same.

CHAPTER V

In what way is the mode of signifying empirically discovered.

9 *In what way is the passive mode of signifying ascertained.* Fifthly, it should be noted that the passive mode of signifying is materially real as it is empirically valable because from the material point of view it is the property of the thing; moreover, the property of the thing exists in that of which it is the property even as it is empirically valable. However, from a formal point of view it is empirically valable in the same way as is the active mode of signifying, because formally it does not differ from the active mode of signifying.

10 *In what way is the active mode of signifying ascertained.* The active mode of signifying, since it may be a property of the significative expression, is materially existent within the significative expression even as it is empirically valable; moreover, it is materially existent in the property of the thing even as some effect is materially existent in the original and abstract cause which effects it in the first place; and it is materially existent in the intellect even as an effect is materially existent in the most immediate cause that effects it; and it is materially existent in the construction, even as a cause capable of being effective is materially existent in its own particular effect.

CHAPTER VI

What is the mutual order of the following designations: sign, word, part of speech, and terminus.

11 *Sign, word, part of speech, terminus.* With reference to these, it must be noted that sign, word, part of speech, and terminus agree and differ. For they can show agreement from the point of view of Proposition and Counterproposition because they can be found in the same Proposition, as for example sign and designate. They differ, however, in terms of their functions,

because a *sign* is specified by means of the faculty of designating or representing something in absolute terms; but a *word* is specified formally by means of the faculty of designating superimposed on the expression, since a word is a significative expression. A *part of speech* exists formally by means of the active mode of signifying superimposed upon the word, because a part of speech is a word inasmuch as it possesses an active mode of signifying. But a *terminus* specifies the faculty of terminating the resolutions of the syllogism, because the dialectician resolves the syllogism into propositions, and propositions into subject and predicate which are said to be termini in logic.

12 *Expression.* Furthermore it should be known that expression, in so far as it is expression, is not considered by the grammarian, but in so far as it is a sign, it is, since grammar deals with the signs of things, and because the expression is the most suitable sign among other signs, therefore expression, in so far as it is a sign, is considered by the grammarian before other signs of things. But because being a sign is a property of the expression, therefore the grammarian, in considering expression, does so accidentally.

You see here how differently Scotus and Ockam regard the same question, how much more simple and lucid Ockam's view is, and how much more certain Scotus's complex theory is to take into account all the facts than Ockam's simple one.

I wish to lean a little towards the side of Scotus in what I say because I fear that you will lean very much the other way. To understand the historical position, you ought not to lean either way.

Chapter 4 is unimportant.

Both spoken and mental terms are subject to yet another division, for some terms are categorematic while others are syncategorematic. Categorematic terms have a definite and determinate signification. Thus, the term 'man' signifies all men; the term 'animal', all animals; and the term 'whiteness', all whitenesses.

Examples of syncategorematic terms are 'every', 'no', 'some', 'all', 'except', 'so much', and 'insofar as'. None of these expressions has a definite and determinate signification, nor does any of them signify anything distinct from what is signified by categorematic terms. The number system provides a parallel here. 'Zero', taken by itself, does not signify anything, but when combined with some other numeral it makes that numeral signify something new.

Chapter 5. Has somewhat more interest. It treats of the distinction between concrete terms such as *man, horse, white,* and abstract terms such as *humanity, horseness, whiteness.*

The distinction was first made a matter of some prominence in logic by Scotus, as I think. You may find his treatment of it in his 8th question on the predicaments.

He defines a concrete term as one which signifies an essence in
so far as it informs a subject and an abstract term as one which
signifies an essence as such.

Ockam by way of definition says that a concrete term and its
corresponding abstract term are two nouns which have the same
beginning and different terminations and that the one which usually
has the most syllables and is a substantive is called the abstract and
the one which usually has the fewer syllables and is an adjective is
called the concrete.

Those definitions put the realist and the nominalist in unusually
strong contrast.

[Read *Nominum autem* &c. down to *pro distinctis rebus sup-
ponunt.* Explaining that he wishes to avoid saying that a concrete
signifies a thing on account of Scotus's arguments.]

> Concrete and abstract names can function in many ways. Sometimes the
> concrete name signifies, connotes, designates, or expresses and also supposits
> for something, which the abstract name in no way signifies and, conse-
> quently never supposits for. Examples are 'just'—'justice', 'white'—'white-
> ness', etc. 'Just' supposits for men in the proposition 'The just are virtuous';
> it would be incorrect to say that it supposits for justice; for although justice
> is a virtue, it is not virtuous. On the other hand, 'justice' supposits for the
> quality of a man, not the man himself. It is because of this that it is impossible
> to predicate this sort of concrete name of its abstract counterpart: the two
> terms supposit for different things.

This has to do with the distinction of logical Extension and Comprehension which Professor Bowen teaches was discovered by the Port
Royalists although it was pretty well known in the middle ages.
Enough so for John of Salisbury to refer to it as "quod fere in omnium
ore celebre est, aliud scilicet esse quod appellativa *significant,* et
aliud esse quod *nominant.* Nominantur singularia, sed universalia
significantur." By *appellativa* here he means as I take it adjectives
and such like.

Ockam devotes several chapters to the consideration of abstracts
and concretes. You remember that Scotus holds that humanity or the
general essence of man in the various men is not really distinct from
the individual man but is formally distinct and therefore it becomes
important for Ockam to show that he can explain the relation of
concrete and abstract terms without making use of this conception

of a formal distinction, for he is going to deny that there is any such distinction.

He treats the subject at considerable length in the 5th to the 9th chapters inclusive.

I do not think we shall find it advantageous to follow him through this, in which he has to speak with extreme caution and to introduce considerable complications into his theory in order to avoid a heresy concerning the incarnation of Christ.

It is sufficient to say that his theory is or evidently would be if it were not for his fear of this heresy that *humanity* means the same as *man* with some syncategorematic term added, he does not say what; probably no one would constantly serve, but frequently *as such* would do, so that *humanity* means *man as such.* Other abstracts are to be explained in the same way. This therefore is Ockam's substitute for Scotus's formal distinction. Between *man* and *man as such* there is such a distinction that one cannot be predicated of the other for you cannot say

Every man is *man as such*

and yet they both denote the same things namely all men.

We have therefore in Ockam a doctrine of implied *syncategorematics in terms,* which fulfills in large measure the same function as Scotus's *formal distinctions in things.*

And as Scotus's doctrine of *formalitates* is what gives to all Scotism its peculiar character of subtilety, so it is Ockam's doctrine of *terms* with their implied syncategorematics which gives to Ockamistic logic its peculiar character, which is an immense development of an extremely technical doctrine of the properties of terms and a continual reference to it.

For it is plain that if terms are very apt to have these hidden syncategorematics in them, syllogisms will constantly be vitiated by that circumstance. For instance, the syllogism

A rational animal is a man as such
No man as such is blue-eyed
Therefore no rational animal is blue-eyed

is apparently perfect in form but is entirely vitiated by the *as such.*

And if many terms contain latent syncategorematics it must be necessary to have a large addition to the science of logic to inform us of this matter in order that we may avoid fallacies similar in principle to this one.

Passing over Ockam's discussion of abstract and concrete names we come to chapter 10. This treats of the distinction between an absolute and a connotative name. Omitting a part of his explanation, it is as follows.

A connotative name is one which signifies one thing primarily and another secondarily so that in its definition there will generally be one noun in the nominative and another in an oblique case. An absolute name is one which is not connotative.

He gives a good many examples of connotative names among which are *white* which is defined as that which is informed by whiteness—*Just* or that which is informed by justice. Words of office as *king* and the like. The word *cause* or something able to produce something. All relative words also as *like* or that which has a quality such as something else has, are connotative names in the widest sense. *Understanding* is also a connotative name, for it is defined as a *soul able to understand.* So is *intelligible* which is defined as *something apprehensible by thought.*

Chapter 11. The foregoing divisions of terms belong says Ockam as well to terms naturally signifying (that is mental terms) as to those made by an arbitrary convention (vocal and written terms).

We now come to some divisions which belong only to terms *ad placitum institutis*—made by arbitrary convention.

In the first place then there are names of first imposition and names of second imposition.

Names of second imposition are those which signify arbitrary signs and their properties as signs. The term *name of second imposition* may be used, however, in two ways. First in a wide sense, for everything which signifies an arbitrary sign but only when it *is* an arbitrary sign and whether it implies a distinction which belongs also to conceptions of mind which are natural signs or not. Such are the terms *noun, pronoun, conjunction, verb, case, number, mood, time,* etc. These are what the grammarians call *names of names.* Strictly speaking however a name of second imposition signifies nothing but arbitrary signs. In this sense *conjugation* and *declension* are names of second imposition.

Names of first imposition include properly only categorematic terms.

Names of first imposition are divided again into names of first intention and names of second intention. Intention here I will remark means conception. I will also say that there is nothing peculiarly nominalistic about all this. It is old material.

Names of second intention:

But the common term 'name of second intention' has both a broad and a narrow sense. In the broad sense an expression is called a name of second intention if it signifies intentions of the soul, natural signs, whether or not it also signifies conventional signs in their capacity as signs. In this sense names of second intention can be either names of first or second imposition.

Chap. 12. [Read the whole. Explaining Ockam's position concerning the *subjective* existence of conception.]

In the previous chapter I indicated that certain expressions are names of first intention and others, names of second intention. Ignorance of the meanings of these terms is a source of error for many; therefore, we ought to see what names of first and second intention are and how they are distinguished.

First, it should be noted that an intention of the soul is something in the soul capable of signifying something else. Earlier we indicated how the signs of writing are secondary with respect to spoken signs. Among conventional signs spoken words are primary. In the same way spoken signs are subordinated to the intentions of the soul. Whereas the former are secondary, the latter are primary. It is only for this reason that Aristotle says that spoken words are signs of the impressions of the soul. Now, that thing existing in the soul which is the sign of a thing and an element out of which a mental proposition is composed (in the same way as a spoken proposition is composed of spoken words) is called by different names. Sometimes it is called an intention of the soul; sometimes an impression of the soul; and sometimes the similitude of the thing. Boethius, in his commentary on the *De Interpretatione,* calls it an intellect. He does not, of course, mean that a mental proposition is composed of intellects in the sense of intellectual souls. He only means that a mental proposition is composed of those intellective things which are signs in the soul signifying other things. Thus, whenever anyone utters a spoken proposition, he forms beforehand a mental proposition. This proposition is internal and it belongs to no particular spoken language. But it also happens that people frequently form internal propositions which, because of the defect of their language, they do not know how to express externally. The parts of such mental propositions are called concepts, intentions, likenesses, and "intellects."

But with what items in the soul are we to identify such signs? There are a variety of opinions here. Some say a concept is something made or fashioned by the soul. Others say it is a certain quality distinct from the act of the understanding which exists in the soul as in a subject. Others say that it is simply the act of understanding. This last view gains support from the principle that one ought not postulate many items when he can get by with fewer. Moreover, all the theoretical advantages that derive from postulating entities distinct from acts of understanding can be had without making such a distinction, for an act of understanding can signify something and can supposit for something just as well as any sign. Therefore, there is no point in postulating anything over and above the act of understanding. But I shall have more to say about these different views later on. For the moment, we shall simply say that an intention is something in the soul which is either a sign naturally signifying something else (for which it can supposit) or a potential element in a mental proposition.

But there are two kinds of intentions. One kind is called a first intention. This is an intention which signifies something that is not itself an intention of the soul, although it may signify an intention along with this. One example is the intention of the soul predicable of all men; another is the intention that is predicable of all whitenesses, blacknesses, etc.

But the expression 'first intention' can be understood in two senses. In the broad sense an intentional sign in the soul is a first intention if it does not signify only intentions or signs. In this broad sense first intentions include not only intentions which so signify that they can supposit in a proposition for their significata, but also intentions which, like syncategorematic intentions, are only signs in an extended sense. In this sense mental verbs, mental syncategorematic expressions, mental conjunctions, and similar terms are first intentions. In the narrow sense only those mental names that are capable of suppositing for their significata are called first intentions.

A second intention, on the other hand, is an intention of the soul which is a sign of first intentions. Examples are *genus, species,* and the like. One intention common to all men is predicated of all men when we say, "This man is a man; that man is a man; . . ." (and so on for all individual men). In the same way, we predicate an intention common to intentions signifying things when we say, "This species is a species; that species is a species; . . ." (and so on). Again, when we say *"Stone* is a genus," *"Animal* is a genus," and *"Color* is a genus," we predicate one intention of another just as we predicate one name of different names when we say that 'man' is a name, 'donkey' is a name, and 'whiteness' is a name. Now, just as names of second imposition conventionally signify names of first imposition, a second intention naturally signifies a first intention. And just as a name of first imposition signifies something other than names, first intentions signify things that are not themselves intentions.

Still, one could claim that in a strict sense, a second intention is an intention which signifies exclusively first intentions; whereas, in a broad sense a second intention can also be an intention signifying both intentions and conventional signs (if, indeed, there are any such intentions).

Chap. 13. [Read definitions of equivocal and univocal.]

A word is equivocal if, in signifying different things, it is a sign subordinated to several rather than one concept or intention of the soul. This is what Aristotle means when he says that one and the same name applies, but that the account of substance corresponding to the name is different. By "account of substance," he means a concept or intention of the soul including the mental description and definition as well as the simple concept. He wants to say that while these differ, there is just one name. A clear example of equivocality is found in the case of a word belonging to different languages, for in one language the expression is used to signify things signified by one concept; whereas, in the other it is used to signify things signified by some other concept. Thus, the expression is subordinated in signification to several different concepts or impressions of the soul. . . .

Every expression that is subordinated to just one concept is called univocal, whether the term signifies several different things or not. But properly speaking a term is not called univocal unless it signifies or could signify indifferently each of several different things. The term is univocal because all of the several things it signifies are also signified by one concept. Thus, a univocal term is a sign subordinated in signification to one natural sign which is an intention or concept of the soul.

Chaps. 14. 15. 16. 17.

But though Ockam held that only singular things existed, it is not to be supposed that he denied that *form* and *matter* were two really distinct and real things. He held that all forms or characters were really individual but he held that they were real things really different from the matter.

Thus he says of the specific difference

Whence it is not to be imagined that the difference is anything intrinsic to the species by which one species differs from another for then the difference would not be universal but would be *matter* or *form* or a *whole* compounded of matter and form but a difference is something predicable alone of one species and not agreeing with another and it is called an essential difference not because it *is* of the essence of the thing but because it *expresses* a part of the essence of the thing and not extrinsic to the thing. Whence the difference of which we are now speaking always expresses a part of the thing and one difference expresses a material part and another a formal part.

So under the head of *subject* he says that *subject* sometimes means something which really supports another thing inhering in it —and so we may speak of a thing as subject of its accidents or of matter as subject in respect to its substantial forms.

So again in treating of substance he says

In one sense substance is said to be anything that is distinct from other things. Writers use the word 'substance' in this sense when they speak of the substance of whiteness, the substance of color, etc.

In a stricter sense substance is anything which is not an accident inhering in something else. In this sense both matter and form as well as the whole composed of these are called substances.

In the strictest sense substance is that which is neither an accident inhering in another thing nor an essential part of something else, although it can combine with an accident. It is in this sense that substance is said to be a summum genus, and according to Aristotle it is divided into first and second substance.

Again under the head of quality he says

It seems that according to the principles of Aristotle's philosophy, one should say that the category of quality is a concept or sign containing under it all such terms as do not express a substantial part of a substance and can be used to answer the question posed about substance 'How is it qualified?' For the present, I shall not consider whether concrete or abstract terms more properly belong in the category of quality.

In the genus of quality there are certain terms which designate things that are distinct from substances, things that are not themselves substances. Examples are 'whiteness', 'blackness', 'color', 'knowledge', and 'light'.

Thus you perceive that Ockam while he denies that there is any *distinction* except between *things* really and numerically different, yet does allow that there is a real difference between things which are really inseparable.

But as to all *relation* he most emphatically and clearly denies that it exists as something different from the things related. And under relation in this connection he expressly says that he means to include relations of agreement as well as relations of opposition.

Whether similarity or dissimilarity is some little thing distinct from the absolute things.

Affirmative: Because it is impossible for anything to pass from contradictory to contradictory except by a change. But Sortes, from being non-whitelike at first, becomes whitelike. Therefore Sortes is changed; not absolutely, we presume; therefore relatively.

Negative: Those things which cannot by any power be separated from each other are not really distinct. But similarity cannot by any power be separated from two whitenesses, because it is a contradiction that two white things should be equally white and yet not be similar. Therefore, etc.

To this question I answer that neither similarity nor dissimilarity is some little thing distinct from the absolute things.

Therefore while he admits the real existence of qualities he expressly denies that these are the respects in which things agree and differ. For they agree and differ he says in themselves and in nothing else.

Yet while he denies that there is really any similarity in things except the things which are similar and while he denies that there is any real respect in which things do agree, yet it is a mistake to assert that he denies that things apart from the action of the mind are similar. For he says

Sortes and Plato are one in species. That is Sortes and Plato are contained under one species to wit under man or Sortes and Plato are such that one common species can be abstracted from them. And if it is said then they would not be really one, the reply is that they are one really, meaning by one what has been said of them that Sortes and Plato are really such that one species can be abstracted from them and so it is to be conceded that there is a real unity less than a numerical unity so that those individuals are really one in that sense and nothing imaginable distinct from the individual or individuals is one in that sense.

A Scotist would probably reply to this mode of supposing a real specific unity that nothing which is only *in potentia* really exists and that nothing whose existence depends on the mind really exists. The combination of these unrealities does not make a reality and therefore that whose existence depends on the mere possibility of an act of the mind does not really exist, and therefore a unity which consists only in the mind's being able to abstract from the singulars one conception is not properly called a real unity.

I would call your attention however to the fact that as Ockam here makes the essential resemblance, for that is certainly the same as an essential unity, *depend upon* and in fact *consist in* the possibility of the imposition of a common mental sign so he must consider every resemblance. The resemblance therefore consists solely in the property of the mind by which it naturally imposes the same mental sign upon the different things. And I have a strong impression that Ockam somewhere says this explicitly but I haven't been able to find the place and I rather doubt it because he seems to think that things do resemble one another apart from the action of the mind although out of the mind there is no general quality or respect in which they agree, but they simply agree of themselves.

This then is a general sketch of Ockam's nominalism so far as it can be understood apart from his psychological doctrines.

I have thought that as a matter of historical interest, an historical curiosity if you please, the Question of Nominalism and Realism would be one to which you would be willing to devote 3 hours, in view of the frequency of references to it—and the intimate connection between Ockamism and the modern English philosophy of Locke, Berkeley, Hume, Hartley, Brown, the two Mills, and Bain.

You may perhaps think that I have been taking up your time with things dead and gone—and utterly trivial. But in reality the difference between Nominalism and Realism has a relation not remote from that between the Idealism of Berkeley and Mill and the Idealisms of Kant and Hegel. If by calling the Question of Nominalism and Realism trivial it is meant that it has no conceivable application to practical affairs it is nothing but the old objection which ignorance has always brought against all purely scientific studies. And one which for an educated man to recognize is to reject.

But it is not true that it is of no practical moment whether we believe in Nominalism or Realism, whether we believe that eternal verities are confined entirely to the other world (for a Nominalist may certainly be a Spiritualist or even a Platonist) or that they are matters of everyday consequence, whether we believe that the Genus homo has no existence except as a collection of individuals and that therefore individual happiness, individual aspirations, and individual life is alone of account or that men really have something in common—and that their very essence—so that the Community is to be regarded as something of more consequence and of more dignity than any single men.

But perhaps by calling the Controversy of Nominalism and Realism trivial it is meant that any reasonable being can decide it in a jiffy. If you think then that all men who disagree with you on this question are foolish, I can only remark that whichever way your opinion lies there are certainly many men quite as competent in mental power, training, and information, who think that *you* have not fully probed the question.

However though it doesn't seem to me so, yet to others whom I must respect, it does seem easy to decide the question. Let it be so then and let us all come to a unanimous decision upon it, only let our decision rest on a historical basis, the only sound basis for any human institution—philosophy, natural science, government, church, or system of education.

Whewell

MS 162: November–December 1869

There is nothing perhaps which in a university town we feel more strongly than the contrast not to say contradiction between the modes of thought of the scientific and literary men. This divergency has existed throughout modern times and we already have evidence of its existence in the thirteenth century from the poem by Henry d'Andeli called the "Battle of the Seven Liberal Arts." You will find it in the Library. As I am not in the least degree literary it would be impossible, I suppose, for me to state correctly the position of literary men but this position appears to me to be that we cannot regard things as they ought to be regarded unless we look at them broadly and from the entirety of human nature; while the scientific man thinks that things cannot be understood unless they are scrutinized closely and narrowly and with the entire exclusion of the passions and emotional sensibilities.

A literary man thinks a specialist is a piddling pedant—and speaks of "Science peddling with the names of things." A scientific man thinks that in specialty lies the only intellectual salvation.

Which of these views is right 'twould be foolish for me to try to say. But this much I think must be conceded, that be the necessity of breadth of view and of general culture as great as you please, yet to understand science well, its proceeding and its logic, one must have recourse besides to an interior view of science and therefore to a scientific specialist.

This I feel sure is the opinion of scientific men, for I have heard the opinion expressed many times by them and the contrary one never.

In this respect Dr. Whewell's qualifications for treating of science could hardly have been better than they were, for he was not only a scientific specialist but an eminent scientific investigator, his works upon the tides containing a research of no ordinary importance. Indeed they will never be forgotten.

But while he was a specialist *positivè* he was not so *negativè* for he made original researches also into dynamics, conic sections, engineering, meteorology, optics, chemistry, and mineralogy of which last science he was professor for many years at Oxford.

Nor was his knowledge confined to Natural Science for he wrote several works upon Ethics and the history of Ethical doctrines, a number of papers on Metaphysics in which he was well versed, two books on Natural Theology, two on University Education, one of them in 3 volumes, a book of Sermons, a book on the Plurality of Worlds, a work on the architecture of German churches, articles in Encyclopaedias on other subjects, besides many other things.

He was a man who made enemies and it was said of him by one of them that "Knowledge was his forte, but omniscience was his foible," and you can imagine how the man must really have been respected, whose extremely arrogant manners brought down no bitterer satire than this.

[Chinese Music]

But Whewell was not the man to write upon the Logic of Science solely on the basis of *general* qualifications. He prepared himself for his task by an exhaustive study of the history of all Natural Science, and the Results of that study he has embodied in two works. One, *The History of the Inductive Sciences,* is a work which I have never heard spoken of without admiration by anybody acquainted with the subject; the other, *The History of Scientific Ideas,* is also executed with great ability, and I do not think these two books can be rivalled by anything upon the same subjects in any language. He also made a study of all previous attempts to erect a philosophy of the sciences and embodied his strictures upon them in a third work called *The Philosophy of the Inductive Sciences.* And then and then only did he begin the construction of his own Theory.

But when I have stated all these qualifications of Whewell for what he undertook, I have left one condition unmentioned the importance of which relatively is as that one which our Saviour mentioned to the young man who had kept all the commandments from his youth up. For the question comes now to be asked did Dr. Whewell with all his knowledge of the history of science really derive his theory from that, or did he only use his knowledge to give a colour of verisimilitude to a theory which had come down to him as a metaphysical tradition or which he had drawn from Kant or some other metaphysical writer? I have not time to answer this question as it should be answered. You will detect some of the grounds upon which I have formed my opinion, but to state them fully would not be possible at present. I can only give it then as my conviction, which I can truly say is impartial, and which you can take for what it is worth, that when I consider what are the characters which are found associated with real Scientific Induction and exert my best power of distinguishing true scientific work I must say that Whewell's *Novum Organon Renovatum* seems to me to possess every mark of such work. And I think that in running over in my mind such of his works as I have read that I should say that a genuine impartiality—a rare *trait*—was one of his. Indeed I am so forcibly impressed with his work's having all the characters of a Scientific Induction from the History of Science that superior as I think that he is to other English and French writers upon the philosophy of science in point of learning and specially in scientific training, I think that his preëminent superiority lies in the perfect singlemindedness with which he has derived his theories from his facts.

A theory of science which is thus founded on the history of science in a truly scientific spirit and by a genuine inductive method and which does not merely make use of facts of scientific history to support a theory which has really been derived not from these but from a general philosophical doctrine of a metaphysical origin, must be true to the grand features of scientific progress, to all those characters of scientific investigation which leave their mark upon its history, although there is doubtless something else which concerns the individual investigator and which does not appear in his publications which such a theory would be apt to overlook. But scientific progress is to a large extent public and belongs to the community of scientific men of the same department, its conclusions are unanimous, its interpretations of nature are no private interpretations, and so much must always be published to the world as will suffice to enable the world to adopt the individual investigator's conclusions. For this reason, I am inclined to think that a historical theory of science like that of Whewell is likely to contain the most representative conditions of the success of scientific thought. And I think that Whewell's theory in fact does so.

There is one defect which I think belongs to Whewell's system and which I should think would be apt to belong to any systematic exposition of the proceedure of science. Such an exposition must of course divide scientific investigation into different parts, it must separate it into different kinds, and it must also distinguish between the different steps taken. I should think that it was a fault to be expected in any such system and one which is found in Whewell's, that the necessity of making these divisions would lead to drawing the line between them too sharply and to representing them as existing in a degree of isolation in which they neither are nor ought to be found.

Whewell's chief strength was in the physical sciences as distinguished from Natural History—and in the former observation and reasoning are much more separated than in the latter—and his chief work was done in that part of the physical sciences in which they are separated the most. I think that his books show this distinctly. His exposition of astronomy, optics, etc., is most admirable but I should imagine that his treatment of the classificatory sciences was less satisfactory. It seems to me, at least, that he has not represented the importance in all such sciences as chemistry, geology, zoology, &c. of observing and thinking together nor the fusion which there is and ought to be in those fields between observation and analysis.

Whewell's general conception of a science is that a scientific conclusion is composed of facts on the one hand and ideas on the other. This sentence really contains the essence or rather the germ of his theory of science, although it cannot at the outset convey any adequate notion to you. A scientific conclusion is composed of facts and of ideas. To reach it, the facts must be brought together—*colligated* —and the conceptions must be rendered distinct—*explicated.* Then the colligation of facts and the explication of conceptions are the two parts of scientific investigation.

I have stated this as though it were a conclusion *à priori.* I have so set it forth because it admits of such a presentation and because in such a mode of statement the unity of the theory is clearly brought out.

But that is not the way in which Whewell enforces it, for he has shown with great elaboration that in every science two processes have taken place. One, the observation and grouping of facts. The other, *controversies* which resulted in the establishment of clear conceptions.

This I have said is the central point of Whewell's theory; and it has been urged that it has been drawn from the Kantian philosophy.

The distinction in Kantism between the matter and form of cognition.

Double origin of knowledge.

This to be seen in Whewell, but yet common experience in scientific reasoning shows it to hold good.

Example of a *cipher*. Facts easily enough obtained. First difficulty is in getting the appropriate idea.

History of science also shows it.

If then it does happen to be in accord with the results of the profound analysis of cognition by Kant—a result which must be allowed by all who would avoid the extremes of sensualism and absolute idealism—I say if Whewell's theory accords with this—as well as with the History of Science—that ought to be regarded rather as a powerful support of the theory rather than as a disproof of it.

Professor Bowen, for example, has declared that Whewell's Philosophy of Science is "mere Kantism." So far as this means that it receives no support from the experience of scientific men, the question must be decided by those who have such experience. But so far as it is intended that Whewell's theory will not hold true if Kantism is false, I reply that Whewell's theory does not involve the whole of Kantism, but only the general proposition that cognition consists of two elements one of which is idealistic and the other empirical, a proposition which seems to be virtually admitted by Hamiltonians when they hold that all knowledge reposes in part ultimately on "Faith." I admit that besides this general agreement with Kant, Whewell also has the same conception of Space and Time in its most general outlines, but not by any means to such an extent as is peculiar to Kantism,—he goes no further than Cudworth did before Kant or than Sir Wm. Hamilton has since. I do not see therefore what Kantian propositions Whewell holds which Hamilton denies.

The process of explication of conceptions has according to Whewell been effected by means of controversies. And there can be no doubt that to take the controversies concerning the single science of mechanics as an example, men's thoughts were confused and hazy before the controversies about Galileo's time concerning the definition of uniform force, the question concerning the measure of the force of Percussion,—the war of the *vis viva*—the controversy of the centre of oscillation—of the principle of heart Action—&c. &c.—and that at the end of these debates their minds were so much clearer as to make a vast difference in the progress of science.

This calls our attention again to Whewell's theory being drawn from the public history of science. It is I have no doubt true that scientific conceptions have always first become clear in debates. And this is an important truth. But what was the mental process, what was the change and what the law of the change in the individual mind by which an obscure idea became clear? This Whewell tells us nothing of and indeed seems to have no conception of the question. A metaphysician's mind would have been wholly engrossed in *this* question to the entire exclusion of that one about the *public* process of controversy.

The final result of the clearing up of a conception, as it takes place in science along with observation and induction is that the conception is seen to be necessary.

Uniform force.

Parallelogram of forces.

Gravity.

This identification of inductive conclusions with *à priori* truths has been eagerly seized by J. S. Mill who makes his sensualistic theory of knowledge rest in large measure on this result of Whewell's. Others have ignorantly characterized it as mere Kantism to which in truth it bears no analogy.

This is decidedly the most theoretical and the weakest part of Whewell's theory but it is one which no man who moves in metaphysics with scientific caution can peremptorily deny. It should be regarded as an open question still and one to the solution of which we are not very near.

A consideration of Whewell's arguments in the *Cambridge Philosophical Transactions* to show that all matter is heavy leads me to the belief that the more convincing ones only go to show that we may be sure that we can adopt the formula "All matter is heavy" as long as we leave other formulae to be determined as may be necessary in order to be consistent with this one.

And this naturally brings us to Whewell's next remark which is that a clear conception resulting from a discussion is often formulated in a definition, but that in that case some proposition expressed or implied has always gone along with the definition. Thus along with the definition of the uniform force goes the proposition that gravity is a uniform force and along with the definition of the *Vis Viva* and in the whole discussion concerning it it is assumed that in the mutual action of bodies the whole effect of the force is unchanged.

This remark is excellent but somewhat inadequate to the subject. You often hear this and that called a question of words, but there are not nearly as many mere questions of words discussed as smatterers in logic are apt to imagine. As important a practical lesson as any other which I could indicate as derivable from the study of logic is how to distinguish a question of words from a question truly scientific and how to treat that class of questions which are apt to be mistaken for questions of words. In this department of logic, Whewell gives us but little assistance. He remarks however with perfect truth that in default of a definition *Axioms* may be made to fulfill the same function.

But clearness is not the only condition which a conception must satisfy in order that it may contribute to the progress of science. Besides being clear it must be *appropriate.* It seems to me that a good illustration of this is afforded us in chemistry. Chemistry presents the phenomenon of the perpetual recurrence of integral numbers. A few examples of these are the following: When two substances combine with one another in different proportions by weight, those proportions are to one another as two small integral numbers. Equivalent proportions of different vapours are either equal or bear to one another a ratio as between two small integral numbers. The specific heats of different substances divided by their chemical equivalents are in the ratio of two small integral numbers. The differences in the boiling points of adjacent members of two different series of organic compounds are in the ratio of two small integral numbers. The ratio of the equivalents of two elements usually approximates nearly to the ratio of two integral numbers.

It is a great and unsolved problem to find a theory which shall explain these things. In searching for such a theory we must look out for an idea which is appropriate to the subject.

Now the spectroscope has shown us that different chemical substances are distinguished by the greater or less refrangibility of the heat with which they vibrate. This greater or less refrangibility means a greater or less rapidity of vibration. And this again means that the elasticity or force which tends to draw a portion back to its original position when it has been disturbed is greater or less. Different chemical substances are therefore bodies of different elasticity and susceptible of different rates of vibration.

Now there is no part of the pure mathematical theory of force in which integral numbers come in to any great extent except that of vibrations. And then they come in constantly in the whole doctrine of *nodes interferens* etc.

Here then we have an idea appropriate to the subject. Not a clear conception as yet I admit—not a definite theory. But we have indicated to us the direction in which a theory should be sought.

What for example is the combining weight of a body? It is the weight of that body which contains a unit of chemical force.

And what is the specific gravity of a gas? It is the weight of the gas which contains a unit of elastic force. But it is a fact of chemistry that these two are equal. Then the elastic force of a gas is equal to its chemical force. But in certain vapours the specific gravity is only half the combining weight. So that the elasticity seems to be doubled just as if there were a sort of node in the vibration.

I have given this illustration of what appears to me to be an idea appropriate to this subject, in order that you might plainly see that the appropriate idea must contain the notion of elastic force. At least it must contain the idea of force.

But how have chemists endeavored to explain these things? By suppositions regarding the *size, shape,* and *arrangement* of the particles of bodies. Now these are mere geometrical ideas, which have no relation to the facts to be explained. And the consequence is that the atomic theory will not explain a single fact as it appears to me without the aid of subsidiary hypotheses, which subsidiary hypotheses taken by themselves, or else others equally probable, will suffice of themselves to account for all the facts which can be accounted for by the additional supposition of atoms.

No discoveries accidental.

We pass now, with Whewell, from the consideration of Ideas to the consideration of Facts, their observation and colligations. And here our author begins with the very fundamental proposition that all Facts involve Ideas.

This may remind the metaphysician of a metaphysical proposition, but nobody can understand Whewell who cannot look at these things from a practically scientific point of view.

All facts involve Ideas. This is the first lesson a man has to learn in studying science. What, is there not such a thing as pure observation?

[Drawings of nebulae.]

There is probably no one maxim of logic the ignorance of which by ordinary people produces such deplorable results as this that all Facts involve ideas. People detail to you some foolish story about Ghosts or Planchettes and seem to think that you must believe it or doubt their veracity. Now I certainly have no great confidence in the veracity of most people on speculative subjects; because a love of truth is very rarely strong without a really sound mental discipline; and nothing but the amiable desire of men to respect one another prevents this from being more generally perceived. But veracity apart, do these people suppose that they *can* make any pure observation unaffected by fancy passion or accidental moods or states of the nerves? The most trained scientific observers cannot do that; and as for those who are undisciplined and who are unaware of this weakness of human nature, especially when they are dealing with a subject so momentous as the other world, they are incapable of any approximation to it. A physician won't prescribe for himself. And if he has too much interest in the matter to keep his observations cold, ought not any ordinary person to be regarded as incompetent to keep cool when an immortal destiny is in question?

[*Struve and 2nd satellite of Neptune*]

But the influence of the mind upon observations is not necessarily evil. It may almost be said that we can only see what we look for.

[*Rose-coloured protuberances*]

And I only give this as a single instance of a proposition perfectly familiar among observers of all kinds.

Hence *observation* as distinct from mere *gazing* consists in perception in the light of a question.

[Enlarge a little on this—Whewell has not remarked this. Why.]

[PRACTICAL LOGIC]

Lessons in Practical Logic

MS 164: Winter 1869–1870

Lesson 1

The object of this course is to teach something of the art of investigating the truth.

It is really a question of little consequence whether this is a proper definition of logic or not. That is a mere question of words; but men who have not thoroughly studied logic are so apt to confound questions of words and questions of fact—both considering verbal discussions as real discussions and real discussions as merely verbal,—that I shall do well to say a few words in defence of the name that I have given to this course of lessons. And besides, I am perhaps bound to show that the subject to which the instruction is really to relate is the same as that advertized.

Now if you examine Hamilton's logic or any of those logics which are the immediate product of pure Kantianism as his was (—not his peculiar system but his lectures in which his system does not appear as it was worked up later) you will find logic defined as the Science of Thought as Thought—or something of that sort. This is an extremely different conception of the subject from that with which I set out. Take for example Mr. Mansel's admirable *Prolegomena Logica* where the Kantian conception of logic is developed in the most consistent and beautiful manner.

Consequences

A *consequence* is the statement that one fact follows from another. The expression of the former fact is called the *antecedent*. The expression of the latter is termed the *consequent*.

Note. The investigation of consequences constitutes *Logic.* All questions of psychology are therefore irrelevant to the science of logic generally, though they may, no doubt, be of importance with reference to particular kinds of consequences when a psychological fact is explicitly or implicitly involved in the antecedent.

Consequences may be divided in the first place into *material* and *formal.* If the fact expressed in the consequent is the same as that expressed in the antecedent or is a part of it, then the consequence is an empty and meaningless expression unless the forms of expression of the antecedent and consequent differ in which case the consequence is the statement of a fact concerning the relation of these forms of expression. Such a *consequence* is called *formal;* but one which expresses a fact concerning the matters in question and not merely concerning the expression of them is termed *material.*

If Socrates is mortal, Socrates is mortal

this is empty. It is a particular sort of nonsense. It involves no absurdity, it is not meaningless in its grammatical construction or its terms but it fails to say anything.

Take this

Socrates dies; ergo, Socrates is mortal

This is a formal consequence. The meaning of the consequent is involved in the meaning of the antecedent.

Socrates dies bravely; ergo Socrates is mortal
Socrates dies before Plato; ergo Socrates is mortal
Socrates dies and Plato lives; ergo Socrates is mortal
Socrates dies and Plato is a man; ergo Socrates is mortal
Some man dies and another lives; ergo, Some man dies
Some man dies and so does every other; ergo, Some man dies
Every man dies; ergo, some man dies.

These are all formal consequences.

The following is a material consequence

Socrates is a man; therefore, Socrates is mortal

for if a man were to discover the Elixir of Life he would not thereby cease to be a man.

This distinction of formal and material consequences is one of the most practically important in the whole range of Logic.

A Practical Treatise on Logic and Methodology

MS 165: Winter 1869–1870

πάντες ἄνθρωποι τοῦ εἰδέναι ὀρέγονται φύσει

Chapter I. Of the Subject-Matter of this book

Logic or dialectic (for these two terms have often been employed synonymously) has been defined in many different ways. Indeed, the definition which a logician gives of his science will usually indicate to what school he belongs. Some of these variations arise from the different ways in which the sciences have been classified without importing any difference either in the subject-matter of logic or the method of treating it; for since a definition usually refers the word or thing defined to a class, disagreement concerning classification will result in disagreement concerning definitions. Other variations have arisen from different opinions in regard to the method in which Logic ought to be investigated. But there is also a great diversity of opinion as to what ought and what ought not to be treated of in a book upon logic.

It is a historical fact that logic originated in an attempt to discover a method of investigating truth. Moreover, the doctrines of logic, as they exist, centre about the forms of inference. Sebastianus Contus has acutely observed that although Scotus and his school profess to regard logic as a purely speculative science yet in their whole method of treatment of it, they show that they really consider it in a practical point of view; and the same may be said of most of the other writers who term it a purely speculative science. On the whole, therefore, we cannot utterly contemn that definition with which Petrus Hispanus opens his celebrated *Summulae,* the classical work upon logic of the middle ages, "Dialectica est ars artium scientia scientiarum, ad omnium methodorum principia viam habens. Sola enim dialectica probabiliter disputat de principiis omnium aliarum scientiarum." In short, we may state it as a historical fact that logic has been essentially the science of the structure of arguments, whereby we can distinguish good arguments from bad ones, can estimate the value of an argument, can determine upon what conditions it is valid, how it needs to be modified, and what can be inferred from a given state of facts.

Rules for Investigation

Chapter I

All men naturally desire knowledge. This book is meant to minister to this passion primarily and secondarily to all the interests which knowledge subserves.

Here will be found maxims for estimating the validity and strength of arguments, and for deciding what facts ought to be examined in the investigation of a question.

That the student may attain a real mastery of the art of thinking, it is necessary that the reasons for these maxims should be made clear to him, and that the maxims themselves should be woven into a harmonious code so as to be readily grasped by the mind.

Logic or dialectic is the name of the science from which such rules are drawn. Right reasoning has been obviously the aim of Aristotle in all the books of the *Organon* except perhaps the first, as it was also of the Stoics, the Lawyers, the medieval summulists, and the modern students of Inductive reasoning, in their additions to Logic. "Dialectica," says the most celebrated treatise on the subject in the middle ages, "est ars artium, scientia scientiarum, ad omnium methodorum principia viam habens. Sola enim dialectica probabiliter disputat de principiis omnium aliarum scientiarum."

Exercise 1. Let the student here write out a fair discussion of the question whether the principles of right reasoning can be investigated. It would seem that these principles must be known before any investigation can be made. In writing this exercise, precision of thought is the first thing to be aimed at, precision in the order of statement the next. All ornament is inadmissible.

A science by which things are tested is necessarily a classificatory science. Thus, every system of qualitative chemical analysis consists in a classification of chemical substances. Accordingly, what we have to study, in the first place, is the classification of inferences. As there are several different systems of qualitative analysis based on different classifications of chemical substances but all valid, so there are different valid systems of logic based on different classifications of inferences. The accomplished reasoner must be familiar with more than one such system.

Chapter 2

After a question has been started, opinions may for a while differ. If a sufficiently long course of experience and reasoning will produce a settlement of opinion, this final opinion is the only legitimate aim of experience and reasoning. For this is all that experience and reasoning really tend to. If experience and reasoning will not lead to a final settlement of opinion, they lead to nothing, and can have no legitimate object. In any case, therefore, the only legitimate aim of experience and reasoning is to reach the final opinion, or in other words to ascertain what would be the ultimate result of sufficient experience and reasoning. Now there is no reason to think that there is any possible opinion which sufficient observation and reasoning would not reverse; hence, no absolutely final opinion can be aimed at. But at a sufficiently advanced point of time, there must be some opinion concerning the future settled opinion, which would result from proper reasoning concerning all the experience so far had by men. For at that time if no experience has been had of that concerning which the question is, the inference is that none will be had. If some experience concerning it has been had, reasoning will, from the nature of its rules, be able to draw some inference from it,—whether with great or little confidence. At a sufficiently advanced point of time, therefore, there will be an opinion which ought, from all the facts hitherto observed, according to right reasoning, to prevail.

Practical Logic

Chapter I

"All men naturally desire knowledge." This book is meant to minister to this passion primarily and secondarily to all interests that knowledge subserves.

Here will be found maxims for estimating the validity and strength of arguments, and for deciding what facts ought to be examined in the investigation of a question.

That the student may attain a real mastery of the art of thinking, it is necessary that the reasons for these maxims should be made clear to him, and that the maxims themselves should be woven into a harmonious code so as to be readily grasped by the mind.

Logic or dialectic is the name of the science from which such rules are drawn. For right reasoning has evidently been the object of inquiry for Aristotle in all the books of the *Organon* except perhaps the first, as it was also that of the Stoics, of the Lawyers, of the medieval Summulists, and of modern students of Induction, in the additions which they have made to the doctrines of the Stagyrite. "Dialectica," says the most celebrated medieval logic, "est ars artium, scientia scientiarum, ad omnium methodorum principia viam habens. Sola enim dialectica probabiliter disputat de principiis omnium aliarum scientiarum."

Exercise 1. Let the student write out an impartial discussion of the question whether the principles of right reasoning can be investigated. For it would seem that these principles must be known before any investigation whatever can be made. In this writing, let precision of thought be the first object, precision in the order of discussion the next. Let no ornament of style be permitted.

A science by which things are tested is necessarily a classificatory science. Thus, every system of qualitative chemical analysis consists in a classification of chemical substances. Accordingly, we have to study, in the first place, the classification of inferences. Just as there are several different systems of qualitative analysis,—as ordinary analysis by sulphuretted hydrogen, blowpipe analysis, and analysis by carbonate of baryta,—based on different classifications of chemical substances, but all valid, so there are different valid systems of logic, based on different classifications of inferences. The accomplished reasoner will do well to be familiar with more than one such system.

Chapter 2

First of all, the student has to gain a perfectly definite conception of the true function of reasoning.

The following axiom requires no comment, beyond the remark that it seems often to be forgotten. *Where there is no real doubt or disagreement there is no question and can be no real investigation.*

Upon the next point, somewhat more thought must be bestowed. Any useful inquisition must lead to some definite conclusion. A method of investigation which should carry different men to different results without tending to bring them to agreement, would be self-destructive and worthless. But if by a sufficiently long result a settlement of opinion could be reached, this concordance (even if further exploration would disturb it) is all that research really tends towards, and is therefore its only attainable end. *The only legitimate aim of reasoning, then, is to ascertain what decision would be agreed upon if the question were sufficiently ventilated.* To this it may be objected, 1st, that the primary object of an investigation is to ascertain the truth itself and not the opinions which would arise under any particular circumstances; and, 2nd, that the resolution of my own doubt is more my object in an investigation than the production of unanimity among others. Undoubtedly, that which we seek in an investigation is called truth, but what distinct conception ought to be attached to this word it is so difficult to say, that it seems better to describe the object of an investigation by a character which certainly belongs to it and to it alone, and which has nothing mysterious or vague about it. In like manner, it may be admitted that a genuine investigation is undertaken to resolve the doubts of the investigator. But observe this: *no sensible man will be void of doubt as long as persons as competent to judge as himself differ from him.* Hence to resolve his own doubts is to ascertain to what position sufficient research would carry all men.

For attaining this unanimous accord,—this catholic confession,— two plans have been pursued.

The first, simplest, and most usual is to adhere pertinaciously to some opinion and endeavour to unite all men upon it. The means of bringing men to agree to such a fixed opinion are an efficient organization of men who will devote themselves to propagating it, working upon the passions of mankind, and gaining an ascendency over them by keeping them in ignorance. In order to guard against all temptation to abandon his opinion, a man must be careful what he reads and must learn to regard his belief as holy, to be indignant at any questioning of it, and especially to consider the senses as the chief means whereby Satan gains access to the soul and as organs constantly to be mortified, distrusted, and despised. With an unwavering determination thus to shut himself off from all influences external to the society of those who think with him, a man may root //opinions/faith// in himself ineradicably; and a considerable body of such men, devoting all their energies to the spread of their doctrines, may produce a great effect under favourable circumstances. They and their followers may truly be said to be not of this world. Their actions will often be inexplicable to the rest of mankind, since they live in a world, which they will call *spiritual* and others will call *imaginary,* with reference to which their opinions are certainly perfectly true. The belief of one of these men, though perhaps resulting in large measure from the force of circumstances, will also be strengthened by a direct effort of the will, and he should therefore consistently regard it as wrong-willed and wicked to allow one's opinion to be formed, independently of what one wishes to believe, by that play of Sense which the Devil puts in one's way.

This method (which we may term the Divine, Spiritual, or Heavenly method) will not serve the purpose of the Children of This World, since the world in which they are interested has this

peculiarity: that *things are not just as we choose to think them.*
Consequently, the accord of those whose belief is determined by a
direct effort of the will, is not the unanimity which these persons
seek.

Chapter 2

MS 166: Winter 1869–1870

First of all, the student has to gain a perfectly definite conception
of the true function of reasoning.

MAXIM I. *Where there is no real doubt there can be no real investigation.* This seems to be sufficiently obvious, and it is difficult to find
any clearer truth by which to illustrate it. Yet it is often forgotten.
For example the Cartesian method of philosophizing is to begin with
a state of philosophic doubt and requires us to lay aside all our beliefs
and begin the whole process of inference anew. Now there never
would have been any Cartesians in the world if it had been understood that this philosophic doubt must be genuine doubt, and if
students had had any proper self-knowledge. It is plainly impossible
to have an unaffected doubt that fire burns,—and one which will
resist a few experiments,—unless one is incapable of reasoning.

MAXIM II. *What is questioned by instructed persons is not certain.*
If two men think differently either may be right; and that one of
them is I makes no difference for each is in the first person to himself.
If a demonstration appears perfectly conclusive to one person and
not so to another, it may be that there is some fallacy in it. Nevertheless, the opinions of most persons upon most subjects may be entirely
neglected. A child's judgment of a lover's motives should have as
much weight against a grown person's as the judgment of an ordinary
person of intelligence against that of a man who is peculiarly fitted
by natural bent, severe training, and large experience, for judging of
the subject. The belief in the right to a private opinion which is the

essence of protestantism, is carried to a ridiculous excess in our community. Some years ago, an instrument was invented called Hedgecock's Quadrant, by observing a candle with which, as the heavenly bodies are observed with an ordinary quadrant, it was pretended that the latitude and longitude could both be ascertained. Most of the newspapers and several ship-owners thought it a valuable invention; but physicists would not listen to their arguments. It was generally thought that this was very wrong, but the event has justified them.

On the other hand, it is folly in me not to doubt what men as capable as myself of forming a correct conclusion doubt. For Agassiz to attach no weight to the opinion of Darwin or for Darwin to attach no weight to that of Agassiz, would show a narrow-mindedness, most fatal to the sober investigation of truth. No self-evident proposition is more recklessly disregarded than this second maxim. We often hear such terms as *indubitable* applied to propositions which actually are doubted by a large proportion of experts; and such language certainly argues great intemperance and want of discipline in him who uses it.

MAXIM III. *The object of reasoning is to settle questions.*

If anybody objects to this that the object of reasoning is rather to ascertain the truth than to make the peace between disputants, I agree with him entirely. We wish to ascertain the truth, but what is truth? This is an indispensible inquiry if we so define the function of reason, yet it would plunge us at once into a sea of metaphysics from which we could not hope soon to emerge. Opinions upon this subject are various; and it is therefore uncertain what truth is. It is not likely *we* could reconcile those opinions when so many greater men have failed, and therefore we could not obtain any certain answer to this question. By such a method, therefore, we could gain no clear and trustworthy conception of the end of reasoning. Let us then avoid this idea of truth as long as we can and keep in the realm of those everyday and concrete notions about which there can be no mystery nor vagueness.

Any useful inquisition must lead to some definite conclusion, for a method of investigation which should carry different men to different results without tending to bring them to agreement, would be self-destructive and worthless. Consequently, reasoning rightly conducted does tend to produce an agreement among men; and doubt once dispelled investigation must cease. Our maxim, therefore, defines in some degree at least the end of reasoning; that is, it serves to exclude a part of those things which are inconsistent with the true end. We shall see presently what needs to be added to this rule.

This is a maxim constantly neglected. Some persons seem to think the chief use of the power of reasoning is its own exercise. And so they make the object of the process the keeping up of a disputation instead of the bringing of it to a close. The best cure for such a spirit of disputatiousness is the constant practical application of reason where its inferences will be speedily tested, and especially the study of the natural sciences. According to my observation there is not one out of two hundred of those of our graduates who have any intellectual force who escape this cursed disease which has always infected schools. And, therefore, in my opinion the first thing a graduate should do is to put himself under the care of a first-rate teacher in a science of observation.

MAXIM IV. *Things are not just as we choose to think them.*

Description of a Notation for the Logic of Relatives, resulting from an Amplification of the Conceptions of Boole's Calculus of Logic

P 52: Communicated 26 January 1870

Relative terms usually receive some slight treatment in works upon logic, but the only considerable investigation into the formal laws which govern them is contained in a valuable paper by Mr. De Morgan in the tenth volume of the *Cambridge Philosophical Transactions*. He there uses a convenient algebraic notation, which is formed by adding to the well-known *spiculæ* of that writer the signs used in the following examples.

X . . LY signifies that X is some one of the objects of thought which stand to Y in the relation L, or is one of the L's of Y.
X . LMY signifies that X is not an L of an M of Y.
X . . (L,M)Y signifies that X is either an L or an M of Y.
LM′ an L of every M. L,M an L of none but M's.
L$^{[-1]}$Y something to which Y is L. l (small L) non-L.

This system still leaves something to be desired. Moreover, Boole's logical algebra has such singular beauty, so far as it goes, that it is interesting to inquire whether it cannot be extended over the whole realm of formal logic, instead of being restricted to that simplest and least useful part of the subject, the logic of absolute terms, which, when he wrote, was the only formal logic known. The object of this paper is to show that an affirmative answer can be given to this question. I think there can be no doubt that a *calculus*, or art of drawing inferences, based upon the notation I am to describe, would be perfectly possible and even practically useful in some difficult cases, and particularly in the *investigation* of logic. I regret that I am not in a situation to be able to perform this labor, but the account here given of the notation itself will afford the ground of a judgment concerning its probable utility.

In extending the use of old symbols to new subjects, we must of course be guided by certain principles of analogy, which, when formulated, become new and wider definitions of these symbols. As we are to employ the usual algebraic signs as far as possible, it is proper to begin by laying down definitions of the various algebraic relations and operations. The following will, perhaps, not be objected to.

General Definitions of the Algebraic Signs

Inclusion in or *being as small as* is a *transitive* relation. The consequence holds that[1]

If	$x \prec y,$
and	$y \prec z,$
then	$x \prec z.$

Equality is the conjunction of being as small as and its converse. To say that $x = y$ is to say that $x \prec y$ and $y \prec x$.

Being less than is being as small as with the exclusion of its converse. To say that $x < y$ is to say that $x \prec y$, and that it is not true that $y \prec x$.

Being greater than is the converse of being less than. To say that $x > y$ is to say that $y < x$.

ADDITION is an *associative* operation. That is to say,[2]

$$(x +, y) +, z = x +, (y +, z).$$

1. I use the sign $\prec$ in place of $\leqq$. My reasons for not liking the latter sign are that it cannot be written rapidly enough, and that it seems to represent the relation it expresses as being compounded of two others which in reality are complications of this. It is universally admitted that a higher conception is logically more simple than a lower one under it. Whence it follows from the relations of extension and comprehension, that in any state of information a broader concept is more simple than a narrower one included under it. Now all equality is inclusion in, but the converse is not true; hence inclusion in is a wider concept than equality, and therefore logically a simpler one. On the same principle, inclusion is also simpler than being less than. The sign $\leqq$ seems to involve a definition by enumeration; and such a definition offends against the laws of definition.

2. I write a comma below the sign of addition, except when (as is the case in ordinary algebra) the corresponding inverse operation (subtraction) is determinative.

Addition is a *commutative* operation. That is,

$$x +\!\!, y = y +\!\!, x.$$

Invertible addition is addition the corresponding inverse of which is determinative. The last two formulæ hold good for it, and also the consequence that

If	$x + y$	$= z,$
and	$x + y'$	$= z,$
then	y	$= y'.$

MULTIPLICATION is an operation which is *doubly distributive with reference to addition.* That is,

$$x(y +\!\!, z) = xy +\!\!, xz,$$
$$(x +\!\!, y)z = xz +\!\!, yz.$$

Multiplication is almost invariably an *associative* operation.

$$(xy)z = x(yz).$$

Multiplication is not generally commutative. If we write commutative multiplication with a comma, we have

$$x, y = y, x.$$

Invertible multiplication is multiplication whose corresponding inverse operation (division) is determinative. We may indicate this by a dot; and then the consequence holds that

If	$x.y$	$= z,$
and	$x.y'$	$= z,$
then	y	$= y'.$

Functional multiplication is the application of an operation to a function. It may be written like ordinary multiplication; but then there will generally be certain points where the associative principle does not hold. Thus, if we write (sin abc)def, there is one such point. If we write (log $_{(\text{base } abc)}$ def)ghi, there are two such points. The number of such points depends on the nature of the symbol of operation, and is necessarily finite. If there were many such points, in any case, it would be necessary to adopt a different mode of writing such functions from that now usually employed. We might, for example, give to "log" such a meaning that what followed it up to a certain point indicated by a † should denote the base of the system, what followed that to the point indicated by a ‡ should be the function operated on, and what followed that should be beyond the influence of the sign "log." Thus log *abc* † *def* ‡ *ghi* would be (log *abc*)*ghi*, the base being *def.* In this paper I shall adopt a notation very similar to this, which will be more conveniently described further on.

The operation of INVOLUTION obeys the formula[3]

$$(x^y)^z = x^{(yz)}.$$

Involution, also, follows the *indexical principle.*

$$x^{y\,+\!,\,z} = x^y,x^z.$$

Involution, also, satisfies the *binomial theorem.*

$$(x\,+\!,\,y)^z = x^z\,+\!,\,\Sigma_p\, x^{z-p},y^p\,+\!,\,y^z,$$

where Σ_p denotes that p is to have every value less than z, and is to be taken out of z in all possible ways, and that the sum of all the terms so obtained of the form x^{z-p},y^p is to be taken.

SUBTRACTION is the operation inverse to addition. We may write indeterminative subtraction with a comma below the usual sign. Then we shall have that

$$(x\,\mathord{\overline{}}\,y)\,+\!,\,y = x,$$
$$(x - y) + y = x,$$
$$(x + y) - y = x.$$

3. In the notation of quaternions, Hamilton has assumed

$$(x^y)^z = x^{(zy)}, \qquad \text{instead of} \qquad (x^y)^z = x^{(yz)},$$

although it appears to make but little difference which he takes. Perhaps we should assume two involutions, so that

$$(x^y)^z = x^{(yz)}, \qquad\qquad {}^z({}^yx) = {}^{(zy)}x.$$

But in this paper only the former of these is required.

DIVISION is the operation inverse to multiplication. Since multiplication is not generally commutative it is necessary to have two signs for division. I shall take

$$(x{:}y)y \;=\; x,$$
$$x\tfrac{y}{x} \;=\; y.$$

Division inverse to that multiplication which is indicated by a comma may be indicated by a semicolon. So that

$$(x\,;y),y \;=\; x.$$

EVOLUTION and TAKING THE LOGARITHM are the operations inverse to involution.

$$(\sqrt[x]{y})^x \;=\; y,$$
$$x^{\,\log_x y} \;=\; y.$$

These conditions are to be regarded as imperative. But in addition to them there are certain other characters which it is highly desirable that relations and operations should possess, if the ordinary signs of algebra are to be applied to them. These I will here endeavor to enumerate.

1. It is an additional motive for using a mathematical sign to signify a certain operation or relation that the general conception of this operation or relation should resemble that of the operation or relation usually signified by the same sign. In particular, it will be well that the relation expressed by $\prec$ should involve the conception of one member being in the other; addition, that of taking together; multiplication, that of one factor's being taken relatively to the other (as we write 3×2 for a triplet *of* pairs, and $D\varphi$ for the derivative of φ); and involution, that of the base being taken for every unit of the exponent.

2. In the second place, it is desirable that, in certain general circumstances, determinate numbers should be capable of being substituted for the letters operated upon, and that when so substituted the equations should hold good when interpreted in accordance with the ordinary definitions of the signs, so that arithmetical algebra should be included under the notation employed as a special case of it. For this end, there ought to be a number known or unknown,

which is appropriately substituted in certain cases, for each one of, at least, some class of letters.

3. In the third place, it is almost essential to the applicability of the signs for addition and multiplication, that a *zero* and a *unity* should be possible. By a *zero* I mean a term such that

$$x \mathbin{+_{,}} 0 = x,$$

whatever the signification of x; and by a *unity* a term for which the corresponding general formula

$$x \mathbin{/} = x$$

holds good. On the other hand, there ought to be no term a such that $a^x = x$, independently of the value of x.

4. It will also be a strong motive for the adoption of an algebraic notation, if other formulæ which hold good in arithmetic, such as

$$x^z, y^z = (x, y)^z,$$
$$\mathbin{/} x = x,$$
$$x' = x,$$
$$x0 = 0,$$

continue to hold good; if, for instance, the conception of a differential is possible, and Taylor's Theorem holds, and 6 or $(1 + i)^{1/i}$ plays an important part in the system, if there should be a term having the properties of $\ominus$ (3.14159), or properties similar to those of space should otherwise be brought out by the notation, or if there should be an absurd expression having the properties and uses of J or the square root of the negative.

Application of the Algebraic Signs to Logic

While holding ourselves free to use the signs of algebra in any sense conformable to the above absolute conditions, we shall find it convenient to restrict ourselves to one particular interpretation except where another is indicated. I proceed to describe the special notation which is adopted in this paper.

Use of the Letters

The letters of the alphabet will denote logical signs. Now logical terms are of three grand classes. The first embraces those whose logical form involves only the conception of quality, and which there-fore represent a thing simply as "a ———." These discriminate ob-jects in the most rudimentary way, which does not involve any con-sciousness of discrimination. They regard an object as it is in itself as *such* (*quale*); for example, as horse, tree, or man. These are *absolute terms.* The second class embraces terms whose logical form involves the conception of relation, and which require the addition of another term to complete the denotation. These discriminate objects with a distinct consciousness of discrimination. They regard an object as over against another, that is as relative; as father of, lover of, or servant of. These are *simple relative terms.* The third class embraces terms whose logical form involves the conception of bringing things into relation, and which require the addition of more than one term to complete the denotation. They discriminate not only with con-sciousness of discrimination, but with consciousness of its origin. They regard an object as medium or third between two others, that is as conjugative; as giver of ——— to ———, or buyer of ——— for ——— from ———. These may be termed *conjugative terms.* The conjugative term involves the conception of THIRD, the relative that of second or OTHER, the absolute term simply considers AN object. No fourth class of terms exists involving the conception of *fourth,* because when that of *third* is introduced, since it involves the conception of bringing objects into relation, all higher numbers are given at once, inasmuch as the conception of bringing objects into relation is independent of the number of members of the rela-tionship. Whether this *reason* for the fact that there is no fourth class of terms fundamentally different from the third is satisfactory or not, the fact itself is made perfectly evident by the study of the logic of relatives. I shall denote absolute terms by the Roman alpha-bet, a, b, c, d, etc.; relative terms by italics, *a, b, c, d,* etc.; and conjugative terms by a kind of type called Madisonian, a, b, c, d, etc.

I shall commonly denote individuals by capitals, and generals by small letters. General symbols for numbers will be printed in black-letter, thus, a, b, c, d, etc. The Greek letters will denote operations.

To avoid repetitions, I give here a catalogue of the letters I shall use in examples in this paper, with the significations I attach to them.

a. animal.
b. black.
f. Frenchman.
h. horse.
m. man.

p. President of the United States Senate.
r. rich person.
u. violinist.
v. Vice-President of the United States.
w. woman.

a. enemy.
b. benefactor.
c. conqueror.
e. emperor.

h. husband.
l. lover.
m. mother.
n. not.

o. owner.
s. servant.
w. wife.

g. giver to ——— of ———.   *b.* betrayer to ——— of ———.
w. winner over of ——— to   *t.* transferrer from ———
——— from ———.   to ———.

Numbers corresponding to Letters

I propose to use the term "universe" to denote that class of individuals *about* which alone the whole discourse is understood to run. The universe, therefore, in this sense, as in Mr. De Morgan's, is different on different occasions. In this sense, moreover, discourse may run upon something which is not a subjective part of the universe; for instance, upon the qualities or collections of the individuals it contains.

I propose to assign to all logical terms, numbers; to an absolute term, the number of individuals it denotes; to a relative term, the average number of things so related to one individual. Thus in a universe of perfect men, the number of "tooth of" would be 32. The number of a relative with two correlates would be the average number of things so related to a pair of individuals; and so on for relatives of higher numbers of correlates. I propose to denote the number of a logical term by enclosing the term in square brackets, thus, $[t]$.

The Signs of Inclusion, Equality, etc.

I shall follow Boole in taking the sign of equality to signify identity. Thus, if v denotes the Vice-President of the United States, and p the President of the Senate of the United States,

$$v = p$$

means that every Vice-President of the United States is President of the Senate, and every President of the United States Senate is Vice-President. The sign "less than" is to be so taken that

$$f < m$$

means every Frenchman is a man, but there are men besides French-men. Drobisch has used this sign in the same sense.[4] It will follow from these significations of = and < that the sign $\prec$ (or $\leqq$, "as small as") will mean "is." Thus,

$$f \prec m$$

means "every Frenchman is a man," without saying whether there are any other men or not. So,

$$m \prec l$$

will mean that every mother of anything is a lover of the same thing; although this interpretation in some degree anticipates a convention to be made further on. These significations of = and < plainly conform to the indispensable conditions. Upon the transitive character of these relations the syllogism depends, for by virtue of it, from

$$f \prec m$$

and

$$m \prec a,$$

we can infer that

$$f \prec a;$$

that is, from every Frenchman being a man and every man being an animal, that every Frenchman is an animal. But not only do the significations of = and < here adopted fulfil all absolute requirements, but they have the supererogatory virtue of being very nearly the same as the common significations. Equality is, in fact, nothing but the identity of two numbers; numbers that are equal are those which are predicable of the same collections, just as terms that are identical are those which are predicable of the same classes. So, to write 5 < 7 is to say that 5 is part of 7, just as to write f < m is to say that Frenchmen are part of men. Indeed, if f < m, then the

---

4. According to De Morgan, *Formal Logic,* p. 334. De Morgan refers to the first edition of Drobisch's *Logic.* The third edition contains nothing of the sort.

number of Frenchmen is less than the number of men, and if v = p, then the number of Vice-Presidents is equal to the number of Presidents of the Senate; so that the numbers may always be substituted for the terms themselves, in case no signs of operation occur in the equations or inequalities.

The Signs for Addition

The sign of addition is taken by Boole, so that

$$x + y$$

denotes everything denoted by x, and, *besides*, everything denoted by y. Thus

$$m + w$$

denotes all men, and, besides, all women. This signification for this sign is needed for connecting the notation of logic with that of the theory of probabilities. But if there is anything which is denoted by both the terms of the sum, the latter no longer stands for any logical term on account of its implying that the objects denoted by one term are to be taken *besides* the objects denoted by the other. For example,

$$f + u$$

means all Frenchmen besides all violinists, and, therefore, considered as a logical term, implies that all French violinists are *besides themselves.* For this reason alone, in a paper which is published in the Proceedings of the Academy for March 17, 1867, I preferred to take as the regular addition of logic a non-invertible process, such that

$$m \mathbin{+\mkern-8mu,} b$$

stands for all men and black things, without any implication that the black things are to be taken besides the men; and the study of the logic of relatives has supplied me with other weighty reasons for the same determination. Since the publication of that paper, I have found that Mr. W. Stanley Jevons, in a tract called *Pure Logic, or the*

Logic of Quality, had anticipated me in substituting the same operation for Boole's addition, although he rejects Boole's operation entirely and writes the new one with a + sign while withholding from it the name of addition.[5] It is plain that both the regular non-invertible addition and the invertible addition satisfy the absolute conditions. But the notation has other recommendations. The conception of *taking together* involved in these processes is strongly analogous to that of summation, the sum of 2 and 5, for example, being the number of a collection which consists of a collection of two and a collection of five. Any logical equation or inequality in which no operation but addition is involved may be converted into a numerical equation or inequality by substituting the numbers of the several terms for the terms themselves,—provided all the terms summed are mutually exclusive. Addition being taken in this sense, *nothing* is to be denoted by *zero,* for then

$$x +\!\!, 0 = x,$$

whatever is denoted by x; and this is the definition of *zero.* This interpretation is given by Boole, and is very neat, on account of the resemblance between the ordinary conception of *zero* and that of nothing, and because we shall thus have

$$[0] = 0.$$

The Signs for Multiplication

I shall adopt for the conception of multiplication *the application of a relation,* in such a way that, for example, lw shall denote whatever is lover of a woman. This notation is the same as that used by Mr. De Morgan, although he appears not to have had multiplication in his mind. s(m $+\!\!,$ w) will, then, denote whatever is servant of anything of the class composed of men and women taken together. So that

$$s(\text{m} +\!\!, \text{w}) = s\text{m} +\!\!, s\text{w}.$$

($l +\!\!, s$)w will denote whatever is lover or servant to a woman, and

$$(l +\!\!, s)\text{w} = l\text{w} +\!\!, s\text{w}.$$

5. In another book he uses the sign $\cdot\!\!\cdot$ instead of +.

(sl)w will denote whatever stands to a woman in the relation of servant of a lover, and

$$(sl)\mathrm{w} = s(l\mathrm{w}).$$

Thus all the absolute conditions of multiplication are satisfied.

The term "identical with ———" is a unity for this multiplication. That is to say, if we denote "identical with ———" by $\textit{1}$ we have

$$x\,\textit{1} = x,$$

whatever relative term x may be. For what is a lover of something identical with anything, is the same as a lover of that thing.

A conjugative term like *giver* naturally requires two correlates, one denoting the thing given, the other the recipient of the gift. We must be able to distinguish, in our notation, the giver of A to B from the giver to A of B, and, therefore, I suppose the signification of the letter equivalent to such a relative to distinguish the correlates as first, second, third, etc., so that "giver of ——— to ———" and "giver to ——— of ———" will be expressed by different letters. Let $\textit{g}$ denote the latter of these conjugative terms. Then, the correlates or multiplicands of this multiplier cannot all stand directly after it, as is usual in multiplication, but may be ranged after it in regular order, so that

$$\textit{g}xy$$

will denote a giver to x of y. But according to the notation, x here multiplies y, so that if we put for x owner (o), and for y horse (h),

$$\textit{g}o\mathrm{h}$$

appears to denote the giver of a horse to an owner of a horse. But let the individual horses be H, H', H", etc. Then

$$\mathrm{h} = \mathrm{H} +, \mathrm{H'} +, \mathrm{H''} +, \text{etc.}$$

$$\begin{aligned}\textit{g}o\mathrm{h} &= \textit{g}o(\mathrm{H} +, \mathrm{H'} +, \mathrm{H''} +, \text{etc.})\\ &= \textit{g}o\mathrm{H} +, \textit{g}o\mathrm{H'} +, \textit{g}o\mathrm{H''} +, \text{etc.}\end{aligned}$$

Now this last member must be interpreted as a giver of a horse to the owner of *that* horse, and this, therefore, must be the interpretation of $\mathcal{g}o$h. This is always very important. *A term multiplied by two relatives shows that* THE SAME INDIVIDUAL *is in the two relations.* If we attempt to express the giver of a horse to a lover of a woman, and for that purpose write

$$\mathcal{g}l\text{wh},$$

we have written giver of a woman to a lover of her, and if we add brackets, thus,

$$\mathcal{g}(l\text{w})\text{h},$$

we abandon the associative principle of multiplication. A little reflection will show that the associative principle must in some form or other be abandoned at this point. But while this principle is sometimes falsified, it oftener holds, and a notation must be adopted which will show of itself when it holds. We already see that we cannot express multiplication by writing the multiplicand directly after the multiplier; let us then affix subjacent numbers after letters to show where their correlates are to be found. The first number shall denote how many factors must be counted from left to right to reach the first correlate, the second how many *more* must be counted to reach the second, and so on. Then, the giver of a horse to a lover of a woman may be written

$$\mathcal{g}_{12}l_1\text{wh} = \mathcal{g}_{11}l_2\text{hw} = \mathcal{g}_{2-1}\text{h}l_1\text{w}.$$

Of course a negative number indicates that the former correlate follows the latter by the corresponding positive number. A subjacent *zero* makes the term itself the correlate. Thus,

$$l_0$$

denotes the lover of *that* lover or the lover of himself, just as $\mathcal{g}o$h denotes that the horse is given to the owner of itself, for to make a term doubly a correlate is, by the distributive principle, to make each individual doubly a correlate, so that

$$l_0 = L_0 \,\,+\!\!, L_0{}' \,\,+\!\!, L_0{}'' \,\,+\!\!, \text{etc.}$$

A subjacent sign of infinity may indicate that the correlate is indeterminate, so that

$$l_\infty$$

will denote a lover of something. We shall have some confirmation of this presently.

If the last subjacent number is a *one* it may be omitted. Thus we shall have

$$l_1 = l,$$
$$\mathcal{G}_{11} = \mathcal{G}_1 = \mathcal{G}.$$

This enables us to retain our former expressions lw, $\mathcal{G}o$h, etc.

The associative principle does not hold in this counting of factors. Because it does not hold, these subjacent numbers are frequently inconvenient in practice, and I therefore use also another mode of showing where the correlate of a term is to be found. This is by means of the marks of reference, † ‡ ‖ § ¶, which are placed subjacent to the relative term and before and above the correlate. Thus, giver of a horse to a lover of a woman may be written

$$\mathcal{G}_{†‡}{}^{†}l_{‖}{}^{‖}w^{‡}h.$$

The asterisk I use exclusively to refer to the last correlate of the last relative of the algebraic term.

Now, considering the order of multiplication to be:—a term, a correlate of it, a correlate of that correlate, etc.,—there is no violation of the associative principle. The only violations of it in this mode of notation are that in thus passing from relative to correlate, we skip about among the factors in an irregular manner, and that we cannot substitute in such an expression as $\mathcal{G}o$h a single letter for oh. I would suggest that such a notation may be found useful in treating other cases of non-associative multiplication. By comparing this with what was said above concerning functional multiplication, it appears that multiplication by a conjugative term is functional, and that the letter denoting such a term is a symbol of operation. I am therefore using two alphabets, the Greek and Madisonian, where only one was necessary. But it is convenient to use both.

Thus far, we have considered the multiplication of relative terms only. Since our conception of multiplication is the application of a relation, we can only multiply absolute terms by considering them as relatives. Now the absolute term "man" is really exactly equivalent to the relative term "man that is ———," and so with any other. I shall write a comma after any absolute term to show that it is so regarded as a relative term. Then man that is black will be written

$$m,b.$$

But not only may any absolute term be thus regarded as a relative term, but any relative term may in the same way be regarded as a relative with one correlate more. It is convenient to take this additional correlate as the first one. Then

$$l,sw$$

will denote a lover of a woman that is a servant of that woman. The comma here after l should not be considered as altering at all the meaning of l, but as only a subjacent sign, serving to alter the arrangement of the correlates. In point of fact, since a comma may be added in this way to any relative term, it may be added to one of these very relatives formed by a comma, and thus by the addition of two commas an absolute term becomes a relative of two correlates. So

$$m,,b,r,$$

interpreted like $\qquad g o h,$

means a man that is a rich individual and is a black that is that rich individual. But this has no other meaning than

$$m,b,r,$$

or a man that is a black that is rich. Thus we see that, after one comma is added, the addition of another does not change the meaning at all, so that whatever has one comma after it must be regarded as having an infinite number. If, therefore, $l,,sw$ is not the same as l,sw (as it plainly is not, because the latter means a lover and servant of a woman, and the former a lover of and servant of and same as a woman), this is simply because the writing of the comma alters the arrangement of the correlates. And if we are to suppose that absolute terms are multipliers at all (as mathematical generality demands that we should), we must regard every term as being a relative requiring an infinite number of correlates to its virtual infinite series "that is —— and is —— and is —— etc." Now a relative formed by a comma of course receives its subjacent numbers like any relative, but the question is, What are to be the implied subjacent numbers for these implied correlates? Any term may be regarded as having an infinite number of factors, those at the end being *ones*, thus,

$$l,sw = l,sw,\mathit{1},\mathit{1},\mathit{1},\mathit{1},\mathit{1},\mathit{1},\mathit{1}, \text{ etc.}$$

A subjacent number may therefore be as great as we please. But all these *ones* denote the same identical individual denoted by w; what then can be the subjacent numbers to be applied to *s,* for instance, on account of its infinite *"that is"*'s? What numbers can separate it from being identical with w? There are only two. The first is *zero*, which plainly neutralizes a comma completely, since

$$s,_0w = sw ,$$

and the other is infinity; for as 1^∞ is indeterminate in ordinary algebra, so it will be shown hereafter to be here, so that to remove the correlate by the product of an infinite series of *ones* is to leave it indeterminate. Accordingly,

$$m,_\infty$$

should be regarded as expressing *some* man. Any term, then, is properly to be regarded as having an infinite number of commas, all or some of which are neutralized by zeros.

"Something" may then be expressed by

$$\mathit{1}_\infty.$$

I shall for brevity frequently express this by an antique figure one (1).
"Anything" by

$$\mathit{1}_0.$$

I shall often also write a straight 1 for *anything*.

It is obvious that multiplication into a multiplicand indicated by a comma is commutative,[6] that is,

$$s,l = l,s.$$

This multiplication is effectively the same as that of Boole in his logical calculus. Boole's unity is my 1, that is, it denotes whatever is.

The sum $x + x$ generally denotes no logical term. But $x,_\infty + x,_\infty$ may be considered as denoting some two x's. It is natural to write

$$x + x = 2.x,$$
and
$$x,_\infty + x,_\infty = 2.x,_\infty,$$

where the dot shows that this multiplication is invertible. We may also use the antique figures so that

$$2.x,_\infty = 2x,$$
just as
$$1_\infty = 1.$$

Then 2 alone will denote some two things. But this multiplication is not in general commutative, and only becomes so when it affects a relative which imparts a relation such that a thing only bears it to *one* thing, and one thing *alone* bears it to a thing. For instance, the lovers of two women are not the same as two lovers of women, that is,

$$l2.w \text{ and } 2.lw$$

are unequal; but the husbands of two women are the same as two husbands of women, that is,

$$h2.w = 2.hw,$$
and in general,
$$x,2.y = 2.x,y.$$

6. It will often be convenient to speak of the whole operation of affixing a comma and then multiplying as a commutative multiplication, the sign for which is the comma. But though this is allowable, we shall fall into confusion at once if we ever forget that in point of fact it is not a different multiplication, only it is multiplication by a relative whose meaning—or rather whose syntax—has been slightly altered; and that the comma is really the sign of this modification of the foregoing term.

The conception of multiplication we have adopted is that of the application of one relation to another. So, a quaternion being the relation of one vector to another, the multiplication of quaternions is the application of one such relation to a second. Even ordinary numerical multiplication involves the same idea, for 2×3 is a pair of triplets, and 3×2 is a triplet of pairs, where "triplet of" and "pair of" are evidently relatives.

If we have an equation of the form

$$xy = z,$$

and there are just as many x's per y as there are *per* things things of the universe, then we have also the arithmetical equation,

$$[x][y] = [z].$$

For instance, if our universe is perfect men, and there are as many teeth to a Frenchman (perfect understood) as there are to any one of the universe, then,

$$[t][f] = [tf]$$

holds arithmetically. So if men are just as apt to be black as things in general,

$$[m,][b] = [m,b],$$

where the difference between $[m]$ and $[m,]$ must not be overlooked. It is to be observed that

$$[\text{\textit{1}}] = 1.$$

Boole was the first to show this connection between logic and probabilities. He was restricted, however, to absolute terms. I do not remember having seen any extension of probability to relatives, except the ordinary theory of *expectation*.

Our logical multiplication, then, satisfies the essential conditions of multiplication, has a unity, has a conception similar to that of admitted multiplications, and contains numerical multiplication as a case under it.

The Sign of Involution

I shall take involution in such a sense that x^y will denote everything which is an x for every individual of y. Thus l^w will be a lover of every woman. Then $(s^l)^w$ will denote whatever stands to every woman in the relation of servant of every lover of hers; and $s^{(lw)}$ will denote whatever is a servant of everything that is lover of a woman. So that

$$(s^l)^w = s^{(lw)}.$$

A servant of every man and woman will be denoted by $s^{m \,+\!\!, \, w}$, and s^m , s^w will denote a servant of every man that is a servant of every woman. So that

$$s^{m \,+\!\!, \, w} = s^m , s^w.$$

That which is emperor or conqueror of every Frenchman will be denoted by $(e \,+\!\!, c)^f$, and $e^f \,+\!\!, \Sigma_p e^{f-p} , c^p \,+\!\!, c^f$ will denote whatever is emperor of every Frenchman or emperor of some Frenchmen and conqueror of all the rest, or conqueror of every Frenchman. Consequently,

$$(e \,+\!\!, c)^f = e^f \,+\!\!, \Sigma_p e^{f-p} , c^p \,+\!\!, c^f.$$

Indeed, we may write the binomial theorem so as to preserve all its usual coefficients; for we have

$$(e \,+\!\!, c)^f = e^f \,+\!\!, [f] \cdot e^{f \,-\, +\!\!,1} , c^{1+\!\!,} \,+\!\!, \frac{[f] \cdot ([f] - 1)}{2} \cdot e^{f - +\!\!,2} , c^{2+\!\!,} \,+\!\!, \text{ etc.}$$

That is to say, those things each of which is emperor or conqueror of every Frenchman consist, first, of all those individuals each of which is a conqueror of every Frenchman; second, of a number of classes equal to the number of Frenchmen, each class consisting of everything which is an emperor of every Frenchman but some one and is a conqueror of that one; third, of a number of classes equal to half the product of the number of Frenchmen by one less than that number, each of these classes consisting of every individual which is an emperor of every Frenchman except a certain two, and is conqueror of those two, etc. This theorem holds, also, equally well with invertible addition, and either term of the binomial may be negative provided we assume

$$(-x)^y = (-)^{[y]}.x^y.$$

In addition to the above equations which are required to hold good by the definition of involution, the following also holds,

$$(s,l)^w = s^w,l^w,$$

just as it does in arithmetic.

The application of involution to conjugative terms presents little difficulty after the explanations which have been given under the head of multiplication. It is obvious that betrayer to every enemy should be written

$$b^a,$$

just as lover of every woman is written

$$l^w.$$

But $b = b_{11}$ and therefore, in counting forward as the subjacent numbers direct, we should count the exponents, as well as the factors, of the letter to which the subjacent numbers are attached. Then we shall have, in the case of a relative of two correlates, six different ways of affixing the correlates to it, thus,

$b a$m betrayer of a man to an enemy of him;
$(b a)^m$ betrayer of every man to some enemy of him;
$b a^m$ betrayer of each man to an enemy of every man;
b^{am} betrayer of a man to all enemies of all men;
b^am betrayer of a man to every enemy of him;
b^{am} betrayer of every man to every enemy of him.

If both correlates are absolute terms, the cases are
$b$mw betrayer of a woman to a man;
$(b m)^w$ betrayer of each woman to some man;
$b m^w$ betrayer of all women to a man;
b^{mw} betrayer of a woman to every man;
b^mw betrayer of a woman to all men;
b^{mw} betrayer of every woman to every man.

These interpretations are by no means obvious, but I shall show that they are correct further on.

It will be perceived that the rule still holds here that

$$(\ell^a)^m = \ell^{(am)},$$

that is to say, that those individuals each of which stand to every man in the relation of betrayer to every enemy of his are identical with those individuals each of which is a betrayer to every enemy of a man of that man.

If the proportion of lovers of each woman among lovers of other women is equal to the average number of lovers which single individuals of the whole universe have, then

$$[l^w] = [l^{w'},][l^{w''},][l^{w'''},] \text{ etc.} = [l]^{[w]}.$$

Thus arithmetical involution appears as a special case of logical involution.

GENERAL FORMULÆ

The formulæ which we have thus far obtained, exclusive of mere explanations of signs and of formulæ relating to the numbers of classes, are:—

(1.) If $x \prec y$ and $y \prec z$, then $x \prec z$.

(2.) $(x \mathbin{+\!\!\!,} y) \mathbin{+\!\!\!,} z = x \mathbin{+\!\!\!,} (y \mathbin{+\!\!\!,} z)$.   (Jevons.)

(3.) $x \mathbin{+\!\!\!,} y = y \mathbin{+\!\!\!,} x$.   (Jevons.)

(4.) $(x \mathbin{+\!\!\!,} y)z = xz \mathbin{+\!\!\!,} yz$.

(5.) $x(y \mathbin{+\!\!\!,} z) = xy \mathbin{+\!\!\!,} xz$.

(6.) $(xy)z = x(yz)$.

(7.) $x,(y \mathbin{+\!\!\!,} z) = x,y \mathbin{+\!\!\!,} x,z$.   (Jevons.)

(8.) $(x,y),z = x,(y,z)$.   (Boole.)

(9.) $x,y = y,x$.   (Boole.)

(10.) $(x^y)^z = x^{(yz)}$.

(11.) $x^{y \mathbin{+\!\!\!,} z} = x^y, x^z$.

(12.) $(x \mathbin{+\!\!\!,} y)^z = x^z \mathbin{+\!\!\!,} \Sigma_p(x^{z-p}, y^p) \mathbin{+\!\!\!,} y^z$

$$= x^z \mathbin{+\!\!\!,} [z].x^{z-\dagger 1}, y^{\dagger 1} \mathbin{+\!\!\!,} \frac{[z].[z-1]}{2}.x^{z-\ddagger 2}, y^{\ddagger 2}$$

$$\mathbin{+\!\!\!,} \frac{[z].[z-1].[z-2]}{2\cdot3}.x^{z-\|3}, y^{\|3} \mathbin{+\!\!\!,} \text{ etc.}$$

(13.) $(x,y)^z = x^z,y^z$.

(14.) $x + 0 = x$.   (Boole.)

(15.) $x \mathbin{\diagup} = x$.

(16.) $(x + y) + z = x + (y + z)$.   (Boole.)

(17.) $x + y = y + x$.   (Boole.)

(18.) $x + y - y = x$.   (Boole.)

(19.) $x,(y + z) = x,y + x,z$.   (Boole.)

(20.) $(x + y)^z = x^z + [z].x^{z-{}^{\dagger 1}},y^{{}^{\dagger 1}} + $ etc.

We have also the following, which are involved implicitly in the explanations which have been given.

(21.) $x \prec x \mathbin{+\!\!,} y$.

This, I suppose, is the principle of identity, for it follows from this that $x = x$.

(22.) $x \mathbin{+\!\!,} x = x$.   (Jevons.)

(23.) $x,x = x$.   (Boole.)

(24.) $x \mathbin{+\!\!,} y = x + y - x,y$.

The principle of contradiction is

(25.) $x,n^x = 0$,

where n stands for "not." The principle of excluded middle is

(26.) $x \mathbin{+\!\!,} n^x = 1$.

It is an identical proposition, that, if φ be determinative, we have

(27.) If $x = y$ $\varphi x = \varphi y$.

The six following are derivable from the formulæ already given:—

(28.) $(x \mathbin{+\!\!,} y),(x \mathbin{+\!\!,} z) = x \mathbin{+\!\!,} y,z$.

(29.) $(x - y) \mathbin{+\!\!,} (z - w) = (x \mathbin{+\!\!,} z) - (y \mathbin{+\!\!,} w) + y,z,(1 - w)$
$+ x,(1 - y),w$.

In the following, φ is a function involving only the commutative operations and the operations inverse to them.[7]

(30.) $\varphi x = (\varphi 1), x + (\varphi 0), (1 - x)$.   (Boole.)

(31.) $\varphi x = (\varphi 1 \,\mathbin{+\!\!\!,}\, (1 - x)), (\varphi 0 \,\mathbin{+\!\!\!,}\, x)$.

(32.) If $\varphi x = 0$ $(\varphi 1), (\varphi 0) = 0$.   (Boole.)

(33.) If $\varphi x = 1$ $\varphi 1 \,\mathbin{+\!\!\!,}\, \varphi 0 = 1$.

Properties of Zero and Unity

The symbolical definition of zero is

$$x + 0 = x,$$

so that by (19) $x, a = x, (a + 0) = x, a + x, 0$.

Hence, from the invertible character of this addition, and the generality of (14), we have

$$x, 0 = 0.$$

7. The reader may wish information concerning the proofs of formulas (30) to (33). When involution is not involved in a function nor any multiplication except that for which $x, x = x$, it is plain that φx is of the first degree, and therefore, since all the rules of ordinary algebra hold, we have as in that

$$\varphi x = \varphi 0 + (\varphi 1 - \varphi 0), x.$$

We shall find, hereafter, that when φ has a still more general character, we have,

$$\varphi x = \varphi 0 + (\varphi\prime - \varphi 0)x.$$

The former of these equations by a simple transformation gives (30).

If we regard $(\varphi 1), (\varphi 0)$ as a function of x and develop it by (30), we have

$$(\varphi 1), (\varphi 0) = x, (\varphi 1), (\varphi 0) + (\varphi 1), (\varphi 0), (1 - x).$$

Comparing these terms separately with the terms of the second member of (30), we see that

$$(\varphi 1), (\varphi 0) \prec \varphi x.$$

This gives at once (32), and it gives (31) after performing the multiplication indicated in the second member of that equation and equating φx to its value as given in (30). If $(\varphi 1 \,\mathbin{+\!\!\!,}\, \varphi 0)$ is developed as a function of x by (31), and the factors of the second member are compared with those of the second member of (31), we get

$$\varphi x \prec \varphi 1 \,\mathbin{+\!\!\!,}\, \varphi 0,$$

from which (33) follows immediately.

By (24) we have in general,

$$x +, 0 = x + 0 - x, 0 = x,$$

or
$$x +, 0 = x.$$

By (4) we have $ax = (a +, 0)x = ax +, 0x.$
But if a is an absurd relation, $ax = 0,$
so that $\quad\quad\quad\quad\quad 0x = 0,$
which must hold invariably.

From (12) we have $a^x = (a +, 0)^x = a^x +, 0^x +,$ etc.
whence by (21) $\quad\quad 0^x \prec a^x.$

But if a is an absurd relation, and x is not zero,

$$a^x = 0,$$
and therefore, unless $x = 0,\ 0^x = 0.$

Any relative x may be conceived as a sum of relatives X, X', X'', etc., such that there is but one individual to which anything is X, but one to which anything is X', etc. Thus, if x denote "cause of," X, X', X'' would denote different kinds of causes, the causes being divided according to the differences of the things they are causes of. Then we have

$$Xy = X(y +, 0) = Xy +, X0,$$

whatever y may be. Hence, since y may be taken so that

$$Xy = 0,$$
we have $\quad\quad\quad\quad X0 = 0;$
and in a similar way,

$$X'0 = 0,\quad X''0 = 0,\quad X'''0 = 0,\ \text{etc.}$$

We have, then,

$$x0 = (X +, X' +, X'' +, X''' +, \text{etc.})0$$
$$= X0 +, X'0 +, X''0 +, X'''0 +, \text{etc.} = 0.$$

If the relative x be divided in this way into X, X', X'', X''', etc., so that x is that which is either X or X' or X'' or X''', etc., then non-x is that which is at once non-X and non-X' and non-X'', etc.; that is to say,

$$\text{non-}x = \text{non-}X, \text{ non-}X', \text{ non-}X'', \text{ non-}X''', \text{ etc.};$$

where non-X is such that there is something (Z) such that everything is non-X to Z; and so with non-X', non-X'', etc. Now, non-x may be any relative whatever. Substitute for it, then, y; and for non-X, non-X', etc., Y, Y', etc. Then we have

$$y = Y, Y', Y'', Y''', \text{ etc.};$$
and $\quad Y'Z' = 1, \quad Y''Z'' = 1, \quad Y'''Z''' = 1, \text{ etc.},$

where Z', Z'', Z''' are individual terms which depend for what they denote on Y', Y'', Y'''. Then we have

$$1 = Y'Z' = Y'^{Z'} = Y'^{(Z' \,+\, 0)} = Y'^{Z'}, Y'^0 = Y'Z', Y'^0,$$

or $\quad Y'^0 = 1, \quad Y''^0 = 1, \quad Y'''^0 = 1, \text{ etc.}$
Then $\quad y^0 = (Y', Y'', Y''', \text{ etc.})^0 = Y'^0, Y''^0, Y'''^0, \text{ etc.} = 1.$

We have by definition, $\quad x\,/ = x.$
Hence, by (6), $\quad ax = (a\,/)x = a(/x).$

Now a may express any relation whatever, but things the same way related to everything are the same. Hence,

$$x = /x.$$

We have by definition, $\quad 1 = /_0.$

Then if X is any individual $\quad X,1 = X,/_0 = X,/X.$
But $\quad /X = X.$
Hence $\quad X,1 = X,X;$
and by (23) $\quad X,1 = X;$
whence if we take $\quad x = X + X' + X'' + X''' + \text{etc.},$

where X, X' etc. denote individuals (and by the very meaning of a general term this can always be done, whatever x may be)

$$x,1 = (X + X' + X'' + \text{etc.}),1$$
$$= X,1 + X',1 + X'',1 + \text{etc.}$$
$$= X + X' + X'' + \text{etc.}$$
$$= x,$$

or $\quad x,1 = x.$

We have by (24) $\quad x \,+\!\!,\, 1 = x + 1 - x,1 = x + 1 - x = 1,$

or $\qquad\qquad x \,+\!\!,\, 1 = 1.$

We may divide all relatives into limited and unlimited. Limited relatives express such relations as nothing has to everything. For example, nothing is knower of everything. Unlimited relatives express relations such as something has to everything. For example, something is as good as anything. For limited relatives, then, we may write

$$p^1 = 0.$$

The converse of an unlimited relative expresses a relation which everything has to something. Thus, everything is as bad as something. Denoting such a relative by q,

$$q1 = 1.$$

These formulæ remind one a little of the logical algebra of Boole; because one of them holds good in arithmetic only for *zero*, and the other only for *unity*.

We have by (10) $\quad 1^x = (q^0)^x = q^{(0x)} = q^0 = 1,$

or $\qquad\qquad 1^x = 1.$

We have by (4) $\quad 1x = (a \,+\!\!,\, 1)x = ax \,+\!\!,\, 1x,$

or by (21) $\qquad\qquad ax \prec 1x.$

But everything is somehow related to x unless x is 0; hence, unless x is 0,

$$1x = 1.$$

If a denotes "what possesses," and y "character of what is denoted by x,"

$$x = a^y = a^{(y\prime)} = (a^y)' = x',$$

or
$$x' = x.$$

Since ∕ means "identical with," l, ∕w denotes whatever is both a lover of and identical with a woman, or a woman who is a lover of herself. And thus, in general,

$$x, \! \diagup = x_{0,}.$$

Nothing is identical with every one of a class; and therefore ∕ˣ is zero, unless x denotes only an individual when ∕ˣ becomes equal to x. But equations founded on interpretation may not hold in cases in which the symbols have no rational interpretation.

Collecting together all the formulæ relating to *zero* and *unity*, we have

(34.) $x \mathbin{+\!\!,} 0 = x.$ (Jevons.)
(35.) $x \mathbin{+\!\!,} 1 = 1.$ (Jevons.)
(36.) $x0 = 0.$
(37.) $0x = 0.$
(38.) $x, \! 0 = 0.$ (Boole.)
(39.) $x^0 = 1.$
(40.) $0^x = 0$, provided $x > 0.$
(41.) $\diagup x = x.$
(42.) $x, \! \diagup = x_{0,}.$
(43.) $x' = x.$
(44.) $\diagup^x = 0$, unless x is individual, when $\diagup^x = x.$
(45.) $q1 = 1$, where q is the converse of an unlimited relative.
(46.) $1x = 1$, provided $x > 0.$
(47.) $x, \! 1 = x.$ (Boole.)
(48.) $p^1 = 0$, where p is a limited relative.
(49.) $1^x = 1.$

These, again, give us the following:—

(50.) $0 \mathbin{+\!\!,} 1 = 1.$
(51.) $0 \mathbin{+\!\!,} \diagup = \diagup.$
(52.) $0\,0 = 0.$
(53.) $0, \! 0 = 0.$
(54.) $0^0 = 1.$

(55.) $\diagup 0 = 0.$
(56.) $0\diagup = 0.$
(57.) $0, \! \diagup = 0.$
(58.) $0' = 0.$
(59.) $\diagup^0 = 1.$

(60.) $01 = 0$.

(61.) $10 = 0$.

(62.) $0,1 = 0$.

(63.) $1^0 = 1$.

(64.) $0^1 = 0$.

(65.) $\prime\prime = \prime$.

(66.) $\prime,\prime = \prime$.

(67.) $\prime' = \prime$.

(68.) $11 = 1$.

(69.) $1,1 = 1$.

(70.) $1^1 = 1$.

(71.) $1\prime = 1$.

(72.) $\prime 1 = 1$.

(73.) $\prime,1 = \prime$.

(74.) $1' = 1$.

(75.) $\prime^1 = 0$.

(76.) $1, = \prime$.

From (64) we may infer that 0 is a limited relative, and from (60) that it is not the converse of an unlimited relative. From (70) we may infer that 1 is not a limited relative, and from (68) that it is the converse of an unlimited relative.

Formulæ relating to the Numbers of Terms

We have already seen that

(77.) If $x \prec y$, then $[x] \prec [y]$.

(78.) When $x,y = 0$, then $[x \mathrel{+\!,} y] = [x] \mathrel{+\!,} [y]$.

(79.) When $[xy]{:}[n^x y] = [x]{:}[n^x]$, then $[xy] = [x][y]$.

(80.) When $[x \,\textrm{п}\, y] = [x][\textrm{п} y][1]$, then $[x^y] = [x]^{[y]}$.

It will be observed that the conditions which the terms must conform to, in order that the arithmetical equations shall hold, increase in complexity as we pass from the more simple relations and processes to the more complex.

We have seen that

(81.) $[0] = 0$.

(82.) $[\prime] = 1$.

Most commonly the universe is unlimited, and then

(83.) $[1] = \infty$;

and the general properties of 1 correspond with those of infinity. Thus,

$$x \mathbin{+\!\!,} 1 = 1 \quad \text{corresponds to} \quad x + \infty = \infty,$$
$$q1 = 1 \qquad \text{"} \qquad \text{"} \quad q\infty = \infty,$$
$$1x = 1 \qquad \text{"} \qquad \text{"} \quad \infty x = \infty,$$
$$p^1 = 0 \qquad \text{"} \qquad \text{"} \quad p^\infty = 0,$$
$$1^x = 1 \qquad \text{"} \qquad \text{"} \quad \infty^x = \infty.$$

The formulæ involving commutative multiplication are derived from the equation $1, = \text{\i}$. But if 1 be regarded as infinite, it is not an absolute infinite; for $10 = 0$. On the other hand, $\text{\i}^1 = 0$.

It is evident, from the definition of the number of a term, that

(84.) $[x,] = [x]{:}[1]$.

We have, therefore, if the probability of an individual being x to any y is independent of what other y's it is x to, and if x is independent of y,

(85.) $[x^y,] = [x,]^{[y]}$.

GENERAL METHOD OF WORKING WITH THIS NOTATION

Boole's logical algebra contains no operations except our invertible addition and commutative multiplication, together with the corresponding subtraction and division. He has, therefore, only to expand expressions involving division, by means of (30), so as to free himself from all non-determinative operations, in order to be able to use the ordinary methods of algebra, which are, moreover, greatly simplified by the fact that

$$x,x = x.$$

Mr. Jevons's modification of Boole's algebra involves only non-invertible addition and commutative multiplication, without the corresponding inverse operations. He is enabled to replace subtraction by multiplication, owing to the principle of contradiction, and to replace division by addition, owing to the principle of excluded middle. For example, if x be unknown, and we have

$$x \mathbin{+\!\!,} m = a,$$

or what is denoted by x together with men make up animals, we can only conclude, with reference to x, that it denotes (among other things, perhaps) all animals not men; that is, that the x's not men are the same as the animals not men. Let $\overline{m}$ denote non-men; then by multiplication we have

$$x,\overline{m} +\!\!,\, m,\overline{m} = x,\overline{m} = a,\overline{m},$$

because, by the principle of contradiction,

$$m,\overline{m} = 0.$$

Or, suppose, x being again unknown, we have given

$$a,x = m.$$

Then all that we can conclude is that the x's consist of all the m's and perhaps some or all of the non-a's, or that the x's and non-a's together make up the m's and non-a's together. If, then, $\overline{a}$ denote non-a, add $\overline{a}$ to both sides and we have

$$a,x +\!\!,\, \overline{a} = m +\!\!,\, \overline{a}.$$

Then by (28) $$(a +\!\!,\, \overline{a}),(x +\!\!,\, \overline{a}) = m +\!\!,\, \overline{a}.$$

But by the principle of excluded middle,

$$a +\!\!,\, \overline{a} = 1$$

and therefore $$x +\!\!,\, \overline{a} = m +\!\!,\, \overline{a}.$$

I am not aware that Mr. Jevons actually uses this latter process, but it is open to him to do so. In this way, Mr. Jevons's algebra becomes decidedly simpler even than Boole's.

It is obvious that any algebra for the logic of relatives must be far more complicated. In that which I propose, we labor under the disadvantages that the multiplication is not generally commutative, that the inverse operations are usually indeterminative, and that transcendental equations, and even equations like

$$a^{bx} = c^{de^x} + f^x + x,$$

where the exponents are three or four deep, are exceedingly common. It is obvious, therefore, that this algebra is much less manageable than ordinary arithmetical algebra.

We may make considerable use of the general formulæ already

given, especially of (1), (21), and (27), and also of the following, which are derived from them:—

(86.) If $a \prec b$ then there is such a term x that $a +\!\!, x = b$.

(87.) If $a \prec b$ then there is such a term x that $b, x = a$.

(88.) If $b, x = a$ then $a \prec b$.

(89.) If $a \prec b$ $c +\!\!, a \prec c +\!\!, b$.

(90.) If $a \prec b$ $ca \prec cb$.

(91.) If $a \prec b$ $ac \prec bc$.

(92.) If $a \prec b$ $c^b \prec c^a$.

(93.) If $a \prec b$ $a^c \prec b^c$.

(94.) $a, b \prec a$.

There are, however, very many cases in which the formulæ thus far given are of little avail.

Demonstration of the sort called mathematical is founded on suppositions of particular cases. The geometrician draws a figure; the algebraist assumes a letter to signify a single quantity fulfilling the required conditions. But while the mathematician supposes an individual case, his hypothesis is yet perfectly general, because he considers no characters of the individual case but those which must belong to every such case. The advantage of his procedure lies in the fact that the logical laws of individual terms are simpler than those which relate to general terms, because individuals are either identical or mutually exclusive, and cannot intersect or be subordinated to one another as classes can. Mathematical demonstration is not, therefore, more restricted to matters of intuition than any other kind of reasoning. Indeed, logical algebra conclusively proves that mathematics extends over the whole realm of formal logic; and any theory of cognition which cannot be adjusted to this fact must be abandoned. We may reap all the advantages which the mathematician is supposed to derive from intuition by simply making general suppositions of individual cases.

In reference to the doctrine of individuals, two distinctions should be borne in mind. The logical atom, or term not capable of logical division, must be one of which every predicate may be universally affirmed or denied. For, let A be such a term. Then, if it is neither true that all A is X nor that no A is X, it must be true that some A is X and some A is not X; and therefore A may be divided into A that is X and A that is not X, which is contrary to its nature as a logical atom. Such a term can be realized neither in thought nor in sense.

Not in sense, because our organs of sense are special,—the eye, for example, not immediately informing us of taste, so that an image on the retina is indeterminate in respect to sweetness and non-sweetness. When I see a thing, I do not see that it is not sweet, nor do I see that it is sweet; and therefore what I see is capable of logical division into the sweet and the not sweet. It is customary to assume that visual images are absolutely determinate in respect to color, but even this may be doubted. I know no facts which prove that there is never the least vagueness in the immediate sensation. In thought, an absolutely determinate term cannot be realized, because, not being given by sense, such a concept would have to be formed by synthesis, and there would be no end to the synthesis because there is no limit to the number of possible predicates. A logical atom, then, like a point in space, would involve for its precise determination an endless process. We can only say, in a general way, that a term, however determinate, may be made more determinate still, but not that it can be made absolutely determinate. Such a term as "the second Philip of Macedon" is still capable of logical division,—into Philip drunk and Philip sober, for example; but we call it individual because that which is denoted by it is in only one place at one time. It is a term not *absolutely* indivisible, but indivisible as long as we neglect differences of time and the differences which accompany them. Such differences we habitually disregard in the logical division of substances. In the division of relations, etc., we do not, of course, disregard these differences, but we disregard some others. There is nothing to prevent almost any sort of difference from being conventionally neglected in some discourse, and if *I* be a term which in consequence of such neglect becomes indivisible in that discourse, we have in that discourse,

$$[I] = 1.$$

This distinction between the absolutely indivisible and that which is one in number from a particular point of view is shadowed forth in the two words *individual* (τὸ ἄτομον) and *singular* (τὸ καθ' ἕκαστον); but as those who have used the word *individual* have not been aware that absolute individuality is merely ideal, it has come to be used in a more general sense.[8]

8. The absolute individual can not only not be realized in sense or thought, but cannot exist, properly speaking. For whatever lasts for any time, however short, is

The old logics distinguish between *individuum signatum* and *individuum vagum.* "Julius Cæsar" is an example of the former; "a certain man," of the latter. The *individuum vagum,* in the days when such conceptions were exactly investigated, occasioned great difficulty from its having a certain generality, being capable, apparently, of logical division. If we include under the *individuum vagum* such a term as "any individual man," these difficulties appear in a strong light, for what is true of any individual man is true of all men. Such a term is in one sense not an individual term; for it represents every man. But it represents each man as capable of being denoted by a term which is individual; and so, though it is not itself an individual term, it stands for any one of a class of individual terms. If we call a thought about a thing in so far as it is denoted by a term, a *second intention,* we may say that such a term as "any individual man" is individual by second intention. The letters which the mathematician uses (whether in algebra or in geometry) are such individuals by second intention. Such individuals are one in number, for any individual man is one man; they may also be regarded as incapable of logical division, for any individual man, though he may either be a Frenchman or not, is yet altogether a Frenchman or altogether not, and not some one and some the other. Thus, all the formal logical laws relating to individuals will hold good of such individuals by second intention, and at the same time a universal proposition may at any moment be substituted for a proposition about such an individual, for nothing can be predicated of such an individual which cannot be predicated of the whole class.

There are in the logic of relatives three kinds of terms which involve general suppositions of individual cases. The first are *individual* terms, which denote only individuals; the second are those relatives whose correlatives are individual: I term these *infinitesimal relatives;* the third are *individual infinitesimal* relatives, and these I term *elementary* relatives.

---

capable of logical division, because in that time it will undergo some change in its relations. But what does not exist for any time, however short, does not exist at all. All, therefore, that we perceive or think, or that exists, is general. So far there is truth in the doctrine of scholastic realism. But all that exists is infinitely determinate, and the infinitely determinate is the absolutely individual. This seems paradoxical, but the contradiction is easily resolved. That which exists is the object of a true conception. This conception may be made more determinate than any assignable conception; and therefore it is never so determinate that it is capable of no further determination.

Individual Terms

The fundamental formulæ relating to individuality are two. Individuals are denoted by capitals.

(95.)   If $x > 0$ $x = X \,+\!, X' \,+\!, X'' \,+\!, X''' \,+\!,$ etc.
(96.) $y^X = yX.$

We have also the following which are easily deducible from these two:—

(97.) $(y,z)X = (yX),(zX).$ (99.) $[X] = 1.$
(98.) $X,y_0 = X,yX.$ (100.) $\mathit{1}^X = X.$

We have already seen that

$$\mathit{1}^x = 0, \text{ provided that } [x] > 1.$$

As an example of the use of the formulæ we have thus far obtained, let us investigate the logical relations between "benefactor of a lover of every servant of every woman," "that which stands to every servant of some woman in the relation of benefactor of a lover of him," "benefactor of every lover of some servant of a woman," "benefactor of every lover of every servant of every woman," etc.

In the first place, then, we have by (95)

$$sw = s(W' \,+\!, W'' \,+\!, W''' \,+\!, \text{ etc.}) = sW' \,+\!, sW'' \,+\!, sW''' \,+\!, \text{ etc.}$$
$$s^w = s^{W' \,+\!, W'' \,+\!, W''' \,+\!, \text{ etc.}} = s^{W'},s^{W''},s^{W'''}, \text{ etc.}$$

From the last equation we have by (96)

$$s^w = (sW'),(sW''),(sW'''), \text{ etc.}$$

Now by (31) $x' \,+\!, x'' \,+\!,$ etc. $= x',x'',x''',$ etc. $\,+\!,$ etc.,
or
(101.) $\Pi' \prec \Sigma',$

where Π' and Σ' signify that the addition and multiplication with commas are to be used. From this it follows that

(102.) $s^w \prec sw.$

If w vanishes, this equation fails, because in that case (95) does not hold.

From (102) we have

(103.) $$(ls)^w \prec ls\mathrm{w}.$$

Since
$$a = a,b \;+,\; \text{etc.,}$$
$$b = a,b \;+,\; \text{etc.,}$$
we have
$$la = l(a,b \;+,\; \text{etc.}) = l(a,b) \;+,\; l(\text{etc.}),$$
$$lb = l(a,b \;+,\; \text{etc.}) = l(a,b) \;+,\; l(\text{etc.}).$$

Multiplying these two equations commutatively we have

$$(la),(lb) = l(a,b) \;+,\; \text{etc.}$$

or

(104.) $$l\Pi' \prec \Pi'l.$$

Now
$$(ls)^w = (ls)^{W' \;+,\; W'' \;+,\; W''' \;+,\; \text{etc.}} = \Pi'(ls)^W = \Pi'ls\mathrm{W},$$
$$ls^w = ls^{W' \;+,\; W'' \;+,\; W''' \;+,\; \text{etc.}} = l\Pi's^W = l\Pi's\mathrm{W}.$$

Hence,

(105.) $$ls^w \prec (ls)^w,$$

or every lover of a servant of all women stands to every woman in the relation of lover of a servant of hers.

From (102) we have

(106.) $$l^s{}^w \prec ls^w.$$

By (95) and (96) we have

$$l^s\mathrm{w} = l^s(\mathrm{W'} \;+,\; \mathrm{W''} \;+,\; \mathrm{W'''} \text{ etc.})$$
$$= l^s\mathrm{W'} \;+,\; l^s\mathrm{W''} \;+,\; l^s\mathrm{W'''} \;+,\; \text{etc.}$$
$$= l^{s\mathrm{W'}} \;+,\; l^{s\mathrm{W''}} \;+,\; l^{s\mathrm{W'''}} \;+,\; \text{etc.}$$

Now
$$s^w = s^{W' \;+,\; W'' \;+,\; W''' \;+,\; \text{etc.}} = s^{W'}, s^{W''}, s^{W'''}, \text{etc.}$$

So that by (94) $$s^w \prec s^{W'} \prec s\mathrm{W'}.$$
Hence by (92)

$$l^{s\mathrm{W'}} \prec l^{s\mathrm{w}}, \qquad l^{s\mathrm{W''}} \prec l^{s\mathrm{w}}, \qquad l^{s\mathrm{W'''}} \prec l^{s\mathrm{w}}.$$

Adding, $$l^{s\mathrm{W'}} \;+,\; l^{s\mathrm{W''}} \;+,\; l^{s\mathrm{W'''}} \prec l^{s\mathrm{w}};$$

or

(107.) $$l^s\mathrm{w} \prec l^{s\mathrm{w}}.$$

That is, every lover of every servant of any particular woman is a lover of every servant of all women.

By (102) we have

(108.) $l^{sw} \prec l^s w.$

Thus we have

$$l^{sw} \prec l^s w \prec l^{sw} \prec ls^w \prec (ls)^w \prec lsw.$$

By similar reasoning we can easily make out the relations shown in the following table. It must be remembered that the formulæ do not generally hold when exponents vanish.

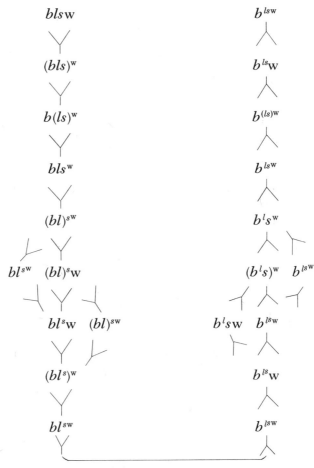

It appears to me that the advantage of the algebraic notation already begins to be perceptible, although its powers are thus far very imperfectly made out. At any rate, it seems to me that such a *prima facie* case is made out that the reader who still denies the utility of the algebra ought not to be too indolent to attempt to write down the above twenty-two terms in ordinary language with logical precision. Having done that, he has only to disarrange them and then restore the arrangement by ordinary logic, in order to test the algebra so far as it is yet developed.

Infinitesimal Relatives

We have by the binomial theorem by (49) and by (47),

$$(1 + x)^n = 1 + \Sigma_p x^{n-p} + x^n.$$

Now, if we suppose the number of individuals to which any one thing is x to be reduced to a smaller and smaller number, we reach as our limit

$$x^2 = 0,$$
$$\Sigma_p x^{n-p} = [n].1^{n-\dagger_1}, x^{\dagger_1} = xn,$$
$$(1 + x)^n = 1 + xn.$$

If, on account of the vanishing of its powers, we call x an infinitesimal here and denote it by i, and if we put

$$xn = in = y,$$

our equation becomes

(109.) $$(1 + i)^{\frac{y}{i}} = 1 + y.$$

Putting $y = \prime$, and denoting $(1 + i)^{\frac{\prime}{i}}$ by Θ, we have

(110.) $$\Theta = (1 + i)^{\frac{\prime}{i}} = 1 + \prime.$$

In fact, this agrees with ordinary algebra better than it seems to do; for $\prime$ is itself an infinitesimal, and Θ is Θ'. If the higher powers of $\prime$ did not vanish, we should get the ordinary development of Θ.

Positive powers of 6 are absurdities in our notation. For negative powers we have

(111.) $6^{-x} = 1 - x.$

There are two ways of raising 6^{-x} to the yth power. In the first place, by the binomial theorem,

$$(1 - x)^y = 1 - [y].1^{y - \dagger_1},x^{\dagger_1} + \tfrac{[y].[y - 1]}{2}.1^{y - \ddagger_2},x^{\ddagger_2} - \text{etc.};$$

and, in the second place, by (111) and (10).

$$6^{-xy} = 1 - xy.$$

It thus appears that the sum of all the terms of the binomial develop-ment of $(1 - x)^y$, after the first, is $- xy$. The truth of this may be shown by an example. Suppose the number of y's are four, viz. Y', Y'', Y''', and Y''''. Let us use x', x'', x''', and x'''' in such senses that

$$xY' = x', \qquad xY'' = x'', \qquad xY''' = x''', \qquad xY'''' = x''''.$$

Then the negatives of the different terms of the binomial develop-ment are,

$$[y].1^{y - \dagger_1},x^{\dagger_1} = x' + x'' + x''' + x''''.$$
$$- \tfrac{[y].[y - 1]}{2}.1^{y - \ddagger_2},x^{\ddagger_2} = - x',x'' - x',x''' - x',x'''' - x'',x'''$$
$$- x'',x'''' - x''',x''''.$$
$$+ \tfrac{[y].[y - 1].[y - 2]}{2\cdot3}.1^{-\|_3},x^{\|_3} = x',x'',x''' + x',x'',x'''' + x',x''',x''''$$
$$+ x'',x''',x''''.$$
$$x^y = - x',x'',x''',x''''.$$

Now, since this addition is invertible, in the first term, x' that is x'', is counted over twice, and so with every other pair. The second term subtracts each of these pairs, so that it is only counted once. But in the first term the x' that is x'' that is x''' is counted in three times only, while in the second term it is subtracted three times; namely, in (x',x'') in (x',x''') and in (x'',x'''). On the whole, therefore, a triplet would not be represented in the sum at all, were it not added by the third term. The whole quartette is included four times in the first term, is subtracted six times by the second term, and is added four times in the third term. The fourth term subtracts it once, and thus in the sum of these negative terms each combination occurs once, and once only; that is to say the sum is

$$x' \,\barwedge\, x'' \,\barwedge\, x''' \,\barwedge\, x'''' \;=\; x(Y' \,\barwedge\, Y'' \,\barwedge\, Y''' \,\barwedge\, Y'''') \;=\; xy.$$

If we write $(ax)^3$ for $[x]\cdot[x-1]\cdot[x-2]\cdot1^x - {}^{\dagger}3, a\,{}^{\dagger}3$, that is for whatever is a to any three x's, regard being had for the order of the x's; and employ the modern numbers as exponents with this significa-tion generally, then

$$1 - ax + \tfrac{1}{2!}(ax)^2 - \tfrac{1}{3!}(ax)^3 + \text{etc.}$$

is the development of $(1-a)^x$ and consequently it reduces itself to $1-ax$. That is,

(112.) $\qquad x = x - \tfrac{1}{2!}x^2 + \tfrac{1}{3!}x^3 - \tfrac{1}{4!}x^4 + \text{etc.}$

$1-x$ denotes everything except x, that is, whatever is other than every x; so that 6^- means "not." We shall take $\log x$ in such a sense that

$$6^{\log x} = x.\,^{9}$$

I define the first difference of a function by the usual formula,

(113.) $\qquad \Delta\varphi x = \varphi(x + \Delta x) - \varphi x,$

where Δx is an indefinite relative which never has a correlate in common with x.
So that

(114.) $\qquad x \,,(\Delta x) = 0 \qquad x + \Delta x = x \,\barwedge\, \Delta x.$

Higher differences may be defined by the formulæ

(115.) $\qquad\qquad \Delta^n x = 0 \text{ if } n > 1.$
$$\Delta^2 \varphi x = \Delta\Delta x = \varphi(x + 2.\Delta x) - 2.\varphi(x + \Delta x) + \varphi x,$$
$$\Delta^3 \varphi x = \Delta\Delta^2 x = \varphi(x + 3.\Delta x) - 3.\varphi(x + 2.\Delta x)$$
$$+ 3.\varphi(x + \Delta x) - \varphi x.$$

9. It makes another resemblance between 1 and infinity that $\log 0 = -1$.

(116.) $\Delta^{n} \cdot \varphi x = \varphi(x + n.\Delta x) - n \cdot \varphi(x + (n - 1).\Delta x)$
$$+ \frac{n.(n - 1)}{2} \cdot \varphi(x + (n - 2).\Delta x) - \text{etc.}$$

The exponents here affixed to Δ denote the number of times this operation is to be repeated, and thus have quite a different signification from that of the numerical coefficients in the binomial theorem. I have indicated the difference by putting a period after exponents significative of operational repetition. Thus, m^2 may denote a mother of a certain pair, $m^{2 \cdot}$ a maternal grandmother.

Another circumstance to be observed is, that in taking the second difference of x, if we distinguish the two increments which x successively receives as $\Delta'x$ and $\Delta''x$, then by (114)

$$(\Delta'x),(\Delta''x) = 0$$

If Δx is relative to so small a number of individuals that if the number were diminished by one $\Delta^{n} \cdot \varphi x$ would vanish, then I term these two corresponding differences *differentials,* and write them with d instead of Δ.

The difference of the invertible sum of two functions is the sum of their differences; for by (113) and (18),

(117.) $\Delta(\varphi x + \psi x) = \varphi(x + \Delta x) + \psi(x + \Delta x) - \varphi x - \psi x$
$$= \varphi(x + \Delta x) - \varphi x + \psi(x + \Delta x) - \psi x = \Delta \varphi x + \Delta \psi x.$$

If a is a constant, we have

(118.) $\Delta a \varphi x = a(\varphi x + \Delta \varphi x) - a \varphi x = a \Delta \varphi x - (a \Delta \varphi x), a \varphi x,$
$\Delta^2 a \varphi x = -\Delta a \varphi x, a \Delta x,$ etc.
$\Delta(\varphi x)a = (\Delta \varphi x)a - ((\Delta \varphi x)a), \varphi x a,$
$\Delta^{2 \cdot}(\varphi x)a = -\Delta(\varphi x)a,$ etc.

(119.) $\Delta(a, \varphi x) = a, \Delta \varphi x.$

Let us differentiate the successive powers of x. We have in the first place,

$$\Delta(x^2) = (x + \Delta x)^2 - x^2 = 2.x^{2 - \dagger 1}, (\Delta x)^{\dagger 1} + (\Delta x)^2.$$

Here, if we suppose Δx to be relative to only one individual, $(\Delta x)^2$ vanishes, and we have, with the aid of (115),

$$d(x^2) = 2.x^1, dx.$$

Considering next the third power, we have, for the first differential,

$$\Delta(x^3) = (x + \Delta x)^3 - x^3$$
$$= 3.x^{3-\dagger_1},(\Delta x)^{\dagger_1} + 3.x^{3-\ddagger_2},(\Delta x)^{\ddagger_2} + (\Delta x)^3,$$
$$d(x^3) = 3.x^2,(dx).$$

To obtain the second differential, we proceed as follows:—

$$\Delta^2(x^3) = (x + 2.\Delta x)^3 - 2.(x + \Delta x)^3 + x^3$$
$$= x^3 + 6.x^{3-\dagger_1},(\Delta x)^{\dagger_1} + 12.x^{3-\ddagger_2},(\Delta x)^{\ddagger_2}$$
$$+ 8.(\Delta x)^3 - 2.x^3 - 6.x^{3 - \|_1},(\Delta x)^{\|_1}$$
$$- 6.x^{3 - \S_2},(\Delta x)^{\S_2} - 2.(\Delta x)^3 + x^3$$
$$= 6.x^{3-\ddagger_2},(\Delta x)^{\ddagger_2} + 6.(\Delta x)^3.$$

Here, if Δx is relative to less than two individuals, $\Delta\varphi x$ vanishes. Making it relative to two only, then, we have

$$d^2(x^3) = 6.x^1,(dx)^2.$$

These examples suffice to show what the differentials of x^n will be. If for the number $\mathfrak{n}$ we substitute the logical term n, we have

$$\Delta(x^n) = (x + \Delta x)^n - x^n = [n].x^{n-\dagger_1},(\Delta x)^{\dagger_1} + \text{etc.}$$
$$d(x^n) = [n].x^{n - 1},(dx).$$

We should thus readily find

(120.) $\quad d^{\mathfrak{m}}(x^n) = [n].[n - 1].[n - 2]$
$$\dots \dots [n - \mathfrak{m} + 1].x^{n - \dagger_{\mathfrak{m}}},(dx)^{\dagger_{\mathfrak{m}}}.$$

Let us next differentiate l^x. We have, in the first place,

$$\Delta l^x = l^{x +, \Delta x} - l^x = l^x, l^{\Delta x} - l^x = l^x,(l^{\Delta x} - 1).$$

The value of $l^{\Delta x} - 1$ is next to be found.

We have by (111) $\qquad 6^{l^{\Delta x} - 1} = l^{\Delta x}.$
Hence, $\qquad\qquad\quad l^{\Delta x} - 1 = \log l^{\Delta x}.$
But by (10) $\qquad\qquad \log l^{\Delta x} = (\log l)\Delta x.$

Substituting this value of $l^{\alpha} - 1$ in the equation lately found for $\mathcal{A}^x$ we have

(121.) $\mathcal{A}^x = l^x,(\log,l)\ dx = l^x,(l - 1)dx$
$$= -\ l^x,(1 - l)dx.$$

In printing this paper, I here make an addition which supplies an omission in the account given above of involution in this algebra. We have seen that every term which does not vanish is conceivable as logically divisible into individual terms. Thus we may write

$$s = S' +, S'' +, S''' +, \text{etc.}$$

where not more than one individual is in any one of these relations to the same individual, although there is nothing to prevent the same person from being so related to many individuals. Thus, "bishop of the see of" may be divided into first bishop, second bishop, etc., and only one person can be n^{th} bishop of any one see, although the same person may (where translation is permitted) be n^{th} bishop of several sees. Now let us denote the converse of x by $\mathcal{K}x$; thus, if s is "servant of," $\mathcal{K}s$ is "master or mistress of." Then we have

$$\mathcal{K}s = \mathcal{K}S' +, \mathcal{K}S'' +, \mathcal{K}S''' +, \text{etc.};$$

and here each of the terms of the second member evidently expresses such a relation that the same person cannot be so related to more than one, although more than one may be so related to the same. Thus, the converse of "bishop of the see of ——" is "see one of whose bishops is ——," the converse of "first bishop of ——" is "see whose first bishop is ——," etc. Now, the same see cannot be a see whose n^{th} bishop is more than one individual, although several sees may be so related to the same individual. Such relatives I term infinitesimal on account of the vanishing of their higher powers. Every relative has a converse, and since this converse is conceivable as divisible into individual terms, the relative itself is conceivable as divisible into infinitesimal terms. To indicate this we may write

(122.)   If $x > 0$ $x = X_, +, X_{,,} +, X_{,,,} +, \text{etc.}$

As a term which vanishes is not an individual, nor is it composed of individuals, so it is neither an infinitesimal nor composed of infinitesimals.

As we write $\qquad lS', lS'', lS'''$, etc. $= l^s,$

so we may write

(123.) $\qquad\qquad L_{,}s, L_{,,}s, L_{,,,}s$, etc. $= {}^l s.$

But as the first formula is affected by the circumstance that *zero* is not an individual, so that l^sw does not vanish on account of no woman having the particular kind of servant denoted by S'', l^sw denoting merely every lover of whatever servant there is of any woman; so the second formula is affected in a similar way, so that the vanishing of $L_{,}s$ does not make ${}^l s$ to vanish, but this is to be interpreted as denoting everything which is a lover, *in whatever way it is a lover at all,* of a servant. Then just as we have by (112), that

(124.) $\qquad\qquad l^s = 1 - (1 - l)s;$

so we have

(125.) $\qquad\qquad {}^l s = 1 - l(1 - s).$

Mr. De Morgan denotes l^s and ${}^l s$ by LS' and $L_{,}S$ respectively, and he has traced out the manner of forming the converse and negative of such functions in detail. The following table contains most of his results in my notation. For the converse of *m,* I write ꞷ; and for that of *n, u.*

x	$\mathscr{K}x$	G^{-x}	$\mathscr{K}\,\mathsf{G}^{-x}$
mn	$u\text{ꞷ}$	$(1-m)^n = {}^m(1-n)$	${}^{u\text{ꞷ}}(1-u) = (1-u\text{ꞷ})^u$
$m^n = {}^{(1-m)}(1-n)$	${}^u\text{ꞷ} = (1-u)^{(1-\text{ꞷ})}$	$(1-m)n$	$\text{ꞷ}(1-u)$
${}^m n = (1-m)^{(1-n)}$	$u^\text{ꞷ} = {}^{(1-u)}(1-\text{ꞷ})$	$m(1-n)$	$(1-\text{ꞷ})u$

I shall term the operation by which w is changed to ^{l}w, *backward involution.* All the laws of this but one are the same as for ordinary involution, and the one exception is of that kind which is said to prove the rule. It is that whereas with ordinary involution we have,

$$(l^s)^w = l^{(sw)};$$

in backward involution we have

(126.) $$l^{(sw)} = {}^{(ls)}w;$$

that is, the things which are lovers to nothing but things that are servants to nothing but women are the things which are lovers of servants to nothing but women.

The other fundamental formulæ of backward involution are as follows:—

(127.) $$l +\!\!, {}^sw = {}^lw,{}^sw,$$

or, the things which are lovers or servants to nothing but women are the things which are lovers to nothing but women and servants to nothing but women.

(128.) $$l^{(f,u)} = {}^lf,{}^lu,$$

or, the things which are lovers to nothing but French violinists are the things that are lovers to nothing but Frenchmen and lovers to nothing but violinists. This is perhaps not quite axiomatic. It is proved as follows. By (125) and (30)

$$l^{(f,u)} = 6^{-l(1 - f,u)} = 6^{-(l(1 - f) +\!\!, l(1 - u))}$$

By (125), (13), and (7),

$${}^lf,{}^lu = 6^{-l(1 - f)},6^{-l(1 - u)} = 6^{-(l(1 - f) +\!\!, l(1 - u))}.$$

Finally, the binomial theorem holds with backward involution. For those persons who are lovers of nothing but Frenchmen and violinists consist first of those who are lovers of nothing but Frenchmen; second, of those who in some ways are lovers of nothing but Frenchmen and in all other ways of nothing but violinists, and finally of those who are lovers only of violinists. That is,

(129.) $$l^{(u +\!\!, f)} = {}^lu +\!\!, \Sigma_p {}^{l-p}u,{}^pf +\!\!, {}^lf.$$

In order to retain the numerical coefficients, we must let $\{l\}$ be the number of persons that one person is lover of. We can then write

$${}^{l}(u + f) = {}^{l}u + \{l\}^{l} - {}^{\dagger_1}u, {}^{\dagger_1}f + \frac{\{l\}\cdot\{l - 1\}}{2}l - {}^{\ddagger_2}u, {}^{\ddagger_2}f + \text{etc.}$$

We have also the following formula which combines the two involutions:—

(130.) $$\qquad\qquad {}^{l}(s^{w}) = ({}^{l}s)^{w};$$

that is, the things which are lovers of nothing but what are servants of all women are the same as the things which are related to all women as lovers of nothing but their servants.

It is worth while to mention, in passing, a singular proposition derivable from (128). Since, by (124) and (125)

$${}^{x}y = (1 - x)^{(1 - y)},$$

and since

$$1 - (u \,+\!\!, f) = 6^{-(u \,+\!\!, f)} = 6^{-u}, 6^{-f} = (1 - u), (1 - f),$$

(128) gives us,

$$(1 - l)^{(1 - u),(1 - f)} = (1 - l)^{(1 - u)}$$
$$+\!\!, \ \Sigma_{p}(1 - (l - p))^{(1 - u)}, (1 - p)^{(1 - f)}$$
$$+\!\!, \ (1 - l)^{(1 - f)}.$$

This is, of course, as true for u and f as for $(1 - u)$ and $(1 - f)$. Making those substitutions, and taking the negative of both sides, we have, by (124)

(131.) $$\qquad l(u,f) = (lu), \Pi'_{p}((l - p)u \,+\!\!, pf), (lf),$$

or, the lovers of French violinists are those persons who, in reference to every mode of loving whatever, either in that way love some violinists or in some other way love some Frenchmen. This logical proposition is certainly not self-evident, and its practical importance is considerable. In a similar way, from (12) we obtain

(132.) $$\qquad (e,c)f = \Pi'_{p}(e(f - p) \,+\!\!, cp),$$

that is, to say that a person is both emperor and conqueror of the same Frenchman is the same as to say that, taking any class of

Frenchmen whatever, this person is either an emperor of some one of this class, or conqueror of some one among the remaining French-men.

The properties of zero and unity, with reference to backward involution, are easily derived from (125). I give them here in compar-ison with the corresponding formulæ for forward involution.

(133.) $\quad\quad\quad\quad^{0}x = 1 \quad\quad\quad\quad x^{0} = 1.$

(134.) $\quad\quad\quad\quad^{q}0 = 0 \quad\quad\quad\quad 0^{r} = 0,$

where q is the converse of an unlimited relative, and r is greater than zero.

(135.) $\quad\quad\quad\quad{}'x = x \quad\quad\quad\quad x{}' = x.$

(136.) $\quad\quad\quad\quad{}^{y}{}_{/} = y \quad\quad\quad\quad {}_{/}{}^{z} = z,$

where y is infinitesimal, and z is individual. Otherwise, both vanish.

(137.) $\quad\quad\quad\quad{}^{1}s = 0 \quad\quad\quad\quad p^{1} = 0,$

where s is less than unity and p is a limited relative.

(138.) $\quad\quad\quad\quad{}^{x}1 = 1 \quad\quad\quad\quad 1^{x} = 1.$

In other respects the formulæ for the two involutions are not so analogous as might be supposed; and this is owing to the dissimilarity between individuals and infinitesimals. We have, it is true, if $X_{,}$ is an infinitesimal and X' an individual,

(139.) $X_{,}(y_{,}z) = X_{,}y_{,}X_{,}z$ like $(y_{,}z)X' = yX',zX';$

(140.) $X_{,,}y_{0} = X_{,,}X_{,}y$ " $X',y_{0} = X',yX';$

(141.) $\{X_{,}\} = 1$ " $[X'] = 1.$

We also have

(142.) $\quad\quad\quad\quad\quad X_{,}y \prec {}^{X}{}_{,}y.$

But we have *not* ${}^{X}{}_{,}y = X_{,}y$, and consequently we have *not* ${}^{s}w \prec sw$, for this fails if there is anything which is not a servant at all, while the corresponding formula $s^{w} \prec sw$ only fails if there is not anything which is a woman. Now, it is much more often the case that there is something which is not x, than that there is not anything which is x. We have with the backward involution, as with the forward, the formulæ

(143.)   If $x \prec y$ $^y z \prec {}^x z$;

(144.)   If $x \prec y$ $^z x \prec {}^z y$.

The former of these gives us

(145.) $^{ls}w \prec {}^{(ls)}w$,

or, whatever is lover to nothing but what is servant to nothing but women stands to nothing but a woman in the relation of lover of every servant of hers. The following formulæ can be proved without difficulty.

(146.) $l^s w \prec {}^{ls}w$,

or, every lover of somebody who is servant to nothing but a woman stands to nothing but women in the relation of lover of nothing but a servant of them.

(147.) $^l sw \prec {}^l(sw)$,

or, whatever stands to a woman in the relation of lover of nothing but a servant of hers is a lover of nothing but servants of women.
    The differentials of functions involving backward involution are

(148.) $d^n x = \{n\}^{n-1} x , dx.$

(149.) $d^x l = {}^x l , dx \ \log.x.$

In regard to powers of 6 we have

(150.) $^x 6 = 6^x.$

Exponents with a dot may also be put upon either side of the letters which they affect.

    The greater number of functions of x in this algebra may be put in the form

$$\varphi x = \Sigma_p \ \Sigma_q \ {}_p A_q \ {}^{Px^q} \ {}_p B_q.$$

For all such functions Taylor's and Maclaurin's theorems hold good in the form,

(151.) $\quad \boxed{\begin{array}{c|c} y & 0 \\ \hline dx & y \end{array}} \; \sum\limits_{0}^{\infty} \frac{1}{p!\,p!} \cdot d^{p\cdot} = \text{\emph{1}}.$

The symbol $\boxed{\begin{array}{c} a \\ \hline b \end{array}}$ is used to denote that a is to be substituted for b in what follows. For the sake of perspicuity, I will write Maclaurin's theorem at length.

$$\varphi x \; = \; \boxed{\begin{array}{c|c} x & 0 \\ \hline dx & x \end{array}} \left(\tfrac{1}{0!} \cdot d^{0\cdot} + \tfrac{1}{1!} \cdot d^{1\cdot} + \tfrac{1}{2!} \cdot d^{2\cdot} + \tfrac{1}{3!} \cdot d^{3\cdot} + \text{etc.} \right) \varphi x.$$

The proof of these theorems is very simple. The $(p+q)^{\text{th}}$ differential of $^{p}x^{q}$ is the only one which does not vanish when x vanishes. This differential then becomes $[p+q]!.^{p}(dx)^{q}$. It is plain, therefore, that the theorems hold when the coefficients $^{p}A^{q}$ and $^{p}B^{q}$ are _1_. But the general development, by Maclaurin's theorem, of $a\varphi x$ or $(\varphi x)a$ is in a form which (112) reduces to identity. It is very likely that the application of these theorems is not confined within the limits to which I have restricted it. We may write these theorems in the form

(152.) $\quad \boxed{\begin{array}{c|c} y & 0 \\ \hline dx & y \end{array}} \; 6^{d} = \text{\emph{1}},$

provided we assume that when the first differential is positive

$$6^{d} = \tfrac{1}{0!} d^{0} + \tfrac{1}{1!} d^{1} + \tfrac{1}{2!} d^{2} + \text{etc.},$$

but that when the first differential is negative this becomes by (111),

$$6^{d} = 1 + d.$$

As another illustration of the use which may be made of differentiation in logic, let us consider the following problem. In a certain institution all the officers (x) and also all their common friends (f) are privileged persons (y). How shall the class of privileged persons be reduced to a minimum? Here we have

$$y = x + f^{x},$$
$$dy = dx + df^{x} = dx - f^{x},(1 - f)dx.$$

When y is at a minimum it is not diminished either by an increase or diminution of x. That is,

$$[\rlap{/}dy] \succ 0,$$

and when [x] is diminished by one,

$$[\rlap{/}dy] \prec 0.$$

When x is a minimum, then

$$[\rlap{/}dx - f^x,(1 - f)\rlap{/}dx] \succ 0 \qquad [\rlap{/}dx - f^{x-1},(1 - f)\rlap{/}dx] \prec 0$$
$$\text{(A.) } [\rlap{/}dx] - [f^x,(1 - f)\rlap{/}dx] \succ 0 \qquad [\rlap{/}dx] - [f^{x-1},(1 - f)\rlap{/}dx] \prec 0.$$

Now we have by (30)

$$f^x,(1 - f)\rlap{/}dx = f^x - (0;0),(1 - f)\rlap{/}dx.$$

Hence,

$$[f^x] \prec [\rlap{/}dx] + [0;0,].[(1 - f)\rlap{/}dx]$$
$$[f^{x-1}] \succ [\rlap{/}dx] + [0;0,].[(1 - f)\rlap{/}dx].$$

But $[0;0,]$ lies between the limits 0 and 1, and

$$(153.) \qquad\qquad [\rlap{/}dx] = 1.$$

We have, therefore,

$$[f^x] \prec 1 + [(1 - f)1] \qquad [f^{x-1}] \succ 1.$$

This is the general solution of the problem. If the event of a person who may be an official in the institution being a friend of a second such person is independent of and equally probable with his being a friend of any third such person, and if we take p, or the whole class of such persons, for our universe, we have,

$$p = 1;$$

$$[f^x,] = \frac{[f^x]}{[p]} = \left(\frac{[f]}{[p]}\right)^{[x]},$$

$$[(1 - f)\rlap{/}dx] = [1 - f].[\rlap{/}dx] = ([p] - [f]).[\rlap{/}dx],$$

$$[f^x,(1 - f)\rlap{/}dx] = \left(\frac{[f]}{[p]}\right)^{[x]}.([p] - [f]).[\rlap{/}dx].$$

Substituting these values in our equations marked (A) we get, by a little reduction,

$$[x] \;\succ\; \frac{\log\,([p] - [f])}{\log\,[p] - \log\,[f]},$$

$$[x] \;\prec\; \frac{\log\,([p] - [f])}{\log\,[p] - \log\,[f]} + 1.$$

The same solution would be reached through quite a different road by applying the calculus of finite differences in the usual way.

Elementary Relatives

By an elementary relative I mean one which signifies a relation which exists only between mutually exclusive pairs (or in the case of a conjugative term, triplets, or quartettes, etc.) of individuals, or else between pairs of classes in such a way that every individual of one class of the pair is in that relation to every individual of the other. If we suppose that in every school, every teacher teaches every pupil (a supposition which I shall tacitly make whenever in this paper I speak of a school), then *pupil* is an elementary relative. That every relative may be conceived of as a logical sum of elementary relatives is plain, from the fact that if a relation is sufficiently determined it can exist only between two individuals. Thus, a *father* is either father in the first ten years of the Christian era, or father in the second ten years, in the third ten years, in the first ten years, B.C., in the second ten years, or the third ten years, etc. Any one of these species of father is father for the first time or father for the second time, etc. Now such a relative as "father for the third time in the second decade of our era, of ———" signifies a relation which can exist only between mutually exclusive pairs of individuals, and is therefore an elementary relative; and so the relative *father* may be resolved into a logical sum of elementary relatives.

The conception of a relative as resolvable into elementary relatives has the same sort of utility as the conception of a relative as resolvable into infinitesimals or of any term as resolvable into individuals.

Elementary simple relatives are connected together in systems of four. For if A:B be taken to denote the elementary relative which multiplied into B gives A, then this relation existing as elementary, we have the four elementary relatives

A:A   A:B   B:A   B:B.

An example of such a system is—colleague: teacher: pupil: school-mate. In the same way, obviously, elementary conjugatives are in systems the number of members in which is $(n + 1)^{n+1}$ where n is the number of correlates which the conjugative has. At present, I shall consider only the simple relatives.

The existence of an elementary relation supposes the existence of mutually exclusive pairs of classes. The first members of those pairs have something in common which discriminates them from the second members, and may therefore be united in one class, while the second members are united into a second class. Thus *pupil* is not an elementary relative unless there is an absolute distinction between those who teach and those who are taught. We have, therefore, two general absolute terms which are mutually exclusive, "body of teachers in a school," and "body of pupils in a school." These terms are general because it remains undetermined what school is referred to. I shall call the two mutually exclusive absolute terms which any system of elementary relatives supposes, the *universal extremes* of that system. There are certain characters in respect to the possession of which both members of any one of the pairs between which there is a certain elementary relation agree. Thus, the body of teachers and the body of pupils in any school agree in respect to the country and age in which they live, etc., etc. Such characters I term *scalar characters* for the system of elementary relatives to which they are so related; and the relatives written with a comma which signify the possession of such characters, I term *scalars* for the system. Thus, supposing French teachers have only French pupils and *vice versa,* the relative

$$f,$$

will be a scalar for the system "colleague:teacher:pupil:schoolmate." If r is an elementary relative for which s, is a scalar,

(154.) $$s,r = rs,.$$

Let c, t, p, s, denote the four elementary relatives of any system; such as colleague, teacher, pupil, schoolmate; and let a,, b,, c,, d,, be scalars for this system. Then any relative which is capable of expression in the form

$$a,c + b,t + c,p + d,s$$

I shall call a *logical quaternion*. Let such relatives be denoted by q, q', q'', etc. It is plain, then, from what has been said, that any relative may be regarded as resolvable into a logical sum of logical quaternions.

The multiplication of elementary relatives of the same system follows a very simple law. For if u and v be the two universal extremes of the system c, t, p, s, we may write

$$c = \text{u:u} \quad t = \text{u:v} \quad p = \text{v:u} \quad s = \text{v:v},$$

and then if w and w' are each either u or v, we have

(155.) $$(\text{w':w})6^{-\text{w}} = 0.$$

This gives us the following multiplication-table, where the multiplier is to be entered at the side of the table and the multiplicand at the top, and the product is found in the middle:—

	c	t	p	s
c	c	t	0	0
t	0	0	c	t
p	p	s	0	0
s	0	0	p	s

(156.)

The sixteen propositions expressed by this table are in ordinary language as follows:—

The colleagues of the colleagues of any person are that person's colleagues;

The colleagues of the teachers of any person are that person's teachers;

There are no colleagues of any person's pupils;

There are no colleagues of any person's schoolmates;

There are no teachers of any person's colleagues;

There are no teachers of any person's teachers;

The teachers of the pupils of any person are that person's colleagues;

The teachers of the schoolmates of any person are that person's teachers;

The pupils of the colleagues of any person are that person's pupils;

The pupils of the teachers of any person are that person's schoolmates;

There are no pupils of any person's pupils;

There are no pupils of any person's schoolmates;

There are no schoolmates of any person's colleagues;

There are no schoolmates of any person's teachers;

The schoolmates of the pupils of any person are that person's pupils;

The schoolmates of the schoolmates of any person are that person's schoolmates.

This simplicity and regularity in the multiplication of elementary relatives must clearly enhance the utility of the conception of a relative as resolvable into a sum of logical quaternions.

It may sometimes be convenient to consider relatives each one of which is of the form

$$a_i + b_j + c_k + d_l + \text{etc.}$$

where $a_,$, $b_,$, $c_,$, $d_,$, etc. are scalars, and i, j, k, l, etc. are each of the form

$$m_u + n_v + o_w + \text{etc.}$$

where $m_,$, $n_,$, $o_,$, etc. are scalars, and u, v, w, etc. are elementary relatives. In all such cases (155) will give a multiplication-table for i, j, k, l, etc. For example, if we have three classes of individuals, u_1, u_2, u_3, which are related to one another in pairs, we may put

$$u_1{:}u_1 = i \qquad u_1{:}u_2 = j \qquad u_1{:}u_3 = k$$
$$u_2{:}u_1 = l \qquad u_2{:}u_2 = m \qquad u_2{:}u_3 = n$$
$$u_3{:}u_1 = o \qquad u_3{:}u_2 = p \qquad u_3{:}u_3 = q$$

and by (155) we get the multiplication-table

	i	j	k	l	m	n	o	p	q
i	i	j	k	0	0	0	0	0	0
j	0	0	0	i	j	k	0	0	0
k	0	0	0	0	0	0	i	j	k
l	l	m	n	0	0	0	0	0	0
m	0	0	0	l	m	n	0	0	0
n	0	0	0	0	0	0	l	m	n
o	o	p	q	0	0	0	0	0	0
p	0	0	0	o	p	q	0	0	0
q	0	0	0	0	0	0	o	p	q

If we take

$$i = \mathrm{u}_1{:}\mathrm{u}_2 + \mathrm{u}_2{:}\mathrm{u}_3 + \mathrm{u}_3{:}\mathrm{u}_4,$$
$$j = \mathrm{u}_1{:}\mathrm{u}_3 + \mathrm{u}_2{:}\mathrm{u}_4,$$
$$k = \mathrm{u}_1{:}\mathrm{u}_4,$$

we have

	i	j	k
i	j	k	0
j	k	0	0
k	0	0	0

If we take

$$i = u_1{:}u_2 + u_2{:}u_3 + u_3{:}u_4 + u_5{:}u_6 + u_7{:}u_8,$$
$$j = u_1{:}u_3 + u_2{:}u_4,$$
$$k = u_1{:}u_4,$$
$$l = u_6{:}u_8 + \mathfrak{a}.u_5{:}u_7 + \mathfrak{b}.u_1{:}u_9 + u_9{:}u_4 + \mathfrak{c}.u_5{:}u_6,$$
$$m = u_5{:}u_8,$$

we have

	i	j	k	l	m
i	j	k	0	m	0
j	k	0	0	0	0
k	0	0	0	0	0
l	$\mathfrak{a}.m$	0	0	$\mathfrak{b}.k + \mathfrak{c}.m$	0
m	0	0	0	0	0

These multiplication-tables have been copied from Professor Peirce's monograph on Linear Associative Algebras.[10] I can assert, upon reasonable inductive evidence, that all such algebras can be interpreted on the principles of the present notation in the same way as those given above. In other words, all such algebras are complications and modifications of the algebra of (156). It is very likely that this is true of all algebras whatever. The algebra of (156), which is of such a fundamental character in reference to pure algebra and our logical notation, has been shown by Professor Peirce to be the algebra of Hamilton's quaternions. In fact, if we put

$$1 = i + l.$$
$$i' = \sqrt{1 - b^2}\, Ji - (\sqrt{1 - a^2}\,b + ab\,J)j$$
$$+ (\sqrt{1 - a^2}\,b - ab\,J)k - \sqrt{1 - b^2}\, Jl.$$

10. *Linear Associative Algebra.* By BENJAMIN PEIRCE. 4to, lithographed. Washington. 1870.

$$j' = - b\sqrt{1 - c^2}\mathbf{J}i + (ac - \sqrt{1 - a^2}\sqrt{1 - b^2}\sqrt{1 - c^2}$$
$$-(\sqrt{1 - a^2}c + a\sqrt{1 - b^2}\sqrt{1 - c^2})\mathbf{J})j$$
$$- (ac - \sqrt{1 - a^2}\sqrt{1 - b^2}\sqrt{1 - c^2} + (\sqrt{1 - a^2}c$$
$$+ a\sqrt{1 - b^2}\sqrt{1 - c^2})\mathbf{J})k + b\sqrt{1 - c^2}\mathbf{J}l.$$
$$k' = bc\mathbf{J}i + (\sqrt{1 - a^2}\sqrt{1 - b^2}c + a\sqrt{1 - c^2}$$
$$+ (a\sqrt{1 - b^2}c - \sqrt{1 - a^2}\sqrt{1 - c^2})\mathbf{J})j$$
$$- (\sqrt{1 - a^2}\sqrt{1 - b^2}c + a\sqrt{1 - c^2} - (a\sqrt{1 - b^2}c$$
$$- \sqrt{1 - a^2}\sqrt{1 - c^2})\mathbf{J})k - bc\mathbf{J}l.$$

where a, b, c, are scalars, then $1, i', j', k'$ are the four fundamental factors of quaternions, the multiplication-table of which is as follows:—

	1	i'	j'	k'
1	1	i'	j'	k'
i'	i'	-1	k'	$-j'$
j'	j'	$-k'$	-1	i'
k'	k'	j'	$-i'$	-1

It is no part of my present purpose to consider the bearing upon the philosophy of space of this occurrence, in pure logic, of the algebra which expresses all the properties of space; but it is proper to point out that one method of working with this notation would be to transform the given logical expressions into the form of Hamilton's quaternions (after representing them as separated into elementary relatives), and then to make use of geometrical reasoning. The following formulæ will assist this process. Take the quaternion relative

$$q = xi + yj + zk + wl,$$

where x, y, z, and w are scalars. The conditions of q being a *scalar, vector,* etc. (that is, being denoted by an algebraic expression which denotes a scalar, a vector, etc., in geometry), are

(157.) Form of a scalar: $x(i + l)$.

(158.) Form of a vector: $xi + yj + zk - xl$.

(159.) Form of a versor:

$$\tfrac{x}{y}\left(\tfrac{x}{z}-1\right)^{-\tfrac{1}{2}i}i+\tfrac{y}{x}\left(\tfrac{x}{z}-1\right)^{-\tfrac{1}{2}j}j+\tfrac{z}{y}\left(\tfrac{z}{x}-1\right)^{-\tfrac{1}{2}k}k+\tfrac{y}{z}\left(\tfrac{z}{x}-1\right)^{-\tfrac{1}{2}l}l.$$

(160.) Form of zero: $xi + xyj + \tfrac{z}{y}k + zl.$
(161.) Scalar of q: $Sq = \tfrac{1}{2}(x + w)(i + l).$
(162.) Vector of q: $Vq = \tfrac{1}{2}(x - w)i + yj + zk + \tfrac{1}{2}(w - x)l.$
(163.) Tensor of q: $Tq = \sqrt{xw - yz}(i + l).$
(164.) Conjugate of q: $Kq = wi - yj - zk + xl.$

In order to exhibit the logical interpretations of these functions, let us consider a universe of married monogamists, in which husband and wife always have country, race, wealth, and virtue, in common. Let i denote "man that is ———," j "husband of ———," k "wife of ———," and l "woman that is ———"; x Negro that is ———, y rich person that is ———, z American that is ———, and w thief that is ———. Then, q being defined as above, the q's of any class will consist of so many individuals of that class as are Negro-men or women-thieves together with all persons who are rich husbands or American wives of persons of this class. Then, $2Sq$ denotes, by (160), all the Negroes and besides all the thieves, while Sq is the indefinite term which denotes half the Negroes and thieves. Now, those persons who are self-q's of any class (that is, the q's of themselves among that class) are $xi + wl$; add to these their spouses and we have $2Sq$. In general, let us term $(j + k)$ the "correspondent of ———." Then, the double scalar of any quaternion relative, q, is that relative which denotes all self-q's, and, besides, "all correspondents of self-q's of ———." $(Tq)^2$ denotes all persons belonging to pairs of corresponding self-q's *minus* all persons belonging to pairs of corresponding q's of each other.

As a very simple example of the application of geometry to the logic of relatives, we may take the following. Euclid's axiom concerning parallels corresponds to the quaternion principle that the square of a vector is a scalar. From this it follows, since by (157) $yj + zk$ is a vector, that the rich husbands and American wives of the rich husbands and American wives of any class of persons are wholly contained under that class, and can be described without any discrimination of sex. In point of fact, by (156), the rich husbands and American wives of the rich husbands and American wives of any class of persons, are the rich Americans of that class.

Lobatchewsky has shown that Euclid's axiom concerning parallels may be supposed to be false without invalidating the propositions of spherical trigonometry. In order, then, that corresponding propositions should hold good in logic, we need not resort to elementary relatives, but need only take S and V in such senses that every relative of the class considered should be capable of being regarded as a sum of a scalar and a vector, and that a scalar multiplied by a scalar should be a scalar, while the product of a scalar and a vector is a vector. Now, to fulfil these conditions we have only to take Sq as "self-q of," and Vq as "alio-q of" (q of another, that other being ——), and q may be any relative whatever. For, "lover," for example, is divisible into self-lover and alio-lover; a self-lover of a self-benefactor of persons of any class is contained under that class, and neither the self-lover of an alio-benefactor of any persons nor the alio-lover of the self-benefactor of any persons are among those persons. Suppose, then, we take the formula of spherical trigonometry,

$$\cos a = \cos b \ \cos c + \cos A \ \sin b \ \sin c.$$

In quaternion form, this is,

(165.) $S(pq) = (Sp)(Sq) + S((Vp)(Vq)).$

Let p be "lover," and q be "benefactor." Then this reads, lovers of their own benefactors consist of self-lovers of self-benefactors together with alio-lovers of alio-benefactors of themselves. So the formula

$$\sin b \ \cos pb' = - \sin a \ \cos c \ \cos pa' - \sin c \ \cos a \ \cos pc'$$
$$+ \sin a \ \sin c \ \sin b \ \cos pb,$$

where A', B', C', are the positive poles of the sides a, b, c, is in quaternions

(166.) $V(pq) = (Vp)(Sq) + (Sp)(Vq) + V((Vp)(Vq)),$

and the logical interpretation of this is: lovers of benefactors of others consist of alio-lovers of self-benefactors, together with self-lovers of alio-benefactors, together with alio-lovers of alio-benefactors of others. It is a little striking that just as in the non-Euclidean or imaginary geometry of Lobatchewsky the axiom concerning parallels holds good only with the ultimate elements of space, so its logical equivalent holds good only for elementary relatives.

It follows from what has been said that for every proposition in geometry there is a proposition in the pure logic of relatives. But the method of working with logical algebra which is founded on this principle seems to be of little use. On the other hand, the fact promises to throw some light upon the philosophy of space.[11]

PROPERTIES OF PARTICULAR RELATIVE TERMS

Classification of Simple Relatives

Any particular property which any class of relative terms may have may be stated in the form of an equation, and affords us another premise for the solution of problems in which such terms occur. A good classification of relatives is, therefore, a great aid in the use of

11. The researches of Lobatchewsky furnish no solution of the question concerning the apriority of space. For though he has shown that it is conceivable that space should have such properties that two lines might be in a plane and inclined to one another without ever meeting, however far produced, yet he has not shown that the facts implied in that supposition are inconsistent with supposing space to retain its present nature and the properties only of the things in it to change. For example, in Lobatchewsky's geometry a star at an infinite distance has a finite parallax. But suppose space to have its present properties, and suppose that there were one point in the universe towards which anything being moved should expand, and away from which being moved should contract. Then this expansion and contraction might obey such a law that a star, the parallax of which was finite, should be at an infinite distance measured by the number of times a yard-stick must be laid down to measure off that distance. I have not seen Beltrami's investigations, but I understand that they do show that something of this sort is possible. Thus, it may be that, make what suppositions you will concerning phenomena, they can always be reconciled to our present geometry or be shown to involve implicit contradictions. If this is so,—and whether it is or not is a completely open question,—then the principles of geometry are necessary, and do not result from the specialities of any object cognized, but from the conditions of cognition in general. In speaking of the conditions of cognition, in general, I have in view no psychological conception, but only a distinction between principles which, if the facts should present a sufficient difficulty, I may always logically doubt, and principles which it can be shown cannot become open to doubt from any difficulty in my facts, as long as they continue to be supposed in all logical procedure.

But, waiving this point, Lobatchewsky's conclusions do not positively overthrow the hypothesis that space is *a priori.* For he has only shown that a certain proposition, *not usually believed to be axiomatical,* is conceivably false. That people may be doubtful or even mistaken about *a priori* truth does not destroy all important practical distinction between the two kinds of necessity. It may be said that if Lobatchewsky's geometry is the true one, then space involves an arbitrary constant, which value cannot be given *a priori.* This may be; but it may be that the general properties of space, with the general fact that there is such a constant, are *a priori,* while the value of the constant is only empirically determined.

It appears to me plain that no geometrical speculations will settle the philosophy of space, which is a logical question. If space is *a priori,* I believe that it is in some recondite way involved in the logic of relatives.

this notation, as the notation is also an aid in forming such a classification.

The first division of relatives is, of course, into simple relatives and conjugatives. The most fundamental divisions of simple relatives are based on the distinction between elementary relatives of the form (A:A), and those of the form (A:B). These are divisions in regard to the amount of opposition between relative and correlative.

a. Simple relatives are in this way primarily divisible into relatives all of whose elements are of the form (A:A) and those which contain elements of the form (A:B). The former express a mere agreement among things, the latter set one thing over against another, and in that sense express an opposition (ἀντικεῖσθαι); I shall therefore term the former *concurrents,* and the latter *opponents.* The distinction appears in this notation as between relatives with a comma, such as (w,), and relatives without a comma, such as (*w*); and is evidently of the highest importance. The character which is signified by a concurrent relative is an absolute character, that signified by an opponent is a relative character, that is, one which cannot be prescinded from reference to a correlate.

b. The second division of simple relatives with reference to the amount of opposition between relative and correlative is into those whose elements may be arranged in collections of squares, each square like this,

A:A	A:B	A:C
B:A	B:B	B:C
C:A	C:B	C:C

and those whose elements cannot be so arranged. The former (examples of which are, "equal to ———," "similar to ———") may be called *copulatives,* the latter *non-copulatives.* A copulative multiplied into itself gives itself. Professor Peirce calls letters having this property, *idempotents.* The present distinction is of course very important in pure algebra. All concurrents are copulatives.

c. Third, relatives are divisible into those which for every element of the form (A:B) have another of the form (B:A), and those which want this symmetry. This is the old division into *equiparants* and *disquiparants,* [12] or in Professor De Morgan's language, convertible

12. "Quædam sunt relationes equiparantiæ, quædam disquiparantiæ. Primæ sunt relationes similium nominum, secundæ relationes dissimilium nominum. Exemplum primi est quando idem nomen ponitur in recto et in obliquo, sicut simile simili

and inconvertible relatives. Equiparants are their own correlatives. All copulatives are equiparant.

d. Fourth, simple relatives are divisible into those which contain elements of the form (A:A) and those which do not. The former express relations such as a thing may have to itself, the latter (as cousin of ——, hater of ——) relations which nothing can have to itself. The former may be termed *self-relatives,* the latter *alio-relatives.* All copulatives are self-relatives.

e. The fifth division is into relatives some power (i.e. repeated product) of which contains elements of the form (A:A), and those of which this is not true. The former I term *cyclic,* the latter *non-cyclic* relatives. As an example of the former, take

$$(A:B) + (B:A) + (C:D) + (D:E) + (E:C).$$
The product of this into itself is
$$(A:A) + (B:B) + (C:E) + (D:C) + (E:D).$$
The third power is
$$(A:B) + (B:A) + (C:C) + (D:D) + (E:E).$$
The fourth power is
$$(A:A) + (B:B) + (C:D) + (D:E) + (E:C).$$
The fifth power is
$$(A:B) + (B:A) + (C:E) + (D:C) + (E:D).$$
The sixth power is
$$(A:A) + (B:B) + (C:C) + (D:D) + (E:E),$$

where all the terms are of the form (A:A). Such relatives, as *cousin of* ——, are cyclic. All equiparants are cyclic.

f. The sixth division is into relatives no power of which is zero, and relatives some power of which is zero. The former may be termed *inexhaustible,* the latter *exhaustible.* An example of the former is "spouse of ——," of the latter, "husband of ——." All cyclics are inexhaustible.

g. Seventh, simple relatives may be divided into those whose products into themselves are not zero, and those whose products into themselves are zero. The former may be termed *repeating,* the

---

est simile. . . . Exemplum secundi est quando unum nomen ponitur in recto sed aliud in obliquo, sicut pater est filii pater et non oportet quod sit patris pater." Ockham *Quodlibetum* 6, qu. 20. See also his *Summa Logices,* pars 1, cap. 52. "Relativa equipa-rantiæ: quæ sunt synonyma cum suis correlativis. . . . Relativa disquiparantiæ: quæ non sunt synonyma cum suis correlativis." Pschlacher in *Petrus Hispanus.* The same defini-tions substantially may be found in many late mediæval logics.

latter, *non-repeating* relatives. All inexhaustible relatives are repeating.

h. Repeating relatives may be divided (after De Morgan) into those whose products into themselves are contained under themselves, and those of which this is not true. The former are well named by De Morgan *transitive*, the latter *intransitive.* All transitives are inexhaustible; all copulatives are transitive; and all transitive equiparants are copulative. The class of transitive equiparants has a character, that of being self-relatives, not involved in the definitions of the terms.

i. Transitives are further divisible into those whose products by themselves are equal to themselves, and those whose products by themselves are less than themselves; the former may be termed *continuous,* the latter *discontinuous.* An example of the second is found in the pure mathematics of a continuum, where if *a* is greater than *b* it is greater than something greater than *b;* and as long as *a* and *b* are not of the same magnitude, an intervening magnitude always exists. All concurrents are continuous.

j. Intransitives may be divided into those the number of the powers (repeated products) of which not contained in the first is infinite, and those some power of which is contained in the first. The former may be called *infinites,* the latter, *finites.* Infinite inexhaustibles are cyclic.

In addition to these, the old divisions of relations into relations of reason and real relations, of the latter into aptitudinal and actual, and of the last into extrinsic and intrinsic, are often useful.[13]

"Not"

We have already seen that "not," or "other than," is denoted by $6^{-\prime}$. It is often more convenient to write it, *n.* The fundamental property of this relative has been given above (111). It is that,

---

13. "Duplex est relatio: scilicet rationis et realis. Unde relatio rationis est quæ fit per actum comparativum intellectus, ut sunt secundæ intentiones; sed relatio realis est duplex, scilicet aptitudinalis et actualis. Aptitudinalis est quæ non requirit terminum actu existere sed solum in aptitudine; cujusmodi sunt omnes propriæ passiones, omnes aptitudines, et omnes inclinationes; et tales sunt in illo prædicamento reductive in quo sunt illa quorum sunt propriæ passiones. Sed relatio actualis est duplex, scilicet, intrinsecus adveniens, et extrinsecus adveniens. Intrinsecus adveniens est quæ necessario ponitur positis extremis in quacunque etiam distantia ponantur, ut similitudo, paternitas, equalitas. Extrinsecus adveniens est quæ necessario non ponitur, positis extremis, sed requiritur debita approximatio extremorum; cujusmodi sunt sex ultima prædicamenta, scilicet, actio, passio, quando, ubi, situs, et habitus." Tartaretus.

$$6^{-x} = 1 - x.$$

Two other properties are expressed by the principles of contradiction and excluded middle. They are,

$$x , 6^{-x} = 0;$$
$$x \,\dot{+}\, 6^{-x} = 1.$$

The following deduced properties are of frequent application:—

(167.) $\qquad\qquad 6^{-(x,y)} = 6^{-x} \,\dot{+}\, 6^{-y};$

(168.) $\qquad\qquad 6^{-x^y} = 6^{-x}y.$

The former of these is the counterpart of the general formula, $z^{x+y} = z^x , z^y$. The latter enables us always to bring the exponent of the exponent of 6^- down to the line, and make it a factor. By the former principle, objects not French violinists consist of objects not Frenchmen, together with objects not violinists; by the latter, individuals not servants of all women are the same as non-servants of some women.

Another singular property of 6^- is that,

(169.) $\qquad\qquad$ If $[x] > 1 \qquad\qquad 6^{-\prime x} = 1.$

"Case of the existence of ———," and "case of the non-existence of ———."

That which first led me to seek for the present extension of Boole's logical notation was the consideration that as he left his algebra, neither hypothetical propositions nor particular propositions could be properly expressed. It is true that Boole was able to express hypothetical propositions in a way which answered some purposes perfectly. He could, for example, express the proposition, "Either the sun will shine, or the enterprise will be postponed," by letting x denote "the truth of the proposition that the sun will shine," and y "the truth of the proposition that the enterprise will be postponed"; and writing,

$$x \,\dot{+}\, y = 1,$$

or, with the invertible addition,

$$x + (1 - x) , y = 1.$$

But if he had given four letters denoting the four terms, "sun," "what is about to shine," "the enterprise," and "what is about to be postponed," he could make no use of these to express his disjunctive proposition, but would be obliged to assume others. The imperfection of the algebra here was obvious. As for particular propositions, Boole could not accurately express them at all. He did undertake to express them, and wrote

Some Y's are X's: $v,y = v,x;$
Some Y's are not X's: $v,y = v,(1 - x).$

The letter v is here used, says Boole, for an "indefinite class symbol." This betrays a radical misapprehension of the nature of a particular proposition. To say that some Y's are X's, is not the same as saying that a logical species of Y's are X's. For the logical species need not be the name of anything existing. It is only a certain description of things fully expressed by a mere definition, and it is a question of fact whether such a thing really exist or not. St. Anselm wished to infer existence from a definition, but that argument has long been exploded. If, then, v is a mere logical species in general, there is not necessarily any such thing, and the equation means nothing. If it is to be a logical species, then, it is necessary to suppose in addition that it exists, and further that *some v is y*. In short, it is necessary to assume concerning it the truth of a proposition, which, being itself particular, presents the original difficulty in regard to its symbolical expression. Moreover, from

$$v,y = v,(1-x)$$

we can, according to algebraic principles, deduce successively

$$v,y = v - v,x$$
$$v,x = v - v,y = v,(1 - y).$$

Now if the first equation means that some Y's are not X's, the last ought to mean that some X's are not Y's; for the algebraic forms are the same, and the question is, whether the algebraic forms are adequate to the expression of particulars. It would appear, therefore, that the inference from Some Y's are not X's to Some X's are not Y's, is good; but it is not so, in fact.

What is wanted, in order to express hypotheticals and particulars analytically, is a relative term which shall denote "case of the existence of ———," or "what exists only if there is any ———"; or else "case of the non-existence of ———," or "what exists only if there is not ———." When Boole's algebra is extended to relative terms, it is easy to see what these particular relatives must be. For suppose that having expressed the propositions "it thunders," and "it lightens," we wish to express the fact that "if it lightens, it thunders." Let

$$A = 0 \quad \text{and} \quad B = 0,$$

be equations meaning respectively, it lightens and it thunders. Then, if φx vanishes when x does not and *vice versa*, whatever x may be, the formula

$$\varphi A \prec \varphi B$$

expresses that if it lightens it thunders; for if it lightens, A vanishes; hence φA does not vanish, hence φB does not vanish, hence B vanishes, hence it thunders. It makes no difference what the function φ is, provided only it fulfils the condition mentioned. Now, 0^x is such a function, vanishing when x does not, and not vanishing when x does. *Zero*, therefore, may be interpreted as denoting "that which exists if, and only if, there is not ———." Then the equation

$$0^0 = 1$$

means, everything which exists, exists only if there is not anything which does not exist. So,

$$0^x = 0$$

means that there is nothing which exists if, and only if, *some x* does not exist. The reason of this is that *some x* means some existing x.

It "lightens" and "it thunders" might have been expressed by equations in the forms

$$A = 1, \quad B = 1.$$

In that case, in order to express that if it lightens it thunders, in the form

$$\varphi A \prec \varphi B,$$

it would only be necessary to find a function, φx, which should vanish unless x were 1, and should not vanish if x were 1. Such a function is ^1x. We must therefore interpret 1 as "that which exists if, and only if, there is ———," ^1x as "that which exists if, and only if, there is nothing but x," and $1x$ as "that which exists if, and only if, there is some x." Then the equation

$$1^x = 1,$$

means everything exists if, and only if, whatever x there is exists.

Every hypothetical proposition may be put into four equivalent forms, as follows:—

> If X, then Y.
> If not Y, then not X.
> Either not X or Y.
> Not both X and not Y.

If the propositions X and Y are $A = 1$ and $B = 1$, these four forms are naturally expressed by

$$^1A \prec {}^1B,$$
$$1(1 - B) \prec 1(1 - A),$$
$$1(1 - A) +, {}^1B = 1,$$
$$^1A, 1(1 - B) = 0.$$

For ^1x we may always substitute $0^{(1 - x)}$.

Particular propositions are expressed by the consideration that they are contradictory of universal propositions. Thus, as $h,(1 - b) = 0$ means every horse is black, so $0^{h,(1 - b)} = 0$ means that some horse is not black; and as $h,b = 0$ means that no horse is black, so $0^{h,b} = 0$ means that some horse is black. We may also write the particular affirmative $1(h,b) = 1$, and the particular negative $1(h,n^b) = 1$.

Given the premises, every horse is black, and every horse is an animal; required the conclusion. We have given

$$h \prec b;$$
$$h \prec a.$$

Commutatively multiplying, we get

$$h \prec a,b.$$

Then, by (92) or by (90),

$$0^{a,b} \prec 0^h, \quad \text{or} \quad 1h \prec 1(a,b).$$

Hence, by (40) or by (46),

$$\text{If } h > 0 \quad 0^{a,b} = 0, \quad \text{or} \quad 1(a,b) = 1;$$

or if there are any horses, some animals are black. I think it would be difficult to reach this conclusion, by Boole's method unmodified.

Particular propositions may also be expressed by means of the signs of inequality. Thus, some animals are horses, may be written

$$a,h > 0;$$

and the conclusion required in the above problem might have been obtained in this form, very easily, from the product of the premises, by (1) and (21).

We shall presently see that conditional and disjunctive propositions may also be expressed in a different way.

Conjugative Terms

The treatment of conjugative terms presents considerable difficulty, and would no doubt be greatly facilitated by algebraic devices. I have, however, studied this part of my notation but little.

A relative term cannot possibly be reduced to any combination of absolute terms, nor can a conjugative term be reduced to any combination of simple relatives; but a conjugative having more than two correlates can always be reduced to a combination of conjugatives of two correlates. Thus for "winner over of ———, from ———, to ———," we may always substitute w, or "gainer of the advantage ——— to ———," where the first correlate is itself to be another conjugative v, or "the advantage of winning over of ——— from ———." Then we may write,

$$w = uv.$$

It is evident that in this way all conjugatives may be expressed as production of conjugatives of two correlates.

The interpretation of such combinations as ℓ^{am}, etc., is not very easy. When the conjugative and its first correlative can be taken together apart from the second correlative, as in $(\ell a)m$ and $(\ell a)^m$ and $(\ell^a)m$ and $(\ell^a)^m$, there is no perplexity, because in such cases (ℓa) or (ℓ^a) is a simple relative. We have, therefore, only to call the betrayer to an enemy an inimical betrayer, when we have

$(\ell a)m$ = inimical betrayer of a man = betrayer of a man to an enemy of him,

$(\ell a)^m$ = inimical betrayer of every man = betrayer of every man to an enemy of him.

And we have only to call the betrayer to every enemy an unbounded betrayer, in order to get

$(\ell^a)m$ = unbounded betrayer of a man = betrayer of a man to every enemy of him,

$(\ell^a)^m$ = unbounded betrayer of every man = betrayer of every man to every enemy of him.

The two terms ℓa^m and ℓ^{am} are not quite so easily interpreted. Imagine a separated into infinitesimal relatives, $A_{,}$, $A_{,,}$, $A_{,,,}$, etc., each of which is relative to but one individual which is m. Then, because all powers of $A_{,}$, $A_{,,}$, $A_{,,,}$, etc., higher than the first, vanish, and because the number of such terms must be [m], we have,

$$a^m = (A_{,} +\!\!, A_{,,} +\!\!, A_{,,,} +\!\!, \text{etc.})^m = (A_{,}\text{m}),(A_{,,}\text{m}),(A_{,,,}\text{m}), \text{etc.}$$

or if M′, M″, M‴, etc., are the individual m's,

$$a^m = (A_{,}\text{M}′),(A_{,,}\text{M}″),(A_{,,,}\text{M}‴), \text{etc.}$$

It is evident from this that ℓa^m is a betrayer to an $A_{,}$ of M′, to an $A_{,,}$ of M″, to an $A_{,,,}$ of M‴, etc., in short of all men to some enemy of them all. In order to interpret ℓ^{am} we have only to take the negative of it. This, by (124), is $(1 - \ell)a^m$, or a non-betrayer of all men to some enemy of them. Hence, ℓ^{am}, or that which is *not* this, is a betrayer of some man to each enemy of all men. To interpret $^\ell(a\text{m})$, we may put it in the form $(1 - \unicode{x142})^{(1 - a)\mathrm{m}}$. This is "non-betrayer of a man to all non-enemies of all men." Now, a non-betrayer of some X to every Y, is the same as a betrayer of all X's to nothing but what is not Y; and the negative of "non-enemy of all men," is "enemy of a man." Thus, ${}^{\unicode{x142}}(a\mathrm{m})$ is, "betrayer of all men to nothing but an enemy of a man." To interpret ${}^{\unicode{x142}}a\mathrm{m}$ we may put it in the form $(1 - \unicode{x142})^{(1 - a)}\mathrm{m}$, which is, "non-betrayer of a man to every non-enemy of him." This is a logical sum of terms, each of which is "non-betrayer of an individual man M to every non-enemy of M." Each of these terms is the same as "betrayer of M to nothing but an enemy of M." The sum of them, therefore, which is ${}^{\unicode{x142}}a\mathrm{m}$ is "betrayer of some man to nothing but an enemy of him." In the same way it is obvious that ${}^{\unicode{x142}a}\mathrm{m}$ is "betrayer of nothing but a man to nothing but an enemy of him." We have $\unicode{x142}^{a}\mathrm{m} = \unicode{x142}(1 - a)^{(1 - \mathrm{m})}$, or "betrayer of all non-men to a non-enemy of all non-men." This is the same as "that which stands to something which is an enemy of nothing but a man in the relation of betrayer of nothing but men to what is not it." The interpretation of ${}^{\unicode{x142}a}\mathrm{m}$ is obviously "betrayer of nothing but a man to an enemy of him." It is equally plain that ${}^{\unicode{x142}}a^{\mathrm{m}}$ is "betrayer of no man to anything but an enemy of him," and that ${}^{\unicode{x142}a}\mathrm{m}$ is "betrayer of nothing but a man to every enemy of him." By putting $\unicode{x142}^{a\mathrm{m}}$ in the form $\unicode{x142}^{(1 - a)(1 - \mathrm{m})}$ we find that it denotes "betrayer of something besides a man to all things which are enemies of nothing but men." When an absolute term is put in place of a, the interpretations are obtained in the same way, with greater facility.

The sign of an operation is plainly a conjugative term. Thus, our commutative multiplication might be denoted by the conjugative

$$\mathit{1},.$$

For we have,

$$l,s\mathrm{w} = \mathit{1},l,s\mathrm{w}.$$

As conjugatives can all be reduced to conjugatives of two correlates, they might be expressed by an operative sign (for which a Hebrew letter might be used) put between the symbols for the two correlates. There would often be an advantage in doing this, owing to the intricacy of the usual notation for conjugatives. If these operational signs happened to agree in their properties with any of the signs of algebra, modifications of the algebraic signs might be used in place of Hebrew letters. For instance, if κ were such that

$$\kappa x \kappa y z = \kappa_{13} \kappa x y z,$$

then, if we were to substitute for κ the operational sign ד we have

$$x ד (y ד z) = (x ד y) ד z,$$

which is the expression of the associative principle. So, if

$$\kappa x y = \kappa y x$$

we may write,

$$x ד y = y ד x$$

which is the commutative principle. If both these equations held for any conjugative, we might conveniently express it by a modified sign $+$. For example, let us consider the conjugative "what is denoted by a term which either denotes ——— or else ———." For this, the above principles obviously hold, and we may naturally denote it by $+$. Then, if p denotes Protestantism, r Romanism, and f what is false,

$$p + r \prec f$$

means either all Protestantism or all Romanism is false. In this way it is plain that all hypothetical propositions may be expressed. Moreover, if we suppose any term as "man" (m) to be separated into its individuals, M′, M″, M‴, etc., then,

$$M′ + M″ + M‴ + \text{etc.,}$$

means "some man." This may very naturally be written

$$‘m’$$

and this gives us an improved way of writing a particular proposition; for

$$‘x’ \prec y$$

seems a simpler way of writing "Some X is Y" than

$$0^{x,y} = 0.$$

Converse

If we separate *lover* into its elementary relatives, take the reciprocal of each of these, that is, change it from

$$A:B \quad \text{to} \quad B:A,$$

and sum these reciprocals, we obtain the relative *loved by*. There is no such operation as this in ordinary arithmetic, but if we suppose a science of discrete quantity in quaternion form (a science of equal intervals in space), the sum of the reciprocals of the units of such a quaternion will be the conjugate-quaternion. For this reason, I express the conjugative term "what is related in the way that to —— is ——, to the latter" by $\mathscr{K}$. The fundamental equations upon which the properties of this term depend are

(169.) $\qquad\qquad \mathscr{K}\mathscr{K} = 1.$

(170.) $\qquad$ If $x < y^z \qquad$ then $\qquad z \prec (\mathscr{K}y)^x$,

or $\qquad\qquad\qquad l(x,yz) = l(z,\mathscr{K}yx).$

We have, also,

(171.) $\qquad\qquad \mathscr{K}\Sigma = \Sigma\mathscr{K},$

(172.) $\qquad\qquad \mathscr{K}\Pi = {}_\Pi\mathscr{K},$

where ${}_\Pi$ denote the product in the reverse order. Other equations will be found in Mr. De Morgan's table, given above.

Conclusion

If the question is asked, What are the axiomatic principles of this branch of logic, not deducible from others? I reply that whatever rank is assigned to the laws of contradiction and excluded middle belongs equally to the interpretations of all the general equations given under the head of "Application of the Algebraic Signs to Logic," together with those relating to backward involution, and the principles expressed by equations (95), (96), (122), (142), (156), (25), (26), (14), (15), (169), (170).

But these axioms are mere substitutes for definitions of the universal logical relations, and so far as these can be defined, all axioms may be dispensed with. The fundamental principles of formal logic are not properly axioms, but definitions and divisions; and the only *facts* which it contains relate to the identity of the conceptions resulting from those processes with certain familiar ones.

A System of Logic

MS 169: Winter–Spring 1870

Chapter I. Syllogism

§1. Why we begin with syllogism

The cause of the existence of logic has as a historical fact been a desire to have a science for testing inferences. That logic serves other ends and is susceptible of a higher definition I admit; but that cannot be understood at the beginning.

Before Aristotle, logic consisted of an inductive method of reaching definitions and a large quantity of sophisms. The former was a mode of drawing inferences so that they should be certain. And what was the interest of these sophisms? To prove, perhaps, that things were self-contradictory. But so far they created no logical knowledge; only when the interest in them came to be the trying of the sufficiency and validity of adopted forms of thought did it at once become necessary to have a science of the syllogism. I think that it must have been that the consideration of such sophisms did much to creating Aristotle's syllogistic theory. In so far as this is a true account of the origin of logic, it originated in a desire to form a theory of inference.

But, as Duns Scotus shows,[1] whatever logic treats of besides inferences, that is to say, propositions and terms, are only parts of syllogisms and these are only treated in logic in their reference to syllogism. Why is the grammatical treatment of propositions so different from that of logic? Merely because logic only considers those differences between propositions upon which differences between syllogisms depend. Logic says nothing about interrogative, imperative, and optative sentences which are of fundamental importance in the

---

1. *Super Universalia*, quaestio 3. Scotus maintains that the object of logic is the syllogism.

general theory of propositions; but on the other hand the distinctions of affirmative and negative, universal and particular which are hardly worth mentioning in grammar are always allowed to be of the highest importance in logic. The reason plainly is that interrogations, commands, and wishes can form no part of a syllogism, while the difference between a valid and an invalid syllogism will often depend on the difference between a universal and a particular or on that between an affirmative and a negative proposition. The same thing may be said of terms. The principles of extension and comprehension, distinctness and confusion, which logic considers, are of importance relatively to the theory of inferences, while the distinctions of noun and adjective, compound names and simple names, singulars and plurals, together with the innumerable distinctions of verbs which it omits have no apparent bearing upon inference.

Having this conviction, I believe it to be altogether wrong to treat propositions and terms before syllogism; for since no distinctions of propositions and terms are to be introduced which the theory of syllogism does not require, none ought to be introduced before the theory of syllogism has shown the necessity of it.

[See Note A. On the Definition of Logic.]

§2. On the Essential Characters of an Argument

During the thirteenth century, a form of argument different from the syllogism came into use, which was called the *consequentia* and which deserves consideration. Here is an actual example of such an argument which I copy from Duns Scotus and which I will make the text of an explanation.

It is an argument to show that the subject of Aristotle's book of the categories is not the ten categories, founded on the assumption that it is a logical work. I abridge the argument a little.

De istis est scientia realis; non ergo Logica. Consequentia patet per Aristotelem 3. de Anima, cont. 38. *Scientiae secantur, ut res;* sed Logica est diversa ab omni scientia reali; ergo subiectum eius a subiecto cuiuslibet scientiae realis est diversum. Probatio antecedentis; quia de istis determinat Metaphysicus, ut patet 5 Metaph. cont. 14. et inde, et 7. Metaphysicae, cont. 1. et inde.

This I should translate as follows. A real science treats of the ten categories; logic, therefore, does not. The consequence (the validity of bond between antecedent and consequent) appears from what Aristotle says in the third book *De Anima* contextus 38. "The divisions of the sciences follow the divisions of the objects to which they relate." Now logic is other than any real science and consequently its subject is other than that of any real science. Proof of the antecedent: metaphysics treats of the ten categories, as appears from two passages in Aristotle.

It will be perceived that this form of setting forth an argument supposes that an argument is composed of an antecedent or premiss and a consequent *(consequens)* or conclusion; while the validity of the argument depends on the truth of a general principle called the *consequence (consequentia)*.

[Henry James's The Secret of Swedenborg*]*

P 54: North American Review *110*
(April 1870):463–68

The Secret of Swedenborg: being an Elucidation of his Doctrine of the Divine Natural Humanity. By Henry James. Boston: Fields, Osgood, & Co. 8vo. pp. 243. 1869.

Though this book presents some very interesting and impressive religious views, and the spiritual tone of it is in general eminently healthy, it is altogether out of harmony with the spirit of this age. If we understand the theory which is here presented as Swedenborg's, it is essentially as follows:—

Philosophy and religion are one. The matter of deepest moment to the heart is the matter of deepest moment to the head. That root of existence for which metaphysics inquires is God. The business of philosophy is to explain the relation between being and appearing; but that which alone has existence independent of everything else is God, while all that appears is relative to the human mind, and so is only man; thus, what is and what appears are God and man, and it is the relations of God and man that philosophy has to expound.

In any real object, that is, any permanent appearance, we may distinguish two elements, the permanence and the appearance. The permanence, the reality, is called by Mr. James the *being;* the appearance or emergence into the world of phenomena is called the *existence.* This distinction is no mere logical convenience or necessity, but is a real partition, for it lies in the very *esse* of a thing. The reality is that on which the appearance is founded, and, therefore, the "being" of a thing is its creator, while the "existence" is the creature in himself. But the creature, because he does not contain within his own self the essence of his being, is, in himself, a mere phantom and no reality.

But if an underlying being is essential to existence, no less is manifestation essential to being. It can make no difference whatever whether a thing is or is not, if it is never to any mind to give any sign of its being. Hence, to *be* without being manifested is a kind of being which does not differ from its negative, but is a meaningless form of words. Thus, it is of the very essence of being that it shall come forth into appearance, of the very essence of God that he shall create.

An appearance is only in consciousness. To create, therefore, or cause an appearance, is to awaken a consciousness, to vivify. To give being is to give life, or being is life. God's being, then, is creation; is vivifying other things, is living in others.[1] Now, to have one's life in others is to love. So the essence of God is love. The creature's being also lies in another, namely, in God; and, therefore, his life too is love; only as he does not confer this life upon that other, but receives it from him, it is receptive or selfish love, while the Creator's is perfect and unselfish love. Since, therefore, the Creator is perfect love, the creation is to be explained on the principle of love.

The Creator, then, cannot have made his creatures for his own sake (for love does nothing for its own sake), but for theirs. Accordingly, he must seek to make them, as much as possible, independent. As long as their being is in God, it is true that any independence they can seem to have will be a mere illusion, but that illusion God must grant. So he gives them a world of phenomena in which and relatively to which they have a reality and a self-determination.

But as all removal from God, all disparateness to his being, is mere self and nothingness, the Creator could not be satisfied with a creation which should stop short at this point, but must institute another movement in creation whereby the creature may be brought back into harmony with him, and thus really appropriate his Creator's being. This return movement is called redemption.

The machinery of this process is man's history, and is, therefore, naturally extremely complex. It has two parts, the redemption of the race, and the redemption of the private man. The redemption of the race is effected by the history of the race, by the breaking down of governmental forms, the development of the family relationship, and above all by the vicissitudes of the Church which culminate in the incarnation of our Lord. By these means a brotherhood is produced among men, such that every man without constraint obeys the

1. Swedenborg holds time to be an illusory appearance, and therefore it does not follow that God cannot be without at the same time creating.

laws of society. The redemption of the individual man is produced by his life and the influence of conscience, which lead him to a perception of the truths of religion. In this redemption creation reaches completion.

These things, however, are not scientifically established. Mr. James says that "no cordial lover of truth can long endure to reason about it"; and he himself is a very cordial lover of truth, in that sense. That his doctrines are incapable of being established by reasoning is, in fact, plainly stated by him more than once. This being so, why call them philosophy? The "sanction of the heart" he rightly says is their only voucher. "We need not expect," he says, "to find Swedenborg justifying himself in a strictly ratiocinative way, or as men deal with what they feel to be matter of opinion merely, but affirmatively rather, or as what they feel to be matter of precise knowledge." This is not the language of a philosopher. Aristotle, Euclid, and Newton did not apply strict ratiocination to logic, geometry, and gravitation, because they did not feel them to be subjects of precise knowledge. What men treat by mere affirmation are matters which they do not believe will be questioned, together with such as they conceive cannot be questioned. But what is in the mind of a writer who talks of *justifying himself affirmatively?* His affirmative justification can amount to nothing but energetic assertion, or energetic denunciation of others. Hence we cannot be surprised at meeting frequently in Mr. James's writings such phrases as, "incorrigible fool," "abject blunder," "transparent quibble," "silly," "impossible for human fatuity ever to go a step farther," "these disputatious gentlemen," "not honest," "utter unscrupulous abandonment of himself to," "flat-footed and flat-headed," "wilful and wicked antediluvian,"—epithets harmless enough, but not wisely applied to thoughts and men that are great historical factors.

Perhaps Mr. James is of opinion that to appeal to the "sanction of the heart" is to appeal to experience, namely, to religious experience. Anybody who can make the truth of this evident will do a good thing for religion; but, as yet, it has not been made out. The reasoning of natural science is valid because it proceeds from outward appearances only to outward appearances. If religion could, in a parallel way, restrict its conclusions to spiritual experiences, it might find a scientific foundation in spiritual experiences. But it cannot. Religion must be supreme or it is nothing. It has to assert, not only that such and such a proposition is one altogether delightful and comforting, but that outward appearances will always be found to conform to it. Religion may be made to rest on religious faith, and a philosophical justification may be given of such a procedure; but it fails to be philosophy while it appeals not to the head, but only to the heart. In saying this, we do not in the least oppose the Scotch philosophy which makes all knowledge finally to repose on what are sometimes called ultimate beliefs; because these beliefs are the common sense of mankind which belong to all men and which no man can resist. If religion can be traced to such premises, it becomes truly philosophical. But to rest it upon propositions which appear to be doubted by sane minds is, until that appearance is proved to be illusory, a procedure which, even if philosophically shown to be worthy of a rational being, nevertheless fails to satisfy that impulse in man which gives rise to science and philosophy. Mr. James, therefore, whose doctrine has "no other voucher but what it finds in every man's unforced delight in the truth," has no right to call his work philosophy. The very distinction between reality and fiction rests on the fact that our taking delight in a belief is, in itself, no sign that the thing believed in is true.

Though deficient in argumentation, the book contains some interesting philosophical doctrines. The most prominent of these is a theory of the relation of matter and form. The form is represented as the archetypal, creative idea; the matter as that in virtue of which a thing attains actual existence. The former gives the thing all its qualities, the latter its mere quantity. The form is the essential element which belongs to the thing even in its mere potentiality; the matter is the element of actuality, which is merely contingent. So far the view is sufficiently familiar. But it is less usual to add, as Mr. James does, that since actuality is only the bringing of a thing into the realm of possible experience, while the potential essence is eternal and absolute, therefore the form is the real and objective element, while the matter is phenomenal and subjective. Moreover, the matter is not only in Aristotelian fashion made the generic element which the form differentiates, but also the principle of individuation (a doctrine maintained by very few). In the case of man, the matter is what sets him off from God and gives him being in himself and consciousness, while the form is the Divine element in him, whereby he is brought back into harmony with his Creator; that is, it is his conscience of good and evil. The form is the element of love in man, the matter the element of self.

Distinct traces of the influence of Platonism upon Swedenborg appear in this philosophy. What Mr. James calls the form is the Platonic idea or form, and the doctrine that God is the highest idea or form, the idea of good, and the form of forms, belongs of course to Plato. The singular conception that form is from its nature living is decidedly Platonic. So also is making numerical unity to depend upon form, and quantity upon matter. The statement that matter, or what exists besides God, is nonentity, is made with equal clearness by Mr. James and by Plato. The doctrines that there is a spiritual perception which is at the same time an act of abstraction of quantities from qualities, that nature is a mere manifestation or revelation of the Divine idea, that this manifestation is, in some sense, an inverted one, that there is a world-soul or *maximus homo,* and that the divine part of the human soul corresponds to it, that the Divinity in the soul is to be compared to the sun shining on the world, that our cognition of necessary truths is a sort of memory, are doctrines which are to be found both in this book and in Plato or Plotinus; though they doubtless occupy very different positions and have very different colors in the two theosophies.

We must fairly warn our readers that all the hard study we have devoted to an attempt to understand this book may have gone for nothing, for it is terribly difficult. Not to mention the fact that we have not the thread of close argumentation to guide us, Mr. James uses terms so peculiarly that we stumble at the commonest words, which often receive meanings apparently quite unrelated to those we are accustomed to attach to them. All philosophers use words in peculiar senses, but they usually define their terms at the outset, and that Mr. James seldom does; even when he does, his definition often only substitutes several mysterious symbols for one. In first opening the book we are puzzled at finding identity attributed to things of which it would seem more consonant to the general drift of the author's thought to deny it. But after being confounded repeatedly by such statements, we begin to see—or think we see—that Mr. James, by saying that A and B are identical, means little more than that they coexist in nature. In like manner we find it difficult to comprehend our author's opposition to idealism until he gives us as its synonyme, "the invention of the world of things-in-themselves." So incessant is this cryptic use of terms, that the reader finally comes to lose all assurance that the commonest word is used in a sense analogous to its usual one. We read of the social destiny of woman, but whether by *woman* is meant those singular creatures whom we ordinarily so designate, or whether man is not meant, or some faculty of the mind, or merely the Aristotelian matter, is a question far beyond our humble powers. It is true that Mr. James supplies us with a synonyme for "woman," namely, "vir"; but it must be allowed that this does not in itself fully clear up the difficulty. On page 49 there is an attempt to explain the words *male* and *female*. "Male and female; *that is to say,* organic and functional, static and dynamic, generic and specific, universal and particular, public and private, outward and inward, common and proper, objective and subjective." From this we should incline to think that form was intended by *woman.* But a little below we find another definition: "Woman as woman or, what is the same thing, . . . the subjective . . . and moral content of human nature." This inclines us to think that by *woman* is meant a certain faculty of the mind. But further on we read of "the *minimus homo,* the moral or conscious Eve, the petty, specific, domestic *vir* of our actual bosoms, who embraces in himself the entire spiritual world, the universe of affection and thought, and to whom all the facts of life, i.e. all the events of history, great and small, public and private, and all the results of experience, good and evil, true and false, exclusively pertain." A missionary from China some years ago, on his return to this country, in order to illustrate the difficulty of making the Chinese comprehend Christianity, told how the "inner man" throughout the New Testament is supposed by the Chinese to mean the woman, it being the idiom in their language. This seemed to us at the time to argue want of acquaintance with Chinese on the part of the translators; yet here is Mr. James, to whom English is vernacular, whose English is extraordinarily idiomatic and racy, who yet constantly, without any explanation, but as the most natural thing in the world, uses *woman* and *inward man* as synonymous. We cannot, however, close without saying that it is our firm conviction that this book can be understood by the right mind with the right preparation, and that, to many a man who cannot fully understand it, it will afford, as it has to us, much spiritual nutriment.

Notes for Lectures on Logic to be given 1st term 1870–71

MS 171: Spring 1870

1. Truth belongs to signs, particularly, and to thoughts as signs.[1] Truth is the agreement of a meaning with a reality.

2. The meaning—τὸ λεκτόν—is the respect in which signs which translate each other are conceived to agree. It is something independent of how the thing signified really is and depends only on what is conveyed to whoever interprets the sign rightly. Whether this meaning is something out of the mind or only in the mind or nothing at all (as the Stoics who originated the term λεκτόν maintained) is a question which cannot affect the propriety of the definition of truth here given.

3. The meaning must be carefully distinguished from the sign itself and from the thing signified.

A real thing is something whose characters are independent of how any representation represents it to be.

Independent, therefore, of how any number of men think it to be. Idealism does not falsify definition.

The next question is in what sense can two things as incommensurable as a meaning and a reality be said to agree.

The point of contact is the living mind which is affected in a similar way by real things and by their signs. And this is the only possible point of contact.

I say "a certain thing is blue." The image of blueness this excites in the mind is not a copy of any blueness in the sentence. Therefore, even if the sensation of blue be a copy of an external blue in the blue thing, there can be no other agreement between the sentence and the thing than that they convey the same notion to the mind.

---

1. True sign is that which means as something really is.

4.[2] The agreement between the meaning of a sign and a reality consists in the former's exciting the same notion in the mind that the reality does.

This is obviously much too vague and shows us the necessity of beginning with a systematic analysis of the conception of a sign.

But before proceeding to such an analysis we may make a certain use of this vague proposition.

This shows that we must come to an idealistic doctrine concerning truth. We must mean by how things are, how we are affected by them.

Yet there is a distinction between a true and false idea, also. Then by the truth concerning a thing we do not mean how any man is affected by a thing.

Nor how a majority is affected.

But how a man would be affected after sufficient experience, discussion, and reasoning.

5.[3] That there is a truth about everything implies that sufficient experience, discussion, and reasoning would lead a man to a certain opinion.[4]

Then since to say that a thing is so and so is the same as to say that it is true that it is so and so it follows that

6. The Real thing is the ultimate opinion about it.

About *it* that is about the ultimate opinion, but not involving the reflection that the opinion is itself that ultimate one and is the real thing. Indeed this opinion is in one sense an ideal inasmuch as *more* experience and reasoning may always be had.

2. The doctrine of individuality should come in here.
3. The doctrine of contradiction should come before this.
4. Final cause acts in history of opinion.

Bain's Logic[1]

P 53: Nation *11(4 August 1870):77–78*

Many works on logic have lately appeared in our language, and a few of them are of considerable importance. The one before us is a school-book of the dryest description, but it is impossible that the best living English psychologist should produce any book which has not the stamp of originality, and which is not deserving of attention. In point of fact, Mr. Bain distinctly proclaims himself a rival, although also a follower, of Mr. Mill. The first thing that we notice in all the English logicians, and Mr. Bain is no exception, is their ignorance or ignoring of all logical writings not English. This is the more reprehensible, as logic has by no means received its greatest development in England. Nothing in the present work will lead the student to suspect that there are any such writers as Trendelenburg or Beneke, although the latter entertains opinions which are more or less in harmony with Bain's own. Trendelenburg has made an elaborate study of Aristotle's categories, the results of which are undeniably of high importance, even if they are not to be regarded as fully established. But Professor Bain does not find it worth while so much as to mention them in his account of the same subject. The exclusively English character of Mr. Bain's work is well illustrated by his making the old distinction of extension and comprehension belong to Hamilton, and by his giving the same writer credit for the symbols S, M, and P, for the three terms of a syllogism.

The chief peculiarity of this treatise is its elaborate treatment of applied logic. One-fourth of the whole book is taken up with "Logic of Mathematics," "Logic of Physics," "Logic of Chemistry," "Logic of Biology," "Logic of Psychology," "Sciences of Classification,"

---

1. *Logic,* by Alexander Bain, LL.D., Professor of Logic in the University of Aberdeen. Part First, Deduction. Part Second, Induction. 2 vols. 8vo. London: Longmans. New York: D. Appleton & Co.

"Logic of Practice," "Logic of Politics," and "Logic of Medicine." The word *logic* in these phrases is taken in a very much wider sense than that in which Dr. Whewell spoke of the logic of induction. Logic in general is defined by Mr. Bain as "a body of doctrines and rules having reference to truth." He regards logic, therefore, not merely as the *via veritatis,* but as including everything which bears upon truth, whether it relates to the investigation of it or to the testing of it, or simply to what may be called its statical characters. Accordingly, the logic of a particular science is the general description of the nature of that science, including not merely its methods, but also its fundamental conceptions and doctrines. As an example, let us take the logic of chemistry. The author begins by stating the essential characters of chemical attraction. They are three: first, that the proportions (misprinted *properties;* the book is full of misprints) are definite; second, that in combination heat is evolved; third, that the chief properties of the elements disappear. He next divides the propositions of chemistry into two classes: first, those which relate to the general conditions of chemical change; second, those which relate to the chemical changes of special substances. He next divides chemistry into organic and inorganic. (Few chemists would now maintain that this division has more than a temporary validity.) He then proceeds to the classification of the elements. The first great division is into metals and non-metals (this is antiquated). The general properties of each group are enumerated, as, for example, that no opaque non-metal has lustre except selenium (forgetting iodine and carbon). He then gives a classification (very unscientific) of the non-metals. He then says how he thinks a chemical substance should be described in a text-book. He seems to be thinking all along of how a text-book should be written, and not of how the subject should be investigated or conceived in the mind of the chemist, for he urges it as a recommendation to the uniting of oxygen and nitrogen in one class that it gives an opportunity for dwelling on the mechanical peculiarities of gaseous elements. He then states the characters of chemical laws. They are two. The first is that such laws are empirical. As an example, he cites the so-called law of Berthollet, in evident ignorance that this law has been entirely disproved. The other property of chemical laws is that they must express the most general conditions of the redistribution of chemical force. He next remarks that most of the hypotheses of chemistry are representative fictions, and concludes with a few elementary observations upon chemical notation. Such an account of a science as Mr. Bain here attempts would certainly be of the greatest value. It is very unlikely that any one man could successfully accomplish the task for all the sciences. At any rate, he must be profoundly versed in them, and must have quite another than a schoolmaster's conception of science in order to make his work of any use at all. But to attempt to write the logic of mathematics, for example, when one is so ignorant of the work of mathematicians as to be capable of saying that the celebrated axiom concerning parallels is "deducible from the definition of parallel lines, and ought to appear among the theorems of the first book," we must say, smacks of conceit.

Another principal feature in the book is the treatment of definition. Like many of the old logicians, the author separates the process of forming a definition from reasoning, a separation which ought not to be made, because analysis of the former proceeding shows it to contain the same elements as the latter. His attaching a very high importance to definition is more in accordance with the tendencies of natural science than it is with the doctrines of that nominalistic school of metaphysics with which Mr. Bain is affiliated. He rightly insists that the characters of the object which are enumerated in the definition should be such as are *important,* but his analysis (usually weak) fails to detect in what the *importance* of a character consists. A sentence which he has quoted from Sir George Cornewall Lewis might have furnished him with a hint. "By including in monarchies," says that writer, "and excluding from republics, every government of which a king is the head, *we make every true general proposition respecting monarchies and republics impossible.*" An *important* character is obviously one upon which others depend, that is, one the inclusion of which in a definition renders true general propositions concerning the object defined possible; and the more such propositions a character renders possible, the more important it is. In the same way, a natural class is one which can be so defined that something can be predicated of it which cannot be predicated of the genera included in its definition. Mr. Bain endeavors to make the logical definition identical with the scientific definition—a most worthy aim; but we fancy that zoölogists and botanists are already so much advanced in the knowledge of classification beyond the mere logician, that Mr. Bain's maxims will have little weight with them.

In treating of causation, Mr. Bain includes in the pure logical principle the law of the conservation of force, which according to him, in opposition to the physicists, refers not to *vis viva* but to *momentum.*

He gives a long account of the systems of De Morgan and Boole, but not such a one as they would approve, and he makes some serious mistakes.

As a school-book the work has some advantages, but even where the author's thought is perhaps not itself vague, his manner of expressing it is not calculated to inculcate precision in the mind of the pupil.

Letter, Peirce to W. S. Jevons

L 227: W. S. Jevons Papers

Pesth. 1870 Aug. 25

Dear Sir

I received a few days ago your gratifying letter from England and as you are the only active worker now I suppose upon mathematical logic I wish very much to set my views before you in their true colours and shall therefore reply to two of the points contained in your letter.

It appears that you do not accept my extended definitions of the mathematical operations. The validity of that generalization it will be for mathematicians to decide and I myself think they will accept my definitions. With regard to addition and multiplication, indeed, the only novelty in my views is that I do not regard it as essential to these operations that they should be "invertible." Now it appears to me that the study of the calculus of functions does not lead us to regard this character as very significant, but on the contrary an operation's being invertible is usually owing to a restriction of its application. Thus, when we take no account of negative and imaginary quantities, involution is invertible. If addition be considered as essentially invertible then the operation is applicable to some logical terms and not to others. Now I greatly mistake the spirit of modern algebra if it is not contrary to it not to extend the definition of addition under these circumstances. Observe, that you cannot shut addition out of logic altogether, for the moment you take = as the sign of identity, that is conceive of equality as a case of identity, you thereby make addition applicable to mutually exclusive terms.

Of course if addition is not essentially invertible multiplication is not either. I do not quite see how you can say that I use the term *multiplication* in a manner quite unconnected with its original meaning. Take my definition on page 3 of my paper. In no respect does this differ from the now universally admitted conceptions, except in regard to the "invertible" character. But take my usual logical multiplication. On p. 15 I think I have shown that the conception of multiplication in quaternions is exactly the same as mine and that numerical multiplication is merely a case of my operation.

I believe that you hold that all reasoning is by substitutions (in which I agree with you); that all substitutions when algebraically denoted appear as the substitution of equals for equals, that, therefore, the copula signifies equality and the theory of the quantified predicate holds. But I fancy the second premise would be hard to make out. You will observe that in a note on p. 2 I have shown rigidly that according to admitted principles, the conception of = is compounded of those of $\prec$ and $\succ$ (or $\leqq$ and $\geqq$). This being so the substitution-syllogism

$$A = B \quad B = C$$
$$\therefore A = C$$

is a compound of the two

$$A \prec B \quad B \prec C \qquad \text{and} \qquad A \succ B \quad B \succ C$$
$$\therefore A \prec C \qquad\qquad\qquad \therefore A \succ C$$

and the logician in analyzing inferences ought to represent it so. What reply is there to my note or to the conclusion I draw from it? Practically it is much easier to manipulate the logical calculus with $\prec$ as a copula than with =.

I especially doubt the possibility of a successful treatment of the substitutions of scientific reasoning upon the principles of the theory of the quantified predicate. In a former paper I have endeavored to prove that all inference proceeds by the substitution of one sign for another on the principle that a sign of a sign is a sign, and that reasoning differs according to the different kinds of signs with which it deals, and that signs are of three kinds, first, things similar to their objects, second, things physically connected with their objects, as blushing is a sign of shame, third, general signs. The substitution of a general sign gives deductive reasoning; the substitution of similars gives reasoning to an hypothesis, as for example if I say This man's coat, hat, mode of speaking, etc. are like a Quaker, therefore I suppose he is one; the substitution of physical signs gives induction, as for example if I say All these samples have been drawn at random from this collection and so the manner in which they have been drawn out physically necessitates their being a sign of what the collection consists of, since therefore these are red balls all the collection are red balls.

I trust you will feel enough interest in this discussion to continue it and I remain with great respect

Yours faithfully
C. S. Peirce

Letters addressed to Robt. Thode and Co. Berlin will reach me.

[Augustus De Morgan]

P 56: Nation 12(13 April 1871):258
and 12(20 April 1871):276

Professor De Morgan was born at Madura, in Southern India, in June, 1806, of a family distinguished in the military service. His mother's grandfather, however, who was a mathematical teacher of some eminence, may be supposed to have predetermined his career. In 1827, he gained at Cambridge the first place in the mathematical tripos of that year, but declined to subscribe to the religious tests necessary to obtain either the degree of M.A., or a college fellowship. In 1828, he accepted the professorship of mathematics in the London University, the principles on which that institution was founded being in accord with his religious independence; and he abandoned this position in 1866 when, as he thought, in violation of those principles, James Martineau was refused a professorship on account of his theological opinions. In the service of the London insurance companies, "he raised the actuary's vocation to the dignity of a profession," and was almost to his last day the confidential adviser of several associations. His *Essay on Probabilities, Elements of Algebra, Formal Logic, or the Calculus of Inference Necessary and Probable,* and *Differential and Integral Calculus,* are among the works which made him distinguished, but which show but a small part of his intellectual activity. He was a constant contributor to various periodicals, to the *Athenæum* from 1840; and by no means on mathematical subjects alone. His contributions to Knight's *Penny Cyclopædia* are a considerable proportion of the entire work. "He passed for diversion's sake from one arduous study to another"; but found time to acquire a good degree of proficiency as an instrumental performer, and was a habitual and eager reader of novels, especially of humorous novels. As a mathematician he had the rare merit of not overestimating his favorite science, though he proved by his *Formal Logic* that it was not incompatible for a mathematician to be also a logician; and he was accordingly one of the weightiest adherents that Spiritualism has ever won over. A treatise of his on these manifestations, entitled *From Matter to Spirit*, was written in 1863. As a writer and a teacher, he was one of the clearest minds that ever gave instruction, while his genial and hearty manners in private and in the school-room strongly attached to him all who came in contact with him. He was a man of full habit, much given to snuff-taking; and those who have seen him at the blackboard, mingling snuff and chalk in equal proportions, will not soon forget the singular appearance he often presented.

We need not apologize for adding to the sketch we gave last week of the late Professor De Morgan a few remarks of a more critical nature. Among mathematicians he was distinguished more for the completeness of his logic than for analytical facility. His pupils speak of him with warm admiration, but it may be presumed that they gained from him even more of general skill in accurate reasoning than of specific mathematical power. His elementary books, which are not enough known, are excellent, especially for students who have no natural turn for mathematics; and his work on the calculus is unusually complete, and its demonstrations particularly instructive. Of his researches, one of the most noticeable is his paper on triple algebra, which traces out the consequences of certain definitions of symbols in a manner much like that of his formal logic; but for this difficult subject De Morgan's analysis was not sufficiently subtle, and he can only be said to have started the enquiry without having arrived at any valuable results. His best contributions were to mathematical logic. In his controversy with Sir William Hamilton, in 1847, both disputants fought in the dark, because Hamilton's system had never been published, and Hamilton had never patiently examined De Morgan's. All the points of Hamilton's attack were, however, completely disproved. Upon the publication of Hamilton's works, De Morgan renewed the controversy with Mr. Thomas Spencer Baynes, who, after an unconditional pledge to produce proof of his position, was compelled to abandon the field. Since that time Hamilton's once celebrated system has fallen into neglect, while De Morgan's commands more and more respect. In point of fact, Hamilton's system, like De Morgan's, is mathematical, but is the work of a mind devoid of mathematical training. It would be premature to try to say what the final judgment of De Morgan's system will be, but it may at least be confidently predicted that the logic of relatives, which he was the first to investigate extensively, will eventually be recognized as a part of logic. The best statement of De Morgan's system is contained in his *Syllabus of a Proposed System of Logic,* but his fourth and fifth papers on the syllogism are of later date. De Morgan was a deep student of the history of the sciences to which he was devoted. He wrote many biographical notices of mathematicians in the *Penny Cyclopædia* and the *English Cyclopædia,* as well as a bibliography of arithmetic. Indeed, the amount of his writing upon various subjects in the two cyclopædias, in the *Athenæum,* in the *Companion to the British Almanac,* in seventeen or more separate books, and in various scientific periodicals, including the *Journal of the Philological Society,* is enormous, and it is all very pleasant reading for its perspicacity, vigor of thought, wit, and a certain peculiar flavor of style. The last qualities are well seen in his "Budget of Paradoxes," published in the *Athenæum.*

Of the Copulas of Algebra

MS 175

1871 April 27

An algebra according as it employs only one copula or more than one I call single-copula'd or multi-copula'd.

I first consider single-copula'd algebra. This employs only one copula (which may be denoted by $\curvearrowright$) and its negative which may be denoted by $\curlywedge$. Some sort of syllogism is valid with this copula or there is no algebra. This syllogism may be in either of the four figures and each of the three propositions may be affirmative or negative. This gives 32 possible different forms of syllogism; but the theory of the reduction of syllogism by contraposition of propositions (developed in my paper on the Classification of Arguments, *Proceedings of the Academy* Vol. 7) shows that all these forms are reducible to the following four.

1st	2nd	3rd	4th
$a \curvearrowright_1 b$	$a \curvearrowright_2 b$	$a \curvearrowright_3 b$	$a \curvearrowright_4 b$
$b \curvearrowright_1 c$	$a \curvearrowright_2 c$	$b \curvearrowright_3 c$	$b \curvearrowright_4 c$
$\therefore a \curvearrowright_1 c$	$\therefore b \curvearrowright_2 c$	$\therefore a \curlywedge_3 c$	$\therefore c \curvearrowright_4 a$

But a further reduction may be made. For consider first the second copula. From $a \curvearrowright_2 x$ and $a \curvearrowright_2 x$ it follows that $x \curvearrowright_2 x$. This therefore will hold of any term x which can be so related to any other a, and of course this will be true of almost all terms, or no algebra is possible. From $x \curvearrowright_2 y$ and $x \curvearrowright_2 x$ it follows that $y \curvearrowright_2 x$; therefore if $x \curvearrowright_2 y$ and x is not one of the few terms of which $a \curvearrowright_2 x$ cannot be true then $y \curvearrowright_2 x$. Therefore, if $x \curvearrowright_2 y$ and $y \curvearrowright_2 z$ we have $x \curvearrowright_2 z$ unless x is one of the exceptiona[l] terms. This copula therefore reduces to a special case of the first copula. In fact if $x \curvearrowright_2 y$, then $x \curvearrowright_1 y$ and $y \curvearrowright_1 x$. The second copula therefore disappears as a fundamental one.

Consider next the fourth copula. I assume that in general every expression has some relation to itself expressible by the copula. For if not then the expressions do not denote the objects whose relations to one another are determinate and therefore a new set of expressions should be taken which do denote these objects. We have then in the case of any copula either

$$x \cap x$$

whatever x may be or

$$x \curlywedge x$$

whatever x may be. Of course in every algebra there may be absurd expressions which violate any of the conditions of the algebra; but these need not be taken account of in the present investigation. We have then in the case of copula number four two cases. In the first $x \cap {}_4x$ and in the second $x \curlywedge {}_4x$. In the first case from $x \cap {}_4x$ and $x \cap {}_4y$ it follows that $y \cap {}_4x$ and therefore we have the syllogism

$$x \cap {}_4y$$
$$y \cap {}_4z$$
$$\therefore x \cap {}_4z$$

Therefore in this case the fourth copula is reducible to the first. Suppose next that $x \curlywedge {}_4x$. Now the doctrine of the reduction of syllogisms gives the forms

$$x \cap {}_4y \qquad\qquad\qquad x \curlywedge {}_4y$$
$$y \curlywedge {}_4z \qquad\qquad\qquad y \cap {}_4z$$
$$\therefore z \curlywedge {}_4x \qquad\qquad\qquad \therefore z \curlywedge {}_4x$$

We have then in general if $x \cap {}_4y$ then $y \curlywedge {}_4z$. We have therefore the syllogism

$$x \cap {}_4y$$
$$y \cap {}_4z$$
$$\therefore x \curlywedge {}_4z$$

which reduces this case to the third copula. The first and third copulas therefore are the only fundamental ones of single-copula'd algebras. In the case of the third we have the forms

$$x \cap {}_3y \qquad\qquad x \cap {}_3z$$
$$x \cap {}_3z \qquad\qquad y \cap {}_3z$$
$$\therefore y \curlywedge {}_3z \qquad\qquad \therefore x \curlywedge {}_3y$$

whence $x \curlywedge {}_3x$. We have therefore here no case of $x \cap x$ and therefore there are but three fundamental single-copula'd algebras.

Denoting their copulas by $<$ $\prec$ $\lhd$, these may be defined as follows.

If $x \prec y$ and $y \prec z$ then $x \prec z$. And $x \prec x$.
If $x < y$ and $y < z$ then $x < z$. And $x \not< x$.
If $x \lhd y$ and $y \lhd z$ then $x \not\lhd z$.

Here the vertical line through a copula sign negatives the copula.

If the only copula of an algebra is $\prec$ then all its expressions may be thrown into classes so that
1. If x and y belong to the same class $x \prec y$ and $y \prec x$
2. These classes form an indefinite number of series so that for the same series

$$x \prec y \prec z \prec w \prec \text{etc.}$$

and these different series may be connected so that if x and y are expressions in different series we may have $x \prec y$. If there is but one such series we have a single algebra. If there are more than one, we have a multiple algebra.

If the copula of an algebra is $<$ all its expressions belong to one series of classes such that
1. If x and y belong to the same class $x < y$ and $y < x$
2. The series of classes are such that

$$a < b < c < d < e \text{ etc.}$$

and if $x < y$ then $y \not< x$.

Let us consider next the algebra whose copula is $\lhd$. The forms of inference are only—

$$x \lhd y \qquad\qquad x \lhd z \qquad\qquad x \lhd y$$
$$y \lhd z \qquad\qquad y \lhd z \qquad\qquad x \lhd z$$
$$\therefore x \not\lhd z \qquad\qquad \therefore x \not\lhd y \qquad\qquad \therefore y \not\lhd z$$

Every premise is affirmative and every conclusion negative. Therefore no algebra worth consideration results unless there be some
additional condition. Every such condition involving only two terms
would contradict the given conditions. It must therefore be a syllogistic condition. The only such condition which would not reduce this
algebra to one of the others is

$$x \lhd y$$
$$y \lhd z$$
$$\therefore z \lhd x$$

Then this condition together with the condition $x \not\lhd x$ include those
above given. In this algebra all quantities are in three classes such
that
1. If a and b belong to the same class $a \not\lhd b$ $\quad b \not\lhd a$
2. If a and b belong to different classes, we may have

$$a \lhd b \text{ and } b \not\lhd a$$
$$\text{or} \quad b \lhd a \text{ and } a \not\lhd b$$
$$\text{or} \quad a \not\lhd b \text{ and } b \not\lhd a$$

Only if $a \lhd b$ or $b \lhd a$ then if c belongs to the same class as b
and is not everywhere substitutable for b, $a \not\lhd c$ and $c \not\lhd a$.
Let $a = b$ denote that in any proposition of the forms

$$a \cap x \qquad x \cap a \qquad b \cap x \qquad x \cap b$$
$$a \curlywedge x \qquad x \curlywedge a \qquad b \curlywedge x \qquad x \curlywedge b$$

a may be substituted for b or b for a.
In the algebra whose single copula is $\prec$

$$a = b \text{ if and only if } a \prec b \text{ and } b \prec a$$

In the algebra whose single copula is $<$

$$a = b \text{ if and only if } a \not< b \text{ and } b \not< a$$

In the algebra whose single copula is $\lhd$

$$a = b \text{ if and only if}$$
$$a \not\lhd b \text{ and } b \not\lhd a \text{ and if further } a \lhd c \text{ or } c \lhd a$$

while $b \lhd c$ or $c \lhd b$.

Of the fundamental operations
of the 3 single-copula'd algebras

If ϕ denotes such an operation that if $a = b$ $\phi a = \phi b$ it is said to be an *operation on values* otherwise an *operation on forms.*

Let us consider first operations on values or *material operations.*

1 Algebra whose copula is $\prec$.

Two quantities not equal are related to one another in one of two ways either

$$a \prec b \qquad b \;{+}\!\!\!\prec\; a$$

or

$$a \;{+}\!\!\!\prec\; b \qquad b \;{+}\!\!\!\prec\; a$$

In either case we must have fundamental operations which will convert either into the other.

Suppose $a \prec b$.

Then let us suppose that $+$ denotes such an operation that
$$x + a = b$$
If $a = b$ then let the special form x takes be 0.
$$0 + a = a$$
$$0 + b = b$$
And we may assume that $0 = 0$.

If $y + b = c$

and $x + a = b$

we may write $y + (x + a) = c$

and then if we have written $z + a = c$ we may write
$$y + x = z \text{ whence } y + (x + a) = (y + x) + a$$
If we have had reason to write

$$y + x = z$$
$$y + u = v$$

then we may conveniently write

$$w + x = u$$

$$w + z = v$$

$$v = y + w + x$$
$$v = w + y + x$$
$$y + w = w + y$$

We may conveniently write with reference to some series $a\ b\ c$ $d\ e\ f\ g$ &c. where

$$a \prec b \prec c \prec d \prec e \prec f \prec g \prec \text{etc.}$$

$$b = x + a$$
$$c = x + b = (x + x) + a$$
$$d = x + c = (x + x) + b = (x + x + x) + a$$
$$e = x + d = (x + x) + c = (x + x + x) + b$$
$$f = x + e = (x + x) + d = (x + x + x) + c$$
$$g = x + f = (x + x) + e = (x + x + x) + d$$
etc.

etc.

Then we may put $x + x = 2x$
$$x + x + x = 3x \text{ etc.}$$

If then we have another series

$$a' \prec b' \prec c' \prec d' \prec e' \prec f' \text{ etc.}$$

and write

$$b' = x + a' \qquad c' = x + b' \qquad d' = x + c' \qquad \text{etc.}$$

and put α also $\quad d' = \alpha d$

$$x + c' = \alpha(x + c)$$

[Charles Babbage]

P 57: Nation *13(9 November 1871):307–8*

The death of Mr. Charles Babbage, the inventor of calculating machines, is announced. He was born December 26, 1792. The analytical power of his mind was early manifested. In 1815, when he was only twenty-two years old, appeared his remarkable *Essay towards the Calculus of Functions,* a very general and profound sort of algebra, of which he was the chief author. About 1822, he made his first model of a calculating machine. It was a "difference engine," that is, the first few numbers of a table being supplied to it, it would go on and calculate the others successively according to the same law. This, at least, is as correct as so short and easy a statement can be. In the following year, at the request of the Royal Society, the Government made a grant of £1,500 to enable Mr. Babbage to proceed with the construction of his machine. In 1829, the Government largely increased this sum, and in 1830 assumed the property of the machine, and declared their intention of defraying the cost of completing it. This Mr. Brunel estimated at £12,000 at a time (February, 1831) when from £8,000 to £9,000 must have been spent. It was in 1830 that Babbage published his *Reflections on the Decline of Science in England, and on Some of Its Causes,* a savage attack on the management of the Royal Society; on Mr. Pond, the Astronomer-Royal; on Captain Sabine, and other influential scientific men. But it was after the publication of this book that Government agreed to furnish the engine. In 1833, a portion of the engine, sufficient to illustrate the working of the whole, was put together. It was a wonderful piece of workmanship, of a precision then unknown, and since unrivalled. To make it, it had been necessary not only to contrive new tools, but to lay a scientific foundation of the principles of tools, and to educate the mechanics who were to use them. Not a penny of the money paid by the Government ever went into Mr. Babbage's pocket, but, on the contrary, he had always advanced the money to pay the workmen until the Treasury warrants were issued, so that he was usually in advance from £500 to £1,000. In 1833, Mr. Babbage declined to continue this system, and, in consequence, the engineer discontinued the construction of the engine, dismissed the workmen, and took away all the tools. During the suspension of the work caused by this circumstance, the great misfortune of his life befell Mr. Babbage. He discovered the possibility of a new *analytical* engine, to which the difference engine was nothing; for it would do all the *arithmetical* work that that would do, but infinitely more; it would perform the most complicated *algebraical* processes, elimination, extraction of roots, integration, and it would find out for itself what operations it was necessary to perform; and the principle of this machine was such as immensely to simplify the means of attaining the object of a difference machine. One would suppose that, finding himself so unlucky as to have thought of such a thing, Babbage would at least have had the sense to keep it strictly to himself. Instead of that, he wrote immediately and communicated it to the Government! Before that, all was going smoothly; after that, they never would advance another penny. But it must be admitted that Mr. Babbage himself does not seem to have been very ardent to go on with the old machine after the new one was invented. Of course, neither has been constructed. Another difference engine has since been made by a Swede, named Scheutz. This machine is now at the Albany Observatory, and a duplicate of it is used in the office of the Registrar-General in London. Recently, an important new plan for such an engine has been invented in this country; and careful estimates show that it could be constructed for at most $5,000. But the analytical engine is, beyond question, the most stupendous work of human invention. It is so complicated that no man's mind could trace the manner of its working through drawings and descriptions, and its author had to invent a new notation to keep account of it. This mechanical notation has been found very serviceable for simpler cases.

Mr. Babbage wrote some works which come within the department of political economy. He has introduced several principles of rather subsidiary importance; but his books are more valuable for the striking facts which they contain. He was also the author of one of the Bridgewater Treatises. He was a single-minded and honorable man of science, who hated intrigues and charlatanry. He was witty and entertaining, and knew how to make himself agreeable to the public, but he did not do it by anything verging upon claptrap. He would invent a ballet or invent an automaton to play *tit-tat-too,* but he did not confound such things with his scientific claims. He was a real genius, but with a not infrequent fault of genius, an egregious and lamentable vanity. There is a trace of it, perhaps, in the following sentence, which may be taken as his epitaph: "If," he says, "it is the will of that Being who gave me the endowments which led to the discovery of the analytical engine that I should not live to complete my work, I bow to that decision with intense gratitude for those gifts, conscious that through life I have never hesitated to make the severest sacrifices of fortune, and even of feelings, in order to accomplish my imagined mission."

A very handsomely printed and well-arranged collection of *Three and Four Place Tables of Logarithmic and Trigonometric Functions,* by Professor James Mills Peirce (published by Ginn Brothers, Boston), which lies upon our table for notice, reminds us of another debt which the world owes to Mr. Babbage. The publication of his logarithms in 1826 makes an era in the art of computation. They were the first ones in which the proper pains were taken to avoid errors, especially by the thorough examination of the stereotype plates. They were also the first ones of which the arrangement, shape, and size of type, manner of ruling, and color of ink and paper, had been determined upon only after careful experimentation. Babbage tried fifty different colors of paper and ten of ink, and found that the blackest ink upon light buff paper was the least fatiguing to the eye. Much attention has since been paid to all such points which facilitate or expedite computation, and some principles of dividing the page by ruled lines have been discovered which were unknown to Babbage. In 1841, Mr. De Morgan called attention to the great advantages of four-place tables. They can be used with twice the speed of five-place tables, and with four times the speed of seven-place tables, and, as De Morgan pointed out, for navigation and most ordinary purposes have all the accuracy which is desirable. Three-place tables are a later notion. They were strongly advocated by Mr. T. Chappelier in 1863; and we know those who have used them for the last four years with unspeakable comfort for all rough approximate work. For ordinary people who do not have enough calculations to make to keep them in practice in using even five-place tables, the three- and four-place tables may, in many cases, be of real utility, if the use of them is once learned.

[THE BERKELEY REVIEW]

[Fraser's The Works of George Berkeley]

P 60: North American Review
113(October 1871):449–72

The Works of George Berkeley, D.D., formerly Bishop of Cloyne: including many of his Writings hitherto unpublished. With Prefaces, Annotations, his Life and Letters, and an Account of his Philosophy. By Alexander Campbell Fraser, M.A., Professor of Logic and Metaphysics in the University of Edinburgh. In Four Volumes. Oxford: At the Clarendon Press. 8vo. 1871.

This new edition of Berkeley's works is much superior to any of the former ones. It contains some writings not in any of the other editions, and the rest are given with a more carefully edited text. The editor has done his work well. The introductions to the several pieces contain analyses of their contents which will be found of the greatest service to the reader. On the other hand, the explanatory notes which disfigure every page seem to us altogether unnecessary and useless.

Berkeley's metaphysical theories have at first sight an air of paradox and levity very unbecoming to a bishop. He denies the existence of matter, our ability to see distance, and the possibility of forming the simplest general conception; while he admits the existence of Platonic ideas; and argues the whole with a cleverness which every reader admits, but which few are convinced by. His disciples seem to think the present moment a favorable one for obtaining for their philosophy a more patient hearing than it has yet got. It is true that we of this day are sceptical and not given to metaphysics, but so, say they, was the generation which Berkeley addressed, and for which his style was chosen; while it is hoped that the spirit of calm and thorough inquiry which is now, for once, almost the fashion, will save the theory from the perverse misrepresentations which formerly assailed it, and lead to a fair examination of the arguments which, in the minds of his sectators, put the truth of it beyond all doubt. But above all it is anticipated that the Berkeleyan treatment of that question of the validity of human knowledge and of the inductive process of science, which is now so much studied, is such as to command the attention of scientific men to the idealistic system. To us these hopes seem vain. The truth is that the minds from whom the spirit of the age emanates have now no interest in the only problems that metaphysics ever pretended to solve. The abstract acknowledgment of God, Freedom, and Immortality, apart from those other religious beliefs (which cannot possibly rest on metaphysical grounds) which alone may animate this, is now seen to have no practical consequence whatever. The world is getting to think of these creatures of metaphysics, as Aristotle of the Platonic ideas: τερετίσματα γάρ ἐστι, καὶ εἰ ἔστιν, οὐδὲν πρὸς τὸν λόγον ἐστίν. The question of the grounds of the validity of induction has, it is true, excited an interest, and may continue to do so (though the argument is now become too difficult for popular apprehension); but whatever interest it has had has been due to a hope that the solution of it would afford the basis for sure and useful maxims concerning the logic of induction,—a hope which would be destroyed so soon as it were shown that the question was a purely metaphysical one. This is the prevalent feeling, among advanced minds. It may not be just; but it exists. And its existence is an effectual bar (if there were no other) to the general acceptance of Berkeley's system. The few who do now care for metaphysics are not of that bold order of minds who delight to hold a position so unsheltered by the prejudices of common sense as that of the good bishop.

As a matter of history, however, philosophy must always be interesting. It is the best representative of the mental development of each age. It is so even of ours, if we think what really is our philosophy. Metaphysical history is one of the chief branches of history, and ought to be expounded side by side with the history of society, of government, and of war; for in its relations with these we trace the significance of events for the human mind. The history of philosophy in the British Isles is a subject possessing more unity and entirety within itself than has usually been recognized in it. The influence of Descartes was never so great in England as that of traditional conceptions, and we can trace a continuity between modern and mediæval thought there, which is wanting in the history of France, and still more, if possible, in that of Germany.

From very early times, it has been the chief intellectual characteristic of the English to wish to effect everything by the plainest and directest means, without unnecessary contrivance. In war, for example, they rely more than any other people in Europe upon sheer hardihood, and rather despise military science. The main peculiarities of their system of law arise from the fact that every evil has been rectified as it became intolerable, without any thoroughgoing measure. The bill for legalizing marriage with a deceased wife's sister is yearly pressed because it supplies a remedy for an inconvenience actually felt; but nobody has proposed a bill to legalize marriage with a deceased husband's brother. In philosophy, this national tendency appears as a strong preference for the simplest theories, and a resistance to any complication of the theory as long as there is the least possibility that the facts can be explained in the simpler way. And, accordingly, British philosophers have always desired to weed out of philosophy all conceptions which could not be made perfectly definite and easily intelligible, and have shown strong nominalistic tendencies since the time of Edward I, or even earlier. Berkeley is an admirable illustration of this national character, as well as of that strange union of nominalism with Platonism, which has repeatedly appeared in history, and has been such a stumbling-block to the historians of philosophy.

The mediæval metaphysic is so entirely forgotten, and has so close a historic connection with modern English philosophy, and so much bearing upon the truth of Berkeley's doctrine, that we may perhaps be pardoned a few pages on the nature of the celebrated controversy concerning universals. And first let us set down a few dates. It was at the very end of the eleventh century that the dispute concerning nominalism and realism, which had existed in a vague way before, began to attain extraordinary proportions. During the twelfth century it was the matter of most interest to logicians, when William of Champeaux, Abélard, John of Salisbury, Gilbert de la Porrée, and many others, defended as many different opinions. But there was no historic connection between this controversy and those of scholasticism proper, the scholasticism of Aquinas, Scotus, and Ockam. For about the end of the twelfth century a great revolution of thought took place in Europe. What the influences were which produced it requires new historical researches to say. No doubt, it was partly due to the Crusades. But a great awakening of intelligence did take place at that time. It requires, it is true, some examination to distinguish this particular movement from a general awakening which had begun a century earlier, and had been growing stronger ever since. But now there was an accelerated impulse. Commerce was attaining new importance, and was inventing some of her chief conveniences and safeguards. Law, which had hitherto been utterly barbaric, began to be a profession. The civil law was adopted in Europe, the canon law was digested; the common law took some form. The Church, under Innocent III, was assuming the sublime functions of a moderator over kings. And those orders of mendicant friars were established, two of which did so much for the development of the scholastic philosophy. Art felt the spirit of a new age, and there could hardly be a greater change than from the highly ornate round-arched architecture of the twelfth century to the comparatively simple Gothic of the thirteenth. Indeed, if any one wishes to know what a scholastic commentary is like, and what the tone of thought in it is, he has only to contemplate a Gothic cathedral. The first quality of either is a religious devotion, truly heroic. One feels that the men who did these works did really believe in religion as we believe in nothing. We cannot easily understand how Thomas Aquinas can speculate so much on the nature of angels, and whether ten thousand of them could dance on a needle's point. But it was simply because he held them for real. If they are real, why are they not more interesting than the bewildering varieties of insects which naturalists study; or why should the orbits of double stars attract more attention than spiritual intelligences? It will be said that we have no means of knowing anything about them. But that is on a par with censuring the schoolmen for referring questions to the authority of the Bible and of the Church. If they really believed in their religion, as they did, what better could they do? And if they found in these authorities testimony concerning angels, how could they avoid admitting it. Indeed, objections of this sort only make it appear still more clearly how much those were the ages of faith. And if the spirit was not altogether admirable, it is only because faith itself has its faults as a foundation for the intellectual character. The men of that time did fully believe and did think that, for the sake of giving themselves up absolutely to their great task of building or of writing, it was well worth while to resign all the joys of life. Think of the spirit in which Duns Scotus must have worked, who wrote his thirteen volumes in folio, in a style as condensed as the most condensed parts of Aristotle, before the age of thirty-four. Nothing is more striking in either of the great intellectual products of that age, than the complete absence of

466 WRITINGS OF CHARLES S. PEIRCE, 1867–1871

self-conceit on the part of the artist or philosopher. That anything of value can be added to his sacred and catholic work by its having the smack of individuality about it, is what he has never conceived. His work is not designed to embody *his* ideas, but the universal truth; there will not be one thing in it however minute, for which you will not find that he has his authority; and whatever originality emerges is of that inborn kind which so saturates a man that he cannot himself perceive it. The individual feels his own worthlessness in comparison with his task, and does not dare to introduce his vanity into the doing of it. Then there is no machine-work, no unthinking repetition about the thing. Every part is worked out for itself as a separate problem, no matter how analogous it may be in general to another part. And no matter how small and hidden a detail may be, it has been conscientiously studied, as though it were intended for the eye of God. Allied to this character is a detestation of antithesis or the studied balancing of one thing against another, and of a too geometrical grouping,—a hatred of posing which is as much a moral trait as the others. Finally, there is nothing in which the scholastic philosophy and the Gothic architecture resemble one another more than in the gradually increasing sense of immensity which impresses the mind of the student as he learns to appreciate the real dimensions and cost of each. It is very unfortunate that the thirteenth, fourteenth, and fifteenth centuries should, under the name of Middle Ages, be confounded with others, which they are in every respect as unlike as the Renaissance is from modern times. In the history of logic, the break between the twelfth and thirteenth centuries is so great that only one author of the former age is ever quoted in the latter. If this is to be attributed to the fuller acquaintance with the works of Aristotle, to what, we would ask, is this profounder study itself to be attributed, since it is now known that the knowledge of those works was not imported from the Arabs? The thirteenth century was realistic, but the question concerning universals was not as much agitated as several others. Until about the end of the century, scholasticism was somewhat vague, immature, and unconscious of its own power. Its greatest glory was in the first half of the fourteenth century. Then Duns Scotus,[1] a Briton (for whether Scotch, Irish, or English is disputed), first stated the realistic position consistently, and developed it with great fulness and applied it to all the different questions which

1. Died 1308.

depend upon it. His theory of "formalities" was the subtlest, except perhaps Hegel's logic, ever broached, and he was separated from nominalism only by the division of a hair. It is not therefore surprising that the nominalistic position was soon adopted by several writers, especially by the celebrated William of Ockam, who took the lead of this party by the thoroughgoing and masterly way in which he treated the theory and combined it with a then rather recent but now forgotten addition to the doctrine of logical terms. With Ockam, who died in 1347, scholasticism may be said to have culminated. After him the scholastic philosophy showed a tendency to separate itself from the religious element which alone could dignify it, and sunk first into extreme formalism and fancifulness, and then into the merited contempt of all men; just as the Gothic architecture had a very similar fate, at about the same time, and for much the same reasons.

The current explanations of the realist-nominalist controversy are equally false and unintelligible. They are said to be derived ultimately from Bayle's *Dictionary;* at any rate, they are not based on a study of the authors. "Few, very few, for a hundred years past," says Hallam, with truth, "have broken the repose of the immense works of the schoolmen." Yet it is perfectly possible so to state the matter that no one shall fail to comprehend what the question was, and how there might be two opinions about it. Are universals real? We have only to stop and consider a moment what was meant by the word *real,* when the whole issue soon becomes apparent. Objects are divided into figments, dreams, etc., on the one hand, and realities on the other. The former are those which exist only inasmuch as you or I or some man imagines them; the latter are those which have an existence independent of your mind or mine or that of any number of persons. The real is that which is not whatever we happen to think it, but is unaffected by what we may think of it. The question, therefore, is whether *man, horse,* and other names of natural classes, correspond with anything which all men, or all horses, really have in common, independent of our thought, or whether these classes are constituted simply by a likeness in the way in which our minds are affected by individual objects which have in themselves no resemblance or relationship whatsoever. Now that this is a real question which different minds will naturally answer in opposite ways, becomes clear when we think that there are two widely separated points of view, from which *reality,* as just defined, may be regarded.

Where is the real, the thing independent of how we think it, to be found? There must be such a thing, for we find our opinions constrained; there is something, therefore, which influences our thoughts, and is not created by them. We have, it is true, nothing immediately present to us but thoughts. Those thoughts, however, have been caused by sensations, and those sensations are constrained by something out of the mind. This thing out of the mind, which directly influences sensation, and through sensation thought, because it *is* out of the mind, is independent of how we think it, and is, in short, the real. Here is one view of reality, a very familiar one. And from this point of view it is clear that the nominalistic answer must be given to the question concerning universals. For, while from this standpoint it may be admitted to be true as a rough statement that one man is like another, the exact sense being that the realities external to the mind produce sensations which may be embraced under one conception, yet it can by no means be admitted that the two real men have really anything in common, for to say that they are both men is only to say that the one mental term or thought-sign "man" stands indifferently for either of the sensible objects caused by the two external realities; so that not even the two sensations have in themselves anything in common, and far less is it to be inferred that the external realities have. This conception of reality is so familiar, that it is unnecessary to dwell upon it; but the other, or realist conception, if less familiar, is even more natural and obvious. All human thought and opinion contains an arbitrary, accidental element, dependent on the limitations in circumstances, power, and bent of the individual; an element of error, in short. But human opinion universally tends in the long run to a definite form, which is the truth. Let any human being have enough information and exert enough thought upon any question, and the result will be that he will arrive at a certain definite conclusion, which is the same that any other mind will reach under sufficiently favorable circumstances. Suppose two men, one deaf, the other blind. One hears a man declare he means to kill another, hears the report of the pistol, and hears the victim cry; the other sees the murder done. Their sensations are affected in the highest degree with their individual peculiarities. The first information that their sensations will give them, their first inferences, will be more nearly alike, but still different; the one having, for example, the idea of a man shouting, the other of a man with a threatening aspect; but their final conclusions, the thought the remotest from sense, will be identical and free from the one-sidedness of their idiosyncrasies. There is, then, to every question a true answer, a final conclusion, to which the opinion of every man is constantly gravitating. He may for a time recede from it, but give him more experience and time for consideration, and he will finally approach it. The individual may not live to reach the truth; there is a residuum of error in every individual's opinions. No matter; it remains that there is a definite opinion to which the mind of man is, on the whole and in the long run, tending. On many questions the final agreement is already reached, on all it will be reached if time enough is given. The arbitrary will or other individual peculiarities of a sufficiently large number of minds may postpone the general agreement in that opinion indefinitely; but it cannot affect what the character of that opinion shall be when it is reached. This final opinion, then, is independent, not indeed of thought in general, but of all that is arbitrary and individual in thought; is quite independent of how you, or I, or any number of men think. Everything, therefore, which will be thought to exist in the final opinion is real, and nothing else. What is the POWER of external things, to affect the senses? To say that people sleep after taking opium because it has a soporific *power,* is that to say anything in the world but that people sleep after taking opium because they sleep after taking opium? To assert the existence of a power or potency, is it to assert the existence of anything actual? Or to say that a thing has a potential existence, is it to say that it has an actual existence? In other words, is the present existence of a power anything in the world but a regularity in future events relating to a certain thing regarded as an element which is to be taken account of beforehand, in the conception of that thing? If not, to assert that there are external things which can be known only as exerting a power on our sense, is nothing different from asserting that there is a general *drift* in the history of human thought which will lead it to one general agreement, one catholic consent. And any truth more perfect than this destined conclusion, any reality more absolute than what is thought in it, is a fiction of metaphysics. It is obvious how this way of thinking harmonizes with a belief in an infallible Church, and how much more natural it would be in the Middle Ages than in Protestant or positivist times.

This theory of reality is instantly fatal to the idea of a thing in itself,—a thing existing independent of all relation to the mind's conception of it. Yet it would by no means forbid, but rather encourage us, to regard the appearances of sense as only signs of the realities. Only, the realities which they represent would not be the unknowable cause of sensation, but *noumena,* or intelligible conceptions which are the last products of the mental action which is set in motion by sensation. The matter of sensation is altogether accidental; precisely the same information, practically, being capable of communication through different senses. And the catholic consent which constitutes the truth is by no means to be limited to men in this earthly life or to the human race, but extends to the whole communion of minds to which we belong, including some probably whose senses are very different from ours, so that in that consent no predication of a sensible quality can enter, except as an admission that so certain sorts of senses are affected. This theory is also highly favorable to a belief in external realities. It will, to be sure, deny that there is any reality which is absolutely incognizable in itself, so that it cannot be taken into the mind. But observing that "the external" means simply that which is independent of what phenomenon is immediately present, that is of how we may think or feel; just as "the real" means that which is independent of how we may think or feel *about it;* it must be granted that there are many objects of true science which are external, because there are many objects of thought which, if they are independent of that thinking whereby they are thought (that is, if they are real), are indisputably independent of all *other* thoughts and feelings.

It is plain that this view of reality is inevitably realistic; because general conceptions enter into all judgments, and therefore into true opinions. Consequently a thing in the general is as real as in the concrete. It is perfectly true that all white things have whiteness in them, for that is only saying, in another form of words, that all white things are white; but since it is true that real things possess whiteness, whiteness is real. It is a real which only exists by virtue of an act of thought knowing it, but that thought is not an arbitrary or accidental one dependent on any idiosyncrasies, but one which will hold in the final opinion.

This theory involves a phenomenalism. But it is the phenomenalism of Kant, and not that of Hume. Indeed, what Kant called his Copernican step was precisely the passage from the nominalistic to the realistic view of reality. It was the essence of his philosophy to regard the real object as determined by the mind. That was nothing else than to consider every conception and intuition which enters necessarily into the experience of an object, and which is not transitory and accidental, as having objective validity. In short, it was to regard the reality as the normal product of mental action, and not as the incognizable cause of it.

This realistic theory is thus a highly practical and common-sense position. Wherever universal agreement prevails, the realist will not be the one to disturb the general belief by idle and fictitious doubts. For according to him it is a consensus or common confession which constitutes reality. What he wants, therefore, is to see questions put to rest. And if a general belief, which is perfectly stable and immovable, can in any way be produced, though it be by the fagot and the rack, to talk of any error in such belief is utterly absurd. The realist will hold that the very same objects which are immediately present in our minds in experience really exist just as they are experienced out of the mind; that is, he will maintain a doctrine of immediate perception. He will not, therefore, sunder existence out of the mind and being in the mind as two wholly improportionable modes. When a thing is in such relation to the individual mind that that mind cognizes it, it is in the mind; and its being so in the mind will not in the least diminish its external existence. For he does not think of the mind as a receptacle, which if a thing is in, it ceases to be out of. To make a distinction between the true conception of a thing and the thing itself is, he will say, only to regard one and the same thing from two different points of view; for the immediate object of thought in a true judgment *is* the reality. The realist will, therefore, believe in the objectivity of all necessary conceptions, space, time, relation, cause, and the like.

No realist or nominalist ever expressed so definitely, perhaps, as is here done, his conception of reality. It is difficult to give a clear notion of an opinion of a past age, without exaggerating its distinctness. But careful examination of the works of the schoolmen will show that the distinction between these two views of the real—one as the fountain of the current of human thought, the other as the unmoving form to which it is flowing—is what really occasions their disagreement on the question concerning universals. The gist of all the nominalist's arguments will be found to relate to a *res extra animam,* while the realist defends his position only by assuming that the immediate object of thought in a true judgment is real. The notion that the controversy between realism and nominalism had anything to do with Platonic ideas is a mere product of the imagination, which the slightest examination of the books would suffice to disprove. But to prove that the statement here given of the essence of these positions is historically true and not a fancy sketch, it will be well to add a brief analysis of the opinions of Scotus and Ockam.

Scotus sees several questions confounded together under the usual *utrum universale est aliquid in rebus.* In the first place, there is the question concerning the Platonic forms. But putting Platonism aside as at least incapable of proof, and as a self-contradictory opinion if the archetypes are supposed to be strictly universal, there is the celebrated dispute among Aristotelians as to whether the universal is really in things or only derives its existence from the mind. Universality is a relation of a predicate to the subjects of which it is predicated. That can exist only in the mind, wherein alone the coupling of subject and predicate takes place. But the word *universal* is also used to denote what are named by such terms as *a man* or *a horse;* these are called universals, because a man is not necessarily this man, nor a horse this horse. In such a sense it is plain universals are real; there really is a man and there really is a horse. The whole difficulty is with the actually indeterminate universal, that which not only is not necessarily *this,* but which, being one single object of thought, is predicable of many things. In regard to this it may be asked, first, is it necessary to its existence that it should be in the mind; and, second, does it exist *in re?* There are two ways in which a thing may be in the mind,—*habitualiter* and *actualiter.* A notion is in the mind *actualiter* when it is actually conceived; it is in the mind *habitualiter* when it can directly produce a conception. It is by virtue of mental association (we moderns should say), that things are in the mind *habitualiter.* In the Aristotelian philosophy, the intellect is regarded as being to the soul what the eye is to the body. The mind *perceives* likenesses and other relations in the objects of sense, and thus just as sense affords sensible images of things, so the intellect affords intelligible images of them. It is as such a *species intelligibilis* that Scotus supposes that a conception exists which is in the mind *habitualiter,* not *actualiter.* This *species* is in the mind, in the sense of being the immediate object of knowledge, but its existence in the mind is independent of *consciousness.* Now that the *actual* cognition of the universal is necessary to its existence, Scotus denies. The subject of science is universal; and if the existence of universal were dependent upon what we happened to be thinking, science would not relate to anything real. On the other hand, he admits that the universal must be in the mind *habitualiter,* so that if a thing be considered as it is independent of its being cognized, there is no universality in it. For there is *in re extra* no one intelligible object attributed to different things. He holds, therefore, that such natures (i.e. sorts of things) as a *man* and a *horse,* which are real, and are not of themselves necessarily *this* man or *this* horse, though they cannot exist *in re* without being some particular man or horse, are in the *species intelligibilis* always represented positively indeterminate, it being the nature of the mind so to represent things. Accordingly any such nature is to be regarded as something which is of itself neither universal nor singular, but is universal in the mind, singular in things out of the mind. If there were nothing in the different men or horses which was not of itself singular, there would be no real unity except the numerical unity of the singulars; which would involve such absurd consequences as that the only real difference would be a numerical difference, and that there would be no real likenesses among things. If, therefore, it is asked whether the universal is in things, the answer is, that the nature which in the mind is universal, and is not in itself singular, exists in things. It is the very same nature which in the mind is universal and *in re* is singular; for if it were not, in knowing anything of a universal we should be knowing nothing of things, but only of our own thoughts, and our opinion would not be converted from true to false by a change in things. This nature is actually indeterminate only so far as it is in the mind. But to say that an object is in the mind is only a metaphorical way of saying that it stands to the intellect in the relation of known to knower. The truth is, therefore, that that real nature which exists *in re,* apart from all action of the intellect, though in itself, apart from its relations, it be singular, yet is actually universal as it exists in relation to the mind. But this universal only differs from the singular in the manner of its being conceived (*formaliter*), but not in the manner of its existence (*realiter*).

Though this is the slightest possible sketch of the realism of Scotus, and leaves a number of important points unnoticed, yet it is sufficient to show the general manner of his thought and how subtle and difficult his doctrine is. That about one and the same nature being in the grade of singularity in existence, and in the grade of universality in the mind, gave rise to an extensive doctrine concerning the various kinds of identity and difference, called the doctrine of the *formalitates;* and this is the point against which Ockam directed his attack.

Ockam's nominalism may be said to be the next stage in English opinion. As Scotus's mind is always running on forms, so Ockam's is on logical terms; and all the subtle distinctions which Scotus effects by his *formalitates,* Ockam explains by implied syncategorematics (or adverbial expressions, such as *per se,* etc.) in terms. Ockam always thinks of a mental conception as a logical term, which, instead of existing on paper, or in the voice, is in the mind, but is of the same general nature, namely, a *sign.* The conception and the word differ in two respects: first, a word is arbitrarily imposed, while a conception is a natural sign; second, a word signifies whatever it signifies only indirectly, through the conception which signifies the same thing directly. Ockam enunciates his nominalism as follows:

It should be known that *singular* may be taken in two senses. In one sense, it signifies that which is one and not many; and in this sense those who hold that the universal is a quality of mind predicable of many, standing however in this predication, not for itself, but for those many (i.e. the nominalists), have to say that every universal is truly and really singular; because as every word, however general we may agree to consider it, is truly and really singular and one in number, because it is one and not many, so every universal is singular. In another sense, the name *singular* is used to denote whatever is one and not many, is a sign of something which is singular in the first sense, and is not fit to be the sign of many. Whence, using the word *universal* for that which is not one in number,—an acceptation many attribute to it,—I say that there is no universal; unless perchance you abuse the word and say that *people* is not one in number and is universal. But that would be puerile. It is to be maintained, therefore, that every universal is one singular thing, and therefore there is no universal except by signification, that is, by its being the sign of many.

The arguments by which he supports this position present nothing of interest.[2] Against Scotus's doctrine that universals are without the mind in individuals, but are not really distinct from the individuals, but only formally so, he objects that it is impossible there should be any distinction existing out of the mind except between things really distinct. Yet he does not think of denying that an individual consists of matter and form, for these, though inseparable, are really distinct things; though a modern nominalist might ask in what sense things could be said to be distinct independently of any action of the mind, which are so inseparable as matter and form. But as to *relation,* he

---

2. The *entia non sunt multiplicanda præter necessitatem* is the argument of Durand de St. Pourçain. But any given piece of popular information about scholasticism may be safely assumed to be wrong.

most emphatically and clearly denies that it exists as anything differ- ent from the things related; and this denial he expressly extends to relations of agreement and likeness as well as to those of opposition. While, therefore, he admits the real existence of qualities, he denies that these real qualities are respects in which things agree or differ; but things which agree or differ agree or differ in themselves and in no respect *extra animam.* He allows that things without the mind are similar, but this similarity consists merely in the fact that the mind can abstract one notion from the contemplation of them. A resem- blance, therefore, consists solely in the property of the mind by which it naturally imposes one mental sign upon the resembling things. Yet he allows there is something in the things to which this mental sign corresponds.

This is the nominalism of Ockam so far as it can be sketched in a single paragraph, and without entering into the complexities of the Aristotelian psychology nor of the *parva logicalia.* He is not so thoroughgoing as he might be, yet compared with Durandus and other contemporary nominalists he seems very radical and profound. He is truly the *venerabilis inceptor* of a new way of philosophizing which has now broadened, perhaps deepened also, into English em- piricism.

England never forgot these teachings. During that Renaissance period when men could think that human knowledge was to be advanced by the use of Cicero's *Commonplaces,* we naturally see little effect from them; but one of the earliest prominent figures in modern philosophy is a man who carried the nominalistic spirit into everything,—religion, ethics, psychology, and physics, the *plusquam nominalis,* Thomas Hobbes of Malmesbury. His razor cuts off, not merely substantial forms, but every incorporeal substance. As for universals, he not only denies their real existence, but even that there are any universal conceptions except so far as we conceive names. In every part of his logic, names and speech play an extraor- dinarily important part. Truth and falsity, he says, have no place but among such creatures as use speech, for a true proposition is simply one whose predicate is the name of everything of which the subject is the name. "From hence, also, this may be deduced, that the first truths were arbitrarily made by those that first of all imposed names upon things, or received them from the imposition of others. For it is true (for example), that *man is a living creature,* but it is for this *reason* that it pleased men to impose both those names on the same thing." The difference between true religion and superstition is simply that the state recognizes the former and not the latter.

The nominalistic love of simple theories is seen also in his opinion, that every event is a movement, and that the sensible qualities exist only in sensible beings, and in his doctrine that man is at bottom purely selfish in his actions.

His views concerning matter are worthy of notice, because Berkeley is known to have been a student of Hobbes, as Hobbes confesses himself to have been of Ockam. The following paragraph gives his opinion:—

And as for that matter which is common to all things, and which philosophers, following Aristotle, usually call *materia prima,* that is, *first matter,* it is not a body distinct from all other bodies, nor is it one of them. What then is it? A mere name; yet a name which is not of vain use; for it signifies a conception of body without the consideration of any form or other accident except only magnitude or extension, and aptness to receive form and other accident. So that whensoever we have use of the name *body in general,* if we use that of *materia prima,* we do well. For when a man, not knowing which was first, water or ice, would find out which of the two were the matter of both, he would be fain to suppose some third matter which were neither of these two; so he that would find out what is the matter of all things ought to suppose such as is not the matter of anything that exists. Wherefore *materia prima* is nothing; and therefore they do not attribute to it form or any other accident, besides quantity; whereas all singular things have their forms and accidents certain.

Materia prima therefore is body in general, that is, body considered universally, not as having neither form nor any accident, but in which no form nor any other accident but quantity are at all considered, that is, they are not drawn into argumentation. (p. 118)

The next great name in English philosophy is Locke's. His philosophy is nominalistic, but does not regard things from a logical point of view at all. Nominalism, however, appears in psychology as sensationalism; for nominalism arises from taking that view of reality which regards whatever is in thought as caused by something in sense, and whatever is in sense as caused by something without the mind. But everybody knows that this is the character of Locke's philosophy. He believed that every idea springs from sensation and from his (vaguely explained) reflection.

Berkeley is undoubtedly more the offspring of Locke than of any other philosopher. Yet the influence of Hobbes with him is very evident and great; and Malebranche doubtless contributed to his thought. But he was by nature a radical and a nominalist. His whole philosophy rests upon an extreme nominalism of a sensationalistic type. He sets out with the proposition (supposed to have been already proved by Locke), that all the ideas in our minds are simply reproductions of sensations, external and internal. He maintains, moreover, that sensations can only be thus reproduced in such combinations as might have been given in immediate perception. We can conceive a man without a head, because there is nothing in the nature of sense to prevent our seeing such a thing; but we cannot conceive a sound without any pitch, because the two things are necessarily united in perception. On this principle he denies that we can have any abstract general ideas, that is, that universals can exist in the mind; if I think of a man it must be either of a short or a long or a middle-sized man, because if I see a man he must be one or the other of these. In the first draft of the Introduction of the *Principles of Human Knowledge,* which is now for the first time printed, he even goes so far as to censure Ockam for admitting that we can have general terms in our mind; Ockam's opinion being that we have in our minds conceptions, which are singular themselves, but are *signs* of many things.[3] But Berkeley probably knew only of Ockam from hearsay, and perhaps thought he occupied a position like that of Locke. Locke had a very singular opinion on the subject of general conceptions. He says:—

If we nicely reflect upon them, we shall find that general ideas are fictions, and contrivances of the mind, that carry difficulty with them, and do not so easily offer themselves as we are apt to imagine. For example, does it not require some pains and skill to form the general idea of a triangle (which is none of the most abstract, comprehensive, and difficult); for it must be neither oblique nor rectangle, neither equilateral, equicrural, nor scalenon, but all and none of these at once? In effect, is something imperfect that cannot exist, an idea wherein some parts of several different and inconsistent ideas are put together.

To this Berkeley replies:—

3. The sole difference between Ockam and Hobbes is that the former admits the universal signs in the mind to be natural, while the latter thinks they only follow instituted language. The consequence of this difference is that, while Ockam regards all truth as depending on the mind's naturally imposing the same sign on two things, Hobbes will have it that the first truths were established by convention. But both would doubtless allow that there is something *in re* to which such truths corresponded. But the sense of Berkeley's implication would be that there are no universal thought-signs at all. Whence it would follow that there is no truth and no judgments but propositions spoken or on paper.

Much is here said of the difficulty that abstract ideas carry with them, and the pains and skill requisite in forming them. And it is on all hands agreed that there is need of great toil and labor of the mind to emancipate our thoughts from particular objects, and raise them to those sublime speculations that are conversant about abstract ideas. From all which the natural consequence should seem to be, that so difficult a thing as the forming of abstract ideas was not necessary to communication, which is so easy and familiar to all sort of men. But we are told, if they seem obvious and easy to grown men, it is only because by constant and familiar use they are made so. Now, I would fain know at what time it is men are employed in surmounting that difficulty. It cannot be when they are grown up, for then it seems they are not conscious of such painstaking; it remains, therefore, to be the business of their childhood. And surely the great and multiplied labor of framing abstract notions will be found a hard task at that tender age. Is it not a hard thing to imagine that a couple of children cannot prate together of their sugar-plums and rattles, and the rest of their little trinkets, till they have first tacked together numberless inconsistencies, and so formed in their minds abstract general ideas, and annexed them to every common name they make use of?

In his private note-book Berkeley has the following:—"*Mem.* To bring the killing blow at the last, e.g. in the matter of abstraction to bring Locke's general triangle in the last."

There was certainly an opportunity for a splendid blow here, and he gave it.

From this nominalism he deduces his idealistic doctrine. And he puts it beyond any doubt that, if this principle be admitted, the existence of matter must be denied. Nothing that we can know or even think can exist without the mind, for we can only think reproductions of sensations, and the *esse* of these is *percipi.* To put it another way, we cannot think of a thing as existing unperceived, for we cannot separate in thought what cannot be separated in perception. It is true, I can think of a tree in a park without anybody by to see it; but I cannot think of it without anybody to imagine it; for I am aware that I am imagining it all the time. Syllogistically: trees, mountains, rivers, and all sensible things are perceived; and anything which is perceived is a sensation; now for a sensation to exist without being perceived is impossible; therefore, for any sensible thing to exist out of perception is impossible. Nor can there be anything out of the mind which *resembles* a sensible object, for the conception of likeness cannot be separated from likeness between ideas, because that is the only likeness which can be given in perception. An idea can be nothing but an idea, and it is absurd to say that anything inaudible can resemble a sound, or that anything invisible can resemble a color. But what exists without the mind can neither be heard nor seen; for we perceive only sensations within the mind. It is said that *Matter* exists without the mind. But what is meant by matter? It is acknowledged to be known only as *supporting* the accidents of bodies; and this word 'supporting' in this connection is a word without meaning. Nor is there any necessity for the hypothesis of external bodies. What we observe is that we have ideas. Were there any use in supposing external things it would be to account for this fact. But grant that bodies exist, and no one can say how they can possibly affect the mind; so that instead of removing a difficulty, the hypothesis only makes a new one.

But though Berkeley thinks we know nothing out of the mind, he by no means holds that all our experience is of a merely phantasmagoric character. It is not all a dream; for there are two things which distinguish experience from imagination: one is the superior vividness of experience; the other and most important is its connected character. Its parts hang together in the most intimate and intricate conjunction, in consequence of which we can infer the future from the past. "These two things it is," says Berkeley, in effect, "which constitute reality. I do not, therefore, deny the reality of common experience, although I deny its externality." Here we seem to have a third new conception of reality, different from either of those which we have insisted are characteristic of the nominalist and realist respectively, or if this is to be identified with either of those, it is with the realist view. Is not this something quite unexpected from so extreme a nominalist? To us, at least, it seems that this conception is indeed required to give an air of common sense to Berkeley's theory, but that it is of a totally different complexion from the rest. It seems to be something imported into his philosophy from without. We shall glance at this point again presently. He goes on to say that ideas are perfectly inert and passive. One idea does not make another and there is no power or agency in it. Hence, as there must be some cause of the succession of ideas, it must be *Spirit*. There is no *idea* of a spirit. But I have a consciousness of the operations of my spirit, what he calls a *notion* of my activity in calling up ideas at pleasure, and so have a relative knowledge of myself as an active being. But there is a succession of ideas not dependent on my will, the ideas of perception. Real things do not depend on my thought, but have an existence distinct from being perceived by me; but the *esse* of everything is *percipi;* therefore, *there must be some other mind wherein they exist.* "As sure, therefore, as the sensible world really exists, so sure do there an infinite omnipotent Spirit who contains and supports it." This puts the keystone into the arch of Berkeleyan idealism, and gives a theory of the relation of the mind to external nature which, compared with the Cartesian Divine Assistance, is very satisfactory. It has been well remarked that, if the Cartesian dualism be admitted, no divine *assistance* can enable things to affect the mind or the mind things, but divine power must do the whole work. Berkeley's philosophy, like so many others, has partly originated in an attempt to escape the inconveniences of the Cartesian dualism. God, who has created our spirits, has the power immediately to raise ideas in them; and out of his wisdom and benevolence, he does this with such regularity that these ideas may serve as signs of one another. Hence, the laws of nature. Berkeley does not explain how our wills act on our bodies, but perhaps he would say that to a certain limited extent we can produce ideas in the mind of God as he does in ours. But a material thing being only an idea, exists only so long as it is in some mind. Should every mind cease to think it for a while, for so long it ceases to exist. Its permanent existence is kept up by its being an idea in the mind of God. Here we see how superficially the just-mentioned theory of reality is laid over the body of his thought. If the reality of a thing consists in its harmony with the body of realities, it is a quite needless extravagance to say that it ceases to exist as soon as it is no longer thought of. For the coherence of an idea with experience in general does not depend at all upon its being actually present to the mind all the time. But it is clear that when Berkeley says that reality consists in the connection of experience, he is simply using the word *reality* in a sense of his own. That *an object's independence of our thought about it* is constituted by its connection with experience in general, he has never conceived. On the contrary, that, according to him, is effected by its being in the mind of God. In the usual sense of the word *reality,* therefore, Berkeley's doctrine is that the reality of sensible things resides only in their archetypes in the divine mind. This is Platonistic, but it is not realistic. On the contrary, since it places reality wholly out of the mind in the cause of sensations, and since it denies reality (in the true sense of the word) to sensible things in so far as they are sensible, it is distinctly nominalistic. Historically there have been prominent examples of an alliance between nominalism and Platonism. Abélard and John of Salisbury, the only two defenders of nominalism of the time of the great controversy whose works remain to us, are both Platonists; and Roscellin, the famous author of the *sententia de flatu vocis,* the first man in the Middle Ages who carried attention to nominalism, is said and believed (all his writings are lost) to have been a follower of Scotus Erigena, the great Platonist of the ninth century. The reason of this odd conjunction of doctrines may perhaps be guessed at. The nominalist, by isolating his reality so entirely from mental influence as he has done, has made it something which the mind cannot conceive; he has created the so often talked of "improportion between the mind and the thing in itself." And it is to overcome the various difficulties to which this gives rise, that he supposes this *noumenon,* which, being totally unknown, the imagination can play about as it pleases, to be the emanation of archetypal ideas. The reality thus receives an intelligible nature again, and the peculiar inconveniences of nominalism are to some degree avoided.

It does not seem to us strange that Berkeley's idealistic writings have not been received with much favor. They contain a great deal of argumentation of doubtful soundness, the dazzling character of which puts us more on our guard against it. They appear to be the productions of a most brilliant, original, powerful, but not thoroughly disciplined mind. He is apt to set out with wildly radical propositions, which he qualifies when they lead him to consequences he is not prepared to accept, without seeing how great the importance of his admissions is. He plainly begins his principles of human knowledge with the assumption that we have nothing in our minds but sensations, external and internal, and reproductions of them in the imagination. This goes far beyond Locke; it can be maintained only by the help of that "mental chemistry" started by Hartley. But soon we find him admitting various *notions* which are not *ideas,* or reproductions of sensations, the most striking of which is the notion of a cause, which he leaves himself no way of accounting for experientially. Again, he lays down the principle that we can have no ideas in which the sensations are reproduced in an order or combination different from what could have occurred in experience; and that therefore we have no abstract conceptions. But he very soon grants that we can consider a triangle, without attending to whether it is equilateral, isosceles, or scalene; and does not reflect that such exclusive attention constitutes a species of abstraction. His want of profound study is also shown in his so wholly mistaking, as he does, the function of the hypothesis of matter. He thinks its only purpose is to account for the production of ideas in our minds, so occupied is he with the Cartesian problem. But the real part that material substance has to play is to account for (or formulate) the constant connection between the accidents. In his theory, this office is performed by the wisdom and benevolence of God in exciting ideas with such regularity that we can know what to expect. This makes the unity of accidents a rational unity, the material theory makes it a unity not of a *directly* intellectual origin. The question is, then, which does experience, which does science decide for? Does it appear that in nature all regularities are directly rational, all causes final causes; or does it appear that regularities extend beyond the requirement of a rational purpose, and are brought about by mechanical causes? Now science, as we all know, is generally hostile to the final causes, the operation of which it would restrict within certain spheres, and it finds decidedly an other than directly intellectual regularity in the universe. Accordingly the claim which Mr. Collyns Simon, Professor Fraser, and Mr. Archer Butler make for Berkeleyanism, that it is especially fit to harmonize with scientific thought, is as far as possible from the truth. The sort of science that his idealism would foster would be one which should consist in saying what each natural production was made for. Berkeley's own remarks about natural philosophy show how little he sympathized with physicists. They should all be read; we have only room to quote a detached sentence or two:—

To endeavor to explain the production of colors or sound by figure, motion, magnitude, and the like, must needs be labor in vain. . . . In the business of gravitation or mutual attraction, because it appears in many instances, some are straightway for pronouncing it *universal;* and that to attract and be attracted by every body is an essential quality inherent in all bodies whatever. . . . There is nothing necessary or essential in the case, but it depends entirely on the will of the Governing Spirit, who causes certain bodies to cleave together or tend towards each other according to various laws, whilst he keeps others at a fixed distance; and to some he gives a quite contrary tendency, to fly asunder just as he sees convenient. . . . First, it is plain philosophers amuse themselves in vain, when they inquire for any natural efficient cause, distinct from *mind* or *spirit.* Secondly, considering the whole creation is the workmanship of a *wise and good Agent,* it should seem to become philosophers to employ their thoughts (contrary to what some hold) about the final causes of things; and I must confess I see no reason why pointing out the various ends to which natural things are adapted, and for which they were originally with unspeakable wisdom contrived, should not be thought one good way of accounting for them, and altogether worthy of a philosopher. (Vol. I, p. 466)

After this how can his disciples say *"that the true logic of physics is the first conclusion from his system!"*

As for that argument which is so much used by Berkeley and others, that such and such a thing cannot exist because we cannot so much as frame the idea of such a thing,—that matter, for example, is impossible because it is an abstract idea, and we have no abstract ideas,—it appears to us to be a mode of reasoning which is to be used with extreme caution. Are the facts such, that if we could have an idea of the thing in question, we should infer its existence, or are they not? If not, no argument is necessary against its existence, until something is found out to make us suspect it exists. But if we ought to infer that it exists, if we only could frame the idea of it, why should we allow our mental incapacity to prevent us from adopting the proposition which logic requires? If such arguments had prevailed in mathematics (and Berkeley was equally strenuous in advocating them there), and if everything about negative quantities, the square root of *minus,* and infinitesimals, had been excluded from the subject on the ground that we can form no idea of such things, the science would have been simplified no doubt, simplified by never advancing to the more difficult matters. A better rule for avoiding the deceits of language is this: Do things fulfil the same function practically? Then let them be signified by the same word. Do they not? Then let them be distinguished. If I have learned a formula in gibberish which in any way jogs my memory so as to enable me in each single case to act as though I had a general idea, what possible utility is there in distinguishing between such a gibberish and formula and an idea? Why use the term *a general idea* in such a sense as to separate things which, for all experiential purposes, are the same?

The great inconsistency of the Berkeleyan theory, which prevents his nominalistic principles from appearing in their true colors, is that he has not treated mind and matter in the same way. All that he has said against the existence of matter might be said against the existence of mind; and the only thing which prevented his seeing that, was the vagueness of the Lockian *reflection,* or faculty of internal perception. It was not until after he had published his systematic exposition of his doctrine, that this objection ever occurred to him. He alludes to it in one of his dialogues, but his answer to it is very lame. Hume seized upon this point, and, developing it, equally denied the existence of mind and matter, maintaining that only appearances exist. Hume's philosophy is nothing but Berkeley's, with this change made in it, and written by a mind of a more sceptical tendency. The innocent bishop generated Hume; and as no one disputes that Hume gave rise to all modern philosophy of every kind, Berkeley ought to have a far more important place in the history of philosophy than has usually been assigned to him. His doctrine was the half-way station, or necessary resting-place between Locke's and Hume's.

Hume's greatness consists in the fact that he was the man who had the courage to carry out his principles to their utmost consequences, without regard to the character of the conclusions he reached. But neither he nor any other one has set forth nominalism in an absolutely thoroughgoing manner; and it is safe to say that no one ever will, unless it be to reduce it to absurdity.

We ought to say one word about Berkeley's theory of vision. It was undoubtedly an extraordinary piece of reasoning, and might have served for the basis of the modern science. Historically it has not had that fortune, because the modern science has been chiefly created in Germany, where Berkeley is little known and greatly misunderstood. We may fairly say that Berkeley taught the English some of the most essential principles of that hypothesis of sight which is now getting to prevail, more than a century before they were known to the rest of the world. This is much; but what is claimed by some of his advocates is astounding. One writer says that Berkeley's theory has been accepted by the leaders of all schools of thought! Professor Fraser admits that it has attracted no attention in Germany, but thinks the German mind too *a priori* to like Berkeley's reasoning. But Helmholtz, who has done more than any other man to bring the empiricist theory into favor, says: "Our knowledge of the phenomena of vision is not so complete as to allow only one theory and exclude every other. It seems to me that the choice which different *savans* make between different theories of vision has thus far been governed more by their metaphysical inclinations than by any constraining power which the facts have had." The best authorities, however, prefer the empiricist hypothesis; the fundamental proposition of which, as it is of Berkeley's, is that the sensations which we have in seeing are signs of the relations of things whose interpretation has to be discovered inductively. In the enumeration of the signs and of their uses, Berkeley shows considerable power in that sort of investigation, though there is naturally no very close resemblance between his and the modern accounts of the matter. There is no modern physiologist who would not think that Berkeley had greatly exaggerated the part that the muscular sense plays in vision.

Berkeley's theory of vision was an important step in the development of the associationalist psychology. He thought all our conceptions of body and of space were simply reproductions in the imagination of sensations of touch (including the muscular sense). This, if it were true, would be a most surprising case of mental chemistry, that is of a sensation being felt and yet so mixed with others that we cannot by an act of simple attention recognize it. Doubtless this theory had its influence in the production of Hartley's system.

Hume's phenomenalism and Hartley's associationalism were put forth almost contemporaneously about 1750. They contain the fundamental positions of the current English "positivism." From 1750 down to 1830—eighty years—nothing of particular importance was added to the nominalistic doctrine. At the beginning of this period Hume's was toning down his earlier radicalism, and Smith's theory of Moral Sentiments appeared. Later came Priestley's materialism, but there was nothing new in that; and just at the end of the period, Brown's *Lectures on the Human Mind.* The great body of the philosophy of those eighty years is of the Scotch common-sense school. It is a weak sort of realistic reaction, for which there is no adequate explanation within the sphere of the history of philosophy. It would be curious to inquire whether anything in the history of society could account for it. In 1829 appeared James Mill's *Analysis of the Human Mind,* a really great nominalistic book again. This was followed by Stuart Mill's *Logic* in 1843. Since then, the school has produced nothing of the first importance; and it will very likely lose its distinctive character now for a time, by being merged in an empiricism of a less metaphysical and more working kind. Already in Stuart Mill the nominalism is less salient than in the classical writers; though it is quite unmistakable.

Thus we see how large a part of the metaphysical ideas of to-day have come to us by inheritance from very early times, Berkeley being one of the intellectual ancestors whose labors did as much as any one's to enhance the value of the bequest. The realistic philosophy of the last century has now lost all its popularity, except with the most conservative minds. And science as well as philosophy is nominalistic. The doctrine of the correlation of forces, the discoveries of Helmholtz, and the hypotheses of Liebig and of Darwin, have all that character of explaining familiar phenomena apparently of a peculiar kind by extending the operation of simple mechanical principles, which belongs to nominalism. Or if the nominalistic character of these doctrines themselves cannot be detected, it will at least be admitted that they are observed to carry along with them those daughters of nominalism,—sensationalism, phenomenalism, individualism, and materialism. That physical science is necessarily connected with doctrines of a debasing moral tendency will be believed by few. But if we hold that such an effect will not be produced by these doctrines on a mind which really understands them, we are accepting this belief, not on experience, which is rather against it, but on the strength of our general faith that what is really true it is good to believe and evil to reject. On the other hand, it is allowable to suppose that science has no essential affinity with the philosophical views with which it seems to be every year more associated. History cannot be held to exclude this supposition; and science as it exists is certainly much less nominalistic than the nominalists think it should be. Whewell represents it quite as well as Mill. Yet a man who enters into the scientific thought of the day and has not materialistic tendencies, is getting to be an impossibility. So long as there is a dispute between nominalism and realism, so long as the position we hold on the question is not determined by any proof *indisputable*, but is more or less a matter of inclination, a man as he gradually comes to feel the profound hostility of the two tendencies will, if he is not less than man, become engaged with one or other and can no more obey both than he can serve God and Mammon. If the two impulses are neutralized within him, the result simply is that he is left without any great intellectual motive. There is, indeed, no reason to suppose the logical question is in its own nature unsusceptible of solution. But that path out of the difficulty lies through the thorniest mazes of a science as dry as mathematics. Now there is a demand for mathematics; it helps to build bridges and drive engines, and therefore it becomes somebody's business to study it severely. But to have a philosophy is a matter of luxury; the only use of that is to make us feel comfortable and easy. It is a study for leisure hours; and we want it supplied in an elegant, an agreeable, an interesting form. The law of natural selection, which is the precise analogue in another realm of the law of supply and demand, has the most immediate effect in fostering the other faculties of the understanding, for the men of mental power succeed in the struggle for life; but the faculty of philosophizing, except in the literary way, is not called for; and therefore a difficult question cannot be expected to reach solution until it takes some practical form. If anybody should have the good luck to find out the solution, nobody else would take the trouble to understand it. But though the question of realism and nominalism has its roots in the technicalities of logic, its branches reach about our life. The question whether the *genus homo* has any existence except as individuals, is the question whether there is anything of any more dignity, worth, and importance than individual happiness, individual aspirations, and individual life. Whether men really have anything in common, so that the *community* is to be considered as an end in itself, and if so, what the relative value of the two factors is, is the most fundamental practical question in regard to every public institution the constitution of which we have it in our power to influence.

[Peirce's Berkeley Review], by Chauncey Wright

O 58: Nation *13(30 November 1871):355–56*

Mr. Charles S. Peirce, in his review of Berkeley in the last *North American,* to which we promised to return, takes the occasion to trace out in the history of philosophical thought in Great Britain the sources of Berkeley's doctrines and of later developments in English philosophy. These he traces back to the famous disputes of the later schoolmen on the question of realism and nominalism—that question on which each new-fledged masculine intellect likes to try its powers of disputation. But the motive of the schoolmen who started this question or gave it prominence, was not in any sense egotistical, however pugilistic it may have been, but was profoundly religious—more religious, in fact, than anything modern, and, perhaps, more fitly to be compared to the devotion that produced the Gothic architecture than to anything else. The most remarkable thing in the essay is Mr. Peirce's interpretation of the actual question so earnestly agitated. This, it should seem, is not at all what has become the universally accepted account of this voluminous dispute—an account derived, it appears, from Bayle's *Dictionary*. The realistic schoolmen were not such dolts as to contend for an incognizable reality beyond any powers we have for apprehending it, nor for the existence of universals as the objects of general conceptions existing outside of the mind. They only contended (against the sceptical or nominalistic tendency) that reality, or the truth of things, depends on something besides the actual courses of experience in individual minds, or is independent of differences and accidents in these; and that truth is not determined by the conventions of language, or by what men choose to mean by their words. So far from being the reality commonly supposed—that is to say, the vivid, actual, present contact with things—the reality of the realists was the final upshot of experience, the general agreement in all experience, as far removed as possible from any particular body's sight, or hearing, or touch, or from the accidents which are inseparable from these. Yet it is essentially intelligible, and, in fact, is the very most intelligible, and is quite independent of conventions in language. The faith of the realists (for theirs was a philosophy of faith) was that this result of all men's experience would contain agreements not dependent on the laws and usages of language, but on truths which determine these laws and usages. Modern science affords ample evidence of the justness of this position.

That this truly was the position of the realistic schoolmen, Mr. Peirce contends; and he bases his opinion and belief on an original examination of their works, such as has not, we venture to say, been undertaken, outside of Germany, for a very long time. In spite of the confirmation of this position which modern science gives, the course of the development of modern science has, nevertheless, as Mr. Peirce points out, been closely associated with the opposite doctrine—nominalism, the representative of the sceptical spirit. This appears in Berkeley's philosophy, who is a nominalist, notwithstanding his *penchant* for Platonic ideas or spiritual archetypes. Hume, a complete representative of the nominalistic and sceptical spirit, is an historical product of Berkeley's nominalism; and, though commonly regarded as the author of modern philosophical movements, was not, historically considered, so different from Berkeley but that

Mr. Peirce regards the latter as entitled to "a far more important place in the history of philosophy than has usually been
assigned to him." So far as Berkeley was a link in the chain, this
is undoubtedly true. So far as Hume (in common with all independent thinkers of the sceptical type) was not such a link, he
was, we think, a starting-point in the movement of thought
which has resulted in English empiricism, or the so-called "Positivism" of modern science, which Mr. Peirce seems inclined to
attribute to a regular development of philosophical thought.
Scepticism, though perhaps never original, as we are taught by
orthodoxy, and only a revival of old and the oft-exploded errors,
is, nevertheless, by its criticism, the source of most of the impulses which the spirit of enquiry has received in the history of
philosophy. The results of modern science, the establishment of
a great body of undisputed truths, the questions settled beyond
debate, may be testimony in favor of the realistic schoolmen;
but this settlement was the work, so far as it depended on the
impulse of philosophy, of the nominalistic or sceptical tendencies of modern thought, which has put itself in opposition, not
to the faith of the realists, as Mr. Peirce understands them, but
to their conservatism and dogmatism, to their desire to agree
with authority—that admirable devotion of theirs. It is curious
that these things, the most certain of all on which the actual arts
of life are now dependent, should be the results equally of the
faith of the realists and the sceptical enquiries of the nominalists. But this is enough to account for the gratitude and the
indifference which we owe to both of them, especially as the
confirmation which science has afforded is not of the sort which
the realists anticipated. It is the empirical conjectures of the
visionary, not the inspired teachings of the wise, that have established realities for themselves and for truth in general.
There are many other curious points of history and criticism in
this article which will engage the scrutiny of the student of
metaphysics, and doubtless afford him great delight. We are
afraid to recommend it to other readers, as Mr. Peirce's style
reflects the difficulties of the subject, and is better adapted for
persons who have mastered these than for such as would rather
avoid them.

Mr. Peirce and the Realists

P 59: Nation *13(14 December 1871):386*

To the Editor of the *Nation:*

Sir: In your far too flattering notice of my remarks upon mediæ-val realism and nominalism, you have attributed to me a degree of originality which is not my due. The common view that realism is a modified Platonism has already been condemned by the most thorough students, such as Prantl and Morin. The realists certainly held (as I have said) that universals really exist in external things. The only feature of the controversy which has appeared to me to need more emphasis than has hitherto been put upon it is that each party had its own peculiar ideas of what it is that is real, the realists assuming that reality belongs to what is present to us in true knowledge of any sort, the nominalists assuming that the absolutely external causes of perception are the only realities. This point of disagreement was never argued out, for the reason that the mental horizon of each party was too limited for it to comprehend what the conception of the other side was. It is a similar narrowness of thought which makes it so hard for many persons to understand one side or the other, at this day.

WASHINGTON, D.C., Dec. 10, 1871.

APPENDIX

Letter, J. E. Oliver to Peirce

L 322

4
53 Green St. Lynn 1871.
21

Dear Sir.

I want to thank you for the pleasure that a partial perusal of your admirable memoir has given me: only wishing that I had the time, at present, to do justice to it all. What you say of Logical Quaternions,—of the Lobatchewsky Geometry,—of the Classification of Relatives,—&c.,—is very suggestive.

In your note, you speak of the fundamental operations of Algebra:—and of Notation. In defining the old Algebraic Symbols and Operations [with the $\succ$ or $\prec$ that is so much needed] primarily by their laws of combination; and only secondarily, if at all, by their relation to subject-matter;—you seem to have done the best thing of the kind that I have seen. I understand you to say, "It is IMPERATIVE that THESE conditions, and *desirable* that these *others*,—be observed whenever either the *[old]* SIGNS or the old NAMES of Algebraic operations are used." And probably you would add, with me, "When these conditions are violated, new signs must be employed; and the new signs would best *resemble* the old ones, or not, according as the new *operations* do or don't resemble the old in t/heir/ laws of combination or in their relation to subject-matter or to formulas." Thus, one might invent a ~{~ if he has to write p ~{~ q = log pq ≠ log qp = q ~{~ p—Yet a few open questions, perhaps, remain; though some of them pertain merely to *notation*. Why not make p. 5, ¶2, line 3 stronger, thus:—"and IT IS IMPERATIVE that when numbers are so substituted for *all* the letters, the equations should hold good" &c. Again, why not recognize that your pretty distinction of invertible vs. non-invertible multiplication, gives 4 kinds,

$$\left\{ \begin{array}{ll} \text{invertible,} & \text{faciend-invertible} \\ \text{facient-invertible,} & \text{non-invertible} \end{array} \right\} ; \text{ whereof,}$$

for convenience you denote all but the first by one sign; while addition, being commutative, is of only 2 kinds? And here is a question of notation: your $(x^y)^z = x^{yz}$ is far more neatly written than Hamilton's $(x^y)^z = x^{zy}$; but is not his the most natural in its relation to the usual subject-matter?—These are the chief questions that I would care to raise now, concerning pp. 1–5; though there are 1 or 2 others that I must look at again.

As regards *notation,* your $^z(^yx) = {}^{zy}x$ is very neat, if you write $(x^y)^z = x^{yz}$. So is $\succ$ or $\prec$. I had abandoned it for γ or ζ, as easier written; but $\succ$ lends itself better to work like that [on p.] 31. Of $+$, and $\div$ we will speak presently. [And] the new notation on these pages, is apparently well-suited for your present purpose, but I agree with you in not recommending it for GENERAL Algebra. Thus, the comma can hardly be spared from its old use as a *non-commutative* mark of *mere collection;*

$$\left(\text{e.g.} \left\{ \begin{array}{l} (x,y) = (a,b) \quad \text{when } x = a, \ y = b; \\[4pt] f(x,yz) \neq f(yz,x); \end{array} \right. \right.$$

$$(a,b,c)(x,y)^2 = ax^2 + 2bxy + cy^2;$$

$$\begin{vmatrix} a,b \\ c,d \end{vmatrix}(w,x)(y,z) = awy + bxy + cwz + dxz;$$

$$\begin{vmatrix} a,b \\ c,d \end{vmatrix}(w,x) = (aw + bx, \ cw + dx);$$

$$\left. \begin{pmatrix} w & y \\ x & z \end{pmatrix} \cdot w^{xyz} = x^{wzy}; \qquad\qquad \right) -$$

for any PERMANENT employment in commutative multiplication.

You speak of the suggestion which was made, 6 or 8 years ago, in my unpublished paper on "Notation," and which I've since made a very slight use of in print;—I will send you a specimen if I can find it. The paper itself, is likely to lie another year before I get ready to revise and print it. But the suggestion is this.

One often invents, for temporary use, a new sig[n] of operation which more or less resembles in its meaning the old $+$, $-$, $\times$, &c.; or a new sign of relation that more or less resembles some old copula $=$, $\succ$, $>$, $\equiv$, $\bowtie$, &c. The sign of operation may thus be varied without the copula, or vice versâ; but in many cases when the SIGN of relation is thus unchanged, the RELATION ITSELF is changed so that it would be allowable though needless to write a different copula. Thus your excellent sign $+$, [when used as you chiefly intend] gives to the sign $=$ used with it a further meaning than $=$ would otherwise have in the same treatise, or in a treatise on the same subject-matter. By a + b = c you commonly express merely a numerical relation; and by a $+$, b = c,—a modified form of that relation, and MOREOVER a relation of IDENTITY that INCLUDES the modified numerical relation. Hence it is merely for simplicity that you have written a $+$, b = c and not a $+$, b $=$ c. All this is much like what you say to me in your note.

Now my suggestion is, that whenever the modification of signs or of copula is such as to give to the *copula* an *additional* meaning, which *includes and implies* the old meaning, as in the above example,—such modification be denoted by marks written BELOW the old symbol; but that when, on the other han[d], the new meaning *is included in* the old one, the modifying marks be written *above* the symbol. The cases that have oftenest occurred in my own studies, have belonged clearly to one class or the other, so that the rule has proved to be a very useful one. It is equally [suffici]ent, now and then, for relations that clearly belong to both classes at once. See $\doteq$ below. In most other cases, I think the position of the modifier would be determined from analogy; while in yet others, as e.g. $+$, $\equiv$, for *not =*, *not* $\equiv$, or the $\sim$ or $+$ or $\ne$ or $+$ which I happened to use above, or the familiar and useful $\sim$, the symbol shows that it neither includes nor is included by the normal one.

Examples. $+$ $-$ $=$ may denote GEOMETRIC addition &c., so that

(1)   a + b $=$ c   when lines *a, b, c* form ,
(2)   a + b = c'   " line c = line c' in length,
      a + b = c"   " length c" = sum of lengths of a and b.
In this case, we had to employ $=$ in (1) to distinguish it from (2). In many other cases, there is no such necessity.

    U $=$ V   when functions U and V agree in *form* as well as in value; for instance, when $D_xU = D_xV$, $D_yU = D_yV$, &c.

$$\begin{bmatrix} a = b \\ c = d \\ e = f \end{bmatrix} = [x = y, z = 0] \text{ when the equations}$$
$$[a = b, c = d, e = f]$$

are together necessary and sufficient to the truth of [x − y = z = 0].

     a ⋈ b   *a* is proportional to *b*

     a ⋈ b   *a* is proportional to *b* and has also the same sign.

+, ×   Completely non-invertible addition and multiplication.

× ×   facient-non-invertible and faciend-non-invertible multip. i.e. faciend-invertible and facient-invertible.

   × could mean × or × or ×

     √x the **positive** √x. Here the mark is below rather than above, because the statement y = √x includes the statement y = √x

     ±   ambiguous sign

     $\pm_1, \pm_2$ particular ambiguous signs

     $\pm_{12}$ their product.

⪰   >

≐   is nearly equal to

≏   is very roughly equal to

$\overset{n}{=}$ is equal to, as far as terms of *n*th order inclusive

≑   is nearly the geometric sum ◺

$\underset{m}{\equiv}$ is congruous to,—the modulus being *m*.

$\underset{m,\,n}{\equiv}$ . . . . . . for modulus *m;* also nearly so, for modulus *n*.

$\underset{+}{\overset{\alpha \quad \beta}{\equiv}}$ congruous on condition α. Has same sign on condition β.

$\underset{+}{\overset{\alpha}{\equiv}}$ is congruous, and has the same sign, if condition α be fulfilled

$\underset{+}{\overset{\beta}{\equiv}}$ $\underset{+\ m}{\overset{\beta}{\equiv}}$ $\underset{m\ n}{\overset{\alpha\ \beta}{\equiv}}$ explain themselves.

H + Cl = HCl . . . 1 . . .H and Cl combine into HCl

H + Cl $\underset{1}{\doteq}$ HCl . . . 3 . . . . . . DO NOT COMBINE; but if they did, they would make HCl. Here the additional information is indicated by subscript mark of negation (|)

H + Cl $\doteq$ HCl . . . 2 . . .H and Cl present in just sufficient
quantities to make HCl; but no asser-
tion is made concerning the reaction's actual occurrence.

These HCl examples belong to a subject where the usual sense
of the algebraic signs is one that INCLUDES the arithmetical
sense; hence we denote the arithmetical sense by a superscript
modifier.

Many of the above, I use in actual work, and find them very
serviceable. Others, like the $\overset{\alpha \quad \beta}{\underset{+}{=\!\!=}}$, the $\overset{\cdot}{\times} \overset{\cdot}{\times} \overset{\cdot}{\times}$ &c., are extem-
porized for illustration, just as one would extemporize them in
actual work. These SYMBOLS of course are not recommended
for adoption: only the PRINCIPLE. For I think good rules for
making temporary symbols when needed, are [a]lmost as important as good permanent symbols. The above system cannot
always dispense with a *definition* for each new symbol; but I
think it conduces to perspicuity, and sometimes the symbol, by
aid of the context, will even explain itself.

The system is almost inapplicable to *letters,* as a_1 a_2 a' a'',
a''' &c.; and to cases like $\underset{m}{\overset{n}{\int}}$, $\pm$, angle $\binom{b}{a}$, permutation $\binom{b}{a}$, $\frac{a}{b}$, &c.
It is meant chiefly for modified *connective* symbols. Possibly
a_0, a_1, a_2, which seem to me to denote SPECIAL values of *a,* while
a', a'', rather denote DERIVATIVES of *a,* values coordinate with
a; and the expression log $_a$x, which is more special than log x
unless the latter be defined as e.g. log $_6$ x; harmonize with it, and
are not offset by x^a; for since in x^a no exponent is thought of
unless written, the effect of writing the a in x^a is merely to
complicate the function, while its effect in log $_a$x is to *define,* or
in one sense to *specialize* it. But this is "drawing it too fine"—
a sure sign that I have written too much. Twice as much as I
intended. But the previous paragraphs are less fanciful while
this one gives but the suggestion of the moment. Indeed, until
within 6 weeks, I used this notation upsidedown,—$\doteq$ for $=$ &c.;
—and so the paper had it; but I reverse it now, chiefly to bring
it into harmony with your own printed $+$, and $-$. Hence the
length at which I now describe it to you.

Yours,

J. E. Oliver.

P.S. On re-reading your letter, some points appear which
were forgotten in writing the above. 1° What you say is true:

quaternion and common addition ar[e] equally definite, whether identical or not; and in one sense the latter is more special than the former, and than +,; but my criterion, as you see, rests on a different consideration from that. 2° You are also right in saying that signs whose laws of combination are alike should commonly be written alike, even though the meaning be varied, *"unless they are to be used* TOGETHER." By "to-gether," of course you mean "in the same *discussion*" and not merely "in the same *equation.*"

3° You speak of "second Multiplication." Defining +, ×, &c. as you do, may not various *additions* coexist; various multiplica-tions for each addition; and so on? Are these multiplications equivalent to units of a multiple algebra? If so, what pretty multiple algebra have you got out of conjugatives?

Happy to accept yr. invitation some day, and call. Fear that you don't lose much in missing my lectures; but they give me some pleasant study &c., and if ever anywhere repeated, they will be better.

J.E.O.

Editorial Notes

The functions of these notes, which are keyed to page and line numbers, are generally self-explanatory. But three kinds of notes require brief explanation.

The first of these is the initial note to each selection which serves as a headnote and provides a brief description of the copy-text, whether manuscript or published article, and, when possible, the reasons for its composition.

The second kind identifies the names not found in the standard reference works for our edition. These works include the *Dictionary of American Biography*, the *Dictionary of National Biography*, the *Dictionary of Scientific Biography*, the 15th edition of the *Encyclopaedia Britannica*, *The Encyclopedia of Philosophy*, the *National Cyclopedia of American Biography*, and the *New Century Cyclopedia of Names*.

The third kind identifies the source of quotations. Scarcely anything in the present volume that was not published by Peirce was intended for publication in anything like the form in which he left it. He was not consistent in his use of source material. He rarely cited his source fully and often omitted documentation altogether. Sometimes he used quotation marks when he was merely paraphrasing, at other times he omitted them when transcribing verbatim. It was originally our intention to identify only those passages quoted verbatim, but it was soon clear that Peirce paraphrased and interpreted the work of others extensively in these early years and that knowing the sources for these materials would be of help to the reader. Consequently, we now identify paraphrases as well.

Material in quotation marks that was found to be verbatim copy, or very close paraphrase of a specific passage, is identified. When Peirce put in quotation marks what is not a quotation but his own interpretation of the author referred to or when without using quotation marks he offered a summary statement of the general view of an author on a certain point, we provide a reference to the passage in which the author comes nearest to saying what Peirce reported. In the case of a rhetorical flourish in quotation marks we of course supply no note. Unless otherwise indicated, all translations in the editorial notes are by the editors.

Every effort is made to cite the editions that Peirce owned or that we know he used. When we cannot provide such information or when the edition he used was not available to us, we cite one that was accessible to Peirce. In some cases we add in brackets a more general reference as to book or chapter number or a reference to an edition more readily available to the modern reader. References to volume 1 of the present edition appear as $W1$, followed by a colon and page number.

Citations are generally given in shortened form; full bibliographic information is provided in the bibliography that follows the editorial notes. Works we know Peirce owned are identified in the bibliography by the degree symbol (°).

Logic Notebook

The so-called Logic Notebook is Peirce's single most fruitful unpublished manuscript. Inscribed during the course of nineteen years between 12 November 1865 and 1 November 1909, it contains 340 pages of text. The entries for 1867, inscribed between 23 March and 7 December, cover 52 pages. Printed here are the first eight pages (17r–20v) and the last nineteen (30r–42r); of what is deleted (20v–29v and 36v) six pages are blank, and the others contain trial lists of syllogisms.

5.29   Berkeley says. . . .] The idea is expressed in the second of Berkeley's *Three Dialogues between Hylas and Philonous* [Fraser's *Works*, 1: 310–11].

9.11   In a smaller and fainter hand and perhaps as a note to himself, Peirce has written the following to the right of this premise:

Not-P is not-S
Some P is S

Boole's Calculus of Logic

Peirce was elected a member of the American Academy of Arts and Sciences on 30 January 1867. Within less than a year he presented five papers now generally known as the American Academy series. These were published in the Academy's *Proceedings* in 1868. (Academy *Proceedings,* as well as *Memoirs,* were published in bound volumes when finances permitted and the quantity of material dictated; but offprints of single papers, bound in their own covers, were usually available to authors shortly after the presentation and submission of papers.) No later than December of 1867, Peirce had offprints of the first three bound together as "Three Papers on Logic," which he distributed among friends and other interested persons. On 21 May 1868, Augustus De Morgan received one of these collective offprints, which were deposited in the library of the University of London after his death. It contains some pencil annotations and corrections in Peirce's hand, and the following is printed on a sheet facing the last page of the third paper: "Students of logic (and persons who will study it) will be supplied, upon application to the author by letter, with copies of these papers and of others which are to follow. The latter will be sent only to those who express a wish to make use of them." Guided by Venn's frequency theory of probability (see item 8 below), Peirce extends Boole's calculus in his first paper— published in the *Proceedings of the American Academy of Arts and Sciences* 7(1868):250–61—in order to make that calculus more readily applicable to problems concerning probability. (See Notes 1–5 in MS 152, item 7 below, pp. 87–93.)

15.30   Note 1 in MS 152 belongs here; see 87.3–88.12.
16.6   Note 2 in MS 152 belongs here; see 88.13–15.
19.2   Note 3 in MS 152 belongs here; see 88.16–22.
19.14   Peirce substitutes r for Boole's $\frac{Prob.\ xy}{c'}$.
21.26–29   Let i . . . some $a.$] Note 4 in MS 152 belongs here; see 88.23–92.24.
22.6   Note 5 in MS 152 belongs here; see 93.1–3.
22.37–40   Suppose . . . Englishman?] Venn, *Logic of Chance,* pp. 183–87.
23n.1–2   For Peirce's notice of Venn's *Logic of Chance,* see item 8 below, pp. 98–102.

Classification of Arguments

Presented on 9 April 1867, the second paper was published in the *Proceedings of the American Academy of Arts and Sciences* 7(1868): 261–87. (See Notes 6–10 in MS 152, item 7 below, p. 93.)

28.21   Note 6 in MS 152 belongs here; see 93.4–6. For the discussion of contradictories, see item 6 below, 83.30–38.
31.26   Note 7 in MS 152 belongs here; see 93.7–11.
32.8–9   There are . . . figures.] Note 8 in MS 152 belongs here; see 93.12–20.
32.10–14   The short . . . conclusion.] Note 9 in MS 152 belongs here; see 93.21–23.
32.23–24   The names . . . moods] See *W*1:508.
35.34   Note 10 in MS 152 belongs here; see 93.24–27.
39.26   The verses of Shyreswood] Reproduced from *W*1:508.

> *Barbara: Celarent: Darii: Ferio: Baralipton:*
> *Celantes: Dabitis: Fapesmo: Frisesomorum.*
> *Cesare: Camestres: Festino: Baroco. Darapti:*
> *Felapton: Disamis: Datisi: Bocardo: Ferison.*

45n.15–16   "that no. . . ."] Comte, *Cours,* 2:434 [Martineau translation, 1:255].
45n.22–23   "An hypothesis. . . ."] Kant, *Werke,* 3:262 [*Logik,* Einleitung X].
46n.3–4   Mr. Venn. . . .] Venn, *Logic of Chance,* chap. 5.

New List of Categories

"On May 14, 1867, after three years of almost insanely concentrated thought, hardly interrupted even by sleep, I produced my one contribution to philosophy in the 'New List of Categories'." Published in the *Proceedings of the American Academy of Arts and Sciences* 7(1868):287–98, the New List is "perhaps the least unsatisfactory, from a logical point of view, that I ever succeeded in producing" and (with "Some Consequences of Four Incapacities," item 22 below) one of his two "strongest philosophical works." Presenting the categories in close conjunction with his theory of signs and of perceptual judgment, the New List is the culmination of a ten-year effort and the keystone of the American Academy series and indeed of Peirce's (early) philosophy as a whole. For some of its earlier stages, see the following items in *W*1: 3, 13, 14, 17, 18, 21, 27, 28, 33, 34,

37, 38, 40, 48, and 52. (See also Notes 11 and 12 in MS 152, item 7 below, p. 94.)

50.25, 30, 38 and 51.62 prescision] See Note 11 in MS 152 below, 94.1–4. The
    word *prescision* has been emended according to the note.
53.6–8   Empirical. . . .] Note 12 in MS 152 belongs here; see 94.5–7.
57n.1–5   Herbart, *Lehrbuch,* p. 77. (See also *W*1:484.)

> All our thoughts may be considered from two points of view; partly as activities
> of our mind, partly in relation to what is thought through them. In the latter
> respect they are called *concepts,* which term, by signifying *what is conceived,*
> requires us to abstract from the mode and manner in which we might receive,
> produce, or reproduce the thought.

Logic of Mathematics

Presented on 10 September 1867 by title only—did Peirce attend
a birthday-party instead, his own twenty-eighth?—the paper was
published in the *Proceedings of the American Academy of Arts and
Sciences* 7(1868):402–12. Peirce said in 1904 that "the curious contrast between all the operations of arithmetic when viewed mul-
titudinally and when viewed ordinally is . . . worth showing"; but also
that this is "by far the worst paper I ever published" and that "it is
now utterly unintelligible to me." (See Note 13 in MS 152, item 7
below, pp. 94–97.)

60.4–8   See item 2 above, pp. 12–23.
64.19–31   In order . . . stated above.] Note 13 in MS 152 belongs here; see
    94.8–97.24.
69n.3   with De Morgan] See De Morgan, *Formal Logic,* p. 59.

Logical Comprehension and Extension

This important paper was published in the *Proceedings of the
American Academy of Arts and Sciences* 7(1868):416–32. Peirce later
intended to use it, in modified form and with a new title ("Upon
Breadth and Depth"), as essay 3 of the 1893 "Search for a Method"
and as chapter 15 of the 1894 "How to Reason: A Critick of Argu-
ments." (The latter is now generally but falsely called the 'Grand
Logic'.) Volume 8 of the present edition will consist exclusively of
"How to Reason," including chapter 15 contained in Robin MS 421.
As that manuscript was not written until 1893, we disregard it for the

present. But Peirce set to reworking his fifth American Academy paper as early as the spring of 1870, in a notebook consisting of pasted-on parts of an offprint and numerous additions and annotations written in ink in the margins and on preceding and following blank pages. The relevant parts of this notebook, MS 170, are reproduced in the notes that follow.

70.7–11   "that the. . . ."] The actual citation begins with "distinction," and Peirce's "announced" is "enounced" in the original.

70.15–16   A German logician] Identified as Lotze in the left-hand margin in MS 170.

70.23–27   That work . . . Bible.] Written in the right-hand margin in MS 170, Peirce has the following as a note to this passage:

> See Boëthius page 645 toward the bottom. "Genus in divisione totum est, in diffinitione pars" etc.

70n.1–2   Peirce expands this note in MS 170, in two paragraphs written on the preceding and following versos.

> Aristotle remarks in several places that genera (and differences) may be regarded as parts of species and species as parts of genera. Thus in the 5th of Metaph (1023b22) he says: ἔτι τὰ ἐν τῷ λόγῳ τῷ δηλοῦντι ἕκαστον, καὶ ταῦτα μόρια τοῦ ὅλου. διὸ τὸ γένος τοῦ εἴδους καὶ μέρος λέγεται, ἄλλως δὲ τὸ εἶδος τοῦ γένους μέρος.
>
> The Greek commentator to whom Baynes refers may possibly be Alexander Aphrodisiensis who has the following:—ἔτι φησὶ τὰ ἐν τῷ λόγῳ τῷ δηλοῦντι ἕκαστον καὶ ταῦτα μόρια τοῦ ὅλου μέρη φησὶν εἶναι ἑκάστου, καὶ τὰ τοῦ λόγου τοῦ δηλοῦντος αὐτοῦ τὸ τί ἦν εἶναι μέρη. τὰ γὰρ μέρη τοῦ ὁρισμοῦ εἴη ἄν, ἀλλὰ παρὰ τοῦ εἴδους μέρη, ὅτι ὁ τοῦ συναμφοτέρου ὁρισμὸς κατὰ μὲν τὸ εἶδος γίνεται, προσσημαίνει μέντοι καὶ τὴν ὕλην, ὡς δῆλον εὐθὺς ἐκ τοῦ γένους οὕτω φησὶ γίνεσθαι μέρος τὸ γένος τοῦ εἴδους, ἐπεὶ μέρος ἐστὶ τοῦ ὁρισμοῦ αὐτοῦ. But there is nothing here not found in medieval writers of every age.

70n.3   Peirce expands this note in MS 170, in two paragraphs written on the preceding verso.

> The grand idea of the Isagoge of Porphyry is the discrimination of different kinds of predication. The conception of the Port-Royalists is the equivalence of all essential predicates and the fusion of genera and differences. Still, that does not prevent Porphyry's having this wider notion and he does have it.
>
> As early as Scotus Erigena we read of "ars illa quae dividit genera in species et species in genera resolvit."

71.15–19   "we owe . . . it."] The quotation appears on p. 114 of the Lectures. Hamilton has "come" instead of "came."

71n.1–2   3. The . . . wholes.] See *Ouvrages inédits d'Abélard*, p. 548.

71n.3   est, aliud] We have corrected the punctuation; the comma appears
after the second word in the *PAAAS*.

71n.3–5   "quod fere. . . ."] "that is well known to nearly everyone, namely
that what common names (appellativa) mean and what they name are
not identical. They name particular things, but their meaning is universal." (See 328.28–31 below.)

71n.5   In the left-hand margin in MS 170, Peirce adds the following:

> By appellativa are meant, as I take it, adjectives, and such like.

71n.7–10   "Si vero . . . subjectivam."] "If indeed it be asked whether this
universal 'man' is in any man whatever as a whole or in part, the answer
is as a whole, that is according to any definitive part of itself whatever.
. . . Not however according to any subjective part whatever."

71n.11–13   "totalitatem . . . partiuntur."] "the same whole, which consists
of parts of reason or of definition, and those parts are genus and differences; on the other hand, the parts are the individuals of the species,
because they in turn are always distributed into the species itself, when
it is predicated of them."

71n.13   partiuntur] We have corrected the nonsensical "partiunter" that
appears in the *PAAAS*.

71n.14   In the left-hand margin in MS 170, Peirce adds the following:

> See Also Duns Scotus Opera i.137 a secundum.

The final reference in the printed note is not quite clear, but presumably there were such commentaries on the first book of Aristotle's *Physics*.

71n.16   Peirce expands this note in MS 170, in a paragraph written on the
preceding verso.

> Descartes has the following "Etenim ad perceptionem cui certum et in-
> dubitatum judicium possit inniti, non modo requiritur ut sit clara, sed etiam ut
> sit distincta. Claram voco illam, quae menti attendenti praesens et aperta est;
> sicut ea clare a nobis videri dicimus, quae oculo intuenti praesentia, satis for-
> titur et aperte illum movent. Distinctam autem illam, quae, cum clara sit, ab
> omnibus aliis ita sejuncta est et praecisa, ut nihil plane aliud, quam quod claram
> est, in se contineat. Ita dum quis magnum aliquem sentit dolorem etc."

71n.17   Peirce expands this note in MS 170, in a paragraph written on the
preceding verso.

> Leibniz (Ed. Dutens vol 6. p 267) says "*M. Descartes* avoit déja remarqué,
> comme vous trouverez, qu'il y a difference entre les idées claires et distinctes
> . . . . . . il suffit qu'elles soient distinctes mais il ne suffit pas qu'elles soient claires
> au sens que M. Descartes prend ses termes et d'autres après lui."

In Dutens, and also in Gerhardt [3:223–24], Burnet is identified as
Thomas Burnett de Kemney, a Scottish nobleman; in a more recent
English edition of Leibnizian writings, as Thomas Burnet, or Burnett
(1635–1715), a Scots lawyer and divine.

72.12–13   *intension . . . comprehension;*] At the bottom of the page in MS
170, Peirce writes

But *intension* was so used by Leibnizians

72.33–73.6   Mill, *System of Logic,* 1:43n [b. 1, chap. 2, §5].

72n.1–2   Peirce expands this note in MS 170, in four paragraphs written at
the bottom of the page and on the preceding verso.

Thomas Aquinas (In sentent. 1.d.8.q 1 art 1) has the following. In secundum
dicendum quod ex creaturis contigit Deum nominari tripliciter. Uno modo
quando nomen ipsum actualiter connotat effectum in creatura propter relationem ad creaturam importatam in nomine, sicut Creator et Dominus.

Of *Connotare,* Morin says "On employait ce verbe pour indiquer la fonction
logique d'un terme qui en suppose un autre, comme, par example, l'accident
suppose le sujet."

Prantl notes upon *suppositum* "i.e. den abgeleiteten secundären Wortfor-
men."

Chauvin in his first ed. says "Connotativum illud est cujus significatum non
sistit in se, sed necessariò ad aliud refertur, vel aliud connotat: v.g. *Rex, magis-
ter, primus."* In his second edition, he says, "Connotare est praeter id, quod
directe sive in casu recto significatur, aliud quiddam indirecte sive in obliquo
importare: sicut *dives* in recto *hominem* in obliquo divitias."

Peirce bought Eustachius's *Summa* on 29 March 1867 and wrote on the
inside cover that "This is a valuable work for terminology." Eustachius,
or Eustace de St. Paul (1573–1640), was a French Cistercian scholar and
a friend of Pope Paul V.

73.9   But the celebrated Prantl] In the right-hand margin in MS 170, Peirce
adds

If I understand him. He expresses himself in his usual enigmatical style.

73.16   Written on the preceding verso in MS 170, Peirce has the following
as a note:

I do not undertake to state precisely what the conception of connotation
(which was a part of the doctrine of *appellatio*) actually was. That would
require too long an explanation.

73.20–38   Peirce has slightly rearranged the order here, for the last sentence should come at the beginning, followed by an ellipsis.

A connotative name, on the other hand, is one that signifies one thing primarily
and another thing secondarily. Connotative names have what is, in the strict

sense, called a nominal definition. In the nominal definition of a connotative term it is frequently necessary to put one expression in the nominative case and another in one of the oblique cases. The term 'white' provides an example. The term has a nominal definition, one expression of which is in the nominative case and another, in one of the oblique cases. Thus, if someone should ask for the nominal definition of 'white', the answer would be "something informed with whiteness" or "something having whiteness." It is clear that here we have one term in the nominative case and another in an oblique case. . . . All the concrete names functioning in the first way outlined are connotative terms, for all those concrete names signify something in the nominative case and something else in an oblique case; that is, in the nominal definition of those names, an expression signifying one thing is in the nominative case and an expression signifying something else is in one of the oblique cases. This is clear with names like the following: 'just', 'white', 'besouled', 'human', and with other such names as well. Likewise, all relative names are connotative, because in the definition of a relative name, there are different expressions which signify different things or the same thing in different modes. The name 'similar' provides an example. . . . Purely absolute names are those which do not signify something principally and another thing (or the same thing) secondarily. Rather, everything signified by an absolute name is signified primarily. The name 'animal' provides an example. (*Ockham's Theory of Terms*, pp. 70, 70–71, 69.)

73.35   We have added the ellipsis missing in the *PAAAS*. (See the beginning of the preceding editorial note.)

73n.3   Peirce expands this note in MS 170, in a paragraph written on the preceding verso.

> The *Summa* of Alexander of Ales was certainly written in the 13th century before 1280 because Roger Bacon refers to it at the same time that he says that Albert is alive. He says of Alexander. Ex suo ingressu (into the order) fratres et alii exultaverunt in coelum et ei dederunt auctoritatem totius studii et ascripserunt ei magnam summam illam, quae est plusquam pondus unius equi, quam ipse non fecit, sed alii, et tamen propter reverentiam ei ascripta fuit, et vocatur summa fratris Alexandri.

Peirce used the 1482 Nuremberg edition of Alexander's work; more usually, his name is given as Alexander de Hales, and sometimes as Alexander Alesius.

74.15–24   Peirce's references in this paragraph are to Rösling's *Lehren;* Überweg, *System der Logik,* §§50 and 53; Baumgarten, *Acroasis Logica,* §24; Fowler, *Elements,* p. 1, chap. 2; Spalding, *Introduction,* §§7, 30, 31; Shedden, *Elements,* p. 10; McGregor, *System of Logic,* p. 191; Jevons's *Pure Logic;* and De Morgan, *Syllabus,* §131. Christian Lebrecht Rösling (1774–1836) was a German logician and mathematician who wrote on logic, mechanics, and architecture. Thomas Shedden (fl. 1860), an Englishman, wrote three books on logic and philosophy.

74.25–27   "those attributes. . . ."] *Port-Royal Logic,* p. 49 [p. 1, chap. 6]. Peirce's "an idea" is "it" in the original.

74n.1   Tartaretus] Petrus Tartaretus (fl. end of 15th century), rector of the

University of Paris and a distinguished scholastic philosopher, wrote commentaries on Aristotle, Duns Scotus, and Petrus Hispanus.

74n.1–2   Peirce expands this note in MS 170, in two paragraphs written on the preceding verso.

> I copy here a part of Eck's remarks "Primo adverte duplicem esse terminum, scilicet absolutum et connotativum. Absolutus est qui sua significata aeque principaliter significat et in recto: ut elephas, cedrus. Vel est terminus qui nihil connotat. Connotativus est qui significat unum in recto et aliud in obliquo. Vel est qui ultra principale significatum aliquid connotat: ut *dulce* significat rem, puta lac vel pomum, et connotat dulcedinem. . . . . Secundo tunc mente, terminum connotativum habere duplex significatum: *formale,* quod in diffinitione quid nominis ponitur in obliquo, *materiale* quod in diffinitione quid nominis ponitur in recto . . ."
>
> Tartaretus speaks of connotative being. "Nulla relativa secundum se habent contrarium cum non sint qualitates primae; sed solum relativa secundum dici, et hoc secundum esse absolutum et significatum principale eorum et non secundum esse respectivum et connotativum." This, in my copy is misprinted *cognotativum* (fol 24a). In another place he has the following "Terminus absolutus est terminus qui nihil connotat, ut sunt termini praedicamenti substantiae. . . . sed connotativus est qui ultra illud pro quo supponit aliquid importat sub habitudine essentiali vel accidentali . . . et habet duplex significatum . . ." (fol 58d) In another place he has the following "Terminus connotativus habet duplex significatum, scilicet materiale et formale. . . . Formale est quod . . . connotat alteri adjacere *vel non adjacere. . . . Et adverte quod de connotatione termini diversitas est inter doctores. Dicunt enim aliqui quod terminus connotat significatum materiale et non formale.* Alii dicunt econtra . . ." (fols. 72. 73) Compare this with the statement I have quoted from Mill.

74n.3–5   The work referred to is Aquinas' opusculum 48, chap. 3, fol. 183a. "Every form having many things under it, that is which is taken universally, has a certain *latitude* (breadth); for it is found in many and predicated of many."

75.11–12   Gerlach and Sigwart] See Gerlach, *Grundriss,* §29, and Sigwart's *Handbuch.* Gottlieb Wilhelm Gerlach (1786–1864), a German librarian and philosopher, wrote numerous books on philosophy.

75.14–18   Peirce's references in this paragraph are to Drobisch, *Neue Darstellung,* §23; Bachmann, *System der Logik,* p. 1, §48; Trendelenburg, *Logische Untersuchungen,* pp. xv and 4; Shedden, *Elements,* pp. 10 and 39; Spalding, *Introduction,* §31; Devey, *Logic,* p. 42; De Morgan, *Syllabus,* §131; Jevons's *Pure Logic;* McGregor, *System of Logic,* p. 191; and Fowler, *Elements,* p. 1, chap. 2. Karl Friedrich Bachmann (1785–1855), a German philosopher, wrote on logic, especially that of Hegel. Joseph Devey (1825–1897), an English scholar, wrote books on Locke, logic, and several other subjects.

75.20–21   Shedden defines. . . .] Shedden, *Elements,* pp. 15–16 and 39–42.

75.31–32   "those *subjects.* . . ."] *Port-Royal Logic,* p. 49 [p. 1, chap. 6].

75.35–36   Watts . . . Fischer] See Watts, *Logick,* p. 1, chap. 1, §3; Fischer,

Lehrbuch, chap. 3, §37. Friedrich Fischer (1801–1853), a German philosopher, wrote many books on logic, philosophy, and psychology.

75n.1–2 Peirce expands this note in MS 170, in two paragraphs written on the preceding verso.

> Scotus thus explains the differences between virtual, habitual, and actual cognition:—"Quantum ad notitiam habitualem sive virtualem, primo expono quid intelligo per terminos. Habitualem notitiam voco, quando obiectum sic est praesens intellectui in ratione intelligibilis actu, ut intellectus statim possit habere actum elicitum circa illud objectum. Virtualem voco, quando aliquid intelligitur in aliquo, ut pars primi intellecti, non autem ut primum intellectum sive ut totale terminans intellectionem. Sicut, cum intelligitur homo, intelligitur animal in homine ut pars intellecti, non ut intellectum primum sive totale terminans intellectionem. Hoc satis proprie vocatur intellectum virtualiter. Quia est satis proximum intellectui in actu. Non enim esse posset actualius intellectum nisi esset propria intellectione intellectum, quae esset ipsius primi ut termini totalis." Tartaretus remarks "Breviter loquendo, notitia habitualis est memoria foecunda." (Reportata Ed. 1583 vol 1. p 147a)
>
> This distinction arose from a mixture of Aristoteleanism and Neo-Platonism. Aristotle distinguished actual and potential thought. Alexander Aphrodisiensis distinguished material intellect (νοῦς ὑλικός), habitual intellect (νοῦς κατὰ ἕξιν) and *intellectus adeptus* (νοῦς ἐπικτητός). These two distinctions have nothing to do with one another. They were nevertheless confounded by the Arabians and their confused doctrine suggested to Scotus his most philosophical division.

76.2 See Bachmann, *System der Logik,* p. 1, §48; Esser, *System der Logik,* p. 1, §34; and Schulze, *Grundsätze,* §29. Wilhelm Esser (1798–1854) was a German philosopher who wrote on logic, psychology, and moral philosophy.

76.7–18 For Peirce's references in this table, excluding those already cited above, see Kant, *Logik,* I, i, §§1–7; Reinhold, *Logik,* p. 115; Fries, *System der Logik,* §20; Bowen, *Treatise on Logic,* p. 67; De Morgan, *Formal Logic,* p. 234; Thomson, *Outline,* pp. 99–102; Mahan, *Intellectual Philosophy,* chap. 7 and 8; Herbart, *Lehrbuch,* II, i, §40; Vorländer, *Wissenschaft der Erkenntniss,* II, i, 2, b; Strümpell, *Entwurf,* chap. 4; and Ritter, *Abriss,* p. 79. Ernst Christian Gottlieb Reinhold (1793–1855), a German Kantian philosopher, wrote numerous works on philosophy and logic. Franz Vorländer (1806–1867) was a German philosopher who wrote on Schleiermacher and Hegel, as well as on ethics, epistemology, and jurisprudence. Ludwig Strümpell (1812–1899) wrote on his teacher Herbart and on Kant and Fichte, as well as on logic, ethics, religion, psychology, and several philosophical subjects.

76.12 In the right-hand margin in MS 170, Peirce adds "Arnauld" to Drobisch and De Morgan.

76.13 At the bottom of the page in MS 170, Peirce adds "Objects of perception ⸻ Baynes" to be inserted between 76.13 and 76.14.

76.22 Kiesewetter] See his *Grundriss,* pp. 26–29 and 86–92. Johann Gottfried Karl Christian Kiesewetter (1766–1819) was a German Kantian philosopher who wrote many books on philosophy and logic.

76.23   Duncan] William Duncan (1717–1760), whose *Elements of Logick* (1748) was many times reprinted.

76.23   At the end of the line in MS 170, Peirce adds "Beneke."

76.29   Peirce intended an additional paragraph here, written on the preceding verso in MS 170.

Dressler, following a hint from Beneke, distinguishes *real* and *ideal* extension and comprehension. I have not his book at hand but think they nearly correspond to my informed and essential breadth and depth. The law of Kant holds only for the ideal quantities.

76.34   Peirce intended an additional paragraph here, written on the preceding verso in MS 170.

Hoppe reverses the law of Kant and maintains that the wider the concept the greater its content. His idea, translated into Aristotelian phraseology, is this. He admits the second antepraedicamental rule, that the differences of different genera are different. (This, of itself, removes him widely from logicians for whom the distinction of comprehension and extension, is the turning-point of logic.) Negro is not a conception formed by the union of the two concepts *man* and *black*, but the peculiar differences of Negro belong to Negroes alone of all beings. This being so, he naturally proceeds a step further, and says that the difference is itself sufficient to constitute the pure concept, and that genus is in fact not an essential predicable. For, on his doctrine, *Negro-man* is a different concept from *Negro*, but no narrower. Thirdly, he finds that the characters of the narrower difference are fewer and less important (!) than those of the higher one—less *wirkungsreich*, and also fewer.

Janus Hoppe (fl. 1850) was a German author who wrote on logic and medicine.

76.35–77.1   Drobisch, *Neue Darstellung*, pp. 208–9; see also pp. 28–32 and 38–39.

77.2–6   Lotze, *Logik*, pp. 63–83 [p. 1, chap. 3].

77.13–23   It is . . . comprehension.] Vorländer, *Wissenschaft der Erkenntniss*, pp. 104–7.

78.4   less *extensive*] This is "more extensive" in De Morgan.

79.5–7   those things. . . .] In MS 170 Peirce has crossed out "not" both times, and in the left-hand margin has written "only" to replace the first "not."

79n.1–2   Peirce expands this note in MS 170, in a passage written on the preceding verso.

Scotus thus distinguishes extensive and comprehensive distinctness:—"Confusum idem est, quod indistinctum. Et sicut est duplex indistinguibilitas ad propositum scilicet totius essentialis in partes essentiales et totius universalis in partes subjectivas; ita est duplex distinctio duplicis totius praedicti ad suas partes."

The work referred to is Scotus's *In sententiarum.*

80.21–25   We may. . . .] In the right-hand margin in MS 170, Peirce writes

Did Aristotle call the negative term ἀόριστος because it has no ὁρισμός?

81.10–12   As Sir William Hamilton. . . .] The reference is given in the
left-hand margin in MS 170 as

Discussions. Am. Ed. p 630.

81.23–25   See Hamilton, *Lectures on Logic,* pp. 516–17.

81n.1   Peirce expands this note in MS 170, with the following quotation
written at the bottom of the page:

"Illud humanitatis quod in me est, non est illud humanitatis quod in te est."

82.26   In a paper . . . ,] The reference is to the "New List of Categories,"
item 4 above.

83.22   Peirce intended an additional paragraph here, written on the
preceding verso in MS 170.

Corresponding to increase of information in us there is a change in the
external world,—developement,—by which many things come to have many
characters involved in few.

83.30–38   This latter . . . it bounds.] This is the discussion of contradictories
referred to in Note 6 in MS 152 (93.4–6), which belongs with item 3
above (28.21).

86.28   Peirce adds a new, six-page section in MS 170, misnumbered because
sections 4 and 5 were both numbered "§4" in the original printing.

§6. *Of Natural Classification.*

Classes are divided into natural and artificial. This doctrine which is the
essense of the doctrine of the Predicables and which was implied in the system
of scholastic realism, which indeed it may be said to constitute, was thought of
little moment by the nominalists and finally slipped out of the logical treatises.
But the students of Botany and Zoölogy revived the conception, and have re-
established a doctrine of natural classes very similar to that of Aristotle, especially in the feature of ranging classes in a sort of hierarchy. The doctrine
of a hierarchy of classes is contained in the second antepraedicamental
rule: τῶν ἑτέρων γενῶν καὶ μὴ ὑπ᾽ἄλληλα τεταγμένων. ἕτεραι τῷ εἴδει
καὶ αἱ διαφοραί, οἷον ζῴον καὶ ἐπιστήμης. "The differences of different & not
subordinated genera are different."

This plainly forbids cross-classification and hence ranges classes in hierarchy.

I do not know that any successful attempt has hitherto been made to say
in what a *natural class* consists. In order to investigate the matter we may take
the two classes

Cows
& Red Cows.

The former is a natural class, the latter is not. Now one predicate more may be attached to Red Cows than to Cows; hence Mr. Mill's attempt to analyze the difference between natural & artificial classes is seen to be a failure. For, according to him, the difference is that a real kind is distinguished by unknown multitudes of properties while an artificial class has only a few determinate ones. Again there is an unusual degree of accordance among naturalists in making Vertebrates a natural class. Yet the number of predicates proper to it is comparatively small.

As Mr. Mill is an extremely popular writer and therefore numbers among his followers many men who have read but little else in logic & philosophy and who have therefore not acquired the calmness and impartiality of mind which comes from large reading, it is not to be expected that this objection to Mr. Mill's position will satisfy the smaller men among his followers. They will argue as though he were *creating* a distinction and not endeavoring to *analyze* one. He may have erected two classes of classes, but are they *real kinds* among classes, either according to an estimate formed after the manner of the naturalists, or *even according to his own definition?*

What are the innumerable properties or some of them, which belong to that class of classes which is defined as consisting of classes of which innumerable properties may be truly asserted?—to that class which includes trout, bees, cows whose tails are two feet 3 inches long, men with their hands behind their backs, &c and excludes vertebrates, radiates, mollusks, articulates, monocotyledonous plants, &c?

Why is *red cows* not a natural class, while *cows* is one? Because the former can be defined as the common extent of the classes *red* and *cows* and nothing can be universally predicated of *red cows* which is not predicable either of *red* or *cows;* whereas *cows* cannot be defined as the common extent of two or more classes such that nothing can be universally predicated of the former which is not predicable of one or other of the latter. In other words *cow* is a term which has an area; *red cow* has no area, except that area which every term has, namely that it excites a particular emotion in the mind.

I now propose to show by ocular demonstration that a class which has an area is one which is marked in nature, and that the more area it has, the more it is marked in nature.

Let the classes by defined thus
1 Circles not shaded
2 Circles shades
3 "   with a horizontal line across
4 "   without "   "   "
5 "   with a vertical line across
6 "   without "   "   "

Then follow one and one-half pages of variously marked circles arranged in three groups, entitled respectively "1st Case No class has an area," "2nd Case One class has a small area," and "3rd Case One class has a larger area." The remaining four pages of the notebook are covered with what appear to be neatly drawn doodles.

Notes

These notes to the first four of the five American Academy Series papers are very carefully written. There are a few minor revisions and corrections in the twenty pages of text. Not published here are four pages at the end of the manuscript, two of trial notations and two of an unfinished earlier version of part of the first note. Notes 1–5 belong with item 2 in the present volume; notes 6–10 with item 3; notes 11–12 with item 4; note 13 with item 5.

87.3–88.12   Note 1 belongs at the end of 15.30.
88.13–15   Note 2 belongs at the end of 16.6.
88.16–22   Note 3 belongs at the end of 19.2.
88.23–92.24   Note 4 belongs with 21.26–29 (Let *i* be . . . some *a*.).
92.1   Sophroniscus] Fifth-century Greek sculptor and father of Socrates.
93.1–3   Note 5 belongs at the end of 22.6.
93.4–6   Note 6 belongs at the end of 28.21. For the discussion of contradictories see 83.30–38 (This latter . . . it bounds.).
93.7–11   Note 7 belongs at the end of 31.22.
93.9–11   "If No B. . . ."] Aristotle, *Prior Analytics*, 1.2.25a15.
93.12–20   Note 8 belongs with 32.8–9 (There are . . . figures.).
93.21–23   Note 9 belongs with 32.10–14 (The short reduction . . . conclusion.).
93.22–23   The reference is to Aristotle's *Prior Analytics*, 1.6.
93.24–27   Note 10 belongs at the end of 35.34.
93.26   See 47.11 for Part III, §4.
94.1–4   Note 11 belongs with 50.25, 30, 38, and 51.6. The word *prescision* has been emended in the present volume.
94.5–7   Note 12 belongs with 53.6–8 (Empirical psychology. . . .).
94.8–97.24   Note 13 belongs with 64.19–31 (In order . . . as stated above.).

Venn's Logic of Chance

There is an unfinished and very short earlier version of this unsigned review in MS 141. The finished review is noteworthy for two reasons: it shows how Venn's book marks a major shift in probability theory—from the Laplacean to a frequency theory—and it gives, in embryonic form, the general outlines of Peirce's own dispositional relative frequency theory. (See the final paragraph and note in item 2 above, 22.31–23.3 and 23n.1–2.)

98.10–12 Mr. Venn . . . stages.] Venn, *Logic of Chance,* preface and chap. 1, §§1–3.

98.20 Bernouilli] Jakob (or Jacques) Bernoulli (1654–1705), Swiss mathematician and scientist, whose *Ars conjectandi*—published posthumously in 1713 and first translated into English in 1795—is one of the most important early works on the doctrine of chances; one of his doctrines is now known as Bernoulli's Law of High Numbers. Peirce got the less usual spelling of the name with the medial *i* from an errata list in Venn's book.

98.28 This is. . . .] The word *nominalistic* does not appear in Venn, who calls the view he maintains 'material' or 'phenomenalist'. Peirce says in MS 141 that "Mr. Venn's book is the most nominalistic of any which has yet appeared."

98.30–99.1 The theory. . . .] Mill, *System of Logic,* 2:62–78 [bk. 3, chap. 18].

99.6 Locke. . . .] This is in vol. 3 of Locke's *Essay.*

99.12 Bacon suggests] See the preface to his *Novum Organum.*

100.25–27 But Boole . . . independent,] Boole, *Laws of Thought,* chap. 17, §4.

100.28–29 Mr. Venn. . . .] Venn, *Logic of Chance,* chap. 7, §§6–8.

100.31–32 "applications. . . ."] Taken from the subtitle of Venn's book.

101.21–24 Hence. . . .] Venn, *Logic of Chance,* chap. 16, §6.

101n.1–9 Venn's analysis is indeed in error, but so is Peirce: both in his own analysis and in his cavalier waiver of objection to Venn's error. Peirce says the amount paid would be

$$\tfrac{1}{10}(c,\bar{e}) + \tfrac{9}{10}(\bar{c},e) + x(c,e), \text{ and } x \text{ is unknown.}$$

But the actual payment would be $x(c,\bar{e}) + y(\bar{c},e) + z(c,e)$ and x, y, and z are unknown. This is because the assumption of the problem says that 1/10 of the consumptives die and that 9/10 of the Englishmen die. These ought to be represented as

$$\tfrac{1}{10}[(c,e) + (c,\bar{e})] \text{ and } \tfrac{9}{10}[(c,e) + (\bar{c},e)].$$

If Peirce's formula were correct, x would have to be both 1/10 and 9/10. [Proof: If $\tfrac{1}{10}(c,\bar{e})$ die and $\tfrac{1}{10}[(c,e) + (c,\bar{e})]$ die, then $\tfrac{1}{10}(c,e)$ must die and $x = \tfrac{1}{10}$; but if $\tfrac{9}{10}(\bar{c},e)$ die and $\tfrac{9}{10}[(c,e) + (\bar{c},e)]$ die, then $x = \tfrac{9}{10}$.]

One, Two, and Three

This manuscript consists of (1) the five pages published here, bearing Peirce's page numbers in the upper right-hand corner; (2) two consecutive pages of an earlier variant with the same title (except for *and*); and (3) two single pages of yet earlier variants of parts of (2). The pages published here are carefully inscribed and contain but a few minor revisions. It is not known of which projected logic book this was to be the first chapter.

104.19–22   Thomas Gray, *Poetical Works,* p. 56 ["Elegy Written in a Country Churchyard," stanza 14].

Dictionary of Logic

Peirce's interest in lexicography was intimated in *W*1:17–19; here it finds its first extensive and detailed expression. Very neatly inscribed, the manuscript consists of a title page; a separate first page; thirteen folded sheets on whose inside versos and rectos are the definitions through 'abundant'; a single sheet of "List of words, beginning with AC"; and three large folded sheets containing the remainder of the text beginning with "Academic. A platonist." Four of the works used in preparing the dictionary (Stewart, Conimbricensis, Cousin, St. Anselm) are listed, but crossed out, at the top of the first page. "Wright's Copy of Wymans Pamphlet to be returned" appears in pencil in the lower center of the title page; in the upper right-hand corner Peirce has written in pencil, in large letters, "Dictionary."

105.18–21   Prantl shows. . . .] Prantl, *Geschichte,* 2:274–77.
105.22–106.2   Hamilton, *Discussions,* p. 619.
106.34   Hollmann] On the flyleaf of his copy of *Logica et philosophia prima,* Peirce wrote that Samuel Christian Hollmann was "born at Stettin 1696, taught in Greifswald, Jena, Wittenberg, and Göttingen, and died 1787. According to Bricker, his *Prima Philosophia* contains the best history of philosophy which his time possessed. He was an eclectic."
106.40   are] We have emended the nonsensical "and" in Peirce's manuscript.
107.13–16   "The rules. . . ."] Kant, *Werke,* 3:171.
107.17–25   "Although. . . ."] Ibid., 2:695, 696 [B1, 2].
107.27–28   The reference is to the first edition; *Werke,* 2:94.
107.29–31   Hamilton, *Metaphysics,* p. 285 [lect. 21]. Hamilton has "faculties of observation and thought."
107.32–36   The reference is to vol. 1 of *Opera philosophica.*
107.38   *Abdicatio* . . . Erigena.] Not located.
108.2–3   Peirce got the information from Prantl, *Geschichte,* 1:521 and 676; Appuleius is further discussed on pp. 580–81.
108.5–6   Julius Pacius, *Operum Aristotelis nova editio,* 1:171–72. An Italian philosopher who taught in France, Germany, and Italy, Giulio Pace (1550–1635) edited works by Aristotle and Raymond Lullius.
108.9–30   "Abduction. . . ."] Aristotle, *Prior Analytics,* 2.25.69a20–37.

109.3–6 Chauvin, *Lexicon rationale*, under *absens*. A French theologian and philosopher, Etienne Chauvin (1640–1725) left France for religious reasons and taught for many years in Rotterdam and Berlin. Not to be confused with Pierre Chauvin, whose *De religione naturali* is falsely attributed to Etienne Chauvin.

109.13–14 Burgersdicius, *Metaphysica*, p. 26.

109.22–27 Calderwood, *Philosophy of the Infinite*, pp. 36–37.

109.28–30 Mansel, *Philosophy of the Conditioned*, p. 66n, and *Limits*, pp. 75–77.

109.31–35 Hamilton, *Discussions*, p. 21n. (Hamilton's definition seems to come from Fleming's *Vocabulary.*)

109.36–110.4 Ibid.

110.5–6 Abbot, "The Conditioned and the Unconditioned," 417.

110.7–9 Fleming's quotation [*Vocabulary*, p. 2] is from Knox's preface. A British theologian and philosopher, William Fleming (1791–1866) wrote a manual of moral philosophy, a book on political economy, and the *Vocabulary*.

110.10–14 See 109.28–29 above.

110.15–18 Furtmair, *Real-Lexikon*, 1:11. Max Furtmair, who flourished in the first half of the nineteenth century, was a German aesthetician whose major work is the one here cited. His reference is to Carl Adolph von Eschenmayer (1768–1852), a German scholar who wrote numerous works on philosophy, religion, and psychology.

110.25–28 Burgersdicius, *Logica*, p. 80; see also *Metaphysica*, p. 198.

110.29–30 Chauvin, *Lexicon rationale*, under *affectio*. (Affection is here divided into absolute and respective.)

111.4–5 Kant, *Werke*, 4:53.

111.11–13 Hamilton, *Discussions*, p. 61; also in *Reid*, p. 749.

111.14–17 Schelling, *Ideen*, p. 56 [vol. 2 of *Werke*].

111.18–19 Burgersdicius, *Logica*, p. 133; see also *Metaphysica*, p. 208.

111.20–24 Chauvin, *Lexicon rationale*, under *independens*. (Independence is here divided into absolute and relative.)

111.25–26 Ibid., under *indivisible* (with a cross-reference to *atomus*).

111.29–30 Scotus. . . .] The reference is to the 1477 Venice edition.

112.3–4 Newton, *Principia*, 1:9 [#4].

112.10–11 Burgersdicius, *Logica*, p. 129; see also *Metaphysica*, p. 205.

112.13–14 "That to which. . . ."] Burgersdicius, *Metaphysica*, p. 223.

112.17–18 Newton, *Principia*, 1:9 [#3].

112.19–22 Hamilton, *Metaphysics*, p. 578.

112.27–29 Absolute principles. . . ."] Hamilton, *Logic*, p. 187.

112.30–32 Burgersdicius, *Logica*, p. 209. ("to which . . . the most" defines 'comparative problem'.)

112.34 *categorical proposition*] See Petrus Hispanus, *Summulae*, tract. 4.

112.35 Mocenicus] Phillippus Mocenicus of Venice, later archbishop of Nicosia, wrote numerous books; his major work is *Universales institutiones ad hominum perfectionem* (1581).

112.36–38 Kant, *Werke*, 2:44–45.

113.3 "to inquire. . . ."] Montaigne, *Works,* 2:207 ["Apology for Raimond Sebond"].

113.10–11 Kant, *Werke,* 3:262.

113.13 Seydel] A theologian and Schellingian philosopher, Rudolph Seydel (1835–1892) was professor of philosophy and comparative religion at Leipzig and the author of numerous books on religious and philosophical subjects.

113.14–15 Newton, *Principia,* 1:8–9 [#2].

113.16–18 Kant, *Werke,* 5:320.

113.19–20 See 74.1–3 above.

113.21–23 Newton, *Principia,* 1:8 [#1].

113.26–27 Überweg, *System der Logik,* p. 3.

113.28–30 Hamilton, *Metaphysics,* p. 15. Hamilton has "the name of absolute or General."

113.33 Kant, *Werke,* 3:265 [*Logik,* Einleitung at end].

113.34–39 Burgersdicius, *Metaphysica,* p. 196.

114.1–2 Kant, *Werke,* 2:24 [*Kritik,* A11].

114.3–5 Fleming, *Vocabulary,* p. 4. (The quotation is from bk. 3, chap. 16 of Elyot's *Governour.*)

114.20–115.3 Schmid, *Wörterbuch,* p. 21. A prolific German philosopher, Carl Christian Erhard Schmid (1761–1812) is best known for his lexicon of Kant.

115.11–18 Überweg, *System der Logik,* pp. 99–100.

115.19–21 Hegel, *Werke,* 18:5 [*Philosophische Propädeutik*].

115.28–116.3 Mill, *System of Logic,* 1:29 [bk. 1, chap. 2, §4].

116.4–6 Hamilton, *Logic,* p. 38. Peirce has added the definite article in "all the arts."

116.10–21 Kant, *Werke,* 1:312 [sec. 2, §6].

116.27 τὰ . . . ,] Aristotle, *Physics,* 190b7–8 ("the taking away or abstracting, as when from a rock a Hermes [is cut]").

116.31–32 "Intellectus . . ."] Duns Scotus, *Quaestiones quodlibetales,* qu. 13, art. 2, §2 ("Our intellect in knowing abstracts from the here-and-now").

116.32–34 "Prius cognoscit. . . ."] Vital du Four, *Quaestiones disputatae de rerum principio,* qu. 13, n. 44 ("The intellect knows the singular before the universal; for it is not possible that the universal abstract meaning from anything unless it knows beforehand that from which it abstracts"). A French Franciscan theologian and philosopher, Vital du Four (1260–1327) wrote numerous philosophical books and commentaries. His *De rerum principio* was formerly attributed to Duns Scotus; see vol. 3 of the Wadding edition.

116.38–117.2 Aristotle, *De anima,* 3.7.431b13, or *Metaphysics,* 11.3.1061a29.

117.16–18 The reference is to *In sententiarum* [in the Vatican *Ordinatio* edition, 7:553].

117.22 eclipse] We have corrected Peirce's misspelled "ecclipse."

117.29–30 *De intellectibus*] Attributed to Abelard.

117.30–32   Kant has. . . .] See 116.10–21 above.
117.35–37   Yet the two. . . .] See Hegel, *Werke*, 3:78 [*Logik*, bk. 1, sec. 1, chap. 1, B–C].
118.8–10   Chauvin, *Lexicon rationale*, under *absurditas*.
119.37–38   Aristotle, *Topics*, 1.5.102b4.
120.4–5   Not located in Ockham's *Summa*, though it might be read between the lines in chapters 25–26 of the first part. According to MS 91, 'accidental definition' is in "Eck, *In summulas*, fol. 59c, note 2."
120.12–32   See also *Logica*, pp. 25 and 62.
120.33–36   Esser, *System der Logik*, p. 194. Wilhelm Esser (1798–1854) was professor of philosophy in Münster and wrote works on logic, moral philosophy, and psychology.
120.37–39   Burgersdicius, *Metaphysica*, p. 237.
120.40–121.2   See Thomas of Erfurt, *Grammatica Speculativa* (1972), from chapter 7 on.
121.3–5   Burgersdicius, *Metaphysica*, p. 225.
121.6–11   See Thomas Aquinas, *Opuscula*, fol. 183 [opusculum 48, chap. 6, col. 2]. Prantl, who calls him Pseudo-Thomas, suggests that several of the *opuscula* that were once attributed to Thomas Aquinas were in fact written by someone who defended Thomistic doctrines against attack.
121.13   Hamilton, *Metaphysics*, pp. 105–6.
121.15–17   "Accidental supposition. . . ."] Petrus Hispanus, *Summulae*, tract. 6 [par. 4]; see Bocheński, p. 58.
121.16   its] We have emended the nonsensical "it" in Peirce's manuscript.
121.18–20   "The supposition. . . ."] Eck, *In summulas*, fol. 86a.

Critique of Positivism

This interesting treatment of positivism is written on both sides of nine sheets; the outline at the beginning appears on the recto of a separate sheet. The manuscript is carefully inscribed, though there are some revisions and corrections. Sometime after its composition, which may have been as early as the spring of 1867, Peirce underlined in red ink the word *metaphysician* and all sentences, clauses, and phrases appearing in italics in the printed text. Page numbers in the upper right- and left-corners of the manuscript are not Peirce's.

123.1–4   This was. . . .] Peirce may be referring to F. E. Abbot's "Positivism in Theology," published in the March 1866 *Christian Examiner*.
125.38–126.1   Bernardus . . . corruptam"] Bernard of Chartres (d. 1130), none of whose writings survives, is quoted in John of Salisbury, *Metalogicus*, p. 134 [bk. 3, chap. 2] ("that whiteness signifies an undefiled virgin, 'is white' the virgin entering the bedroom or lying down on a sofa, and 'white' the girl herself after having been defiled"). Peirce probably found the quotation in Prantl, *Geschichte*, 2:126n93.

125.40   eandem introeuntem] We have corrected Peirce's inaccurate "eam introentem."

126.2–4   It is true. . . .] Peirce may be referring to F. E. Abbot or to John Fiske.

Harris's Janet and Hegel

The following six items represent an exchange between Peirce and W. T. Harris, founding editor of the *Journal of Speculative Philosophy,* on issues of logic and speculative metaphysics emerging from the philosophy and logic of Hegel. Occasioned by "Paul Janet and Hegel," and marked by Harris's sympathy with the dialectical logic of the Hegelian tradition and by Peirce's own employment of ordinary formal logic, the exchange consists entirely of letters. Harris transformed two of Peirce's letters into dialectically structured discussion articles and published them in his journal as "Nominalism *versus* Realism" and "What Is Meant by 'Determined'." In the last letter in the exchange, Peirce responds to Harris's request for something for his journal dealing with the rationale of the objective validity of the laws of logic, which request led to three of Peirce's most important publications (see items 21–23 below). In other words, the Peirce-Harris exchange on Hegel led directly to the so-called *Journal of Speculative Philosophy* series. Though only a single letter from Harris to Peirce survives, there are twenty letters from Peirce to Harris, dated between 1 January 1868 and 8 December 1869. The latter are deposited in the W. T. Harris collection in the Hoose Library of the School of Philosophy of the University of Southern California in Los Angeles. The letters included in the present volume are reprinted by permission of the Hoose Library; for further letters, see the *Personalist* 43(1962):35–45.

132.20   Bénard] Charles Magloire Bénard (1807–1898).

132.22   Vera] Augusto Vera (1813–1885).

133.7   Seelye] Julius Hawley Seelye (1824–1895).

133.19   Morell] John Daniel Morell (1816–1891).

134.32–36   Sir William Hamilton. . . .] Hamilton, *Reid,* p. 129n.

135.6–7   *to think . . . Him;*] Hamilton, *Discussions,* pp. 20–21.

136.8–10   He traces . . . Scotch."] Janet, *Etudes,* pp. 298–300.

136.27–30   "Hegel has . . . *thought,"*] Ibid., pp. 305–6.

137.25–27   "The principal . . . system."] Ibid., p. 306.

137.26–27   *The . . . Reason*] The title of Kant's work is not italicized in Harris's article.

137.32–33   "Kant sees. . . ."] Ibid., pp. 307–8.
137.33–36   This he says . . . experience"!] Ibid., p. 309.
138.6–14   This syllogism . . . *experience.*] Ibid., pp. 310–14.
138.16–18   "the determined . . . knowing!"] Ibid., p. 317.
138.37–38   "The pure. . . ."] Ibid., p. 318.
140.2   (p. 340)] The reference is to Janet's *Etudes.*
140.4–21   Both citations are from the work and section given in 140.8.
140.22–24   "Such . . . Hegel."] Janet, *Etudes,* p. 341.
142.8–9   *"Du gleichst. . . .*] Goethe, *Faust,* I:512–13 ("You are like the spirit you comprehend,/Not me").
142.15   "What need . . . Nature?"] Janet, *Etudes,* p. 375.
142.25–26   "But in Plato. . . ."] Ibid., pp. 386–87.

Peirce to Harris, 1/24/1868

This letter is particularly important in that it contained what Harris, adding his own replies and commentary, published in his journal as "Nominalism *versus* Realism," the very next item in the present volume.

144.6   The missing text, indicated by ellipsis in italic brackets, appears as Peirce's part in the immediately following item.

Nominalism versus Realism

In his letter of 24 January 1868, Peirce had taken issue with Harris's account of the Hegelian relation of Being and Nothing as presented in "Paul Janet and Hegel," item 12 above. Harris took parts of Peirce's letter, added his own replies and commentary, provided the title, and published all that in his journal.

144.20–32   This editorial note is by Harris, and the reference at the beginning is to his "Paul Janet and Hegel," item 12 above.
145.1   The salutation is by Harris, not Peirce.
146.14–15   "whose extension . . . ,"] Harris is quoting Peirce; see 145.8–9.
149.7–9   (See chapter. . . .)] Harris's "Introduction to Philosophy" was a regular feature of the *Journal of Speculative Philosophy* from its inception. Marietta Kies compiled a number of chapters of these Introductions and published them in 1889 as *Introduction to the Study of Philosophy.*
150.7–8   for Albertus . . . effect] Albertus Magnus, *Commentarii,* p. 256 [dist. 8, art. 25].

153.1–3 "The self. . . ."] Not located.
153.3 "When me . . . Brahma] See stanza 3, line 2 in "Brahma," a poem by Emerson.

Peirce to Harris, 3/16/1868

This letter is interesting because of its "two unimportant errata" and because it shows Peirce's early interest in political economy or mathematical economics.

154.10 the proof sheets] Proof-sheets of "Nominalism *versus* Realism," the immediately preceding item here.
154.16 your own statement on p. 117] The reference is to chapter 3 of Harris's "Introduction to Philosophy" in volume 1 of his journal. See also 157.23–25.
154.24–27 Harris must have received Peirce's letter too late, for the errata remain in "Nominalism *versus* Realism" as published in the *Journal of Speculative Philosophy.*
154.28 Mr. Kroeger's pamphlet] The reference is to *Our Form of Government and the Problems of the Future* (1862), by Adolph Ernst Kroeger (1837–1882), a journalist and city official in St. Louis and a minor figure in the Philosophical Society there.

What Is Meant by "Determined"

Peirce thought that Harris had quite missed the point in his replies in "Nominalism *versus* Realism"—due probably to unclarities regarding the term 'determined'—and therefore sent further remarks in a letter toward the end of April 1868. Harris took Peirce's letter, added his own replies (in editorial footnotes), provided the title, and published all that in his journal.

155.11–15 This editorial note is by Harris, who gives an inaccurate title to the earlier discussion.
155.16 The salutation is by Harris, not Peirce.
156.31 Hegel's *Werke.* . . .] The reference is to the second edition of the first volume of three of Hegel's *Wissenschaft der Logik* [p. 113 in the first edition]. Peirce owned a complete set of Hegel's *Werke: Vollständige Ausgabe,* but some volumes were from the first, others from the second edition.
157.16–17 Trendelenburg . . . note;] Verified in fifth edition, pp. 112–13.
157n.1–7 The passage . . . of all.] In a letter of 12/10/1867, Harris told

Peirce that in that chapter he "discussed a problem that is related to the one you discuss in" the "New List of Categories."

157n.7–8   Just as . . . sees;] See W1:156–58.

158n.9   older than Plato] The reference is probably to Heraclitus.

Peirce to Harris, 4/9/1868

This letter antedates the one incorporated in the immediately preceding item, but it is placed here because it serves as a good transition or introduction to the so-called Journal of Speculative Philosophy Series. The overriding focus or concern of the series is here announced as "the rationale of the objective validity of logical laws." Also interesting is Peirce's remark that he prefers Harris's journal to other periodicals and the *Proceedings* of the American Academy of Arts and Sciences.

158.16   two letters] These have not been found.

158.17–18   your printed reply to my letter] The reference is to "Nominalism *versus* Realism," item 14 above.

159.2   three articles] See items 21–23 below.

159.6–9   I should cut . . . digression.] The page references are to Peirce's manuscript, which is no longer extant. Obviously Harris was not bothered by the digression or the long footnote, for he published both; see 197.37–199.31 for the passage, and note 4 on pp. 199–200 for the long footnote.

Questions on Reality

Occasioned by the Peirce-Harris exchange on Hegel, the *Journal of Speculative Philosophy* series consists of the six items that follow, especially the three published papers on cognition and reality that have been considered the key to Peirce's overall philosophical orientation. As it is our policy to leave series of papers intact, the order of the six items is not entirely chronological. It might be well to read them in the following order: 18, 21, 19, 20, 22, 23. An early version of the first of the three published papers, item 18 is an heroic attempt to treat in a unified way all the issues that were eventually divided among the three *JSP* papers. It treats cognition, truth and reality, and finally some issues of formal logic. MS 148 consists of four sections, the first three of which are published here: (1) one folded sheet with two pages of the outline of twelve questions; (2) two folded sheets with three pages of text on questions 6, 7, and 8; (3) three sheets, with one page of text each, numbered 1 through 3 in the upper right-hand corner; eight large folded sheets, with thirty-two pages of text, numbered 4 through 10 in the upper right-hand corner of the first recto —page numbers 11 through 14 are by a later reader of the manuscript—one folded sheet, with text on one recto and verso only; and two large folded sheets, with eight pages of text—there are forty-five pages of text in all; and (4) one folded sheet and three single sheets, with six pages of text, none of them consecutive. The pages in this last section represent discarded earlier variants of parts of the third section. The three sections of the manuscript published here are carefully inscribed, with only occasional revisions and corrections, both in ink and pencil.

166.4–5   the truth . . . inference,] Berengarius, *De sacra coena*, pp. 100–101. Peirce probably got this information from Prantl, *Geschichte*, 2:72–75.

167.28–32   It has. . . .] See Kant, *Werke*, 7 (2):11–12 [*Anthropologische Didaktik*].

172.38   Thought. . . .] Plato, *Works*, 1:428–29 [*Theaetetus*, 189E] and 3:178 [*Sophist*, 262E].

184.7   Herbart's explanation] Herbart, *Lehrbuch*, p. 230 [p. 4, chap. 3, §139].

185.2–6   Mill . . . term,] Mill, *System of Logic*, 1:188ff. [b. 2, chaps. 2 and 3].

185.12–13   Leibnitz. . . .] In his letter to Burnet; see 71.22–24 above.

Potentia ex Impotentia

This interesting manuscript consists of two variants, the first of three and the second of six pages. (Page numbers in the top right corner of the manuscript, running from 1 to 9, are not by Peirce.) Written in August or September of 1868, with many revisions and crossed out and rewritten sections, they represent two early versions of item 22, the second of the three *JSP* articles. In the first, Peirce says that philosophizing should be consonant with our common-sense ways of dealing with the world about us; in the second, he emphasizes that probable forms of reasoning, which have been so fruitful in the physical sciences, might enable us to reduce the uncertainties of metaphysics. This same speculative spirit pervades the sweeping theory of mental activity articulated in the final version of the second *JSP* article. The meaning of the title might be that from our *not* having the faculties the first article argued we did not have, it follows that we *do* have a faculty previously denied, namely that of knowing the very things themselves.

187.16–17   In the last . . . man."] See item 21 below, pp. 193–211.
189.6–7   To attempt . . . done,] Peirce's reference is to Hegel's 'objective method' as described in the preface to the *Phenomenology of the Mind* or in *Wissenschaft der Logik,* p. 1, b. 1 [*Werke,* 3:59–79].
190.9–23   It was. . . .] See item 21 below, pp. 193–211.
191.7   Here follows an interesting paragraph in the manuscript, which Peirce however deleted.

> The first consequence is a very obvious one. If we can not only have no knowledge of things-in-themselves as the sceptics and critics maintain, but cannot even conceive of them at all, so the word is simply devoid of meaning, then they do not exist, and consequently we can attain to a knowledge of the very things themselves. So that by simply denying to man one more faculty we restore (practically) to him the most important of those of which he he has been stripped by scepticism.

Peirce to Harris, 11/30/1868

This letter is somewhat out of place here, for while it properly follows item 19, it should precede item 22 rather than item 21; but the series of three published articles (items 21–23) was to be left intact. The letter is reprinted by permission of the Hoose Library of the University of Southern California.

192.5   two proof-sheets] Proof-sheets of item 22, "Some Consequences of Four Incapacities."
192.7–8   paragraph referring to Hegelians] As there is neither manuscript nor printer's copy for the second of the three published articles, we can only guess at the content of this paragraph on Hegelians.
192.16   your remark] Harris's remark, which came with the proof-sheets of the second article, does not survive.

Questions Concerning Certain Faculties

According to the last letter in the Peirce-Harris exchange on Hegel, Peirce sent this paper to Harris on 9 April 1868. In 1893 he intended to use the three *Journal of Speculative Philosophy* papers as essays 4, 5, and 6 of his "Search for a Method," and in 1904 he said that in them he "endeavored to prove and to trace the consequences of certain propositions in epistemology tending toward the recognition of the reality of continuity and of generality and going to show the absurdity of individualism and of egoism." The thrust of the three papers is, their titles notwithstanding, primarily metaphysical.

193n.1–5   The word . . . *intuition.*] Anselm, *Monologium,* pp. 89–90, 95 [chaps. 66, 70]. The saying of St. Paul ("For now we see in a mirror, darkly; but then face to face"), which Peirce quotes from the Vulgate, is in 1 Cor. 13:12.

195n.1–5   The proposition . . . *dei."*] Berengarius, *De sacra coena,* p. 101; quoted in Prantl, *Geschichte,* 2:72–75. ("Clearly it is characteristic of a great soul to take refuge in dialectic in all circumstances, because to take refuge in it is to take refuge in reason, and whoever does not take refuge there, since it is in respect of reason that he is made in the image of God, gives up his honor; nor can he be renewed from day to day in the image of God.")

195n.6–10   When Fredegisus. . . .] Peirce read this in Prantl, *Geschichte,* 2:17–19. Fredegisus (d. 834) was an English monk and Alcuin's successor at the court of Charlemagne; his best-known work is *De nihilo et tenebris.*

195n.10–12   Abelard. . . .] Abelard, *Ouvrages inédits,* p. 179.

195n.12–19   The author . . . *exceptis.*] See *De generibus et speciebus,* pp. 528, 517, 535.

195n.23–25   *"Sunt et. . . ."*] John of Salisbury, *Metalogicus,* p. 213 [bk. 4, chap. 27]. ("Although there are many mistakes in Aristotle, as is evident from the writings of Christians and pagans alike, his equal in logic has yet to be found.")

195n.25–27   *"Sed nihil . . . recepimus?"*] Abelard, *Ouvrages inédits,* pp. 293, 204. ("But nothing against Aristotle," and "But if we can find fault with Aristotle the prince of the Peripatetics, what *can* we trust in this art?")

196.4   McAlister] Almost certainly the reference is to J. M. Macallister, a New England magican.

199n.1   See pp. 50–51 above.

208.24–25   Berkeley . . . seeing,] See Berkeley, *Principles of Human Knowledge,* §§1–6.

Consequences of Four Incapacities

This second of the three *Journal of Speculative Philosophy* papers, which Peirce sent to Harris toward the end of October of 1868, begins by formulating the "spirit of Cartesianism" in four points and then contrasts them to four points of what Peirce later called 'critical common-sensism'. The paper, which with the "New List of Categories" (item 4 above) is one of his two "strongest philosophical works," ends with the first published declaration of Peirce's scholastic realism.

213.15–17   In the last. . . .] See the immediately preceding item in the present volume.

217.33–35   induction. . . .] Aristotle, *Prior Analytics*, 68b15–17 or 69a16–19, for examples.

218n.1–2   Several. . . .] There is no such published objection, but people like Chauncey Wright or F. E. Abbot might have objected to Peirce's argument after presentation of his "Classification of Arguments" (item 3 above) before the American Academy of Arts and Sciences.

218n.6–7   D. Stewart. . . .] This is the second volume of Stewart's *Elements . . . of the Human Mind*, where (pp. 305–16) in addition to the four authors mentioned, he also discusses Bacon, Fontenelle, D'Alembert, Reid, and Prevost.

218n.9–10   Aristotle. . . .] Aristotle, *Posterior Analytics*, 1.2.72a15.

218n.16   *Synopsis* of Psellus] Peirce did not know that this is a translation, by George Scholarios (1400–1464), of the *Summulae* of Petrus Hispanus.

219n.6–11   "An hypothesis is a proposition that is assumed in order to test the truth of what is not yet known to be true. Many demand that for an hypothesis to be identified as being true, no matter how true it appears before, other things must be deducible from it. But others say that for an hypothesis to be true, this one thing is required; namely, that such things must be deducible from it as correspond to phenomena and as satisfy all the difficulties encountered, on the one hand, in the thing itself and, on the other, in such as arise from it."

219n.7   probandam] We have corrected the inaccurate "probandum" that appears in the *JSP.*

219n.12–17   From Newton's "General Scholium" [*Principia,* 2:201–2]: "I have thus far explained the phenomena of the heavens and sea by the force of gravity, but have not yet assigned the cause of gravity. . . . I have not yet been able to deduce from the phenomena the reason for these properties of gravity, and I do not invent hypotheses. Whatever cannot be deduced from the phenomena should be called an *hypothesis.* . . . In this philosophy, propositions are deduced from phenomena and are rendered general by induction."

219n.26   provisionally] In the original, this is "provisorily."

219n.44   Jäsche] Gottlieb Benjamin Jäsche (1762–1842), German philosopher and theologian who, upon Kant's recommendation, edited the latter's *Logik* (1800).

219n.49   *Einleitung*] Peirce's short title for Herbart's *Lehrbuch zur Einleitung in die Philosophie.*

226n.1–3   See item 6 above, pp. 70–86.

227n.3–4   See item 4 above, pp. 49–59.

233.14   Hermolaus Barbarus] Or Ermolao Barbaro (1454–1493), Italian poet and savant and translator of Aristotle.

233.19–21 "must be. . . ."] Berkeley, *Works* (1843), 1:76 [*Principles of Human Knowledge,* §10 of introduction].

233.23–26 No statement. . . .] See Locke, *Human Understanding,* pp. 82–83 [vol. 3, b. 4, chap. 7, §9].

233.40–234.2 "The colors. . . ."] Hume, *Enquiry,* p. 29 [p. 18 in Selby-Bigge]. Peirce's "the memory" is "it" in the original, and "compared with" is "in comparison of."

234n.15–19 "to include. . . ."] Mansel, *Prolegomena,* p. 9n. Peirce's "space and time" is "space or time" in the original.

234n.19–20 we have . . . *Intuitus;*] In Kant's doctoral dissertation, *De mundi sensibilis atque intelligibilis forma et principiis* [*Werke,* 1: 301–41].

240n.1–3 "It is the same nature that in existence is determinate through the grade of singularity and that in the intellect, that is as having to the intellect the relation of known to knower, is indeterminate."

240n.4 See *Ockham's Theory of Terms,* pp. 82–84.

242.4–6 Shakespeare, *Measure for Measure,* 2.2.117–20. As usual, Peirce leaves out line 118 ("Drest in a little brief authority").

Validity of the Laws of Logic

Written between 5 and 20 December 1868, this third and most important of the three *Journal of Speculative Philosophy* papers comes to grips with the issue initially proposed by Harris—the rationale for the objective validity of the laws of logic—and in the process articulates a theory of truth and reality. This is also the first of Peirce's writings containing a reference to De Morgan's paper on the logic of relations.

242.11 an article . . . Journal,] The reference is to the immediately preceding item in the present volume.

243.5–6 having put . . . research,] See items 14, 16, 21, and 22 in the present volume.

243n.3–4 *Significatio* is. . . ."] Petrus Hispanus, *Summulae,* tract. 6 (signification is "the representation, established by convention, of a thing by an utterance").

243n.7–244n.1 "Unde significatio. . . ."] Ibid. ("Signification is thus prior to supposition, and they differ in that signification belongs to the word, whereas supposition belongs to the term already composed of the word and its signification").

244.10–11 in the article. . . .] See editorial note 242.11 above.

245n.1–4 The quotation appears on page 337 of De Morgan's paper. Peirce's "ordinary" is "such" in the original.

247.32–33 in an article. . . .] See editorial note 242.11 above.

248n.1 See Mill, *System of Logic,* 1:204 [b. 2, chap. 3].

249.3–6 Swift, *Gulliver's Travels,* p. 322 [b. 3].

250.18   Hegel taught. . . .] The idea is expressed in several places, as for example in *Werke*, 5:124 [*Wissenschaft der Logik*, p. 2, sec. 1, chap. 3]; see 252n.1–3.

252.10–254.9   Of this. . . .] See Hegel, *Werke*, 5:118–71.

252n.1–3   The reference is to the second edition [pp. 127–8 in first edition].

254.32–255.13   Zeno's arguments. . . .] See Aristotle, *Physics*, 6.9.239b5, or Plutarch, *Moralia*, 6:167 [chap. 43].

256.8–11   Another . . . moves.] Ibid.

261n.13–14   Hobbes. . . .] Hobbes, *Leviathan*, p. 85 [chap. 11]. In MS 199, to be published in volume 3 of the present edition, Peirce puts it thus: "no man can act otherwise than for the sake of pleasure."

263n.2   *Pauli*. . . .] Sophism 50 is the last in the book, which Peirce acquired on 20 May 1867. On the inside cover, he wrote that Paulus Venetus (or Paul of Venice) "studied in Oxford in 1390, and also in Padua, was Doctor of Theology and Philosophy in the latter university in 1408 and of Medicine and Logic in 1411, in 1422 was Doctor at Sienna, in 1423 was Rector of the university in Perugia, and died at Padua in 1429. He wrote many works on Logic. This is the first & only edition of the present work."

263n.3–4   *Sophistici Elenchi*, cap. 25.] 180a23–180b39 in Bekker.

266n.5   in] We have restored this word that, for whatever reason, was left out in the *JSP*.

266n.9–12   The remainder of the paragraph reads thus: "if a human being were miraculously kept alive to witness this change, he surely would soon cease to believe in any uniformity, the uniformity itself no longer existing. If this be admitted, the belief in uniformity either is not an instinct, or it is an instinct conquerable, like all other instincts, by acquired knowledge."

267.32–268.1   "How are . . . ?"] Kant, *Werke*, 2:705 [*Critique*, B19].

270.33–34   What shall . . . soul?] See Matthew 16:26, Mark 8:36, or Luke 9:25.

Porter's Human Intellect

Haskell's *Index to the Nation* identifies Peirce as the author of this unsigned review of Porter's very highly regarded and influential book.

273.14–16   "is somewhat. . . ."] Porter, *Human Intellect*, p. i.

275.3–5   Either. . . .] See Hamilton, *Reid*, pp. 804ff.

277.17–23   The Thomistic . . . itself.] See Thomas Aquinas, *Summa theologica*, 1.1 [qu. 3, art. 2].

277.23–37   Scotus . . . thing.] This is an excellent summary of Scotus's basic position as expressed in *Quaestiones subtilissimae super libros metaphysicorum Aristotelis*, b. 7, qu. 18 [Vivès, 7:452–61] or in *Ordinatio*, b. 2, dist. 3, p. 1, qu. 1–6 [Vatican, 7:391–494].

277.39   Occam's attack] The reference is to Ockham's *Scriptum in librum*

primum sententiarum Ordinatio, dist. 2, qu. 6, where he summarizes
the extended argument of Scotus's *Ordinatio.*

278.11–12   to what . . . know] These are Porter's words: "The facts which
the philosopher seeks to discover are the facts or phenomena which are
common to all men, and of which all men are actually conscious."

278.26–27   "Should you. . . ."] Not located.

278.28–30   "to hope . . . states,"] Porter, *Human Intellect,* p. 118.

279.12–13   "entirely. . . ."] Ibid., p. 481.

279.16–22   These intuitions. . . .] Ibid., pp. 482–92.

279.24–25   "not . . . processes,"] Ibid., p. 499. The original reads, after the
first comma, "but they are *involved in* these processes."

Pairing of the Elements

Peirce's authorship of this unsigned letter to the editor is
confirmed by a report in the 11 September 1869 *Scientific American.*
The title is no doubt the editor's. Not printed here are two paragraphs that precede, and three that follow, Peirce's letter in the
Chemical News. The table of Perissads and Artiads is inserted toward
the end of the final editorial paragraph.

282.1   The two editorial paragraphs between title and the beginning of
Peirce's letter:

> The table of paired elements which appeared in the April *Supplement,* and
> the remarks we made about it in the May *Supplement,* have attracted consider-
> able attention among those who are interested in chemical philosophy. The
> prevailing opinion appears to be that the pairing, which at present may not be
> regarded as anything beyond a curious fact, may be found at last to be allied
> or dependent upon some as yet undefined law of matter.
>
> Of the letters which we have received upon the subject, the following is the
> most important.

282.3–4   Your remarks . . . News] One of these remarks was Charles A.
Seeley's "The Numerical Relations of Atoms, New Elements Predicted." His basic idea was that in most cases a given element has a
partner of about the same atomic weight, having a different atomicity
but similar properties.

282.4   enclosed table] Peirce did not hit upon the periodic table discovered
by Dmitri Mendeleyev in 1869, but his own table was one of the best
for its time, and it shows that he was working along the same lines as
the Russian chemist. Mendeleyev's Groups II, III, V, and VIII ([Li, Na,
K . . .], [. . . Mg, Ca, . . . Sr . . .], [C, Si, Ti . . .], and [Fl, Cl, Br . . .]) are
the same as the groups in Peirce's table as we read up along ordinates.
Both Peirce and Mendeleyev were probably influenced by Jean Bap-
tiste Dumas's work on triads, homologous series, and parallelism. Like
Dumas, William Odling had worked on natural chemical triads; but

unlike Dumas, he had emphasized the twinning of elements. That may have inspired Peirce to concentrate on the pairing of the elements.

283.11   Here follow three editorial paragraphs. The first indicates that Peirce's table was drawn on engineers' profile paper and is thus "easier to be understood and to be verified than the engraving" in the *Chemical News*. (On the next page Peirce's table is reproduced as it would have appeared on engineers' profile paper rather than on the unlined —and thus difficult to verify—*Chemical News* engraving.) The second reads as follows:

> Our correspondent's table, besides being a very admirable exposition of the facts of pairing, at the same time illustrates almost everything of value which has been written on the classification of the elements and the numerical relations of the atomic weights. It will well repay a careful study.

The final paragraph remarks upon the probable number of elements, cites William Odling, and concludes with this sentence: "If it be determined that the pairing is an order of nature, and that the known elements are nearly all paired, and that the known groups appear filled, we ought not to expect many new elements."

284.table   Mg appears twice under Artiads, though one should probably be Al (Aluminum). It is not known whether the error is Peirce's or the editor's.

Roscoe's Spectrum Analysis

Haskell's *Index to the Nation* identifies Peirce as the author of this unsigned review. Sir Henry Enfield Roscoe (1833–1915) was a famous chemist who worked for a time with Bunsen in Germany.

288.2–5   In addition . . . spring,] The most notable scientific observations made by Peirce on a single occasion, and his earliest single-handed scientific achievement, took place on 15 April 1869 when he observed the auroral spectrum with the large telescope of the Harvard Observatory and determined the places of seven lines. (See also P 36, not printed here.)

288.20–21   "serve. . . ."] Roscoe, *Spectrum Analysis*, p. vi.

288.26   Thalén] (Tobias) Robert Thalén (1827–1905), a Swedish physicist best known for his work on magnetism and the wave-length of light.

288.31   Dr. Gibbs's] Oliver Wolcott Gibbs's.

Solar Eclipse

Peirce's letter is addressed not, as one might expect, to Benjamin Peirce, who served as superintendent of the Coast Survey from 1867 to 1874, but to Joseph Winlock, director of the Harvard Observatory, under whose direction Peirce worked from 1869 to 1875. The letter was not published until 1872—all *Coast Survey Reports* appeared two or three years after the year reported—by which time Peirce had already seen his second total solar eclipse. (See P 76, not published here.) In 1895 he remembered his first eclipse and the first time he saw helium:

> I remember, as if it were yesterday, the first time I saw helium. It was in 1869. Astronomical spectroscopy was then in its earliest infancy. There was to be a total eclipse of the sun. Such events were, in those days, of great importance for fixing the longitude; and I, as an employee of the Coast Survey, was ordered to Kentucky to observe the eclipse. There were not very many men in those days who were proficient, at once with the astronomical telescope and with the spectroscope. The protuberances, or prominences, of the Sun had then never been seen, except during a total eclipse. It was in August. The sky was at its bluest and most cloudless. My telescope, with a spectroscope attached to it, was set up in an open field, where there was a wide horizon. I had never seen a total eclipse before; and those who have never seen high noon changed to night over a wide expanse in one second, can have as little idea of it as,—well, there really is no experience whatever at all comparable to it. . . . I found yellow protuberances to give the most surprizing multitude of lines, among which a yellow one was very prominent. Mr. Lockyer had already seen it in another eclipse some months before; but of that I was unaware. I felt as certain that I was gazing upon a chemical element previously unknown, as I am today. It was *helium,* so named about that time by Lockyer. (Robin MS 1036)

291.29–31   These were. . . .] Given the limitations of his instruments, Peirce seems to describe accurately all that could be seen. He probably saw C, 1017K, 1474K, 1608K, and F. (On 15 April he had seen 1247K, 1351K, 1474K, 1608K, near F, 2640H, and near G. See editorial note 288.2–5.) At Bardstown he saw two of the lines he had measured in the Aurora Borealis; other observers measured lines at 1247K, 1351K, 1474K, and b. What all these observations seem to prove is that the corona and the aurora have a number of lines in common.

291.30   the well-known yellow line] If we consider Peirce's words in Robin MS 1036, this is a puzzling phrase indeed.

Sketch of Logic

This carefully inscribed sketch, with just a few minor revisions, covers the first nine pages of a notebook. The remainder of the notebook is blank, except for the final page. It contains a brief logical notation, and an apparent title ("Argument-Kinds") is followed by the beginning of a paragraph: "That Propositions & Terms are necessarily considered." The sketch of logic may have been written somewhat earlier than the fall of 1869.

295n.1   Aristotle. . . .] See, for examples, *Posterior Analytics*, 1.1.71a1–10; *Prior Analytics*, 2.23.68b10–14; or *Rhetoric*, 1.1.1355a7ff. or 1.2.1358a10ff.

Logic Notebook

The Logic Notebook entries for 1869, particularly interesting for the section on the map-coloring (or four-color) problem, cover less than two weeks and only twelve pages, of which five are blank. The remaining seven pages, inscribed between 6 and 15 October, are printed here in their entirety. (For more information on the Logic Notebook, see the first headnote above.)

English Doctrine of Ideas

Haskell's *Index to the Nation* identifies Peirce as the author of this unsigned review. It focuses on what Peirce considers to be the typically English way of thinking, for further discussions of which see items 8, 24, 31–33, 43, and 48 in the present volume.

302.27   a great German metaphysician] Hegel.

303.25–26   virtue is. . . .] James Mill, *Human Mind*, 2:288–89, 292–93 [chap. 23].

303.37–38   some German psychologists] Fechner, Helmholtz, and Wundt, for examples.

304.6–13   This is a summary of chap. 2 of James Mill's *Human Mind* [1 :51–62].

304.32–34   Hume. . . .] Hume differentiates between idea and impression, the latter being subdivided into sensation and reflection. See his *Treatise of Human Nature* [bk. 1, pt. 1, sec. 1] or his *Enquiry Concerning Human Understanding* [sec. 2]. James Mill's sensation is equivalent to Hume's impression.

304.38–40   "must be. . . ."] Berkeley, *Works* (1843), 1:76 [*Principles of Human Knowledge*, §10 of introduction].

305.19   Mill repeats the verb *is* after both "every size" and "every shape."

305.24–26   "It is . . . resemblance."] James Mill, *Human Mind*, 1:270 [chap. 8].

306.38–307.3   Wundt's remark. . . .] Wundt, *Vorlesungen*, 1:iv [preface].

307.10–12   Hamilton has. . . .] Hamilton, *Reid*, pp. 889ff.

307.19–20   But this. . . .] Aristotle, *De memoria et reminiscentia*, 2.451a18.

307n.1–2   See lectures 4, 19, 43, and especially 49 [*Vorlesungen*, 2: 311ff.].

Early nominalism and realism

The 1869–70 Harvard University Lectures, later called "the germ of the graduate school," focused on philosophy and modern literature. Francis G. Peabody attended all six series of philosophical lectures and later gave his "Notes of lectures on Philosophy by Francis Bowen, John Fiske, Charles S. Peirce, J. Elliot Cabot, Ralph Waldo Emerson, Frederic H. Hedge, George P. Fisher, delivered to graduate students in Harvard College, 1869–70" to the Harvard University Archives. These notes are our primary source of information for Peirce's lectures, regarding which he had written to Charles W. Eliot, Harvard president, on 2 September 1869: "I shall be glad to give some lectures on 'British Logicians' if that meets the terms of the invitation. I shall not write the lectures." It is not surprising, then, that there are manuscripts for only three of these lectures in the Peirce Papers. (But he probably used MSS 124 and 125—see the two headnotes in *W*1:558—and some no longer extant manuscript of item 39 below.) Peirce was scheduled to give nine lectures, but actually gave fifteen: 1 and 2 on early nominalism and realism (12/14 & 16); 3 and 4 on Duns Scotus (12/17 & 21); 5 on Ockham (12/23); 6 on Whewell (12/24); 7 on Mill (12/28); 8, 9, and 10 on De Morgan and the logic of relations (12/30 & 31 and 1/4); 11, 12, and 13 on Boole and an amplification of his calculus applied to the logic of relations (1/6, 7, & 11); 14 on Mill on induction and hypothesis (1/14); and 15 on Bacon on induction and hypothesis (1/18). The course of lectures inaugurated Peirce's lifelong championship of Whewell over Mill in the logic of science and contains the first public exposition of his work in the logic of relations. "Lecture I. Early nominalism and realism" (MS 158) consists of fourteen pages, numbered consecutively in the upper right-hand corner by Peirce. Though there are a number of corrections and revisions, the manuscript is generally well written; there are also three time notations. (For an earlier, less finished attempt see MS 157, which is not included in the present volume.) There are some pencil remarks of a more general nature on the final verso of MS 158, closely resembling Peabody's notes. Peirce must have used them at the beginning of his first lecture:

Excuse necessary for so wide a subject. A limitation of a wide one. Original request. Extensive literature of logic. Young man. Even as now stands too much for nine lectures. Must therefore be *fragmentary*. Some features of a system here & there.

Subject dry. Haven't come to be entertained but because you have an interest in the subject. No graces of style or delivery. No gift of speech & I do not write out what I have to say for I find interest on audience even less (if that be possible) when I read written lectures. Besides I wish them to be Conversational. So that questions may be asked & doubts raised by you. Let us then call them Conversations not Lectures.

Extra lectures after these.—

But I presume that nine lectures upon this subject is as much as you will desire, & I do not mean to exceed that number, unless you take more interest in the matter than I at all expect.

311.23–25   his own. . . .] For a discussion of Hamilton's doctrine of the quantified predicate, see *W*1:295–301 or his *Lectures on Logic,* pp. 509–58.

311.29   *Parva Logicalia*] For a discussion of this interesting branch of scholastic logic, see Peirce's entry in Baldwin's *Dictionary of Philosophy and Psychology* (P 857). William of Sherwood is no longer regarded as the earliest writer of *parva logicalia.*

311.32–33   *Synopsis* . . . Psellus] See editorial note 218n.16.

312.20–21   Jourdain . . . *age,*] The proper title of Charles Gabriel Brechillet Jourdain's work is *Recherches critiques sur l'age et l'origine des traductions latines d'Aristote, et sur des commentaires grecs ou arabes employés par les docteurs scholastiques* (1843).

312.21–22   Barach . . . *Roscellinus*] The full and proper title of Carl Sigmund Barach's work is *Zur Geschichte des Nominalismus vor Roscellin* (1866).

312.24–26   the *Liber* . . . Boethius,] Peirce owned *Boethi opera omnia* (Basel, 1570), containing *Gilberti Porretae . . . de Trinitate commentarii.* Gilbertus Porretanus (1076–1154) was Bishop of Poitiers. Boethius is now thought to have written *De Trinitate* after all.

312.28–30   The best. . . .] Prantl, *Geschichte,* 2:98–260.

312.37–313.8   "The sacred . . . Dei."] Berengarius, *De sacra coena,* pp. 99–101. For a translation of the Latin passage, see editorial note 195n.1–5.

314.28   "Study. . . ."] Not located.

315.7   George . . . Aristotle] The reference is to Lewes's *Aristotle: A Chapter from the History of Science, including Analyses of Aristotle's Scientific Writings* (London, 1864).

315.27–28   Algebra . . . eye] As there is no evidence that Peirce had read Gauss at this time, it is safe to assume that Sylvester, a frequent visitor to the Peirce house, gave him the information. See Sylvester's August 1869 address to the British Association for the Advancement of Science (in the Association's *Report,* where however we have "mathematics" instead of "algebra").

316.7–8   Porphyry's . . . categories] The reference is of course to Porphyry's *Isagoge,* in the fourth of the five volumes of *Aristotelis opera* (1836–1870), the famous Berlin edition. Peirce owned the first four volumes in 1869.

316.11–13   A sentence. . . .] Cousin, *Fragments philosophiques,* p. 77 [in a section entitled "Que la philosophie scholastique est sortie d'une phrase de Porphyre, traduite par Boèce"].

316.34–35   Hjort. . . .] The following six authors published at least one book each on Erigena: Peder Hjort (1793–1871), Danish philologist and historian; Franz Anton Staudenmaier (1800–1856), German theologian; René Taillandier (1817–1879), French scholar; Nicolaus Möller (fl. 1850), Belgian scholar; Theodor Christlieb (1833–1889), German theologian; and Johannes Nepomuk Huber (1830–1879), German theologian and philosopher.

317.7–9   no philosopher. . . .] Erigena, *De divisione naturae,* p. 155 [b. 2, §29].

317.10–12   the ancient. . . .] The ancient philosopher is Parmenides, whose statement Peirce no doubt found in Hegel, *Wissenschaft der Logik,* pp. 79–80 [b. 1, p. 1, chap. 1, §C1, Anmerkung 1].

317.12–15   the name. . . .] Erigena, *De divisione naturae,* p. 240 [b. 3, §19]. The Latin might be translated as "when it is thought of with regard to its own nature."

317.18–20   "Darkness. . . ."] Ibid., p. 62 [b. 1, §60].

Ockam

The subtitle of MS 160 notwithstanding, this is actually the fifth lecture on "British Logicians." Peirce had continued his presentation of nominalism and realism in lectures 2 and 3; had discussed John of Salisbury and the weight given to authority, as well as questions of signification and reality; and toward the end of the third lecture, had turned to universals and Duns Scotus. He devoted lecture 4 entirely to Duns Scotus, and lecture 5 entirely to Ockham; he knows less of the latter, he says, than he does of the former. MS 160 is a notebook, with "Ockam" inscribed on a label on the outside cover, consisting of a first page entitled "Lecture 3" and thirty-three pages of text all written on the rectos. There are a number of corrections and revisions, as well as notes to himself on some of the versos. Some of the quotations in the published text appear as bibliographic references or instructions in the manuscript. (See MS 159 for a three-page "Abstract of Occam's Summa Logices.") All translations of Ockham's *Summa* are from *Ockham's Theory of Terms* and are printed here by permission of the publisher. All translations from Thomas of Erfurt's *Grammatica Speculativa* are printed here by permission of the publisher and the editor-translator.

318.7   the first 17 chapters] These are the ones outlined in MS 159.

318.23–319.35   *Ockham's Theory of Terms,* pp. 49–51.

320.33–36   "However, since there is no reason to postulate irrelevant elements among mental terms, one might wonder whether, among intentions, participles constitute a separate part of speech over and above verbs in the way that they do in spoken and written language" (*Ockham's Theory of Terms,* p. 52).

321.32   Martin Grabmann showed in 1922 that the work is by Thomas of Erfurt rather than Scotus; Grabmann's findings are now universally accepted.

321.37–327.16   *Thomas of Erfurt: Grammatica Speculativa,* pp. 135–49 (odd numbers only, the Latin text is on even-numbered pages).

323.37–38   Hence . . . God,] This replaces "Hence, although *in Deo,* in reality is not a passive property" in the printed book. (Personal communication from Professor Bursill-Hall.)

326.18   This replaces *"In what way is the mode of signifying so to speak empirically ascertained"* in the printed book. (Personal communication from Professor Bursill-Hall.)

327.25–36   *Ockham's Theory of Terms,* p. 55.

328.15–24   Ibid., p. 56.

328.28–31   "quod fere . . . significantur."] John of Salisbury, *Metalogicus,* p. 111 [b. 2, chap. 20]. "It is well known that what common names mean and what they name are not identical. They name particular things, but their meaning is universal." (See 71n.1–14 above.)

330.8–11   See *Ockham's Theory of Terms,* pp. 69–71.

331.6–10   *Ockham's Theory of Terms,* p. 73.

331.13–332.42   Ibid., pp. 73–75.

332.44–333.17   Ibid., pp. 75–76.

333.25–33   Peirce's translation of part of chap. 23; see *Ockham's Theory of Terms,* pp. 99–100.

333.34–37   Peirce's paraphrase of part of chap. 30; see *Ockham's Theory of Terms,* pp. 110–11.

333.39–334.8   *Ockham's Theory of Terms,* p. 131.

334.10–18   Ibid., p. 178.

334.27–38   Editors' translation of Ockham, *Quodlibeta septem,* p. 6, qu. 8.

335.8–16   Peirce's translation of part of chap. 39 of Ockham's *Summa;* see *Ockham's Theory of Terms,* p. 125.

335.11   one really,] We have added the comma to clarify the meaning of the sentence.

335.14   numerical] We have emended Peirce's nonsensical "numeral."

Whewell

This must have been the sixth lecture, delivered on Christmas Eve 1869: Peabody was absent that day, and Whewell does not appear in the notes for the other fourteen lectures. Peirce's lecture is contained in a notebook, with "Whewell" inscribed on a label on the outside cover. The text appears on rectos 1 through 17, with occasional notes and revisions on the versos; 18v that replaces the crossed out 18r; recto and verso of both 19 and 20; and rectos 21 through 33, again with occasional revisions and notes. There is a time notation, "30m," on 23v. Not published here are the first three pages of the notebook, a "General Outline" containing remarks on Whewell and summarizing chapters 1–7 of book 2 and chapter 5 of book 3 of the *Novum Organon Renovatum.* The following are among the more interesting remarks: "Whewell's Theory based on the study of the history of science"; "on the whole his work of eternal value"; and Whewell "a truly scientific man" and his investigations "more true to science than those of the positivists." The lecture itself gives us not only Peirce's views on Whewell, but his thoughts on the difference between a scientific and a literary mentality, the role of the *a priori* in science, and the importance of as well as the necessary qualifications for doing the philosophy of science.

337.7–8   the poem. . . .] MS 147 indicates that Peirce read the poem "in Ruteboeuf," *Oeuvres complètes de Rutebeuf* (Paris: E. Pannier, 1839), 2:415. Henri d'Andeli was a thirteenth-century trouvère from Normandy.

337.18   "Science. . . ."] Not located, though there may be no such quotation.

337.31–32   his works upon the tides] See "On the Results of an Extensive System of Tide Observations made on the Coast of Europe and America in June 1835" (1836) and "On the Tides of the Pacific and on the Diurnal Inequality" (1848).

338.4   Oxford] Peirce is wrong; Whewell was professor at Cambridge.

338.13–14   "Knowledge . . . foible,"] Not located.

338.17   The reference may be to something contained in *A memorial Poem, suggested by the lamented death of Dr. Whewell . . .* by a Cambridge Master of Arts (London, 1866), which however could not be checked. Whewell was quite interested in music, as is evident from his 1863 paper read before the Royal Institute of British Architects, "Of Certain Analogies between Architecture and the Other Fine Arts."

338.33–35   that one. . . .] See Mark 10:21.

340.20–21   Whewell, *Novum Organon,* b. 2, chap. 3.

341.15–16   Professor . . . Kantism."] See Bowen's *Treatise on Logic.*

342.14–16   Whewell, *Novum Organon,* b. 2, chap. 6.

342.17–19   This identification. . . .] See Mill, *System of Logic,* 1:327ff. [b. 3, chaps. 1 and 2].

342.27–32   The reference is to Whewell's article entitled "Demonstration that all Matter is heavy."

342.33–40   This is a paraphrase of Whewell, *Novum Organon,* pp. 30 and 36 [b. 2, chap. 2, aph. 2 and §2].

343.9–11   He remarks. . . .] Ibid., p. 40 [b. 2, chap. 2, §3].

344.28–31   See editorial note 340.20–21 above.

344.38   This is the first of three examples (see also the next two editorial notes) from nineteenth-century astronomy to illustrate various aspects of the proposition that all facts involve ideas. Though it is uncertain how Peirce planned to proceed in his explanation—he may have guessed that not all the drawings of nebulae are resolvable into collections of separate stars—he used the example of the "Drawings of nebulae" to explain why there is no such thing as pure observation.

345.20   The details of the second example from nineteenth-century astronomy are even more uncertain than those of the first. The first satellite of Neptune was discovered in 1846, the second more than a century later. The Struve family produced four generations of astronomers; their interest in binary stars may have disposed Otto Wilhelm Struve (1819–1905) to think that Neptune must have a second satellite, though there was no empirical evidence for its existence. In any case, Peirce used the example of "Struve and 2nd satellite of Neptune" to illustrate that predispositions, desires, and emotions can affect observations.

345.23   The third example from nineteenth-century astronomy refers to the prominences, or rose-colored protuberances, within the corona of the sun. These prominences first received attention during the total solar eclipse of 1842; they became the center of attention during the eclipses of 1851, 1860, 1867, 1868, and 1869. The study of prominences became particularly intense in 1868–69, because by use of the spectroscope they could now be observed daily. In any case, Peirce used the example of the "Rose-coloured protuberances" to illustrate that we tend to see only what we look for, but that the influence of the mind upon observations is not necessarily bad. (For the solar eclipse of 1869 and Peirce's remarks on the prominences, see item 27 above.)

Lessons in Logic

The following five items belong to some unidentified project here called "Practical Logic." Perhaps Peirce's Lectures on British Logicians of 1869 (items 31–33) or his Lectures on Logic of 1870–71 (item 42) were originally intended to be on practical logic; and when the topic of his lectures changed, he decided to make that the title of a book? Not published here is MS 163, which consists of a single sheet containing two very sketchy outlines for either a book or a series of lectures, both entitled "Practical Logic." MS 164, published here in its entirety, is obviously a lecture or a part of one, and consists of three pages, the last two of which are on both sides of the second sheet. It is on the whole carefully written.

348.13–14 the subject. . . .] No such advertisement has been found.
348.18–19 logic defined . . . Thought—] Hamilton, *Lectures on Logic,* p. 3.

Logic and Methodology

MS 165 consists of the three items printed here, as well as ten separate pages of carelessly written earlier versions of parts of the three items. On the first of these ten pages, logic is defined as "the science of general principles by which inferences are tested," and methodology as "the general science by which we are enabled to conduct an investigation wisely." With only three minor revisions, "Logic and Methodology" is carefully inscribed on both sides of a single sheet.

350.6 πάντες . . .] Aristotle, *Metaphysics,* 1.1.980a22.
350.23–351.3 Sebastianus . . . view;] In his *Commentarii in universam dialecticam Aristotelis,* the eighth and last of the Conimbricensis treatises (1592–1606). Sebastianus Contus (1567–1639?) was a Portuguese theologian and philosopher and one of the masters of the Coimbra Colegio das Artes.
351.7–10 "Dialectica. . . ."] "Logic is the art of arts, the science of sciences, showing the way to the principles of the methods of them all. For logic alone properly examines the principles of all other sciences."

Rules for Investigation

This three-page item is written on two sheets. There are a few minor revisions, and Chapter 2 represents a rewriting of three crossed-out paragraphs, two of them very short. In the title, "Rules for" has replaced the crossed-out "The Laws of."

351.18 All men. . . .] Translation of Aristotle, *Metaphysics,* 1.1.980a22. See 350.6.
352.3–7 "Dialectica. . . ."] See 351.5–10 above, as well as the accompanying editorial note.

Practical Logic

These three and one-half pages appear on two sheets and, except for three minor revisions, are more carefully inscribed than either of the two preceding items.

353.10   "All men. . . ."] See editorial note 351.18.
353.26–29   "Dialectica. . . ."] See 351.5–10 above, as well as the accompanying editorial note.

Chapter 2

This five-page manuscript represents a more polished version of
the immediately preceding item. There are a number of minor revisions, and two of the maxims have been entirely, and more concisely,
rewritten. Peirce's page numbers appear in the upper right-hand
corner of the five sheets.

357.2–3   Hedgecock's Quadrant] The invention of Thomas Hedgecock, a
British scientist who flourished in the first half of the nineteenth century.

Logic of Relatives

According to Chauncey Wright's manuscript minutes of the
616th meeting of the American Academy of Arts and Sciences, in
Boston on 26 January 1870, "The President also communicated by
title . . . a paper 'On the Extension of Boole's System to the Logic of
Relations by C. S. Peirce'." Peirce's paper appeared, with a different
title, in the Academy's *Memoirs* (vol. 9, p. 2) in 1873. (Academy
Memoirs and *Proceedings* were published in bound volumes whenever finances permitted and the quantity of material dictated.) But
like all other papers submitted to the Academy, Peirce's was typeset,
printed, and bound in its own covers not long after the meeting. He
began circulating it no later than the beginning of June. The first
public comment upon the paper was made in September by Robert
Harley, an English mathematician, who called it "the most remarkable amplification of Boole's conceptions which [he had] hitherto
met with." Not all reactions have been favorable since. The 1870
"Logic of Relatives" is no doubt one of Peirce's most difficult papers,
published or unpublished; its particular formulas and its complex
mathematical analogies are at times obscure or puzzling, and it is not
always clear whether he is dealing with relations or relatives. But as
the first attempt by anyone at expanding Boole's algebra of logic to
include the logic of relations, Peirce's paper remains one of the most
important works in the history of modern logic. His annotations in
four offprints of the paper—one in MS 168, one in the Johns Hopkins

University Archives (JHU), and two in Robin MS 1600—are reproduced in the notes that follow.

359.8–18   a valuable paper. . . .] De Morgan, "On the Syllogism, No. IV."
362.21–26   In the left-hand margin in JHU, Peirce writes:

> Additional notation for inverse operations needed. Given x = y:z required a
> function of x such that φx = z:y

In MS 168 he writes

> The subject of inverse operations requires further development; Because the
> inverse of the inverse processes is needed. Thus given x = y:z we seek a
> function K such that Kx = z:y

362n.1   Hamilton] Sir William Rowan Hamilton. See his *Lectures on Quaternions*.
362n.6   At the bottom of this page in MS 168, Peirce writes:

> Farther on (p 36 et seqq) both operations are used

In JHU he writes

> Both are needed. See p. 36.

The reference is, of course, to p. 36 in the original offprint; see 400.5ff.
364.19   Taylor's Theorem] See editorial note 406.1.
366.16   The universe . . . De Morgan's] See De Morgan, *Formal Logic*, p. 37.
366.21–29   In the right-hand margin in MS 168, Peirce writes:

> This is vague and imperfect. I dont say what I would do about the number of
> lovers etc. where the same man may love several women

366.31–32   I shall. . . .] See Boole, *Laws of Thought*, pp. 27 and 61–62.
367n.1–2   Peirce owned only the third edition of Drobisch's work.
368.7–10   The sign. . . .] Boole, *Laws of Thought*, p. 33.
368.22–28   in a paper . . . men;] See item 2 above, 12.24ff.
368.30–369.4   Since. . . .] See Jevons, *Pure Logic*, chapters 15 and 6.
369n.1   Jevons's other book is *The Substitution of Similars*.
376.9   In the right-hand margin, beginning here but extending to the bottom of the page, Peirce writes in MS 168:

> This is an error. Thus let g denote God of. Then, there are just as many God's
> per French man as per non French man, namely 1. But the number of 'Gods
> of' multiplied by the number of Frenchmen does not give the number of God's
> of Frenchmen. The true condition is as follows The relative number of t per

f is not $\frac{[tf]}{[f]}$ as I have assumed incautiously. If this were so my conclusion would be right. But is $\frac{\Sigma_i[tF_i]}{[f]}$

376.22 The symbol to the right of the equation sign represents the numeral one; the symbol to the left the identity relation. (Also, the Arabic one represents 'anything'; the antique one 'something'.)

376.23–24 Boole. . . .] Boole, *Laws of Thought,* pp. 243ff.

377.1–378.7 This is p. 16 in the original offprint; at the bottom of this page in JHU, Peirce writes

See addition at p. 36.

for which see 400.5ff.

378.20–32 In the right-hand margin in MS 168, Peirce writes sideways:

betrayer to every enemy of a man of a man of whom he is enemy

It is not clear how and where this fits; nor can it be put into a notation.

378.21–31 In MS 168, a bracket to the left connects lines 21 and 23, and 22 and 24; a smaller bracket connects lines 30 and 31, which is connected by another bracket with line 28.

378.22 In JHU and MS 168, Peirce writes "all men" for "each man"; and in Robin MS 1600 (2), "the same" for "an."

378.23 In Robin MS 1600 (2), Peirce writes "some" for "a"; both here and in JHU, "every enemy" for "all enemies"; and in MS 168, "each enemy" for "all enemies."

378.27–32 In MS 168 Peirce writes the following figure to the right of the second set of six cases:

$$bmw$$

$$bm^w \qquad\qquad (bm)^w$$

$$b^m w \qquad\qquad b^{m^w}$$

$$b^{mw}$$

The figure seems to represent the cyclic property of the inclusion relation or to demonstrate the inclusion relation for conjugative terms whose correlates are restricted to absolute terms.

378.30 In Robin MS 1600 (2) immediately following the case, Peirce writes

follows from last because neg. of $\overline{bm}^w$

380.12–13 $x = x$ follows from (21.) in several ways by using various combinations of the first twenty-three formulas. The two lines are not quite satisfactorily placed.

382.10–11   In Robin MS 1600 (2) Peirce draws a bracket connecting the end of the two lines, and writes

This is not so.

It is not clear what Peirce meant or why he thought so.

385.19, 25   In Robin MS 1600 (2) Peirce writes to the left of both lines "Wr" (meaning 'wrong'), crosses out "x > 0", and replaces that with "x is an unlimited relative." He probably saw later that "x > 0" is not restricted enough.

394.6   This is the last line of p. 30 in the original offprint. At the bottom of that page in Robin MS 1600 (1) Peirce writes

$$l +\!\!, \bar{s} +\!\!, \overline{w} \prec (l +\!\!, \bar{s})w \prec l +\!\!, \bar{s}w \prec l(s +\!\!, \overline{w}) \prec ls +\!\!, \overline{w} \prec lsw$$

unless	unless	unless
$w \prec 0$	$s + \overline{w} \prec 0$	$w \prec 0$

In Robin MS 1600 (2) Peirce adds the following under the last line (here reproduced):

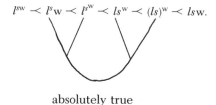

$$l^{sw} \prec l^{s}w \prec l^{sw} \prec ls^{w} \prec (ls)^{w} \prec lsw.$$

absolutely true

394.10–27   In Robin MS 1600 (2) Peirce writes to the right of the two columns, "Crossed are not universally true"; he crosses, in both columns, the first and fourth forks, the innermost of the sixth forks, and the outer of the seventh forks; also crossed is the connecting line at the end.

401.17–19   Mr. De Morgan. . . .] De Morgan, *Formal Logic,* p. 341.

401.29   ordinary] Here ends page 37 of the original offprint; at the bottom of this page in Robin MS 1600 (2) Peirce writes

$$K(^{l}{}^{s}) = {}^{K-s}K - l^{K-l}$$

The notation seems to exemplify backward and converse involution, though it does not seem to be related to anything in the text; it is not clear whether the three signs on the right-hand side of the equation are dots or dashes.

406.1–7   For a modern version of the Taylor-Maclaurin Theorem, see Richard Stevens Burington, *Handbook of Mathematical Tables and Formulas,* 5th edition (New York: McGraw-Hill, 1973), pp. 56, 245.

413.14–15   These multiplication-tables. . . .] Presumably Peirce refers to the four tables on the last four pages; but only the small table at the bottom of the preceding page appears exactly as in his father's work, while the others are modified or corrected. (See P 188, Peirce's corrected and enlarged edition of the *Linear Associative Algebra.*)

413.20–23   The algebra. . . .] See P 188, p. 161.

416.1–3   Lobatchewsky. . . .] See Lobatchewsky's *Geometrische Untersuchungen.*

417n.13   Beltrami's investigations] The reference is to Eugenio Beltrami, "Saggio di interpretazione della geometrica non-euclidea," *Giornale di Matematica* 6(1868):248–312.

418.10–13   The former. . . .] As a note to this sentence, Peirce writes in the left-hand margin in Robin MS 1600 (2):

> As we speak of *self-loving* etc. the former of these classes should be called *self-relatives*

418.27–29   The former. . . .] As a note to this sentence, Peirce writes in the left-hand margin in Robin MS 1600 (2):

> The idea of a copula is different. These should be called *assimilative.*

418.30–31   Professor Peirce. . . .] Benjamin Peirce, *Linear Associative Algebra*, §25.

418.33–35   *c.* Third. . . .] As a note to this sentence, Peirce writes in the left-hand margin in Robin MS 1600 (2):

> If such reciprocation is admissible but not necessary they may be called *reciprocable.*

By *reciprocable* Peirce seems to mean what is today meant by 'non-symmetrical', as contradistinguished from 'asymmetrical'.

418.36–419.1   convertible. . . .] De Morgan, *Formal Logic,* p. 345.

418n.1–419n.5   Ockham:

> There are relations of equiparance and relations of disquiparance. The first relations are of similar names, the second relations of dissimilar names. An example of the first is when the same name appears in the nominative and in an oblique case, as what is similar to the similar is similar (to what it is similar to). . . . An example of the second is when one name appears in the nominative case but another in an oblique case, as father is father of son and not properly father of father.

Petrus Hispanus, *Compendiarius,* leaf 77v:

> Relatives of equiparance are synonymous with their correlates. . . . Relatives of disquiparance are not synonymous with their correlates.

419.7   self-relatives] In the right-hand margin in Robin MS 1600 (2), Peirce writes: "Instead of self-relatives, better concurrents."

419.10–11   In Robin MS 1600 (2) Peirce inserts "only" between 'contains' and 'elements', and writes "acyclic" over 'non-cyclic'.

419.33–420.1   The former. . . .] In Robin MS 1600 (2) Peirce adds the following in the right-hand margin: "or *iterative* and *final.*"

419n.4   disquiparantiae] We have inserted the medial *s* that was left out in the *Memoirs.*

419n.5   Pschlacher] Konrad Pschlacher (fl. 1512), a Viennese author, wrote several philosophical works as well as commentaries on Petrus Hispanus and Aristotle's *Posterior Analytics.*

420.5–6   The former. . . .] De Morgan, *Formal Logic,* p. 346.

420.14   *continuous*] In the left-hand margin in Robin MS 1600 (2), Peirce writes

Should be called *concatenated*

420n.1–12   Tartaretus, *Expositio,* fol. 23c:

Relation is twofold: namely, relation of reason and real relation. The relation of reason is that which is made by a comparative act of the intellect, as are second intentions; but real relation is twofold: namely, aptitudinal and actual. Aptitudinal relation is that which does not require its term to exist actually but only in aptitude; such are all proper passions, all aptitudes, and all inclinations; and these are in that reductive predicament in which are the things whose private passions they are. But actual relation is twofold; namely, intrinsically advenient and extrinsically advenient. Intrinsically advenient is that which is necessarily posited when the extremes are posited at whatever distance, as in likeness, paternity, equality. Extrinsically advenient is that which is not necessarily posited when the extremes are posited, but requires a suitable proximity of the extremes; such are the six last categories; namely action, passion, time, place, position, and habit.

422.5–10   As for . . . symbol."] Boole, *Laws of Thought,* pp. 228, 62.

428.23   In MS 168 Peirce has written to the right, "Objection to this."— perhaps because these two commas might be misread as apostrophes.

429.14   In MS 168 Peirce has written to the right, "For"—a false start for what he writes below.

429.20   This is the last line on p. 61 of the original offprint; at the bottom of this page in the offprint in MS 168, Peirce has written the following, the exact meaning and placement of which is not clear:

If $S = \frac{1}{2} + \frac{1}{2}K$ $V = \frac{1}{2} - \frac{1}{2}K$ For Conjugatives if $A = qBC$ take HJK such that $A = JqCB$

$S^2 = S$ $V^2 = V$ $SV = VS = 0$ $C = HqBA$ $B = KqAC$ $C = MqAB$ $B = NqCA$

429.21–35   These are lines 1–12 at the top of page 62 of the original offprint.

Peirce fills the remainder of the page both in JHU and in MS 168. In JHU he writes:

A better list of Axioms—(not properly Axioms or synthetic propositions)

Formulae defining copula
(1) $x \prec x$ The *Principle of Identity*
(2) If $x \prec y$ and $y \prec z$ then $x \prec z$ The *Dictum de Omni* or *Nota notae*
Formulae defining $+$,
(3) $x \prec x +, y$
(4) $y \prec x +, y$
(5) If $x \prec z$ and $y \prec z$, then $x +, y \prec z$
Formulae defining ,
(6) $x,y \prec x$
(7) $x,y \prec y$
(8) If $x \prec y$ and $x \prec z$ then $x \prec y,z$
Formula defining Zero
(9) $0 \prec x$
Formula defining Unity
(10) $x \prec 1$
Formulae defining Multiplication
(11) If $x \prec y$ then $zx \prec zy$
(12) If $x \prec y$ then $xz \prec yz$
(13) $x(y +, z) \prec xy +, xz$
(14) $(x +, y)z \prec xz +, yz$
(15) $x(yz) \prec (xy)z$
(16) $(xy)z \prec x(yz)$
Formulae defining forward Involution
(17) If $Y \prec y$ then either $x^y \prec xY$ or $Y \prec 0$
(18) If it follows from $Y \prec y$ that either $a \prec xY$ or $Y \prec 0$ then $a \prec x^y$
Formulae defining backward Involution
(19) If $a \prec {}^x y$ and $a \prec xz$ then $z \prec y$
(20) If it follows from $a \prec xz$ that $z \prec y$ then $a \prec {}^x y$
Formulae defining $\ominus$
(21) $x,6^{-x} \prec 0$ Principle of Contradiction
(22) $1 \prec x +, 6^{-x}$ Principle of Excluded Middle.

In MS 168 he writes:

The fundamental formulae are all definitions. No axioms or postulates needed.

They are as follows.
    Two formulae defining $\prec$
        (1) $x \prec x$
        (2) If $x \prec y$ and $y \prec z$, then $x \prec z$
    Two formulae defining $>$
        (1) If $x \prec y$ and not $y \prec x$ then $y > x$
        (2) If $y > x$ then $x \prec y$ and not $y > x$

Three formulae defining $+,$
   (1) $x \prec x + y$
   (2) $y \prec x + y$
   (3) If $x \prec z$ and $y \prec z$ $x + y \prec z$
Three formulae defining ,
   (1) $x,y \prec x$
   (2) $x,y \prec y$
   (3) If $x \prec y$ $x \prec z$ then $x \prec y,z$
One formula defining 0
   $0 \prec x$ whatever x may be
One formula defining 1
   $x \prec 1$ whatever x may be

On the flyleaf following page 62 in MS 168, Peirce writes the following (which may fit with the material in the section on 'Individual Terms', pp. 392–395 above):

Taking s to mean "some ———" or "whatever has certain character X not determined and also those of an ———" we have

$$slw = l^{sw}$$
$$n^{ls} = ln^{s}$$
$$n^{ls} = {}^{l}ns$$

But I doubt the legitimacy of this.

System of Logic

This rather inchoate system of logic is contained in a carefully written manuscript of a little more than five pages. There are a few minor revisions, and two paragraphs (a Duns Scotus quotation and Peirce's explanatory translation) have been crossed out on pp. 4–5. Peirce's page numbers appear in the upper right-hand corner.

430n.1–2 "Dicendum ergo quod subiectum primum et proprium Logicae est syllogismus." (See the Vivès edition, 1:70.)
431.20 This note has not been found.
431.26 Here follow the two crossed-out paragraphs in the manuscript. After a brief quotation from Scotus's *Quaestiones in metaphysicam Aristotelis,* the second paragraph reads as follows:

I should translate this as follows. *Universal* is predicated of the five predicables (genus, species, difference, property, and accident) in its name and in its meaning, and therefore it is predicated of them univocally. The consequence (i.e. the necessity of the connection between the antecedent and consequent) appears from what Aristotle says in the beginning of his book upon the categories. (He says that whatever is predicated in its name and in its meaning is predicated univocally.) The antecedent (that *Universal* is so predicated of the five predicables) is manifest because each of the five predicables is from its essential meaning capable of signifying a plurality, and to be thus capable of signifying many is to be universal according to the definition of this term which is given in the 5th chapter of the 1st book *de interpretatione.*

431.30–35   Not located, though almost certainly from Scotus's *Quaestiones in metaphysicam Aristotelis.*

James's Secret of Swedenborg

Haskell's *Index to the Nation* identifies Peirce as the author of this unsigned review. Peirce first met Henry James the Elder in 1866, and he remembered him warmly as late as 1911. In 1892 he had said that "James is the most ill-mannered and insulting to his reader possible; but he is so outrageously and grotesquely so, that the offensiveness is swallowed up in the farce of it" (Robin MS 957). And referring to the *Secret of Swedenborg, Substance and Shadow,* and *Spiritual Creation,* he says in 1911 that from their study he has "profitted concerning morality and otherwise. . . . The fact that I have been unable to agree with much, not to say *most,* of the author's opinions, while not quite confident of my own, has, no doubt, increased their utility to me. Much that they contain enlightened me greatly" (Robin MS 675).

435.6–7   "no cordial . . ."] James, *Swedenborg,* p. 122. James says "no cordial, disinterested lover."

435.10–11   "sanction . . . voucher.] Ibid., p. 21.

435.11–14   "We need. . . ."] Ibid., p. 90. James has "as I have already said" for Peirce's "he says"; "him" for "Swedenborg"; "or as they deal with what they feel" for "or as what they feel."

436.15–16   "no other . . . ,"] Ibid., p. 11. James has "no voucher but what it found."

437.37   "the invention. . . ."] Ibid. James has "the invention of another or *noumenal* world, the world of 'things-in-themselves'."

438.7–10   "Male and. . . ."] Peirce has deleted "physical and moral, cosmical and domestic," which in James follows "generic and specific."

438.12–14   "Woman. . . ."] Excerpted from the following sentence (p. 49): "This spontaneous marriage of man as man with woman as woman— or, what is the same thing, of the objective and subjective, or physical and moral, contents of human nature—is what is meant by society, which is the consummation of human destiny."

438.15–21   "the *minimus.* . . ."] James, *Swedenborg,* p. 137.

Lectures on Logic

These rough and hastily inscribed notes appear on the first five recto pages of a notebook, with four brief notes on preceding versos. The final verso in the notebook, not printed here, contains a list of articles on astronomical observations. Peirce had been appointed (Harvard) University Lecturer on Logic for 1870–71 on 6 January 1870, the lectures to begin on 3 October. But on 18 June he sailed for Europe as a member of the Coast Survey eclipse expedition, and did not return until 7 March 1871. His lectures were at first postponed to the second term, to begin on 13 February 1871, but were then canceled altogether. It appears that the lectures were to develop the theory of signs within the framework of the logic of relations and then to focus on the problems of meaning, truth, and reality within the framework of the theory of signs.

439.6 τὸ λεκτόν] First used in this sense, as Peirce says below, by the Stoics. (See Cleanthes, *Stoicus,* 1.109.)

Bain's Logic

Though Haskell's *Index to the Nation* leaves this review unassigned, Peirce is no doubt the author. He reviewed numerous logic books for the *Nation,* and the attitudes toward British logicians as well as the kinds of themes and subjects treated and referred to in the review are thoroughly Peircean. For further discussions of Peirce's view of British logicians, see items 8, 24, 30–33, and 48 in the present volume.

442.3 Dr. Whewell. . . .] Whewell, *Novum Organon,* pp. 97–98 [aphs. 17–23].
442.4–5 "a body. . . ."] Bain, *Logic,* 1:1.
442.12–16 The author . . . disappear.] Ibid., 2:243.
442.35 he cites . . . Berthollet] Ibid., 2:254.
443.9–10 "deducible . . . ,"] Ibid., 2:210.
443.24–27 "By including. . . ."] Ibid., 2:158.

Peirce to Jevons

This is the only extant letter in the correspondence between Peirce and Jevons, deposited in the W. S. Jevons Papers in the Manchester University Library in England. There are no letters or letter drafts among the Peirce Papers. Printed by permission of the Manchester University Library.

445.31 Take my....] This and the following two references are to "Description of a Notation for the Logic of Relatives," item 39 in the present volume. See 361.9–10 above.

446.2–4 On p. 15....] See p. 376 above.

446.10 a note on p. 2] See note 1 on p. 360 above.

446.26 In a former paper] The reference is to "Some Consequences of Four Incapacities," item 22 above. Peirce's argument is summarized at the beginning of item 23 and it appears, less clearly, in item 4.

447.9 Peirce had sailed for Europe on 18 June 1870; he returned on 7 March 1871.

De Morgan

Haskell's *Index to the Nation* does not identify the author of this two-part obituary, which appeared in two successive issues of the *Nation*. The second part is almost certainly by Peirce; the first less certainly so. Peirce had met De Morgan in London on 11 July 1870, less than a year before the latter's death.

448.17 "he raised ...,"] Not located.

448.26–27 "He passed ..."] Not located.

449.2–3 A treatise....] This treatise "by C. D. with a Preface by A. B." was written by De Morgan's wife, Sophia Elizabeth De Morgan.

449.20–22 one of ... logic;] The reference is to De Morgan's "On the Syllogism, No. IV" of 1859.

449.26 his controversy ...,] See De Morgan, *Formal Logic*, pp. 297–323 ["Account of a controversy between the Author of this Work and Sir William Hamilton of Edinburgh; and final reply to the latter"].

450.9–10 bibliography of arithmetic] De Morgan, *Arithmetical Books from the Invention of Printing to the Present Time: Being Brief Notices of a Large Number of Works drawn up from Actual Inspection* (London: Taylor and Walton, 1847).

450.16–17 "Budget....] This was published separately, with author's additions, by De Morgan's widow in 1872. A second edition appeared in 1915 (Chicago: Open Court).

Copulas of Algebra

This brief though interesting treatment of the copulas of algebra appears on both sides of four large sheets. Though there are some revisions (and doodles on the penultimate page) and several lines and clauses are crossed out, the manuscript is carefully inscribed on the whole. What occasioned its writing is not known.

451.13–14   (developed in . . .)] See item 3 above, pp. 32–42.

Babbage

Though Haskell's *Index to the Nation* does not identify the author of this obituary, both internal and external evidence suggests that it was written by Peirce. No one else in his time had the expertise to write the obituary, to understand all the technical and mechanical requirements of the machine, and to realize that it could be accomplished only by upgrading the tool-maker's art. Peirce's authorship seems to be further substantiated by the reference to his elder brother, James Mills Peirce.

458.23   Scheutz] Georg Scheutz (1785–1873), a Swedish engineer, built a machine of modest capacity working from a magazine account of Babbage's project. It was used for many years at the Dudley Observatory in Albany, New York.

458.33–34   Mr. Babbage. . . .] See his *A Comparative View of the Various Institutions for the Assurance of Lives* (1826), *Thoughts on the Principles of Taxation* (1848), and *On the Economy of Machinery and Manufactures* (1832), to mention only three.

458.36–37   He was. . . .] There are eight Bridgewater Treatises, written between 1833 and 1840, so called after Francis Henry Egerton, 8th Earl of Bridgewater (1756–1829), who at his death left £8,000 to the authors of the best treatises "On the Power, Wisdom, and Goodness of God, as manifested in the Creation." According to the preface of the second edition (1838), Babbage's *The Ninth Bridgewater Treatise: A Fragment* (London: J. Murray, 1837) "does not form a part of that series [of Bridgewater Treatises]."

459.5–11   "If. . . ."] Not located.

459.16–17   The publication . . . 1826] Babbage's *Table of Logarithms of the Natural Numbers, from 1 to 108000* was published by J. Murray in London in 1827.

459.28–29   In 1841. . . .] See De Morgan's "On the Use of Small Tables of Logarithms in Commercial Calculations, and on the Practicability of Decimal Coinage," published in *Contributions to the British Almanac.*

459.33–34   Mr. T. Chappelier] Not identified. Perhaps the reference is to Jean-Charles Chapellier, who in 1848 published *Eléments d'arithmétique théorique.*

Fraser's Berkeley

Peirce's untitled 'critical notice' of Fraser's edition of the works of Berkeley is, in the words of Chauncey Wright, "much more than a mere notice" and probably the most important such notice he ever wrote. Here, he later said, he "first declared" for realism, a modified scholastic realism, and here we find the germ of pragmatism. Peirce intended to use this notice as essay 7 for his "Search for a Method" in 1893. For other discussions of the nominalist-realist controversy, see items 8, 14, 22, 30–33, and 42 in the present volume. See also the two immediately following items as well as P 791, "Berkeley's Works," Peirce's review of the 1901 edition published in the *Nation* 73(1 August 1901):95–96.

463.14   Aristotle, *Posterior Analytics*, 83a33–34 ("they are mere prattle or twitterings, and even if they exist, they are irrelevant").

464.17   the time of Edward I] Edward reigned 1272–1307.

467.19–21   "Few. . . ."] Hallam, *View of Europe*, p. 684.

470.37   Copernican step] See Kant, *Werke*, 2:670, 673n2 [*Critique*, B16, 22n2].

472.5–473.31   See 277.23–37 and the accompanying editorial note.

474.13–28   Ockham, *Summa logicae*, p. 1, chap. 13, fol. 8a.

474n.1–2   The *entia*. . . .] The exact phrase (in Berkeley's *Works*, 4:384) has not been found in Durandus, though the idea occurs several times; see, for example, *In sententias*, b. 2, dist. 6, qu. 5, §4, fol. 139a.

475.17   Durandus] See footnote 2 on the preceding page.

475.36–476.1   "From hence . . . thing."] Hobbes, *English Works*, 1:36 [*Elements of Philosophy*].

476.13   a body] "any body" in the original.

476.18   For when] "For as when" in the original.

476.23   to it form] "to it either form" in the original.

477.24–32   Locke, *Human Understanding*, pp. 82–83 [vol. 3, b. 4, chap. 7, §9]. (See 233.23–26.)

478.1–19   Berkeley, *Works*, 1:146 [*Principles of Human Knowledge*, §14 of introduction].

478.20–22   "Mem. . . ."] Ibid., 4:448 ["Metaphysical Commonplace Book"].

479.13–481.16   For Berkeley's views on reality, existence, and experience, see especially his *Principles of Human Knowledge*, §89, and his "Commonplace Book," §§29–33.

479.20–22   "These two . . . externality."] Not located.

480.2–4   "As sure. . . ."] Berkeley, *Works*, 1:304 [*Second Dialogue between Hylas and Philonous*].

481.29   "mental chemistry"] The reference is to David Hartley's 'white medullary substance' and the related theories on sensation and imagination; see especially his *Observations on Man, His Frame, His Duty and His Expectations* (London, 1749).

482.25–43 Berkeley, *Works*, 1:208, 210–11 [*Principles of Human Knowledge*, §§102, 106, 107]. The parenthetical reference is to an older edition, but not to that of 1784 or that of 1843.

483.1–2 *"that the. . . ."*] Archer Butler in an article in the *Dublin University Magazine* 7:538–39; quoted in Fraser's *Life and Letters of George Berkeley* [*Works*, 4:407].

484.23–25 Professor Fraser. . . .] See Berkeley, *Works*, 1:3 [Fraser's preface to Berkeley's *Vision*].

484.27–32 "Our knowledge . . . had."] Helmholtz, *Optik*, p. 796.

Wright on the Berkeley Review

Haskell's *Index to the Nation* identifies Chauncey Wright as the author of this untitled note. Wright had commented briefly on No. 233 of the *North American Review* in the 2 November issue of the *Nation,* and concerning Peirce's review, had concluded that "The initials 'C.S.P.' are appended to the review of Berkeley, and, doubtless, they stand for Mr. Charles S. Peirce, who, it is probable, has of all men paid most attention to the subject which he handles in this essay. It is much more than a mere notice of Mr. Fraser's volumes, and we must reserve till next week what we have to say about it" (*Nation* 13:294). Wright had his say not the following week but four weeks later.

489.1–3 "a far more. . . ."] See 484.3–4 above.

Peirce and the Realists

The preceding item in the present volume shows that Peirce's letter should have been addressed to Chauncey Wright rather than Wendell Phillips Garrison, the editor of the *Nation.* Garrison provided the title for the present item.

490.8 Prantl and Morin] See Prantl, *Geschichte*, 2:8–11, and Morin, *Dictionnaire*, under *réalisme*.

Oliver to Peirce

This is the first of three letters from the American mathematician James Edward Oliver (1829–1895) to Peirce contained in the Peirce Papers. No letters from Peirce to Oliver, or other letters from Oliver to Peirce, have been found. The letter here printed is written on very thin paper and consists of four folded sheets with eight pages of text and an additional smaller sheet containing the last part of the postscript. Because of bleed-throughs, water stains, and holes (where the sheets were sewn together), parts of the letter are nearly illegible. The "admirable memoir" referred to at the beginning is "Description of a Notation for the Logic of Relatives," item 39 in the present volume.

Bibliography of Peirce's References*

Abbot, Francis Ellingwood. "The Conditioned and the Unconditioned." *North American Review* 99(1864):402–48.

°Abelard, Peter. *Ouvrages inédits d'Abélard pour servir à l'histoire de la philosophie scolastique en France.* Edited by Victor Cousin. Paris: Imprimerie Royale, 1836.

———. *Opera.* Vol. 1. Edited by Victor Cousin. Paris: Imprimerie Royale, 1849. (Reprinted Hildesheim and New York: Georg Olms, 1970.)

Albertus Magnus. *Commentarii in primum librum sententiarum (dist. I–XXV).* Vol. 25 of *Opera omnia.* Edited by Auguste Borgnet. Paris: Ludovicus Vivès, 1893.

Aldrich, Henry. *Artis logicæ rudimenta.* 4th ed. Edited by H. L. Mansel. London: Rivingtons, 1862.

Alexander of [H]Ales. *Summa theologica.* Edited by Bernardinus Klumper. Ad Claras Aquas: Collegium S. Bonaventurae, 1924.

°Andrews, Ethan Allen, and Solomon Stoddard. *A Grammar of the Latin Language, for the Use of Schools and Colleges.* 18th ed. Boston: Crocker and Brewster, 1850.

Anselm. *Monologium et proslogion nec non liber pro insipiente cum libro apologetico.* Vol. 1 of *Sancti Anselmi Contuariensis opuscula philosophico-theologica selecta.* Edited by Carolus Haas. Tübingen, 1863.

°Aristotle. *Aristoteles Graece.* 2 vols. Edited by Immanuel Bekker. Berlin: Georg Reimer, 1831. (Vols. 1 and 2 of *Aristotelis opera,* the famous five-volume Berlin edition.)

°———. *Aristotelis Organon graece.* 2 vols. Edited by Theodor Waitz. Leipzig: Hahn, 1844–46.

———. *Operum Aristotelis Stagiritæ philosophorum omnium longè principis nova editio, græcè & latiné.* Edited by Giulio Pace. Genevæ, 1597.

Bachmann, Karl Friedrich. *System der Logik: Ein Handbuch zum Selbststudium.* Leipzig, 1828.

°Bacon, Francis. *Novum Organum; or, True Suggestions for the Interpretation of Nature.* Translated by Andrew Johnson. London: Bell & Daldy, 1859.

°Bain, Alexander. *Logic.* 2 vols. London: Longmans, Green, Reader, & Dyer, 1870.

*The degree symbol (°) identifies works Peirce is known to have owned.

Baumgarten, Alexander Gottlieb. *Acroasis Logica.* 2nd ed. Halle, 1773.

Beneke, Friedrich Eduard. *System der Logik als Kunstlehre des Denkens.* 2 vols. Berlin: Ferdinand Dümmler, 1842.

°Berengarius (of Tours). *De sacra coena adversus Lanfrancum liber posterior.* Edited by A. F. and F. Th. Vischer. Berlin: Haude and Spener, 1834.

°Berkeley, George. *The Works of George Berkeley.* 2 vols. Edited by G. N. Wright. London: Printed for Thomas Tegg, 1843.

°———. *The Works of George Berkeley.* 4 vols. Edited by Alexander Campbell Fraser. Oxford: Clarendon, 1871.

Bernoulli, Jakob. *Ars conjectandi.* Edited by Nicolas Bernoulli. Basel, 1713.

°Boole, George. *An Investigation of the Laws of Thought, on which are founded the Mathematical Theories of Logic and Probabilities.* London: Walton and Maberly, 1854.

Bowen, Francis. *A Treatise on Logic; or, The Laws of Pure Thought—Comprising both the Aristotelic and Hamiltonian Analyses of Logical Forms, and Some Chapters of Applied Logic.* Cambridge, MA: Sever & Francis, 1864.

°Burgersdicius. *Institutionum logicarum libri duo.* Cambridge: Joann. Hayes, 1680.

°———. *Institutionum metaphysicarum lib. II.* Oxford: H. Hall, 1675.

Calderwood, Henry. *The Philosophy of the Infinite; with Special Reference to the Theories of Sir William Hamilton and M. Cousin.* Edinburgh: Thomas Constable and Co., 1854.

Chauvin, Etienne. *Lexicon philosophicum.* Leonardiae: Franciscus Halma, 1713. [2nd ed. of following item.]

———. *Lexicon rationale sive thesaurus philosophicus.* Rotterdam: Petrus vander Slaart, 1692.

Comte, Auguste. *Cours de philosophie positive.* 2 vols. Paris: Bachelier, 1835.

———. *The Positive Philosophy of Auguste Comte.* Translated and condensed by Harriet Martineau. Vol. 1. New York: D. Appleton and Co., 1854.

Conimbricenses. *Commentarii collegii conimbricensis societatis Iesu, in tres libros De anima Aristotelis Stagiritae.* 3rd ed. Cologne: Lazarus Zetzner, 1600.

Cousin, Victor. *Fragments philosophiques: philosophie scholastique.* 2nd ed. Paris: Ladrange, 1840.

Cudworth, Ralph. *A Treatise Concerning Eternal and Immutable Morality.* London: Printed for James and John Knapton, at the Crown in St. Paul's Church-yard, 1731.

De Morgan, Augustus. *Formal Logic: or The Calculus of Inference, Necessary and Probable.* London: Taylor and Walton, 1847.

———. "On the Syllogism, No. IV, and on the Logic of Relations." *Transactions of the Cambridge Philosophical Society* 10(1864):331–58.

———. *Syllabus of a Proposed System of Logic.* London: Walton and Maberly, 1860.

°Descartes, René. *Œuvres choisies.* New ed. Paris: Garnier Frères, 1865.

————. *Principia philosophiae.* Amsterdam: Ludovicus Elzevirius, 1650.

Devey, Joseph. *Logic, or The Science of Inference: A Systematic View of the Principles of Evidence, and the Methods of Inference in the Various Departments of Human Knowledge.* London: H. G. Bohn, 1854.

Drobisch, Moritz Wilhelm. *Neue Darstellung der Logik nach ihren einfachsten Verhältnissen: mit Rücksicht auf Mathematik und Naturwissenschaft.* 3rd ed. Leipzig: Leopold Voss, 1863.

Duncan, William. *The Elements of Logic: In Four Books.* Edinburgh: Printed for Bell & Bradfute, Peter Hill & Co. and Ogle, Allardice, & Thomson, 1819.

Duns Scotus. *Opera omnia.* 12 vols. Edited by Luke Wadding. Lugduni, 1639. (The Wadding edition.)

————. *Opera omnia.* 26 vols. Paris: Ludovicus Vivès, 1891–95. (The Vivès edition, a revised version of Wadding's.)

————. *Opera omnia.* Edited by Charles Balić et al. Vatican City, 1950–. (The Vatican edition; so far only the *Lecturae* and the first two parts of the *Ordinatio* have appeared.)

°————. *Oxoniense scriptum in librum primum Sententiarum Magistri Petri Lombardi.* Edited by Joannes ab Incarnatione. Conimbricae, 1609.

°————. *Quaestiones quatuor voluminum scripti Oxoniensis super Sententias.* Venice, 1580.

°————. *Quaestiones quodlibetales.* Edited by Thomas Penketh. Venice, 1477.

————. *Quaestiones Scoti super Universalia Porphyrij: necnon Aristotelis Praedicamenta ac Peryarmenias.* Venice: B. Locatellus, 1508.

°————. *Quaestiones subtilissimae Scoti in metaphysicam Aristotelis.* Venice, 1497.

°————. *Scriptum in quatuor libros Sententiarum.* 2 vols. Venice, 1477.

Durandus a Sancto Porciano. *In Petri Lombardi Sententias theologicas commentariorum libri quarti.* Venice, 1571.

°Eck, Johann. *In summulas Petri Hispani extemporaria et succincta sed succosa explanatio.* Augustae Vindelicorum, 1516.

Emerson, Ralph Waldo. "Brahma." In *May-Day and Other Pieces.* Boston: Ticknor and Fields, 1867.

Erigena, John Scotus. *De divisione naturae: libri quinque.* Edited by C. B. Schlüter. Monasterium Guestphalorum: Aschendorff, 1838.

Esser, Wilhelm. *System der Logik.* 2nd ed. Münster: In der Theissingschen Buchhandlung, 1830.

°Eustachius a Sancto Paulo. *Summa philosophiae quadripartita, de rebus dialecticis, moralibus, physicis, & metaphysicis.* Cologne: Lazarus Zetzner, 1620.

Fischer, Friedrich. *Lehrbuch der Logik, für academische Vorlesungen und Gymnasialvorträge.* Stuttgart, 1838.

°Fleming, William. *The Vocabulary of Philosophy, Mental, Moral, and Metaphysical; with Quotations and References; for the Use of Students.* London and Glasgow: Richard Griffin and Company, 1857.

Fowler, Thomas. *The Elements of Deductive Logic, Designed Mainly for the Use of Junior Students in the Universities.* Oxford: Clarendon, 1867.

Fries, Jakob Friedrich. *System der Logik: Ein Handbuch für Lehrer und zum Selbstgebrauch.* 3rd ed. Heidelberg: C. F. Winter, 1837.

°Furtmair, Max. *Philosophisches Real-Lexikon.* 4 vols. Augsburg: Verlag der Karl Kollmann'schen Buchhandlung, 1853.

Gerlach, Gottlieb Wilhelm. *Grundriss der Logik, zum Gebrauch bei Vorlesungen.* 2nd ed. Halle: Gebauersche Buchhandlung, 1822.

Gray, Thomas. "Elegy Written in a Country Churchyard." In *The Poetical Works of Thomas Gray.* [Cambridge, MA:] Sever and Francis, [n.d.].

Hallam, Henry. *View of the State of Europe during the Middle Ages.* 4th ed. London: Alex. Murray & Son, 1869.

°Hamilton, William. *Discussions on Philosophy and Literature, Education and University Reform.* New York: Harper & Brothers, 1853.

°————. *Lectures on Logic.* Edited by Henry L. Mansel and John Veitch. Boston: Gould and Lincoln, 1859.

°————. *Lectures on Metaphysics.* Edited by Henry L. Mansel and John Veitch. Boston: Gould and Lincoln, 1859.

Hamilton, William Rowan. *Lectures on Quaternions.* Dublin: Hodges and Smith, 1853.

°Hegel, Georg Wilhelm Friedrich. *Encyclopädie der philosophischen Wissenschaften im Grundrisse.* 2nd ed. Heidelberg: August Osswald, 1827.

°————. *Philosophische Propädeutik.* Vol. 18 of *Werke,* 1840.

°————. *Wissenschaft der Logik.* Vols. 3–5 of *Werke,* 1833–34.

°————. *Werke: Vollständige Ausgabe durch einen Verein des Verewigten.* 18 vols. Edited by Philipp Marheineke et al. Berlin: Duncker and Humblot, 1832–1840; 2nd ed., 1840–1844. (Peirce owned vols. 1, 7, 16, 17, and 18 of the first edition, all others of the second.)

Helmholtz, H[ermann Ludwig Ferdinand von]. *Handbuch der physiologischen Optik.* Leipzig: Leopold Voss, 1867. [Vol. 9 of *Allgemeine Encyklopädie der Physik.* Edited by Gustav Karsten.]

°Herbart, Johann Friedrich. *Lehrbuch zur Einleitung in die Philosophie.* Vol. 1 of *Sämmtliche Werke.* Edited by G. Hartenstein. Leipzig: Leopold Voss, 1850.

°Hobbes, Thomas. *The English Works of Thomas Hobbes of Malmesbury.* 6 vols. Edited by Sir William Molesworth. London: John Bohn, 1839–1841. (Peirce owned only the first volume.)

°Hollmann, Samuel Christian. *Logica et philosophia prima.* Vol. 1 of *In universam philosophiam introductio.* Wittemberg: Karl Sigmund Henning, 1734.

°Hoppe, J[anus]. *Die gesammte Logik: Ein Lehr- und Handbuch, aus den Quellen bearbeitet, vom Standpunkte der Naturwissenschaften, und gleichzeitig als Kritik der bisherigen Logik; in allgemein verständlicher Darstellung.* Paderborn: Ferdinand Schöningh, 1868.

°Hume, David. *An Enquiry Concerning Human Understanding.* In vol. 2 of *Essays and Treatises on Several Subjects.* New ed. London: Printed for T. Cadell [et al.], 1788.

————. *An Enquiry Concerning Human Understanding.* In *Hume's Enquiries.* 2nd ed. Edited by L. A. Selby-Bigge. Oxford: Clarendon, 1902.

————. *A Treatise of Human Nature: Being an Attempt to Introduce the Experimental Method of Reasoning into Moral Subjects.* New ed. 2 vols. London: Printed for Thomas and Joseph Allman, 1817.

————. *A Treatise of Human Nature.* Edited by L. A. Selby-Bigge. Oxford: Clarendon, 1896.

°James, Henry [Sr.]. *The Secret of Swedenborg: Being an Elucidation of His Doctrine of the Divine Natural Humanity.* Boston: Fields, Osgood, & Co., 1869.

Jevons, W. Stanley. *Pure Logic or the Logic of Quality apart from Quantity: with Remarks on Boole's System and on the Relation of Logic and Mathematics.* London: Edward Stanford, 1864.

————. *The Substitution of Similars: The True Principle of Reasoning, Derived from a Modification of Aristotle's Dictum.* London: Macmillan, 1869.

John of Salisbury. *The Metalogicon of John of Salisbury: A Twelfth-Century Defense of the Verbal and Logical Arts of the Trivium.* Translated by Daniel D. McGarry. Berkeley and Los Angeles: University of California Press, 1955. (Reprinted Gloucester, MA: Peter Smith, 1971.)

°————. *Metalogicus.* Paris: Apud Hadrianum Beys, 1610.

°Kant, Immanuel. *Anthropologie in pragmatischer Hinsicht.* Part 7:2 of *Sämmtliche Werke,* 1838.

————. *Critik der reinen Vernunft.* Riga: Johann Friedrich Hartknoch, 1781; 2nd ed., 1787.

°————. *De mundi sensibilis atque intelligibilis forma et principiis.* In part 1 of *Sämmtliche Werke,* 1838.

°————. *Kritik der reinen Vernunft.* Part 2 of *Sämmtliche Werke,* 1838.

°————. *Kritik der Urtheilskraft und Beobachtungen über das Gefühl des Schönen und Erhabenen.* Part 4 of *Sämmtliche Werke,* 1838.

°————. *Logik.* In part 3 of *Sämmtliche Werke,* 1838.

°————. *Prolegomena zu einer jeden künftigen Metaphysik, die als Wissenschaft wird auftreten können.* In part 3 of *Sämmtliche Werke,* 1838.

°————. *Schriften zur Philosophie der Natur.* Part 5 of *Sämmtliche Werke,* 1839.

°————. *Immanuel Kant's sämmtliche Werke.* 12 parts in 14 vols. Edited by Karl Rosenkranz and Friedrich Wilhelm Schubert. Leipzig: Leopold Voss, 1838–1842.

Kiesewetter, J. G. C. C. *Grundriss einer allgemeinen Logik nach Kantischen Grundsätzen: zum Gebrauch für Vorlesungen.* 4th ed. Leipzig: H. A. Köchly, 1824.

°Lambert, J[ohann] H[einrich]. *Neues Organon oder Gedanken über die Erforschung und Bezeichnung des Wahren und dessen Unterscheidung vom Irrthum und Schein.* 2 vols. Leipzig: Johann Wendler, 1764. (Reprinted Hildesheim: Georg Olms, 1965.)

Leibniz, Gottfried Wilhelm. *Opera omnia, nunc primum collecta, in classes distributa, praefationibus et indicibus exornata.* Vol. 6. Edited by Ludwig Dutens. Geneva: Apud Fratres de Tournes, 1768.

———. *Opera philosophica quae exstant latina gallica germanica omnia.* Vol. 1. Edited by Johannes Eduard Erdmann. Berlin: G. Eichler, 1840.

———. *Die philosophischen Schriften.* Vol. 3. Edited by C. J. Gerhardt. Berlin: Weidmannsche Buchhandlung, 1887.

Lobatchewsky, Nikolai. *Geometrische Untersuchungen zur Theorie der Parallellinien.* Berlin: G. Fincke, 1840.

°Locke, John. *An Essay Concerning Human Understanding; with Thoughts on the Conduct of the Understanding.* 3 vols. London: Printed for C. Bathurst [et al.], 1795.

Lotze, R. Hermann. *Logik.* Leipzig: Weidmann'sche Buchhandlung, 1843.

°McGregor, P. *A System of Logic, comprising a Discussion of the Various Means of Acquiring and Retaining Knowledge, and Avoiding Error.* New York: Harper & Brothers, 1862.

Mahan, Asa. *The Science of Logic; or, The Analysis of the Laws of Thought.* New York: A. S. Barnes, 1857.

°Mansel, Henry Longueville. *The Limits of Religious Thought.* Boston: Gould and Lincoln, 1859.

° ———. *The Philosophy of the Conditioned: Comprising some Remarks on Sir William Hamilton's Philosophy and on Mr. J. S. Mill's Examination of that Philosophy.* London and New York: Alexander Strahan, 1866.

———. *Prolegomena Logica: An Inquiry into the Psychological Character of Logical Processes.* 2nd ed. Oxford: Henry Hammans, 1860.

°Mill, James. *Analysis of the Phenomena of the Human Mind.* 2 vols. A new edition with notes by Alexander Bain, Andrew Findlater, and George Grote; edited with additional notes by John Stuart Mill. London: Longmans Green Reader and Dyer, 1869.

°Mill, John Stuart. *A System of Logic, Ratiocinative and Inductive: Being a Connected View of the Principles of Evidence, and the Methods of Scientific Investigation.* 2 vols. 6th ed. London: Longmans, Green, and Co., 1865.

Montaigne, Michel Eyquem de. *Works of Michael de Montaigne.* By W. Hazlitt. New ed. by O. W. Wight. Vol. 2. New York: Hurd and Houghton, 1864.

Morin, Frédéric. *Dictionnaire de philosophie et de théologie scolastiques, ou études sur l'enseignement philosophique et théologique au moyen âge.* 2 vols. Paris: J.-P. Migne, 1856.

Newton, Isaac. *Philosophiae naturalis principia mathematica.* 2 vols. Edited by Thomas Le Seur and Franciscus Jacquier. Glasgow: T. T. and J. Tegg, 1833.

°Paulus Venetus. *Sophismata aurea et perutilia.* Pavia, 1483.

°Peirce, Benjamin. *Linear Associative Algebra.* Washington, D.C., 1870.

°Petrus Hispanus. *Compendiarius parvorum logicalium continens perutiles Petri Hispani tractatus priores sex & clarissimi philosophi Marsilij dialectices documenta.* Edited by Konrad Pschlacher. Vienna, 1512.

———. *Summulae logicales.* Venice, 1597.

————. *Summulae Logicales.* Edited by I. M. Bocheński. Turin: Marietti, 1947.

————. *The Summulae logicales of Peter of Spain.* Edited by Joseph P. Mullaly. Notre Dame, IN: University of Notre Dame Press, 1945.

°Plato. *The Sophist.* In vol. 3 of *The Works of Plato.* Edited and translated by George Burges. London: Henry G. Bohn, 1854.

°————. *Theaetetus.* In vol. 1 of *The Works of Plato.* Edited and translated by Henry Cary. London: Henry G. Bohn, 1852.

Plutarch. *Varia scripta quae Moralia vulgo vocantur.* Vol. 6. Leipzig: Karl Tauchnitz, 1829.

°Porphyry. *Isagoge.* In *Scholia in Aristotelem.* Edited by Christian August Brandis. Berlin: Georg Reimer, 1836. (Vol. 4 of the famous Berlin edition of Aristotle.)

°Porter, Noah. *The Human Intellect: With an Introduction upon Psychology and the Soul.* 4th ed. New York: Charles Scribner's Sons, 1868.

[Port-Royal Logic]. *Logique de Port-Royal.* Edited by Charles Jourdain. Paris: Hachette, 1854.

°*The Port-Royal Logic, by Antoine Arnauld and Pierre Nicole.* 2nd ed. Translated by Thomas Spencer Baynes. Edinburgh: Sutherland and Knox, 1851.

°Prantl, Carl. *Geschichte der Logik im Abendlande.* 3 vols. Leipzig: S. Hirzel, 1855–1867.

°Reid, Thomas. *The Works of Thomas Reid: Now Fully Collected, with Selections from His Unpublished Letters.* 5th ed. Edited by William Hamilton. Edinburgh: Maclachlan and Stewart, 1858.

Reinhold, Ernst Christian Gottlieb. *Die Logik oder die allgemeine Denkformenlehre.* Jena: Cröker, 1827.

Ritter, Heinrich. *Abriss der philosophischen Logik: Für Vorlesungen.* 2nd ed. Berlin: T. Trautwein, 1829.

Rösling, Christian Lebrecht. *Die Lehren der reinen Logik.* Ulm, 1826.

°Roscoe, Henry E. *Spectrum Analysis: Six Lectures, Delivered in 1868, Before the Society of Apothecaries of London.* New York: D. Appleton and Co., 1869.

Schelling, Friedrich Wilhelm Joseph von. *Ideen zu einer Philosophie der Natur als Einleitung in das Studium dieser Wissenschaft.* In vol. 2 of *Sämmtliche Werke.* Edited by Karl Friedrich August Schelling. Stuttgart and Augsburg: J. G. Cotta, 1856. (In vol. 1 of *Schellings Werke.* Edited by Manfred Schröter. Munich: C. H. Beck, 1927.)

°Schmid, Carl Christian Erhard. *Wörterbuch zum leichtern Gebrauch der Kantischen Schriften nebst einer Abhandlung.* 2nd ed. Jena: Crökersche Buchhandlung, 1788.

Schulze, Gottlob Ernst. *Grundsätze der allgemeinen Logik.* 5th ed. Göttingen: Vandenhoeck and Ruprecht, 1831.

Seydel, Rudolf. *Logik oder Wissenschaft vom Wissen, mit Berücksichtigung des Verhältnisses zwischen Philosophie und Theologie im Umrisse dargestellt.* Leipzig: Breitkopf and Härtel, 1866.

Shedden, Thomas. *The Elements of Logic.* London: Longman, Green, Longman, Roberts, & Green, 1864.

Sigwart, Heinrich Christoph Wilhelm. *Handbuch zu Vorlesungen über die Logik.* 3rd ed. Tübingen: Osiander, 1835.

Spalding, William. *An Introduction to Logical Science* (being a reprint of the article "Logic" from the 8th ed. of Encyclopædia Britannica). Edinburgh: A. and C. Black, 1857.

°Stewart, Dugald. *Elements of the Philosophy of the Human Mind.* Vol. 3 of *The Collected Works of Dugald Stewart.* Edited by William Hamilton. Edinburgh: Thomas Constable and Co., 1854.

Strümpell, Ludwig. *Entwurf der Logik.* Mitau and Leipzig, 1846.

Swift, Jonathan. *Travels into Several Remote Nations of the World, by Lemuel Gulliver.* Philadelphia: Porter & Coates, [n.d.].

Sylvester, J. J. Address to the Mathematics and Physics Section, Thirty-Ninth Meeting of the British Association for the Advancement of Science, Exeter, August 1869. *Report of the Thirty-Ninth Meeting of the British Association for the Advancement of Science,* pp. 1–8. London: John Murray, 1870.

°Tartaretus, Petrus. *Expositio magistri Petri Tatareti in summulas Petri Hyspani.* Lugduni, 1509.

°Thomas Aquinas. *Opuscula Sancti Thome: quibus alias impressis nuper hec addidimus. vz. Summam totius logice. Tractatum celeberrimum de usuris nusquam alias impressum.* Venice, 1508.

———. *Summa theologica.* 17th ed. Edited by Nicolai [et al.]. Paris: Bloud and Barral, [1856].

———. *Summa totius theologiae.* Vols. 10–16 of *Opera.* Naples: Virgiliana, 1845–1858.

Thomas of Erfurt. *De modis significandi, sive grammatica speculativa.* In vol. 1 of the Wadding edition of Duns Scotus' *Opera omnia.* Lugduni, 1639.

———. *Thomas of Erfurt: Grammatica speculativa—An Edition with Translation and Commentary.* By G. L. Bursill-Hall. London: Longman, 1972.

°Thomson, William. *An Outline of the Necessary Laws of Thought: A Treatise on Pure and Applied Logic.* 4th ed. London: W. Pickering, 1857.

°Trendelenburg, Friedrich Adolph. *Elementa Logices Aristoteleae: in usum scholarum.* 5th ed. Berlin: Gustav Bethge, 1862.

———. *Logische Untersuchungen.* Berlin: Gustav Bethge, 1840; 2nd ed., 1862.

Überweg, Friedrich. *System der Logik und Geschichte der logischen Lehren.* Bonn: Adolph Marcus, 1857.

°Venn, John. *The Logic of Chance: An Essay on the Foundations and Province of the Theory of Probability, with Especial Reference to Its Application to Moral and Social Science.* London and Cambridge: Macmillan and Co., 1866.

Vincent of Beauvais. *Speculum doctrinale.* Venetiis: Hermann Lichtenstein, 1494.

Vital du Four. *Quaestiones disputatae de rerum principio.* In vol. 3 of the Wadding, vol. 4 of the Vivès edition of Duns Scotus' *Opera omnia.*

Vorlaender, Franz. *Wissenschaft der Erkenntniss: Im Abriss systematisch entworfen.* Marburg and Leipzig: Elwert'sche Universitäts-Buchhandlung, 1847.

Watts, Isaac. *Logick, or The Right Use of Reason in the Enquiry after Truth.* 5th American ed. Boston: West & Richardson, 1812.

Whewell, William. "Demonstration that All Matter is Heavy." *Transactions of the Cambridge Philosophical Society* 7(1842):197–207.

°————. *Novum Organon Renovatum.* 3rd ed. London: John W. Parker and Son, 1858.

William of Ockham. *Ockham's Theory of Terms: Part I of the 'Summa Logicae'.* Translated and Introduced by Michael J. Loux. Notre Dame, IN: University of Notre Dame Press, 1974.

°————. *Quodlibeta septem una cum tractatu de sacramento altaris.* Argentiae, 1491.

°————. *Summa logicae.* Paris: Johannes Higman, 1488.

Wilson, W. D. *An Elementary Treatise on Logic; Part I. Analysis of Formulae, Part II. Method. With an Appendix of Examples for Analysis and Criticism. And a Copious Index of Terms and Subjects.* New York: D. Appleton and Company, 1857.

Wundt, Wilhelm. *Vorlesungen über die Menschen- und Thierseele.* 2 vols. Leipzig: Leopold Voss, 1863.

CHRONOLOGICAL LIST
1867–1871

Three kinds of materials are included here:

1. All of Peirce's known publications, identified by P followed by a number. For these numbers and for further bibliographical information, see *A Comprehensive Bibliography and Index of the Published Works of Charles Sanders Peirce with a Bibliography of Secondary Studies,* ed. Kenneth L. Ketner et al. (Greenwich, CT: Johnson Associates, 1977).

2. All of Peirce's known manuscripts and annotated offprints, identified by MS followed by a number. These numbers reflect the Kloesel rearrangement and chronological ordering of the Peirce Papers, the originals of which are in The Houghton Library of Harvard University, and of papers found in other collections. Parentheses after the MS number give either the name or location of those collections, or they identify the Robin manuscript number. See Richard S. Robin, *Annotated Catalogue of the Papers of Charles S. Peirce* (Amherst: University of Massachusetts Press, 1967), and "The Peirce Papers: A Supplementary Catalogue," *Transactions of the Charles S. Peirce Society* 7(1971):37–57.

3. Selected letters and letter drafts, identified by L followed by a (Robin) number. Parentheses give the location of letters not contained in the Peirce Papers.

Not included here, or in future lists, are (1) those items in *A Comprehensive Bibliography and Index* that merely make mention of Peirce's Coast Survey duties and observations (in the annual *Report of the Superintendent of the United States Coast Survey*) or give brief descriptive notes of papers which were presented at professional meetings or on other occasions, but for which there are no manuscripts, and (2) those manuscript items that are of purely biographical interest, such as address books or diaries.

Manuscripts and a few rarely republished items that have appeared in earlier editions are identified in brackets at the end of the entry. CP refers to the *Collected Papers,* while other references are given in full.

Dates of publication or composition appear to the right; those in italics are Peirce's own. Descriptive or supplied titles appear in italic brackets. Journal titles are abbreviated. Items marked with an asterisk are published in the present volume.

*P 30   12 March 1867
   "On an Improvement in Boole's Calculus of Logic." *Proc of the
   Am Acad of Arts and Sciences* 7, 250–261. [CP 3.1–19.]
*MS 140 (339)   *23 March–7 December 1867*
   [The Logic Notebook].
*P 31   9 April 1867
   "On the Natural Classification of Arguments." *Proc of the Am
   Acad of Arts and Sciences* 7, 261–287. [CP 2.461–516.]
*P 32   14 May 1867
   "On a New List of Categories." *Proc of the Am Acad of Arts and
   Sciences* 7, 287–298. [CP 1.545–559.]
MS 141 (762)   May–June 1867
   [Draft of Venn Review (P 21)].
P 35   5 June 1867
   "Deposition of Charles Saunders Peirce [in the Howland Will
   Case]." In *Supreme Court of the United States, in Equity. Hetty
   H. Greene & Edward H. Greene, in Equity, vs. Thomas Mandell
   and Others: Appeal from the Circuit Court of the District of
   Massachusetts, filed Dec. 17, 1868,* pp. 761–765. [Unmarked copy
   in MS 142.]
*P 21   July 1867
   ["Venn's *The Logic of Chance*"]. *North Am R* 105, 317–321. [CP
   8.1–6.]
MS 143 (722, 719, 396)   summer–fall 1867
   Chapter I. Fundamental Notions.
*MS 144 (721)   summer–fall 1867
   Chapter I. *One, Two,* and *Three.*
*P 33   10 September 1867
   "Upon the Logic of Mathematics." *Proc of the Am Acad of Arts
   and Sciences* 7, 402–412. [CP 3.20–44.]
*P 34   13 November 1867
   "Upon Logical Comprehension and Extension." *Proc of the Am
   Acad of Arts and Sciences* 7, 416–432. [CP 2.391–426.]
*MS 145 (1174)   *November 1867*
   Specimen of a Dictionary of the Terms of Logic and allied
   Sciences: A to ABS.
*MS 146 (970)   winter 1867–68
   [Critique of Positivism]. [Published in parts in *Values in a Uni-*

verse of Chance, ed. Philip P. Wiener (Garden City, NY: Double-
day, 1958), pp. 137–141; rpt. as Charles S. Peirce: Selected Writings (New York: Dover, 1966).]

O 1247   1867
"A Philosopher's Political Diagnosis." In New York: A Symphonic
Study, by Melusina Fay Peirce (New York: Neale, 1918), pp. 100–
104. [Cf. P 89.]

P 23–24   1868
["Atlantic Almanac Calendars, Tables, Notes"]. Boston: Ticknor
and Fields, 1868. ("Entered according to Act of Congress, in the
year 1867, by Ticknor.")

MS 147 (1549)   1 January 1868
Catalogue of Books on Mediaeval Logic which are available in
Cambridge.

*L 183 (Harris Collection)   24 January 1868
[Letter, Peirce to W. T. Harris]. [This letter, three further letters
listed below, and several others, were first published by Wallace
Nethery, "C. S. Peirce to W. T. Harris," Personalist 43(1962):-
35–45.]

*P 25   1868
"Nominalism versus Realism." J of Speculative Phil 2, 57–61. [CP
6.619–624.]

*L 183 (Harris Collection)   16 March 1868
[Letter, Peirce to W. T. Harris].

*MS 148 (931, 396)   winter–spring 1868
Questions on Reality.

*L 183 (Harris Collection)   9 April 1868
[Letter, Peirce to W. T. Harris].

*P 26   1868
"Questions Concerning Certain Faculties Claimed for Man." J of
Speculative Phil 2, 103–114. [CP 5.213–263.]

*MS 149 (932)   summer 1868
Potentia ex Impotentia.

MS 150 (1535)   fall 1868
Transformations of Cards.

MS 151 (339)   2–15 November 1868
[The Logic Notebook].

*L 183 (Harris Collection)   30 November 1868
[Letter, Peirce to W. T. Harris].

*MS 152 (785)   November–December 1868
Notes [to PAAAS series].

*P 27   1868
"Some Consequences of Four Incapacities." J of Speculative Phil
2, 140–157. [CP 5.264–317.]

*P 28   1868
"What Is Meant by 'Determined'." J of Speculative Phil 2, 190–
191. [CP 6.625–630.]

MS 153 (225) 1868
    Memoranda of How To Do Things.
P 37–38 1869
    ["Atlantic Almanac Calendars, Tables, Notes"]. Boston: Ticknor
    and Fields, 1869.
*P 43 18 March 1869
    "Professor Porter's *Human Intellect."* Nation 8, 211–213.
*P 41 1869
    "Grounds of Validity of the Laws of Logic: Further Consequences
    of Four Incapacities." *J of Speculative Phil* 2, 193–208. [CP 5.
    318–357.]
*P 40 June 1869
    "The Pairing of the Elements." *Chemical News, Am Supplement*
    4, 339–340.
*P 44 22 July 1869
    "Roscoe's *Spectrum Analysis."* Nation 9, 73–74.
*P 70 *20 August 1869*
    ["The Solar Eclipse of 7 August 1869"]. Coast Survey Report 1869,
    126–127.
*MS 154 (742) fall 1869
    Preliminary Sketch of Logic.
*MS 155 (339) *6–15 October 1869*
    [The Logic Notebook].
*P 45 25 November 1869
    "The English Doctrine of Ideas." *Nation* 9, 461–462.
MS 156 (584) November–December 1869
    List of British Logicians.
MS 157 (584) November–December 1869
    Lectures on British Logicians.
*MS 158 (584) November–December 1869
    Lecture I. Early nominalism and realism.
MS 159 (585) November–December 1869
    Abstract of Occam's *Summa Logices.*
*MS 160 (585) November–December 1869
    Ockam. Lecture 3.
MS 161 (585) November–December 1869
    History of Logic in England from Ockam to Bacon.
*MS 162 (586) November–December 1869
    Whewell.
MS 163 (697) winter 1869–70
    Practical Logic.
*MS 164 (697) winter 1869–70
    Lessons in Practical Logic.
*MS 165 (695, 1573) winter 1869–70
    A Practical Treatise on Logic and Methodology.
    Rules for Investigation.
    Practical Logic.

*MS 166 (365, 698)   winter 1869–70
  Chapter 2.
MS 167 (529)   winter 1869–70
  [Non-commutative multiplication and other topics in logical alge-
  bra].
P 49–51   1870
  ["Atlantic Almanac Calendars, Tables, Notes"]. Boston: Fields,
  Osgood & Co., 1870. (See especially "The Spectroscope," p. 62.)
*P 52   26 January 1870
  "Description of a Notation for the Logic of Relatives, Resulting
  from an Amplification of the Conceptions of Boole's Calculus of
  Logic." Memoirs of the Am Acad of Arts and Sciences n.s. 9,
  317–378. [CP 3.45–149. MS 168 (572) contains a copy with a few
  annotations by Peirce.]
*MS 169 (723)   winter–spring 1870
  A System of Logic.
*P 54   April 1870
  ["Henry James's The Secret of Swedenborg"]. North Am R 110,
  463–468.
MS 170 (725)   spring 1870
  [Annotated copy of "Upon Logical Comprehension and Exten-
  sion" (P 34)].
*MS 171 (587)   spring 1870
  Notes for Lectures on Logic: to be given first term 1870–71.
*P 53   4 August 1870
  "Bain's Logic." Nation 11, 77–78.
*L 227 (Jevons Papers)   25 August 1870
  [Letter, Peirce to W. S. Jevons].
*P 56   13 and 20 April 1871
  ["Augustus De Morgan"]. Nation 12, 258 and 276.
*MS 175 (576)   27 April 1871
  Of the Copulas of Algebra.
*P 60   October 1871
  ["Fraser's The Works of George Berkeley"]. North Am R 113,
  449–472. [CP 8.7–38.]
*P 57   9 November 1871
  ["Charles Babbage"]. Nation 13, 307–308.
*P 59   14 December 1871
  "Mr. Peirce and the Realists." Nation 13, 386.
MS 176 (S 86)   December 1871
  Calculus of Wealth.
MS 177 (155)   winter 1871–72
  [Physical Constants].
MS 178 (1574)   1871
  [On Logical Algebra].

Essay on Editorial Method

The writings by Peirce contained in this volume are of two kinds: those that were published during his lifetime and those he left only in manuscript form. Of the 48 Peirce items included here, 23 were published by Peirce, and they run the gamut from articles in major journals or proceedings to book reviews, two obituaries, and one Coast Survey report. The different publication sources for the 23 items number seven in all. Though seven different sources present us with seven different house publication styles, only two of the 23 items pose textual complications and are discussed at length below.

The remaining 25 Peirce texts in this volume exist in manuscripts never before published (excepting only item 11, parts of which have in fact appeared). The problems they pose derive chiefly from their physical state and from Peirce's working methods. Though widely scattered runs of manuscript pages had first to be reassembled, and in three instances pages appear to be irretrievably lost,[1] most of the manuscripts included in this volume are in good physical condition. In a few cases, portions of words are obliterated by frayed or torn edges, burns, ink stains, or water damage, but these are easily restored.

Peirce's working methods, on the other hand, present an altogether different set of problems. Most of the manuscripts included in this volume are unfinished, or at the very least must be considered unpolished. Some are carelessly inscribed or hurriedly written, and, as in the case of the lecture notes for the British Logicians series, are nothing more than abbreviated, at times cryptic, outlines. Others contain what at first glance seem to be different "drafts" of the same

---

[1]These "lost" pages occur in MSS 140, 148, and L 183 (Peirce's letter to W. T. Harris of 24 January 1868), though to call this last "irretrievably lost" is not quite accurate. The pages were removed from the letter and presumably used as printer's copy for "Nominalism *versus* Realism."

piece. On closer scrutiny, it becomes apparent that this is not the case. Peirce seldom created "drafts" by copying out an earlier version. Rather, he was more likely to begin anew, repeating perhaps the same or a similar first sentence but then going in a different direction, and thus creating several versions of a single composition. More often than not, these several versions cannot be confidently dated regarding the order in which they were written, nor can they be collated; as a result, all become justifiable candidates for publication.[2]

Many of the manuscripts published here may fairly be called "working copies." As pointed out in the discussion of the manuscripts published in volume 1, Peirce seemed to be concerned with getting his thoughts on paper, and spent his composition time searching for the most appropriate and precise words in order to achieve a lucid expression of his ideas. This is still true for the manuscripts contained in this volume, but we begin to see a marked difference between the manuscripts published in volume 1 and those published here. The early 1857–66 manuscripts exhibit a most negligent attitude on Peirce's part for such formal matters as punctuation, spelling, and paragraphing. By the late 1860s, however, he seems to be giving these matters more attention. Though the manuscripts still show much self-editing (deletions, insertions, transpositions, false starts, incomplete revisions, notes to himself, and alternative words left undecided), there are fewer and fewer characteristic misspellings, and punctuation is used more accurately. Even so, many of the manuscripts still require editorial intervention. Peirce continues to succumb to his self-proclaimed "inveterate habit of leaving letters [and syllables] out of words," for example. But a change in punctuation that he requests in a letter to one of his editors demonstrates an awareness on Peirce's part of the difference in meaning which can be brought about by a misplaced or misinterpreted point of punctuation.[3] Peirce's new attitude or level of awareness can be attributed to the fact that during the years covered by this volume, he is writing with the goal of publication in mind, and indeed is beginning to gain recognition in print.

----

[2]MS 148 provides a good example of Peirce's working methods. A large part of what appears in the three sections of this manuscript included here may also be compared to Peirce's final version in his published "Questions Concerning Certain Faculties Claimed for Man."

[3]See Peirce's letter of 16 March 1868 to W. T. Harris, pages 154–55 above.

The first, crucial step in preparing manuscripts for editing and subsequent publication lies in the transcription process. To assure the reader that he has before him what Peirce actually wrote, we have established certain transcription guidelines based on editorial theory and on the available working materials.

The Peirce Edition Project owns two sets of photocopies of the Peirce manuscripts deposited in The Houghton Library, Harvard University. These were not made directly from the originals; they are third-generation copies, made from an electroprint copy, which, in turn, was printed from the negative microfilm copy at Harvard.[4] The legibility of our photocopies is generally good, partly because Peirce used black ink as his basic writing medium. When he used lead pencil or different colors of ink and pencil for revisions and annotations, the legibility of our copies falls away sharply. For this reason, after the initial transcripts are made, they are read at least two times, by two different editors, against the photocopies. During these readings, the more difficult to read and questionable passages are marked. One of the editors then takes the transcripts to The Houghton Library and, with the help of a local person, re-reads them a third time against the originals, paying careful attention to those "questionable" or "difficult to read" passages. Also such features are noted as holes, inkblots, or colored pencil contained in the originals but not distinguishable on the copies. Upon return to the Project, the transcripts are revised to coincide with the Harvard originals.

Certain points of editorial policy concerning the transcribing of manuscripts to typewritten copies need to be stated. Peirce's incomplete revisions, misspellings, misplaced or omitted punctuation, etc., are typed exactly as they appear on the manuscript page. The underlinings (single, double, and even triple) that Peirce used for emphasis are included also, but are later interpreted as modern copy-editing instructions and are printed in the volume as italic, small capital letters, and regular capital letters respectively. As mentioned above, Peirce made many internal revisions in his manuscripts, usually during the process of composition. All such revisions are interpreted as Peirce's final intention and are incorporated into the initial transcriptions. Material that Peirce crossed out is omitted, including accompa-

---

[4]The electroprint copies were checked against the original manuscripts, and pages that had been omitted from the microfilm copy were added to make our photocopy complete.

nying punctuation that he failed to cross out; his careted-in revisions
are inserted, passages he marked for transposition are transposed,
and his instructions for moving large blocks of material are followed.[5]
For the most part, Peirce clearly marked such revisions and marginal
annotations. When he did not, we use the following established
guidelines for resolving the difficulty.

When the context permits, the questionable material is inserted
into the text. When marginal material seems better suited to a footnote, again according to context, we create a footnote for Peirce. In
either case, these are instances of editorial intervention and we record them in the Emendations list with an accompanying textual
note indicating the original placement of the material on the manuscript page. When the questionable revision or marginal annotation
cannot be incorporated into the text or placed as a footnote without
creating a nonsensical reading, it is reproduced in the Editorial
Notes, again with an explanation of its placement on the manuscript
page. The only material on the manuscript page that the reader will
not find reproduced are Peirce's page numbers and doodles, or later
annotations by other persons. Of the more than 300 manuscript
pages published in this volume, there are only four instances in
which Peirce's intended revisions and marginal annotations are unclear. All appear in MS 171 and have been placed as footnotes, specifically at 439.4, 440.1, 440.17, and 440.19.

One final point of editorial policy regarding the transcription of
manuscripts and the interpretation of Peirce's intention must be
noted. As Peirce's placement of quotation marks (both single and
double) when used in combination with a period, comma, colon, or
semi-colon is rarely precise enough to make his intention clear, we
interpret all such combinations by modern standard punctuation
practices.

Three sets of symbols have been adopted and incorporated into
the text to reflect the physical limitations of the manuscripts. In the
three cases where pages are lost, three ellipsis points within italic
brackets mark the absence. Where manuscripts are partially destroyed and words or portions of them are editorially recon-
structed, the reconstructions appear in italic brackets also; to give

---

[5]Peirce's alterations in the manuscripts are so numerous that a complete record
of them would greatly increase the size and cost of the volume. In view of the
accessibility of the microfilm edition and other photocopies of the original papers, we
supply such information only when his final intentions remain unclear.

the reader some hint as to manuscript content, we have supplied titles within italic brackets to papers that Peirce left untitled. The third symbol combination incorporated into the text is that of double and single slashes used to alert the reader to cases where Peirce left choices of words or phrases undecided. The double slash signals the beginning and ending of the undecided choice, and the single slash divides the two alternatives. The reading to the left of the single slash is the original inscription, and that to the right the interlined alternative.

Determining copy-text for Peirce's unpublished manuscripts did not prove problematical. Because his working method created variant texts which cannot be collated, each variant text theoretically stands as a separate item. Choice among these alternative texts was made with the advice of at least one of the contributing editors, and that text was chosen for publication that seemed most carefully written and most fully developed and best argued. When a contributing editor thought more than one version worth publishing, more than one is published. Each version, then, serves as its own copy-text, and no other version of the same paper is considered as having any textual authority for that one, though we may refer to others for helpful information. In the very few cases where we do have successively written collatable drafts of a single paper, the latest is considered to reflect the closest approach to Peirce's final intention and is chosen as copy-text. All earlier drafts are considered to be pre-copy-text forms without textual authority.

Nor did Peirce's published articles included in this volume pose problems regarding the choice of copy-text. Three sight collations of each article were performed using journal copies and original offprint copies (when available) obtained from three different sources. With the exception of two articles, collation indicated that each went through but a single printing.

A curious problem developed, however, with the American Academy of Arts and Sciences publications, both the *Memoirs* and the *Proceedings*. When offprint copies of Peirce's six papers were collated against their respective *Memoirs* and *Proceedings* publication copies, it was noted that three titles had been reset, one article contained renumbered signatures and pages, and, most important, five differences in punctuation were found within the text of two of the articles.

One of these differences appears in "Description of a Notation for the Logic of Relatives" (item 39), presented to the Academy on 26 January 1870, and published in its *Memoirs,* new series, volume 9, part 2. The title page of the *Memoirs* carries the imprint of Welch, Bigelow, and Company, 1873. The complete title of Peirce's paper along with his name and communication date appears at the top of the first full page of the article, recto page 317. The article itself runs through page 378 and, beginning on page 317, bears the signature numbers 44 through 51 accompanied by the volume number in the lower left-hand corner of every eighth page. The three *Memoirs* copies collated show no differences within the text and display the same instances of broken or battered type and printing flaws. In addition to these same instances of broken and battered type and printing flaws, the offprint contains a comma at 424.5 which the *Memoirs* copies do not. The offprint copy has pages numbered 1 through 62, the signatures are numbered 1 through 8, without the volume number, and the title on the first full page of text reads only "The Logic of Relatives" in large bold type. A title page has been glued on to the first signature giving the full title, author's name, and the information "Extracted from the Memoirs of the American Academy, Vol. IX." The imprint again is Welch, Bigelow, and Company, but the year given with it is 1870.

As there are substantive typographical errors within the text of the article, it hardly seems likely this single change in punctuation was requested by Peirce, an editor, or a proofreader. More probably, since it does occur at the end of a line in the copy-text, it can be attributed to dropped or battered type.

The five papers Peirce presented to the Academy between March and November of 1867 were printed in volume 7 (May 1865 to May 1868) of the Academy's *Proceedings,* published in 1868. A collective offprint of the first three papers appeared late in 1867 under the title "Three Papers on Logic." The fourth and fifth papers were also made available as a collective offprint, probably by mid-1868.

The first three papers run consecutively in the *Proceedings,* separated only by brief minutes of the meetings at which the second and third papers were read. Collation of three *Proceedings* copies of each paper and one complete offprint copy indicated no differences within the text of the articles and in fact revealed that offprint as well as *Proceedings* pages were made from the same type, with no alteration in titles, or page and signature numbers, and without deletion of the minutes. The added title page to the offprint gives only the author's name, the collective title, and the information "Read before the American Academy of Arts and Sciences, 1867."

When three *Proceedings* copies of each of the final two papers were collated, again no differences were found. But a collation of the collective offprint copy against the *Proceedings* publications disclosed four differences in punctuation within the text of the fourth paper, "Upon the Logic of Mathematics." Moreover, the process of creating the collective offprint was a matter of splicing together two separate sections of the *Proceedings*. The fourth paper appears on pages 402 through 412, the fifth on pages 416 through 432, and each is preceded by relatively lengthy meeting minutes. In refashioning the pages for the offprint, Peirce's titles were reset in large, bold type, presumably to take up extra space created by the reduction of both sets of minutes to two lines each. The lower two-thirds of page 416, containing the reduced 13 November minutes and the beginning of the fifth paper, is printed on page 412, immediately following the end of the fourth paper. The next (facing) page is 417. All other page numbers have been retained as they appear in the *Proceedings*, including the erroneous number 232 instead of 432. Signature numbers are also the same. The recto of page 402 is used as a title page for the offprint and, aside from author's name and source information, contains the title of both papers in an emended form. The titles on the interior of the offprint begin with the word *Upon*, just as in the *Proceedings*. The word *On* has been substituted in both cases on the title page.

All this evidence suggests that the pages for the *Proceedings* were run off prior to recomposition for the collective offprint. Consequently, one of the internal changes in punctuation, a quotation mark at 68.38, can be attributed to simple replacement of dropped type at the end of a line, but the other three alterations indicate purposeful intervention in the text.

A request for information on publishing procedures to the American Academy of Arts and Sciences brought this reply from Nicholas Ziegler, Research Associate at the Academy:

Regarding the general publication and distribution procedures for the *Memoirs*. My understanding is that articles were typeset and printed separately (or in batches of two or three) and bound together in volumes when the quantity of material dictated and finances permitted. Such a procedure is suggested for volume 9, n.s., (1867–1873) by the signature markings, initial recto paging for most articles, and by the errata sheets. Full distribution to the membership and exchange institutions apparently had to wait until the volumes were bound. Individual authors, however, had customarily been able to distribute their articles in offprint form without waiting for full volumes to be completed. This offprint policy was formalized at the meeting of 24 May 1864, when the Fellows voted that, "One hundred extra copies of each paper accepted for the Memoirs of the Academy shall be separately printed, of which fifty shall be placed at the disposal of the author, free of charge" [*Proceedings* 6(1862–1865):321]. I interpret 'separately printed' to mean that special title pages were supplied for the authors' offprints; other evidence suggests that the text pages for offprints and bound volumes were printed at the same time. An editorial note following the title page for part 2 of the *Memoirs*, n.s. volume 10 (1868–1882) confirms this seriatim printing procedure.[6] The note also indicates that the Academy considered the publication date of a paper synonymous with the date of printing. The date at which sheets were bound into a volume varied widely and was not considered important in establishing priority or chronology.

The practice for the *Proceedings* was somewhat less clear because papers were interspersed with the minutes until volume 9 (1873–1874), when the *Proceedings* began to appear annually and when the minutes for the year were segregated in the final section of the bound volumes. It is likely that the first eight volumes of the *Proceedings* (1846–1873) were produced in much the same way as the *Memoirs*, with minutes and papers typeset and printed on a seriatim basis. Offprints were apparently given to authors of papers for the *Proceedings* on an ad hoc basis until 24 May 1874, when the Secretaries were formally authorized to give the authors 50 extra copies free [*Proceedings* 10(1874–1875):465].

Given the above information and the evidence within the off-prints themselves, it was decided to use the *Memoirs* publication

---

[6]The note, signed by the Publishing Committee and dated 1 June 1885, reads, "From want of funds applicable to the purpose, this Academy published no Memoirs in quarto from 1874 to 1881, and during this period the sheets of the paper of Mr. Alexander Agassiz on the 'Embryology of the Ctenophoræ', printed in August, 1874, and intended to stand as Number 3 in Volume X, were laid aside for the completion of the volume.

"On resuming the quarto publications with the Memoir of Mr. Henry W. Haynes on the 'Discovery of Palæolithic Flint Implements in Upper Egypt', printed January, 1881, the paper of Mr. Agassiz was overlooked, and not only were its folios duplicated, but the volume was also completed, bound, and distributed without it. The Publishing Committee greatly regret this oversight; but as numerous copies of the Memoir on the Ctenophoræ were distributed by the author immediately after it was printed, and since this paper is referred to as an important stage in the development of the subject on which it treats, the Committee do not feel at liberty to alter the paging, and now distribute the Memoir of Mr. Agassiz to its correspondents without alteration, as a Supplement to Part II of Volume X, together with a new table of contents. It has been determined in future to distribute the quarto Memoirs of the Academy as often as the successive papers are published."

copy as copy-text for "Description of a Notation for the Logic of Relatives," but with the additional comma which appears in the offprint emended into the text. In the case of "Upon the Logic of Mathematics," copy-text is the article as it appeared in the *Proceedings*, with only the missing quotation mark replaced. Though Peirce may have had to request production of the collective offprint, there is no evidence that he authorized the other three alterations to the text.

The large number of published items included here requires a further word concerning offprints and emendation policy.

Peirce meticulously collected offprints of his published papers, sent some to his friends and colleagues and retained others for his personal use which included binding them into collected volumes. Many of these offprints are extant, a few being catalogued within the main body of the Peirce Papers, others scattered throughout the thirteen boxes of miscellaneous materials labeled Robin MS 1600, and still others in collections of papers, deposited in libraries worldwide, of several of Peirce's correspondents. Some of the offprints are important because Peirce corrected and annotated them. They contain (a) corrections of typographical errors; (b) annotations that take the form of queries, critical comments, or further in-depth explanations; and (c) additional notes and reworking of the texts for incorporation into later, larger works, specifically the 1893 "Search for a Method" and the 1894 "How to Reason." Consequently, we have developed a general policy to deal with such corrections and annotations.

Typographical corrections are accepted as emendations to the text, and in listing these we indicate the source.

Annotations tend to be more problematical. We have, for example, not one but four offprints of "Description of a Notation for the Logic of Relatives" (item 39), annotated at various times up to ten years after its publication. Some of the annotations overlap or show but slight differences in wording or phrasing. Others are found in only one (sometimes two) of the four copies. But none bears a close enough relationship to the text as it originally appeared to warrant emendation. In fact, many of these annotations appear at first sight to be typographical corrections but upon further examination seem to reflect relatively later changes of mind concerning the structure of the logic and the notation used. And as with some of the marginalia in the manuscripts, Peirce gives no clear indication of how, where, or even if these annotations should be incorporated into the text. We reproduce all such material, without changes, in the Editorial Notes.

Those offprints which Peirce revised for inclusion in his projected books of 1893 and 1894 will be published in later volumes in their reworked state.

One last, unique feature of Peirce's published papers required an adjustment to our general policy of including only Peirce materials within the text. Any items by another author which we deem necessary to a clearer understanding of Peirce's writings are usually relegated to appendixes following the main body of the text. Two articles, "Nominalism *versus* Realism" (item 14) and "What Is Meant by 'Determined' " (item 16), contain Harris's responses to Peirce's queries and statements. In item 14 Harris published his answers directly after each of Peirce's numbered queries. In item 16 his responses appear as footnotes to Peirce's text. To have conformed to our usual policy would no doubt have destroyed the continuity of the articles themselves as well as that of the full exchange of ideas between Peirce and Harris. We therefore publish items 14 and 16 as they originally appeared in the *Journal of Speculative Philosophy* along with Harris's "Paul Janet and Hegel" in its proper chronological sequence. We have added vertical marginal lines to the text to indicate non-Peirce material. Chauncey Wright's critique of Peirce's Berkeley review is treated in the same way.

As our purpose in this volume is not to reproduce handwritten documents nor to represent the individual and sometimes antiquated printing styles of different publishing houses, but to offer readable and reliable texts for the further study of Peirce's life and thought, the following guidelines are used in emending the texts.

Any spellings not accepted in the nineteenth century are considered to be in error and are corrected. The *Oxford English Dictionary* is our standard reference for determining correctness of spelling, and no attempt is made to regularize Peirce's spelling when more forms than one were acceptable in his day. Similarly, alternative spellings of a given proper name are allowed to stand if they were once acceptable.

Closely related to the spelling problem is that of hyphenated words. When Peirce's intentions cannot be made out, the *Oxford English Dictionary* again serves as our guide, and hyphens are inserted or deleted accordingly.

Whatever Peirce marks as direct quotation is allowed to stand as he gives it, even if it differs from the original. In those cases where

Peirce's own oversight or a printer's error results in nonsensical readings, the text is emended, and the entry in the list of emendations includes a reference to the Editorial Notes, where all information on his quotations and their sources may be found.

Though no attempt is made to modernize or regularize his citations, they are corrected when erroneous or unintelligible, and appropriate punctuation is added.

With few exceptions, such common abbreviations as Ch., Chap., Bk., etc., are retained, though missing periods are added. Uncommon or unclear abbreviations are expanded.

Peirce often wrote notes to himself as reminders to include or expand on certain points. His usual practice was to enclose these notes in brackets. In the few cases where he failed to do this, the editors do it for him.

Periods are added at the ends of sentences where Peirce's pen skipped or he inadvertently omitted them. Periods are deleted after the phrase "per cent" and after Roman numerals used as parts of titles. (Such periods are archaic printing practices to which Peirce does not adhere in his manuscripts.)

Except in special cases, commas are added to divide parts of a series, including a comma before the conjunction (which seems to be Peirce's more usual practice). A comma, dash, parenthesis, or quotation mark is added when it is the missing half of a pair, and apostrophes are inserted in possessives and contractions where Peirce carelessly omitted them.

Italics or quotation marks are added or changed to conform to modern usage in book, play, article, chapter, and other titles. Quotation marks are deleted where lengthy quotations are treated as extracts, and in cases of papers published by Peirce where the house style differs from our own.

When in referring to another of his published writings Peirce gives specific page or volume numbers, we replace these with the appropriate page number(s) in the present volume; the numbers are retained when the publication does not appear in the present volume.

Peirce uses several methods for the treatment of special terms and phrases. When his practice within a single paper can be established, we emend his oversights to accord with it. When his practice within a given paper cannot be established, we emend the text to conform to modern standards.

When Peirce is inconsistent in his use of paragraphing or when ragged margins make his intention unclear, we paragraph according to the context of Peirce's argument. All such questionable cases are listed as emendations.

Other changes are of course required from time to time, and in many cases the need for them arises from Peirce's revising of his work. In the very process of revision, for example, he sometimes creates grammatical errors. In other cases, he fails to complete his intended revision by crossing out a necessary word or phrase but not going back to replace it. In such instances we usually return to his original word or phrase, citing each occurrence of it in the Emendations. And we often find Peirce adding introductory clauses to already inscribed sentences but not going back to lowercase the first word of the original sentence. Again, we emend such misplaced capitalization for him.

The few manuscript notes we have for Peirce's British Logicians lecture series present one feature beyond those we have so far mentioned. They did evolve into a final form, of sorts—the spoken word. So far as possible, we treat these manuscripts like all others in the present volume. The chief exception is the lecture titled "Ockam," in which Peirce quoted extensively from Ockham's *Summa logicae* and Thomas of Erfurt's *Grammatica speculativa*. As was his established practice, he carried the books to the lecture and read directly from them. At such points the manuscript contains only the bracketed instruction to himself to read a specific passage to his audience. Moreover, these instructions clearly indicate Peirce was using Latin editions of both these works. Following Peirce's instructions, we insert into the text those quoted passages for which the manuscript gives only references, though we use standard English translations rather than the Latin editions Peirce used.

All emendations and editorial additions to the text discussed above are listed in the Emendations. The following modifications, however, are mainly concerned with the mechanical presentation of the printed material and are made silently.

All titles, heads, subheads, and dates used as subheads are printed here without periods. Such phrases as "By Charles Peirce," which may appear after the title of published papers or on the cover pages of manuscripts, are not reproduced.

The symbols or page-by-page numbering systems Peirce or his publishers used for footnotes are replaced by a single series of Arabic numerals for each paper.

Unless the material calls for other special treatment, all the papers begin with a paragraph indention.

In place of varying numbers of ellipsis points to mark omissions, modern standard form is followed.

For the convenience of the printer and our budget, superscribed portions of abbreviations such as M^r or 1st (Peirce's nineteenth-century practice) are placed on line.

Those points of punctuation which Peirce used with single and double quotation marks and which were modernized in transcribing his manuscripts, are modernized in the previously published papers as well, to achieve conformity between the two kinds of materials.

Except in "Description of a Notation for the Logic of Relatives" and J. E. Oliver's letter to Peirce, all variables appearing in the logic and mathematics are italicized. Peirce was aware of this practice but did not follow it with any consistency. The instances in which we perform this task for him are too numerous to enter as emendations.

LYNN ZIEGLER

Explanation of Symbols

Within the Text

Titles supplied by the editors appear in italic brackets.

Ellipsis points within italicized brackets indicate the loss of at least one full manuscript page.

Italicized brackets surrounding only a few words or parts of words indicate an editorial reconstruction of a damaged portion of manuscript.

Sets of slashes are used to signal Peirce's unresolved alternative readings. The double slashes mark the beginning and ending of such a reading, while the single slash divides the two alternatives.

Portions of text marked by vertical lines in the margins are by someone other than Peirce.

Within the Apparatus

All page and line numbers refer to the present edition with each line of text, excluding running heads, counted. Footnotes are lined separately from the text and are indicated by an *n* following the page number. Number(s) within parentheses following a line number indicate the first, second, or third appearance of the key word within that line. The use of *Also* following a complete entry indicates the same emendation occurs at the listed places within that selection.

Page and line numbers preceded by an asterisk (*) indicate a reference to a textual note in which that particular reading is discussed more fully.

A double dagger (‡) preceding a page and line number alerts the reader to the presence of an editorial note explaining an unavoidable change in a direct quotation.

All readings to the left of the square bracket (]) are from the present edition, and the source of these readings is given in the headnote for each selection.

Not present signifies a word, phrase, or passage which does not appear in the copy-text or any other authoritative text prior to the accepted emendation.

The use of the abbreviations *ital.* or *rom.* to the right of the square bracket indicates that the listing to the left of the bracket was originally printed in italic (in the case of manuscripts, underlined) or roman (not underlined in the manuscripts) type.

The simple entry *extract* given with inclusive line numbers indicates the quotation which appears between those lines is printed as an extract to conform to our own style, and quotation marks have been removed.

The term *reinstate* to the right of the bracket applies to manuscript material only and signifies that the reading to the left of the bracket was deleted by Peirce in the original but is reinstated by the editors.

Supplied signals those cases in the lectures in which Peirce read from volumes but did not include the quotation in the manuscript. The editors have supplied the quotation.

Two common conventions are used here which pertain to punctuation and paragraphing changes only, the curved dash ($\sim$) and inferior caret ($_\wedge$). The caret signals the absence of punctuation, and the curved dash is used in emendations of punctuation to indicate repetition to the right of the bracket of the word which appears to the left of the bracket.

A vertical stroke (|) indicates a line-end break and is used in cases where it helps to clarify an emendation.

Textual Notes

25.9   The numbering of the sections for Part I is not correct. The original has §1, §2, §4, §5, with no §3. Hence the change here and at 26.6.

31.23 and 32.2   In the University of London offprint, Peirce has placed an asterisk after "defined" at 31.23 and at 32.2 but has given a single footnote at the bottom of the page to be used for both. Since it is our policy to number footnotes consecutively, we have duplicated Peirce's footnote, giving each a separate number.

78.32   This article was originally printed with a duplicated number (4) on two different sections.

103.16   The word *time* actually appears at this point in the manuscript, interlined in red pencil; but the handwriting is not Peirce's. The editors have included it as an emendation to the text in order to avoid a nonsensical reading.

122.21   This emendation is necessitated by Peirce's incomplete revision at the beginning of the manuscript. The rejected reading "Its" refers to "The positive philosophy" in what was originally the first sentence; Peirce later deleted it.

162.29   Peirce's original placement of the question marks is directly above the phrase "hypothetical propositions." The editors have moved the question marks to follow this phrase for the convenience of the printer.

180.35   Peirce penciled in the word *that* directly above the original ink-inscribed *which*. The editors have interpreted this as an incomplete revision on Peirce's part rather than alternative readings which would normally be printed here with sets of double slashes.

189.22   This emendation is the result of several layers of incomplete and muddled revisions in the manuscript.

318.22   Although Peirce's instructions are "Read three whole chapter," we supply only the first chapter. The word *three* appears to be part of an incomplete revision. The original line reads "Read three definitions." Peirce crossed out *definitions* and inscribed "whole chapter" above it.

349.17   The word *grammatical* has been removed editorially, because it appears to be the result of an incomplete revision on Peirce's part. The original inscription reads "un-|grammatical." Peirce deleted "un-" but did not drop to the next line to complete the deletion.

412.14   Only the antique twos are crossed out by Peirce in the JHU and 168 offprints. The editors have removed the multiplication signs following these twos in order to avoid a nonsensical reading.

424.5(2)   This comma does not appear in any of the published copies collated by the editors. The offprint copies do contain this comma, however, and the editors have inserted it here as an emendation on the basis that its absence in the *Memoir* copies could be due to dropped or battered type.

439.4, 440.1, 440.17, and 440.19   These are editorially created footnotes. All were inscribed on otherwise blank verso pages approximately opposite to their present placement as footnotes. Peirce gave no indication of actual placement or intention.

448.4   The first of the two parts of this obituary appears in the "Notes" section of the *Nation*, sandwiched between two paragraphs discussing the deaths of two of De Morgan's contemporaries, Robert Chambers and George Gottfried Gervinus. The three paragraphs are written as a single obituary in which references are made in each paragraph to at least one of the other men. The "scarcely less voluminous writer" is, of course, De Morgan who is being compared here to Robert Chambers.

Emedations

Logic Notebook

Copy-text for "The Logic Notebook" is MS 140. All readings to the left of the brackets are emendations supplied by the editors. All readings to the right of the brackets are rejected readings from MS 140.

1.12	and] & *Also* 1.23, 2.1, 2.23, 3.4, 3.27, 3.28, 4.11, 4.12, 4.21, 4.37, 5.11, 5.27, 5.33, 6.2, 6.14, 6.27(2), 7.4, 7.5, 7.8, 7.11, 7.14, 7.16, 7.31, 8.30
1.14	one;] ∼ₐ
1.23	vice versa.] ∼ ∼ₐ
1.27	Whatever has] Whatever is has
2.13	than] that
2.17	way.] ∼ₐ
2.35	yet,] ∼ₐ
3.5	(necessary).] (∼)ₐ
4.9	Or this—] or This∧
4.10	eclipse] ecclipse
4.17	And] &
4.19	representation] represention *Also* 4.21
4.28	representation] represtation
4.33	eclipsed—the] ecclipsed. The
5.1	*truth*] rom.
5.6	Sep.] ∼ₐ *Also* 5.21
5.29	says] say
6.1	quality.] ∼ₐ
6.1(2,3)	inconceivable] inconceiveable *Also* 6.4
6.28	"Englishman" is] "Englishman"
7.1	"magnanimous hero"] ₐ∼ ∼ₐ
7.1	"hero"] ₐ∼ₐ
7.4	"man John"] ₐ∼ ∼ₐ
7.4	"man."] ₐ∼·ₐ
7.6	predication] predcation

7.8–9	Comprehension.] $\sim_\wedge$
7.15	*and*] *&*
7.18	extension.] $\sim_\wedge$
7.29	Oct.] $\sim_\wedge$ *Also* 9.8
7.31	affirmatives] affirmative
8.8	them,] $\sim_\wedge$
8.14	it.] $\sim_\wedge$
8.21	laugher,] $\sim_\wedge$
8.21	one-eyed] $\sim_\wedge\sim$
8.21	man,] $\sim_\wedge$
8.21	person,] $\sim_\wedge$
8.27	predicate.] $\sim_\wedge$
8.28	&c.] $\sim_\wedge$ *Also* 8.30
8.29	$P,$] $\sim_\wedge$
8.30	make] may
9.3	has no] $\begin{array}{l}\text{has no}\\\text{has no}\end{array}$
9.14	$P_\wedge$] $\sim.$
9.16	$S.$] $\sim_\wedge$
9.19	not-$P.$] $\sim_\wedge\sim_\wedge$
10.6	representation.] $\sim_\wedge$
10.10	necessary'.] $\sim'_\wedge$
10.14	why] which
10.19	imagination.] $\sim_\wedge$

Boole's Calculus of Logic

Copy-text is the publication of this article in *Proceedings of the American Academy of Arts and Sciences* 7(1868):250–61. The emendations to the text appear to the left of the square brackets and are from two sources. Those labeled E are supplied by the editors. Those labeled UL are from a Peirce-corrected offprint deposited in the philosophy section of the main library at the University of London. All readings to the right of the semicolons are rejected readings from the copy-text.

13.14	analogy$_\wedge$] E; $\sim,$
13.14	other),] E; $\sim,$)
13.21	$c \mp a$] E; $\sim = \sim$
14.7	$c) \mp a'$] E; $\sim)$ = $\sim$
14.24	$x = x - x$] UL; $\sim \mp \sim - \sim$
15.8	$x = x{:}x$] UL; $\sim \mp \sim{:}\sim$
15.32	is nothing] UL; is equal to nothing
19.2	given,] E; $\sim.$
19.2	not less than $p + q - 1$] UL; *not present*

19.2	$p + q - 1$.] E; $\sim + \sim - \sim_\wedge$
19.34	Negro] E; negro
20.2	Yp] UL; Y_p
20.3	Zq] UL; Z_q
20.4	Zr] UL; Z_r
20.8	$(\bar{p}',\bar{q}')$] UL; (p',q')
20.14	$p'_{q'},q'$] UL; $\sim_\wedge\sim$
20.14	$\bar{q}'_{\bar{p}'},\bar{p}'$] UL; $\sim_\wedge\sim$
20.15	$q'_{p'},p'$] UL; $\sim_\wedge\sim$
20.15	$\bar{p}'_{\bar{q}'},\bar{q}'$] UL; $\sim_\wedge\sim$
22.38	nine-tenths] E; $\sim_\wedge\sim$ *Also* 22.39
23n.1	*North American Review*] E; rom.

Classification of Arguments

Copy-text is the publication of this article in *Proceedings of the American Academy of Arts and Sciences* 7(1868):261–87. The emendations to the text appear to the left of the square brackets and are from two sources. Those labeled E are supplied by the editors. Those labeled UL are from a Peirce-corrected offprint deposited in the philosophy section of the main library at the University of London. All readings to the right of the semicolons are rejected readings from the copy-text.

23.10	down$_\wedge$] E; $\sim$,
23.11	sign),] E; $\sim$,)
*25.9	3] E; 4
26.6	4] E; 5
26.10	is] E; *ital.*
*31.23	defined[4]] UL; defined
*32.2	defined[5]] UL; defined
33.12	$M_\wedge$] E; $\sim$,
34.32	some-S] E; some-S'
35.9(1)	S] E; S'
36.16	table, where] E; $\sim$. Where
36.17	E] E; *ital. Also* 36.19, 42.19, 42.23, 42.25, 42.26(1,2)
36.18	I] E; *ital. Also* 36.20, 42.19, 42.23, 42.25, 42.26, 42.27
36.19	A] E; *ital. Also* 36.20, 42.16, 42.19, 42.26(1,2)
36.20	contraposition of] E; contraposition
37.16	figure,] E; $\sim_\wedge$
39.2	Bocardo] UL; Bocadro
42.23	O] E; *ital. Also* 42.24, 42.25(1,2), 42.26, 42.27
43.16	M,] E; $\sim$.
45n.23	*Logic*] E; rom.
45n.24	III,] E; $\sim$.

45n.24	XIV,] E; ∼.
46.26	induction∧)] E; ∼,)
47.2	Deductively∧)] E; ∼,)
47.6	hypothesis∧)] E; ∼,)
47.8	Deductively∧)] E; ∼,)
48.3	S''] E; S'

New List of Categories

Copy-text is the publication of this article in *Proceedings of the American Academy of Arts and Sciences* 7(1868):287–98. The emendations to the text appear to the left of the square brackets and are from two sources. Those labeled E are supplied by the editors. Those labeled UL are from a Peirce-corrected offprint deposited in the philosophy section of the main library at the University of London. Though not listed as a source of emendation, the reader is directed to MS 152 ("Notes"), 194.1–4 in the text. All readings to the right of the semicolons are rejected readings from the copy-text.

50.25	prescision] UL; precision *Also* 50.30
50.38	prescision] E; precision
51.6	Prescision] UL; Precision
52n.1	∧*De Generibus et Speciebus,*∧] E; "De Generibus et Speciebus,"
52n.1–2	*Ouvrages Inédits d'Abélard*] E; Ouvrages Inédits d'Abelard
54.2–3	"representation"] E; ∧∼∧
54.23	this] E; the
55.10–11	an other] E; another
56.38(1)	former∧] E; ∼,
56.39	limitation),] E; ∼,)
57n.3	letzterer] E; letzerer
58.26	P',] E; ∼∧

Logic of Mathematics

Copy-text is the publication of this article in *Proceedings of the American Academy of Arts and Sciences* 7(1868):402–12. All readings to the left of the brackets are emendations supplied by the editors. All readings to the right of the brackets are rejected readings from the copy-text.

60.27	B_1] B_2
60.31	respectively.)] ∼).
60.34	B).] ∼)∧

64.13	VIII$_\wedge$] ~.
64.13	IX$_\wedge$] ~.
64.14	VI$_\wedge$] ~.
64.14	VII$_\wedge$] ~.
64.14	IX$_\wedge$] ~.
64.15	VI$_\wedge$] ~.
65.14	VII$_\wedge$] ~.
65.29	IX$_\wedge$] ~.
65.33	IX$_\wedge$] ~.
66.29	IX$_\wedge$] ~.
67.10	X$_\wedge$] ~.
68.28	States] State
68.38	cube,"] ~,$_\wedge$
69.29	55] 293

Logical Comprehension and Extension

Copy-text is the publication of this article in the *Proceedings of the American Academy of Arts and Sciences* 7(1868):416–32. All emendations are supplied by the editors and appear to the left of the square brackets. All readings to the right of the brackets are rejected readings from the copy-text.

70.11	*Port-Royal Logic*] Port$_\wedge$Royal Logic *Also* 70n.1, 71.17
70.16	logician$_\wedge$] ~,
70.23	*Isagoge*] rom.
70n.1	Baynes] Baines
70n.1	ed.,] ~.$_\wedge$
70n.1	xxxiii$_\wedge$] ~.
71.19	*Lectures on Logic*] rom.
71n.1	$_\wedge$*De Generibus et Speciebus*$_\wedge$] "De Generibus et Speciebus"
71n.3	est$_\wedge$] ~,
71n.3	aliud,] ~$_\wedge$
71n.5	*Metalogicus*] rom.
71n.5	1610] 1620
71n.6	III,] ~.
71n.10	III,] ~.
‡71n.13	partiuntur] partiunter
71n.14	*Physics,*] Phys.
71n.15	I,] ~.
71n.16	I,] ~.
72.11	*Extension*] rom.
72.11	*comprehension*] rom. *Also* 72.13
72.14	*intensity*] rom.

72.33–73.6	*extract*
72n.1	I,] ∼.
72n.1	p. 685] col. 684
72n.2	I,] ∼.
72n.2	I,] ∼.
73.14	Hales] Ales
73.16	*creator*] rom.
73.20–38	*extract*
73.26	"aliquid] '∼
73.26	albedine"] ∼'
73.26	"aliquid] '∼
73.26–27	albedinem"] ∼'
‡73.35	simile. . . .] ∼.ᴧ
73n.1	III,] ∼.
73n.2	*Quodlibeta,*] *Quodlib.*
73n.3	I,] ∼.
73n.4	I,] ∼.
74.13	Extension] *ital. Also* 78.33
74.14	Comprehension] *ital. Also* 78.32
74.24	*Syllabus*] rom.
74n.1	Tartaretus'] Tatareti
74n.1	*Expositio in summulas Petri Hispani*] Expositio in Petr. Hisp.
74n.3	*Logic*] rom.
77.27–33	*extract*
77n.1	*Logik*] rom.
77n.1	Aufl.,] ∼.ᴧ
77n.2	*Formal Logic*] rom.
77n.2	*Syllabus*] rom.
78.1–5	*extract*
78.1	"man] '∼
78.3	America,"] ∼,'
78.3	"man] '∼
78.4	Europe"] ∼'
78.32	5] 4
78n.1	*Laws of Thought*] rom.
78n.2	*Logic*] rom.
78n.2	I,] ∼.
78n.2	ii,] ∼.
79.18	is said] is
79n.2	i,] ∼.
79n.2	2,] ∼.
80.18	not-*T*] ∼ᴧ∼
82.24	6] 5
82.33	1stᴧ] ∼.
82.35	2dᴧ] ∼.
82.37	3dᴧ] ∼.

83.2	1st$_\wedge$] $\sim$.
83.3	2d$_\wedge$] $\sim$.
83.4	3d$_\wedge$] $\sim$.
83.13	1st$_\wedge$] $\sim$.
83.15	2d$_\wedge$] $\sim$.
83.17	3d$_\wedge$] $\sim$.
85.5	S',] $\sim_\wedge$

Notes

Copy-text for "Notes" is MS 152. All readings to the left of the brackets are emendations supplied by the editors. All readings to the right of the brackets are rejected readings from MS 152.

87.15	$+, a_1$.] $+, \sim_\wedge$
88.3	$\bar{x}$.] $\sim_\wedge$
88.4	only] on
88.10	subtractions] subtactions
88.10(1)	and$_\wedge$] $\sim$,
88.26	Another] Other
89.16	familiar-looking] $\sim_\wedge\sim$
89.27	∓ 0,] $\mp \sim_\wedge$
90.23	&c.] $\sim_\wedge$
90.24	k_{-n}.] $\sim_\wedge$
90.25	$= 0$.] $= \sim_\wedge$
91.24	killer,] $\sim_\wedge$
91.25	himself.] $\sim_\wedge$
92.12	∓ 0.] $\mp \sim_\wedge$
93.3	$_\wedge$*Pure Logic, . . . of Quality.*$_\wedge$] "Pure Logic, . . . of Quality."
93.14	Long$_\wedge$] $\sim$.
93.16	Fig.] $\sim_\wedge$ *Also* 93.19
93.23	28a24.] $\sim_\wedge$
93.26	III,] $\sim_\wedge$
94.3	proof-sheets] $\sim_\wedge\sim$
94.3	*Metaphysics*] metaphysics
94.3	and] & *Also* 95.2, 95.4, 95.6, 95.10, 97.13, 97.20, 97.21, 97.22(2)
94.4	*Lexicon*] rom.
94.12	fatiguing] fatigueing
94.12	abbreviated] abbrieviated
94.18	B_n).] $\sim$)$_\wedge$
94.24	def.] $\sim_\wedge$ *Also* 94.28, 95.8, 95.21, 96.8, 96.21, 96.23, 97.1, 97.6, 97.8, 97.9, 97.13, 97.16
94.28	2$_\wedge$,] $\sim$.,
95.2	3$_\wedge$] $\sim$.
95.2	*Barbara,*] $\sim$.
95.15	3$_\wedge$] $\sim$.

95.17	Def.] $\sim_\wedge$
95.17	cond.] $\sim_\wedge$ *Also* 97.1, 97.9, 97.16
96.6	on p. 64] at the bottom of p. 406
97.8	B_n.] $\sim_\wedge$
97.9	A_a.] $\sim_\wedge$
97.12	belongs.] $\sim_\wedge$
97.15	individual.] $\sim_\wedge$
97.20	exists] exist

Venn's Logic of Chance

Copy-text is the publication of this article in *North American Review* 105(July 1867):317–21. All emendations are supplied by the editors and appear to the left of the square brackets. All readings to the right of the brackets are rejected readings from the copy-text.

99.6	*Understanding*] *rom.*
99.6	IV,] $\sim$.
99.6	15] 14
99.32	two-thirds] $\sim_\wedge\sim$
100.33	"On the Credibility of Extraordinary Stories"] "on the credibility of extraordinary stories"
101.25	*probability*] *rom.*

One, Two, and Three

Copy-text for this item is MS 144. All emendations are supplied by the editors and appear to the left of the brackets. All readings to the right of the brackets are rejected readings from the copy-text.

103.1	I. One] $\sim_\wedge|\sim$
103.9	name,] name to,
*103.16	same time] same
103.26	*entity*] *rom. Also* 103.31
104.5	non-existent] nonexistent
104.13	whether] whether whether
104.19–22	*extract*

Dictionary of Logic

Copy-text for this item is MS 145. All emendations are supplied by the editors and appear to the left of the square brackets. The readings to the right of the brackets are rejected readings from the copy-text.

105.2	Sciences:] ∼.
105.10	*Analytics*] rom.
106.9	*A parte.*] ∼ ∼ᴧ
106.11	*Universal.*] ∼ᴧ
106.14	*Consequence.*] ∼ᴧ
106.18	prior] rom.
106.18	posterior] rom.
106.21	Aquinas,] ∼.
106.21	*Summa,*] Summa.
106.21	prim.,] ∼.ᴧ
106.21	quaest. 2,] q 2.
106.22	follows.] ∼,
106.26	cause.] ∼ᴧ
106.26	Hamilton,] ∼.
106.26	*Reid's Works,*] Reid's Works.
106.27	p.] ∼ᴧ *Also* 107.12, 108.12, 110.39, 111.36, 112.35, 112.38, 114.22, 115.22
106.27	also,] ∼.
106.27	Trendelenburg,] ∼.
106.27	*Elementa Logices Aristoteleae,*] El. Log. Ar.ᴧ
106.28	Wolffians] Wolfians
106.31	Hollmann,] ∼.
106.32(1,2)	3,] ∼.
‡106.37	are] and
107.3	Cudworth,] ∼.
107.3	*Eternal and Immutable Morality,*] Etern. and Imm. Mor.ᴧ
107.4	3,] ∼.
107.4	§5,] ∼.
107.12	*a priori.*] ∼ ∼ᴧ
107.12	Lambert,] ∼.
107.12	Book 1,] ∼ ∼ᴧ
107.12	9,] ∼.
107.12	§637,] ∼ᴧ
107.12	vol. 1,] ∼ᴧ ∼.
107.17	*Logik,*] Logik.
107.17	Einleitung] Einl.
107.25	*a posteriori.*"] ∼ ∼.ᴧ
107.25	*Kritik d. reinen Vernunft,*] Kritik d. reinen Vernunft.
107.26	Ed.,] ∼.ᴧ
107.26	Einleitung] Einl *Also* 113.11
107.28	Kant,] ∼ᴧ
107.28	*Kritik,*] Kritikᴧ
107.31	exercise.] ∼ᴧ
107.31	Hamilton.] Ham.
107.36	Leibniz,] ∼.
107.38	*Abdication.*] ∼ᴧ
107.38	*Abdicatio*] rom.

107.38	Scotus Erigena.] $\sim$ $\sim_\wedge$
108.6	ἀπαγωγή$_\wedge$] $\sim$,
108.6	*Prior Analytics,*] Pr. An.$_\wedge$
108.6	lib. 2,] $\sim_\wedge$ $\sim_\wedge$
108.6	cap.] $\sim_\wedge$ *Also* 112.2, 112.26
108.11	*Analytica Posteriora,*] An. Post.$_\wedge$
108.11	lib. i,] $\sim_\wedge$ $\sim_\wedge$
108.11–12	ch. 21,] $\sim_\wedge$ $\sim$.
108.32	Waitz,] $\sim$.
108.32	*Organon,*] Organon.
109.8	metaphorically] metaphorical$_\wedge$|ly
109.11	Aquinas,] $\sim$.
109.12	prim. prim.,] pr. pr.$_\wedge$
109.12	9,] $\sim$.
109.12	art.] $\sim_\wedge$
109.19	*absolute distribution*] rom.
109.19	*absolute scepticism*] rom.
109.20–21	*absolute proposition*] rom.
109.21	*absolute necessity*] rom.
109.28	Mansel] Mansell
109.29	*Philosophy of Conditioned*] Phil. of Conditioned
109.30	*Limits of Religious Thought*] rom.
109.35	Hamilton.] $\sim_\wedge$
110.6	indivisibility)] $\sim_\wedge$
110.8	Knox,] $\sim$.
110.8	*History of Reform.*] History of Reform$_\wedge$
110.9	*Vocabulary*] rom.
110.14	Mansel,] Mansell.
110.14	*Philosophy of Conditioned*] Phil. of Cond.
110.21	*tree,*] $\sim$.
110.38–39	propagation] propogation
110.39	Hamilton,] $\sim$.
110.39	Metaphysical Lecture] Metaph. Lect.
110.39	46,] $\sim$.
111.1	*Philargyrus.*] $\sim_\wedge$
111.3	Eck,] $\sim$.
111.3	*In summulas Petri Hispani,*] In summul. Petr. Hisp.$_\wedge$
111.5	Kant,] $\sim$.
111.5	*Kritik d. Urtheilskraft,*] Kritik d. Urtheilskraft.
111.9	Kant,] $\sim$.
111.10	*Logik,*] Logik.
111.10	Einleitung VI,] Einl V.
111.17	Schelling.] $\sim_\wedge$
111.18	*impossibility.*] $\sim_\wedge$
111.19	Burgersdicius.] $\sim_\wedge$
111.24	none.] $\sim_\wedge$
111.25	*indivisibility.*] $\sim_\wedge$

111.29	*intellectus)*.] intellectus)ₐ
111.29	Scotus,] ∼.
111.29–30	*In sententiarum,*] In sentent.ₐ
111.30	lib. 2,] ∼ₐ ∼.
111.30	dist. 6,] ∼ₐ ∼.
111.30	qu. 1,] ∼ₐ ∼.
111.30	vol. 2,] ∼ₐ ∼.
111.30	p. 242.] ∼ₐ ∼ₐ
111.35	Burgersdicius,] Burgersdicii.
111.35	*Institutionum Logicarum,*] Instit. Log.ₐ
112.1	Burgersdicius,] Burgersdicii.
112.1–2	*Institutionum Metaphysicarum,*] Metaph.ₐ
112.2	lib. 1,] ∼ₐ ∼ₐ
112.9	Occam.] ∼ₐ
112.9	Prantl,] ∼.
112.9	iii,] ∼.
112.14	belongs.] ∼ₐ
112.14	Burgersdicius.] Burgersd.
112.21–22	Hamilton,] ∼.
112.22	Metaphysical] Metaph
112.25	Burgersdicius,] Burgersdiciiₐ
112.25–26	*Institutionum Metaphysicarum,*] Metaphₐ
112.26	lib. 2,] ∼ₐ ∼.
112.35	*Logic,*] Logic.
112.35	13,] ∼.
112.38	*Kritik d. r. Vernunft,*] Kritik d. r. Vernunft.
112.38	Ed.,] ∼.ₐ
113.6–7	Montaigne's] Montaine's
113.7	*Essays,*] Essays.
113.7	2,] ∼.
113.10	illusion.] ∼ₐ
113.10	Kant,] ∼.
113.11	*Logik,*] Logik.
113.13	Seydel,] ∼.
113.13	*Logik,*] Logik.
113.14	*space*ₐ] ∼.
113.14–15	immovable.] ∼ₐ
113.17	space.] ∼ₐ
113.17	Kant,] ∼.
113.17–18	*Anfangsgründe der Naturwissenschaft*] rom.
113.20	Eck,] ∼.
113.20	*In summulas Petri Hispani,*] In summul. Petr. Hisp.ₐ
113.20	Tractatus] Tr.
113.20(1,2)	2,] ∼ₐ
113.23	duration.] ∼ₐ
113.39	body)] ∼ₐ
113.39	Burgersdicius.] Burg.

114.2	mixed.] $\sim_\wedge$
114.5	Elyot,] $\sim$.
114.5	*Governour*] rom.
114.12	*ex abstractione,*] $\sim \sim_\wedge$
114.19	Schmid.] $\sim$,
114.21	abstracted$_\wedge$] $\sim$,
114.21–22	*Critik d. r. Vernunft,*] Critik d. r. Vernunft.
114.22	Ed.,] $\sim._\wedge$
115.6	attribute,] $\sim$.
115.14	*Logik,*] Log.$_\wedge$
115.18	things.] $\sim_\wedge$
115.21	Hegel.] $\sim_\wedge$
115.22	*Reid,*] Reid$_\wedge$
115.24	1.] $\sim_\wedge$
115.25	Scotus,] $\sim$.
115.26	*Quaestiones in Praedicamentis,*] Quaes. in Praedicamentis.
115.26	Qu.] $\sim_\wedge$
115.26	*Abstract*] rom.
115.30	'abstract name'] "$\sim \sim$"
115.37	'general name'] $_\wedge\sim \sim_\wedge$
116.3	Mill,] $\sim$.
116.3	*Logic*] rom.
116.20–21	*De mundi sensibilis atque intellegibilis forma et principii.*] De mundi sensib. atque intell. forma et princip.
116.26	*abstrahere*] rom.
116.31	*abstractio*] rom.
116.35	*ratio universalis*] rom.
117.14	*Monologium,*] Monologium:
117.14–15	62, 63, 66,] $\sim$. $\sim$. $\sim$.
117.17	quiddity] quidity
117.18	Scotus,] $\sim_\wedge$
117.18	lib. 2,] $\sim_\wedge \sim_\wedge$
117.18	dist. 3,] $\sim_\wedge \sim_\wedge$
117.18	9,] $\sim$.
117.19	2.] $\sim_\wedge$
117.22	eclipse] ecclipse
117.27	Conimbricenses,] Conimbr.$_\wedge$
117.27	*De Anima,*] De An.$_\wedge$
117.27	lib. 2,] $\sim_\wedge \sim_\wedge$
117.27	cap. 6,] $\sim_\wedge \sim_\wedge$
117.27	3,] $\sim_\wedge$
117.27	art.] $\sim_\wedge$
117.29–30	*De intellectibus.*] $\sim \sim_\wedge$
117.30	Cousin,] $\sim$.
117.30	*Fragments Philosophiques,*] Frag. Philos.$_\wedge$
117.30	p. 481).] $\sim_\wedge \sim$.)
118.12	*Simple.*] $\sim_\wedge$

118.14	*Reductio.*] ~_∧

118.14   *Reductio.*] ~ˏ
118.25   —mode] ˏ~
119.15   *Old, Middle, New*] rom.
119.20   used,] ~ˏ
119.24   ACCEPTILATION.] ~ˏ
119.26   Quintilian] Quinctilian
119.35   *property*),] ~,)
119.38   subject.] ~ˏ
119.39   *Accident*] Ac.
120.2   *Agreement*ˏ] ~.
120.5   sense).] ~.)
120.8   *distinction.*] ~ˏ
120.31   Burgersdicius,] ~.
120.31   *Institutionum Metaphysicarum,*] Metaph.ˏ
120.32   lib. i,] ~ˏ ~.
120.32   25,] ~.
120.39   Burgersdicius.] ~ˏ
120.40   *signifying*ˏ] ~.
121.3   *perfection*ˏ] ~.
121.4–5   ornament'.] ~'ˏ
121.10–11   Pseudo-Aquinas,] ~-~.
121.11   *Summa logices*] rom.
121.13   *quality.*] ~ˏ
‡121.16   its] it
121.17   taken.] ~ˏ
121.20   die'."] ~'ˏˏ

Critique of Positivism

Copy-text for "Critique of Positivism" is MS 146. All readings to the left of the square brackets are emendations supplied by the editors. All readings to the right of the brackets are rejected readings from the copy-text.

122.4   Philosophies.] ~ˏ
122.16   §7.] ~ˏ
122.17   §7½.] ~ˏ
122.17   positivism.] ~ˏ
122.18   §8.] ~ˏ
122.20   §9.] ~ˏ
*122.21   The] Its
123.9   believers] beleivers
123.9   even if] even
123.13   Freedom,] ~ˏ

123.17	belief] beleif *Also* 123.24, 124.22, 127.23, 128.1, 128.7, 128.37
123.24	inspiriting] enspiriting
123.30	it,] ~ₐ
124.10	and] & *Also* 124.33, 124.34, 126.39, 127.2, 129.33(2)
124.15	all] All
124.22	annihilated;] ~,
124.30	within] with in
124.31(1)	our] or
124.31	wherever] where ever
124.38	*idiosyncracy*] *idyosyncracy*
125.12	idiosyncracy] idiosyncrasy
125.31	*implies,*] ~ₐ
125.31	*knowledge,*] ~ₐ
125.33–34	Positivists] Positist
‡125.40	eandem] eam
‡125.40	introeuntem] introentem
126.10	That] There
126.17	titillation] titi|lation
126.17	this or that] this that
127.9	metaphysical] metaphical
127.14	there] There
127.24	discussion of] discussion
127.26	ourselves),] ~,)
127.33	to such] to the such
127.40	metaphysics,] ~ₐ
128.4	produce] produces
128.22	reason,] ~ₐ
128.25	end?] ~.
128.27	considered] consided
128.35	believe] beleive *Also* 128.39, 130.2
129.3	in] is
129.4(2)	from] of
129.15	men's] mens
129.17	believing] beleiving
129.27	They] The
129.29	determination of] determination
129.38	are] are to
129.38	supposably] supposeably
129.38–39	possible,] ~ₐ
130.18	intuition] intuition on

Harris's Janet and Hegel

Copy-text is the publication of this article in the *Journal of Specu-lative Philosophy* 1(1867):250–56. All emendations are supplied by

the editors and appear to the left of the square brackets. All readings
to the right of the square brackets are rejected readings from the
copy-text.

132.14	I. H. Fichte] J. H. Fichte
132.19	*Æsthetics*] *rom.*
132.21	*Encyclopædia*] *rom.*
132.23	₍*Philosophy of Nature*₎] "Philosophy of Nature"
132.24	₍*Philosophy of Spirit,*₎] "Philosophy of Spirit,"
132.28	₍*Philosophy of History*₎₎] "Philosophy of History,"
132n.1	₍*Etudes . . . dans Hegel,*₎] "Essai . . . dans Hegel,"
132n.2	Paris:] ∼,
132n.2	₍Ladrange,₎] (∼,)
133.1	Library);] ∼;)
133.2	*Logic*₎] Logic,
133.3–4	₍*The Secret of Hegel,*₎] "The Secret of Hegel,"
133.5	*History of Philosophy*] *rom.*
133.8	₍*Secret of Hegel.*₎] "Secret of Hegel."
133.14	common-sense] ∼₎∼ *Also* 137.21
133.19	Mansel] Mansell
133.32	*Philosophy of Art*] *rom.*
133.34	*Logic*] *rom. Also* 133.37, 138.2
133.35–36	*Philosophy of History*] *rom.*
133.36–37	*Philosophy of Religion*] *rom.*
133.38	*The History of Philosophy*] *rom.*
134.34	*Menschen*₎] ∼,
134.35	one-sided] onesided
134.35	downfall),] ∼,)
135.37	₍*Etudes*] "Essai
135.38	*Hegel.*₎] ∼."
137.1	₍*Logik*₎] "Logik"
137.2	₍*Phänomenologie des Geistes*₎] "Phänomenologie des Geistes"
‡137.26–27	*The Critique of Pure Reason*] *rom.*
137.39	*Dialectic*] *rom.*
139.3	*Philosophy*] *rom.*
139.34	P.] p.
140.4–7	*extract*
140.8	₍and] (∼
140.8	₍*Logik und Metaphysik,*₎] "Logik und Metaphysik₎"
140.8	II,] ∼.
140.8	§29₎:] ∼):
140.9–21	*extract*
140.34	*Sophist*] *rom.*
141.3	determination₎] ∼,
141.38	*Spirit*] *rom.*

142.10	asks$_\wedge$] ~,
142.31	*alone*$_\wedge$] ~,
142.32	itself$_\wedge$] ~,

Peirce to Harris, 1/24/1868

Copy-text for this item is L 183. All emendations are supplied by the editors and appear to the left of the square brackets. The readings to the right of the brackets are rejected readings from L 183.

143.13	Jan. 24] ~$_\wedge$ ~.
143.15	your] you
144.5	p. 140] p. 255
144.8	and] &
144.8–9	unmistakable] unmiskeable

Nominalism versus Realism

Copy-text for "Nominalism *versus* Realism" is the publication of this article in *Journal of Speculative Philosophy* 2(1868):57–61. There are, however, two sources of emendation for this item. The first is a letter from Peirce to W. T. Harris (see p. 154–55 of this volume) in which Peirce requests two changes after having seen the proof-sheets. The letter is dated 16 March 1868 but apparently did not reach Harris in time for the requested changes to be made. The letter is deposited in the W. T. Harris Collection, Hoose Library, and the emendations appearing to the left of the brackets and marked HL are from this letter. All other emendations are supplied by the editors and are marked E. The readings to the right of the semicolons are rejected readings from the copy-text.

145.3	p. 140] E; vol. i., p. 255
145.41	same$_\wedge$] E; ~,
146.15	*existence*$_\wedge$] E; ~,
146.16	*Being*),] E; ~,)
146.28-29	two-foldness$_\wedge$] E; ~-~,
146.29	nature),] E; ~,)
148.30	Nothing$_\wedge$] E; ~,
149.7	VIII$_\wedge$] E; ~.
149.8	"Introduction to Philosophy,"] E; $_\wedge$~ ~ ~,$_\wedge$
149.8	X$_\wedge$] E; ~.
150.7	new$_\wedge$] E; ~,
150.8	effect),] E; ~,)

150.14	Being-not] HL; ~—~
151.31	humanity, or] HL; humanity, or that being, in the sense intended, is humanity, or
152.3	criticism,] E; ~,
152.3	(p. 141),] E; (vol. i. of the present Journal, p. 255,)
154.2	*evanescent*] E; *rom.*
154.5	Eternity."]] E; ~."‸

Peirce to Harris, 3/16/1868

Copy-text for this letter is L 183. All emendations are supplied by the editors and appear to the left of the square brackets. All readings to the right of the brackets are rejected readings from the copy-text.

154.8	16,] ~.
154.12	*abstract*] *rom.*
154.12	*concrete*] *rom.*
154.26	and] & *Also* 155.2(1)
154.28–29	attention,] ~‸
154.29	interest,] ~‸
155.6	&c.] ~‸

What Is Meant by "Determined"

Copy-text is the publication of this article in *Journal of Speculative Philosophy* 2(1868):190–91. All emendations are supplied by the editors and appear to the left of the square brackets. The readings to the right of the brackets are rejected readings from the copy-text.

156.1	other)."] ~).‸
156.8	page 151] page 60, column 1
156.31	*Werke*] *rom.*
157.7	p. 151] p. 60
157.10	p. 145] p. 57
157.13	qu. 8;] *ital.*
157.14	*In Sententias*] *In Sentent.*
157.14	lib. 1, . . . 1;] *ital.*
157.15	pars . . . 5;] *ital.*
157.15	*sub v.*] *sub.* V.
157.16	Bk. 1, . . . 4;] *ital.*
157.16–17	*Elementa Logices Aristoteleae*] *Elementa Logices Arist.*
157.17	6th . . . note;] *ital.*
157.21	*Pure Being*] *rom.*
157.24	I,] ~.

157.25	p. 146] Vol. II., p. 57
157n.1	III$_\wedge$] $\sim$.

Peirce to Harris, 4/9/1868

Copy-text for this letter is L 183. All readings to the left of the square brackets are emendations supplied by the editors. All readings to the right of the brackets are rejected readings from the copy-text.

158.14	Apr.] $\sim_\wedge$
158.16	received] rec'd
158.17	and] & *Also* 159.4(1), 159.7
159.13	American] Amer.
159.16	MS$_\wedge$] $\sim$.

Questions on Reality

Copy-text for each of the three discrete texts is MS 148. All emendations are supplied by the editors and appear to the left of the square brackets. All readings to the right of the brackets are rejected readings from MS 148.

162.3	Qu.] $\sim_\wedge$ *Also* 162.9, 162.16, 162.22, 162.25, 162.27, 162.31, 163.1, 163.3, 163.5, 163.6, 163.7
162.19(2)	and] &
162.19	believed] beleived
162.24	No.] $\sim_\wedge$
162.25	5.] $\sim_\wedge$
162.26	Corollary] Corrollarry
162.28	*Ans.*] $\sim_\wedge$
	? ?
*162.29	hypothetical propositions (??)] hypothetical propositions

Questions on Reality (A)

163.10	*Qu.*] $\sim_\wedge$ *Also* 163.16, 164.35
163.18	believed] beleived
163.25	every] previous to every
164.10	incognizable] incognizeable
164.15	is its cause] its cause is
164.25	holding] hold
164.26	in] that

Questions concerning Reality

165.8	and] & *Also* 177.24, 179.33(2), 181.12, 181.38, 183.1, 183.5, 185.26, 186.4, 186.10, 186.11
165.23	arbitrarily),] ~,)
165.23	seem] seems
166.8(2)	he] it
166.17	4th‸] ~.
167.18	believe] beleive *Also* 170.12, 170.17, 170.18, 172.40, 174.16, 178.39, 181.15, 182.3, 182.4, 182.6, 182.9
167.19(1)	not‸] ~,
167.21	for).] ~‸.
167.29	*I*] rom.
167.34	children] childen
168.8	is it] is
168.13	unsupported by] unsupported for by
168.17	Johnny] Johny
168.18	correlation] correllation
169.17–18	self-consciousness] ~‸~ *Also* 169.38
169.18	details.] ~‸
169.20	self-conscious] self-consciousness
170.4	believed] beleived *Also* 170.14–15
170.13	any way] any
170.37	it is] is
171.1	unquestionably] unquestionable
171.8	it‸] ~,
171.22	¶*Question*] ‸~
171.34	the constitution] constitution
171.38	an inference] in inference
172.14	called] call
172.23	¶It remains] ‸~ ~
172.31	that] than
172.33	*Qu.*] ~‸ *Also* 174.1
172.33	5.] ~‸
173.2	an instant] instant
173.15	the] then
174.8	universal] univesal
174.9	inexhaustible] inexaustible
174.10	cloven-hoofed] ~‸~
174.27	incognizable] incognizeable *Also* 183.3
174.28	'If . . . *B*'] ‸~ . . . ~‸
174.29	'whenever . . . *B*'] ‸~ . . . ~‸
174.30–31	'If . . . mark'] ‸~ . . . ~‸
174.32–33	'whenever . . . mark'] ‸~ . . . ~‸
174.36	contradictory,] ~‸

174.40	cognizable] cognizeable *Also* 175.5
174.40–175.1	uncognizable] uncognizeable
175.2	copula$_\wedge$)] $\sim$,)
175.2–3	self-contradictory] $\sim_\wedge\sim$
175.4	syncategorematic] syncategoreumatic
175.4–5	term, so] $\sim$. So
175.10	suppose.] supposes$_\wedge$
175.11	this] the
175.11	(Answer] [$\sim$
175.11	Q.] $\sim_\wedge$
175.30	way] way, then,
176.3	that] than
176.6	the] The
177.14	strengthened] strengthen$_\wedge$|ed
177.22	that] than
177.22	even if] even
177.30	least$_\wedge$] $\sim$,
177.30	application,] $\sim_\wedge$
178.13	which is less] less
178.28	no one] one
178.33	to fall] fall
179.10	individuation.] $\sim_\wedge$
179.38	selves$_\wedge$] $\sim$,
180.15	between] been
180.23	this] This
180.24	this is] this
180.27	determined it] determined
*180.35	that is] that / which is
181.10	is,] $\sim_\wedge$
181.25	be,] $\sim_\wedge$
181.26	that] that that
182.9	which I] which
182.9	believing] beleiving
182.29–30	'If ... D'] $_\wedge\sim$ ... $\sim_\wedge$
182.31–32	'If ... D'] $_\wedge\sim$ ... $\sim_\wedge$
182.33	B,] $\sim_\wedge$
182.33	X,] $\sim_\wedge$
182.34	'If ... D'] $_\wedge\sim$ ... $\sim_\wedge$
182.39	on] On
183.31	spilt.] $\sim_\wedge$
184.7	that] than
184.17	breathe] breath
185.1	ones,—] $\sim,_\wedge$
185.21	not] no

186.8   shall] sall
186.9   proposition).] ~.)

Potentia ex Impotentia

Copy-text for the two texts of "Potentia ex Impotentia" is MS 149. All readings to the left of the square brackets are emendations supplied by the editors. All readings to the right of the brackets are rejected readings from the copy-text.

188.5–6   astronomy] astromy
188.20   symptoms] symtoms
188.32   contemn] contemp
188.38   bearings] bearing
188.39   religion,] ~ₐ

Potentia ex Impotentia

189.12   *believe*] *beleive*
189.19   psychological] psycholical
*189.22   mistrust.] mistrust. in a
189.22   to] To
190.8   and] &
190.10–11   "Questions . . . for man,"] '~ . . . ~ ~,'
190.21–22   incognizable] incognizeable *Also* 191.1, 191.2, 191.10–11
190.23   7th,] ~.
190.26–27   cognizable] cognizeable *Also* 190.40, 190.40–191.1, 191.1,
               191.2, 191.12
190.39   *cognizable*] *cognizeable*
191.11   Hence if] Hence whatever if
191.30   contiguous,] ~ₐ
191.39   *externality*] rom.
191.39   *reality*] rom.
191.40   *figment*] rom.

Peirce to Harris, 11/30/1868

Copy-text for this letter is L 183. The emendations are supplied by the editors and appear to the left of the square brackets. The readings to the right of the brackets are rejected readings from L 183.

| 192.3 | 30$_\wedge$] ∼. |
| 192.12 | and] & *Also* 192.23(1,2), 192.24 |

Questions Concerning Certain Faculties

Copy-text is the publication of this article in *Journal of Speculative Philosophy* 2(1868):103–14. All emendations are supplied by the editors and appear to the left of the square brackets. All readings to the right of the brackets are rejected readings from the copy-text.

193n.1	*Monologium*] rom.
193n.11	*In sententias,*] In sentent.
193n.13	*Werke*] rom. *Also* 201n.1
193n.15	*Reid*] rom.
195n.6	Fredegisus] Fredigisus
197.6	left-hand] ∼$_\wedge$∼ *Also* 197.8
197.9	right-hand] ∼$_\wedge$∼
198.10	nerve-points] ∼$_\wedge$∼
198.12	impression$_\wedge$] ∼,
198.13	system),] ∼,)
199n.1	*Proceedings of the American Academy*] rom.
199n.7	*Critik d. reinen Vernunft*] rom.
199n.9	"Transcendental Æsthetic"] $_\wedge$∼ ∼$_\wedge$
201n.1	vii$_\wedge$] ∼.
203.3	himself$_\wedge$] ∼,
203.4	etc.).] ∼.)$_\wedge$
203.18	then] them
205.35	*facts.*] ∼?
208.23	syncategorematic] syncategoreumatic
210.39	dipped$_\wedge$] ∼.

Consequences of Four Incapacities

Copy-text is the publication of this article in *Journal of Speculative Philosophy* 2(1868):140–57. The emendations to the text appear to the left of the square brackets and are from two sources. Those labeled E are supplied by the editors. Those labeled MF are from an errata list published on the inside back cover of the *Journal.* Extant copies of this published errata list are rare, and the only copy the editors were able to obtain is privately owned by Max Fisch. All readings to the right of the semicolons are rejected readings from the copy-text.

215.30	about.] E; $\sim_\wedge$
216.17	*per cent*$_\wedge$] E; $\sim \sim$. *Also* 216.18(1,2), 216.18–19, 216.33, 216.34(1,2), 217.30, 217.33, 218.9, 218.14
216.26	*F,*] E; $\sim_\wedge$
216.35	*a,*] E; $\sim_\wedge$
217.31	*F,*] E; $\sim_\wedge$
217.32	*F,*] E; $\sim_\wedge$
218n.4	10,] E; $\sim_\wedge$
218n.4	*Œuvres choisies*] E; rom.
218n.5	*Nouveaux Essais*] E; Nouv. Ess.
218n.6	*Works*] E; rom.
218n.7	G. L.] E; $\sim_\wedge \sim$.
218n.7	*Hypothesis*] E; rom.
218n.12	conditionally.] E; $\sim_\wedge$
218n.16	*Synopsis*] E; rom.
219n.6	*Lexicon Rationale*] E; rom.
‡219n.7	probandam] E; probandum
219n.17	*Principia*] E; rom.
219n.20	*Lectures on Logic*] E; rom.
219n.23	Ibid.] E; $\sim_\wedge$ *Also* 219n.30, 219n.46
219n.30	*Lectures on Metaphysics*] E; rom.
219n.35	*Logic*] E; rom.
219n.43	*Logik*] E; rom.
219n.44	Jäsche,] E; $\sim_\wedge$
219n.44	*Werke,*] E; Werke;
219n.44	ed.] E; Ed.
219n.44	Rosenkranz] E; Rosenk.
219n.44	Schubert] E; Sch.
219n.49	*Einleitung;*] E; rom.
219n.49	*Werke*] E; rom.
219n.51	*System der Logik*] E; rom.
224.30	*Negro*] E; negro *Also* 224.31, 224.33
224.35	Negro] E; negro
226n.2–3	*Proceedings . . . Sciences*] E; rom. *Also* 227n.3–4
227.19	thought] E; thonght
228.1	page 197] E; page 105 of this volume
230.27	etc.,] E; $\sim._\wedge$
232.33	*b,*] E; $\sim_\wedge$
234n.4–5	*Essay concerning Human Understanding*] E; rom.
234n.5	II$_\wedge$] E; $\sim$. *Also* 234n.7
234n.6	again$_\wedge$] E; $\sim$,
234n.7	§1),] E; $\sim)_\wedge$
234n.13	insuperable] MF; insufferable
235.5	isosceles] E; isoceles *Also* 235.6–7
238.20	noologists] E; no-ologists
239.18	an indefinite] MF; a definite
239.21	reaffirm] E; re-affirm

240.36	this] MF; the
240n.3	*Quæstiones Subtillissimæ*] E; Quæst. Subtillissimæ
240n.4	part‸] E; ∼.
242.4–6	*extract*

Validity of the Laws of Logic

Copy-text is the publication of this article in *Journal of Specula-tive Philosophy* 2(1869):193–208. All emendations are supplied by the editors and appear to the left of the square brackets. All readings to the right of the brackets are rejected readings from the copy-text.

242.15	argument] argu|gument
244n.4	"writing-table‸"] "∼-∼' "
245.3	*P.*] ∼;
245n.3–4	"On . . . Relations."] ‸∼ . . . ∼.‸
245n.3	IV,] ∼.
249.3–6	*extract*
252n.2	*Werke*] rom.
252n.2	v‸] ∼.
255.10	smallest‸] ∼,
255.11	finite),] ∼,)
255.16–17	distances] distancs
261n.3	causes‸] ∼,
261n.4	irrefragable),] ∼,)
263n.2	Sophisma] *Soph.*
263n.3	*Sophistici Elenchi*] Sophist. Elench.
263n.3	cap.] *ital.*
263n.10	3d part . . . , cap.] *ital.*
263n.11	Mansel's] Mansell's
263n.11	Aldrich] *ital.*
265.33	increased‸] ∼,
265.33	distinct),] ∼,)
266n.1	*Logic*] rom.
‡266n.5	in some one] some one
266n.9	"Were] ‸∼
267.12	*probability*] rom.
268.9	handfuls] hand|fulls
268.20	first] flrst
268.29	p. 239] p. 155
269.10	sufficiently] snfficiently
270.14	benevolence] be|evolence
272.6	*con*‸—] ∼.—
272.10	sufficient] sufflcient

Porter's Human Intellect

Copy-text is the publication of this review in the *Nation* 8(18 March 1869):211–13. All emendations are supplied by the editors and appear to the left of the square brackets. All readings to the right of the brackets are rejected readings from the copy-text.

273.1	‸Human Intellect‸] "∼ ∼"
273n.1	‸*The Human . . . Soul*] "The Human . . . Soul
273n.3	College.‸] ∼.'
274.38	"external] ‸∼
274.38	perception"] ∼‸
277.23	admitted] admit‸|ted
280.40	assurance] assu‸|rance
281.6	*con*‸] ∼.

Pairing of the Elements

Copy-text is the publication of this article in the American Supplement to *Chemical News and Journal of Physical Science* 4(June 1869):339–40. All emendations are supplied by the editors and appear to the left of the square brackets. The readings to the right of the brackets are rejected readings from the copy-text.

282.3	‸Your] "∼
282.3–4	*Chemical News*] Chemical News
282.14	‸You] "∼
283.1	‸I] "∼
283.8	‸Finally] "∼
283.11	&c.‸] ∼."

Roscoe's Spectrum Analysis

Copy-text is the publication of this review in the *Nation* 9(22 July 1869):73–74. All emendations are supplied by the editors and appear to the left of the square brackets. The readings to the right of the brackets are rejected readings from the copy-text.

285.12	W. H. F. Talbot] H. F. Talbot
285.17	absorption-lines] absorp‸|tion-lines
285n.1–2	‸*Spectrum Analysis. . . . London*] "Spectrum Analysis. . . . London
285n.3	Manchester.‸] ∼."

286.23	Plattner] Platner *Also* 286.25, 286.28
286.24	per cent‚] ~ ~‚ *Also* 286.26, 287.40

Solar Eclipse

Copy-text is the publication of this report in *Coast Survey Report 1869.* The emendation which appears to the left of the square bracket is supplied by the editors. The reading to the right of the bracket is the rejected reading from the copy-text.

290.3	1869‚] ~.

Sketch of Logic

Copy-text for this item is MS 154. All emendations are supplied by the editors and appear to the left of the square brackets. All readings to the right of the brackets are rejected readings from the copy-text.

294.3	¶§1.] ‚~.
294.5	and] & *Also* 294.26, 294.29, 295.23, 296.36, 297.8, 297.35, 297.37
294.7(2)	bank-note] ~‚~
294.13	facts,] ~‚
294.14	taken,] ~‚
294.14	determines] determine
294.18(2)	the] The
294.20(1)	the] to
294.21–22	*leading‚principle*] ~-~
294.28	§4.] ~‚
294.29	leading‚principle] ~-~ *Also* 295.2, 295.8, 296.7
294n.2	it] in
294n.2	diallele.] ~‚
296.26	together—] ~‚
296.35	§8.] ~‚
296.36	one] to one
296.37	it it] it
297.5–6	determined by] determined
297.16	substitutions] substititutions
297.20	§9.] ~‚
297.26	substituted.] ~‚
297.34	*deduction.*] ~‚
297.35	¶§10.] ‚~‚
297.35	figure,] ~‚

Logic Notebook

Copy-text for this portion of "The Logic Notebook" is MS 155. All emendations are supplied by the editors and appear to the left of the square brackets. The readings to the right of the brackets are rejected readings from MS 155.

298.4	and] & *Also* 298.16, 300.9
298.23	$\overline{n}_\wedge +$,] $\sim$, +;
299.7	Oct.] $\sim_\wedge$ *Also* 301.1
299.10	d,] $\sim_\wedge$
299.10	&c.] $\sim_\wedge$ *Also* 299.12, 299.14, 299.24(1,2), 300.3(1,2), 301.21(1,2)
299.10	countries.] $\sim_\wedge$
299.11	colour.] $\sim_\wedge$
299.20(2)	∓ 0] = $\sim$
299.22(1)	l^e] d^e
300.7	A,] $\sim_\wedge$
300.7	B,] $\sim_\wedge$
300.7	C.] $\sim_\wedge$
300.8	$\mp 0).)$] $\mp \sim)_\wedge$)
300.9	A,] $\sim_\wedge$
300.9	B,] $\sim_\wedge$
300.10(1,2)	= 0,] = $\sim_\wedge$
300.11	A,] $\sim_\wedge$
300.11	B,] $\sim_\wedge$
300.11	then the] Then The
300.11–12	= 1.|When] = 1 when|when
300.12	equations] eq.
300.18	above.] $\sim_\wedge$
300.24	C.] $\sim_\wedge$
300.27	let us] let
300.29	proposition.] $\sim_\wedge$
300.30	− C).] − $\sim)_\wedge$
301.14	$l^{a,b}$.] $\sim_\wedge$
301.15	l^a.] $\sim_\wedge$
301.16	l'.] $\sim_\wedge$
301.17	not.] $\sim_\wedge$

English Doctrine of Ideas

Copy-text is the publication of this review in the *Nation* 9(25 November 1869):461–62. All emendations are supplied by the editors and appear to the left of the square brackets. The readings to the right of the brackets are rejected readings from the copy-text.

302.3	∧*Analysis of . . . Mind*∧] "Analysis of . . . Mind"
302n.1	∧*Analysis of . . . Mind*] "Analysis of . . . Mind
302n.2	Findlater] Finlater
302n.3	Mill.∧] ∼."
302n.3–4	Longmans,] ∼.
303.14	∧*Analysis*∧] "Analysis" *Also* 307.21
305.22	i∧,] ∼.,
306.4	ii∧,] ∼.,
306.11	i∧,] ∼.,
306.19	i∧,] ∼.,
307.6	conceive] cenceive
307n.1–2	∧*Vorlesungen über . . . Thierseele.*∧] "Vorle|ungen über . . . Thierseelen."

Early nominalism and realism

Copy-text for this lecture is MS 158. All emendations are supplied by the editors and appear to the left of the square brackets. The readings to the right of the brackets are rejected readings from MS 158.

310.14	as the] as which the
311.4	Englishman,] ∼∧
311.5	Scotus,] ∼∧
311.6	name,] ∼∧
311.9	the profoundest] profoundest
311.16	*Novum Organum*] rom.
311.18	Herschel] Herschell
311.18	some of] some
311.22	Wm.] ∼∧
311.27	scholastics] scolastics
311.29	*Parva Logicalia*] rom. *Also* 311.30
311.32–33	*Synopsis* Ἀριστοτελόος Ὀργάνου] Synopsis Αριστοτελ-όος Orgavou
311.33	Englishman,] ∼—
311.33–34	William of Sherwood] William Shirwood
311.39	to devote] devote
312.4	relations] relalations
312.8	Scholasticism] Scolasticism
312.9	and] & *Also* 313.9, 314.10(2), 314.18, 314.20, 314.32, 314.39, 315.3, 315.6, 315.11, 315.12(1,2), 315.13, 315.17, 315.25, 315.28, 315.31, 316.2, 316.8, 316.26(1,2)
312.16	*Ouvrages Inédits d'Abélard*] Ouvrages Inédits d'Abelard
312.17	*Documents . . . de France*] rom.
312.18–19	*Fragments Philosophiques: Philosophie Scholastique*] rom.

312.19	Hauréau] Haureau *Also* 316.31
312.19–20	*Histoire de la philosophie scholastique*] rom.
312.20	de Rémusat] de Remusat
312.20	*Abélard*] Abelard
312.20–21	*Recherches critiques . . . dans le moyen age*] rom.
312.21	*la*] le
312.22	*Nominalismus vor Roscellinus*] rom.
312.23	Anselm,] ∼∧
312.24	*Liber sex principiorum*] rom.
312.25	author's] authors
312.25	*De∧Trinitate*] de-|Trinitate
312.26	Abaelard's] Abaelards
312.27	*Introductio in Theologiam*] rom.
312.27	—works] ∧∼
312.28	history—] ∼∧
312.29–30	*Geschichte der Logik im Abendlande,*] Geschichte der Logik im Abendlande.
312.33	two] too
313.1	reasons."] ∼.∧
313.2	St. Augustine] St. Augustin
313.2–3	*De doctrina christiana*] rom.
313.9	Bible,] bible∧
313.9	church,] ∼∧
313.34	others'] others
314.3	hand.] ∼;
314.19	makes] make
314.20	extensive,] ∼∧
314.21	strict∧] ∼,
314.21	have] has
314.25	has] as
314.29	possibly] possible
314.30	words∧] ∼—
314.31	Latin] latin
314.34	to the] to the the
314.37	so-called] ∼∧∼
314.37	philosophers.] ∼∧
314.38–39	everywhere,] ∼∧
315.9(1)	it] is
315.10	way:] ∼∧
315.20	overbalanced] over balanced
315.23	which] with
315.32–33	indefinitely] indefitely
316.5	sixtieth] sixtyeth
316.7	*Prior Analytics*] prior Analytics
316.17–18	excusable] excuseable
316.30	*De Divisione Naturae*] rom.
316.31	*Notices*] rom.

316.34	Hjort,] ~‸
317.5	non-existences] nonexistences
317.5–6	*De divisione naturae*] de divisione naturae
317.6	by dividing] He begins by dividing
317.12	*Nothing*] rom.
317.13	incomprehensible,] ~‸
317.19	'and] "~
317.20	night'."] ~‸."

Ockam

Copy-text for these lecture notes is MS 160. All emendations are supplied by the editors and appear to the left of the square brackets. The readings to the right of the brackets are the rejected readings from the copy-text.

318.3	method,] ~‸
318.3	commentaries,] ~‸
318.6	and] & *Also* 319.43, 320.5, 320.6, 320.7, 320.8, 320.10, 320. 11, 320.18(1,2), 320.23(1,2), 320.26, 320.39, 321.6, 321.12, 321.13, 321.15, 321.16, 321.17, 321.18, 321.20, 327.17, 327. 18(1), 328.2, 328.8, 328.10, 328.25, 328.32, 329.6, 329.15, 330.4, 330.8, 330.15, 330.23, 330.26, 330.32, 330.37, 331.2, 332.43, 333.20, 333.21, 333.28, 333.29(1,2), 333.31, 333. 33(1,2), 334.20, 334.23, 334.40, 335.1(1,2), 335.4, 335.8(1,2), 335.9, 335.12, 335.13, 335.15, 335.22, 335.27, 335.33, 335.40, 336.3, 336.6(1,2), 336.7, 336.8(1), 336.9(1,2), 336.19, 336.20, 336.22, 336.23, 336.25, 336.30, 336.34
318.10	"Omnes] ‸~
318.12–13	propositionis."] ~.‸
318.15(1)	propositions] propopositions
318.21	"Triplex] ‸~
*318.22	conceptus."] ~.‸ [Read three whole chapter]
318.23–319.35	The written term . . . anything.] *supplied*
319.38	in] in in
319.38	senses.] ~‸
319.39	categorical] cathegorical
319.39	proposition.] ~‸
319.41	proposition.] ~‸
319.42	propositions.] ~‸
319.44	proposition.] ~‸
320.2	*significative sumptum*] rom.
320.3	*simpliciter*] rom.
320.3	*materialit[er]*] rom.
320.3	phraseology.] phras.

320.4	¶On] ₐ~
320.5	conceived, but] ~. But
320.6	together.] ~ₐ
320.10	written,] ~ₐ
320.10	vocal,] ~ₐ
320.12	terms.] ~ₐ
320.14	and] are
320.15	*verb:*] ~.
320.31	it] is
320.32–33	says "Utrum] ~|ₐ~
320.36	terminis."] ~.ₐ
320.40	language.] ~ₐ
321.9	signifying,] ~ₐ
321.21	*distinctio realis*] rom.
321.23	believe] beleive *Also* 336.15(1,2)
321.32	*Grammatica Speculativa*] rom.
321.35	Ockam.] ~ₐ
321.36	chapters.] chapters [Read them.]
321.37–327.16	THE AUTHOR'S PREAMBLE . . . accidentally.] *supplied*
‡323.37	there is,] although *in Deo,*
‡323.37	no] is not a
‡323.37–38	property in God,] property,
‡326.18	*signifying*] *signifying so to speak*
‡326.18	*discovered*] *ascertained*
327.18	question,] ~ₐ
327.18	is,] ~ₐ
327.20	Ockam's] Ockams
327.24	unimportant.] unimportant. [Read it to bottom of column]
327.25–36	Both spoken . . . new.] *supplied*
327.38	*man, horse,*] rom.
327.38	*white,*] white_ₐ
327.39	*humanity, horseness, whiteness*] rom.
328.4	that] than
328.12	&c.] ~ₐ
328.13(1)	that] that that
328.14	arguments.]] ~.ₐ
328.15–24	Concrete and abstract . . . things.] *supplied*
328.28	as "quod] ~|¶"~
328.30	*nominant.*] ~ₐ
328.31	significantur.] ~ₐ
328.31	*appellativa*] rom.
329.7	complications] comₐ|plications
329.11	syncategorematic] syncategoreumatic
329.12	what;] ~,
329.20–21	*syncategorematics*] *syncategoreumatics*
329.25	syncategorematics] syncategoreumatics *Also* 329.30, 329.36
329.30	them,] ~ₐ

329.33	blue-eyed] $\sim_\wedge\sim$ *Also* 329.34
329.35	*such.*] $\sim_\wedge$
330.1	inform] informs
330.7	follows.] $\sim_\wedge$
330.13–14	whiteness] white$_\wedge$|ness
330.16	something.] $\sim_\wedge$
330.18	name,] $\sim_\wedge$
330.23	terms).] $\sim)_\wedge$
330.29–30	*name of second imposition*] rom.
330.30	a wide] wide
330.34	terms] term
330.34	*noun,*] $\sim_\wedge$
330.34	*pronoun,*] $\sim_\wedge$
330.34	*conjunction,*] $\sim_\wedge$
330.34	*verb,*] $\sim_\wedge$
330.34	*case,*] $\sim_\wedge$
330.34	*number,*] $\sim_\wedge$
330.34	*mood,*] $\sim_\wedge$
330.34	*time,*] $\sim_\wedge$
330.36	name] names
330.38	imposition.] $\sim_\wedge$
330.39	categorematic] categoreumatic
331.5	intention:] intention [read to end of chapter] [bottom of 2nd colum of fol VII]
331.6–10	But the common term . . . imposition.] *supplied*
331.11	Chap.] $\sim_\wedge$
331.13–332.42	In the previous . . . intentions).] *supplied*
332.43	Chap. 13.] $\sim_\wedge \sim_\wedge$
332.44–333.17	A word is . . . the soul.] *supplied*
333.3	substance] substnace
333.18	Chaps.] $\sim_\wedge$
333.18	17.] $\sim_\wedge$
333.25–33	*extract*
333.37	its] it
333.38	says] says [XXIX c cap xlii Vno° dicit subā down to p̣mas ⱬ secūdas"]
333.39–334.8	In one sense . . . substance.] *supplied*
334.9	says] says [cap lv. down to lux scientia et huiusmodi]
334.10–18	It seems that . . . 'light'.] *supplied*
334.26	opposition.] opposition [Read from quodlibeta
334.27–38	Whether similarity or . . . absolute things.] *supplied*
335.7	similar.] $\sim_\wedge$
335.8–16	*extract*
335.9	Sortes] sortes *Also* 335.12
335.9	Plato] plato *Also* 335.12
‡335.11	really,] $\sim_\wedge$
‡335.14	numerical] numeral

335.23	mind's] minds
335.26(1)	the] the an
335.26	resemblance,] ~∧
335.27	unity,] ~∧
336.4	Mills] Mill's
336.5-6	with things] withings
336.6	trivial.] ~—
336.9	Hegel.] ~∧
336.18	everyday] every day
336.22	common—] ~∧
336.22	essence—] ~∧
336.33	seem] seems

Whewell

Copy-text for this lecture is MS 162. All emendations are supplied by the editors and appear to the left of the square brackets. The readings to the right of the brackets are rejected readings from MS 162.

337.4	than] that
337.6	and] & *Also* 337.15(1,2), 337.16, 337.17, 337.22, 337.23, 337. 27, 338.3, 338.6, 338.12, 338.21, 338.25, 338.28, 339.8, 339. 16, 339.17, 339.21(1,2), 339.28, 339.32, 340.3, 340.5, 340. 10(2), 340.18(1,2), 340.19, 340.21, 340.24, 340.27, 340.30, 340.35, 341.1, 341.11, 341.26, 341.34, 342.5, 342.12, 342.22, 342.25, 342.38(2), 343.2, 343.7, 343.28, 343.38, 344.19, 344. 29, 345.13
337.8	"Battle of . . . Arts."] ∧~ ~ . . . ~.∧
337.10	literary] leterary
337.18	things.] ~∧
337.19	salvation.] ~∧
337.25	specialist.] ~∧
337.29	Dr.] ~∧
337.33	forgotten] fogotten
338.4	professor] proffessor
338.8	Education,] ~∧
338.10	churches,] ~∧
338.11	subjects,] ~.
338.12	it] It
338.16	this.] ~∧
338.21	works. One,] ~∧one∧
338.22	*The History of . . . Sciences,*] The History of . . . Sciences∧
338.24	subject;] ~,
338.24	other,] ~∧

338.24	*The History of Scientific Ideas,*] The History of Scientific Ideas‸
338.27	sciences] science
338.28–29	*The Philosophy of . . . Sciences*] the Philosophy of . . . Sciences
339.9	Whewell's‸] ∼—
339.9–10	*Novum Organon Renovatum*] rom.
339.17	training,] ∼‸
339.18	superiority lies] superiority
339.25	scientific] sci|entic
339.36	representative] repre|sent
340.3	kinds,] ∼‸
340.5	Whewell's,] ∼‸
340.13	that] the
340.14	astronomy] astromy
340.14	etc.] ∼‸
340.15–16	satisfactory.] ∼‸
340.17	zoology,] ∼‸
340.17	&c.] ∼‸
340.35	facts.] ∼‸
341.7	appropriate] appropiate
341.7	idea.] ∼‸
341.10	which] *reinstate*
341.12	if] If
341.13	Science—] ∼‸
341.25	Kant,] ∼‸
341.29	Hamilton] Hamil‸|ton
341.34	example,] ∼‸
342.15	forces.] ∼‸
342.16	Gravity.] ∼‸
342.27–28	*Cambridge Philosophical Transactions*] rom.
343.18	weight,] ∼‸
343.23	numbers.] ∼‸
343.25	The ratio] The the ratio
343.26	approximates] approximate
343.38	vibration.] ∼‸
344.7	force.] ∼‸
344.8	gas?] ∼.
344.9	force.] ∼‸
344.11	is] *reinstate*
344.12	weight.] ∼‸
344.16	of] *reinstate*
344.18	things?] ∼.
344.27	accidental.] ∼‸
344.30	that] the
344.36	What,] ∼‸
344.38	[Drawings] ‸∼

344.38	nebulae.]] ~.ˆ
345.4	believe] beleive
345.11	nerves?] ~.
345.12	observers] observors
345.20	[Struve] ˆ~
345.20	and] &
345.20	Neptune]] neptuneˆ
345.22	It] In
345.23	[Rose-] ˆ~-
345.23	protuberances]] ~ˆ

Lessons in Logic

Copy-text is MS 164 for the first lesson in practical logic. All emendations are supplied by the editors and appear to the left of the square brackets. The readings to the right of the brackets are rejected readings from MS 164.

348.21	Mansel's] Mansell's
348.21–22	*Prolegomena Logica*] rom.
349.10	and] & *Also* 349.13, 349.25, 349.26, 349.27, 349.28
349.14	concerning] concernning
*349.17	terms] terms grammatical

Rules for Investigation

Copy-text for this item is MS 165. It is one of three discrete texts within this manuscript, all of which are published here. The first, "A Practical Treatise on Logic and Methodology," contains no emendations. Emendations for "Rules for Investigation," and for the third text, "Practical Logic," are supplied by the editors and appear to the left of the square brackets. The readings to the right of the brackets are rejected readings from MS 165.

352.1	*Organon*] rom.
352.11	exercise] excercise
352.26	this] This
353.1	at that time] at time

Practical Logic

353.22	*Organon*] rom.
354.12	sulphuretted] sulphurrhetted
355.22	despised] dispised

Chapter 2

Copy-text for this chapter of a *[Practical Logic]* is MS 166. All emendations are supplied by the editors and appear to the left of the square brackets. The readings to the right of the brackets are rejected readings from the copy-text.

356.27	person's] persons
357.2–3	Hedgecock's] Hedgcock's
357.3	Quadrant] Qudrant
357.13	proposition] propo|sion
357.15	hear] *reinstate*
357.15	terms,] ~—
357.26	are] a
357.29	and] &
358.8	tested,] ~,
358.13	first-rate] ~,~
358.15	IV.] ~,

Logic of Relatives

Copy-text for this item is the publication of it in *Memoirs of the American Academy of Arts and Sciences* n.s. 9(1873):317–78. The emendations to the text appear to the left of the square brackets and are from four sources. The editors have supplied those emendations labeled E. The other three sources are individual Peirce-corrected and -annotated offprints, and the emendations taken from them are labeled as follows:

JHU, an offprint deposited in The Ferdinand Hamburger, Jr. Archives of The Johns Hopkins University. An inscription on the front cover reads, "D. C. Gilman|from the author|Baltimore, January 1878" and is in Gilman's hand.

168, an offprint contained within the main collection of the Peirce Papers and given manuscript number 168.

1600², the second of two additional offprints in the Peirce Papers listed as Robin manuscript number 1600 (13 boxes of uncatalogued offprints and other miscellaneous materials). The first of these two offprints (1600¹) contains marginal annotations only.

All readings to the right of the semicolons are rejected readings from the copy-text. For a further discussion of the editorial handling of this item, see the Essay on Editorial Method. The reader is also directed to the Editorial Notes section for a listing and discussion of Peirce's marginal annotations which are not entered into the text as emendations.

359.9–10	*Cambridge Philosophical Transactions*] E; *rom.*
366.24	men,] 168; men (men),
367n.1	*Formal Logic*] E; *rom.*
367n.2	*Logic*] E; *rom.*
368.31–369.1	$_\wedge$*Pure Logic, . . . of Quality,*$_\wedge$] E; "Pure Logic, . . . of Quality,"
376.11	arithmetical] 168; arithmethical
379.30	y^z] 168; y^p
382.11	$= 0,$] E; $= \sim$.
385.34(2)	$= 1.$] E; $= \sim_\wedge$
392.20(1,2)	W‴] E; W″
393.13	W‴] E; W″
393.14	$l\Pi's^{\mathrm{W}}$] 168; $l\Pi's^{\mathrm{W'}}$
393.23	+, etc.] E; $+ \sim$. *Also* 393.24
399.8(1)	†1] E; †1
399.24	$l^{\triangle x}$] E; $l^{\triangle'x}$
401.3	etc.] E; $\sim_\wedge$ *Also* 401.5
401.7	l^sw] E; $l^s w$ *Also* 401.8
402.27	^{p}f] E; Pf
403.17(1,2)	u] E; *ital. Also* 403.20(3)
403.17(1,2)	f] E; *ital.*
409.36	+ d,$s_\wedge$] E; $+ \sim$.
*412.14	$k = u_1$] JHU,168; $k = 2.u_1$ *Also* 413.4
413.5	+ ƀ] JHU,168; + 2 ƀ
413.5	u₆,] E; $\sim$.
414.29	yj] E; yi
415.12	Negro] E; negro
415.15	Negro-men] E; negro-men
415.18	Negroes] E; negroes *Also* 415.19
415.24	"all] E; $_\wedge\sim$
415.31	yj] E; yz
419.23	(E:E),] E; ($\sim$).
419n.3	*Quodlibetum*] E; *rom.*
419n.3	qu.] E; $\sim_\wedge$
419n.3	*Summa Logices*] E; *rom.*
‡419n.4	disquiparantiæ] E; diquiparantiæ
419n.5	*Petrus Hispanus.*] E; Petr. Hisp.
422.27	x] JHU,168; *ital. Also* 422.28
423.24	0^x] E; $0x$
*424.5(2)	if,] E; $\sim_\wedge$
424.19	$1(1 - B) \prec 1(1 - A)$] E; $1(1 - A) \prec 1(1 - B)$
424.20	¹B] JHU; B
427.12	^lam] E; ^{ba}m

427.19	$^{\flat}a^{\text{m}}$] E; $^{\flat}a^{\text{m}}$
427.21	him."] E; $\sim._{\wedge}$
428.3	$^{\kappa}{}_{13}{}^{\kappa}xyz$] JHU,168; $^{\kappa}{}_{13}{}^{\kappa}yz$
429.15	x).] JHU,1600^2; $\sim_{\wedge}$.

System of Logic

Copy-text for "A System of Logic" is MS 169. All emendations are supplied by the editors and appear to the left of the square brackets. The readings to the right of the brackets are rejected readings from the copy-text.

430.27	imperative,] $\sim_{\wedge}$
430n.1	*Super Universalia*] *rom.*
431.10	considers,] $\sim_{\wedge}$
431.15	believe] beleive
431.30–35	*extract*
432.1	antecedent] antecent
432.10	the] The

James's Secret of Swedenborg

Copy-text is the publication of this review in *North American Review* 110(April 1870):463–68. All emendations are supplied by the editors and appear to the left of the square brackets. The readings to the right of the brackets are rejected readings from the copy-text.

438.1	*woman*] *rom. Also* 438.12, 438.14, 438.30
438.7	*male*] *rom.*
438.7	*female*] *rom.*
438.30	*inward man*] *rom.*

Lectures on Logic

Copy-text for this item is MS 171. The readings to the left of the square brackets are emendations supplied by the editors. The readings to the right of the brackets are rejected readings from MS 171.

439.4	1.] $\sim_{\wedge}$
439.4	and] & *Also* 439.23, 440.4, 440.18, 440.20, 440.21, 440.24, 440.26
*439.4	signs.[1]] signs$_{\wedge}$

439.6	2.] ∼ₐ
439.6	λεκτόv] λέκτοv *Also* 439.11
439.14	3.] ∼ₐ
439.19	definition.] ∼ₐ
439.20–21	incommensurable] incommsurable
*440.1	4.²] 4ₐ
440.2	former's] formers
440.14	affected.] ∼ₐ
440.15	experience,] ∼ₐ
*440.17	5.³] 5ₐ
440.18	experience,] ∼ₐ
440.18	discussion,] ∼ₐ
*440.19	opinion.⁴] opininion.
440.22	6.] ∼ₐ
440n.2	this.] ∼ₐ

Bain's Logic

Copy-text is the publication of this review in the *Nation* 11(4 August):77–78. The three emendations are supplied by the editors and appear to the left of the square brackets. The readings to the right of the brackets are the rejected readings from the copy-text.

441n.1	ₐ*Logic*] "Logic
441n.1–2	Aberdeen.ₐ] ∼."
442.2	*logic*] rom.

Peirce to Jevons

Copy-text for this letter is L 227. All emendations are supplied by the editors and appear to the left of the square brackets. The readings to the right of the brackets are rejected readings from L 227.

445.3	Aug.] ∼ₐ
445.8	and] & *Also* 445.12, 445.19, 445.22, 446.3, 446.8, 446.19, 446.27, 446.29, 447.1, 447.6, 447.9
445.18	operation's] operations
445.26(2)	identity,] ∼ₐ
445.30	*multiplication*] rom.
446.2	p.] ∼ₐ
446.8	copula] compula
446.10	p. 2ₐ] ∼ₐ ∼.
446.31	third,] ∼ₐ
446.33	This] this

446.34	coat,] $\sim_\wedge$
446.34	hat,] $\sim_\wedge$
446.34	speaking,] $\sim_\wedge$
446.34	etc.] $\sim_\wedge$
446.34	Quaker,] quaker$_\wedge$
446.36	All] all
447.1	they have] have

De Morgan

Copy-text for this two-part obituary is the publication of it in two successive issues of the *Nation* 12(13 April 1871):258 and 12(20 April):276. The first two pages are from the 13 April issue, and the last two and a half pages are from the 20 April issue. All emendations are supplied by the editors.

*448.4	Professor De Morgan was] A scarcely less voluminous writer was Professor De Morgan, who was
448.19	$_\wedge$*Essay on Probabilities,*$_\wedge$] "Essay on Probabilities,"
448.19	$_\wedge$*Elements of Algebra,*$_\wedge$] "Elements of Algebra,"
448.19–20	$_\wedge$*Formal Logic, . . . Probable,*$_\wedge$] "Formal Logic, . . . Probable,"
448.21	$_\wedge$*Differential . . . Calculus,*$_\wedge$] "Differential . . . Calculus,"
448.25	$_\wedge$His] "$\sim$
448.31	$_\wedge$*Formal Logic*$_\wedge$] "Formal Logic"
449.3	$_\wedge$*From Matter to Spirit,*$_\wedge$] "From Matter to Spirit,"
449.31	Thomas Spencer Baynes] Spencer Baynes
450.5	$_\wedge$*Syllabus of . . . Logic,*$_\wedge$] "Syllabus of . . . Logic,"
450.8–9	$_\wedge$*Penny Cyclopædia*$_\wedge$] "Penny Cyclopædia"
450.9	$_\wedge$*English Cyclopædia*$_\wedge$] "English Cyclopædia"

Copulas of Algebra

Copy-text for this item is MS 175. The readings to the left of the square brackets are emendations supplied by the editors. The readings to the right of the brackets are the rejected readings from MS 175.

451.4	according as] according
451.13–14	*Proceedings of the Academy*] rom.
451.14	Vol. 7$_\wedge$] $\sim_\wedge$ $\sim$.
451.23	and] & *Also* 452.4, 452.14(1), 453.18(1), 454.1, 454.13, 454.14, 454.15, 454.16, 454.17, 454.19(1), 454.30(2), 455.23, 456.20, 456.22
452.15	$_4x_\wedge$] $\sim$.

452.31	single-copula'd] $\sim_\wedge\sim$ *Also* 453.5, 455.2
453.8(4)	*x.*] $\sim_\wedge$
453.17	etc.] $\sim_\wedge$ *Also* 453.26, 456.7, 456.12, 456.15, 456.19, 456.21
453. 28	$\lhd$.] $\sim_\wedge$
454.6	algebra] algbra
454.10	include] in$_\wedge$|clude
454.14	2.] $\sim_\wedge$
454.19	*b*,] $\sim_\wedge$
454.19	*a.*] $\sim_\wedge$
454.27	$a \not\Subset b$ and] $a \not\Subset b$
455.4	*forms.*] $\sim_\wedge$
455.13	*b.*] $\sim_\wedge$
455.19	0.] $\sim_\wedge$
456.5	conveniently] conviently
456.6	&c.] $\sim_\wedge$

Babbage

Copy-text for this obituary notice is the publication of it in the *Nation* 13(9 November 1871):307–8. The emendations are supplied by the editors and appear to the left of the square brackets. The readings to the right of the brackets are the rejected readings from the copy-text.

457.6–7	$_\wedge$*Essay towards the Calculus of Functions,*$_\wedge$] "Essay towards the Calculus of Functions,"
457.20–21	$_\wedge$*Reflections on the Decline of Science in England, and on Some of Its Causes,*$_\wedge$] "Enquiry into the Causes, of the Decay of Science in England,"
458.23	Scheutz] Scheütz
459.12–13	$_\wedge$*Three and Four Place . . . Functions,*$_\wedge$] "Three and Four Place . . . Functions,"
459.37	three-] $\sim_\wedge$

Fraser's Berkeley

Copy-text for this review is the publication of it in *North American Review* 113(October 1871):449–72. All emendations are supplied by the editors and appear to the left of the square brackets. The readings to the right of the brackets are the rejected readings from the copy-text.

463.14	εἰ ἔστιν] ἐι ἐστιν
464.17	I.ₐ] ∼.
465.7	III.ₐ] ∼.
467.18	*Dictionary*] rom.
468.13	standpoint] stand-point
469.17	number] numbor
472.15	as] a
474.13–28	*extract*
474n.2	de St. Pourçain] de St. Pourcain
475.24	*Commonplaces*] rom.
476.11–29	*extract*
476.29	(p. 118)] —∼. ∼.
477.15–16	*Principles of Human Knowledge*] rom.
477.24–32	*extract*
478.1–19	*extract*
478.20	following:—"Mem.] ∼:—|¶"∼
482.13	causes?] ∼.
482.25–43	*extract*
482.43	(Vol. I,] —∼. ∼.
482.43	466)] ∼.
484.26	Helmholtz] Helmholz *Also* 485.37
485.17	*Lectures on the Human Mind*] rom.
485.22–23	*Analysis of the Human Mind*] rom.
485.24	*Logic*] rom.

Wright on the Berkeley Review

Copy-text for this article by Chauncey Wright is the publication of it in the *Nation* 13(30 November 1871):355–56. The only emendation to this article is supplied by the editors and appears to the left of the square bracket. The reading to the right of the bracket is the rejected reading from the copy-text.

488.2–3	*Dictionary*] rom.

Peirce and the Realists

Copy-text for this letter is the publication of it in the *Nation* 13(14 December 1871):386. The only emendation to this article is supplied by the editors and appears to the left of the bracket. The reading to the right of the bracket is the rejected reading from the copy-text.

490.3	*Nation*] NATION

Oliver to Peirce

Copy-text for this letter is L 322. The two emendations which appear to the left of the square brackets are supplied by the editors. The readings to the right of the brackets are the rejected readings from the copy-text.

492.29   5,] ~ₐ
492.29   2,] ~ₐ

Word-Division

The following list records the editors' resolutions of compounds or possible compounds hyphenated at the end of a line in the copy-texts.

28.20–21	well-known
70.25	overlooked
75.29	coextensive
89.13	wiser-than-some-|man
103.6	four-sided
103.13	schoolmen
111.23	non-ens
134.38–39	self-refutation
135.17	unthinkable
141.25	deep-seated
142.31	self-relation
148.4	self-relation
148.8	self-transcending
150.6	*nicht-seiende*
150.17	self-contradictory
152.3	oversight
152.27	self-contradictory
158.4–5	self-contradictory
158n.5–6	self-contradictory
159.8	footnote
162.11	self-consciousness
166.17	self-contemplation
167.25	self-consciousness
167.30	self-consciousness
176.8	sulphur-like
176.27	cloven-hoofed
192.5	proof-sheets
194.28	"evidence-proof"
195n.8	nominalistic-Platonistic
201.19	self-consciousness

203.20	self-consciousness
208.32	not-*A*
217.9	text-books
221.31	over-estimated
223.32–33	thought-sign
225.15	weathercock
230.10	thought-sign
233.21	middle-sized
234n.23	countrymen
235.24	needle-points
242.14	self-contradictory
255.19	non-finite
256.31	outside
258.7	inkstand
258.10	inkstand
259.9	non-white
260.8(2)	black-white
261n.2	overlaid
269.1	policy-holder
290.24	binding-screw
314.7	schoolmen
322.35	cosign
356.17	self-knowledge
372.26	non-associative
416.30	alio-lovers
416.32	non-Euclidean
426.30	non-betrayer
442.35	so-called
457.22	Astronomer-Royal
459.1	*tit-tat-|too*
459.30	seven-place
465.26	schoolmen
465.39	thirty-four
466.10	machine-work
467.6	thoroughgoing
488.29	outside
496.33	upsidedown

The following is a list of those words which are broken at the end of a line in the present text and which should be transcribed as hyphenated. All other ambiguously broken compound words or possible compound words should be transcribed as single words.

28.20	well-known
33.24	not-*P*
121.10	Pseudo-Aquinas

148.3	self-relation
149.16	pre-supposes
150.5	non-being
158.8	non-contradiction
165.21	self-evident
176.8	so-called
181.6	self-contradictory
198.27	nerve-points
206.19	self-evident
223.32	thought-sign
233.25	right-angled
238.1	logic-book
271.20	self-sacrifice
274.11	sense-perception
290.20	flint-glass
292.40	nesting-cries
314.36	world-wide
326.41	Counter-proposition
365.34	black-letter
367.2	Vice-President
387.24	non-invertible
416.12	self-benefactor
419.7	*alio-relatives*
435.27	flat-footed
477n.7	thought-signs
487.20	new-fledged

Index

Abbot, Francis Ellingwood, 110
Abduction, 108
Abelard, Peter, 195n, 276, 277, 464, 481; *Introductio in theologiam,* 312; *Ouvrages inédits d'Abélard,* 52n, 312
Absence, 109
Absolute: predication of, 135; various senses of, 109–14
Abstinence, 114
Abstract: vs. abstraction, 157; vs. concrete, 157; vs. general, 154; modes of signification or representation, 114–15
Abstracting, 116, 172, 335
Abstraction, 50, 81, 84, 103, 117, 148, 151; and agreement of things, 52–53; as attention, 231–32; and being, 145–48; as formation of concepts, 174, 208; as formation of habit, 233; as formation of ideas, 481; as generalization, 190; and nothing, 145–48; in perception, 236; pure, 52–53; and similarity, 475; various senses of, 116–17. *See also* Precision
Abstrahent, 117
Absurd, 118
Acatalepsy, 119
Acceptation, 119
Acceptilation, 119
Accident, 55, 119, 121, 482; grammatical, 320–21
Accidental: various senses of, 120–21
Achilles and the Tortoise, paradox of, 163, 173, 178, 207, 211, 254–56. *See also* Paradox
Act, pure, 138, 142
Action: instinctive, 233; rational, 272; voluntary, 233
Addition: algebraic, 360–61; arithmetical, 12, 60, 64, 65, 66; geometric, 494; invertible, 361, 445; logical, 13, 15, 21, 60, 61, 368–69, 445; non-invertible, 494
Adjunct, absolutely proper, 113

Affection, absolute, 110
Agassiz, Louis, 357
Agreement: accidental, 120; constituting reality, xli; in science, 212, 313–14
Alain de Lille, 312
Albertus Magnus, 150, 277
Alexander of Hales, 73; *Summa theologica,* 73n
Algebra: application of algebraic signs, 363–71, 377–79, 492–97; logical, xxxiii, xlii, xlvi, 359–60, 384, 387–88, 417; multi-copula, 451–53; operations of extended, 492–97; signs of defined, 360–63; single-copula, 451–56. *See also* Boole, George
American Academy of Arts and Sciences, xxv, xxxii
Analogy: argument from, 46–47, 48, 218n, 220; and hypothesis, 47; and induction, 47; and syllogism, 48
Analysis: limit of, 147; mental, 303; as method of positivism, 303; process of, 147–48; vs. synthesis, 147–48
Anaxagoras, 134
Andrews, Ethan Allen, and Solomon Stoddard: *A Grammar of the Latin Language,* 157
Anger, 172
Ångström, Anders Jöns, 288
Anschauung, 234n
Anselm, 117, 276, 312, 422; *Monologium,* 117, 193n
Antecedent: of an argument, 432; of a consequence, 348
Antithesis, 141
Anything: in logic of relatives, 374. *See also* Some
Apagogical: argument, 27, 29–30; proof, 48, 108
A posteriori: various senses of, 106–7. *See also* A priori
Appearance: vs. fact, 168–69; and reality, 470; in Swedenborg, 433–34

bility, xxvi, 98; scholastic, 239, 391n; as theory of reality, 175, 468, 470, 479, 488, 490. *See also* Conceptualism; Nominalism; Reality; Universals

Reality, 112, 127, 163, 175, 180, 252, 270; Berkeley's conception of, 479–80; constituted by consensus, xli, 471; existence of, 104, 269–70; external, 191, 470; vs. fiction, 104, 191; and final opinion, 470; as independent of representation, 439; involving community, xxviii, 239, 241; and mind, 470–71; nominalistic theory of, 175, 181–82, 468, 470–71, 479, 490; realistic theory of, 175, 468, 470, 479, 488, 490; and validity of induction, 269–70. *See also* Idealism

Reason, 126, 134, 358; vs. authority, 194–95, 312

Reasoning, 243, 354; and breadth and depth, 84–86; deductive, 263, 446; fallacious, 221–23; from definition to definitum, 85–86; hypothetical, 177, 187–88, 213, 446; inductive, 187–88, 279, 446–47; kinds of, 217, 446; object of, 357–58; probable, 263–64; as settlement of opinion, 357–58; synthetic, 268, 269. *See also* Inference

Redemption, 434–35

Reductio: ad absurdum, 257, 260–61; *per impossibile,* 37–38

Reduction: of manifold to unity, 45, 49–52, 54, 91, 199, 217, 218; of syllogism, 32–37, 39–42

Reference: to correlate, 53–56, 57, 82; direct, 82; to ground, 53–56, 59, 82; to interpretant, 162; to relate, 55–56; of thought-sign, 224. *See also* Representation; Sign

Regularity: frequency of, 264–65; in future events, 469; in nature, 264–66. *See also* Induction

Reid, Thomas, 134; *The Works of Thomas Reid,* 106, 115, 193n. *See also* Hamilton, William

Reinhold, Ernst Christian Gottlieb, 76

Relate, 53, 55–56. *See also* Being; Category; Correlate

Relation, xlii–xliii, xlv, xlvii, 409, 420; applicability of algebraic signs to, 363–64; category of, xxviii, xxxi, 54–55; cognition of, 164, 177, 210; existence of, 475; logical division of, 390; negation as, 420–21; numerical, 494; objectivity of, 471; quantified, xliv–xlv; vs. relative, xlviii; self-relation, 137, 141, 142, 148; vs. sign for relation, 494

Relatives: classification of, 418–20, 492; converse of, 429; elementary, xlv, 391,

408–14; inferences involving, 245; infinitesimal, 391, 395, 400–401, 408, 426; limited, 384, 386; simple, 417–20, 425; universal extremes of, 409; unlimited, 384, 386

Religion: basis of, 280–81, 435–36; positivist approach to, 122–23, 125–28; religious experience, 435; and science, 280, 435

Rémusat, François Marie Charles de: *Abélard,* 312

Representamen, 55. *See also* Category; Representation; Sign

Representation, xxviii, xxxi, 4, 10, 173, 233, 236, 439; abstract, 114–15; comprehension of, 4, 74; correlate of, 53; determined, 3; extension of, 4, 74; ground of, 53; material quality of, 228; mediating, 53–54; and proposition, 2; psychological, 274–75; as reference to interpretant, 53–54, 162; relate of, 53; three kinds of, 56. *See also* Meaning; Representamen; Sign

Resemblance: association by, 237, 238; between individuals, 467; denotation by, 237; imposed by mind, 475. *See also* Likeness; Similarity

Respect: as correlate of sign, 223–25; as object of consciousness, 224–25. *See also* Representation; Sign

Restriction, 84. *See also* Breadth; Depth

Rhetoric: formal, 57; rhetorical argument, 24, 24n–25n, 295

Ritter, Heinrich, 76

Roscelin, 239, 276, 317, 481

Roscoe, Henry Enfield, 288, 289; *Spectrum Analysis,* xxii, 285n

Rosenkranz, Johann Karl Friedrich, 132, 193n, 219n

Rösling, Christian Lebrecht, 74

Russell, Bertrand, xxxi

Sabine, Edward, 457

Satan, 355

Scalar, 409, 411, 414–15

Scepticism: absolute, 112–13, 242–43, 247; initial, 212; vs. theism, 123

Schelling, Friedrich Wilhelm Joseph von, 111, 135

Scheutz, Georg, 458

Schmid, Carl Christian Erhard, 114

Scholasticism, 137, 314; and authority, 312, 314; vs. Cartesianism, 211–13; nature of, 465–67; and nominalism-realism controversy, 464, 487–88; and science, 314–15; spirit of, 465–66, 467

Schröder, Ernst, xxxi

Volition: as abstracting, 207; nature of, 172, 207

Vorländer, Franz, 76, 77, 84

Vox, 276–77. *See also Flatus vocis;* Nominalism; *Sermo*

Waitz, Theodor, 108

Walker, Robert James, xxii

Watts, Isaac, 75, 76

Weber, Wilhelm Eduard, xxx

What is, 55. *See also* Being; Category; It

Whately, Richard: *Elements of Logic,* xxvi, xxviin

Whewell, William, 311, 442, 486; his conception of science, 339–40; on concepts in science, 342–44; his historical theory of science, 339; Kantianism of, 340–42; as a man of science, 337–39; *The History of the Inductive Sciences,* 338; *The History of Scientific Ideas,* 338; *Novum Organon Renovatum,* 339; *The Philosophy of the Inductive Sciences,* 338

Whitehead, Alfred North, xxxi

Will, 135, 179

William of Auvergne, 71n

William of Champeaux, 464

William of Ockham, xxv, 73, 239, 311, 312, 336, 464, 472, 476, 477; on association of ideas, 306; on conception, 331–32; on the doctrine of *formalitates,* 473–75; on equivocality, 332–33; vs. Hobbes, 477n; on *Insolubilia,* 263n; on intention, 331–32; on mental distinction, 320; on names, 112, 330–33; nominalism of, 335, 467, 474–75; on quality, 278, 334–35, 475; razor of, 303; on real distinction, 240; on reality, 227–28; on relation, 278, 334, 474–75; on signification, 318–20, 330–31; on similarity, 334–35; on substance, 333–34; on terms, 317–20, 327–30, 474; *Quodlibeta,* 418n–419n; *Summa logicae,* 73, 157, 240n, 263n, 419n

William of Sherwood (Shyreswood), 32, 39, 311

Wilson, William Dexter, 78; *An Elementary Treatise on Logic,* 78n

Wolff, Christian, 136, 157; *Logik,* 115

Winlock, Joseph, xxii, xxiii, xxxii, 288n

Word: comprehension of, 74; extension of, 74; general meaning of, 305; signification of, 474; in Thomas of Erfurt, 326–27. *See also* Name; Term

World: external, 162, 213; internal, 162, 206, 213

Wright, Chauncey, xxiv, xxxii, 487–89

Wundt, Wilhelm, xxx, 276, 306–7; *Vorlesungen über die Menschen- und Thierseele,* xxx, 307n

Zeno, paradox of, 173, 178, 184, 254, 256–57. *See also* Paradox

Zero class. *See* Class, zero